WILLIAM
SHAKESPEARE

WILLIAM SHAKESPEARE

A CRITICAL STUDY

BY

GEORGE BRANDES

NEW YORK

THE MACMILLAN COMPANY

1911

PRINTED IN ENGLAND

CONTENTS

BOOK FIRST

CONTENTS

BOOK SECOND

CONTENTS

BOOK THIRD

WILLIAM SHAKESPEARE

BOOK FIRST

THE same year which saw the death of Michael Angelo in Rome, saw the birth of William Shakespeare at Stratford-on-Avon. The great artist of the Italian Renaissance, the man who painted the ceiling of the Sistine Chapel, was replaced, as it were, by the great artist of the English Renaissance, the man who wrote *King Lear*.

Death overtook Shakespeare in his native place on the same date on which Cervantes died in Madrid. The two great creative artists of the Spanish and the English Renaissance, the men to whom we owe Don Quixote and Hamlet, Sancho Panza and Falstaff, were simultaneously snatched away.

Michael Angelo has depicted mighty and suffering demigods in solitary grandeur. No Italian has rivalled him in sombre lyrism or tragic sublimity.

The finest creations of Cervantes stand as monuments of a humour so exalted that it marks an epoch in the literature of the world. No Spaniard has rivalled him in type-creating comic force.

Shakespeare stands co-equal with Michael Angelo in pathos and with Cervantes in humour. This of itself gives us a certain standard for measuring the height and range of his powers.

It is three hundred years since his genius attained its full development, yet Europe is still busied with him as though with a contemporary. His dramas are acted and read wherever civilisation extends. Perhaps, however, he exercises the strongest fascination upon the reader whose natural bent of mind leads him to delight in searching out the human spirit concealed and revealed in a great artist's work. "I will not let you go until you have confessed to me the secret of your being"—these are the words that rise to the lips of such a reader of Shakespeare. Ranging the plays in their probable order of production, and reviewing the poet's life-work as a whole, he feels constrained to form for himself some image of the spiritual experience of which it is the expression.

A

I

A BIOGRAPHY OF SHAKESPEARE DIFFICULT
BUT NOT IMPOSSIBLE

WHEN we pass from the notabilities of the nineteenth century to Shakespeare, all our ordinary critical methods leave us in the lurch. We have, as a rule, no lack of trustworthy information as to the productive spirits of our own day and of the past two centuries. We know the lives of authors and poets from their own accounts or those of their contemporaries; in many cases we have their letters; and we possess not only works attributed to them, but works which they themselves gave to the press. We not only know with certainty their authentic writings, but are assured that we possess them in authentic form. If disconcerting errors occur in their works, they are only misprints, which they themselves or others happen to have overlooked. Insidious though they may be, there is no particular difficulty in correcting them. Bernays, for example, has weeded out not a few from the text of Goethe.

It is otherwise with Shakespeare and his fellow-dramatists of Elizabethan England. He died in 1616, and the first biography of him, a few pages in length, dates from 1709. This is as though the first sketch of Goethe's life were not to be written till the year 1925. We possess no letters of Shakespeare's, and only one (a business letter) addressed to him. Of the manuscripts of his works not a single line is extant. Our sole specimens of his handwriting consist of five or six signatures, three appended to his will, two to contracts, and one, of very doubtful authenticity, on the copy of Florio's translation of Montaigne, which is shown at the British Museum. We do not know exactly how far several of the works attributed to Shakespeare are really his. In the case of such plays as *Titus Andronicus*, the trilogy of *Henry VI.*, *Pericles*, and *Henry VIII.*, the question of authorship presents great and manifold difficulties. In his youth Shakespeare had to adapt or retouch the plays of others; in later life he sometimes collaborated with younger men. And worse than this, with the exception of two short narrative poems, which Shakespeare himself gave to the press, not one of his works is known to have been published under his own supervision. He seems never to have sanctioned any publication, or to have read a single proof-sheet. The 1623 folio of his plays, issued after his death by two of his actor-friends, purports to be printed "according to the True Originall Copies;" but this assertion is demonstrably false in numerous instances in which we can test it—where the folio, that is to say, presents a simple reprint, often with additional blunders, of the old pirated quartos, which must have been based either on the surreptitious notes of stenographers or on "prompt copies" dishonestly acquired.

It has become the fashion to say, not without some show of justice, that we know next to nothing of Shakespeare's life. We do not know for certain either when he left Stratford or when he returned to Stratford from London. We do not know for certain whether he ever went abroad, ever visited Italy. We do not know the name of a single woman whom he loved during all his years in London. We do not know for certain to whom his Sonnets are addressed. We can see that as he advanced in life his prevailing mood became gloomier, but we do not know the reason. Later on, his temper seems to grow more serene, but we cannot tell why. We can form but tentative conjectures as to the order in which his works were produced, and can only with the greatest difficulty determine their approximate dates. We do not know what made him so careless of his fame as he seems to have been. We only know that he himself did not publish his dramatic works, and that he does not even mention them in his will.

On the other hand, enthusiastic and indefatigable research has gradually brought to light a great number of indubitable facts, which furnish us with points of departure and of guidance for an outline of the poet's life. We possess documents, contracts, legal records; we can cite utterances of contemporaries, allusions to works of Shakespeare's and to passages in them, quotations, fierce attacks, outbursts of spite and hatred, touching testimonies to his worth as a man and to the lovableness of his nature, evidence of the early recognition of his talent as an actor, of his repute as a narrative poet, and of his popularity as a dramatist. We have, moreover, one or two diaries kept by contemporaries, and among others the account-book of an old theatrical manager and pawnbroker, who supplied the players with money and dresses, and who has carefully dated the production of many plays.

To these contemporary evidences we must add that of tradition. In 1662 a clergyman named John Ward, Vicar of Stratford, took some notes of information gathered from the inhabitants of the district; and in 1693 a Mr. Dowdall recorded some details which he had learnt from the octogenarian sexton and verger of Stratford Church. But tradition is mainly represented by Rowe, Shakespeare's first tardy biographer. He refers in particular to three sources of information. The earliest is Sir William Davenant, Poet Laureate, who did nothing to discountenance the rumour which gave him out to be an illegitimate son of Shakespeare. His contributions, however, can have reached Rowe only at second hand, since he died before Rowe was born. Naturally enough, then, the greater part of what is related on his authority proves to be questionable. Rowe's second source of information was Aubrey, an antiquary after the fashion of his day, who, half a century after Shakespeare's death, visited Stratford on one of his riding-tours. He wrote numerous short biographies, all of which contain gross and demonstrable errors, so that we can scarcely put implicit faith in the insignificant anecdotes about Shakespeare preserved in his manuscript of 1680. Rowe's most important source of information, however, is Betterton the actor, who, about 1690, made a journey to Warwickshire for the express purpose of collecting whatever oral traditions with regard to Shakespeare might linger in the district. His gleanings form the most valuable part of Rowe's biography; contemporary documents subsequently discovered have in several instances lent them curious confirmation.

We owe it, then, to a little group of worthy but by no means brilliant men that we are able to sketch the outline of Shakespeare's career. They have preserved for us anecdotes of little worth, even if they are true, while leaving us entirely in the dark as to important points in his outward history, and throwing little or no light upon the course of his inner life.

It is true that we possess in Shakespeare's Sonnets a group of poems which bring us more directly into touch with his personality than any of his other works. But to determine the value of the Sonnets as autobiographical documents requires not only historical knowledge but critical instinct and tact, since it is by no means self-evident that the poet is, in a literal sense, speaking in his own name.

II

STRATFORD—PARENTAGE—BOYHOOD

WILLIAM SHAKESPEARE was a child of the country. He was
born in Stratford-on-Avon, a little town of fourteen or fifteen
hundred inhabitants, lying in a pleasant and undulating tract of
country, rich in green meadows and trees and leafy hedges, the
natural features of which Shakespeare seems to have had in his
mind's eye when he wrote the descriptions of scenery in *A Midsummer Night's Dream, As You Like It,* and *A Winter's Tale.*
His first and deepest impressions of nature he received from this
scenery; and he associated with it his earliest poetical impressions, gathered from the folk-songs of the peasantry, so often
alluded to and reproduced in his plays. The town of Stratford
lies upon the ancient high-road from London to Ireland, which
here crosses the river Avon. To this circumstance it owes its
name (Street-ford). A handsome bridge spanned the river. The
picturesque houses, with their gable-roofs, were either wooden
or frame-built. There were two handsome public buildings, which
still remain: the fine old church close to the river, and the Guildhall, with its chapel and Grammar School. In the chapel, which
possessed a pleasant peal of bells, there was a set of frescoes
—probably the first and for long the only paintings known to
Shakespeare.

For the rest, Stratford-on-Avon was an insanitary place of
residence. There was no sort of underground drainage, and
street-sweepers and scavengers were unknown. The waste water
from the houses flowed out into badly kept gutters; the streets
were full of evil-smelling pools, in which pigs and geese freely
disported themselves; and dunghills skirted the highway. The
first thing we learn about Shakespeare's father is that, in April
1552, he was fined twelvepence for having formed a great midden
outside his house in Henley Street—a circumstance which on the
one hand proves that he kept sheep and cattle, and on the other
indicates his scant care for cleanliness, since the common dunghill
lay only a stone's-throw from his house. At the time of his
highest prosperity, in 1558, he, along with some other citizens, is
again fined fourpence for the same misdemeanour.

The matter is not without interest, since it is in all probability

5

to these defects of sanitation that Shakespeare's early death is to be ascribed.

Both on his father's and his mother's side, the poet was descended from yeoman families of Warwickshire. His grandfather, Richard Shakespeare, lived at Snitterfield, where he rented a small property. Richard's second son, John Shakespeare, removed to Stratford about 1551, and went into business in Henley Street as a tanner and glover. In the year 1557 his circumstances were considerably improved by his marriage with Mary Arden, the youngest daughter of Robert Arden, a well-to-do yeoman in the neighbourhood, who had died a few months before. On his death she had inherited his property of Asbies at Wilmecote; and she had, besides, a reversionary interest in a larger property at Snitterfield. Asbies was valued at £224, and brought in a rental of £28, or about £140 of our modern money. The inventory appended to her father's will gives us a good insight into the domestic economy of a rich yeoman's family of those days: a single bed with two mattresses, five sheets, three towels, &c. Garments of linen they do not seem to have possessed. The eating utensils were of no value: wooden spoons and wooden platters. Yet the home of Shakespeare's mother was, according to the standard of that day, distinctly well-to-do.

His marriage enabled John Shakespeare to extend his business. He had large transactions in wool, and also dealt, as occasion offered, in corn and other commodities. Aubrey's statement that he was a butcher seems to mean no more than that he himself fattened and killed the animals whose skins he used in his trade. But in those days the different occupations in a small English country town were not at all strictly discriminated; the man who produced the raw material would generally work it up as well.

John Shakespeare gradually rose to an influential position in the little town in which he had settled. He first (in 1557) became one of the ale-tasters, sworn to look to the quality of bread and beer; in the following year he was one of the four " petty constables " of the town. In 1561 he was Chamberlain, in 1565 Alderman, and finally, in 1568, High Bailiff.

William Shakespeare was his parents' third child. Two sisters, who died in infancy, preceded him. He was baptized on the 26th of April 1564; we do not know his birthday precisely. Tradition gives it as the 23rd of April; more probably it was the 22nd (in the new style the 4th of May), since, if Shakespeare had died upon his birthday, his epitaph would doubtless have mentioned the circumstance, and would not have stated that he died in his fifty-third year [*Ætatis* 53].

Neither of Shakespeare's parents possessed any school education; neither of them seems to have been able to write his or her own name. They desired, however, that their eldest son should not lack the education they themselves had been denied, and therefore sent the boy to the Free School or Grammar School of Stratford, where children from the age of seven upwards were grounded in Latin grammar, learned to construe out of a school-book called *Sententiæ Pueriles*, and afterwards read Ovid, Virgil, and Cicero. The school-hours, both in summer and winter, occupied the whole day, with the necessary intervals for meals and recreation. An obvious reminiscence of Shakespeare's schooldays is preserved for us in *The Merry Wives of Windsor* (iv. 1), where the schoolmaster, Sir Hugh Evans, hears little William his *Hic, Hæc, Hoc*, and assures himself of his knowledge that *pulcher* means fair, and *lapis* a stone. It even appears that his teacher was in fact a Welshman.

The district in which the child grew up was rich in historical memories and monuments. Warwick, with its castle, renowned since the Wars of the Roses, was in the immediate neighbourhood. It had been the residence, in his day, of the Earl of Warwick who distinguished himself at the battle of Shrewsbury and negotiated the marriage of Henry V. The district was, however, divided during the Wars of the Roses. Warwick for some time sided with York, Coventry with Lancaster. With Coventry, too, a town rich in memories of the period which he was afterwards to summon to life on the stage, Shakespeare must have been acquainted in his boyhood. It was in Coventry that the two adversaries who appear in his *Richard II.* Henry Bolingbroke and the Duke of Norfolk, had their famous encounter. But in another respect as well Coventry must have had great attractions for the boy. It was the scene of regular theatrical representations, which, at first organised by the Church, afterwards passed into the hands of the guilds. Shakespeare must doubtless have seen the half-mediæval religious dramas sometimes alluded to in his works—plays which placed before the eyes of the audience Herod and the Massacre of the Innocents, souls burning in hell, and other startling scenes of a like nature[1] (*Henry V.*, ii. 3 and iii. 3).

Of royal and princely splendour Shakespeare had probably certain glimpses even in his childhood. When he was eight years old Elizabeth paid a visit to Sir Thomas Lucy of Charlecote, in the immediate neighbourhood of Stratford — the Sir Thomas Lucy who was to have such a determining influence upon Shakespeare's career. In any case, he must doubtless have visited the neighbouring castle of Kenilworth, and seen something of the great festivities organised by Leicester in Elizabeth's honour, during her visit to the castle in 1575. We know that the Shakespeare family possessed a near and influential kinsman in

---

[1] We find reminiscences of these scenes in Hamlet's expression, "He out-herods Herod," and in the comparison of a flea on Bardolph's nose to a black soul burning in hell-fire.

Leicester's trusted attendant, Edward Arden, who soon afterwards, apparently on account of the strained relations which
arose between the Queen and Leicester after the fêtes, incurred
the suspicion or displeasure of his master, and was ultimately
executed.

Nor was it only mediæval mysteries that the future poet, during
his boyhood, had opportunities of seeing. The town of Stratford
showed a marked taste for secular theatricals. The first travelling
company of players came to Stratford in the year when Shakespeare's father was High Bailiff, and between 1569 and 1587 no
fewer than twenty-four strolling troupes visited the town. The
companies who came most frequently were the Queen's Men and
the servants of Lord Worcester, Lord Leicester, and Lord Warwick. Custom directed that they should first wait upon the High
Bailiff to inform him in what nobleman's service they were en-
rolled; and their first performance took place before the Town
Council alone. A writer named Willis, born in the same year
as Shakespeare, has described how he was present at such a
representation in the neighbouring town of Gloucester, standing
between his father's knees; and we can thus picture to ourselves
the way in which the glories of the theatre were for the first time
revealed to the future poet.

As a boy and youth, then, he no doubt had opportunities of
making himself familiar with the bulk of the old English repertory, partly composed of such pieces as he afterwards ridicules—
for instance, the *Cambyses*, whose rant Falstaff parodies—partly
of pieces which subsequently became the foundation of his own
plays, such as *The Supposes*, which he used in *The Taming of
the Shrew*, or *The Troublesome Raigne of King John*, or the
Famous Victories of Henry the Fifth, which supplied some of the
material for his *Henry IV*.

Probably Shakespeare, as a boy and youth, was not content
with seeing the performances, but sought out the players in the
different taverns where they took up their quarters, the "Swan,"
the "Crown," or the "Bear."

The school course was generally over when a boy reached his
fourteenth year. It appears that when Shakespeare was at this
age his father removed him from the school, having need of him
in his business. His father's prosperity was by this time on the
wane.

In the year 1578 John Shakespeare mortgaged his wife's
property, Asbies, for a sum of £40, which he seems to have
engaged to repay within two years, though this he himself denied.
In the same year the Town Council agrees that he shall be
required to pay only one-half of a tax (6s. 8d. in all) for the
equipment of soldiers, and absolves him altogether from payment
of a poor-rate levied on the other Aldermen. In the following
year he cannot pay even his half of the pikemen-tax. In 1579

he sold the reversion of a piece of land falling to him on his mother-in-law's death. In the following year he wanted to pay off the mortgage on Asbies; but the mortgagee, a certain Edmund Lambert, declined to receive the money, for the reason, or under the pretext, that it had not been tendered within the stipulated time, and that Shakespeare had, moreover, borrowed other sums of him. In the course of the consequent lawsuit, John Shakespeare described himself as a person of "small wealthe, and verey fewe frends and alyance in the countie." The result of this lawsuit is unknown, but it seems as though the father, and the son after him, took it much to heart, and felt that a great injustice had been done them. In the Induction to *The Taming of the Shrew*, Christopher Sly calls himself "Old Sly's son of Burton Heath." But Barton-on-the-Heath was precisely the place where lived Edmund Lambert and his son John, who, after his death in 1587, carried on the litigation. And this utterance of the chief character in the Induction is, significantly enough, one of the few which Shakespeare added to the Induction to the old play he was here adapting.

From this time forward John Shakespeare's position goes from bad to worse. In the year 1586, when his son was probably already in London, his goods are distrained upon, and no fewer than three warrants are issued for his arrest; he seems for a time to have been imprisoned for debt. He is removed from his position as Alderman because he has not for a long time attended the meetings at the Guildhall. He probably dared not put in an appearance for fear of being arrested by his creditors. He seems to have lost a considerable sum of money by standing surety for his brother Henry. There was, moreover, a commercial crisis in Stratford. The cloth and yarn trade, in which most of the citizens were engaged, had become much less remunerative than before.

We find evidence of the painful position in which John Shakespeare remained so late as the year 1592, in Sir Thomas Lucy's report with reference to the inhabitants of Stratford who did not obey her Majesty's order that they should attend church once a month. He is mentioned as one of those who "coom not to Churche for fear of processe for debtte."

It is probable that the young William, when his father removed him from the Grammar School, assisted him in his trade; and it is not impossible that, as a somewhat dubious allusion in a contemporary seems to imply, he was for some time a clerk in an attorney's office. His great powers, at any rate, doubtless revealed themselves very early; he must have taken early to writing verses, and, like most men of genius, must have ripened early in every respect.

III

MARRIAGE—SIR THOMAS LUCY—DEPARTURE FROM STRATFORD

IN December 1582, being then only eighteen, William Shake-speare married Anne Hathaway, daughter of a well-to-do yeoman, recently deceased, in a neighbouring hamlet of the same parish. The marriage of a boy not yet out of his teens, whose father was in embarrassed circumstances, while he himself had probably nothing to live on but such scanty wages as he could earn in his father's service, seems on the face of it somewhat precipitate ; and the arrangements for it, moreover, were unusually hurried. In a document dated November 28, 1582, two friends of the Hathaway family give a bond to the Bishop of Worcester's Court, declaring, under relatively heavy penalties, that there is no legal impediment to the solemnisation of the marriage after one publication of the banns, instead of the statutory three. So far as we can gather, it was the bride's family that hurried on the marriage, while the bridegroom's held back, and perhaps even opposed it. This haste is the less surprising when we find that the first child, a daughter named Susanna, was born in May 1583, only five months and three weeks after the wedding. It is probable, however, that a formal betrothal, which at that time was regarded as the essential part of the contract, had preceded the marriage.

In 1585 twins were born, a girl, Judith, and a boy, Hamnet (the name is also written Hamlet), no doubt called after a friend of the family, Hamnet Sadler, a baker in Stratford, who is mentioned in Shakespeare's will. This son died at the age of eleven.

It was probably soon after the birth of the twins that Shake-speare was forced to quit Stratford. According to Rowe he had "fallen into ill company," and taken part in more than one deer-stealing raid upon Sir Thomas Lucy's park at Charlecote. "For this he was prosecuted by that gentleman, as he thought, some-what too severely, and in order to revenge that ill-usage he made a ballad upon him. . . . It is said to have been so very bitter that it redoubled the prosecution against him to that degree that he was obliged to leave his business and family in Warwickshire for some time and shelter himself in London." Rowe believed this

ballad to be lost, but what purports to be the first verse of it has
been preserved by Oldys, on the authority of a very old man
who lived in the neighbourhood of Stratford.   It may possibly be
genuine.   The coincidence between it and an unquestionable gibe
at Sir Thomas Lucy in *The Merry Wives of Windsor* renders it
probable that it has been more or less correctly remembered.[1]
Although poaching was at that time regarded as a comparatively
innocent and pardonable misdemeanour of youth, to which the
Oxford students, for example, were for many generations greatly
addicted, yet Sir Thomas Lucy, who seems to have newly and
not over-plentifully stocked his park, deeply resented the depreda-
tions of young Stratford.   He was, it would appear, no favourite
in the town.   He never, like the other landowners of the district,
requited with a present of game the offerings of salt and sugar
which, as we learn from the town accounts, the burgesses were in
the habit of sending him.   Shakespeare's misdeeds were not at
that time punishable by law; but, as a great landowner and justice
of the peace, Sir Thomas had the young fellow in his power, and
there is every probability in favour of the tradition, preserved by
the Rev. Richard Davies, who died in 1708, that he "had him oft
whipt and sometimes imprisoned."   It is confirmed by the substantial correctness of Davies' further statement: "His reveng
was so great, that he is his Justice Clodpate [Shallow], . . . that
in allusion to his name bore three louses rampant for his arms."
We find, in fact, that in the opening scene of *The Merry Wives*,
Justice Shallow, who accuses Falstaff of having shot his deer,
has, according to Slender's account, a dozen white luces (pikes)
in his coat-of-arms, which, in the mouth of the Welshman, Sir
Hugh Evans, become a dozen white louses—the word-play being
exactly the same as that in the ballad.   Three luces argent were
the cognisance of the Lucy family.

    The attempt to cast doubt upon this old tradition of Shake-
speare's poaching exploits becomes doubly unreasonable in face
of the fact that precisely in 1585 Sir Thomas Lucy spoke in
Parliament in favour of more stringent game-laws.

    The essential point, however, is simply this, that at about the
age of twenty-one Shakespeare leaves his native town, not to
return to it permanently until his life's course is nearly run.
Even if he had not been forced to bid it farewell, the impulse to
develop his talents and energies must ere long have driven him

---

[1] It runs :—

> " A parliament member, a justice of peace,
> At home a poor scare-crow, at London an asse ;
> If lowsie is Lucy, as some volke miscalle it,
> Then Lucy is lowsie, whatever befall it ;
> > He thinkes himself greate
> > Yet an asse in his state
> We allowe by his eares but with asses to mate.
> If Lucy is lowsie, as some volke miscalle it,
> Sing lowsie Lucy, whatever befalle it.

forth. Young and inexperienced as he was, at all events, he had now to betake himself to the capital to seek his fortune.

Whether he left any great happiness behind him we cannot tell; but it is scarcely probable. There is nothing to show that in the peasant girl, almost eight years older than himself, whom he married at the age of eighteen, Shakespeare found the woman who, even for a few years, could fill his life. Everything, indeed, points in the opposite direction. She and the children remained behind in Stratford, and he saw her only when he revisited his native place, as he did at long intervals, probably, at first, but afterwards annually. Tradition and the internal evidence of his writings prove that he lived, in London, the free Bohemian life of an actor and playwright. We know, too, that he was soon plunged in the business cares of a theatrical manager and part-proprietor. The woman's part in this life was not played by Anne Hathaway. On the other hand, there can be no doubt that Shakespeare never for a moment lost sight of Stratford, and that he had no sooner made a footing for himself in London than he set to work with the definite aim of acquiring land and property in the town from which he had gone forth penniless and humiliated. His father should hold up his head again, and the family honour be re-established.

IV

LONDON—BUILDINGS, COSTUMES, MANNERS

SO the young man rode from Stratford to London. He probably, according to the custom of the poorer travellers of that time, sold his horse on his arrival at Smithfield; and, as Halliwell-Phillips ingeniously suggests, he may have sold it to James Burbage, who kept a livery stable in the neighbourhood. It may have been this man, the father of Richard Burbage, afterwards Shakespeare's most famous fellow-actor, who employed Shakespeare to take charge of the horses which his customers of the Smithfield district hired to ride to the play. James Burbage had built, and now owned, the first playhouse erected in London (1576), known as *The Theatre;* and a well-known tradition, which can be traced to Sir William Davenant, relates that Shakespeare was driven by dire necessity to hang about the doors of the theatre and hold the horses of those who had ridden to the play. The district was a remote and disreputable one, and swarmed with horse-thieves. Shakespeare won such favour as a horseholder, and was in such general demand, that he had to engage boys as assistants, who announced themselves as "Shakespeare's boys," a style and title, it is said, which long clung to them. A fact which speaks in favour of this much-ridiculed legend is that, at the time to which it can be traced back, well on in the seventeenth century, the practice of riding to the theatres had entirely fallen into disuse. People then went to the play by water.

A Stratford tradition represents that Shakespeare first entered the theatre in the character of "servitor" to the actors, and Malone reports "a stage tradition that his first office in the theatre was that of prompter's attendant," whose business was to give the players notice of the time for their entrance. It is evident, however, that he soon rose above these menial stations.

The London to which Shakespeare came was a town of about 300,000 inhabitants. Its main streets had quite recently been paved, but were not yet lighted; it was surrounded with trenches, walls, and gates; it had high-gabled, red-roofed, two-story wooden houses, distinguished by means of projecting signs, from which they took their names—houses in which benches did duty for chairs, and the floors were carpeted with rushes. The streets were usually thronged, not with wheel-traffic, for the first carriage was imported into England in this very reign, but with people on foot, on horseback, or in litters; while the Thames, still blue and clear, in spite of the already large consumption of coal, was alive with thousands of boats threading their way, amid the watermen's shrill cries of "Eastward hoe!" or "Westward hoe!" through bevies of swans which put forth from, and returned to, the green meadows and beautiful gardens bordering the steam.

There was as yet only one bridge over the Thames, the mighty London Bridge, situated not far from that which now bears the name. It was broad, and lined with buildings; while on the tall gate-towers heads which had fallen on the block were almost always displayed. In its neighbourhood lay Eastcheap, the street in which stood Falstaff's tavern.

The central points of London were at that time the newly erected Exchange and St. Paul's Church, which was regarded not only as the Cathedral of the city, but as a meeting-place and promenade for idlers, a sort of club where the news of the day was to be heard, a hiring-fair for servants, and a sanctuary for debtors, who were there secure from arrest. The streets, still full of the many-coloured life of the Renaissance, rang with the cries of 'prentices inviting custom and hawkers proclaiming their wares; while through them passed many a procession, civil, ecclesiastical, or military, bridal companies, pageants, and troops of crossbow-men and men-at-arms.

Elizabeth might be met in the streets, driving in her huge State carriage, when she did not prefer to sail on the Thames in her magnificent gondola, followed by a crowd of gaily decorated boats.

In the City itself no theatres were tolerated. The civic authorities regarded them with an unfriendly eye, and had banished them to the outskirts and across the Thames, together with the rough amusements with which they had to compete: cock-fighting and bear-baiting with dogs.

The handsome, parti-coloured, extravagant costumes of the period are well known. The puffed sleeves of the men, the women's stiff ruffs, and the fantastic shapes of their hooped skirts, are still to be seen in stage presentations of plays of the time. The Queen and her Court set the example of great and unreasonable luxury with respect to the number and material of costumes. The ladies rouged their faces, and often dyed their hair. Auburn, as the Queen's colour, was the most fashionable. The conveniences of daily life were very meagre. Only of late had fireplaces begun to be substituted for the open hearths. Only of late had proper bedsteads come into general use; when Shakespeare's well-to-do grandfather, Richard Arden, made his will, in the year 1556, there was only one bedstead in the house where he lived with his seven daughters. People slept on straw mattresses, with a billet of wood under their heads and a fur rug over them. The only decoration of the rooms of the wealthier classes was the tapestry on the walls, behind which people so often conceal themselves in Shakespeare's plays.

The dinner-hour was at that time eleven in the morning, and it was reckoned fashionable to dine early. Those who could afford it ate rich and heavy dishes; the repasts would often last an inordinate time, and no regard whatever was paid to the minor decencies of life. Domestic utensils were very mean. So late as 1592, wooden trenchers, wooden platters, and wooden spoons were in common use. It was just about this time that tin and silver began to supplant wood. Table-knives had been in general use since about 1563; but forks were still unknown in Shakespeare's time—fingers supplied their place. In a description of five months' travels on the Continent, published by Coryat in 1611, he tells how surprised he was to find the use of forks quite common in Italy :—

"I obserued a custome in all those Italian Cities and Townes through which I passed, that is not vsed in any other country that I saw in my trauels, neither doe I thinke that any other nation of Christendome doth vse it, but only Italy. The Italian and also most strangers that are commorant in Italy doe alwaies at their meales vse a little forke when they cut their meate. For while with their knife which they hold in one hand they cut the meate out of the dish, they fasten their forke which they hold in their other hand vpon the same dish, so that whatsoeuer he be that sitting in the company of any others at meale, should vnaduisedly touch the dish of meate with his fingers from which all at the table doe cut, he will giue occasion of offence vnto the company, as hauing transgressed the lawes of good manners, in so much that for his error he shall be at the least brow-beaten, if not reprehended in wordes. . . . The reason of this their curiosity is, because the Italian cannot by any means indure to haue his dish touched with fingers, seing all men's fingers are not alike cleane." [1]

We see, too, that Coryat was the first to introduce the new appliance into his native land. He tells us that he thought it best to imitate the Italian fashion not only in Italy and Germany, but "often in England" after his return; and he relates how a learned and jocular gentleman of his acquaintance rallied him on that account and called him "Furcifer." In one of Ben Jonson's plays, *The Devil is an Ass*, dating from 1614, the use of forks is mentioned as lately imported from Italy, in order to save napkins. We must conceive, then, that Shakespeare was as unfamiliar with the use of the fork as a Bedouin Arab of to-day.

He does not seem to have smoked. Tobacco is never mentioned in his works, although the people of his day gathered in tobacco-shops where instruction was given in the new art of smoking, and although the gallants actually smoked as they sat on the stage of the theatre.

---

[1] *Coryat's Crudities*, ed. 1776, vol. i. p. 106.

V

POLITICAL AND RELIGIOUS CONDITIONS—
ENGLAND'S GROWING GREATNESS

THE period of Shakespeare's arrival in London was momentous both in politics and religion. It is the period of England's development into a great Protestant power. Under Bloody Mary, the wife of Philip II. of Spain, the government had been Spanish-Catholic; the persecutions directed against heresy brought many victims, and among them some of the most distinguished men in England, to the scaffold, and even to the stake. Spain made a cat's-paw of England in her contest with France, and reaped all the benefit of the alliance, while England paid the penalty. Calais, her last foothold on the Continent, was lost.

With Elizabeth, Protestantism ascended the throne and became a power in the world. She rejected Philip's courtship; she knew how unpopular the Spanish marriage had made her sister. In the struggle with the Papal power she had the Parliament on her side. Parliament had at once recognised her as Queen by the law of God and the country whilst the Pope, on her accession, denied her right to the throne. The Catholic world took his part against her; first France, then Spain. England supported Protestant Scotland against its Catholic Queen and her Scottish-French army, and the Reformation triumphed in Scotland. Afterwards, when Mary Stuart had ceased to rule over Scotland and taken refuge in England, in the hope of there finding help, it was no longer France but Philip of Spain who stood by her. He saw his despotism in the Netherlands threatened by the victory of Protestantism in England.

Political interest led Elizabeth's Government to throw Mary into prison. The Pope excommunicated Elizabeth, absolved her subjects from their oath of allegiance, and declared her a usurper in her own kingdom. Whoever should obey her commands was excommunicated along with her, and for twenty years on end one Catholic conspiracy against Elizabeth treads on another's heels, Mary Stuart being involved in almost all of them.

In 1585 Elizabeth opened the war with Spain by sending her fleet to the Netherlands, with her favourite, Leicester, in command of the troops. In the beginning of the following year, Francis Drake, who in 1577–80 had for the first time circumnavigated the world, surprised and took San Domingo and Carthagena. The ship in which he had achieved his great voyage lay at anchor in the Thames as a memorial of the feat; it was often visited by Londoners, and no doubt by Shakespeare among them.

In the years immediately following, the springtide of the national spirit burst into full bloom. Let us try to picture to ourselves the impression it must have made upon Shakespeare in the year 1587. On the 8th of February 1587 Mary Stuart was executed at Fotheringay, and the breach between England and the Catholic world was thus made irreparable. On the 16th of February, England's noblest knight and the flower of her chivalry, Sir Philip Sidney, the hero of Zutphen, and the chief of the Anglo-Italian school of poets, was buried in St. Paul's Cathedral, with a pomp which gave to the event the character of a national solemnity. Sidney was an ideal representative of the aristocracy of the day. He possessed the widest humanistic culture, had studied Aristotle and Plato no less than geometry and astronomy, had travelled and seen the world, had read and thought and written, and was not only a scholar but a soldier to boot. As a cavalry officer he had saved the English army at Gravelines, and he had been the friend and patron of Giordano Bruno, the freest thinker of his time. The Queen herself was present at his funeral, and so, no doubt, was Shakespeare.

In the following year Spain fitted out her great Armada and despatched it against England. As regards the size of the ships and the number of the troops they carried, it was the largest fleet that had ever been seen in European waters. And in the Netherlands, at Antwerp and Dunkerque, transports were in readiness for the conveyance of a second vast army to complete the destruction of England. But England was equal to the occasion. Elizabeth's Government demanded fifteen ships of the city of London ; it fitted out thirty, besides raising a land force of 30,000 men and lending the Government £52,000 in ready money.

The Spanish fleet numbered one hundred and thirty huge galleons, the English only sixty sail, of lighter and less cumbrous build. The young English noblemen competed for the privilege of serving in it. The great Armada was ill designed for defying wind and weather in the English Channel. It manœuvred awkwardly, and, in the first encounters, proved itself powerless against the lighter ships of the English. A couple of fire-ships were sufficient to throw it into disorder; a season of storms set in, and the greater number of its galleons were swept to destruction.

The greatest Power in the world of that day had broken down in its attempt to crush the growing might of England, and the whole nation revelled in the exultant sense of victory.

B

VI

SHAKESPEARE AS ACTOR AND RETOUCHER OF OLD PLAYS—GREENE'S ATTACK

BETWEEN 1586 and 1592 we lose all trace of Shakespeare. We know only that he must have been an active member of a company of players. It is not proved that he ever belonged to any other company than the Earl of Leicester's, which owned the Black-friars, and afterwards the Globe, theatre. It is proved by several passages in contemporary writings that, partly as actor, partly as adapter of older plays for the use of the theatre, he had, at the age of twenty-eight, made a certain name for himself, and had therefore become the object of envy and hatred.

A passage in Spenser's *Colin Clouts Come Home Again*, referring to a poet whose Muse " doth like himself heroically sound," may with some probability, though not with certainty, be applied to Shakespeare. The theory is supported by the fact that the word " gentle " is here, as so often in after-life, attached to his personality. Against it we must place the circumstance that the poem, although not published till 1594, seems to have been composed as early as 1591, when Shakespeare's muse was as yet scarcely heroic, and that Drayton, who had written under the pseudonym of Rowland, may have been the poet alluded to.

The first indubitable allusion to Shakespeare is of a quite different nature. It occurs in a pamphlet written on his deathbed by the dramatist Robert Greene, entitled *A Groat's Worth of Wit bought with a Million of Repentance* (August 1592). In it the utterly degraded and penniless poet calls upon his friends, Marlowe, Lodge or Nash, and Peele (without mentioning their names), to give up their vicious life, their blasphemy, and their " getting many enemies by bitter words," holding himself up as a deterrent example; for he died, after a reckless life, of an illness said to have been induced by immoderate eating, and in such misery that he had to borrow money of his landlord, a poor shoe-maker, while his landlord's wife was the sole attendant of his dying hours. He was so poor that his clothes had to be sold to procure him food. He sent his wife these lines :—

" Doll, I charge thee, by the loue of our youth and by my soules rest, that thou wilte see this man paide ; for if hee and his wife had not succoured me, I had died in the streetes. ROBERT GREENE."

The passage in which he warns his friends and fellow-poets against the ingratitude of the players runs as follows:—

"Yes, trust them not: for there is an upstart crow, beautified with our feathers, that with his *Tygers heart wrapt in a Players hide*, supposes he is as well able to bumbast out a blanke verse as the best of you: and being an absolute *Johannes fac totum*, is in his owne conceit the only Shake-scene in a countrie."

The allusion to Shakespeare's name is unequivocal, and the words about the tiger's heart point to the outburst, "Oh Tyger's hart wrapt in a serpents hide!" which is found in two places: first in the play called *The True Tragedie of Richard Duke of Yorke, and the Death of the good King Henrie the Sixt*, and then (with "womans" substituted for "serpents"), in the third part of *King Henry VI.*, founded on the *True Tragedie*, and attributed to Shakespeare. It is preposterous to interpret this passage as an attack upon Shakespeare in his quality as an actor; Greene's words, beyond all doubt, convey an accusation of literary dishonesty. Everything points to the belief that Greene and Marlowe had collaborated in the older play, and that the former saw with disgust the success achieved by Shakespeare's adaptation of their text.

But that Shakespeare was already highly respected, and that the attack aroused general indignation, is proved by the apology put forth in December 1592 by Henry Chettle, who had published Greene's pamphlet. In the preface to his *Kind-hart's Dreame* he expressly deplores his indiscretion with regard to Shakespeare:—

"I am as sory as if the originall fault had beene my fault, because my selfe haue seene his demeanor no lesse ciuill than he exelent in the qualitie he professes. Besides, diuers of worship haue reported his vprightnes of dealing, which argues his honesty, and his facetious grace in writing, that aprooues his Art."

We see, then, that the company to which Shakespeare had attached himself, and in which he had already attracted notice as a promising poet, employed him to revise and furbish up the older pieces of their repertory. The theatrical announcements of the period would show us, even if we had no other evidence, that it was a constant practice to recast old plays, in order to heighten their powers of attraction. It is announced, for instance, that such-and-such a play will be acted as it was last presented before her Majesty, or before this or that nobleman. Poets sold their works outright to the theatre for such sums as five or ten pounds, or for a share in the receipts. As the interests of the theatre demanded that plays should not be printed, in order that rival companies might not obtain possession of them, they remained in manuscript (unless pirated), and the players could accordingly do what they pleased with the text.

None the less, of course, was the older poet apt to resent the re-touches made by the younger, as we see from this outburst of Greene's, and probably, too, from Ben Jonson's epigram, *On Poet-Ape*, even though this cannot, with any show of reason, be applied to Shakespeare.

In the view of the time, theatrical productions as a whole were not classed as literature. It was regarded as dishonourable for a man to sell his work first to a theatre and then to a book-seller, and Thomas Heywood declares, as late as 1630 (in the preface to his *Lucretia*), that he has never been guilty of this misdemeanour. We know, too, how much ridicule Ben Jonson incurred when, first among English poets, he in 1616 published his plays in a folio volume.

On the other hand, we see that not only Shakespeare's genius, but his personal amiability, the loftiness and charm of his nature, disarmed even those who, for one reason or another, had spoken disparagingly of his activity. As Chettle, after printing Greene's attack, hastened to make public apology, so also Ben Jonson, to whose ill-will and cutting allusions Shakespeare made no retort,[1] became, in spite of an unconquerable jealousy, his true friend and admirer, and after his death spoke of him warmly in prose, and with enthusiasm in verse, in the noble eulogy prefixed to the First Folio. His prose remarks upon Shakespeare's character are introduced by a critical observa-tion:—

"I remember the players have often mentioned it as an honour to Shakespeare, that in his writing (whatsoever he penned) he never blotted out a line. My answer hath been, Would he had blotted a thousand. Which they thought a malevolent speech. I had not told posterity this but for their ignorance, who chose that circumstance to commend their friend by, wherein he most faulted; and to justify mine own candour: for I loved the man, and do honour his memory, on this side idolatry, as much as any. He was (indeed) honest, and of an open and full nature; had an excellent phantasy, brave notions, and gentle expressions; wherein he flowed with that facility, that sometimes it was necessary he should be stopped: *Sufflaminandus erat*, as Augustus said of Haterius."

---

[1] He is said to have procured the production of Jonson's first play.

VII

THE "HENRY VI." TRILOGY

ONE might expect that it would be with the early plays in which Shakespeare only collaborated as with those Italian pictures of the best period of the Renaissance, in which the connoisseur identifies (for example) an angel's head by Leonardo in a Crucifixion of Andrea del Verrocchio's. The work of the pupil stands out sharp and clear, with pure contours, a picture within the picture, quite at odds with its style and spirit, but impressing us as a promise for the future. As a matter of fact, however, there is no analogy between the two cases.

A mystery hangs over the *Henry VI.* trilogy which neither Greene's venomous attack nor Chettle's apology enables us to clear up.

Of all the works attributed to Shakespeare, this is certainly the one whose origin affords most food for speculation. The inclusion of the three plays in the First Folio shows clearly that his comrades, who had full knowledge of the facts, regarded them as his literary property. That the two earlier plays which are preserved, the *First Part of the Contention* and the *True Tragedie* (answering to the second and third parts of *Henry VI.*), cannot be entirely Shakespeare's work is evidenced both by the imprint of the anonymous quartos and by the company which is stated to have produced them; for none of Shakespeare's genuine plays was published by this publisher or played by this company. It is proved quite clearly, too, by internal evidence, by the free and unrhymed versification of these plays. At the period from which they date, Shakespeare was still extremely addicted to the use of rhyme in his dramatic writing.

Nevertheless, the great majority of German Shakespeare students, and some English as well, are of opinion that the older plays are entirely Shakespeare's, either his first drafts or, as is more commonly maintained, stolen texts carelessly noted down.

Some English scholars, such as Malone and Dyce, go to the opposite extreme, and regard the second and third parts of *Henry VI.* as the work of another poet. The majority of English students look upon these plays as the result of Shakespeare's retouching of another man's, or rather other men's, work.

The affair is so complicated that none of these hypotheses is quite satisfactory.

Though there are doubtless in the older plays portions unworthy of Shakespeare, and more like the handiwork of Greene,
while others strongly suggest Marlowe, both in matter, style, and
versification, there are also passages in them which cannot be by
any one else than Shakespeare. And while most of the alterations
and additions which are found in the second and third parts of
Henry VI. bear the mark of unmistakable superiority, and are
Shakespearian in spirit no less than in style and versification,
there are at the same time others which are decidedly un-Shake-
spearian and can almost certainly be attributed to Marlowe. He
must, then, have collaborated with Shakespeare in the adaptation,
unless we suppose that his original text was carelessly printed
in the earlier quartos, and that it here reappears, in the Shakespearian *Henry VI.*, corrected and completed in accordance with
his manuscript.

I agree with Miss Lee, the writer of the leading treatise[1] on
these plays, and with the commentator in the Irving Edition, in
holding that Shakespeare was not responsible for all the alterations in the definitive text. There are several which I cannot
possibly believe to be his.

In the old quartos there appears not a line in any foreign
language. But in the Shakespearian plays we find lines and
exclamations in Latin scattered here and there, along with one in
French.[2] If the early quartos are founded on a text taken down
by ear, we can readily understand that the foreign expressions,
not being understood, should be omitted. Such foreign sentences
are extremely frequent in Marlowe, as in Kyd and the other
older dramatists; they appear in season and out of season, but
always in irreconcilable conflict with the sounder taste of our
time. Marlowe would even suffer a dying man to break out in a
French or Latin phrase as he gave up the ghost, and this occurs
here in two places (at Clifford's death and Rutland's). Shakespeare, who never bedizens his work with un-English phrases,
would certainly not place them in the mouths of dying men, and
least of all foist them upon an earlier purely English text.

Other additions also seem only to have restored the older form
of the plays—those, to wit, which really add nothing new, but
only elaborate, sometimes more copiously than is necessary or
tasteful, a thought already clearly indicated. The original omis-
sion in such instances appears almost certainly to have been
dictated by considerations of convenience in acting. One example
is Queen Margaret's long speech in Part II., Act iii. 2, which is
new with the exception of the first fourteen lines.

But there is another class of additions and alterations which
surprises us by being unmistakably in Marlowe's style. If these

---

[1] *New Shakspere Society's Transactions*, 1875-76, pp. 219-303.

[2] "Tantæne animis cœlestibus iræ !—Medice, te ipsum !—Gelidus timor occupat
artus—La fin couronne les œuvres—Di faciant ! laudis summa sit ista tuæ."

additions are really by Shakespeare, he must have been under the influence of Marlowe to a quite extraordinary degree. Swinburne has pointed out how entirely the verses which open the fourth act of the Second Part are Marlowesque in rhythm, imagination, and choice of words; but characteristic as are these lines—

> " And now loud howling wolves arouse the jades
> That drag the tragic melancholy night,"

they are by no means the only additions which seem to point to Marlowe. We feel his presence particularly in the additions to Iden's speeches at the end of the fourth act, in such lines as—

> " Set limb to limb, and thou art far the lesser;
> Thy hand is but a finger to my fist;
> Thy leg a stick, compared with this truncheon ; "

and especially in the concluding speech :—

> " Die, damned wretch, the curse of her that bare thee !
> And as I thrust thy body in with my sword,
> So wish I, I might thrust thy soul to hell.
> Hence will I drag thee headlong by the heels
> Unto a dunghill, which shall be thy grave,
> And there cut off thy most ungracious head."

There is Marlowesque emphasis in this wildness and ferocity, which reappears, in conjunction with Marlowesque learning, in Young Clifford's lines in the last act :—

> " Meet I an infant of the house of York,
> Into as many gobbets will I cut it,
> As wild Medea young Absyrtus did :
> In cruelty will I seek out my fame "—

and in those which, in Part III., Act iv. 2, are placed in the mouth of Warwick :—

> " Our scouts have found the adventure very easy :
> That as Ulysses, and stout Diomede,
> With sleight and manhood stole to Rhesus' tents,
> And brought from thence the Thracian fatal steeds ;
> So we, well cover'd with the night's black mantle,
> At unawares may beat down Edward's guard,
> And seize himself."

And as in the additions there are passages the whole style of which belongs to Marlowe, or bears the strongest traces of his influence, so also there are passages in the earlier text which in every respect recall the manner of Shakespeare. For example, in Part II., Act iii. 2, Warwick's speech :—

> " Who finds the heifer dead, and bleeding fresh,
>   And sees fast by a butcher with an axe,
>   But will suspect 'twas he that made the slaughter ? "

or Suffolk's to Margaret :—

> " If I depart from thee, I cannot live ;
>   And in thy sight to die, what were it else,
>   But like a pleasant slumber in thy lap ?
>   Here could I breathe my soul into the air,
>   As mild and gentle as the cradle-babe,
>   Dying with mother's dug between its lips."

Most Shakespearian, too, is the manner in which, in Part III., Act ii. 1, York's two sons are made to draw their characters, each in a single line, when they receive the tidings of their father's death :—

> " *Edward.* O, speak no more ! for I have heard too much.
>   *Richard.* Say, how he died, for I will hear it all."

Again, we seem to hear the voice of Shakespeare when Margaret, after they have murdered her son before her eyes, bursts forth (Part III., Act v. 5) :—

> " You have no children, butchers ! if you had
>   The thought of them would have stirred up remorse."

This passage anticipates, as it were, a celebrated speech in *Macbeth.* Most remarkable of all, however, are the Cade scenes in the Second Part. I cannot persuade myself that these were not from the very first the work of Shakespeare. It is evident that they cannot proceed from the pen of Marlowe. An attempt has been made to attribute them to Greene, on the ground that there are other folk-scenes in his works which display a similar strain of humour. But the difference is enormous. It is true that the text here follows the chronicle with extraordinary fidelity; but it was precisely in this ingenious adaptation of material that Shakespeare always showed his strength. And these scenes answer so completely to all the other folk-scenes in Shakespeare, and are so obviously the outcome of the habit of political thought which runs through his whole life, becoming ever more and more pronounced, that we cannot possibly accept them as showing only the trivial alterations and retouches which elsewhere distinguish his text from the older version.

These admissions made, however, there is on the whole no difficulty in distinguishing the work of other hands in the old texts. We can enjoy, point by point, not only Shakespeare's superiority, but his peculiar style, as we here find it in the very process of development; and we can study his whole method of work in the text which he ultimately produces.

We have here an almost unique opportunity of observing him in the character of a critical artist. We see what improvements he makes by a trivial retouch, or a mere rearrangement of words. Thus, when Gloucester says of his wife (Part. II., Act ii. 4)—

> " Uneath may she endure the flinty streets,
> To tread them with her tender-feeling feet,"

all his sympathy speaks in these words. In the old text it is she who says this of herself. In York's great soliloquy in the first act, beginning "Anjou and Maine are given to the French," the first twenty-four lines are Shakespeare's; the rest belong to the old text. From the second "Anjou and Maine" onwards, the verse is conventional and monotonous; the meaning ends with the end of each line, and a pause, as it were, ensues; whereas the verse of the opening passage is full of dramatic movement, life, and fire.

Again, if we turn to York's soliloquy in the third act (sc. I)—

> " Now, York, or never, steel thy fearful thoughts,"

and compare it in the two texts, we find their metrical differences so marked that, as Miss Lee has happily put it, the critic can no more doubt that the first version belongs to an earlier stage in the development of dramatic poetry, than the geologist can doubt that a stratum which contains simpler organisms indicates an earlier stage of the earth's development than one containing higher forms of organic life. There are portions of the Second Part which no one can believe that Shakespeare wrote, such as the old-fashioned fooling with Simpcox, which is quite in the manner of Greene. There are others which, without being unworthy of Shakespeare, not only indicate Marlowe in their general style, but are now and then mere variations of verses known to be his. Such, for example, is Margaret's line in Part III., Act i. :—

> " Stern Faulconbridge commands the narrow seas,"

which clearly echoes the line in Marlowe's *Edward II. :—*

> " The haughty Dane commands the narrow street."

What interests us most, perhaps, is the relation between Shakespeare and his predecessor with respect to the character of Gloucester. It cannot be denied or doubted that this character, the Richard III. of after-days, is completely outlined in the earlier text ; so that in reality Shakespeare's own tragedy of *Richard III.*, written so much later, is still quite Marlowesque in the fundamental conception of its protagonist. Gloucester's two great soliloquies in the third part of *Henry VI.* are especially instructive to study. In the first (iii. 2) the keynote of the passion is indeed struck by Marlowe, but all the finest passages are Shakespeare's. Take, for example, the following :—

> " Why then, I do but dream on sovereignty ;
> Like one that stands upon a promontory,
> And spies a far-off shore where he would tread,
> Wishing his foot were equal with his eye ;
> And chides the sea that sunders him from thence,
> Saying—he'll lade it dry to have his way :
> So do I wish the crown, being so far off,
> And so I chide the means that keep me from it ;
> And so I say—I'll cut the causes off,
> Flattering me with impossibilities."

The last soliloquy (v. 6), on the other hand, belongs entirely to the old play. A thoroughly Marlowesque turn of phrase meets us at the very beginning :—

> " See, how my sword weeps for the poor king's death."

Shakespeare has here left the powerful and admirable text untouched, except for the deletion of a single superfluous and weakening verse, "I had no father, I am like no father," which is followed by the profoundest and most remarkable lines in the play :—

> " I have no brother, I am like no brother ;
> And this word love, which greybeards call divine,
> Be resident in men like one another,
> And not in me : I am myself alone."

VIII

CHRISTOPHER MARLOWE AND HIS LIFE-WORK—
TITUS ANDRONICUS

THE man who was to be Shakespeare's first master in the drama
—a master whose genius he did not at the outset fully understand—was born two months before him. Christopher (Kit)
Marlowe, the son of a shoemaker at Canterbury, was a foundation scholar at the King's School of his native town; matricu-
lated at Cambridge in 1580; took the degree of B.A. in 1583,
and of M.A. at the age of twenty-three, after he had left the
University; appeared in London (so we gather from an old ballad)
as an actor at the Curtain Theatre; had the misfortune to break
his leg upon the stage; was no doubt on that account compelled
to give up acting; and seems to have written his first dramatic
work, *Tamburlaine the Great*, at latest in 1587. His development
was much quicker than Shakespeare's, he attained to comparative
maturity much earlier, and his culture was more systematic. Not
for nothing had he gone through the classical curriculum; the
influence of Seneca, the poet and rhetorician through whom
English tragedy comes into relation with the antique, is clearly
recognisable in him, no less than in his predecessors, the authors
of *Gorboduc* and *Tancred and Gismunda* (the former composed
by two, the latter by five poets in collaboration); only that the
construction of these plays, with their monologues and their
chorus, is directly imitated from Seneca, while the more independent Marlowe is influenced only in his diction and choice of
material.

In him the two streams begin to unite which have their
sources in the Biblical dramas of the Middle Ages and the later
allegorical folk-plays on the one hand, and, on the other hand, in
the Latin plays of antiquity. But he entirely lacks the comic
vein which we find in the first English imitations of Plautus and
Terence—in *Ralph Roister Doister* and in *Gammer Gurton's
Needle*, acted, respectively, in the middle of the century and in
the middle of the sixties, by Eton schoolboys and Cambridge
students.

Kit Marlowe is the creator of English tragedy. He it was
who established on the public stage the use of the unrhymed
iambic pentameter as the medium of English drama. He did not

invent English blank verse—the Earl of Surrey (who died in 1547) had used it in his translation of the *Æneid*, and it had been employed in the old play of *Gorboduc* and others which had been performed at court. But Marlowe was the first to address the great public in this measure, and he did so, as appears from the prologue to *Tamburlaine*, in express contempt for "the jigging veins of rhyming mother-wits" and "such conceits as clownage keeps in pay," seeking deliberately for tragic emphasis and "high astounding terms" in which to express the rage of Tamburlaine.

Before his day, rhymed couplets of long-drawn fourteen-syllable verse had been common in drama, and the monotony of these rhymes naturally hampered the dramatic life of the plays. Shakespeare does not seem at first to have appreciated Marlowe's reform, or quite to have understood the importance of this rejection of rhyme in dramatic writing. Little by little he came fully to realise it. In one of his first plays, *Love's Labour's Lost*, there are nearly twice as many rhymed as unrhymed verses, more than a thousand in all; in his latest works rhyme has disappeared. There are only two rhymes in *The Tempest*, and in *A Winter's Tale* none at all.

Similarly, in his first plays (like Victor Hugo in his first Odes), Shakespeare feels himself bound to make the sense end with the end of the verse; as time goes on, he gradually learns an ever freer movement. In *Love's Labour's Lost* there are eighteen end-stopped verses (in which the meaning ends with the line) for every one in which the sense runs on; in *Cymbeline* and *A Winter's Tale* they are only about two to one. This gradual development affords one method of determining the date of production of otherwise undated plays.

Marlowe seems to have led a wild life in London, and to have been entirely lacking in the commonplace virtues. He is said to have indulged in a perpetual round of dissipations, to have been dressed to-day in silk, to-morrow in rags, and to have lived in audacious defiance of society and the Church. Certain it is that he was killed in a brawl when only twenty-nine years old. He is said to have found a rival in company with his mistress, and to have drawn his dagger to stab him; but the other, a certain Francis Archer, wrested the dagger from his grasp, and thrust it through his eye into his brain. It is further related of him that he was an ardent and aggressive atheist, who called Moses a juggler and said that Christ deserved death more than Barabbas. These reports are probable enough. On the other hand, the assertion that he wrote books against the Trinity and uttered blasphemies with his latest breath, is evidently inspired by Puritan hatred for the theatre and everything concerned with it. The sole authority for these fables is Beard's *Theatre of God's Judgments* (1597), the work of a clergyman, a fanatical Puritan, which appeared six years after Marlowe's death.

There is no doubt that Marlowe led an extremely irregular life, but the legend of his debaucheries must be much exaggerated, if only from the fact that, though he was cut off before his thirtieth year, he has yet left behind him so large and puissant a body of work. The legend that he passed his last hours in blaspheming God is rendered doubly improbable by Chapman's express statement that it was in compliance with Marlowe's dying request that he continued his friend's paraphrase of *Hero and Leander*. The passionate, defiant youth, surcharged with genius, was fair game for the bigots and Pharisees, who found it only too easy to besmirch his memory.

It is evident that Marlowe's gorgeous and violent style, especially as it bursts forth in his earlier plays, made a profound impression upon the youthful Shakespeare. After Marlowe's death, Shakespeare made a kindly and mournful allusion to him in *As You Like It* (iii. 5), where Phebe quotes a line from his *Hero and Leander*:—

> " Dead shepherd ! now I find thy saw of might :
> ' Who ever lov'd, that lov'd not at first sight ? ' "

Marlowe's influence is unmistakable not only in the style and versification but in the sanguinary action of *Titus Andronicus*, clearly the oldest of the tragedies attributed to Shakespeare.

The evidence for the Shakespearian authorship of this drama of horrors, though mainly external, is weighty and, it would seem, decisive. Meres, in 1598, names it among the poet's works, and his friends included it in the First Folio. We know from a gibe in Ben Jonson's Induction to his *Bartholomew Fair* that it was exceedingly popular. It is one of the plays most frequently alluded to in contemporary writings, being mentioned twice as often as *Twelfth Night*, and four or five times as often as *Measure for Measure* or *Timon*. It depicts savage deeds, executed with the suddenness with which people of the sixteenth century were wont to obey their impulses, cruelties as heartless and systematic as those which characterised the age of Machiavelli. In short, it abounds in such callous atrocities as could not fail to make a deep impression on iron nerves and hardened natures.

These horrors are not, for the most part, of Shakespeare's invention.

An entry in Henslowe's diary of April 11, 1592, mentions for the first time a play named *Titus and Vespasian* (" tittus and vespacia "), which was played very frequently between that date and January 1593, and was evidently a prime favourite. In its English form this play is lost ; no Vespasian appears in our *Titus Andronicus*. But about 1600 a play was performed in Germany, by English actors, which has been preserved under the title, *Eine sehr klägliche Tragoedia von Tito Andronico und der hoffertigen Kayserin, darinnen denckwürdige actiones zubefinden*, and in this play a Vespasian duly appears, as well as the Moor Aaron, under the name of Morian; so that, clearly enough, we have here a translation, or rather a free adaptation, of the old play which formed the basis of Shakespeare's.

We see, then, that Shakespeare himself invented only a few of the horrors which form the substance of the play. The action, as he presents it, is briefly this:—

Titus Andronicus, returning to Rome after a victory over the Goths, is hailed as Emperor by the populace, but magnanimously hands over the crown to the rightful heir, Saturninus. Titus even wants to give him his daughter Lavinia in marriage, although she is already betrothed to the Emperor's younger brother Bassianus, whom she loves. When one of Titus's sons opposes this scheme, his father kills him on the spot.

In the meantime, Tamora, the captive Queen of the Goths, is brought before the young Emperor. In spite of her prayers, Titus has ordered the execution of her eldest son, as a sacrifice to the manes of his own sons who have fallen in the war; but as Tamora is more attractive to the Emperor than his destined bride, the young Lavinia, Titus makes no attempt to enforce the promise he has just made, and actually imagines that Tamora is sincere when she pretends to have forgotten all the injuries he has done her. Tamora, moreover, has been and is the mistress of the cruel and crafty monster Aaron, the Moor.

At the Moor's instigation, she induces her two sons to take advantage of a hunting party to murder Bassianus; whereupon they ravish Lavinia, and tear out her tongue and cut off her hands, so that she cannot denounce them either in speech or writing. They remain undetected, until at last Lavinia unmasks them by writing in the sand with a stick which she holds in her mouth. Two of Titus's sons are thrown into prison, falsely accused of the murder of their brother-in-law; and Aaron gives Titus to understand that their death is certain unless he ransoms them by cutting off his own right hand and sending it to the Emperor. Titus cuts off his hand, only to be informed by Aaron, with mocking laughter, that his sons are already beheaded—he can have their heads, but not themselves.

He now devotes himself entirely to revenge. Pretending madness, after the manner of Brutus, he lures Tamora's sons to his house, ties their hands behind their backs, and stabs them like pigs, while Lavinia, with the stumps of her arms, holds a basin to catch their blood. He bakes their heads in a pie, and serves it up to Tamora at a feast given in her honour, at which he appears disguised as a cook.

In the slaughter which now sets in, Tamora, Titus, and the Emperor are killed. Ultimately Aaron, who has tried to save the bastard Tamora has secretly borne him, is condemned to be buried alive up to the waist, and thus to starve to death. Titus's son Lucius is proclaimed Emperor.

It will be seen that not only are we here wading ankle-deep in blood, but that we are quite outside all historical reality. Among the many changes which Shakespeare has made in the old play is the dissociation of this motley tissue of horrors from the name of the Emperor Vespasian. The part which he plays in the older drama is here shared between Titus's brother Marcus and his son Lucius, who succeeds to the throne. The woman who answers to Tamora is of similar character in the old play, but is Queen of Ethiopia. Among the horrors which Shakespeare found ready made are the rape and mutilation of Lavinia and the way in which the criminals are discovered, the hewing off of Titus's hand, and the scenes in which he takes his revenge in the dual character of butcher and cook.

The old English poet evidently knew his Ovid and his Seneca. The mutilation of Lavinia comes from the *Metamorphoses* (the story of Procne), and the cannibal banquet from the same source, as well as from Seneca's *Thyestis*. The German version of the tragedy, however, is written in a wretchedly flat and anti-quated prose, while Shakespeare's is couched in Marlowesque pentameters.

The example set by Marlowe in *Tamburlaine* was no doubt in some measure to blame for the lavish effusion of blood in the play adapted by Shakespeare, which may in this respect be bracketed with two other contemporary dramas conceived under the influence of *Tamburlaine*, Robert Greene's *Alphonsus King of Arragon* and George Peele's *Battle of Alcazar*. Peele's tra-gedy has also its barbarous Moor, Muley Hamet, who, like Aaron, is probably the offspring of Marlowe's malignant Jew of Malta and his henchman, the sensual Ithamore.

Among the horrors added by Shakespeare, there are two which deserve a moment's notice. The first is Titus's sudden and unpremeditated murder of his son, who ventures to oppose his will. Shocking as it seems to us to-day, such an incident did not surprise the sixteenth century public, but rather appealed to them as a touch of nature. Such lives as Benvenuto Cellini's show that even in highly cultivated natures, anger, passion, and revenge were apt to take instantaneous effect in sanguinary deeds. Men of action were in those days as ungovernable as they were barbarously cruel when a sudden fury possessed them.

The other added trait is the murder of Tamora's son. We are reminded of the scene in *Henry VI.*, in which the young Prince Edward is murdered in the presence of Queen Margaret; and Tamora's entreaties for her son are among those verses in the play which possess the true Shakespearian ring.

Certain peculiar turns of phrase in *Titus Andronicus* remind us of Peele and Marlowe.[1]　But whole lines occur which Shakespeare repeats almost word for word.　Thus the verses—

> "She is a woman, therefore may be woo'd;
> She is a woman, therefore may be won,"

reappear very slightly altered in *Henry VI.*, Part I.:—

> "She's beautiful, and therefore to be woo'd;
> She is a woman, and therefore to be won;"

while a similar turn of phrase is found in Sonnet XLI. :—

> "Gentle thou art, and therefore to be won;
> Beauteous thou art, therefore to be assailed;"

and, finally, a closely related distich occurs in Richard the Third's famous soliloquy:

> "Was ever woman in this humour woo'd?
> Was ever woman in this humour won?"

It is true that the phrase "She is a woman, therefore may be won," occurs several times in Greene's romances, of earlier date than *Titus Andronicus*, and this seems to have been a sort of catchword of the period.

Although, on the whole, one may certainly say that this rough-hewn drama, with its piling-up of external effects, has very little in common with the tone or spirit of Shakespeare's mature tragedies, yet we find scattered through it lines in which the most diverse critics have professed to recognise Shakespeare's revising touch, and to catch the ring of his voice.

Few will question that such a line as this, in the first scene of the play—

> "Romans—friends, followers, favourers of my right!"

comes from the pen which afterwards wrote *Julius Cæsar*.　I may mention, for my own part, that lines which, as I read the play through before acquainting myself in detail with English criticism, had struck me as patently Shakespearian, proved to be precisely the lines which the best English critics attribute to Shakespeare. To one's own mind such coincidences of feeling naturally carry conviction.　I may cite as an example Tamora's speech (iv. 4):—

---

[1] "Gallops the zodiac" (ii. 1, line 7) occurs twice in Peele.　The phrase "A thousand deaths" (same scene, line 79) appears in Marlowe's *Tamburlaine*.

" King, be thy thoughts imperious, like thy name.
Is the sun dimm'd, that gnats do fly in it?
The eagle suffers little birds to sing,
And is not careful what they mean thereby;
Knowing that with the shadow of his wings
He can at pleasure stint their melody.
Even so may'st thou the giddy men of Rome."

Unmistakably Shakespearian, too, are Titus's moving lament (iii. 1) when he learns of Lavinia's mutilation, and his half-distraught outbursts in the following scene foreshadow even in detail a situation belonging to the poet's culminating period, the scene between Lear and Cordelia when they are both prisoners. Titus says to his hapless daughter:

" Lavinia, go with me:
I'll to thy closet; and go read with thee
Sad stories chanced in the times of old."

In just the same spirit Lear exclaims:

" Come, let's away to prison . . .
        .   .   .   .   so we'll live,
And pray, and sing, and tell old tales."

It is quite unnecessary for any opponent of blind or exaggerated Shakespeare-worship to demonstrate to us the impossibility of bringing *Titus Andronicus* into harmony with any other than a barbarous conception of tragic poetry. But although the play is simply omitted without apology from the Danish translation of Shakespeare's works, it must by no means be overlooked by the student, whose chief interest lies in observing the genesis and development of the poet's genius. The lower its point of departure, the more marvellous its soaring flight.

IX

SHAKESPEARE'S CONCEPTION OF THE RELATIONS OF THE SEXES—HIS MARRIAGE VIEWED IN THIS LIGHT—LOVE'S LABOUR'S LOST—ITS MATTER AND STYLE—JOHN LYLY AND EUPHUISM—THE PERSONAL ELEMENT

DURING these early years in London, Shakespeare must have been conscious of spiritual growth with every day that passed. With his inordinate appetite for learning, he must every day have gathered new impressions in his many-sided activity as a hard-working actor, a furbisher-up of old plays in accordance with the taste of the day for scenic effects, and finally as a budding poet, in whose heart every mood thrilled into melody, and every conception clothed itself in dramatic form. He must have felt his spirit light and free, not least, perhaps, because he had escaped from his home in Stratford.

Ordinary knowledge of the world is sufficient to suggest that his association with a village girl eight years older than himself could not satisfy him or fill his life. The study of his works confirms this conjecture. It would, of course, be unreasonable to attribute conscious and deliberate autobiographical import to speeches torn from their context in different plays; but there are none the less several passages in his dramas which may fairly be taken as indicating that he regarded his marriage in the light of a youthful folly. Take, for example, this passage in *Twelfth Night* (ii. 4):—

> "*Duke.* What kind of woman is't?
> *Vio.*   Of your complexion.
> *Duke.* She is not worth thee then.   What years, i' faith?
> *Vio.* About your years, my lord.
> *Duke.* Too old, by Heaven.   Let still the woman take
> An elder than herself; so wears she to him,
> So sways she level in her husband's heart:
> For, boy, however we do praise ourselves,
> Our fancies are more giddy and unfirm,
> More longing, wavering, sooner lost and worn,
> Than women's are.
> *Vio.*   I think it well, my lord.

Duke. Then, let thy love be younger than thyself,
Or thy affection cannot hold the bent ;
For women are as roses, whose fair flower,
Being once display'd, doth fall that very hour."

And this is in the introduction to the Fool's exquisite song about the power of love, that song which " The spinsters and the knitters in the sun And the free maids, that weave their thread with bones, Do use to chant "—Shakespeare's loveliest lyric.

There are passages in other plays which seem to show traces of personal regret at the memory of this early marriage and the circumstances under which it came about. In the *Tempest*, for instance, we have Prospero's warning to Ferdinand (iv. 1):—

" If thou dost break her virgin-knot before
All sanctimonious ceremonies may,
With full and holy rite, be minister'd,
No sweet aspersion shall the heavens let fall
To make this contract grow, but barren hate,
Sour-ey'd disdain, and discord, shall bestrew
The union of your bed with weeds so loathly,
That you shall hate it both."

Two of the comedies of Shakespeare's first period are, as we might expect, imitations, and even in part adaptations, of older plays. By comparing them, where it is possible, with these earlier works, we can discover, among other things, the thoughts to which Shakespeare, in these first years in London, was most intent on giving utterance. It thus appears that he held strong views as to the necessary subordination of the female to the male, and as to the trouble caused by headstrong, foolish, or jealous women.

His *Comedy of Errors* is modelled upon the *Menæchmi* of Plautus, or rather on an English play of the same title dating from 1580, which was not itself taken direct from Plautus, but from Italian adaptations of the old Latin farce. Following the example of Plautus in the *Amphitruo*, Shakespeare has supplemented the confusion between the two Antipholuses by a parallel and wildly improbable confusion between their serving-men, who both go by the same name and are likewise twins. But it is in the contrast between the two female figures, the married sister Adriana and the unmarried Luciana, that we catch the personal note in the play. On account of the confusion of persons, Adriana rages against her husband, and is at last on the point of plunging him into lifelong misery. To her complaint that he has not come home at the appointed time, Luciana answers :—

" A man is master of his liberty :
Time is their master ; and, when they see time,
They'll go, or come : if so, be patient, sister.

Adriana. Why should their liberty than ours be more?
Luciana. Because their business still lies out o' door.
Adr. Look, when I serve him so, he takes it ill.
Luc. O! know he is the bridle of your will.
Adr. There's none but asses will be bridled so.
Luc. Why, headstrong liberty is lash'd with woe.
There's nothing situate under heaven's eye
But hath his bound, in earth, in sea, in sky:
The beasts, the fishes, and the winged fowls,
Are their males' subjects, and at their controls.
Men, more divine, the masters of all these,
Lords of the wide world, and wild wat'ry seas,

Are masters to their females, and their lords:
Then, let your will attend on their accords."

In the last act of the comedy, Adriana, speaking to the Abbess accuses her husband of running after other women :—

" *Abbess.* You should for that have reprehended him.
Adriana. Why, so I did.
Abb.   Ay, but not rough enough.
Adr. As roughly as my modesty would let me.
Abb. Haply, in private.
Adr.   And in assemblies too.
Abb. Ay, but not enough.
Adr. It was the copy of our conference.
In bed, he slept not for my urging it:
At board, he fed not for my urging it;
Alone, it was the subject of my theme;
In company, I often glanced it:
Still did I tell him it was vile and bad.
    Abb. And therefore came it that the man was mad:
The venom clamours of a jealous woman
Poison more deadly than a mad dog's tooth.
It seems, his sleeps were hinder'd by thy railing,
And thereof comes it that his head is light.
Thou say'st, his meat was sauc'd with thy upbraidings:
Unquiet meals make ill digestions;
Thereof the raging fire of fever bred:
And what's a fever but a fit of madness?"

At least as striking is the culminating point of Shakespeare's adaptation of the old play called *The Taming of a Shrew.* He took very lightly this piece of task-work, executed, it would seem, to the order of his fellow-players. In point of diction and metre it is much less highly finished than others of his youthful comedies; but if we compare the Shakespearian play (in whose title the Shrew receives the definite instead of the indefinite article) point by point with the original, we obtain an invaluable glimpse into Shakespeare's comic, as formerly into his tragic, workshop. Few examples are so instructive as this.

Many readers have no doubt wondered what was Shakespeare's design in presenting this piece, of all others, in the framework which we Danes know in Holberg's [1] *Jeppe paa Bjerget*. The answer is, that he had no particular design in the matter. He took the framework ready-made from the earlier play, which, how ever, he throughout remodelled and improved, not to say re-crea ted. It is not only far ruder and coarser than Shakespeare's, but does not redeem its crude puerility by any raciness or power.

Nowhere does the difference appear more decisively than in the great speech in which Katharine, cured of her own shrewishness, closes the play by bringing the other rebellious women to reason. In the old play she begins with a whole cosmogony: "The first world was a form without a form," until God, the King of kings, "in six days did frame his heavenly work ":—

> " Then to his image he did make a man,
>   Olde Adam, and from his side asleepe
>   A rib was taken, of which the Lord did make
>   The woe of man, so termd by Adam then,
>   Woman for that by her came sinne to vs,
>   And for her sin was Adam doomd to die.
>   As Sara to her husband, so should we
>   Obey them, loue them, keepe and nourish them
>   If they by any meanes doo want our helpes,
>   Laying our handes vnder theire feete to tread,
>   If that by that we might procure there ease."

And she herself sets the example by placing her hand under her husband's foot.

Shakespeare omits all this theology and skips the Scriptural authorities, but only to arrive at the self-same result:—

> " Fie, fie ! unknit that threatening unkind brow,
>   And dart not scornful glances from those eyes,
>   To wound thy lord, thy king, thy governor.
> .   .   .   .   .   .
>   A woman mov'd is like a fountain troubled,
>   Muddy, ill-seeming, thick, bereft of beauty ;
>   And, while it is so, none so dry or thirsty
>   Will deign to sip, or touch one drop of it.
>   Thy husband is thy lord, thy life, thy keeper,
>   Thy head, thy sovereign ; one that cares for thee,
>   And for thy maintenance ; commits his body
>   To painful labour, both by sea and land,
>   To watch the night in storms, the day in cold,
>   Whilst thou liest warm at home, secure and safe ;

---

[1] Ludvig Holberg (1684-1754), the great comedy-writer of Denmark, and founder of the Danish stage.—(TRANS.)

> And craves no other tribute at thy hands,
> But love, fair looks, and true obedience,
> Too little payment for so great a debt.
> Such duty as the subject owes the prince,
> Even such a woman oweth to her husband ;
> And when she's froward, peevish, sullen, sour,
> And not obedient to his honest will,
> What is she but a foul contending rebel,
> And graceless traitor to her loving lord ? ”

In these adapted plays, then, partly from the nature of their subjects and partly because his thoughts ran in that direction, we find Shakespeare chiefly occupied with the relation between man and woman, and specially between husband and wife. They are not, however, his first works. At the age of five-and-twenty or thereabouts Shakespeare began his independent dramatic production, and, following the natural bent of youth and youthful vivacity, he began it with a light and joyous comedy.

We have several reasons, partly metrical (the frequency of rhymes), partly technical (the dramatic weakness of the play), for supposing *Love's Labour's Lost* to be his earliest comedy. Many allusions point to 1589 as the date of this play in its original form. For instance, the dancing horse mentioned in i. 2 was first exhibited in 1589; the names of the characters, Biron, Longaville, Dumain (Duc du Maine), suggest those of men who were prominent in French politics between 1581 and 1590; and, finally, when we remember that the King of Navarre, as the Princess's betrothed, becomes heir to the throne of France, we cannot but conjecture a reference to Henry of Navarre, who mounted that throne precisely in 1589. The play has not, however, reached us in its earliest form; for the title-page of the quarto edition shows that it was revised and enlarged on the occasion of its performance before Elizabeth at Christmas 1597. There are not a few places in which we can trace the revision, the original form having been inadvertently retained along with the revised text. This is apparent in Biron's long speech in the fourth act, sc. 3:—

> “ For when would you, my lord, or you, or you,
> Have found the ground of study's excellence,
> Without the beauty of a woman's face ?
> From women's eyes this doctrine I derive :
> They are the ground, the books, the academes,
> From whence doth spring the true Promethean fire.”

This belongs to the older text. Farther on in the speech, where we find the same ideas repeated in another and better form, we have evidently the revised version before us:—

> “ For when would you, my liege, or you, or you,
> In leaden contemplation have found out

Such fiery numbers, as the prompting eyes
Of beauty's tutors have enrich'd you with?
    .   .   .   .

From women's eyes this doctrine I derive:
They sparkle still the right Promethean fire,
They are the books, the arts, the academes,
That show, contain, and nourish all the world;
Else none at all in aught proves excellent."

The last two acts, which far surpass the earlier ones, have evidently been revised with special care, and some details, especially in the parts assigned to the Princess and Biron, now and then reveal Shakespeare's maturer style and tone of feeling.

No original source has been found for this first attempt of the young Stratfordian in the direction of comedy. For the first, and perhaps for the last time, he seems to have sought for no external stimulus, but set himself to evolve everything from within. The result is that, dramatically, the play is the slightest he ever wrote. It has scarcely ever been performed even in England, and may, indeed, be described as unactable.

It is a play of two motives. The first, of course, is love— what else should be the theme of a youthful poet's first comedy? —but love without a trace of passion, almost without deep personal feeling, a love which is half make-believe, tricked out in word-plays. For the second theme of the comedy is language itself, poetic expression for its own sake—a subject round which all the meditations of the young poet must necessarily have centred, as, in the midst of a cross-fire of new impressions, he set about the formation of a vocabulary and a style.

The moment the reader opens this first play of Shakespeare's, he cannot fail to observe that in several of his characters the poet is ridiculing absurdities and artificialities in the manner of speech of the day, and, moreover, that his personages, as a whole, display a certain half-sportive luxuriance in their rhetoric as well as in their wit and banter. They seem to be speaking, not in order to inform, persuade, or convince, but simply to relieve the pressure of their imagination, to play with words, to worry at them, split them up and recombine them, arrange them in alliterative sequences, or group them in almost identical antithetic clauses; at the same time making sport no less fantastical with the ideas the words represent, and illustrating them by new and far-fetched comparisons; until the dialogue appears not so much a part of the action or an introduction to it, as a tournament of words, clashing and swaying to and fro, while the rhythmic music of the verse and prose in turns expresses exhilaration, tenderness, affectation, the joy of life, gaiety or scorn. Although there is a certain superficiality about it all, we can recognise in it that exuberance of all the vital spirits which characterises the Renaissance. To the appeal—

" White-handed mistress, one sweet word with thee,"

comes the answer—

" Honey, and milk, and sugar : there are three."

And well may Boyet say (v. 2):—

> " The tongues of mocking wenches are as keen
> As is the razor's edge invisible,
> Cutting a smaller hair than may be seen ;
> Above the sense of sense, so sensible
> Seemeth their conference ; their conceits have wings
> Fleeter than arrows, bullets, wind, thought, swifter things."

Boyet's words, however, refer merely to the youthful gaiety and quickness of wit which may be found in all periods. We have here something more than that: the diction of the leading characters, and the various extravagances of expression cultivated by the subordinate personages, bring us face to face with a linguistic phenomenon which can be understood only in the light of history.

The word Euphuism is employed as a common designation for these eccentricities of style—a word which owes its origin to John Lyly's romance, *Euphues, the Anatomy of Wit*, published in 1578. Lyly was also the author of nine plays, all written before 1589, and there is no doubt that he exercised a very important influence upon Shakespeare's dramatic style.

But it is a very narrow view of the matter which finds in him the sole originator of the wave of mannerism which swept over the English poetry of the Renaissance.

The movement was general throughout Europe. It took its rise in the new-born enthusiasm for the antique literatures, in comparison with whose dignity of utterance the vernacular seemed low and vulgar. In order to approximate to the Latin models, men devised an exaggerated and dilated phraseology, heavy with images, and even sought to attain amplitude of style by placing side by side the vernacular word and the more exquisite foreign expression for the same object. Thus arose the *alto estilo*, the *estilo culto*. In Italy, the disciples of Petrarch, with their *concetti*, were dominant in poetry; in Shakespeare's own time, Marini came to the front with his antitheses and word-plays. In France, Ronsard and his school obeyed the general tendency. In Spain, the new style was represented by Guevara, who directly influenced Lyly.

John Lyly was about ten years older than Shakespeare. He was born in Kent in 1553 or 1554, of humble parentage. Nevertheless he obtained a full share of the literary culture of his time, studied at Oxford, probably by the assistance of Lord Burleigh, took his Master's degree in 1575, afterwards went to Cambridge, and eventually, no doubt on account of the success of his *Euphues*, found a position at the court of Elizabeth. For a period of ten years he was Court Poet, what in our days would be called Poet Laureate. But his position was without emolument. He was always hoping in vain for the post of Master of the Revels, and two touching letters to Elizabeth, the one dated 1590, the other 1593, in which he petitions for this appointment, show that after ten years' labour at court he felt himself a ship-wrecked man, and after thirteen years gave himself up to despair. All the duties and responsibilities of the office he coveted were heaped upon him, but he was denied the appointment itself. Like Greene and Marlowe, he lived a miserable life, and died in 1606, poor and indebted, leaving his family in destitution.

His book, *Euphues*, is written for the court of Elizabeth. The Queen herself studied and translated the ancient authors, and it was the fashion of her court to deal incessantly in mytho-logical comparisons and allusions to antiquity. Lyly shows this tendency in all his writings. He quotes Cicero, imitates Plautus, cites numberless verses from Virgil and Ovid, reproduces almost word for word in his *Euphues* Plutarch's *Treatise on Education*, and borrows from Ovid's *Metamorphoses* the themes of several of his plays. In *A Midsummer Night's Dream*, when Bottom appears with an ass's head and exclaims, "I have a reasonable good ear for music; let's have the tongs and the bones," we may doubtless trace the incident back to the metamorphosis of Midas in Ovid, but through the medium of Lyly's *Mydas*.

It was not merely the relation of the age to antiquity that produced the fashionable style. The new intercourse between country and country had quite as much to do with it. Before the invention of printing, each country had been spiritually isolated; but the international exchange of ideas had by this time become very much easier. Every European nation begins in the sixteenth century to provide itself with a library of translations. Foreign manners and fashions, in language as well as in costume, came into vogue, and helped to produce a heterogeneous and motley style.

In England, moreover, we have to note the very important fact that, precisely at the time when the Renaissance began to bear literary fruit, the throne was occupied by a woman, and one who, without possessing any delicate literary sense or refined artistic taste, was interested in the intellectual movement. Vain, and inclined to secret gallantries, she demanded, and received, incessant homage, for the most part in extravagant mythological terms, from the ablest of her subjects—from Sidney, from Spenser, from Raleigh—and was determined, in short, that the whole litera-ture of the time should turn towards her as its central point. Shakespeare was the only great poet of the period who absolutely declined to comply with this demand.

It followed from the relation in which literature stood to Elizabeth that it addressed itself as a whole to women, and especially to ladies of position. *Euphues* is a ladies' book. The new style may be described, not inaptly, as the development of a more refined method of address to the fair sex.

Sir Philip Sidney, in a masque, had done homage to Elizabeth, then forty-five years old, as "the Lady of the May." A letter which Sir Walter Raleigh, after his disgrace, addressed from his prison to Sir Robert Cecil on the subject of Elizabeth, affords a particularly striking example of the Euphuistic style, admirably fitted as it certainly was to express the passion affected by a soldier of forty for the maiden of sixty who held his fate in her hands :—

"While she was yet nigher at hand, that I might hear of her once in two or three days, my sorrows were the less ; but even now my heart is cast into the depth of all misery. I that was wont to behold her riding like Alexander, hunting like Diana, walking like Venus, the gentle wind blowing her fair hair about her pure cheeks like a nymph ; sometime sitting in the shade like a goddess ; sometime singing like an angel ; sometime playing like Orpheus. Behold the sorrow of this world ! Once amiss, hath bereaved me of all." [1]

The German scholar Landmann, who has devoted special study to Euphuism,[2] has justly pointed out that the greatest extravagances of style, and the worst sins against taste, of that period are always to be found in books written for ladies, celebrating the charms of the fair sex, and seeking to please by means of highly elaborated wit.

This may have been the point of departure of the new style ; but it soon ceased to address itself specially to feminine readers, and became a means of gratifying the propensity of the men of the Renaissance to mirror their whole nature in their speech, making it peculiar to the point of affectation, and affected to the point of the most daring mannerism. Euphuism ministered to their passion for throwing all they said into high and highly coloured relief, for polishing it till it shone and sparkled like real or paste diamonds in the sunshine, for making it ring, and sing, and chime, and rhyme, without caring whether reason took any share in the sport.

As a slight but characteristic illustration of this tendency, note the reply of the page, Moth, to Armado (iii. 1) :—

"*Moth.* Master, will you win your love with a French brawl?
"*Arm.* How meanest thou ? brawling in French ?
"*Moth.* No, my complete master ; but to jig off a tune at the tongue's end, canary to it with your feet, humour it with turning up your eyelids, sigh a note, and sing a note ; sometime through the throat, as if you

---

[1] *Raleigh*, by Edmund Gosse (English Worthies Series), p. 57
[2] *New Shakspere Society's Transactions*, 1880-86, Pt. ii. p. 241.

swallowed love with singing love; sometime through the nose, as if you snuffed up love by smelling love; with your hat, penthouse-like, o'er the shop of your eyes; with your arms crossed on your thin belly-doublet, like a rabbit on a spit; or your hands in your pocket, like a man after the old painting; and keep not too long in one tune, but a snip and away. These are complements, these are humours, these betray nice wenches, that would be betrayed without these, and make them men of note (do you note me?), that most are affected to these."

Landmann has conclusively proved that John Lyly's *Euphues* is only an imitation, and at many points a very close imitation, of the Spaniard Guevara's book, an imaginary biography of Marcus Aurelius, which, in the fifty years since its publication, had been six times translated into English. It was so popular that one of these translations passed through no fewer than twelve editions. Both in style and matter *Euphues* follows Guevara's book, which, in Sir Thomas North's adaptation, bears the title of *The Dial of Princes.*

The chief characteristics of Euphuism were parallel and assonant antitheses, long strings of comparisons with real or imaginary natural phenomena (borrowed for the most part from Pliny's *Natural History*), a partiality for images from antique history and mythology, and a love of alliteration.

Not till a later date did Shakespeare ridicule Euphuism properly so called—to wit, in that well-known passage in *Henry IV.,* Part I., where Falstaff plays the king. In his speech beginning "Peace, good pint-pot! peace, good tickle-brain!" Shakespeare deliberately parodies Lyly's similes from natural history. Falstaff says:—

"Harry, I do not only marvel where thou spendest thy time, but also how thou art accompanied: for though the camomile, the more it is trodden on, the faster it grows, yet youth, the more it is wasted, the sooner it wears."

Compare with this the following passage from Lyly (cited by Landmann):—

"Too much studie doth intoxicate their braines, for (say they) although yron, the more it is used, the brighter it is, yet silver with much wearing doth wast to nothing . . . though the Camomill, the more it is troden and pressed downe, the more it spreadeth, yet the Violet, the oftner it is handeled and touched, the sooner it withereth and decayeth."

Falstaff continues in the same exquisite strain:—

"There is a thing, Harry, which thou hast often heard of, and it is known to many in our land by the name of pitch: this pitch, as ancient writers do report, doth defile; so doth the company thou keepest."

This citation of "ancient writers" in proof of so recondite a phenomenon as the stickiness of pitch is again pure Lyly. Yet again, the adjuration, "Now I do not speak to thee in drink, but in tears; not in pleasure, but in passion; not in words only, but in woes also," is an obvious travesty of the Euphuistic style.

Strictly speaking, it is not against Euphuism itself that Shakespeare's youthful satire is directed in *Love's Labour's Lost*. It is certain collateral forms of artificiality in style and utterance that are aimed at. In the first place, bombast, represented by the ridiculous Spaniard, Armado (the suggestion of the Invincible Armada in the name cannot be unintentional); in the next place, pedantry, embodied in the schoolmaster Holofernes, for whom tradition states that Florio, the teacher of languages and translator of Montaigne, served as a model—a supposition, however, which seems scarcely probable when we remember Florio's close connection with Shakespeare's patron, Southampton. Further, we find throughout the play the over-luxuriant and far-fetched method of expression, universally characteristic of the age, which Shakespeare himself had as yet by no means succeeded in shaking off. Only towards the close does he rise above it and satirise it. That is the intent of Biron's famous speech (v. 2):—

> "Taffata phrases, silken terms precise,
> Three-pil'd hyperboles, spruce affectation,
> Figures pedantical: these summer-flies
> Have blown me full of maggot ostentation.
> I do forswear them; and I here protest,
> By this white glove, (how white the hand, God knows)
> Henceforth my wooing mind shall be express'd
> In russet yeas, and honest kersey noes."

In the very first scene of the play, the King describes Armado, in too indulgent terms, as—

> "A refined traveller of Spain;
> A man in all the world's new fashion planted,
> That hath a mint of phrases in his brain;
> One, whom the music of his own vain tongue
> Doth ravish like enchanting harmony."

Holofernes the pedant, nearly a century and a half before Holberg's Else Skolemesters,[1] expresses himself very much as she does:—

"*Holofernes*. The posterior of the day, most generous sir, is liable, congruent, and measurable for the afternoon: the word is well cull'd, chose; sweet and apt, I do assure you, sir; I do assure."

---

[1] The schoolmaster's wife in Ludvig Holberg's inimitable comedy, *Barselstuen.* —(TRANS.)

Armado's bombast may probably be accepted as a not too extravagant caricature of the bombast of the period. Certain it is that the schoolmaster Rombus, in Sir Philip Sidney's *Lady of the May*, addresses the Queen in a strain no whit less ridiculous than that of Holofernes. But what avails the justice of a parody if, in spite of the art and care lavished upon it, it remains as tedious as the mannerism it ridicules! And this is unfortunately the case in the present instance. Shakespeare had not yet attained the maturity and detachment of mind which could enable him to rise high above the follies he attacks, and to sweep them aside with full authority. He buries himself in them, circumstantially demonstrates their absurdities, and is still too inexperienced to realise how he thereby inflicts upon the spectator and the reader the full burden of their tediousness. It is very characteristic of Elizabeth's taste that, even in 1598, she could still take pleasure in the play. All this fencing with words appealed to her quick intelligence; while, with the unabashed sensuousness characteristic of the daughter of Henry VIII. and Anne Boleyn, she found entertainment in the playwright's freedom of speech, even, no doubt, in the equivocal badinage between Boyet and Maria (iv. 1).

As was to be expected, Shakespeare is here more dependent on models than in his later works. From Lyly, the most popular comedy-writer of the day, he probably borrowed the idea of his Armado, who answers pretty closely to Sir Tophas in Lyly's *Endymion*, copied, in his turn, from Pyrgopolinices, the boastful soldier of the old Latin comedy. It is to be noted, also, that the braggart and pedant, the two comic figures of this play, are permanent types on the Italian stage, which in so many ways influenced the development of English comedy.

The personal element in this first sportive production is, however, not difficult to recognise : it is the young poet's mirthful protest against a life immured within the hard-and-fast rules of an artificial asceticism, such as the King of Navarre wishes to impose upon his little court, with its perpetual study, its vigils, its fasts, and its exclusion of womankind. Against this life of unnatural constraint the comedy pleads with the voice of Nature, especially through the mouth of Biron, in whose speeches, as Dowden has rightly remarked, we can not infrequently catch the accent of Shakespeare himself. In Biron and his Rosaline we have the first hesitating sketch of the masterly Benedick and Beatrice of *Much Ado About Nothing*. The best of Biron's speeches, those which are in unrhymed verse, we evidently owe to the revision of 1598; but they are conceived in the spirit of the original play, and merely express Shakespeare's design in stronger and clearer terms than he was at first able to compass. Even at the end of the third act Biron is still combating as well as he can the power of love :—

> "What! I love! I sue! I seek a wife!
> A woman, that is like a German clock,
> Still a repairing, ever out of frame,
> And never going aright, being a watch,
> But being watch'd that it may still go right!"

But his great and splendid speech in the fourth act is like a hymn to that God of Battles who is named in the title of the play, and whose outpost skirmishes form its matter:—

> "Other slow arts entirely keep the brain,
> And therefore, finding barren practisers,
> Scarce show a harvest of their heavy toil;
> But love, first learned in a lady's eyes,
> Lives not alone immured in the brain,
> But, with the motion of all elements,
> Courses as swift as thought in every power,
> And gives to every power a double power,
> Above their functions and their offices.
> It adds a precious seeing to the eye;
> A lover's eyes will gaze an eagle blind;
> A lover's ear will hear the lowest sound,
> When the suspicious head of theft is stopp'd:
> Love's feeling is more soft, and sensible,
> Than are the tender horns of cockled snails.
>
> .   .   .   .   .   .
>
> Never durst poet touch a pen to write,
> Until his ink were temper'd with Love's sighs;
> O! then his lines would ravish savage ears,
> And plant in tyrants mild humility."

We must take Biron-Shakespeare at his word, and believe that in these vivid and tender emotions he found, during his early years in London, the stimulus which taught him to open his lips in song.

X

LOVE'S LABOUR'S WON: THE FIRST SKETCH OF ALL'S WELL THAT ENDS WELL—THE COMEDY OF ERRORS—THE TWO GENTLEMEN OF VERONA

As a counterpart to the comedy of *Love's Labour's Lost*, Shakespeare soon after composed another, entitled *Love's Labour's Won*. This we learn from the celebrated passage in Francis Meres' *Palladis Tamia*, where he enumerates the plays which Shakespeare had written up to that date, 1598. We know, however, that no play of that name is now included among the poet's works. Since it is scarcely conceivable that a play of Shakespeare's, once acted, should have been entirely lost, the only question is, which of the extant comedies originally bore that title. But in reality there is no question at all: the play is *All's Well that Ends Well*—not, of course, as we now possess it, in a form and style belonging to a quite mature period of the poet's life, but as it stood before the searching revision, of which it shows evident traces.

We cannot, indeed, restore the play as it originally issued from Shakespeare's youthful imagination. But there are passages in it which evidently belong to the older version, rhymed conversations, or at any rate fragments of dialogue, rhymed letters in sonnet form, and numerous details which entirely correspond with the style of *Love's Labour's Lost*.

The piece is a dramatisation of Boccaccio's story of Gillette of Narbonne. Only the comic parts are of Shakespeare's invention; he has added the characters of Parolles, Lafeu, the Clown, and the Countess. Even in the original sketch he no doubt gave new depth and vitality to the leading characters, who are mere outlines in the story. The comedy, as we know, has for its heroine a young woman who loves the haughty Bertram with an unrequited and despised passion, cures the King of France of a dangerous sickness, claims as her reward the right to choose a husband from among the courtiers, chooses Bertram, is repudiated by him, and, after a nocturnal meeting at which she takes the place of another woman whom he believes himself to have seduced, at last overcomes his resistance and is acknowledged as his wife.

Shakespeare has here not only shown the unquestioning acceptance of his original, which was usual even in his riper years,

but has transferred to his play all its peculiarities and impro-
babilities. Even the psychological crudities he has swallowed as
they stand—such, for instance, as the fact of a delicate woman
forcing herself under cover of night upon the man who has
left his home and country for the express purpose of escaping
from her.

Shakespeare has drawn in Helena a patient Griselda, that
type of loving and cruelly maltreated womanhood which reappears
in German poetry in Kleist's *Käthchen von Heilbronn*—the woman
who suffers everything in inexhaustible tenderness and humility,
and never falters in her love until in the end she wins the rebellious heart.

The pity is that the unaccommodating theme compelled Shakespeare to make this pearl among women in the end enforce her
rights, after the man she adores has not only treated her with
contemptuous brutality, but has, moreover, shown himself a liar
and hound in his attempt to blacken the character of the Italian
girl whose lover he believes himself to have been.

It is very characteristic of the English renaissance, and of the
public which Shakespeare had in view in his early plays, that he
should make this noble heroine take part with Parolles in the long
and jocular conversation (i. 1) on the nature of virginity, which is
one of the most indecorous passages in his works. This dialogue
must certainly belong to the original version of the play.

We must remember that Helena, in that version, was in all
probability very different from the high-souled woman she became
in the process of revision. She no doubt expressed herself freely,
according to Shakespeare's youthful manner, in rhyming reveries
on love and fate, such as the following (i. 1) :—

> " Our remedies oft in ourselves do lie
> Which we ascribe to Heaven : the fated sky
> Gives us free scope ; only, doth backward pull
> Our slow designs, when we ourselves are dull.
> What power is it which mounts my love so high ;
> That makes me see, and cannot feed mine eye ?
> The mightiest space in fortune Nature brings
> To join like likes, and kiss like native things.
> Impossible be strange attempts to those
> That weigh their pains in sense, and do suppose,
> What hath been cannot be. Who ever strove
> To show her merit, that did miss her love ? "

Or else he made her pour forth multitudinous swarms of images,
each treading on the other's heels, like those in which she fore-
casts Bertram's love-adventures at the court of France (i. 1) :—

> " There shall your master have a thousand loves,
> A mother, and a mistress, and a friend,
> A phœnix, captain, and an enemy,

A guide, a goddess, and a sovereign,
A counsellor, a traitress, and a dear;
His humble ambition, proud humility,
His jarring concord, and his discord dulcet,
His faith, his sweet disaster; with a world
Of pretty, fond, adoptious christendoms,
That blinking Cupid gossips."

Love's Labour's Won was probably conceived throughout in this lighter tone.

There can be little doubt that the figure of Parolles was also sketched in the earlier play. It forms an excellent counterpart to Armado in *Love's Labour's Lost*. And in it we have undoubtedly the first faint outline of the figure which, seven or eight years later, becomes the immortal Falstaff. Parolles is a humorous liar, braggart, and "misleader of youth," like Prince Henry's fat friend. He is put to shame, just like Falstaff, in an ambuscade devised by his own comrades; and being, as he thinks, taken prisoner, he deserts and betrays his master. Falstaff hacks the edge of his sword in order to appear valiant; and Parolles says (iv. 1), "I would the cutting of my garments would serve the turn, or the breaking of my Spanish sword."

In comparison with Falstaff the character is, of course, meagre and faint. But if we compare it with such a figure as Armado in *Love's Labour's Lost*, we find it sparkling with gaiety. It was, in all probability, touched up and endowed with new wit during the revision.

On the other hand, there is a good deal of quite youthful whimsicality in the speeches of the Clown, especially in the first act, which there is no difficulty in attributing to Shakespeare's twenty-fifth year. The song which the Fool sings at this point (i. 3) seems to belong to the earlier form, and with it the speeches to which it gives rise :—

" *Countess.* What! one good in ten? you corrupt the song, sirrah.

" *Clown.* One good woman in ten, madam, which is a purifying o' the song. Would God would serve the world so all the year! we'd find no fault with the tithe-woman, if I were the parson. One in ten, quoth 'a! an we might have a good woman born but for every blazing star, or at an earthquake, 't would mend the lottery well."

In treating of *Love's Labour's Won*, we must necessarily fall back upon more or less plausible conjecture. But we possess other comedies dating from this early period of Shakespeare's career in which the improvement of his technique and his steady advance towards artistic maturity can be clearly traced.

First and foremost we have his *Comedy of Errors*, which must belong to this earliest period, even if it comes after the two Love's Labour comedies. It is written in a highly polished, poetical style; it contains fewer lines of prose than any other of Shakespeare's

D

comedies; but its diction is full of dramatic movement, the rhymes do not impede the lively flow of the dialogue, and it has three times as many unrhymed as rhymed verses.

Yet it must follow pretty close upon the plays we have just reviewed. Certain phrases in the burlesque portrait of the fat cook drawn by Dromio of Syracuse (iii. 2) help to put us on the track of its date. His remark, that Spain sent whole "armadoes of caracks" to ballast themselves with the rubies and carbuncles on her nose, indicates a time not far remote from the Armada troubles. A more exact indication may be found in the answer which the servant gives to his master's question as to where France is situated upon the globe suggested by the cook's spherical figure. "Where France?" asks Antipholus; and Dromio replies, "In her forehead; arm'd and reverted, making war against her heir." Now, in 1589, Henry of Navarre really ceased to be the heir to the French throne, although his struggle for the possession of it lasted until his acceptance of Catholicism in 1593. Thus we may place the date of the play somewhere between the years 1589 and 1591.

This comedy on the frontier-line of farce shows with what giant strides Shakespeare progresses in the technique of his art. It has the blood of the theatre in its veins; we can already discern the experienced actor in the dexterity with which the threads of the intrigue are involved, and woven into an ever more intricate tangle, until the simple solution is arrived at. While *Love's Labour's Lost* still dragged itself laboriously over the boards, here we have an impetus and a *brio* in all the dramatic passages which reveal an artist and foretell a master. Only the rough outlines of the play are taken from Plautus; and the motive, the possibility of incessant confusion between two masters and two servants, is manipulated with a skill and certainty which astound us in a beginner, and sometimes with quite irresistible whimsicality. No doubt the merry play is founded upon an extreme improbability. So exact is the mutual resemblance of each pair of twins, no less in clothing than in feature, that not a single person for a moment doubts their identity. Astonishing resemblances between twins do, however, occur in real life; and when once we have accepted the premises, the consequences develop naturally, or at any rate plausibly. We may even say that in the art of intrigue-spinning, which was afterwards somewhat foreign and unattractive to him, the poet here shows himself scarcely inferior to the Spaniards of his own or of a later day, remarkable as was their dexterity.

Now and then the movement is suspended for the sake of an exchange of word-plays between master and servant; but it is generally short and entertaining. Now and then the action pauses to let Dromio of Syracuse work off one of his extravagant witticisms, as for example (iii. 2):—

" *Dromio S.* And yet she is a wondrous fat marriage.
" *Antipholus S.* How dost thou mean a fat marriage?
" *Dro. S.* Marry, sir, she's the kitchen-wench, and all grease; and I know not what use to put her to, but to make a lamp of her, and run from her by her own light. I warrant, her rags, and the tallow in them, will burn a Poland winter: if she lives till doomsday, she'll burn a week longer than the whole world."

As a rule, however, the interest is so evenly sustained that the spectator is held in constant curiosity and suspense as to the upshot of the adventure.

At one single point the style rises to a beauty and intensity which show that, though Shakespeare here abandons himself to the light play of intrigue, it is a diversion to which he only condescends for the moment. The passage is that between Luciana and Antipholus of Syracuse (iii. 2), with its tender erotic cadences. Listen to such verses as these:—

" *Ant. S.* Sweet mistress (what your name is else, I know not,
Nor by what wonder you do hit of mine),
Less in your knowledge, and your grace, you show not,
Than our earth's wonder; more than earth divine.
Teach me, dear creature, how to think and speak:
Lay open to my earthy-gross conceit,
Smother'd in errors, feeble, shallow, weak,
The folded meaning of your words' deceit.
Against my soul's pure truth, why labour you
To make it wander in an unknown field?
Are you a god? would you create me new?
Transform me then, and to your power I'll yield."

Since the play was first published in the Folio of 1623, it is, of course, not impossible that Shakespeare may have worked over this lovely passage at a later period. But the whole structure of the verses, with their interwoven rhymes, points in the opposite direction. We here catch the first notes of that music which is soon to fill *Romeo and Juliet* with its harmonies.

The play which in all probability stands next on the chronological list of Shakespeare's works, *The Two Gentlemen of Verona*, is also one in which we catch several anticipatory glimpses of later productions, and is in itself a promising piece of work. It surpasses the earlier comedies in two respects: first, in the beauty and clearness with which the two young women are outlined, and then in the careless gaiety which makes its first triumphant appearance in the parts of the servants. Only now and then, in one or two detached scenes, do Speed and Launce bore us with euphuistic word-torturings; as a rule they are quite entertaining fellows, who seem to announce, as with a flourish of trumpets, that, unlike either Lyly or Marlowe, Shakespeare possesses the inborn gaiety, the keen sense of humour, the sparkling playfulness, which are to enable him, without any strain on his invention, to kindle the laughter of his audiences, and send it flashing round the theatre from the groundlings to the gods. He does not as yet display any particular talent for individualising his clowns. Nevertheless we notice that, while Speed impresses us chiefly by his astonishing volubility, the true English humour makes its entrance upon the Shakespearian stage when Launce appears, dragging his dog by a string.

Note the torrent of eloquence in this speech of Speed's, enumerating the symptoms from which he concludes that his master is in love :—

"First, you have learn'd, like Sir Proteus, to wreath your arms, like a malcontent; to relish a love-song, like a robin-redbreast; to walk alone, like one that had the pestilence; to sigh, like a school-boy that had lost his A B C; to weep, like a young wench that had buried her grandam; to fast, like one that takes diet; to watch, like one that fears robbing; to speak puling, like a beggar at Hallowmas. You were wont, when you laugh'd, to crow like a cock; when you walk'd, to walk like one of the lions; when you fasted, it was presently after dinner; when you look'd sadly, it was for want of money ; and now you are metamorphosed with a mistress, that, when I look on you, I can hardly think you my master."

All these similes of Speed's are apt and accurate; it is only the way in which he piles them up that makes us laugh. But when Launce opens his mouth, unbridled whimsicality at once takes the upper hand. He comes upon the scene with his dog :—

"Nay, 'twill be this hour ere I have done weeping; all the kind of the Launces have this very fault. . . . I think Crab, my dog, be the sourest-natured dog that lives: my mother weeping, my father wailing, my sister crying, our maid howling, our cat wringing her hands, and all our house in a great perplexity, yet did not this cruel-hearted cur shed one tear. He is a stone, a very pebble-stone, and has no more pity in him than a dog; a Jew would have wept to have seen our parting: why, my grandam, having no eyes, look you, wept herself blind at my parting. Nay, I'll show you the manner of it. This shoe is my father: —no, this left shoe is my father;—no, no, this left shoe is my mother;— nay, that cannot be so, neither:—yes, it is so, it is so; it hath the worser sole. This shoe, with the hole in it, is my mother, and this my father. A vengeance on 't! there 't is: now, sir, this staff is my sister; for, look you, she is as white as a lily, and as small as a wand: this hat is Nan, our maid: I am the dog;—no, the dog is himself, and I am the dog, —O! the dog is me, and I am myself: ay, so, so."

Here we have nothing but joyous nonsense, and yet nonsense of a highly dramatic nature. That is to say, here reigns that youthful exuberance of spirit which laughs with a childlike grace, even where it condescends to the petty and low; exuberance as of one who glories in the very fact of existence, and rejoices to feel life pulsing and seething in his veins; exuberance such as belongs of right, in some degree, to every well-constituted man in the light-hearted days of his youth—how much more, then, to one who possesses the double youth of years and genius among a people which is itself young, and more than young : liberated, emancipated, enfranchised, like a colt which has broken its tether and scampers at large through the luxuriant pastures.

The Two Gentlemen of Verona — which, by the way, is Shakespeare's first declaration of love to Italy — is a graceful, entertaining, weakly constructed comedy, dealing with faithful and faithless love, with the treachery of man and the devotion of woman. Its hero, a noble and wrongfully-banished youth, comes to live the life of a robber captain, like Schiller's Karl von Moor two centuries later, but without a spark of his spirit of rebellion. The solution of the imbroglio, by means of the instant and unconditional forgiveness of the villain, is so naïve, so senselessly conciliatory, that we feel it to be the outcome of a joyous, untried, and unwounded spirit.

Shakespeare has borrowed part of his matter from a novel entitled Diana, by the Portuguese Montemayor (1520–1562). The translation, by Bartholomew Yong, was not printed until 1598, but the preface states that it had then been completed for fully sixteen years, and manuscript copies of it had no doubt passed from hand to hand, according to the fashion of the time. On comparing the essential portion of the romance[1] with The Two Gentlemen of Verona, we find that Proteus's infidelity and Julia's idea of following her lover in male attire, with all that comes of it, belong to Montemayor. Moreover, in the novel, Julia, disguised as a page, is present when Proteus serenades Sylvia (Celia in the original). She also goes to Sylvia at Proteus's orders to plead his cause with her ; but in the novel the fair lady falls in love with the messenger in male attire—an incident which Shakespeare reserved for Twelfth Night. We even find in Diana a sketch of the second scene of the first act, between Julia and Lucetta, in which the mistress, for appearance' sake, repudiates the letter which she is burning to read.

One or two points in the play remind us of Love's Labour's Won, which Shakespeare had just completed in its original form ; for example, the journey in male attire in pursuit of the scornful loved one. Many things, on the other hand, point forward to Shakespeare's later work. The inconstancy of the two men in A Midsummer Night's Dream is a variation and parody of Proteus's fickleness in this play. The beginning of the second scene of the first act, where Julia makes Lucetta pass judgment on her different suitors, is the first faint outline of the masterly scene to the same effect between Portia and Nerissa in The Merchant of Venice. The conversation between Sylvia and Julia,

[1] The Shepherdess Felismena in Hazlitt's Shakespeare's Library, Pt. I. vol. i. ed. 1875.

which brings the fourth act to a close, answers exactly to that between Olivia and Viola in the first act of *Twelfth Night*. Finally, the fact that Valentine, after learning the full extent of his false friend's treachery, offers to resign to him his beautiful betrothed, Sylvia, in order to prove by this sacrifice the strength of his friendship, however foolish and meaningless it may appear in the play, is yet an anticipation of the humble renunciation of the beloved for the sake of the friend and of friendship, which impresses us so painfully in Shakespeare's Sonnets.

In almost every utterance of the young women in this comedy we see nobility of soul, and in the lyric passages a certain pre-Raphaelite grace. Take, for example, what Julia says of her love in the last scene of the second act :—

> "The current, that with gentle murmur glides,
> Thou know'st, being stopp'd, impatiently doth rage;
> But, when his fair course is not hindered,
> He makes sweet music with the enamell'd stones,
> Giving a gentle kiss to every sedge
> He overtaketh in his pilgrimage.
>
> .   .   .   .
>
> I'll be as patient as a gentle stream,
> And make a pastime of each weary step,
> Till the last step have brought me to my love;
> And there I'll rest, as, after much turmoil,
> A blessed soul doth in Elysium."

And although the men are here of inferior interest to the women, we yet find in the mouth of Valentine outbursts of great lyric beauty. For example (iii. 1):—

> "Except I be by Silvia in the night,
> There is no music in the nightingale;
> Unless I look on Silvia in the day,
> There is no day for me to look upon.
> She is my essence; and I leave to be,
> If I be not by her fair influence
> Foster'd, illumin'd, cherish'd, kept alive."

Besides the strains of passion and of gaiety in this light acting play, a third note is clearly struck, the note of nature. There is fresh air in it, a first breath of those fragrant midland memories which prove that this child of the country must many a time have said to himself with Valentine (v. 4):—

> "How use doth breed a habit in a man!
> This shadowy desert, unfrequented woods,
> I better brook than flourishing peopled towns."

In many passages of this play we are conscious for the first time of that keen love of nature which never afterwards deserts Shakespeare, and which gives to some of the most mannered of his early efforts, as, for example, to his short narrative poems, their chief interest and value.

XI

VENUS AND ADONIS: DESCRIPTIONS OF NATURE — THE RAPE OF LUCRECE: RELATION TO PAINTING

ALTHOUGH Shakespeare did not publish *Venus and Adonis* until the spring of 1593, when he was twenty-nine years old, the poem must certainly have been conceived, and probably written, several years earlier. In dedicating it to the Earl of Southampton, then a youth of twenty, he calls it "the first heire of my invention;" but it by no means follows that it is literally the first thing he ever wrote. The expression may merely imply that his work for the theatre was not regarded as an independent exercise of his poetic talent. But the over-luxuriant style betrays the youthful hand, and we place it, therefore, among Shakespeare's writings of about 1590–91.

He had at this period, as we have seen, won a firm footing as an actor, and had made himself not only useful but popular as an adapter of old plays and an independent dramatist. But the drama of that time was not reckoned as literature. There was all the difference in the world between a "playwright" and a real poet. When Sir Thomas Bodley, about the year 1600, extended and remodelled the old University Library, and gave it his name, he decreed that no such "riffe-raffes" as playbooks should ever find admittance to it.

Without being actually ambitious, Shakespeare felt the highly natural wish to make a name for himself in literature. He wanted to take his place among the poets, and to win the approval of the young noblemen whose acquaintance he had made in the theatre. He also wanted to show that he was familiar with the spirit of antiquity.

Spenser (born 1553) had just attracted general attention by publishing the first books of his great narrative poem. What more natural than that Shakespeare should be tempted to measure his strength against Spenser, as he already had against Marlowe, his first master in the drama?

The little poem of *Venus and Adonis*, and its companion-piece, *The Rape of Lucrece*, which appeared in the following year, have this great value for us, that here, and here only, are we certain of possessing a text exactly as Shakespeare wrote it, since he himself superintended its publication.

Italy was at this time the centre of all culture. The lyric and minor epic poetry of England were entirely under the influence of the Italian style and taste. Shakespeare, in *Venus and Adonis*, aims at the insinuating sensuousness of the Italians. He tries to strike the tender and languorous notes of his Southern forerunners. Among the poets of antiquity, Ovid is naturally his model. He takes two lines from Ovid's *Amores* as the motto of his poem, which is, indeed, nothing but an expanded version of a scene in the *Metamorphoses*.

The name of Shakespeare, like the names of Æschylus, Michael Angelo, and Beethoven, is apt to ring tragically in our ears. We have almost forgotten that he had a Mozartean vein in his nature, and that his contemporaries not only praised his personal gentleness and "honesty," but also the "sweetness" of his singing.

In *Venus and Adonis* glows the whole fresh sensuousness of the Renaissance and of Shakespeare's youth. It is an entirely erotic poem, and contemporaries aver that it lay on the table of every light woman in London.

The conduct of the poem presents a series of opportunities and pretexts for voluptuous situations and descriptions. The ineffectual blandishments lavished by Venus on the chaste and frigid youth, who, in his sheer boyishness, is as irresponsive as a bashful woman—her kisses, caresses, and embraces, are depicted in detail. It is as though a Titian or Rubens had painted a model in a whole series of tender situations, now in one attitude, now in another. Then comes the suggestive scene in which Adonis's horse breaks away in order to meet the challenge of a mare which happens to wander by, together with the goddess's comments thereupon. Then new advances and solicitations, almost inadmissibly daring, according to the taste of our day.

An element of feeling is introduced in the portrayal of Venus's anguish when Adonis expresses his intention of hunting the boar. But it is to sheer description that the poet chiefly devotes himself —description of the charging boar, description of the fair young body bathed in blood, and so forth. There is a fire and rapture of colour in it all, as in a picture by some Italian master of a hundred years before.

Quite unmistakable is the insinuating, luscious, almost saccharine quality of the writing, which accounts for the fact that, when his immediate contemporaries speak of Shakespeare's diction, honey is the similitude that first suggests itself to them. John Weever, in 1595, calls him "honey-tongued," and in 1598 Francis Meres uses the same term, with the addition of "mellifluous."

There is, indeed, an extraordinary sweetness in these strophes.

Tenderness, every here and there, finds really entrancing utterance. When Adonis has for the first time harshly repulsed Venus, in a speech of some length :—

> " 'What! canst thou talk?' quoth she, 'hast thou a tongue?
> O, would thou hadst not, or I had no hearing !
> Thy mermaid's voice hath done me double wrong ;
> I had my load before, now press'd with bearing :
>   Melodious discord, heavenly tune harsh-sounding,
>   Ear's deep-sweet music, and heart's deep-sore wounding.' "

But the style also exhibits numberless instances of tasteless Italian artificiality. Breathing the "heavenly moisture" of Adonis's breath, she

> "Wishes her cheeks were gardens full of flowers,
>   So they were dew'd with such distilling showers."

Of Adonis's dimples it is said :—

> "These lovely caves, these round enchanting pits,
>   Open'd their mouths to swallow Venus' liking."

"My love to love," says Adonis, "is love but to disgrace it." Venus enumerates the delights he would afford to each of her senses separately, supposing her deprived of all the rest, and concludes thus :—

> " 'But, O, what banquet wert thou to the taste,
> Being nurse and feeder of the other four
> Would they not wish the feast might ever last,
> And bid Suspicion double-lock the door,
>   Lest Jealousy, that sour unwelcome guest,
>   Should, by his stealing in, disturb the feast?' "

Such lapses of taste are not infrequent in Shakespeare's early comedies as well. They answer, in their way, to the riot of horrors in *Titus Andronicus*—analogous mannerisms of an as yet undeveloped art.

At the same time, the puissant sensuousness of this poem is as a prelude to the large utterance of passion in *Romeo and Juliet*, and towards its close Shakespeare soars, so to speak, symbolically, from a delineation of the mere fever of the senses to a forecast of that love in which it is only one element, when he makes Adonis say :—

> " 'Love comforteth like sunshine after rain,
> But Lust's effect is tempest after sun ;
> Love's gentle spring doth always fresh remain,
> Lust's winter comes ere summer half be done :
>   Love surfeits not, Lust like a glutton dies ;
>   Love is all truth, Lust full of forged lies.' "

It would, of course, be absurd to lay too much stress on these edifying antitheses in this unedifying poem. It is more important to note that the descriptions of animal life—for example, that of the hare's flight—are unrivalled for truth and delicacy of observation, and to mark how, even in this early work, Shakespeare's style now and then rises to positive greatness.

This is especially the case in the descriptions of the boar and of the horse. The boar—his back "set with a battle of bristly pikes," his eyes like glow-worms, his snout "digging sepulchres where'er he goes," his neck short and thick, and his onset so fierce that

> "The thorny brambles and embracing bushes,
> As fearful of him, part; through which he rushes"

—this boar seems to have been painted by Snyders in a hunting-piece, in which the human figures came from the brush of Rubens.

Shakespeare himself seems to have realised with what mastery he had depicted the stallion; for he says :—

> "Look, when a painter would surpass the life,
> In limning out a well-proportion'd steed,
> His art with nature's workmanship at strife,
> As if the dead the living should exceed;
> So did this horse excel a common one,
> In shape, in courage, colour, pace, and bone."

We can feel Shakespeare's love of nature in such a stanza as this :—

> "Round-hoof'd, short-jointed, fetlocks shag and long,
> Broad breast, full eye, small head, and nostril wide,
> High crest, short ears, straight legs, and passing strong,
> Thin mane, thick tail, broad buttock, tender hide:
> Look, what a horse should have, he did not lack,
> Save a proud rider on so proud a back."

How consummate, too, is the description of all his movements :—

> "Sometime he scuds far off, and there he stares;
> Anon he starts at stirring of a feather."

We hear "the high wind singing through his mane and tail." We are almost reminded of the magnificent picture of the horse at the end of the Book of Job: "He swalloweth the ground with fierceness and rage. . . . He smelleth the battle afar off, the thunder of the captains, and the shouting." So great is the compass of style in this little poem of Shakespeare's youth: from Ovid to the Old Testament, from modish artificiality to grandiose simplicity.

Lucrece, which appeared in the following year, was, like *Venus and Adonis*, dedicated to the Earl of Southampton, in distinctly more familiar, though still deferential terms. The poem is designed as a counterpart to its predecessor. The one treats of male, the other of female, chastity. The one portrays ungovernable passion in a woman ; the other, criminal passion in a man. But in *Lucrece* the theme is seriously and morally handled. It is almost a didactic poem, dealing with the havoc wrought by unbridled and brutish desire.

It was not so popular in its own day as its predecessor, and it does not afford the modern reader any very lively satisfaction. It shows an advance in metrical accomplishment. To the six-line stanza of *Venus and Adonis* a seventh line is added, which heightens its beauty and its dignity. The strength of *Lucrece* lies in its graphic and gorgeous descriptions, and in its sometimes microscopic psychological analysis. For the rest, its pathos consists of elaborate and far-fetched rhetoric.

The lament of the heroine after the crime has been committed is pure declamation, extremely eloquent no doubt, but copious and artificial as an oration of Cicero's, rich in apostrophes and antitheses. The sorrow of "Collatine and his consorted lords" is portrayed in laboured and quibbling speeches. Shakespeare's knowledge and mastery are most clearly seen in the reflections scattered through the narrative—such, for instance, as the following profound and exquisitely written stanza on the softness of the feminine nature :—

> " For men have marble, women waxen minds,
> And therefore are they form'd as marble will ;
> The weak oppress'd, the impression of strange kinds
> Is form'd in them by force, by fraud, or skill :
> Then call them not the authors of their ill,
>   No more than wax shall be accounted evil,
>   Wherein is stamp'd the semblance of a devil."

In point of mere technique the most remarkable passage in the poem is the long series of stanzas (lines 1366 to 1568) describing a painting of the destruction of Troy, which Lucrece contemplates in her despair. The description is marked by such force, freshness, and naïveté as might suggest that the writer had never seen a picture before :—

> " Here one man's hand leaned on another's head,
> His nose being shadowed by his neighbour's ear."

So dense is the throng of figures in the picture, so deceptive the presentation,

> " That for Achilles' image stood his spear,
> Grip'd in an armed hand : himself behind
> Was left unseen, save to the eye of mind.
>   A hand, a foot, a face, a leg, a head,
>   Stood for the whole to be imagined."

Here, as in all other places in which Shakespeare mentions pictorial or plastic art, it is realism carried to the point of illusion that he admires and praises. The paintings in the Guild Chapel at Stratford were, doubtless, as before mentioned, the first he ever saw. He may also, during his Stratford period, have seen works of art at Kenilworth Castle or at St. Mary's Church in Coventry. In London, in the Hall belonging to the Merchants of the Steel-Yard, he had no doubt seen two greatly admired pictures by Holbein which hung there. Moreover, there were in London at that time not only numerous portraits by Dutch masters, but also a few Italian pictures. It appears, for example, from a list of "Pictures and other Works of Art" drawn up in 1613 by John Ernest, Duke of Saxe-Weimar, that there hung at Whitehall a painting of Julius Cæsar, and another of Lucretia, said to have been "very artistically executed." This picture may possibly have suggested to Shakespeare the theme of his poem. Larger compositions were no doubt familiar to him in the tapestries of the period (the hangings at Theobald's presented scenes from Roman history); and he may very likely have seen the excellent Dutch and Italian pictures at Nonsuch Palace, then in the height of its glory.

His reflections upon art led him, as aforesaid, to the conclusion that it was the artist's business to keep a close watch upon nature, to master or transcend her. Again and again he ranks truth to nature as the highest quality in art. He evidently cared nothing for allegorical or religious painting; he never so much as mentions it. Nor, with all his love for "the concord of sweet sounds," does he ever allude to church music.

The description of the great painting of the fall of Troy is no mere irrelevant decoration to the poem; for the fall of Troy symbolises the fall of the royal house of Tarquin as a consequence of Sextus's crime. Shakespeare did not look at the event from the point of view of individual morality alone; he makes us feel that the honour of a royal family, and even its dynastic existence, are hazarded by criminal aggression upon a noble house. All the conceptions of honour belonging to mediæval chivalry are transferred to ancient Rome. "Knights, by their oaths, should right poor ladies' harms," says Lucrece, in calling upon her kinsmen to avenge her.

In his picture of the sack of Troy, Shakespeare has followed the second book of Virgil's _Æneid;_ for the groundwork of his poem as a whole he has gone to the short but graceful and sympathetic rendering of the story of Lucretia in Ovid's _Fasti_ (ii. 685–852).

A comparison between Ovid's style and that of Shakespeare certainly does not redound to the advantage of the modern poet. In opposition to this semi-barbarian, Ovid seems the embodiment of classic severity. Shakespeare's antithetical conceits and other

lapses of taste are painfully obtrusive. Every here and there we
come upon such stumbling-blocks as these :—

> " Some of her blood still pure and red remain'd,
>   And some look'd black, and that false Tarquin stain'd ; "

or,

> " If children pre-decease progenitors,
>   We are their offspring, and they none of ours."

This lack of nature and of taste is not only characteristic of the
age in general, but is bound up with the great excellences and
rare capacities which Shakespeare was now developing with such
amazing rapidity. His momentary leaning towards this style
was due, in part at least, to the influence of his fellow-poets, his
friends, his rivals in public favour—the influence, in short, of
that artistic microcosm in whose atmosphere his genius shot up
to sudden maturity.

We talk of " schools " in literature, and it is no exaggeration
to say that every period of rich productivity presupposes a school
or schools. But the word " school," beautiful in its original Greek
signification, has been narrowed and specialised by modern usage.
We ought to say " forcing-house " instead of " school "—to talk
of the classic and the romantic forcing-house, the Renaissance
forcing-house,[1] and so forth. In very small communities, where
there is none of that emulation which alone can call forth all an
artist's energies, absolute mastery is as a rule unattainable. Under
such conditions, a man will often make a certain mark early in
life, and find his success his ruin. Others seek a forcing-house
outside their native land—Holberg in Holland, England, and
France ; Thorvaldsen in Rome ; Heine in Paris. The moment
he set foot in London, Shakespeare was in such a forcing-house.
Hence the luxuriant burgeoning of his genius.

He lived in constant intercourse and rivalry with vivid and
daringly productive spirits. The diamond was polished in diamond
dust.

The competitive instinct (as Rümelin has rightly pointed out)
was strong in the English poets of that period. Shakespeare
could not but strive from the first to outdo his fellows in strength
and skill. At last he comes to think, like Hamlet : however deep
they dig—

> " it shall go hard
> But I will delve one yard below their mines "

—one of the most characteristic utterances of Hamlet and of
Shakespeare.

This sense of rivalry contributed to the formation of Shakespeare's early manner, both in his narrative poems and in his

---

[1] The author's idea is, I think, best rendered by this literal translation ; but the
Danish word *Drivhus* is much less cumbrous than its English equivalent.—TRANS.

plays. Hence arose that straining after subtleties, that absorption in quibbles, that wantoning in word-plays, that bandying to and fro of shuttlecocks of speech. Hence, too, that state of over-heated passion and over-stimulated fancy, in which image begets image with a headlong fecundity, like that of the low organisms which pullulate by mere scission.

This man of all the talents had the talent for word-plays and thought-quibbles among the rest; he was too richly endowed to be behind-hand even here. But there was in all this something foreign to his true self. When he reaches the point at which his inmost personality begins to reveal itself in his writings, we are at once conscious of a far deeper and more emotional nature than that which finds expression in the teeming conceits of the narrative poems and the incessant scintillations of the early comedies.

XII

A MIDSUMMER NIGHT'S DREAM—ITS HISTORICAL CIRCUMSTANCES—ITS ARISTOCRATIC, POPULAR, COMIC, AND SUPERNATURAL ELEMENTS

IN spite of the fame and popularity which *Venus and Adonis* and *Lucrece* won for Shakespeare, he quickly understood, with his instinctive self-knowledge, that it was not narrative but dramatic poetry which offered the fullest scope for his powers.

And now it is that we find him for the first time rising to the full height of his genius. This he does in a work of dramatic form; but, significantly enough, it is not as yet in its dramatic elements that we recognise the master-hand, but rather in the rich and incomparable lyric poetry with which he embroiders a thin dramatic canvas.

His first masterpiece is a masterpiece of grace, both lyrical and comic. *A Midsummer Night's Dream* was no doubt written as a festival-play or masque, before the masque became an established art-form, to celebrate the marriage of a noble patron; probably for the May festival after the private marriage of Essex with the widow of Sir Philip Sidney in the year 1590. In Oberon's great speech to Puck (ii. 2) there is a significant passage about a throned vestal, invulnerable to Cupid's darts, which is obviously a flattering reference to Elizabeth in relation to Leicester; while the lines about a little flower wounded by the fiery shaft of love mournfully allude, in the like allegorical fashion, to Essex's mother and her marriage with Leicester, after his courtship had been rejected by the Queen. Other details also point to Essex as the bridegroom typified in the person of Theseus.

How is one to speak adequately of *A Midsummer Night's Dream?* It is idle to dwell upon the slightness of the character-drawing, for the poet's effort is not after characterisation; and, whatever its weak points, the poem as a whole is one of the tenderest, most original, and most perfect Shakespeare ever produced.

It is Spenser's fairy-poetry developed and condensed; it is Shelley's spirit-poetry anticipated by more than two centuries. And the airy dream is shot with whimsical parody. The frontiers of Elf-iand and Clown-land meet and mingle.

We have here an element of aristocratic distinction in the princely couple, Theseus and Hippolyta, and their court. We have here an element of sprightly burlesque in the artisans' performance of Pyramus and Thisbe, treated with genial irony and divinely felicitous humour. And here, finally, we have the element of supernatural poetry, which soon after flashes forth again in *Romeo and Juliet*, where Mercutio describes the doings of Queen Mab. Puck and Pease-blossom, Cobweb and Mustard-seed—pigmies who hunt the worms in a rosebud, tease bats, chase spiders, and lord it over nightingales—are the leading actors in an elfin play, a fairy carnival of inimitable mirth and melody, steeped in a midsummer atmosphere of mist-wreaths and flower-scents, under the afterglow that lingers through the sultry night. This miracle of happy inspiration contains the germs of innumerable romantic achievements in England, Germany, and Denmark, more than two centuries later.

There is in French literature a graceful mythological play of somewhat later date—Molière's *Psyché*—in which the exquisite love-verses which stream from the heroine's lips were written by the sexagenarian Corneille. It is, in its way, an admirable piece of work. But read it and compare it with the nature-poetry of *A Midsummer Night's Dream*, and you will feel how far the great Englishman surpasses the greatest Frenchmen in pure un-rhetorical lyrism and irrepressibly playful, absolutely poetical poetry, with its scent of clover, its taste of wild honey, and its airy and shifting dream-pageantry.

We have here no pathos. The hurricane of passion does not as yet sweep through Shakespeare's work. No; it is only the romantic and imaginative side of love that is here displayed, the magic whereby longing transmutes and idealises its object, the element of folly, infatuation, and illusion in desire, with its consequent variability and transitoriness. Man is by nature a being with no inward compass, led astray by his instincts and dreams, and for ever deceived either by himself or by others. This Shakespeare realises, but does not, as yet, take the matter very tragically. Thus the characters whom he here presents, even, or rather especially, in their love-affairs, appear as anything but reasonable beings. The lovers seek and avoid each other by turns, they love and are not loved again; the couples attract each other at cross-purposes; the youth runs after the maiden who shrinks from him, the maiden flees from the man who adores her; and the poet's delicate irony makes the confusion reach its height and find its symbolic expression when the Queen of the Fairies, in the intoxication of a love-dream, recognises her ideal in a journeyman weaver with an ass's head.

It is the love begotten of imagination that here bears sway. Hence these words of Theseus (v. 1):—

" Lovers and madmen have such seething brains,
Such shaping fantasies, that apprehend
More than cool reason ever comprehends.
The lunatic, the lover, and the poet,
Are of imagination all compact."

And then follows Shakespeare's first deliberate utterance as to
the nature and art of the poet.   He is not, as a rule, greatly concerned with the dignity of the poet as such.   Quite foreign to him
is the self-idolatry of the later romantic poets, posing as the
spiritual pastors and masters of the world.   Where he introduces
poets in his plays (as in *Julius Cæsar* and *Timon*), it is generally
to assign them a pitiful part.   But here he places in the mouth of
Theseus. the famous and exquisite words :—

" The poet's eye, in a fine frenzy rolling,
Doth glance from heaven to earth, from earth to heaven ;
And, as imagination bodies forth
The forms of things unknown, the poet's pen
Turns them to shapes, and gives to airy nothing
A local habitation and a name.
Such tricks hath strong imagination."

When he wrote this he felt that his wings had grown.
As *A Midsummer Night's Dream* was not published until
1600, it is impossible to assign an exact date to the text we
possess.   In all probability the piece was altered and amplified
before it was printed.
Attention was long ago drawn to the following lines in
Theseus's speech at the beginning of the fifth act :—

" *The thrice three Muses mourning for the death
Of Learning, late deceas'd in beggary.*
This is some satire, keen and critical."

Several commentators have seen in these lines an allusion to
the death of Spenser, which, however, did not occur until 1599,
so late that it can scarcely be the event alluded to.   Others have
conjectured a reference to the death of Robert Greene in 1592.
The probability is that the words refer to Spenser's poem, *The
Tears of the Muses*, published in 1591, which was a complaint of
the indifference of the nobility towards the fine arts.   If the play,
as we have so many reasons for supposing, was written for the
marriage of Essex, these lines must have been inserted later, as
they might easily be in a passage like this, where a whole series
of different subjects for masques is enumerated.
The important passage (ii. 2) where Oberon recounts his vision
has already been mentioned.   It follows Oberon's description of
the mermaid seated on a dolphin's back—

E

"Uttering such dulcet and harmonious breath
That certain stars shot madly from their spheres,"

—an allusion, not, as some have supposed, to Mary Stuart, who was married to the Dauphin of France, but to the festivities and firework displays which celebrated Elizabeth's visit to Kenilworth in 1575. The passage is interesting, among other reasons, because we have here one of the few allegories to be found in Shakespeare —an allegory which has taken that form because the matters to which it alludes could not be directly handled. Shakespeare is here referring back, as English criticism has long ago pointed out,[1] to the allegory in Lyly's mythological play, *Endymion*. There can be no doubt that Cynthia (the moon-goddess) in Lyly's play stands for Queen Elizabeth, while Leicester figures as Endymion, who is represented as hopelessly enamoured of Cynthia. Tellus and Floscula, of whom the one loves Endymion's "person," the other his "virtues," represent the Countesses of Sheffield and Essex, who stood in amatory relations to Leicester. The play is one tissue of adulation for Elizabeth, but is so constructed as at the same time to flatter and defend Leicester. In defiance of the actual fact, it exhibits the Queen as entirely inaccessible to her adorer's homage, and Leicester's intrigue with the Countess of Sheffield as a mere mask for his passion for the Queen; in other words, it represents these relations as the Queen would wish to have them understood by the people, and Leicester by the Queen. The Countess of Essex, who was afterwards to play so large a part in Leicester's life, plays a very small part in the drama. Her love finds expression only in one or two unobtrusive phrases, such as her cry of joy on seeing Endymion, after the forty years' sleep in which he has grown an old man, rejuvenated by a single kiss from Cynthia's lips.

The relation between Leicester and Lettice, Countess of Essex, must certainly have made a deep impression upon Shakespeare. By Leicester's contrivance, her husband had been for a long time banished to Ireland, first as commander of the troops in Ulster, and afterwards as Earl-Marshal; and when he died, in 1576— commonly thought, though without proof, to have been poisoned —his widow, after a lapse of only a few days, went through a secret marriage with his supposed murderer. When Leicester, twelve years later, met with a sudden death, also, according to popular belief, by poison, the event was regarded as a judgment on a great criminal. In all probability, Shakespeare found in these events one of the motives of his *Hamlet*. Whether the Countess Lettice was actually Leicester's mistress during her husband's lifetime is, of course, uncertain; in any case, the Countess's relation to Robert, Earl of Essex, her son by her first marriage, was always

---

[1] N. J. Halpin : *Oberon's Vision in the Midsummer Night's Dream, illustrated by a Comparison with Lylie's Endymion*, 1842.

of the best. She was, however, punished by the Queen's displeasure, which was so vehement that she was forbidden to show
herself at court.

Shakespeare has retained Lyly's names, merely translating
them into English. Cynthia has become the moon, Tellus the
earth, Floscula the little flower; and with this commentary, we
are in a position to admire the delicate and poetical way in which
he has touched upon the family circumstances of the supposed
bridegroom, the Earl of Essex :—

> " *Oberon.* That very time I saw (but thou couldst not),
> Flying between the cold moon and the earth,
> Cupid all arm'd : a certain aim he took
> At a fair vestal throned by the west,
> And loos'd his love-shaft smartly from his bow,
> As it should pierce a hundred thousand hearts.
> But I might see young Cupid's fiery shaft
> Quench'd in the chaste beams of the wat'ry moon,
> And the imperial votaress passed on,
> In maiden meditation, fancy-free.
> Yet mark'd I where the bolt of Cupid fell:
> It fell upon a little western flower,
> Before milk-white, now purple with love's wound,
> And maidens call it Love-in-idleness."

It is with the juice of this flower that Oberon makes every one
upon whose eyes it falls dote upon the first living creature they
happen to see.

The poet's design in the flattery addressed to Elizabeth—one
of the very few instances of the kind in his works—was no doubt to
dispose her favourably towards his patron's marriage, or, in other
words, to·deprecate the anger with which she was in the habit
of regarding any attempt on the part of her favourites, or even of
ordinary courtiers, to marry according to their own inclinations.
Essex in particular had stood very close to her, since, in 1587, he
had supplanted Sir Walter Raleigh in her favour; and although
the Queen, now in her fifty-seventh year, was fully thirty-four
years older than her late adorer, Shakespeare did not succeed
in averting her anger from the young couple. The bride was
commanded " to live very retired in her mother's house."

A Midsummer Night's Dream is the first consummate and
immortal masterpiece which Shakespeare produced.

The fact that the pairs of lovers are very slightly individualised,
and do not in themselves awaken any particular sympathy, is a
fault that we easily overlook, amid the countless beauties of
the play. The fact that the changes in the lovers' feelings are
entirely unmotived is no fault at all, for Oberon's magic is simply
a great symbol, typifying the sorcery of the erotic imagination.
There is deep significance as well as drollery in the presentation

of Titania as desperately enamoured of Bottom with his ass's head. Nay, more; in the lovers' ever-changing attractions and repulsions we may find a whole sportive love-philosophy.

The rustic and popular element in Shakespeare's genius here appears more prominently than ever before. The country-bred youth's whole feeling for and knowledge of nature comes to the surface, permeated with the spirit of poetry. The play swarms with allusions to plants and insects, and all that is said of them is closely observed and intimately felt. In none of Shakespeare's plays are so many species of flowers, fruits, and trees men·tioned and characterised. H. N. Ellacombe, in his essay on *The Seasons of Shakspere's Plays*,[1] reckons no fewer than forty-two species. Images borrowed from nature meet us on every hand. For example, in Helena's beautiful description of her school friendship with Hermia (iii. 2), she says:—

> " So we grew together,
> Like to a double cherry, seeming parted,
> But yet an union in partition ;
> Two lovely berries moulded on one stem."

When Titania exhorts her elves to minister to every desire of her asinine idol, she says (iii. 1):—

> " Be kind and courteous to this gentleman :
> Hop in his walks, and gambol in his eyes ;
> Feed him with apricocks, and dewberries,
> With purple grapes, green figs, and mulberries.
> The honey-bags steal from the humble-bees,
> And for night-tapers crop their waxen thighs,
> And light them at the fiery glow-worm's eyes,
> To have my love to bed, and to arise ;
> And pluck the wings from painted butterflies,
> To fan the moonbeams from his sleeping eyes.
> Nod to him, elves, and do him courtesies."

The popular element in Shakespeare is closely interwoven with his love of nature. He has here plunged deep into folk-lore, seized upon the figments of peasant superstition as they survive in the old ballads, and mingled brownies and pixies with the delicate creations of artificial poetry, with Oberon, who is of French descent ("Auberon," from *l'aube du jour*), and Titania, a name which Ovid gives in his *Metamorphoses* (iii. 173) to Diana as the sister of the Titan Sol. *The Maydes Metamorphosis*, a play attributed to Lyly, although not printed till 1600, may be older than *A Midsummer Night's Dream*. In that case Shakespeare may have found the germ of some of his fairy dialogue in the pretty fairy song which occurs in it. There is a marked

---

[1] *New Shakspere Society's Transactions*, 1880–86, p. 67.

similarity even in details of dialogue. For example, this conversation between Bottom and the fairies (iii. 1) reminds us of Lyly [1] :—

"*Bot.* I cry your worship's mercy, heartily.—I beseech your worship's name.

" *Cob.* Cobweb.

" *Bot.* I shall desire you of more acquaintance, good Master Cobweb. If I cut my finger, I shall make bold with you. Your name, honest gentleman?

" *Peas.* Pease-blossom.

" *Bot.* I, pray you, commend me to Mistress Squash, your mother, and to Master Peascod, your father. Good Master Pease-blossom, I shall desire you of more acquaintance too.—Your name, I beseech you, sir.

" *Mus.* Mustard-seed.

" *Bot.* Good Master Mustard-seed, I know your patience well: that same cowardly, giant-like oxbeef hath devoured many a gentleman of your house. I promise you, your kindred hath made my eyes water ere now. I desire you of more acquaintance, good Master Mustard-seed."

The contrast between the rude artisans' prose and the poetry of the fairy world is exquisitely humorous, and has been frequently imitated in the nineteenth century: in Germany by Tieck ; in Denmark by J. L. Heiberg, who has written no fewer than three imitations of *A Midsummer Night's Dream*—*The Elves*, *The Day of the Seven Sleepers*, and *The Nutcrackers*.

The fairy element introduced into the comedy brings in its train not only the many love-illusions, but other and external forms of thaumaturgy as well. People are beguiled by wandering voices, led astray in the midnight wood, and victimised in many innocent ways. The fairies retain from first to last their grace and sportiveness, but the individual physiognomies, in this stage of Shakespeare's development, are as yet somewhat lacking in expression. Puck, for instance, is a mere shadow in comparison with a creation of twenty years later, the immortal Ariel of *The Tempest*.

Brilliant as is the picture of the fairy world in *A Midsummer Night's Dream*, the mastery to which Shakespeare had attained is most clearly displayed in the burlesque scenes, dealing with the little band of worthy artisans who are moved to represent the history of Pyramus and Thisbe at the marriage of Theseus and

[1] The passage in *The Maydes Metamorphosis* runs as follows :—

" *Mopso.* I pray you, what might I call you?
1*st Fairy.* My name is Penny.
Mopso. I am sorry I cannot purse you.
Frisco. I pray you, sir, what might I call you?
2*nd Fairy.* My name is Cricket.
Frisco. I would I were a chimney for your sake."

Hippolyta. Never before has Shakespeare risen to the sparkling and genial humour with which these excellent simpletons are portrayed. He doubtless drew upon childish memories of the plays he had seen performed in the market-place at Coventry and elsewhere. He also introduced some whimsical strokes of satire upon the older English drama. For instance, when Quince says (i. 2), "Marry, our play is—The most lamentable comedy, and most cruel death of Pyramus and Thisby," there is an obvious reference to the long and quaint title of the old play of *Cambyses*: "A lamentable tragedy mixed full of pleasant mirth,"[1] &c.

Shakespeare's elevation of mind, however, is most clearly apparent in the playful irony with which he treats his own art, the art of acting, and the theatre of the day, with its scanty and imperfect appliances for the production of illusion. The artisan who plays Wall, his fellow who enacts Moonshine, and the excellent amateur who represents the Lion are deliciously whimsical types.

It was at all times a favourite device with Shakespeare, as with his imitators, the German romanticists of two centuries later, to introduce a play within a play. The device is not of his own invention. We find it already in Kyd's *Spanish Tragedie* (perhaps as early as 1584), a play whose fustian Shakespeare often ridicules, but in which he nevertheless found the germ of his own *Hamlet*. But from the very first the idea of giving an air of greater solidity to the principal play by introducing into it a company of actors had a great attraction for him. We may compare with the Pyramus and Thisbe scenes in this play the appearance of Costard and his comrades as Pompey, Hector, Alexander, Hercules, and Judas Maccabæus in the fifth act of *Love's Labour's Lost*. Even there the Princess speaks with a kindly tolerance of the poor amateur actors :—

> "That sport best pleases, that doth least know how :
> Where zeal strives to content, and the contents
> Die in the zeal of them which it presents,
> Their form confounded makes most form in mirth ;
> When great things labouring perish in their birth."

Nevertheless, there is here a certain youthful cruelty in the courtiers' ridicule of the actors, whereas in *A Midsummer Night's Dream* everything passes off in the purest, airiest humour. What can be more perfect, for example, than the Lion's reassuring address to the ladies ?—

> " 'You, ladies, you, whose gentle hearts do fear
> The smallest monstrous mouse that creeps on floor,

---

[1] The passion for alliteration in his contemporaries is satirised in these lines of the prologue to *Pyramus and Thisbe* :—

> " Whereat with blade, with bloody blameful blade,
> He bravely broach'd his boiling bloody breast."

May now, perchance, both quake and tremble here,
When lion rough in wildest rage doth roar.
Then know, that I, one Snug the joiner, am
No lion fell, nor else no lion's dam :
For, if I should as lion come in strife
Into this place, 't were pity on my life.' "

And how pleasant, when he at last comes in with his roar, is Demetrius' comment, of proverbial fame, "Well roared, lion !"

It is true that *A Midsummer Night's Dream* is rather to be described as a dramatic lyric than a drama in the strict sense of the word. It is a lightly-flowing, sportive, lyrical fantasy, dealing with love as a dream, a fever, an illusion, an infatuation, and making merry, in especial, with the irrational nature of the instinct. That is why Lysander, turning, under the influence of the magic flower, from Hermia, whom he loves, to Helena, who is nothing to him, but whom he now imagines that he adores, is made to exclaim (ii. 3) :—

"The will of man is by his reason sway'd,
And reason says you are the worthier maid."

Here, more than anywhere else, he is the mouthpiece of the poet's irony. Shakespeare is far from regarding love as an expression of human reason; throughout his works, indeed, it is only by way of exception that he makes reason the determining factor in human conduct. He early felt and divined how much wider is the domain of the unconscious than of the conscious life, and saw that our moods and passions have their root in the unconscious. The germs of a whole philosophy of life are latent in the wayward love-scenes of *A Midsummer Night's Dream*.

And it is now that Shakespeare, on the farther limit of early youth, and immediately after writing *A Midsummer Night's Dream*, for the second time takes the most potent of youthful emotions as his theme, and treats it no longer as a thing of fantasy, but as a matter of the deadliest moment, as a glowing, entrancing, and annihilating passion, the source of bliss and agony, of life and death. It is now that he writes his first independent tragedy, *Romeo and Juliet*, that unique, imperishable love-poem, which remains to this day one of the loftiest summits of the world's literature. As *A Midsummer Night's Dream* is the triumph of grace, so *Romeo and Juliet* is the apotheosis of pure passion.

XIII

ROMEO AND JULIET—THE TWO QUARTOS—ITS ROMANESQUE STRUCTURE—THE USE OF OLD MOTIVES—THE CONCEPTION OF LOVE

Romeo and Juliet, in its original form, must be presumed to date from 1591, or, in other words, from Shakespeare's twenty-seventh year.

The matter was old; it is to be found in a novel by Masuccio of Salerno, published in 1476, which was probably made use of by Luigi da Porta when, in 1530, he wrote his *Hystoria novella-mente ritrovata di dui nobili Amanti.* After him came Bandello, with his tale, *La sfortunata morte di due infelicissimi amanti;* and upon it an English writer founded a play of *Romeo and Juliet,* which seems to have been popular in its day (before 1562), but is now lost.

An English poet, Arthur Brooke, found in Bandello's *Novella* the matter for a poem: *The tragicall Historye of Romeus and Juliet, written first in Italian by Bandell and now in Englishe by Ar. Br.* This poem is composed in rhymed iambic verses of twelve and fourteen syllables alternately, whose rhythm indeed jogs somewhat heavily along, but is not unpleasant and not too monotonous. The method of narration is very artless, loquacious, and diffuse; it resembles the narrative style of a clever child, who describes with minute exactitude and circumstantiality, going into every detail, and placing them all upon the same plane.[1]

Shakespeare founded his play upon this poem, in which the two leading characters, Friar Laurence, Mercutio, Tybalt, the Nurse, and the Apothecary, were ready to his hand, in faint outlines. Romeo's fancy for another woman immediately before he meets Juliet is also here, set forth at length; and the action as a whole follows the same course as in the tragedy.

The First Quarto of *Romeo and Juliet* was published in 1597,

---

[1] Here is a specimen. Romeo says to Juliet—

> " Since, lady, that you like to honor me so much
> As to accept me for your spouse, I yeld my selfe for such.
> In true witness whereof, because I must depart,
> Till that my deed do prove my woord, I leave in pawne my hart.
> Tomorrow eke bestimes, before the sunne arise,
> To Fryer Lawrence will I wende, to learne his sage advise."

with the following title: *An excellent conceited Tragedie of Romeo and Juliet. As it hath been often (with great applause) plaid publiquely, by the right Honourable the L. of Hunsdon his Seruants.* Lord Hunsdon died in July 1596, during his tenure of office as Lord Chamberlain; his successor in the title was appointed to the office in April 1597; in the interim his company of actors was not called the Lord Chamberlain's, but only Lord Hunsdon's servants, and it must, therefore, have been at this time that the play was first acted.

Many things, however, suggest a much earlier origin for it, and the Nurse's allusion to the earthquake (i. 3) is of especial importance in determining its date. She says—

" 'Tis since the earthquake now eleven years;"

and a little later—

" And since that time it is eleven years."

There had been an earthquake in England in the year 1580. But we must not, of course, take too literally the babble of a garrulous old servant.

But even if Shakespeare began to work upon the theme in 1591, there is no doubt that, according to his frequent practice, he went through the play again, revised and remoulded it, somewhere between that date and 1599, when it appeared in the Second Quarto almost in the form in which we now possess it. This Second Quarto has on its title-page the words, "newly corrected, augmented and amended." Not until the fourth edition does the author's name appear.

No one can doubt that Tycho Mommsen and that excellent Shakespeare scholar Halliwell-Phillips are right in declaring the 1597 Quarto to be a pirated edition. But it by no means follows that the complete text of 1599 already existed in 1597, and was merely carelessly abridged. In view of those passages (such as the seventh scene of the second act) where a whole long sequence of dialogue is omitted as superfluous, and where the old text is replaced by one totally new and very much better, this impression will not hold ground.

We have here, then, as elsewhere—but seldom so indubitably and obviously as here—a play of Shakespeare's at two different stages of its development.

In the first place, all that is merely sketched in the earlier edition is elaborated in the later. Descriptive scenes and speeches, which afford a background and foil to the action, are added. The street skirmish in the beginning is much developed; the scene between the servants and the scene with the musicians are added. The Nurse, too, has become more loquacious and much more comic; Mercutio's wit has been enriched by some of its most characteristic touches; old Capulet has acquired a more lifelike physiognomy; the part of Friar Laurence, in particular, has grown to almost twice its original dimensions; and we feel in these amplifications that care on Shakespeare's part, which appears in other places as well, to prepare, in the course of revision, for what is to come, to lay its foundations and foreshadow it. The Friar's reply, for example, to Romeo's vehement outburst of joy (ii. 6) is an added touch :—

> "These violent delights have violent ends,
> And in their triumphs die : like fire and powder,
> Which, as they kiss, consume."

New, too, is his reflection on Juliet's lightness of foot :—

> "A lover may bestride the gossamer
> That idles in the wanton summer air,
> And yet not fall; so light is vanity."

With the exception of the first dozen lines, the Friar's splendidly eloquent speech to Romeo (iii. 3) when, in his despair, he has drawn his sword to kill himself, is almost entirely new. The added passage begins thus :—

> "Why rail'st thou on thy birth, the heaven, and earth?
> Since birth, and heaven, and earth, all three do meet
> In thee at once, which thou at once wouldst lose.
> Fie, fie! thou sham'st thy shape, thy love, thy wit;
> Which, like an usurer, abound'st in all,
> And usest none in that true use indeed
> Which should bedeck thy shape, thy love, thy wit."

New, too, is the Friar's minute description to Juliet (iv. 1) of the action of the sleeping-draught, and his account of how she will be borne to the tomb, which paves the way for the masterly passage (iv. 3), also added, where Juliet, with the potion in her hand, conquers her terror of awakening in the grisly underground vault.

But the essential change lies in the additional earnestness, and consequent beauty, with which the characters of the two lovers have been endowed in the course of the revision. For example, Juliet's speech to Romeo (ii. 2) is inserted :—

> "And yet I wish but for the thing I have.
> My bounty is as boundless as the sea,
> My love as deep; the more I give to thee,
> The more I have, for both are infinite."

In the passage (ii. 5) where Juliet is awaiting the return of the Nurse with a message from Romeo, almost the whole expression of her impatience is new; for example, the lines :—

" Had she affections, and warm youthful blood,
She'd be as swift in motion as a ball ;
My words would bandy her to my sweet love,
And his to me :
But old folks, many feign as they were dead ;
Unwieldy, slow, heavy and pale as lead."

In Juliet's celebrated soliloquy (iii. 2), where, with that mixture of innocence and passion which forms the groundwork of her character, she awaits Romeo's first evening visit, only the four opening lines, with their mythological imagery, are found in the earlier text :—

"*Jul.* Gallop apace, you fiery-footed steeds,
Towards Phœbus' lodging : such a waggoner
As Phaethon would whip you to the west,
And bring in cloudy night immediately."

Not till he put his final touches to the work did Shakespeare find for the young girl's love-longing that marvellous utterance which we all know :—

" Spread thy close curtain, love-performing night !
That runaways' eyes may wink, and Romeo
Leap to these arms, untalk'd-of, and unseen !

.   .   .   .   .   .

Hood my unmann'd blood, bating in my cheeks,
With thy black mantle ; till strange love, grown bold,
Think true love acted simple modesty.
Come, night ! come, Romeo ! come, thou day in night ! "

Almost the whole of the following scene between the Nurse and Juliet, in which she learns of Tybalt's death and Romeo's banishment, is likewise new. Here occur some of the most daring and passionate expressions which Shakespeare has placed in Juliet's mouth :—

" Some word there was, worser than Tybalt's death,
That murder'd me. I would forget it fain.

.   .   .   .   .   .

That 'banished,' that one word 'banished,'
Hath slain ten thousand Tybalts. Tybalt's death
Was woe enough, if it had ended there :
Or,—if sour woe delights in fellowship,
And needly will be rank'd with other griefs,—
Why follow'd not, when she said—Tybalt's dead,
Thy father, or thy mother, nay, or both,
Which modern lamentation might have mov'd ?
But, with a rearward following Tybalt's death,
'Romeo is banished !'—to speak that word,
Is father, mother, Tybalt, Romeo, Juliet,
All slain, all dead."

To the original version, on the other hand, belong not only the highly indecorous witticisms and allusions with which Mercutio garnishes the first scene of the second act, but also the majority of the speeches in which the conceit-virus rages. The uncertainty of Shakespeare's taste, even at the date of the revision, is apparent in the fact that he has not only let all these speeches stand, but has interpolated not a few of equal extravagance.

So little did it jar upon him that Romeo, in the original text, should thus apostrophise love (i. 1)—

> " O heavy lightness ! serious vanity !
> Misshapen chaos of well-seeming forms !
> Feather of lead, bright smoke, cold fire, sick health !
> Still-waking sleep, that is not what it is ! "

that in the course of revision he must needs place in Juliet's mouth these quite analogous ejaculations (iii. 2) :—

> " Beautiful tyrant ! fiend angelical !
> Dove-feather'd raven ! wolvish-ravening lamb !
> Despised substance of divinest show ! "

Romeo in the old text indulges in this deplorably affected outburst (i. 2) :—

> " When the devout religion of mine eye
> Maintains such falsehood, then turn tears to fires ;
> And these, who, often drown'd, could never die,
> Transparent heretics, be burnt for liars."

In the old text, too, we find the barbarously tasteless speech in which Romeo, in his despair, envies the fly which is free to kiss Juliet's hand (iii. 2) :—

> " More validity,
> More honourable state, more courtship lives
> In carrion flies, than Romeo : they may seize
> On the white wonder of dear Juliet's hand,
> And steal immortal blessing from her lips ;
> Who, even in pure and vestal modesty,
> Still blush, as thinking their own kisses sin ;
> But Romeo may not ; he is banished.
> Flies may do this, but I from this must fly : .
> They are free men, but I am banished."

It is astonishing to come upon these lapses of taste, which are not surpassed by any of the absurdities in which the French *Précieuses Ridicules* of the next century delighted, side by side with outbursts of the most exquisite lyric poetry, the most brilliant wit, and the purest pathos to be found in the literature of any country or of any age.

Romeo and Juliet is perhaps not such a flawless work of art

as *A Midsummer Night's Dream.* It is not so delicately, so absolutely harmonious. But it is an achievement of much greater
significance and moment; it is the great and typical love-tragedy
of the world.

It soars immeasurably above all later attempts to approach it.
The Danish critic who should mention such a tragedy as *Axel
and Valborg* in the same breath with this play would show more
patriotism than artistic sense. Beautiful as Oehlenschläger's
drama is, the very nature of its theme forbids us to compare it
with Shakespeare's. It celebrates constancy rather than love;
it is a poem of tender emotions, of womanly magnanimity and
chivalrous virtue, at war with passion and malignity. It is
not, like *Romeo and Juliet,* at once the pæan and the dirge of
passion.

Romeo and Juliet is the drama of youthful and impulsive love-
at-first-sight, so passionate that it bursts every barrier in its path,
so determined that it knows no middle way between happiness
and death, so strong that it throws the lovers into each other's
arms with scarcely a moment's pause, and, lastly, so ill-fated that
death follows straightway upon the ecstasy of union.

Here, more than anywhere else, has Shakespeare shown in
all its intensity the dual action of an absorbing love in filling
the soul with gladness to the point of intoxication, and, at the
same time, with despair at the very idea of parting.

While in *A Midsummer Night's Dream* he dealt with the
imaginative side of love, its fantastic and illusive phases, he here
regards it in its more passionate aspect, as the source of rapture
and of doom.

His material enabled Shakespeare to place his love-story in
the setting best fitted to throw into relief the beauty of the
emotion, using as his background a vendetta between two noble
families, which has grown from generation to generation through
one sanguinary reprisal after another, until it has gradually infected the whole town around them. According to the traditions
of their race, the lovers ought to hate each other. The fact that,
on the contrary, they are so passionately drawn together in
mutual ecstasy, bears witness from the outset to the strength
of an emotion which not only neutralises prejudice in their own
minds, but continues to assert itself in opposition to the prejudices
of their surroundings. This is no peaceful tenderness. It flashes
forth like lightning at their first meeting, and its violence, under
the hapless circumstances, hurries these young souls straight to
their tragic end.

Between the lovers and the haters Shakespeare has placed
Friar Laurence, one of his most delightful embodiments of reason.
Such figures are rare in his plays, as they are in life, but ought
not to be overlooked, as they have been, for example, by Taine
in his somewhat one-sided estimate of Shakespeare's great-

ness.   Shakespeare knows and understands passionlessness; but
he always places it on the second plane.   It comes in very
naturally here, in the person of one who is obliged by his age
and his calling to act as an onlooker in the drama of life.   Friar
Laurence is full of goodness and natural piety, a monk such as
Spinoza or Goethe would have loved, an undogmatic sage, with
the astuteness and benevolent Jesuitism of an old confessor—
brought up on the milk and bread of philosophy, not on the fiery
liquors of religious fanaticism.

It is very characteristic of the freedom of spirit which Shakespeare early acquired, in the sphere in which freedom was then
hardest of attainment, that this monk is drawn with so delicate
a touch, without the smallest ill-will towards conquered Catholicism, yet without the smallest leaning towards Catholic doctrine
—the emancipated creation of an emancipated poet.   The poet
here rises immeasurably above his original, Arthur Brooke, who,
in his naïvely moralising "Address to the Reader," makes the
Catholic religion mainly responsible for the impatient passion of
Romeo and Juliet and the disasters which result from it.[1]

It would be to misunderstand the whole spirit of the play if
we were to reproach Friar Laurence with the not only romantic
but preposterous nature of the means he adopts to help the lovers
—the sleeping-potion administered to Juliet.   This Shakespeare
simply accepted from his original, with his usual indifference to
external detail.

The poet has placed in the mouth of Friar Laurence a tranquil
life-philosophy, which he first expresses in general terms, and
then applies to the case of the lovers.   He enters his cell with a
basket full of herbs from the garden.   Some of them have curative
properties, others contain death-dealing juices; a plant which has
a sweet and salutary smell may be poisonous to the taste; for
good and evil are but two sides to the same thing (ii. 3):—

> " Virtue itself turns vice, being misapplied,
> And vice sometimes 's by action dignified.
> Within the infant rind of this sweet flower
> Poison hath residence, and medicine power:
> For this, being smelt, with that part cheers each part;
> Being tasted, slays all senses with the heart.
> Two such opposed kings encamp them still
> In man as well as herbs,—grace, and rude will;
> And where the worser is predominant,
> Full soon the canker death eats up that plant."

---

[1] "A coople of vnfortunate louers, thralling themselves to vnhonest desire, neglect-
ing the authoritie and aduise of parents and frendes, conferring their principall
counsels with dronken gossyppes and superstitious friers (the naturally fitte instru-
mentes of unchastitie), attemptyng all aduentures of peryll for thattaynyng of their
wished lust, vsyng auriculer confession (the key of whoredom and treason). . . ."

When Romeo, immediately before the marriage, defies sorrow
and death in the speech beginning (ii. 6)—

> " Amen, Amen ! but come what sorrow can,
> It cannot countervail the exchange of joy
> That one short minute gives me in her sight,"

Laurence seizes the opportunity to apply his view of life. He
fears this overflowing flood-tide of happiness, and expounds his
philosophy of the golden mean—that wisdom of old age which is
summed up in the cautious maxim, "Love me little, love me long."
Here it is that he utters the above-quoted words as to the violent
ends ensuing on violent delights, like the mutual destruction
wrought by the kiss of fire and gunpowder. It is remarkable
how the idea of gunpowder and of explosions seems to have
haunted Shakespeare's mind while he was busied with the fate of
Romeo and Juliet. In the original sketch of Juliet's soliloquy in
the fifth scene of the second act we read :—

> " Loue's heralds should be thoughts,
> And runne more swift, than hastie powder fierd,
> Doth hurrie from the fearfull cannons mouth."

When Romeo draws his sword to kill himself, the Friar says
(iii. 3) :—

> " Thy wit, that ornament to shape and love,
> Misshapen in the conduct of them both,
> Like powder in a skilless soldier's flask,
> Is set a-fire by thine own ignorance,
> And thou dismember'd with thine own defence."

Romeo himself, finally, in his despair over the false news of
Juliet's death, demands of the apothecary a poison so strong that

> " the trunk may be discharg'd of breath
> As violently, as the hasty powder fir'd,
> Doth hurry from the fatal cannon's womb."

In other words, these young creatures have gunpowder in their
veins, undamped as yet by the mists of life, and love is the fire
which kindles it. Their catastrophe is inevitable, and it was
Shakespeare's deliberate purpose so to represent it ; but it is
not deserved, in the moral sense of the word : it is not a
punishment for guilt. The tragedy does not afford the smallest
warranty for the pedantically moralising interpretation devised
for it by Gervinus and others.

Romeo and Juliet, as a drama, still represents in many ways
the Italianising tendency in Shakespeare's art. Not only the
rhymed couplets and stanzas and the abounding *concetti* betray

Italian influence: the whole structure of the tragedy is very Romanesque. All Romanesque, like all Greek art, produces its effect by dint of order, which sometimes goes the length of actual symmetry. Purely English art has more of the freedom of life itself; it breaks up symmetry in order to attain a more delicate and unobtrusive harmony, much as an excellent prose style shuns the symmetrical regularity of verse, and aims at a subtler music of its own.

The Romanesque type is apparent in all Shakespeare's earlier plays. He sometimes even goes beyond his Romanesque models. In *Love's Labour's Lost* the King with his three courtiers is opposed to the Princess and her three ladies. In *The Two Gentlemen of Verona* the faithful Valentine has his counterpart in the faithless Proteus, and each of them has his comic servant. In the *Menæchmi* of Plautus there is only one slave; in *The Comedy of Errors* the twin masters have twin servants. In *A Midsummer Night's Dream* the heroic couple (Theseus and Hippolyta) have as a counterpart the fairy couple (Oberon and Titania); and, further, there is a complex symmetry in the fortunes of the Athenian lovers, Hermia being at first wooed by two men, while Helena stands alone and deserted, whereas afterwards it is Hermia who is left without a lover, while the two men centre their suit upon Helena. Finally, there is a fifth couple in Pyramus and Thisbe, represented by the artisans, who in burlesque and sportive fashion complete the symmetrical design.

The French critics who have seen in Shakespeare the antithesis to the Romanesque principle in art have overlooked these his beginnings. Voltaire, after more careful study, need not have expressed himself horrified; and if Taine, in his able essay, had gone somewhat less summarily to work, he would not have found everywhere in Shakespeare a fantasy and a technique entirely foreign to the genius of the Latin races.

The composition of *Romeo and Juliet* is quite as symmetrical as that of the comedies, indeed almost architectural in its equipoise. First, two of Capulet's servants enter, then two of Montague's; then Benvolio, of the Montague party; then Tybalt, of the Capulets; then citizens of both parties; then old Capulet and his wife; then old Montague and his; and finally, as the "keystone of the arch," the Prince, the central figure around whom all the characters range themselves, and by whom the fate of the lovers is to be determined.[1]

But it is not as a drama that *Romeo and Juliet* has won all hearts. Although, from a dramatic point of view, it stands high above *A Midsummer Night's Dream*, yet it is in virtue of its exquisite lyrism that this erotic masterpiece of Shakespeare's youth, like its fantastic predecessor, has bewitched the world. It is from the lyrical portions of the tragedy that the magic

[1] See Dowden: *Shakspere: his Mind and Art*, p. 60.

of romance proceeds, which sheds its glamour and its glory over the whole.

The finest lyrical passages are these : Romeo's declaration of love at the ball, Juliet's soliloquy before their bridal night, and their parting at the dawn.

Gervinus, a conscientious and learned student, in spite of his tendency to see in Shakespeare the moralist specially demanded by the Germany of his own day, has followed Halpin in pointing out that in all these three passages Shakespeare has adopted age-old lyric forms. In the first he almost reproduces the Italian sonnet; in the second he approaches, both in matter and form, to the bridal song, the Epithalamium; in the third he takes as his model the mediæval Dawn-Song, the *Tagelied*. But we may be sure that Shakespeare did not, as the commentators think, deliberately choose these forms in order to give perspective to the situation, but instinctively gave it a deep and distant background in his effort to find the truest and largest utterance for the emotion he was portraying.

The first colloquy between Romeo and Juliet (i. 5), being merely the artistic idealisation of an ordinary passage of ball-room gallantry, turns upon the prayer for a kiss, which the English fashion of the day authorised each cavalier to demand of his lady, and is cast in a sonnet form more or less directly derived from Petrarch. But whereas Petrarch's style is simple and pure, here we have far-fetched turns of speech, quibbling appeals, and expressions of admiration suggested by the intellect rather than the feelings. The passage opens with a quatrain of unspeakable tenderness :—

> "*Romeo.* If I profane with my unworthiest hand
> This holy shrine, the gentle fine is this ;
> My lips, two blushing pilgrims, ready stand
> To smooth that rough touch with a tender kiss."

And though the scene proceeds in the somewhat artificial style of the later Italians—

> "*Romeo.* Thus from my lips, by thine, my sin is purg'd.
> [*Kissing her.*]
> *Juliet.* Then have my lips the sin that they have took.
> *Rom.* Sin from my lips? O trespass sweetly urg'd !
> Give me my sin again.
> *Jul.*   You kiss by the book "

—yet so much soul is breathed into the Italian love-fencing that under its somewhat affected grace we can distinguish the pulse-throbs of awakening desire.

Juliet's soliloquy before the bridal night (iii. 2) lacks only rhyme to be, in good set form, an epithalamium of the period. These compositions spoke of Hymen and Cupid, and told how

Hymen at first appears alone, while Cupid lurks concealed, until, at the door of the bridal chamber, the elder brother gives place to the younger.

It is noteworthy that the mythological opening lines, which belong to the earlier form of the play, contain a clear reminiscence of a passage in Marlowe's *King Edward II*. Marlowe's

"Gallop apace, bright Phœbus, through the sky !"

reappears in Shakespeare in the form of

"Gallop apace, you fiery-footed steeds,
Towards Phœbus' lodging ! "

The rest of the soliloquy, as we have seen above, ranks among the loveliest things Shakespeare ever wrote. One of its most delicately daring expressions is imitated in Milton's *Comus ;* and the difference between the original and the imitation is curiously typical of the difference between the poet of the Renaissance and the poet of Puritanism. Juliet implores love-performing night to spread its close curtain, that Romeo may leap unseen to her arms ; for—

"Lovers can see to do their amorous rites
By their own beauties ; or, if love be blind,
It best agrees with night."

Milton annexes the thought and the turn of phrase ; but the part played by beauty in Shakespeare, Milton assigns to virtue :—

"Virtue could see to do what virtue would
By her own radiant light."

There is in Juliet's utterance of passion a healthful delicacy that ennobles it ; and it need not be said that the presence of this very passion in Juliet's monologue renders it infinitely more chaste than the old epithalamiums.

The exquisite dialogue in Juliet's chamber at daybreak (iii. 5) is a variation on the motive of all the old Dawn-Songs. They always turn upon the struggle in the breasts of two lovers who have secretly passed the night together, between their reluctance to part and their dread of discovery—a struggle which sets them debating whether the light they see comes from the sun or the moon, and whether it is the nightingale or the lark whose song they hear.

How gracefully is this motive here employed, and what added depth is given to the situation by our knowledge that the banished Romeo's life is forfeit if he lingers until day !—

"*Juliet.* Wilt thou be gone ? it is not yet near day :
It was the nightingale, and not the lark,
That pierc'd the fearful hollow of thine ear ;
Nightly she sings on yon pomegranate-tree :
Believe me, love, it was the nightingale.

Romeo. It was the lark, the herald of the morn,
No nightingale: look, love, what envious streaks
Do lace the severing clouds in yonder east."

Romeo is a well-born youth, richly endowed by nature, enthusiastic and reserved. At the beginning of the play we find him indifferent as to the family feud, and absorbed in his hopeless fancy for a lady of the hostile house, Capulet's fair niece, Rosaline, whom Mercutio describes as a pale wench with black eyes. The Rosaline of *Love's Labour's Lost* is also described by Biron, at the end of the third act, as

"A whitely wanton with a velvet brow,
With two pitch-balls stuck in her face for eyes,"

so that the two namesakes may not improbably have had a common model.

Shakespeare has retained this first passing fancy of Romeo's, which he found in his sources, because he knew that the heart is never more disposed to yield to a new love than when it is bleeding from an old wound, and because this early feeling already shows Romeo as inclined to idolatry and self-absorption. The young Italian, even before he has seen the woman who is to be his fate, is reticent and melancholy, full of tender longings and forebodings of evil. Then he is seized as though with an overwhelming ecstasy at the first glimpse of Rosaline's girl-kinswoman.

Romeo's character is less resolute than Juliet's; passion ravages it more fiercely; he, as a youth, has less control over himself than she as a maiden. But none the less is his whole nature elevated and beautified by his relation to her. He finds expressions for his love for Juliet quite different from those he had used in the case of Rosaline. There occur, indeed, in the balcony scene, one or two outbursts of the extravagance so natural to the rhetoric of young love. The envious moon is sick and pale with grief because Juliet is so much more fair than she; two of the fairest stars, having some business, do entreat her eyes to twinkle in their spheres till they return. But side by side with these conceits we find immortal lines, the most exquisite words of love that ever were penned :—

"With love's light wings did I o'erperch these walls;
For stony limits cannot hold love out . . ."

or—

"It is my soul that calls upon my name:
How silver-sweet sound lovers' tongues by night,
Like softest music to attending ears!"

His every word is steeped in a sensuous-spiritual ecstasy.

Juliet has grown up in an unquiet and not too agreeable home. Her testy, unreasonable father, though not devoid of kindliness, is yet so brutal that he threatens to beat her and turn her out of doors if she does not comply with his wishes; and her mother is a cold-hearted woman, whose first thought, in her rage against Romeo, is to have him put out of the way by means of poison. She has thus been left for the most part to the care of the humorous and plain-spoken Nurse, one of Shakespeare's most masterly figures (foretelling the Falstaff of a few years later), whose babble has tended to prepare her mind for love in its frankest manifestations.

Although a child in years, Juliet has the young Italian's mastery in dissimulation. When her mother proposes to have Romeo poisoned, she agrees without moving a muscle, and thus secures the promise that no one but she shall be allowed to mix the potion. Her beauty must be conceived as dazzling. I saw her one day in the streets of Rome, in all the freshness of her fourteen years. My companion and I looked at each other, and exclaimed with one consent, "Juliet!" Romeo's exclamation on first beholding her—

"Beauty too rich for use, for earth too dear,"

conveys an instant impression of nobility, high mental gifts, and unsullied purity, combined with the utmost ardour of temperament. In a few days the child ripens into a heroine.

We make acquaintance with her at the ball in the palace of the Capulets, and in the moonlit garden where the nightingale sings in the pomegranate-tree—surroundings which harmonise as completely with the whole spirit and tone of the play as the biting wintry air on the terrace at Kronborg, filled with echoes of the King's carouse, harmonises with the spirit and tone of *Hamlet*. But Juliet is no mere creature of moonshine. She is practical. While Romeo wanders off into high-strung raptures of vague enthusiasm, she, on the contrary, promptly suggests a secret marriage, and promises on the instant to send the Nurse to him to make a more definite arrangement. After the killing of her kinsman, it is Romeo who despairs and she who takes up the battle, daring all to escape the marriage with Paris. With a firm hand and a steadfast heart she drains the sleeping-potion, and arms herself with her dagger, so that, if all else fails, she may still be mistress of her own person.

How shall we describe the love that indues her with all this strength?

Modern critics in Germany and Sweden are agreed in regarding it as a purely sensual passion, by no means admirable—nay, essentially reprehensible. They insist that there is a total absence of maidenly modesty in Juliet's manner of feeling, thinking, speaking, and acting. She does not really know Romeo, they say; is there anything more, then, in this unbashful love than the attraction of mere bodily beauty?[1]

As if it were possible thus to analyse and discriminate! As if, in such a case, body and soul were twain! As if a love which, from the first moment, both lovers feel to be, for them, the arbiter of life and death, were to be decried in favour of an affection founded on mutual esteem—the variety which, it appears, "our age demands."

Ah no! these virtuous philosophers and worthy professors have no feeling for the spirit of the Renaissance: they are altogether too remote from it. The Renaissance means, among many other things, a new birth of warm-blooded humanity and pagan innocence of imagination.

It is no love of the head that Juliet feels for Romeo, no admiring affection that she reasons herself into; nor is it a sentimental love, a riot of idealism apart from nature. But still less is it a mere ferment of the senses. It is based upon instinct, the infallible instinct of the child of nature, and it is in her, as in him, a vibration of the whole being in longing and desire, a quivering of all its chords, from the highest to the lowest, so intense that neither he nor she can tell where body ends and soul begins.

Romeo and Juliet dominate the whole tragedy; but the two minor creations of Mercutio and the Nurse are in no way inferior to them in artistic value. In this play Shakespeare manifests for the first time not only the full majesty but the many-sidedness of his genius, the suppleness of style which is equal at once to the wit of Mercutio and to the racy garrulity of the Nurse. *Titus Andronicus* was as monotonously sombre as a tragedy of Marlowe's. *Romeo and Juliet* is a perfect orb, embracing the twin hemispheres of the tragic and the comic. It is a symphony so rich that the strain from fairyland in the Queen Mab speech harmonises with the note of high comedy in Mercutio's sparkling, cynical, and audacious sallies, with the wanton flutings of farce in the Nurse's anecdotes, with the most rapturous descants of passion in the antiphonies of Romeo and Juliet, and with the

---

[1] Edward von Hartmann, from the lofty standpoint of German morality, has launched a diatribe against Juliet. He asserts her immeasurable moral inferiority to the typical German maiden, both of poetry and of real life. Schiller's Thekla has undeniably less warm blood in her veins.

A Swedish professor, Henrik Schück, in an able work on Shakespeare, says of Juliet: "On examining into the nature of the love to which she owes all this strength, the unprejudiced reader cannot but recognise in it a purely sensual passion. . . . A few words from the lips of this well-favoured youth are sufficient to awaken in its fullest strength the slumbering desire in her breast. But this love possesses no psychical basis; it is not founded on any harmony of souls. They scarcely know each other. . . . Can their love, then, be anything more than the merely sensual passion aroused by the contemplation of a beautiful body? . . . So much I say with confidence, that the woman who, inaccessible to the spiritual element in love, lets herself be carried away on this first meeting by the joy of the senses . . . that woman is ignorant of the love which our age demands."

deep organ - tones in the soliloquies and speeches of Friar Laurence.

How intense is the life of Romeo and Juliet in their environment! Hark to the gay and yet warlike hubbub around them, the sport and merriment, the high words and the ring of steel in the streets of Verona! Hark to the Nurse's strident laughter, old Capulet's jesting and chiding, the low tones of the Friar, and the irrepressible rattle of Mercutio's wit! Feel the magic of the whole atmosphere in which they are plunged, these embodiments of tumultuous youth, living and dying in love, in magnanimity, in passion, in despair, under a glowing Southern sky, softening into moonlight nights of sultry fragrance—and realise that Shakespeare had at this point completed the first stage of his triumphal progress!

XIV

LATTER-DAY ATTACKS UPON SHAKESPEARE—THE BACONIAN THEORY — SHAKESPEARE'S KNOWLEDGE, PHYSICAL AND PHILOSOPHICAL

IN one of his sonnets Robert Browning says that Shakespeare's name, like the Hebrew name of God, ought never to be taken in vain. A timely monition to an age which has seen this great name besmirched by American and European imbecility! It is well known that in recent days a troop of less than half-educated people have put forth the doctrine that Shakespeare lent his name to a body of poetry with which he had really nothing to do — which he could not have understood, much less have written. Literary criticism is an instrument which, like all delicate tools, must be handled carefully, and only by those who have a vocation for it. Here it has fallen into the hands of raw Americans and fanatical women. Feminine criticism on the one hand, with its lack of artistic nerve, and Americanism on the other hand, with its lack of spiritual delicacy, have declared war to the knife against Shakespeare's personality, and have within the last few years found a considerable number of adherents. We have here another proof, if any were needed, that the judgment of the multitude, in questions of art, is a negligible quantity.[1]

Before the middle of this century, it had occurred to no human being to doubt that—trifling exceptions apart—the works attributed to Shakespeare were actually written by him. It has been reserved for the last forty years to see an ever-increasing stream of obloquy and contempt directed against what had hitherto been the most honoured name in modern literature.

At first the attack upon Shakespeare's memory was not so dogmatic as it has since become. In 1848 an American, Hart by name, gave utterance to some general doubts as to the origin of the plays. Then, in August 1852, there appeared in *Chambers's*

---

[1] According to W. H. Wyman's *Bibliography of the Bacon-Shakespeare Controversy* (Cincinnati, 1884), there had been published up to that date 255 books, pamphlets, and essays as to the authorship of Shakespeare's plays. In America 161 treatises of considerable bulk had been devoted to the question, and in England 69. Of these, 73 were decidedly opposed to Shakespeare's authorship, while 65 left the question undetermined. In other words, out of 161 books, only 23 were in favour of Shakespeare. And since then the proportion has no doubt remained much the same.

Edinburgh Journal an anonymous article, the author of which declared his conviction that William Shakespeare, uneducated as he was, must have hired a poet, some penniless famished Chatterton, who was willing to sell him his genius, and let him take to himself the credit for its creations. We see, he says, that his plays steadily improve as the series proceeds, until suddenly Shakespeare leaves London with a fortune, and the series comes to an abrupt end. In the case of so strenuously progressive a genius, can we account for this otherwise than by supposing that the poet had died, while his employer survived him ?

This is the first definite expression of the fancy that Shakespeare was only a man of straw who had arrogated to himself the renown of an unknown immortal.

In 1856 a Mr. William Smith issued a privately-printed letter to Lord Ellesmere, in which he puts forth the opinion that William Shakespeare was, by reason of his birth, his upbringing, and his lack of culture, incapable of writing the plays attributed to him. They must have been the work of a man educated to the highest point by study, travel, knowledge of books and men—a man like Francis Bacon, the greatest Englishman of his time. Bacon had kept his authorship secret, because to have avowed it would have been to sacrifice his position both in his profession and in Parliament; but he saw in these plays a means of strengthening his economic position, and he used the actor Shakespeare as a man of straw. Smith maintains that it was Bacon who, after having fallen into disgrace in 1621, published the First Folio edition of the plays in 1623.

If there were no other objection to this far-fetched theory, we cannot but remark that Bacon was scrupulously careful as to the form in which his works appeared, rewrote them over and over again, and corrected them so carefully that scarcely a single error of the press is to be found in his books. Can he have been responsible for the publication of these thirty-six plays, which swarm with misreadings and contain about twenty thousand errors of the press !

The delusion did not take serious shape until, in the same year, a Miss Delia Bacon put forward the same theory in American magazines: her namesake Bacon, and not Shakespeare, was the author of the renowned dramas. In the following year she published a quite unreadable book on the subject, of nearly 600 pages. And close upon her heels followed her disciple, Judge Nathaniel Holmes, also an American, with a book of no fewer than 696 pages, full of denunciations of the ignorant vagabond William Shakespeare, who, though he could scarcely write his own name and knew no other ambition than that of money-grubbing, had appropriated half the renown of the great Bacon.

The assumption is always the same: Shakespeare, born in a

provincial town, of illiterate parents, his father being, among other things, a butcher, was an ignorant boor, a low fellow, a " butcher-boy," as his assailants currently call him. In Holmes, as in later writers, the main method of proving Bacon's authorship of the Shakespearian plays is to bring together passages of somewhat similar import in Bacon and Shakespeare, in total disregard of context, form, or spirit.

Miss Delia Bacon literally dedicated her life to her attack upon Shakespeare. She saw in his works, not poetry, but a great philosophico-political system, and maintained that the proof of her doctrine would be found deposited in Shakespeare's grave. She had discovered in Bacon's letters the key to a cipher which would clear up everything; but unfortunately she became insane before she had imparted this key to the world.[1] She went to Stratford, obtained permission to have the grave opened, hovered about it day and night, but at last left it undisturbed, as it did not appear to her large enough to contain the posthumous papers of the Elizabeth Club. She did not, however, expect to find in the grave the original manuscripts of Shakespeare's plays. No ! she exclaims in her article on " William Shakespeare and his Plays" (*Putnam's Magazine*, January 1856), Lord Leicester's groom, of course, cared nothing for them, but only for the profit to be made out of them. What was to prevent him from lighting the fire with them ? "He had those manuscripts ! . . . He had the original *Hamlet* with its last finish; he had the original *Lear* with his own final readings; he had them all, as they came from the gods. . . . And he left us to wear out our youth and squander our lifetime in poring over and setting right the old garbled copies of the playhouse ! . . . Traitor and miscreant ! what did you do with them ? You have skulked this question long enough. You will have to account for them. . . . The awakening ages will put you on the stand, and you will not leave it until you answer the question, 'What did you do with them ?' "

It is hard to be the greatest dramatic genius in the world's

---

[1] One of her many followers, an American lawyer, Ignatius Donelly formerly Member of Congress and Senator from Minnesota, claims to have found the key. His crazy book is called *The Great Cryptogram : Francis Bacon's Cipher in the so-called Shakespeare Plays.* Donelly claims that among Bacon's papers he has discovered a cipher which enables him to extract here and there from the First Folio letters which form words and phrases distinctly stating that Bacon is the author of the dramas, and how Bacon embodied in the First Folio a cipher-confession of his authorship. Apart from the general folly of such a proceeding, Bacon must thus have made the editors, Heminge and Condell, his accomplices in his meaningless deception, and must even have induced Ben Jonson to confirm it by his enthusiastic introductory poem. Donelly has the impudence to declare that he won't communicate the key, lest anybody else shall be able to read the parts of the Cryptogram not yet interpreted, and in that way deprive him of his remuneration. During the first three months of publication of this two-volume work, no less than 20,000 copies were sold at two pounds.

history, and then, two centuries and a half after your death, to be called to account in such a tone as this for the fact that your manuscripts have disappeared. As regards purely external evidence, it is worth mentioning that the greatest student of Bacon's works, his editor and biographer, James Spedding, being challenged by Holmes to give his opinion, made a statement which begins thus:—" I have read your book on the authorship of Shakespeare faithfully to the end, and . . . I must declare myself not only unconvinced but undisturbed. To ask me to believe that ' Bacon was the author of these dramas ' is like asking me to believe that Lord Brougham was the author not only of Dickens' novels, but of Thackeray's also, and of Tennyson's poems besides. I deny," he concludes, "that a *primâ facie* case is made out for questioning Shakespeare's title. But if there were any reason for supposing that somebody else was the real author, I think I am in a condition to say that, whoever it was, it was not Bacon " (*Reviews and Discussions*, 1879, pp. 369–374).

What most amazes a critical reader of the Baconian impertinences is the fact that all the different arguments for the impossibility of attributing these plays to Shakespeare are founded upon the universality of knowledge and insight displayed in them, which must have been unattainable, it is urged, to a man of Shakespeare's imperfect scholastic training. Thus all that these detractors bring forward to Shakespeare's dishonour serves, rightly considered, to show in a clearer light the wealth of his genius.

On the other hand, the arguments adduced in support of Bacon's authorship are so ridiculous as almost to elude criticism. Opponents of the doctrine have dwelt upon such details as the philistinism of Bacon's essays "Of Love," "Of Marriage and Single Life," contrasted with the depth and the wit of Shakesperian utterances on these subjects; or they have cited certain lines from the miserable translations of seven Hebrew psalms which Bacon produced in the last years of his life, contrasting them with passages from *Richard III.* and *Hamlet*, in which Shakespeare has dealt with exactly similar ideas — the harvest that follows from a seed-time of tears, and the leaping to light of secret crimes. But it is a waste of time to go into details. Any one who has read even a few of Bacon's essays or a stanza or two of his verse translations, and who can discover in them any trace of Shakespeare's style in prose or verse, is no more fitted to have a voice on such questions than an inland bumpkin is fitted to lay down the law upon navigation.

Even putting aside the conjecture with regard to Bacon, and looking merely at the theory that Shakespeare did not write the plays, we cannot but find it unrivalled in its ineptitude. How can we conceive that not only contemporaries in general, but those with whom Shakespeare was in daily intercourse — the players. to whom he gave these dramas for production, who received his instructions about them, who saw his manuscripts and have described them to us (in the foreword to the First Folio) ; the dramatists who were constantly with him, his rivals and afterwards his comrades, like Drayton and Ben Jonson ; the people who discussed his works with him in the theatre, or, over the evening glass, debated with him concerning his art ; and, finally, the young noblemen whom his genius attracted and who became his patrons and afterwards his friends—how can we conceive that none of these, no single one, should ever have observed that he was not the man he pretended to be, and that he did not even understand the works he fraudulently declared to be his ! How can we conceive that none of all this intelligent and critical circle should ever have discovered the yawning gulf which separated his ordinary thought and speech from the thought and style of his alleged works !

In sum, then, the only evidence against Shakespeare lies in the fact that his works give proof of a too many-sided knowledge and insight !

The knowledge of English law which Shakespeare displays is so surprising as to have led to the belief that he must for some time in his youth have been a clerk in an attorney's office—a theory which was thought to be supported by the belief, now discredited, that an attack by the satirist Thomas Nash upon lawyers who had deserted the law for poetry was directed against him.[1]

Shakespeare shows a quite unusual fondness for the use of legal expressions. He knows to a nicety the technicalities of the bar, the formulas of the bench.   While most English writers of his period are guilty of frequent blunders as to the laws of marriage and inheritance, lawyers of a later date have not succeeded in finding in Shakespeare's references to the law a single error or deficiency. Lord Campbell, an eminent lawyer, has written a book on *Shakespeare's Legal Acquirements*.   And it was not through the lawsuits of Shakespeare's riper years that he attained this knowledge.   It is to be found even in his earliest works.   It appears, quaintly enough, in the mouth of the goddess in *Venus and Adonis* (verse 86, &c.), and it obtrudes itself in Sonnet xlvi., with its somewhat tasteless and wire-drawn description of a formal lawsuit between the eye and the heart.   It is characteristic that

---

[1] The passage runs thus : " It is a common practice now a days among a sort of shifting companions that run through every art and thrive by none, to leave the trade of *noverint*, whereto they were born, and busy themselves with the endeavours of art, that could scarcely latinize their neck-verse if they should have need ; yet English Seneca, read by candlelight, yields many good sentences, as *Blood is a beggar*, and so forth ; and if you entreat him fair in a frosty morning, he will afford you whole *Hamlets*, I should say handfuls, of tragical speeches." Although this passage seems at first sight an evident gibe at Shakespeare, it has in reality no reference to him, since *An Epistle to the Gentlemen Students of both Universities*, by Thomas Nash, although not printed till 1589, can be proved to have been written as early as 1587, many years before Shakespeare so much as thought of *Hamlet*.

his knowledge does not extend to the laws of foreign countries; otherwise we should scarcely find *Measure for Measure* founded upon such an impossible state of the law as that which is described as obtaining in Vienna. Shakespeare's accurate knowledge begins and ends with what comes within the sphere of his personal observation.

He seems equally at home in all departments of human life. If we might conclude from his knowledge of law that he had been a lawyer, we might no less confidently infer from his knowledge of typography that he had been a printer's devil. An English printer named Blades has written an instructive book, *Shakespeare and Typography*, to show that if the poet had passed his whole life in a printing-office he could not have been more familiar with the many peculiarities of nomenclature belonging to the handicraft. Bishop Charles Wordsworth has written a highly esteemed, very pious, but, I regret to say, quite unreadable work, *Shakespeare's Knowledge and Use of the Bible*, in which he makes out that the poet was impregnated with the Biblical spirit, and possessed a unique acquaintance with Biblical forms of expression.

Shakespeare's knowledge of nature is not simply such as can be acquired by any one who passes his childhood and youth in the open air and in the country. But even of this sort of knowledge he has an astonishing store. Whole books have been written as to his familiarity with insect life alone (R. Patterson: *The Natural History of the Insects mentioned by Shakespeare;* London, 1841), and his knowledge of the characteristics of the larger animals and birds seems to be inexhaustible. Appleton Morgan, one of the commentators of the Baconian theory, adduces in *The Shakespearean Myth* a whole series of examples.

In *Much Ado* (v. 2) Benedick says to Margaret—

" Thy wit is as quick as the greyhound's mouth ; it catches."

The greyhound alone among dogs can seize its prey while in full career.

In *As You Like It* (i. 2) Celia says—

" Here comes Monsieur Le Beau.
   Rosalind. With his mouth full of news.
   Celia. Which he will put on us as pigeons feed their young."

Pigeons have a way, peculiar to themselves, of passing food down the throats of their young.

In *Twelfth Night* (iii. 1) the Clown says to Viola—

" Fools are as like husbands, as pilchards are to herrings,—the husband's the bigger."

The pilchard is a fish of the herring family, which is caught in the Channel; it is longer and has larger scales.

In the same play (ii. 5) Maria says of Malvolio—

" Here comes the trout that must be caught with tickling."

When a trout is tickled on the sides or the belly it becomes so stupefied that it lets itself be caught in the hand.

In *Much Ado* (iii. 1) Hero says—

" For look where Beatrice, like a lapwing, runs
Close by the ground, to hear our conference."

The lapwing, which runs very swiftly, bends its neck towards the ground in running, in order to escape observation.

In *King Lear* (i. 4) the Fool says—

" The hedge-sparrow fed the cuckoo so long,
That it had its head bit off by its young."

In England, it is in the hedge-sparrow's nest that the cuckoo lays its eggs.

In *All's Well that Ends Well* (ii. 5) Lafeu says—

" I took this lark for a bunting."

The English bunting is a bird of the same colour and appearance as the lark, but it does not sing so well.

It would be easy to show that Shakespeare was as familiar with the characteristics of plants as with those of animals. Strangely enough, people have thought this knowledge of nature so improbable in a great poet, that in order to explain it they have jumped at the conclusion that the author must have been a man of science as well.

More comprehensible is the astonishment which has been awakened by Shakespeare's insight in other domains of nature not lying so open to immediate observation. His medical knowledge early attracted attention. In 1860 a Doctor Bucknill devoted a whole book to the subject, in which he goes so far as to attribute to the poet the most advanced knowledge of our own time, or, at any rate, of the 'sixties, in this department. Shakespeare's representations of madness surpass all those of other poets. Alienists are full of admiration for the accuracy of the symptoms in Lear and Ophelia. Nay, more, Shakespeare appears to have divined the more intelligent modern treatment of the insane, as opposed to the cruelty prevalent in his own time and long after. He even had some notions of what we in our days call medical jurisprudence; he was familiar with the symptoms of violent death

in contradistinction to death from natural causes.   Warwick says
in the second part of *Henry VI.* (iii. 2):—

> " See, how the blood is settled in his face.
>   Oft have I seen a timely-parted ghost,
>   Of ashy semblance, meagre, pale, and bloodless,
>   Being all descended to the labouring heart."

These lines occur in the oldest text.   In the later text, undoubtedly the result of Shakespeare's revision, we read :—

> " But see, his face is black, and full of blood ;
>   His eye-balls further out than when he liv'd,
>   Staring full ghastly like a strangled man :
>   His hair uprear'd, his nostrils stretch'd with struggling ;
>   His hands abroad display'd, as one that grasp'd
>   And tugg'd for life, and was by strength subdued.
>   Look, on the sheets, his hair, you see, is sticking ;
>   His well-proportion'd beard made rough and rugged,
>   Like to the summer's corn by tempest lodg'd.
>   It cannot be but he was murder'd here ;
>   The least of all these signs were probable."

Shakespeare seems, in certain instances, to be not only abreast
of the natural science of his time, but in advance of it.   People
have had recourse to the Baconian theory in order to explain the
surprising fact that although Harvey, who is commonly represented as the discoverer of the circulation of the blood, did not
announce his discovery until 1619, and published his book upon it
so late as 1628, yet Shakespeare, who, as we know, died in 1616,
in many passages of his plays alludes to the blood as circulating
through the body.   Thus, for example, in *Julius Cæsar* (ii. 1),
Brutus says to Portia—

> " You are my true and honourable wife ;
>   As dear to me as are the ruddy drops
>   That visit my sad heart."

Again, in *Coriolanus* (i. 1) Menenius makes the belly say of
its food—

> " I send it through the rivers of your blood,
>   Even to the court, the heart, to the seat o' the brain ;
>   And, through the cranks and offices of man,
>   The strongest nerves, and small inferior veins,
>   From me receive that natural competency
>   Whereby they live."

But apart from the fact that the highly gifted and unhappy
Servetus, whom Calvin burned, had, between 1530 and 1540, made
the discovery and lectured upon it, all men of culture in England
knew very well before Harvey's time that the blood flowed, even
that it circulated, and, more particularly, that it was driven from

the heart to the different limbs and organs; only, it was generally conceived that the blood passed from the heart through the veins, and not, as is actually the case, through the arteries. And there is nothing in the seventy-odd places in Shakespeare where the circulation of the blood is mentioned to show that he possessed this ultimate insight, although his general understanding of these questions bears witness to his high culture.

Another point which some people have held inexplicable, except by the Baconian theory, may be stated thus: Although the law of gravitation was first discovered by Newton, who was born in 1642, or fully twenty-six years after Shakespeare's death, and although the general conception of gravitation towards the centre of the earth had been unknown before Kepler, who discovered his third law of the mechanism of the heavenly bodies two years after Shakespeare's death, nevertheless in *Troilus and Cressida* (iv. 2) the heroine thus expresses herself:—

> " Time, force, and death,
> Do to this body what extremes you can,
> But the strong base and building of my love
> Is as the very centre of the earth,
> Drawing all things to it."

So carelessly does Shakespeare throw out such an extraordinary divination. His achievement in thus, as it were, rivalling Newton may seem in a certain sense even more extraordinary than Goethe's botanical and osteological discoveries; for Goethe had enjoyed a very different education from his, and had, moreover, all desirable leisure for scientific research. But Newton cannot rightly be said to have discovered the law of gravitation; he only applied it to the movements of the heavenly bodies. Even Aristotle had defined weight as "the striving of heavy bodies towards the centre of the earth." Among men of classical culture in England in Shakespeare's time, the knowledge that the centre point of the earth attracts everything to it was quite common. The passage cited only affords an additional proof that several of the men whose society Shakespeare frequented were among the most highly-developed intellects of the period. That his astronomical knowledge was not, on the whole, in advance of his time is proved by the expression, "the glorious planet Sol" in *Troilus and Cressida* (i. 3). He never got beyond the Ptolemaic system.

Another confirmation of the theory that Bacon must have written Shakespeare's plays has been found in the fact that the poet clearly had some conception of geology; whereas geology, as a science, owes its origin to Niels Steno, who was born in 1638, twenty-two years after Shakespeare's death. In the second part of *Henry IV.* (iii. 1), King Henry says:—

> " O God ! that one might read the book of fate,
> And see the revolution of the times
> Make mountains level, and the continent,
> Weary of solid firmness, melt itself
> Into the sea ! and, other times, to see
> The beachy girdle of the ocean
> Too wide for Neptune's hips ; how chances mock,
> And changes fill the cup of alteration
> With divers liquors ! "

The purport of this passage is simply to show that in nature, as in human life, the law of transformation reigns ; but no doubt it is implied that the history of the earth can be read in the earth itself, and that changes occur through upheavals and depressions. It looks like a forecast of the doctrine of Neptunism.

Here, again, people have gone to extremities in order artificially to enhance the impression made by the poet's brilliant divination. It was Steno who first systematised geological conceptions ; but he was by no means the first to hold that the earth had been formed little by little, and that it was therefore possible to trace in the record of the rocks the course of the earth's development. His chief service lay in directing attention to stratification, as affording the best evidence of the processes which have fashioned the crust of the globe.

It is, no doubt, a sign of Shakespeare's many-sided genius that here, too, he anticipates the scientific vision of later times ; but there is nothing in these lines that presupposes any special or technical knowledge. Here is an analogous case : In Michael Angelo's picture of the creation of Adam, where God wakens the first man to life by touching the figure's outstretched finger-tip with his own, we seem to see a clear divination of the electric spark. Yet the induction of electricity was not known until the eighteenth century, and Michael Angelo could not possibly have any scientific understanding of its nature.

Shakespeare's knowledge was not of a scientific cast. He learned from men and from books with the rapidity of genius. Not, we may be sure, without energetic effort, for nothing can be had for nothing ; but the effort of acquisition must have come easy to him, and must have escaped the observation of all around him. There was no time in his life for patient research ; he had to devote the best part of his days to the theatre, to uneducated and unconsidered players, to entertainments, to the tavern. We may fancy that he must have had himself in mind when, in the introductory scene to *Henry V.*, he makes the Archbishop of Canterbury thus describe his hero, the young king :—

> " Hear him but reason in divinity,
> And, all-admiring, with an inward wish
> You would desire the king were made a prelate :
> Hear him debate of commonwealth affairs,

You would say, it hath been all-in-all his study:
List his discourse of war, and you shall hear
A fearful battle render'd you in music:
Turn him to any cause of policy,
The Gordian knot of it he will unloose,
Familiar as his garter; that, when he speaks,
The air, a charter'd libertine, is still,
And the mute wonder lurketh in men's ears,
To steal his sweet and honey'd sentences;
So that the art and practic part of life
Must be the mistress to this theoric:
Which is a wonder, how his grace should glean it,
Since his addiction was to courses vain;
His companies unletter'd, rude, and shallow;
His hours fill'd up with riots, banquets, sports;
And never noted in him any study,
Any retirement, any sequestration
From open haunts and popularity."

To this the Bishop of Ely answers very sagely, "The straw-berry grows underneath the nettle." We cannot but conceive, however, that, by a beneficent provision of destiny, Shakespeare's genius found in the highest culture of his day precisely the nourishment it required.

G

XV

*THE THEATRES—THEIR SITUATION AND ARRANGEMENTS—
THE PLAYERS—THE POETS—POPULAR AUDIENCES—THE
ARISTOCRATIC PUBLIC—SHAKESPEARE'S ARISTOCRATIC
PRINCIPLES*

ON swampy ground beside the Thames lay the theatres, of which
the largest were wooden sheds, only half thatched with rushes,
with a trench around them and a flagstaff on the roof. After
the middle of the fifteen-seventies, when the first was built, they
shot up rapidly, and in the early years of the new century
theatre-building took such a start that, as we learn from Prynne's
Histriomastix, there were in 1633 no fewer than nineteen permanent theatres in London, a number which no modern town of
300,000 inhabitants can equal. These figures show how keen
and how widespread was the interest in the drama.

More than a hundred years before the first theatre was built
there had been professional actors in England. Their calling had
developed from that of the travelling jugglers, who varied their
acrobatic performances with "plays." The earliest scenic representations had been given by the Church, and the Guilds had
inherited the tradition. Priests and choir-boys were the first
actors of the Middle Ages, and after them came the mummers of
the Guilds. But none of these performers acted except at periodical festivals; none of them were professional actors. From
the days of Henry the Sixth onwards, however, members of the
nobility began to entertain companies of actors, and Henry VII.
and Henry VIII. had their own private comedians. A "Master of
the Revels" was appointed to superintend the musical and dramatic
entertainments at court. About the middle of the sixteenth century, Parliament begins to keep an eye upon theatrical representations. It forbids the performance of anything conflicting with the
doctrines of the Church, and prohibits miracle-plays, but does
not object to songs or plays designed to attack vice and represent
virtue. In other words, dramatic art escapes condemnation when
it is emphatically moral, and thrives best when it keeps to purely
secular matters.

Under Mary, religious plays once more came into honour.
Elizabeth began by strictly prohibiting all dramatic representations, but sanctioned them again in 1560, subjecting them, how-

ever, to a censorship. This measure was dictated at least as
much by political as by religious motives. The censorship must,
however, have been exercised somewhat loosely, since a statute
of 1572 declared that all actors who were not attached to the
service of a nobleman should be treated as "rogues and vagabonds," or, in other words, might be whipped out of any town in
which they appeared. This decree, of course, compelled all actors
to enter the service of one or other great man, and we see that
the aristocracy felt bound to protect their art. A large number
of the first men in the kingdom, during Elizabeth's reign, had
each his company of actors. The player received from the nobleman whose "servant" he was a cloak bearing the arms of the
family. On the other hand, he received no salary, but was simply
paid for each performance given before his patron. We must
thus conceive Shakespeare as bearing on his cloak the arms of
Leicester, and afterwards of the Lord Chamberlain, until about
his fortieth year. From 1604 onwards, when the company was
promoted by James I. to be "His Majesty's Servants," it was the
Royal arms that he wore. One is tempted to say that he exchanged a livery for a uniform.

In 1574 Elizabeth had given permission to Lord Leicester's
Servants to give scenic representations of all sorts for the delectation of herself and her lieges, both in London and anywhere else
in England. But neither in London nor in other towns did the
local authorities recognise this patent, and the hostile attitude
of the Corporation of London forced the players to erect their
theatres outside its jurisdiction. For if they played in the City
itself, as had been the custom, either in the great halls of the
Guilds or in the open inn-yards, they had to obtain the Lord
Mayor's sanction for each individual performance, and to hand
over half their receipts to the City treasury.

It was with anything but satisfaction that the peaceable burgesses of London saw a playhouse rise in the neighbourhood of
their homes. The theatre brought in its train a loose, frivolous,
and rowdy population. Around the playhouses, at the hours of
performance, the narrow streets of that period became so crowded
that business suffered in the shops, processions and funerals were
obstructed, and perpetual causes of complaint arose. Houses
of ill-fame, moreover, always clustered round a theatre; and,
although the performances took place by day, there was always
the danger of fire inseparable from theatres, and especially from
wooden erections with thatched roofs.

But the chief opposition to the theatres did not come from
the mere Philistinism of the industrious middle-class, but from
the fanatical Puritanism which was now rearing its head. It is
the Puritans who have killed the old Merry England, abolishing
its May-games, its popular dances, its numerous rustic sports.
They could not look on with equanimity, and see the drama,

which had once been a spiritual institution, become a platform for mere worldliness.

Their chief accusation against the dramatic poets was that they lied. For intelligences of this order, there was no difference between a fiction and a falsehood. The players they attacked on the ground that when they played female parts they appeared in women's attire, which was expressly forbidden in the Bible (Deut. xxii. 5) as an abomination to the Lord. They saw in this masquerading in the guise of the other sex a symptom of unnatural and degrading vices. They not only despised the actors as jugglers and loathed them as persons living beyond the pale of respectability, but they further accused them of cultivating in private all the vices which they were in the habit of portraying on the stage.

There can be no doubt that from a very early period the influence of Puritanism made itself felt in the attitude of the City authorities.

It can easily be understood, then, that the leaders of the new theatrical industry tried to escape from their jurisdiction; and this they did by choosing sites outside the City, and yet as near its boundaries as possible. To the south of the Thames lay a stretch of land not belonging to the City but to the Bishop of Winchester, a spiritual magnate who tried to make his territory as profitable as he could without inquiring too closely as to the uses to which it was put. Here lay the Bear Garden; here were numerous houses of ill-fame; and here arose the different theatres, the "Hope," the "Swan," the "Rose," &c. When James Burbage's successors, in the year 1598, found themselves compelled, after a lawsuit, to pull down the building known as the Theatre (in Bishopsgate Street), they employed the material to erect on this artistic no-man's-land the celebrated Globe Theatre, which was opened in 1599.

The theatres were of two classes, one known as private, the other as public, a distinction which was at one time rather obscure, since the difference was clearly not that admission to the private theatres took place by invitation, and to the public ones by payment. A nobleman could hire any theatre, whether private or public, and engage the company to give a performance for him and his invited guests. The real distinction was, that the private theatres were designed on the model of the Guildhalls or Town Halls, in which, before the period of special buildings, representations had been given; while the public theatres were constructed on the lines of the inn-yard. The private theatres, then, were fully roofed, and, being the more fashionable, had seats in every part of the house, including the parterre, here known as the pit. Being roofed, they could be used not only in the daytime, but by artificial light. In the public theatres, on the other hand, as in ancient Greece and to this day in the

Tyrol, only the stage was roofed, the auditorium being open to the sky, so that performances could be given only by daylight. But in Greece the air is pure, the climate mild; in the Tyrol performances take place only on a few summer days. Here plays were acted while rain and snow fell upon the spectators, fogs enwrapped them, and the wind plucked at their garments. As the prototype of these theatres was the old inn-yard, in which some of the spectators stood, while others were seated in the open galleries running all round it, the parterre, which retained the name of *yard*, was here devoted to the poorest and roughest of the public, who stood throughout the performance, while the galleries (*scaffolds*), running along the walls in two or three tiers, offered seats to wealthier playgoers of both sexes.

The days of performance at these theatres were announced by the hoisting of a flag on the roof. The time of beginning was three o'clock punctually, and the performance went straight on, uninterrupted by entr'actes. It lasted, as a rule, for only two hours or two hours and a half.

Close to the Globe Theatre lay the Bear Garden, the rank smell from which greeted the nostrils, even before it came in sight. The famous bear Sackerson, who is mentioned in *The Merry Wives of Windsor*, now and then broke his chain and put female theatre-goers shrieking to flight.

Tickets there were none. A penny was the price of admission to standing-room in the yard; and those who wanted better places put their money in a box held out to them for that purpose, the amount varying from a penny to half-a-crown, in accordance with the places required. When we remember that one shilling of Queen Elizabeth's was equivalent to five of Queen Victoria's, the price of the dearer places seems very considerable in comparison with those current to-day. The wealthiest spectators gave more than twelve shillings (in modern money) for their places in the proscenium-boxes on each side of the stage. At the Globe Theatre the orchestra was placed in the upper proscenium-box on the right; it was the largest in London, consisting of ten performers, all distinguished in their several lines, playing lutes, oboes, trumpets, and drums.

The most fashionable seats were on the stage itself, approached, not by the ordinary entrances, but through the players' tiring-room. There sat the amateurs, the noble patrons of the theatre, Essex, Southampton, Pembroke, Rutland; there snobs, upstarts, and fops took their places on chairs or stools; if there were not seats enough, they spread their cloaks upon the pine-sprigs that strewed the boards, and (like Bracchiano in Webster's *Vittoria Corombona*) lay upon them. There, too, sat the author's rivals, the dramatic poets, who had free admissions; and there, lastly, sat the short-hand writers, commissioned by piratical booksellers, who, under pretence of making critical notes, secretly took down the dialogue

—men who were a nuisance to the players and, as a rule, a thorn in the side to the poets, but to whom posterity no doubt owes the preservation of many plays which would otherwise have been lost.

All these notabilities on the stage carry on half-audible conversations, and make the servitors of the theatre bring them drinks and light their pipes, while the actors can with difficulty thread their way among them—arrangements which cannot have heightened the illusion, but perhaps did less to mar it than we might imagine.

For the audience is not easily disturbed, and does not demand any of the illusion which is supplied by modern mechanism. Movable scenery was unknown before 1660. The walls of the stage were either hung with loose tapestries or quite uncovered, so that the wooden doors which led to the players' tiring-rooms at the back were clearly visible. In battle-scenes, whole armies entered triumphant, or were driven off in confusion and defeat, through a single door. When a tragedy was acted the stage was usually hung with black; for a comedy the hangings were blue.

As in the theatre of antiquity, rude machines were employed to raise or lower actors through the stage; trap-doors were certainly in use, and probably "bridges," or small platforms, which could be elevated into the upper regions. In somewhat earlier times still ruder appliances had been in vogue. For example, in the religious and allegorical plays, Hell-mouth was represented by a huge face of painted canvas with shining eyes, a large red nose, and movable jaws set with tusks. When the jaws opened, they seemed to shoot out flames, torches being no doubt waved behind them. The theatrical property-room of that time was incomplete without a "rybbe colleryd red" for the mystery of the Creation. But in Shakespeare's day scarcely anything of this sort was required. It was Inigo Jones who first introduced movable scenery and decorations at the court entertainments. They were certainly not in use at the popular playhouses at any time during Shakespeare's connection with the stage.

Audiences felt no need for such aids to illusion; their imagination instantly supplied the want. They saw whatever the poet required them to see—as a child sees whatever is suggested to its fancy, as little girls see real-life dramas in their games with their dolls. For the spectators were children alike in the freshness and in the force of their imagination. If only a placard were hung on one of the doors of the stage bearing in large letters the name of Paris or of Venice, the spectators were at once transported to France or Italy. Sometimes the Prologue informed them where the scene was placed. Men of classical culture, who insisted on unity of place in the drama, were offended by the continual changes of scene and the pitiful appliances by which they were indicated. Sir Philip Sidney, in his *Defense of Poesy*, published in 1583, ridicules the plays in which "You shall have

Asia of the one side, and Afric of the other, and so many other under-kingdoms, that the player, when he cometh in, must ever begin with telling where he is, or else the tale will not be conceived."

This alacrity of imagination on the part of popular audiences was unquestionably an advantage to the English stage in its youth. If an actor made a movement as though he were plucking a flower, the scene was at once understood to be a garden; as in *Henry VI.*, where the adoption of the red rose and white rose as party badges is represented. If an actor spoke as though he were standing on a ship's deck in a heavy sea, the convention was at once accepted; as in the famous scene in *Pericles* (iii. 2). Shakespeare, though he did not hesitate to take advantage of this accommodating humour on the part of his public, and made no attempt at illusive decoration, nevertheless ridiculed, as we have seen, in *A Midsummer Night's Dream*, the meagre scenic apparatus of his time (especially, we may suppose, on the provincial stage); while in the Prologue to his *Henry V.* he deplores and apologises for the narrowness of his stage and the poverty of his resources :—

> " Pardon, gentles all,
> The flat unraised spirits that have dar'd
> On this unworthy scaffold to bring forth
> So great an object : can this cockpit hold
> The vasty fields of France? or may we cram
> Within this wooden O the very casques,
> That did affright the air at Agincourt?
> O, pardon ! since a crooked figure may
> Attest in little place a million ;
> And let us, ciphers to this great accompt,
> On your imaginary forces work.
> Suppose, within the girdle of these walls
> Are now confin'd two mighty monarchies."

These monarchies, then, were mounted in a frame formed of young noblemen, critics and stage-struck gallants, who bantered the boy-heroines, fingered the embroideries on the costumes, smoked their clay pipes, and otherwise made themselves entirely at their ease.

A curtain, which did not rise, but parted in the middle, separated the stage from the auditorium.

The only extant drawing of the interior of an Elizabethan theatre was recently discovered by Karl Gaedertz in the University Library at Utrecht. It is a sketch of the Swan Theatre, executed in 1596 by the Dutch scholar, Jan de Witt. The stage, resting upon strong posts, has no other furniture than a single bench, on which one of the performers is seated. The background is formed by the tiring-house, into which two doors lead. Over it is a roofed balcony, which could be used, no doubt, both by the players and by the audience. Above the roof of the tiring-house rises a second story, crowned by a sort of hutch, over which waves a flag bearing the image of a swan. At an open door of the hutch is seen a trumpeter giving a signal of some sort. The theatre is oval in shape, and has three tiers of seats, while the pit is left open for the standing " groundlings."

The balcony over the tiring-house answers in this case to the inner stage of other and better-equipped theatres.

This smaller raised platform at the back of the principal stage was exceedingly useful, and, in a certain measure, supplied the place of the scenic apparatus of later times. Tieck, who probably went further than any other critic in his dislike for modern mechanism and his enthusiasm for the primitive arrangements of Shakespeare's day, has elaborately reconstructed it in his novel, *Der junge Tischlermeister.*

In the middle of the deep stage, according to him, rose two wooden pillars, eight or ten feet high, which supported a sort of balcony. Three broad steps led from the front stage to the inner alcove under the balcony, which was sometimes open, sometimes curtained off. It represented, according to circumstances, a cave, a room, a summer-house, a family vault, and so forth. It was here that, in *Macbeth*, the ghost of Banquo appeared seated at the table. Here stood the bed on which Desdemona was smothered. Here, in *Hamlet*, the play within a play was acted. Here Gloucester's eyes were put out. On the balcony above, Juliet waited for her Romeo, and Sly took his place to see *The Taming of the Shrew.* When the siege of a town had to be represented, the defenders of the walls stood and parleyed on this balcony, while the assailants were grouped in the foreground.

It is probable that at each side a pretty broad flight of steps led up to this balcony. Here sat senates, councils, and princes with their courts. It needed but few figures to fill the inner stage, so narrow were its dimensions. Macbeth mounted these stairs, and so did Falstaff in the *Merry Wives.* Melancholy or contemplative personages leaned against the pillars. The structure offered a certain facility for effective groupings, somewhat like that in Raffaelle's " School of Athens." Figures in front did not obstruct the view of those behind, and groups gathered to the right and left of the main stage could, without an overstrain of make-believe, be supposed not to see each other.

The only department of decoration which involved any considerable expense was the costumes of the actors. On these such large sums were lavished that the Puritans made this extravagance one of their chief points of attack upon theatres. In Henslowe's Diary we find such entries as £4, 14s. for a pair of breeches, and £16 for a velvet cloak. It is even on record that a famous actor once gave £20, 10s. for a mantle. In an inventory of the property belonging to the Lord Admiral's Company in the year 1598, we find many splendid dresses enumerated: for example, " 1 payr of carnatyon satten Venesyons [breeches] layd with gold lace," and " 1 orenge taney [tawny] satten dublet, layd thycke with gowld lace."[1]   The sums paid for these costumes are glaringly out of keeping with the paltry fees allotted to the author. Up to the year 1600 the ordinary price of a play was from five to six pounds—scarcely more than the cost of a pair of breeches to be worn by the actor who played the Prince or King.

In the boxes ("rooms") sat the better sort of spectators, officers, City merchants, sometimes with their wives; but ladies always wore a mask of silk or velvet, partly for protection against sun and air, partly in order to blush (or not to blush) unseen, at the frivolous and often licentious things that were said upon the stage.   The mask was then as common an article of female attire as is the veil in our days.   But the front rows of what we should now call the first tier were occupied by beauties who had no desire whatever to conceal their countenances, though they might use the mask (as in later times the fan) for purposes of coquetry. These were the kept mistresses of men of quality, and other gorgeously decked ladies, who resorted to the playhouse in order to make acquaintances.   Behind them sat the respectable citizens. But in the gallery above a rougher public assembled—sailors, artisans, soldiers, and loose women of the lowest class.

No women ever appeared upon the stage.

The frequenters of the pit, with their coarse boisterousness, were the terror of the actors.   They all had to stand—coal-heavers and bricklayers, dock-labourers, serving-men, and idlers. Refreshment-sellers moved about among them, supplying them with sausages and ale, with apples and nuts.   They ate and drank, drew corks, smoked tobacco, fought with each other, and often, when they were out of humour, threw fragments of food, and even stones, at the actors.   Now and then they would come to loggerheads with the fine gentlemen on the stage, so that the performance had to be interrupted and the theatre closed.   The sanitary arrangements were of the most primitive description, and the groundlings resisted all attempts at reform on the part of the management.   When the evil smells became intolerable, juniper-berries were burnt by way of freshening the atmosphere.

The theatrical public made and executed its own laws.   There was no police in the theatre.   Now and then a pickpocket would be caught in the act, and tied to a post at the corner of the stage beside the railing which divided it from the auditorium.

The beginning of the performance was announced by three trumpet-blasts.   The actor who spoke the Prologue appeared in a long cloak, with a laurel-wreath on his head, probably because this duty was originally performed by the poet himself.   After the play, the Clown danced a jig, at the same time singing some comic

---

[1] See Appendix to *Diary of Philip Henslowe* (Shakspere Society's Publications).

jingle and accompanying himself on a small drum and flute.   The Epilogue consisted of, or ended in, a prayer for the Queen, in which all the actors took part, kneeling.

Elizabeth herself and her court did not visit these theatres. There was no Royal box, and the public was too mixed. On the other hand, the Queen could, without derogating from her state, summon the players to court, and the Lord Chamberlain's Company, to which Shakespeare belonged, was very often commanded to perform before her, especially upon festivals such as Christmas Day, Twelfth Night, and so forth.   Thus Shakespeare is known to have acted before the Queen in two comedies presented at Greenwich Palace at Christmas 1594.   He is mentioned along with the leading actors, Burbage and Kemp.

Elizabeth paid for such performances a fee of twenty nobles, and a further gratuity of ten nobles—in all, £10.

As the Queen, however, was not content with thus witnessing plays at rare intervals, she formed companies of her own, the so-called Children's Companies, recruited from the choir-boys ot the Chapels-Royal, whose music-schools thus developed, as it were, into nurseries for the stage.   These half-grown boys, who were, of course, specially fitted to represent female characters, won no small favour, both at court and with the public ; and we see that one such troupe, consisting of the choir-boys of St. Paul's, for some time competed, at the Blackfriars Theatre, with Shakespeare's company.   We may gather from the bitter complaint in *Hamlet* (ii. 2) how serious was this competition :—

"*Hamlet.* Do they [the players] hold the same estimation they did when I was in the city?   Are they so followed?

"*Rosencrantz.* No, indeed, they are not.

"*Ham.* How comes it?   Do they grow rusty?

"*Ros.* Nay, their endeavour keeps in the wonted pace : but there is, sir, an aery of children, little eyases, that cry out on the top of question, and are most tyrannically clapped for 't : these are now the fashion ; and so berattle the common stages (so they call them), that many wearing rapiers are afraid of goose-quills, and dare scarce come thither.

"*Ham.* Do the boys carry it away?

"*Ros.* Ay, that they do, my lord ; Hercules and his load too." [1]

The number of players in a company was not great—not more, as a rule, than eight or ten ; never, probably, above twelve. The players were of different grades.   The lowest were the so-called hirelings, who received wages from the others and were in some sense their servants.   They appeared as supernumeraries or in small speaking parts, and had nothing to do with the man-

---

[1] A figure of Hercules with the globe on his shoulders served as sign to the Globe Theatre.

agement of the theatre. The actors, properly so called, differed in standing according as they shared in the receipts only as actors, or were entitled to a further share as part-proprietors of the theatre. There was no manager. The actors themselves decided what plays should be performed, distributed the parts, and divided the receipts according to an established scale. The most advantageous position, of course, was that of a shareholder in the theatre; for half of the gross receipts went to the shareholders, who provided the costumes and paid the wages of the hirelings.

Shakespeare's comparatively early rise to affluence can be accounted for only by assuming that, in his dual capacity as poet and player, he must quickly have become a shareholder in the theatre.

As an actor he does not seem to have attained the highest eminence—fortunately, for if he had, he would probably have found very little time for writing. The parts he played appear to have been dignified characters of the second order; for there is no evidence that he was anything of a comedian. We know that he played the Ghost in *Hamlet*—a part of no great length, it is true, but of the first importance. It is probable, too, that he played old Adam in *As You Like It*, and pretty certain that he played old Knowell in Ben Jonson's *Every Man in His Humour*. It may possibly be in the costume of Knowell that he is represented in the well-known Droeshout portrait at the beginning of the First Folio. Tradition relates that he once played his own Henry IV. at court, and that the Queen, in passing over the stage, dropped her glove as a token of her favour, whereupon Shakespeare handed it back to her with the words:—

"And though now bent on this high embassy,
Yet stoop we to take up our cousin's glove."

In all lists of the players belonging to his company he is named among the first and most important.

Not least among the marvels connected with his genius is the fact that, with all his other occupations, he found time to write so much. His mornings would be given to rehearsals, his afternoons to the performances; he would have to read, revise, accept or reject a great number of plays; and he often passed his evenings either at the Mermaid Club or at some tavern; yet for eighteen years on end he managed to write, on an average, two plays a year—and such plays!

In order to understand this we have to recollect that although between 1557 and 1616 there were forty noteworthy and two hundred and thirty-three inferior English poets, who issued works in epic or lyric form, yet the characteristic of the period was the immense rush of productivity in the direction of dramatic art. Every Englishman of talent in Elizabeth's time could write a tolerable play, just as every second Greek in the age of Pericles could model a tolerable statue, or as every European of to-day can write a passable newspaper article. The Englishmen of that time were born dramatists, as the Greeks were born sculptors, and as we hapless moderns are born journalists. The Greek, with an inborn sense of form, had constant opportunities for observing the nude human body and admiring its beauty. If he saw a man ploughing a field, he received a hundred impressions and ideas as to the play of the muscles in the naked leg. The modern European possesses a certain command of language, is practised in argument, has a knack of putting thoughts and events into words, and is, finally, a confirmed newspaper-reader—all characteristics which make for the multiplication of newspaper articles. The Englishman of that day was keenly observant of human destinies, and of the passions which, after the fall of Catholicism and before the triumph of Puritanism, revelled in the brief freedom of the Renaissance. He was accustomed to see men following their instincts to the last extremity—which was not infrequently the block. The high culture of the age did not exclude violence, and this violence led to dramatic vicissitudes of fortune. It was but a short way from the palace to the scaffold —witness the fate of Henry VIII.'s wives, of Mary Stuart, of Elizabeth's great lovers, Essex and Raleigh. The Englishman of that age had always before his eyes pictures of extreme prosperity followed by sudden ruin and violent death. Life itself was dramatic, as in Greece it was plastic, as in our days it is journalistic, photographic—that is to say, striving in vain to give permanence to formless and everyday events and thoughts.

A dramatic poet in those days, no less than a journalist in ours, had to study his public closely. All the intellectual conflicts of the period were for sixty years fought out in the theatre, as they are nowadays in the press. Passionate controversies between one poet and another were cast in dramatic form. Rosencrantz says to Hamlet, "There was, for a while, no money bid for argument, unless the poet and the player went to cuffs in the question." The efflorescence of the drama on British soil was of short duration—as short as that of painting in Holland. But while it lasted the drama was the dominant art-form and medium of intellectual expression, and it was consequently supported by a large public.

Shakespeare never wrote a play "for the study," nor could he have imagined himself doing anything of the sort. As playwright and player in one, he had the stage always in his eye, and what he wrote had never long to wait for performance, but took scenic shape forthwith. Although, like all productive spirits, he thought first of satisfying himself in what he wrote, yet he must necessarily have borne in mind the public to whom the play appealed. He could by no means avoid considering the tastes of the average playgoer. The average playgoer, indeed, made no bad audience, but an audience which had to be amused, and which could not, for too long at a stretch, endure unrelieved seriousness or lofty flights of thought. For the sake of the common people, then, scenes of grandeur and refinement were interspersed with passages of burlesque. To please the many-headed, the Clown was brought on at every pause in the action, much as he is in the circus of to-day. The points of rest which are now marked by the fall of the curtain between the acts were then indicated by conversations such as that between Peter and the musicians in *Romeo and Juliet* (iv. 5); it merely implies that the act is over.

For the rest, Shakespeare did not write for the average spectator. He did not value his judgment. Hamlet says to the First Player (ii. 2):—

"I heard thee speak me a speech once,—but it was never acted; or, if it was, not above once; for the play, I remember, pleased not the million; 'twas caviare to the general: but it was (as I received it, and others, whose judgments in such matters cried in the top of mine) an excellent play."

All Shakespeare lies in the words, "It pleased not the million."

The English drama as it took shape under Shakespeare's hand addressed itself primarily to the best elements in the public. But "the best" were the noble young patrons of the theatre, to whom he personally owed a great deal of his culture, almost all his repute, and, moreover, the insight he had attained into the aristocratic habit of mind.

A young English nobleman of that period must have been one of the finest products of humanity, a combination of the Belvedere Apollo with a prize racehorse; he must have felt himself at once a man of action and an artist.

We have seen how early Shakespeare must have made the acquaintance of Essex, before his fall the mightiest of the mighty. He wrote *A Midsummer Night's Dream* for his marriage, and he introduced a compliment to him into the Prologue to the fifth act of *Henry V*. England received her victorious King, he says—

"As, by a lower but loving likelihood,
Were now the general of our gracious empress
(As, in good time, he may) from Ireland coming,
Bringing rebellion broached on his sword,
How many would the peaceful city quit,
To welcome him!"

We have seen, moreover, how early and how intimate was his connection with the young Earl of Southampton, to whom he dedicated the only two books which he himself gave to the press.

It must have been from young aristocrats such as these that Shakespeare acquired his aristocratic method of regarding the course of history. How else could he regard it? A large part of the middle class was hostile to him, despised his calling, and treated him as one outside the pale; the clergy condemned and persecuted him; the common people were in his eyes devoid of judgment. The ordinary life of his day did not, on the whole, appeal to him. We find him totally opposed to the realistic dramatisation of everyday scenes and characters, to which many contemporary poets devoted themselves. This sort of truth to nature was foreign to him, so foreign that he suffered for lack of it. Towards the close of his artistic career he was outstripped in popularity by the realists of the day.

His heroes are princes and noblemen, the kings and barons of England. It is always they, in his eyes, who make history, of which he shows throughout a naïvely heroic conception. In the wars which he presents, it is always an individual leader and hero on whom everything depends. It is Henry V. who wins the day at Agincourt, just as in Homer it is Achilles who conquers before Troy. Yet the whole issue of these wars depended upon the foot-soldiers. It was the English archers, 14,000 in number, who at Agincourt defeated the French army of 50,000 men, with a loss of only 1600, as against 10,000 on the other side. Shakespeare certainly did not divine that it was the rise of the middle classes and their spirit of enterprise that constituted the strength of England under Elizabeth. He regarded his age from the point of view of the man who was accustomed to see in richly endowed and princely young noblemen the very crown of humanity, the patrons of all lofty effort, and the originators of all great achievements. And, with his necessarily scanty historic culture, he saw bygone periods, of Roman as well as of English history, in the same light as his own times.

This tendency appears already in the second part of *Henry VI.* Note the picture of Jack Cade's rebellion (iv. 2), which contains some inimitable touches :—

" *Cade.* Be brave then; for your captain is brave, and vows reformation. There shall be in England seven halfpenny loaves sold for a penny; the three-hooped pot shall have ten hoops; and I will make it felony to drink small beer. All the realm shall be in common, and in Cheapside shall my palfrey go to grass. And, when I am king (as king I will be),—

" *All.* God save your majesty !

" *Cade.* I thank you, good people :—there shall be no money; all shall eat and drink on my score; and I will apparel them all in one livery, that they may agree like brothers, and worship me their lord.

" *Dick.* The first thing we do, let's kill all the lawyers.

"*Cade*. Nay, that I mean to do. Is not this a lamentable thing, that of the skin of an innocent lamb should be made parchment? that parchment, being scribbled o'er, should undo a man?

.   .   .   .

"*Enter some, bringing in the Clerk of Chatham.*

"*Smith*. The clerk of Chatham: he can write and read, and cast accompt.
"*Cade*. O monstrous!
"*Smith*. We took him setting of boys' copies.
"*Cade*. Here's a villain!
"*Smith*. Has a book in his pocket, with red letters in 't.

.   .   .   .

"*Cade*. Let me alone.—Dost thou use to write thy name, or hast thou a mark to thyself, like an honest plain-dealing man?
"*Clerk*. Sir, I thank God, I have been so well brought up, that I can write my name.
"*All*. He hath confessed: away with him! he's a villain and a traitor.
"*Cade*. Away with him, I say: hang him with his pen and ink-horn about his neck."

What is so remarkable and instructive in these brilliant scenes is that Shakespeare here, quite against his custom, departs from his authority.   In Holinshed, Jack Cade and his followers do not appear at all as the crazy Calibans whom Shakespeare depicts. The chief of their grievances, in fact, was that the King alienated the crown revenues and lived on the taxes; and, moreover, they complained of abuses of all sorts in the execution of the laws and the raising of revenue.   The third article of their memorial stands in striking contrast to their action in the play; for it points out that nobles of royal blood (probably meaning York) are excluded from the King's "dailie presence," while he gives advancement to "other meane persons of lower nature," who close the King's ears to the complaints of the country, and distribute favours, not according to law, but for gifts and bribes.   Moreover, they complain of interferences with freedom of election, and, in short, express themselves quite temperately and constitutionally.   Finally, in more than one passage of the complaint, they give utterance to a thoroughly English and patriotic resentment of the loss of Normandy, Gascony, Aquitaine, Anjou, and Maine.

But it did not at all suit Shakespeare to show a Jack Cade at the head of a popular movement of this sort. He took no interest in anything constitutional or parliamentary.   In order to find the colours he wanted for the rebellion, he hunts up in Stow's *Summarie of the Chronicles of England* the picture of Wat Tyler's and Jack Straw's risings under Richard II., two outbursts of wild communistic enthusiasm, reinforced by religious fanaticism. From this source he borrows, almost word for word, some of the rebels' speeches. In these risings, as a matter of fact, all "men of law, justices, and jurors" who fell into the hands of the leaders were beheaded, and all records and muniments burnt, so that owners of property might not in future have the means of establishing their rights.

This contempt for the judgment of the masses, this anti-democratic conviction, having early taken possession of Shakespeare's mind, he keeps on instinctively seeking out new evidences in its favour, new testimonies to its truth ; and therefore he transforms facts, where they do not suit his view, on the model of other facts which do.

XVI

FROM the autumn of 1592 until the summer of 1593 all the London theatres were closed. That frightful scourge, the plague, from which England had so long been free, was raging in the capital. Even the sittings of the Law Courts had to be suspended. At Christmas 1592 the Queen refrained from ordering any plays at court, and the Privy Council had at an earlier date issued a proclamation forbidding all public theatrical performances, on the reasonable ground that convalescents, weary of their long confinement, made haste to resort to such entertainments before they were properly out of quarantine, and thus spread the contagion.

The matter has a particular bearing upon the biography of Shakespeare, since, if he ever travelled on the continent of Europe, it was probably at this period, while the theatres were closed.

That it must have been now, if ever, there can be no great doubt. But it remains exceedingly difficult to determine whether Shakespeare ever crossed the Channel.

We have noticed what an attraction Italy possessed for him, even from the beginning of his career. To this *The Two Gentlemen of Verona* and *Romeo and Juliet* bear witness. But in these plays we as yet find nothing which points definitely to the conclusion that the poet had seen with his own eyes the country in which his action is placed. It is different with the dramas of Italian scene which Shakespeare produces about the year 1596— the adaptation of the old *Taming of a Shrew* and *The Merchant of Venice;* it is different, too, with *Othello*, which comes much later. Here we find definite local colour, with such an abundance of details pointing to actual vision that it is hard to account for them otherwise than by assuming a visit on the poet's part to such cities as Verona, Venice, and Pisa.

It is on the face of it highly probable that Shakespeare should wish to see Italy as soon as he could find an opportunity. To the Englishman of that day Italy was the goal of every longing. It was the great home of culture. Men studied its literature and imitated its poetry. It was the beautiful land where dwelt the joy of life. Venice in especial exercised a fascination stronger than that of Paris. It needed no great wealth to make a pilgrimage to Italy. One could travel inexpensively, perhaps on foot, like that Coryat who discovered the use of the fork ; one could pass the night at cheap hostelries. Many of the distinguished men of the time are known to have visited Italy—men of science, like Bacon, and afterwards Harvey ; authors and poets like Lyly, Munday, Nash, Greene, and Daniel, the form of whose sonnets determined that of Shakespeare's. Among the artists of Shakespeare's time, the widely-travelled Inigo Jones had made a stay in Italy. Most of these men have themselves given us some account of their travels ; but as Shakespeare has left us no biographical records whatever, the absence of any direct mention of such a journey on his part is of little moment, if other significant facts can be adduced in its favour.

And such facts are not wanting.

There were in Shakespeare's time no guide-books for the use of travellers. What he knows, then, of foreign lands and their customs he cannot have gathered from such sources. Of Venice, which Shakespeare has so livingly depicted, no description was published in England until after he had written his *Merchant of Venice*. Lewkenor's description of the city (itself a mere compilation at second hand) dates from 1598, Coryat's from 1611, Moryson's from 1617.

In Shakespeare's *Taming of the Shrew*, we notice with surprise not only the correctness of the Italian names, but the remarkable way in which, at the very beginning of the play, several Italian cities and districts are characterised in a single phrase. Lombardy is "the pleasant garden of great Italy;" Pisa is "renowned for grave citizens;" and here the epithet "grave" is especially noteworthy, since many testimonies concur to show that it was particularly characteristic of the inhabitants of Pisa. C. A. Brown, in *Shakespeare's Autobiographical Poems*, has pointed out the remarkable form of the betrothal of Petruchio and Katherine (namely, that her father joins their hands in the presence of two witnesses), and observes that this form was not English, but peculiarly Italian. It is not to be found in the older play, the scene of which, however, is laid in Athens.

Special attention was long ago directed to the following speech at the end of the second act, where Gremio reckons up all the goods and gear with which his house is stocked :—

> "First, as you know, my house within the city
> Is richly furnished with plate and gold :
> Basins, and ewers, to lave her dainty hands ;
> My hangings all of Tyrian tapestry ;
> In ivory coffers I have stuff'd my crowns ;
> In cypress chests my arras, counterpoints,

Costly apparel, tents, and canopies,
Fine linen, Turkey cushions boss'd with pearl,
Valance of Venice gold in needlework,
Pewter and brass, and all things that belong
To house, or housekeeping."

Lady Morgan long ago remarked that she had seen literally all of these articles of luxury in the palaces of Venice, Genoa, and Florence. Miss Martineau, in ignorance alike of Brown's theory and Lady Morgan's observation, expressed to Shakespeare's biographer, Charles Knight, her feeling that the local colour of *The Taming of the Shrew* and *The Merchant of Venice* displays such an intimate acquaintance, not only with the manners and customs of Italy, but with the minutest details of domestic life, that it cannot possibly have been gleaned from books or from mere conversations with this man or that who happened to have floated in a gondola.

On such a question as this, the decided impressions of feminine readers are not without a certain weight.

Brown has pointed out as specifically Italian such small traits as Iago's scoffing at the Florentine Cassio as "a great arithmetician," "a counter-caster," the Florentines being noted as masters of arithmetic and bookkeeping. Another such trait is the present of a dish of pigeons which Gobbo, in *The Merchant of Venice*, brings to his son's master.

Karl Elze, who has strongly insisted upon the probability of Shakespeare's having travelled Italy in the year 1593, dwells particularly upon his apparent familiarity with Venice. The name of Gobbo is a genuine Venetian name, and suggests, moreover, the kneeling stone figure, "Il Gobbo di Rialto," that forms the base of the granite pillar to which, in former days, the decrees of the Republic were affixed. Shakespeare knew that the Exchange was held on the Rialto island. An especially weighty argument lies in the fact that the study of the Jewish nature, to which his Shylock bears witness, would have been impossible in England, where no Jews were permitted by law to reside since their expulsion, begun in the time of Richard Cœur-de-Lion, and completed in 1290. Not until Cromwell's time was the embargo removed in a few cases. On the other hand, there were in Venice more than eleven hundred Jews (according to Coryat, as many as from five to six thousand).[1]

One of the most striking details as regards *The Merchant of Venice* is this: Portia sends her servant Balthasar with an important message to Padua, and orders him to ride quickly and meet her at "the common ferry which trades to Venice." Now Portia's palace at Belmont may be conceived as one of the

---

[1] A very few Jews were, indeed, tolerated in England in spite of the prohibition, but it is not probable that Shakespeare knew any of them.

summer residences, rich in art treasures, which the merchant princes of Venice at that time possessed on the banks of the Brenta. From Dolo, on the Brenta, it is twenty miles to Venice —just the distance which Portia says that she must "measure" in order to reach the city. If we conceive Belmont as situated at Dolo, it would be just possible for the servant to ride rapidly to Padua, and on the way back to overtake Portia, who would travel more slowly, at the ferry, which was then at Fusina, at the mouth of the Brenta. How exactly Shakespeare knew this, and how uncommon the knowledge was in his day, is shown in the expressions he uses, and in the misunderstanding of these expressions on the part of his printers and editors. The lines in the fourth scene of the third act, as they appear in all the Quartos and Folios, are these :—

> " Bring them, I pray thee, with imagined speed
> Unto the tranect, to the common ferry,
> Which trades to Venice."

" Tranect," which means nothing, is, of course, a misprint for " traject," an uncommon expression which the printers clearly did not understand. This, as Elze has pointed out, is simply the Venetian word *traghetto* (Italian *tragitto*). How should Shakespeare have known either of the word or the thing if he had not been on the spot ?

Other details in the second of these plays, written immediately after his conjectured return, strengthen this impression. In the Induction to *The Taming of the Shrew*, where the nobleman proposes to show Sly his pictures, there occur the lines :—

> " We 'll show thee Io as she was a maid,
> And how she was beguiled and surpris'd,
> As lively painted as the deed was done."

These lines, as Elze has justly urged, convey the impression that Shakespeare had seen Correggio's famous picture of Jupiter and Io. This is quite possible if he travelled in North Italy at the time suggested, for from 1585 to 1600 the picture was in the palace of the sculptor Leoni at Milan, and was constantly visited by travellers. If we add that Shakespeare's numerous references to sea-voyages, storms at sea, the agonies of sea-sickness, &c., together with his illustrations and metaphors borrowed from provisions and dress at sea,[1] point to his having made a sea-passage of some length,[2] we cannot but regard it as highly probable that he possessed a closer knowledge of

---

[1] See *Pericles, The Tempest, Cymbeline* (i. 7), *As You Like It* (ii. 7), *Hamlet* (v. 2).

[2] It must be remembered that the sea route to Italy was practically closed by Spanish cruisers.

Italy than could be gained from oral descriptions and from books.

It is impossible, however, to arrive at any certainty on the point. His pictures of Italy are sometimes notably lacking in traits which could scarcely have been overlooked by one who knew the places. And the reader cannot but feel a certain scepticism when he observes how scholars have converted every seeming piece of ignorance on Shakespeare's part into a proof of his miraculous knowledge.

In virtue of this determination to make every apparent blot in Shakespeare redound to his advantage, it could be shown that he had been in Italy before he began to write plays at all. In *The Two Gentlemen of Verona* it is said that Valentine takes ship at Verona to go to Milan. This seems to betray a gross ignorance of the geography of Italy. Karl Elze, however, has discovered that in the sixteenth century Verona and Milan were actually connected by a canal. In *Romeo and Juliet* the heroine says to Friar Laurence, "Shall I come again at evening mass?" This sounds strange, as the Catholic Church knows nothing of evening masses; but R. Simpson has discovered that they were actually in use at that time, and especially in Verona. Shakespeare probably knew no more of these details than he did of the fact that, about 1270, Bohemia possessed provinces on the Adriatic, so that he could with an easy conscience accept from Greene the voyage to the coast of Bohemia in *The Winter's Tale*.

On the whole, scholars have been far too eager to find confirmation of every trivial detail in Shakespeare's allusions to Italian localities. Knight, for instance, declared that "the Sagittary," mentioned in *Othello*, "was the residence at the arsenal of the commanding officers of the navy and army of the Republic," and that Shakespeare had "probably looked upon" the figure of an archer over the gates; whereas it now appears that the commanding officer never had any residence in the arsenal, and that no figure of an archer ever existed there. Elze, again, has gone into most uncritical raptures over Shakespeare's marvellously exact characterisation of Giulio Romano (*The Winter's Tale*, v. 2) as that "rare Italian master who, had he himself eternity, and could put breath into his works, would beguile Nature of her custom, so perfectly he is her ape." As a matter of fact, Shakespeare has simply attributed to an artist whose fame had reached his ears that characteristic which, as we have seen above, he regarded as the highest in pictorial art. Giulio Romano, with his crude superficiality, could not possibly have aroused his admiration had he known his work. That he did not know it is sufficiently evident from the fact that he has made him a sculptor, and praised him in that capacity, and not as a painter.

Elze, confronted with this fact, takes refuge in a Latin epitaph on Romano, quoted by Vasari, which speaks of "Corpora sculpta pictaque" by him, and here again finds a testimony to Shakespeare's omniscience, since he knew of works of sculpture by Romano which no one else has seen or heard of. We can only see in this a new proof of the fact that critical idolatry of departed greatness can now and then lead the student as far astray as uncritical prejudice.

XVII

ABOUT the age of thirty, even men of an introspective disposition are apt to turn their gaze outwards. When Shakespeare
approaches his thirtieth year, he begins to occupy himself in
earnest with history, to read the chronicles, to project and work
out a whole series of historical plays. Several years had now
passed since he had revised and furbished up the old dramas on
the subject of Henry VI. This task had whetted his appetite,
and had cultivated his sense for historic character and historic
nemesis. Having now given expression to the high spirits,the
lyrism, and the passion of youth, in lyrical and dramatic productions of scintillant diversity, he once more turned his attention to
the history of England. In so doing he obeyed a dual vocation,
both as a poet and as a patriot.

Shakespeare's plays founded on English history number ten
in all, four dealing with the House of Lancaster (*Richard II.*, the
two parts of *Henry IV.* and *Henry V.*), four devoted to the House
of York (the three parts of *Henry VI.* and *Richard III.*), and two
which stand apart from the main series, *King John*, of an earlier
historic period, and *Henry VIII.*, of a later.

The order of production of these plays is, however, totally
unconnected with their historical order, which does not, therefore,
concern us. At the same time it is worthy of remark that all
these plays (with the single exception of *Henry VIII.*) were
produced in the course of one decade, the decade in which
England's national sentiment burst into flower and her pride
was at its highest. These English "histories" are, however,
of very unequal value, and can by no means be treated as standing on one plane.

Henry VI. was a first attempt and a mere adaptation. Now,
in the year 1594, Shakespeare attacks the theme of *Richard II.* ;
and in this, his first independent historical drama, we see his
originality still struggling with the tendency to imitation.

There were older plays on the subject of *Richard II.*, but
Shakespeare does not seem to have made any use of them. The
model he had in his mind's eye was Marlowe's finest tragedy, his

Edward II.   Shakespeare's play is, however, much more than a clever imitation of Marlowe's ; it is not only better composed, with a more concentrated action, but has also a great advantage in the full-blooded vitality of its style.   Marlowe's style is here monotonously dry and sombre.   Swinburne, moreover, has done Shakespeare an injustice in preferring Marlowe's character-drawing to that of *Richard II.*

The first half of Marlowe's drama is entirely taken up with the King's morbid and unnatural passion for his favourite Gaveston ; Edward's every speech either expresses his grief at Gaveston's banishment and his longing for his return, or consists of glowing outbursts of joy on seeing him again.   This passion makes Edward dislike his Queen and loathe the Barons, who, in their aristocratic pride, contemn the low-born favourite.   He will risk everything rather than part from one who is so dear to himself and so obnoxious to his surroundings.   The half-erotic fervour of his partiality renders the King's character distasteful, and deprives him of the sympathy which the poet demands for him at the end of the play.

For in the fourth and fifth acts, weak and unstable though he be, Edward has all Marlowe's sympathies.   There is, indeed, something moving in his loneliness, his grief, and his brooding self-reproach.   " The griefs," he says,

> " of private men are soon allay'd ;
> But not of kings.   The forest deer, being struck,
> Runs to an herb that closeth up the wounds :
> But when the imperial lion's flesh is gor'd,
> He rends and tears it with his wrathful paw."

The simile is not true to nature, like Shakespeare's, but it forcibly expresses the meaning of Marlowe's personage.   Now and then he reminds us of Henry VI.   The Queen's relation to Mortimer recalls that of Margaret to Suffolk.   The abdication-scene, in which the King first vehemently refuses to lay down the crown, and is then forced to consent, gave Shakespeare the model for Richard the Second's abdication.   In the murder-scene, on the other hand, Marlowe displays a reckless naturalism in the description and representation of the torture inflicted on the King, an unabashed effect-hunting in the contrast between the King's magnanimity, dread, and gratitude on the one side, and the murderers' hypocritical cruelty on the other, which Shakespeare, with his gentler nature and his almost modern tact, has rejected. It is true that we find in Shakespeare several cases in which the severed head of a person whom we have seen alive a moment before is brought upon the stage.   But he would never place before the eyes of the public such a murder-scene as this, in which the King is thrown down upon a feather-bed, a table is overturned upon him, and the murderers trample upon it until he is crushed.

Marlowe's more callous nature betrays itself in such details, while something of his own wild and passionate temperament has passed into the minor characters of the play—the violent Barons, with the younger Mortimer at their head—who are drawn with a firm hand. The time had scarcely passed when a murder was reckoned an absolute necessity in a drama. In 1581, Wilson, one of Lord Leicester's men, received an order for a play which should not only be original and entertaining, but should also include " all sorts of murders, immorality, and robberies."

Richard II. is one of those plays of Shakespeare's which have never taken firm hold of the stage. Its exclusively political action and its lack of female characters are mainly to blame for this. But it is exceedingly interesting as his first attempt at independent treatment of a historical theme, and it rises far above the play which served as its model.

The action follows pretty faithfully the course of history as the poet found it in Holinshed's Chronicle. The character of the Queen, however, is quite unhistorical, being evidently invented by Shakespeare for the sake of having a woman in his play. He wanted to gain sympathy for Richard through his wife's devotion to him, and saw an opportunity for pathos in her parting from him when he is thrown into prison. In 1398, when the play opens, Isabella of France was not yet ten years old, though she had nominally been married to Richard in 1396. Finally, the King's end, fighting bravely, sword in hand, is not historical: he was starved to death in prison, in order that his body might be exhibited without any wound.

Shakespeare has vouchsafed no indication to facilitate the spectators' understanding of the characters in this play. Their action often takes us by surprise. But Swinburne has done Shakespeare a great wrong in making this a reason for praising Marlowe at his expense, and exalting the subordinate characters in *Edward II.* as consistent pieces of character-drawing, while he represents as inconsistent and obscure such a personage as Shakespeare's York. We may admit that in the opening scene Norfolk's figure is not quite clear, but here all obscurity ends. York is self-contradictory, unprincipled, vacillating, composite, and incoherent, but in no sense obscure. He in the first place upbraids the King with his faults, then accepts at his hands an office of the highest confidence, then betrays the King's trust, while he at the same time overwhelms the rebel Bolingbroke with reproaches, then admires the King's greatness in his fall, then hastens his dethronement, and finally, in virtuous indignation over Aumerle's plots against the new King, rushes to him to assure him of his fidelity and to clamour for the blood of his own son. There lies at the root of this conception a profound political bitterness and an early-acquired experience. Shakespeare must have studied attentively that portion of English history which lay nearest to him, the shufflings and vacillations that went on under Mary and Elizabeth, in order to have received so deep an impression of the pitifulness of political instability.

The character of old John of Gaunt, loyal to his King, but still more to his country, gives Shakespeare his first opportunity for expressing his exultation over England's greatness and his pride in being an Englishman. He places in the mouth of the dying Gaunt a superbly lyrical outburst of patriotism, deploring Richard's reckless and tyrannical policy. All comparison with Marlowe is here at an end. Shakespeare's own voice makes itself clearly heard in the rhetoric of this speech, which, with its self-controlled vehemence, its equipoise in unrest, soars high above Marlowe's wild magniloquence. In the thunderous tones of old Gaunt's invective against the King who has mortgaged his English realm, we can hear all the patriotic enthusiasm of young England in the days of Elizabeth :—

> " This royal throne of kings, this sceptr'd isle,
> This earth of majesty, this seat of Mars,
> This other Eden, demi-paradise,
> This fortress, built by Nature for herself,
> Against infection, and the hand of war ;
> This happy breed of men, this little world,
> This precious stone set in the silver sea,
> Which serves it in the office of a wall,
> Or as a moat defensive to a house,
> Against the envy of less happier lands ;
> This blessed plot, this earth, this realm, this England,
> This nurse, this teeming womb of royal kings,
> Fear'd by their breed, and famous by their birth,
>
> .   .   .   .
>
> This land of such dear souls, this dear, dear land,
> Dear for her reputation through the world,
> Is now leas'd out, I die pronouncing it,
> Like to a tenement, or pelting farm.
> England, bound in with the triumphant sea,
> Whose rocky shore beats back the envious siege
> Of watery Neptune, is now bound in with shame,
> With inky blots, and rotten parchment bonds :
> That England, that was wont to conquer others,
> Hath made a shameful conquest of itself.
> Ah ! would the scandal vanish with my life,
> How happy then were my ensuing death ! " (ii. 1).

Here we have indeed the roar of the young lion, the vibration of Shakespeare's own voice.

But it is upon the leading character of the play that the poet has centred all his strength ; and he has succeeded in giving a vivid and many-sided picture of the Black Prince's degenerate but interesting son. As the protagonist of a tragedy, however, Richard has exactly the same defects as Marlowe's Edward. In the first half of the play he so repels the spectator that nothing he can do in the second half suffices to obliterate the unfavourable impression. Not only has he, before the opening of the piece, committed such thoughtless and politically indefensible acts as have proved him unworthy of the great position he holds, but he behaves with such insolence to the dying Gaunt, and, after his uncle's death, displays such a low and despicable rapacity, that he can no longer appeal, as he does, to his personal right. It is true that the right of which he holds himself an embodiment is very different from the common earthly rights which he has overridden. He is religiously, dogmatically convinced of his inviolability as a king by the grace of God. But since this conviction, in his days of prosperity, has brought with it no sense of correlative duties to the crown he wears, it cannot touch the reader's sympathies as it ought to for the sake of the general effect.

We see the hand of the beginner in the way in which the poet here leaves characters and events to speak for themselves without any attempt to range them in a general scheme of perspective. He conceals himself too entirely behind his work. As there is no gleam of humour in the play, so, too, there is no guiding and harmonising sense of style.

It is from the moment that the tide begins to turn against Richard that he becomes interesting as a psychological study. After the manner of weak characters, he is alternately downcast and overweening. Very characteristically, he at one place answers Bolingbroke's question whether he is content to resign the crown: "Ay, no;—no, ay." In these syllables we see the whole man. But his temperament was highly poetical, and misfortune reveals in him a vein of reverie. He is sometimes profound to the point of paradox, sometimes fantastically overwrought to the verge of superstitious insanity (see, for instance, Act iii. 3). His brooding melancholy sometimes reminds us of Hamlet's—

> "Of comfort no man speak :
> Let's talk of graves, of worms, and epitaphs ;
> Make dust our paper, and with rainy eyes
> Write sorrow on the bosom of the earth.
> Let's choose executors, and talk of wills :
>
> .   .   .   .   .   .
>
> For God's sake, let us sit upon the ground,
> And tell sad stories of the death of kings :—
> How some have been depos'd, some slain in war,
> Some haunted by the ghosts they have depos'd.
> Some poison'd by their wives, some sleeping kill'd,
> All murder'd :—for within the hollow crown,
> That rounds the mortal temples of a king,

> Keeps Death his court, and there the antick sits,
> Scoffing his state, and grinning at his pomp ;
> Allowing him a breath, a little scene,
> To monarchise, be fear'd, and kill with looks " (iii. 2).

In these moods of depression, in which Richard gives his wit and intellect free play, he knows very well that a king is only a human being like any one else :—

> " For you have but mistook me all this while :
> I live with bread like you, feel want, taste grief,
> Need friends.   Subjected thus,
> How can you say to me, I am a king ? " (iii. 2).

But at other times, when his sense of majesty and his monarchical fanaticism master him, he speaks in a quite different tone :—

> " Not all the water in the rough rude sea
> Can wash the balm from an anointed king ;
> The breath of worldly men cannot depose
> The deputy elected by the Lord.
> For every man that Bolingbroke hath press'd,
> To lift shrewd steel against our golden crown,
> God for his Richard hath in heavenly pay
> A glorious angel " (iii. 2).

Thus, too, at their first meeting (iii. 3) he addresses the victorious Henry of Hereford, to whom he immediately after "debases himself ":—

> " My master, God omnipotent,
> Is mustering in his clouds on our behalf
> Armies of pestilence ; and they shall strike
> Your children yet unborn, and unbegot,
> That lift your vassal hands against my head,   .
> And threat the glory of my precious crown."

Many centuries after Richard, King Frederick William IV. of Prussia displayed just the same mingling of intellectuality, superstition, despondency, monarchical arrogance, and fondness for declamation.

In the fourth and fifth acts, the character of Richard and the poet's art rise to their highest point.   The scene in which the groom, who alone has remained faithful to the fallen King, visits him in his dungeon, is one of penetrating beauty.   What can be more touching than his description of how the " roan Barbary," which had been Richard's favourite horse, carried Henry of Lancaster on his entry into London, " so proudly as if he had disdained the ground."   The Arab steed here symbolises with fine simplicity the attitude of all those who had sunned themselves in the prosperity of the now fallen King.

The scene of the abdication (iv. 1) is admirable by reason of the delicacy of feeling and imagination which Richard displays.

His speech when he and Henry have each one hand upon the crown is one of the most beautiful Shakespeare has ever written:—

> "Now is this golden crown like a deep well,
> That owes two buckets filling one another;
> The emptier ever dancing in the air,
> The other down, unseen, and full of water:
> That bucket down, and full of tears, am I,
> Drinking my griefs, whilst you mount up on high."

This scene is, however, a downright imitation of the abdication-scene in Marlowe. When Northumberland in Shakespeare addresses the dethroned King with the word "lord," the King answers, "No lord of thine." In Marlowe the speech is almost identical: "Call me not lord!"

The Shakespearian scene, it should be mentioned, has its history. The censorship under Elizabeth would not suffer it to be printed, and it first appears in the Fourth Quarto, of 1608.[1] The reason of this veto was that Elizabeth, strange as it may appear, was often compared with Richard II. The action of the censorship renders it probable that it was Shakespeare's *Richard II.* (and not one of the earlier plays on the same theme) which, as appears in the trial of Essex, was acted by the Lord Chamberlain's Company before the conspirators, at their leaders' command, on the evening before the outbreak of the rebellion (February 7, 1601). There is nothing inconsistent with this theory in the fact that the players then called it an old play, which was already "out of use;" for the interval between 1593-94 and 1601 was sufficient, according to the ideas of that time, to render a play antiquated. Nor does it conflict with this view that in the last scenes of the play the King is sympathetically treated. On the very points on which he was comparable with Elizabeth there could be no doubt that he was in the wrong; while Henry of Hereford figures in the end as the bearer of England's future, and, for the not oversensitive nerves of the period, that was sufficient. He, who was soon to play a leading part in two other Shakespearian dramas, is here endowed with all the qualities of the successful usurper and ruler: cunning and insight, power of dissimulation, ingratiating manners, and promptitude in action.

In a single speech (v. 3) the new-made Henry IV. sketches the character of his "unthrifty son," Shakespeare's hero: he passes his time in the taverns of London with riotous boon-companions, who now and then even rob travellers on the highway; but, being no less daring than dissolute, he gives certain "sparks of hope" for a nobler future.

[1] Its title runs, "The Tragedie of King Richard the Second: with new additions of the Parliament Sceane, and the deposing of King Richard, As it hath been lately acted by the Kinges Maiesties Seruantes, at the Globe. By William Shake-speare. At London. Printed by W. W. For Mathew Law, and are to be sold at his shop in Paules Church-yard, at the Signe of the Foxe. 1608."

XVIII

IN the year 1594–95 Shakespeare returns to the material which passed through his hands during his revision of the Second and Third Parts of *Henry VI.* He once more takes up the character of Richard of York, there so firmly outlined; and, as in *Richard II.* he had followed in Marlowe's footsteps, so he now sets to work with all his might upon a Marlowesque figure, but only to execute it with his own vigour, and around it to construct his first historic tragedy with well-knit dramatic action. The earlier "histories" were still half epical; this is a true drama. It quickly became one of the most effective and popular pieces on the stage, and has imprinted itself on the memory of all the world in virtue of the monumental character of its protagonist.

The immediate occasion of Shakespeare's taking up this theme was probably the fact that in the year 1594 an old and worthless play on the subject was published under the title of *The True Tragedy of Richard III.* The publication of this play may have been due to the renewed interest in its hero awakened by the performances of *Henry VI.*

It is impossible to assign a precise date to Shakespeare's play. The first Quarto of *Richard II.* was entered in the Stationers' Register on the 29th August 1597, and the first edition of *Richard III.* was entered on the 20th October of the same year. But there is no doubt that its earliest form is of much older date. The diversities in its style indicate that Shakespeare worked over the text even before it was first printed; and the difference between the text of the first Quarto and that of the first Folio bears witness to a radical revision having taken place in the interval between the two editions. It is certainly to this play that John Weever alludes when, in his poem, *Ad Gulielmum Shake-speare*, written as early as 1595, he mentions Richard among the poet's creations.

From the old play of *Richard III.* Shakespeare took nothing at all, or, to be precise, possibly one or two lines in the first scene of the second act. He throughout followed Holinshed, whose

Chronicle is here copied word for word from Hall, who, in his turn, merely translated Sir Thomas More's history of Richard III. We can even tell what edition of Holinshed Shakespeare used, for he has copied a slip of the pen or error of the press which appears in that edition alone.   In Act v. scene 3, line 324, he writes:—

"Long kept in Bretagne at our *mother's* cost,"

instead of *brother's*.

The text of *Richard III.* presents no slight difficulties to the editors of Shakespeare.   Neither the first Quarto nor the greatly amended Folio is free from gross and baffling errors.   The editors of the Cambridge Edition have attempted to show that both the texts are taken from bad copies of the original manuscripts.   It would not surprise us, indeed, that the poet's own manuscript, being perpetually handled by the prompter and stage-manager, should quickly become so ragged that now one page and now another would have to be replaced by a copy.   But the Cambridge editors have certainly undervalued the augmented and amended text of the First Folio.   James Spedding has shown in an excellent essay (*The New Shakspere Society's Transactions*, 1875–76, pp. 1–119) that the changes which some have thought accidental and arbitrary, and therefore not the work of the poet himself, are due to his desire, sometimes to improve the form of the verse, sometimes to avoid the repetition of a word, sometimes to get rid of antiquated words and turns of phrase.

Every one who has been nurtured upon Shakespeare has from his youth dwelt wonderingly upon the figure of Richard, that fiend in human shape, striding, with savage impetuosity, from murder to murder, wading through falsehood and hypocrisy to ever-new atrocities, becoming in turn regicide, fratricide, tyrant, murderer of his wife and of his comrades, until, besmirched with treachery and slaughter, he faces his foes with invincible greatness.

When J. L. Heiberg refused to produce *Richard III.* at the Royal Theatre in Copenhagen, he expressed a doubt whether "we could ever accustom ourselves to seeing Melpomene's dagger converted into a butcher's knife."   Like many other critics before and after him, he took exception to the line in Richard's opening soliloquy, "I am determined to prove a villain."   He doubted, justly enough, the psychological possibility of this phrase; but the monologue, as a whole, is a non-realistic unfolding of secret thoughts in words, and, with a very slight change in the form of expression, the idea is by no means indefensible.   Richard does not mean that he is determined to be what he himself regards as criminal, but merely declares with bitter irony that, since he cannot "prove a lover To entertain these fair well-spoken days," he will play the part of a villain, and give the rein to his hatred for the "idle pleasures" of the time.

There is in the whole utterance a straightforwardness, as of a programme, that takes us aback. Richard comes forward naïvely in the character of Prologue, and foreshadows the matter of the tragedy. It seems almost as though Shakespeare had determined to guard himself at the outset against the accusation of obscurity which had possibly been brought against his *Richard II.* But we must remember that ambitious men in his day were less composite than in our times, and, moreover, that he was not here depicting even one of his own contemporaries, but a character which appeared to his imagination in the light of a historical monster, from whom his own age was separated by more than a century. His Richard is like an old portrait, dating from the time when the physiognomy of dangerous, no less than of noble, characters was simpler, and when even intellectual eminence was still accompanied by a bull-necked vigour of physique such as in later times we find only in the savage chieftains of distant corners of the world.

It is against such figures as this of Richard that the critics who contest Shakespeare's rank as a psychologist are fondest of directing their attacks. But Shakespeare was no miniature-painter. Minutely detailed psychological painting, such as in our days Dostoyevsky has given us, was not his affair; though, as he proved in *Hamlet,* he could on occasion grapple with complex characters. Even here, however, he gets his effect of complexity, not by unravelling a tangle of motives, but by producing the impression of an inward infinity in the character. It is clear that, in his age, he had not often the chance of observing how circumstances, experience, and changing conditions cut and polish a personality into shimmering facets. With the exception of Hamlet, who in some respects stands alone, his characters have sides indeed, but not facets.

Take, for instance, this Richard. Shakespeare builds him up from a few simple characteristics : deformity, the potent consciousness of intellectual superiority, and the lust for power. His whole personality can be traced back to these simple elements.

He is courageous out of self-esteem; he plays the lover out of ambition; he is cunning and false, a comedian and a bloodhound, as cruel as he is hypocritical—and all in order to attain to that despotism on which he has set his heart.

Shakespeare found in Holinshed's Chronicle certain fundamental traits : Richard was born with teeth, and could bite before he could smile; he was ugly; he had one shoulder higher than another; he was malicious and witty; he was a daring and open-handed general; he loved secrecy; he was false and hypocritical out of ambition, cruel out of policy.

All this Shakespeare simplifies and exaggerates, as every artist must. Delacroix has finely said, " *L'art, c'est l'exagération à propos.*"

The Richard of the tragedy is deformed; he is undersized and crooked, has a hump on his back and a withered arm.

He is not, like so many other hunchbacks, under any illusion as to his appearance. He does not think himself handsome, nor is he loved by the daughters of Eve, in whom deformity is so apt to awaken that instinct of pity which is akin to love.

No, Richard feels himself maltreated by Nature; from his birth upwards he has suffered wrong at her hands, and in spite of his high and strenuous spirit, he has grown up an outcast. He has from the first had to do without his mother's love, and to listen to the gibes of his enemies. Men have pointed at his shadow and laughed. The dogs have barked at him as he halted by. But in this luckless frame dwells an ambitious soul. Other people's paths to happiness and enjoyment are closed to him. But he will rule; for that he was born. Power is everything to him, his fixed idea. Power alone can give him his revenge upon the people around him, whom he hates, or despises, or both. The glory of the diadem shall rest upon the head that crowns this misshapen body. He sees its golden splendour afar off. Many lives stand between him and his goal; but he will shrink from no falsehood, no treachery, no bloodshed, if only he can reach it.

Into this character Shakespeare transforms himself in imagination. It is the mark of the dramatic poet to be always able to get out of his own skin and into another's. But in later times some of the greatest dramatists have shrunk shuddering from the out-and-out criminal, as being too remote from them. For example, Goethe. His wrong-doers are only weaklings, like Weislingen or Clavigo; even his Mephistopheles is not really evil. Shakespeare, on the other hand, made the effort to feel like Richard. How did he set about it? Exactly as we do when we strive to understand another personality; for example, Shakespeare himself. He imagines himself into him; that is to say, he projects his mind into the other's body and lives in it for the time being. The question the poet has to answer is always this: How should I feel and act if I were a prince, a woman, a conqueror, an outcast, and so forth?

Shakespeare takes, as his point of departure, the ignominy inflicted by Nature; Richard is one of Nature's victims. How can Shakespeare feel with him here—Shakespeare, to whom deformity of body was unknown, and who had been immoderately favoured by Nature? But he, too, had long endured humiliation, and had lived under mean conditions which afforded no scope either to his will or to his talents. Poverty is itself a deformity; and the condition of an actor was a blemish like a hump on his back. Thus he is in a position to enter with ease into the feelings of one of Nature's victims. He has simply to give free course to all the moods in his own mind which have been evoked by personal humiliation, and to let them ferment and run riot.

I

Next comes the consciousness of superiority in Richard, and the lust of power which springs from it. Shakespeare cannot have lacked the consciousness of his personal superiority, and, like every man of genius, he must have had the lust of power in his soul, at least as a rudimentary organ. Ambitious he must assuredly have been, though not after the fashion of the actors and dramatists of our day. Their mere jugglery passes for art, while his art was regarded by the great majority as mere jugglery. His artistic self-esteem received a check in its growth; but none the less there was ambition behind the tenacity of purpose which in a few years raised him from a servitor in the theatre to a shareholder and director, and which led him to develop the greatest productive talent of his country, till he outshone all rivals in his calling, and won the appreciation of the leaders of fashion and taste. He now transposed into another sphere of life, that of temporal rule, a habit of mind which was his own. The instinct of his soul, which never suffered him to stop or pause, but forced him from one great intellectual achievement to another, restlessly onward from masterpiece to masterpiece—the fierce instinct, with its inevitable egoism, which led him in his youth to desert his family, in his maturity to amass property without any tenderness for his debtors, and (*per fas et nefas*) to attain his modest patent of gentility—this instinct enables him to understand and feel that passion for power which defies and tramples upon every scruple. And all the other characteristics (for example, the hypocrisy, which in the Chronicle holds the foremost place) he uses as mere instruments in the service of ambition.

Note how he has succeeded in individualising this passion. It is hereditary. In the Second Part of *Henry VI.* (iii. 1) Richard's father, the Duke of York, says—

> " Let pale-fac'd fear keep with the mean-born man,
> And find no harbour in a royal heart.
> Faster than spring-time showers comes thought on thought,
> And not a thought but thinks on dignity.
>
> .   .   .   .
>
> Well, nobles, well ; 't is politicly done,
> To send me packing with an host of men :
> I fear me, you but warm the starved snake,
> Who, cherish'd in your breasts, will sting your hearts."

In the Third Part of *Henry VI.*, Richard shows himself the true son of his father. His brother runs after the smiles of women ; he dreams only of might and sovereignty. If there was no crown to be attained, the world would have no joy to offer him. He says himself (iii. 2)—

" Why, love forswore me in my mother's womb:
And, for I should not deal in her soft laws,
She did corrupt frail nature with some bribe,
To shrink mine arm up like a wither'd shrub ;
To make an envious mountain on my back.

. . . . . .

To disproportion me in every part ;
Like to a chaos, or an unlick'd bear-whelp,
That carries no impression like the dam.
And am I then a man to be belov'd ?
O monstrous fault, to harbour such a thought !
Then, since this earth affords no joy to me
But to command, to check, to o'erbear such
As are of better person than myself,
I 'll make my heaven to dream upon the crown."

The lust of power is an inward agony to him. He compares himself to a man " lost in a thorny wood, That rends the thorns and is rent by the thorns ;" and he sees no way of deliverance except to "hew his way out with a bloody axe." Thus is he tormented by his desire for the crown of England ; and to achieve it he will "drown more sailors than the mermaid shall ; . . . Deceive more slyly than Ulysses could ; . . . add colours to the chameleon ; . . . And send the murd'rous Machiavel to school." (The last touch is an anachronism, for Richard died fifty years before *The Prince* was published.)

If this is to be a villain, then a villain he is. And for the sake of the artistic effect, Shakespeare has piled upon Richard's head far more crimes than the real Richard can be historically proved to have committed. This he did, because he had no doubt of the existence of such characters as rose before his imagination while he read in Holinshed of Richard's misdeeds. He believed in the existence of villains—a belief largely undermined in our days by a scepticism which greatly facilitates the villains' operations. He has drawn more villains than one : Edmund in *Lear*, who is influenced by his illegitimacy as Richard is by his deformity, and the grand master of all evil, Iago in *Othello*.

But let us get rid of the empty by-word villain, which Richard applies to himself. Shakespeare no doubt believed theoretically in the free-will which can choose any course it pleases, and villainy among the rest ; but none the less does he in practice assign a cause to every effect.

On three scenes in this play Shakespeare evidently expended particular care—the three which imprint themselves on the memory after even a single attentive reading.

The first of these scenes is that in which Richard wins over the Lady Anne, widow of one of his victims, Prince Edward, and daughter-in-law of another, Henry VI. Shakespeare has here carried the situation to its utmost extremity. It is while Anne is accompanying the bier of the murdered Henry VI. that the murderer confronts her, stops the funeral procession with drawn sword, calmly endures all the outbursts of hatred, loathing, and contempt with which Anne overwhelms him, and, having shaken off her invectives like water from a duck's back, advances his suit, plays his comedy of love, and there and then so turns the current of her will that she allows him to hope, and even accepts his ring.

The scene is historically impossible, since Queen Margaret took Anne with her in her flight after the battle of Tewkesbury, and Clarence kept her in concealment until two years after the death of Henry VI., when Richard discovered her in London. It has, moreover, something astonishing, or rather bewildering, about it at the first reading, appearing as though written for a wager or to outdo some predecessor. Nevertheless it is by no means unnatural. What may with justice be objected to it is that it is unprepared. The mistake is, that we are first introduced to Anne in the scene itself, and can consequently form no judgment as to whether her action does or does not accord with her character. The art of dramatic writing consists almost entirely in preparing for what is to come, and then, in spite of, nay, in virtue of the preparation, taking the audience by surprise. Surprise without preparation loses half its effect.

But this is only a technical flaw which so great a master would in riper years have remedied with ease. The essential feature of the scene is its tremendous daring and strength, or, psychologically speaking, the depth of early-developed contempt for womankind into which it affords us a glimpse. For the very reason that the poet has not given any individual characteristics to this woman, it seems as though he would say: Such is feminine human nature. It is quite evident that in his younger years he was not so much alive to the beauties of the womanly character as he became at a later period of his life. He is fond of drawing unamiable women like Adriana in *The Comedy of Errors*, violent and corrupt women like Tamora in *Titus Andronicus*, and Margaret in *Henry VI.*, or scolding women like Katherine in *The Taming of the Shrew*. Here he gives us a picture of peculiarly feminine weakness, and personifies in Richard his own contempt for it.

Exasperate a woman against you (he seems to say), do her all the evil you can think of, kill her husband, deprive her thereby of the succession to a crown, fill her to overflowing with hatred and execration—then if you can only cajole her into believing that in all you have done, crimes and everything, you have been actuated simply and solely by burning passion for her, by the hope of approaching her and winning her hand—why, then the game is yours, and sooner or later she will give in. Her vanity cannot hold out. If it is proof against ten measures of flattery, it will succumb to a hundred; and if even that is not enough, then pile on more. Every woman has a price at which her vanity is for sale; you have only to dare greatly and bid high enough. So Shakespeare makes this crookbacked assassin accept Anne's insults without winking and retort upon them his declaration of love—he at once seems less hideous in her eyes from the fact that his crimes were committed for her sake. Shakespeare makes him hand her his drawn sword, to pierce him to the heart if she will; he is sure enough that she will do nothing of the sort. She cannot withstand the intense volition in his glance; he hypnotises her hatred; the exaltation with which his lust of power inspires him bewilders and overpowers her, and he becomes almost beautiful in her eyes when he bares his breast to her revenge. She yields to him under the influence of an attraction in which are mingled dizziness, terror, and perverted sensuality. His very hideousness becomes a stimulus the more. There is a sort of fearful billing-and-cooing in the stichomythy in the style of the antique tragedy, which begins:—

> " *Anne.* I would I knew thy heart.
> *Gloucester.* 'Tis figured in my tongue.
> *Anne.* I fear me both are false.
> *Gloucester.* Then never man was true."

But triumph seethes in his veins—

> " Was ever woman in this humour wooed?
> Was ever woman in this humour won?"

—triumph that he, the hunchback, the monster, has needed but to show himself and use his polished tongue in order to stay the curses on her lips, dry the tears in her eyes, and awaken desire in her soul. This courtship has procured him the intoxicating sensation of irresistibility.

The fact of the marriage Shakespeare found in the Chronicle; and he led up to it in this brilliant fashion because his poetic instinct told him to make Richard great, and thereby possible as a tragic hero. In reality, he was by no means so dæmonic. His motive for paying court to Anne was sheer cupidity. Both Clarence and Gloucester had schemed to possess themselves of the vast fortune left by the Earl of Warwick, although the Countess was still alive and legally entitled to the greater part of it. Clarence, who had married the elder daughter, was certain of his part in the inheritance, but Richard thought that by marrying the younger daughter, Prince Edward's widow, he would secure the right to go halves. By aid of an Act of Parliament, the matter was arranged so that each of the brothers received his share in the booty. For this low rapacity in Richard,

Shakespeare has substituted the hunchback's personal exultation on finding himself a successful wooer.

Nevertheless, it was not his intention to represent Richard as superior to all feminine wiles. This opening scene has its counterpart in the passage (iv. 4) where the King, after having rid himself by poison of the wife he has thus won, proposes to Elizabeth, the widow of Edward IV., for the hand of her daughter.

The scene has the air of a repetition. Richard has made away with Edward's two sons in order to clear his path to the throne. Here again, then, the murderer woos the nearest kinswoman of his victims, and, in this case, through the intermediary of their mother. Shakespeare has lavished his whole art on this passage. Elizabeth, too, expresses the deepest loathing for him. Richard answers that, if he has deprived her sons of the throne, he will now make amends by raising her daughter to it. Here also the dialogue takes the form of a stichomythy, which clearly enough indicates that these passages belong to the earliest form of the play :—

" *King Richard.* Infer fair England's peace by this alliance.
Queen Elizabeth. Which she shall purchase with still lasting war.
K. Rich. Tell her, the king, that may command, entreats.
Q. Eliz. That at her hands, which the kings' King forbids."

Richard not only asserts the purity and strength of his feelings, but insists that by this marriage alone can he be prevented from bringing misery and destruction upon thousands in the kingdom. Elizabeth pretends to yield, and Richard bursts forth, just as in the first act—

" Relenting fool, and shallow changing woman ! "

But it is he himself who is overreached. Elizabeth has only made a show of acquiescence in order immediately after to offer her daughter to his mortal foe.

The second unforgetable passage is the Baynard's Castle scene in the third act. Richard has cleared away all obstacles on his path to the throne. His elder brother Clarence is murdered —drowned in a butt of wine. Edward's young sons are presently to be strangled in prison. Hastings has just been hurried to the scaffold without trial or form of law. The thing is now to avoid all appearance of complicity in these crimes, and to seem austerely disinterested with regard to the crown. To this end he makes his rascally henchman, Buckingham, persuade the simple-minded and panic-stricken Lord Mayor of London, with other citizens of repute, to implore him, in spite of his seeming reluctance, to mount the throne. Buckingham prepares Richard for their approach (iii. 7):—

" Intend some fear ;
Be not you spoke with but by mighty suit :
And look you get a prayer-book in your hand,

> And stand between two churchmen, good my lord:
> For on that ground I'll make a holy descant:
> And be not easily won to our requests;
> Play the maid's part, still answer nay, and take it."

Then come the citizens. Catesby bids them return another time. His grace is closeted with two right reverend fathers; he is "divinely bent to meditation," and must not be disturbed in his devotions by any "worldly suits." They renew their entreaties to his messenger, and implore the favour of an audience with his grace "in matter of great moment."

Not till then does Gloucester show himself upon the balcony between two bishops.

When, at the election of 1868, which turned upon the Irish Church question, Disraeli, a very different man from Richard, was relying on the co-operation of both English and Irish prelates, *Punch* depicted him in fifteenth-century attire, standing on a balcony, prayer-book in hand, with an indescribable expression of sly humility, while two bishops, representing the English and the Irish Church, supported him on either hand. The legend ran, in the words of the Lord Mayor: "See where his grace stands 'tween two clergymen!"—whereupon Buckingham remarks—

> "Two props of virtue for a Christian prince,
>   To stay him from the fall of vanity;
> And, see, a book of prayer in his hand,
>   True ornament to know a holy man."

The deputation is sternly repulsed, until Richard at last lets mercy stand for justice, and recalling the envoys of the City, yields to their insistence.

The third master-scene is that in Richard's tent on Bosworth Field (v. 3). It seems as though his hitherto immovable self-confidence had been shaken; he feels himself weak; he will not sup. "Is my beaver easier than it was? . . . Fill me a bowl of wine. . . . Look that my staves be sound and not too heavy." Again: "Give me a bowl of wine."

> "I have not that alacrity of spirit,
> Nor cheer of mind, that I was wont to have."

Then, in a vision, as he lies sleeping on his couch, with his armour on and his sword-hilt grasped in his hand, he sees, one by one, the spectres of all those he has done to death. He wakens in terror. His conscience has a thousand tongues, and every tongue condemns him as a perjurer and assassin:—

> "I shall despair.—There is no creature loves me;
> And if I die no soul shall pity me."

These are such pangs of conscience as would sometimes beset even the strongest and most resolute in those days when faith and superstition were still powerful, and when even one who scoffed at religion and made a tool of it had no assurance in his heart of hearts. There is in these words, too, a purely human sense of loneliness and of craving for affection, which is valid for all time.

Most admirable is the way in which Richard summons up his manhood and restores the courage of those around him. These are the accents of one who will give despair no footing in his soul :—

> " Conscience is but a word that cowards use,
> Devis'd at first to keep the strong in awe ; "

and there is in his harangue to the soldiers an irresistible roll of fierce and spirit-stirring martial music ; it is constructed like strophes of the *Marseillaise* :—

> " Remember whom you are to cope withal ;—
> A sort of vagabonds, rascals, runaways.
> (*Que veut cette horde d'esclaves ?*)
> You having lands, and bless'd with beauteous wives,
> They would restrain the one, distain the other.
> (*Égorger vos fils, vos compagnes.*)
> Let's whip these stragglers o'er the seas again."

But there is a ferocity, a scorn, a popular eloquence in Richard's words, in comparison with which the rhetoric of the *Marseillaise* seems declamatory, even academic. His last speeches are nothing less than superb :—

> "Shall these enjoy our lands ? lie with our wives ?
> Ravish our daughters ?—[*Drum afar off.*] Hark ; I hear their drum.
> Fight, gentlemen of England ! fight, bold yeomen !
> Draw, archers, draw your arrows to the head !
> Spur your proud horses hard, and ride in blood :
> Amaze the welkin with your broken staves !

> *Enter a Messenger.*

> What says Lord Stanley ? will he bring his power ?
> *Mess.* My lord, he doth deny to come.
> *K. Rich.* Off with his son George's head !
> *Norfolk.* My lord, the enemy is pass'd the marsh :
> After the battle let George Stanley die.
> *K. Rich.* A thousand hearts are great within my bosom.
> Advance our standards ! set upon our foes !
> Our ancient word of courage, fair Saint George,
> Inspire us with the spleen of fiery dragons !
> Upon them ! Victory sits on our helms.

.   .   .   .

K. Rich. A horse! a horse! my kingdom for a horse!
Catesby. Withdraw, my lord; I'll help you to a horse.
K. Rich. Slave! I have set my life upon a cast,
And I will stand the hazard of the die.
I think there be six Richmonds in the field;
Five have I slain to-day, instead of him.—
A horse! a horse! my kingdom for a horse!"

In no other play of Shakespeare's, we may surely say, is the leading character so absolutely predominant as here. He absorbs almost the whole of the interest, and it is a triumph of Shakespeare's art that he makes us, in spite of everything, follow him with sympathy. This is partly because several of his victims are so worthless that their fate seems well deserved. Anne's weakness deprives her of our sympathy, and Richard's crime loses something of its horror when we see how lightly it is forgiven by the one who ought to take it most to heart. In spite of all his iniquities, he has wit and courage on his side —a wit which sometimes rises to Mephistophelean humour, a courage which does not fail him even in the moment of disaster, but sheds a glory over his fall which is lacking to the triumph of his coldly correct opponent. However false and hypocritical he may be towards others, he is no hypocrite to himself. He is chemically free from self-delusion, even applying to himself the most derogatory terms; and this candour in the depths of his nature appeals to us. It must be said for him, too, that threats and curses recoil from him innocuous, that neither hatred nor violence nor superior force can dash his courage. Strength of character is such a rare quality that it arouses sympathy even in a criminal. If Richard's reign had lasted longer, he would perhaps have figured in history as a ruler of the type of Louis XI.: crafty, always wearing his religion on his sleeve, but far-seeing and resolute. As a matter of fact, in history as in the drama, his whole time was occupied in defending himself in the position to which he had fought his way, like a bloodthirsty beast of prey. His figure stands before us as his contemporaries have drawn it: small and wiry, the right shoulder higher than the left, wearing his rich brown hair long in order to conceal this malformation, biting his under-lip, always restless, always with his hand on his dagger-hilt, sliding it up and down in its sheath, without entirely drawing it. Shakespeare has succeeded in throwing a halo of poetry around this tiger in human shape.

The figures of the two boy princes, Edward's sons, stand in the strongest contrast to Richard. The eldest child already shows greatness of soul, a kingly spirit, with a deep feeling for the import of historic achievement. The fact that Julius Cæsar built the Tower, he says, even were it not registered, ought to live from age to age. He is full of the thought that while Cæsar's "valour did enrich his wit," yet it was his wit "that made his valour live," and he exclaims with enthusiasm, "Death makes no conquest of this conqueror." The younger brother is childishly witty, imaginative, full of boyish mockery for his uncle's grimness, and eager to play with his dagger and sword. In a very few touches Shakespeare has endowed these young brothers with the most exquisite grace. The murderers "weep like to children in their death's sad story" :—

> "Their lips were four red roses on a stalk,
>   And, in their summer beauty, kiss'd each other."

Finally, the whole tragedy of Richard's life and death is enveloped, as it were, in the mourning of women, permeated with their lamentations. In its internal structure, it bears no slight resemblance to a Greek tragedy, being indeed the concluding portion of a tetralogy.

Nowhere else does Shakespeare approach so nearly to the classicism on the model of Seneca which had found some adherents in England.

The whole tragedy springs from the curse which York, in the Third Part of *Henry VI.* (i. 4), hurls at Margaret of Anjou. She has insulted her captive enemy, and given him in mockery a napkin soaked in the blood of his son, the young Rutland, stabbed to the heart by Clifford.

Therefore she loses her crown and her son, the Prince of Wales. Her lover, Suffolk, she has already lost. Nothing remains to attach her to life.

But now it is her turn to be revenged.

The poet has sought to incarnate in her the antique Nemesis, has given her supernatural proportions and set her free from the conditions of real life. Though exiled, she has returned unquestioned to England, haunts the palace of Edward IV., and gives free vent to her rage and hatred in his presence and that of his kinsfolk and his courtiers. So, too, she wanders around under Richard's rule, simply and solely to curse her enemies— and even Richard himself is seized with a superstitious shudder at these anathemas.

Never again did Shakespeare so depart from the possible in order to attain a scenic effect. And yet it is doubtful whether the effect is really attained. In reading, it is true, these curses strike us with extraordinary force; but on the stage, where she only disturbs and retards the action, and takes no effective part in it, Margaret cannot but prove wearisome.

Yet, though she herself remains inactive, her curses are effectual enough. Death overtakes all those on whom they fall —the King and his children, Rivers and Dorset, Lord Hastings and the rest.

She encounters the Duchess of York, the mother of Edward IV., Queen Elizabeth, his widow, and finally Anne, Richard's daringly-won and quickly-repudiated wife. And all these women, like a Greek chorus, give utterance in rhymed verse to imprecations and lamentations of high lyric fervour. In two passages in particular (ii. 2 and iv. 1) they chant positive choral odes in dialogue form. Take as an example of the lyric tone of the diction these lines (iv. 1) :—

> " *Duchess of York* [*To Dorset.*] Go thou to Richmond, and good
>   fortune guide thee !—
> [*To Anne.*] Go thou to Richard, and good angels tend thee !—
> [*To Q. Elizabeth.*] Go thou to sanctuary, and good thoughts
>   possess thee !—
> I to my grave, where peace and rest lie with me !
> Eighty odd years of sorrow have I seen,
> And each hour's joy wrack'd with a week of teen."

Such is this work of Shakespeare's youth, firm, massive, and masterful throughout, even though of very unequal merit. Everything is here worked out upon the surface ; the characters themselves tell us what sort of people they are, and proclaim themselves evil or good, as the case may be. They are all transparent, all self-conscious to excess. They expound themselves in soliloquies, and each of them is judged in a sort of choral ode. The time is yet to come when Shakespeare no longer dreams of making his characters formally hand over to the spectators the key to their mystery—when, on the contrary, with his sense of the secrets and inward contradictions of the spiritual life, he sedulously hides that key in the depths of personality.

XIX

SHAKESPEARE LOSES HIS SON—TRACES OF HIS GRIEF IN KING JOHN—THE OLD PLAY OF THE SAME NAME—DISPLACEMENT OF ITS CENTRE OF GRAVITY—ELIMINATION OF RELIGIOUS POLEMICS—RETENTION OF THE NATIONAL BASIS—PATRIOTIC SPIRIT—SHAKESPEARE KNOWS NOTHING OF THE DISTINCTION BETWEEN NORMANS AND ANGLO-SAXONS, AND IGNORES THE MAGNA CHARTA

IN the Parish Register of Stratford-on-Avon for 1596, under the heading of burials, we find this entry, in a clear and elegant handwriting :—

> "*August* 11, *Hamnet filius William Shakespeare.*"

Shakespeare's only son was born on the 2nd of February 1585 ; he was thus only eleven and a half when he died.

We cannot doubt that this loss was a grievous one to a man of Shakespeare's deep feeling ; doubly grievous, it would seem, because it was his constant ambition to restore the fallen fortunes of his family, and he was now left without an heir to his name.

Traces of what his heart must have suffered appear in the work he now undertakes, *King John*, which seems to date from 1596–97.

One of the main themes of this play is the relation between John Lackland, who has usurped the English crown, and the rightful heir, Arthur, son of John's elder brother, in reality a boy of about fourteen at the date of the action, but whom Shakespeare, for the sake of poetic effect, and influenced, perhaps, by his private preoccupations of the moment, has made considerably younger, and consequently more childlike and touching.

The King has got Arthur into his power. The most famous scene in the play is that (iv. 1) in which Hubert de Burgh, the King's chamberlain, who has received orders to sear out the eyes of the little captive, enters Arthur's prison with the irons, and accompanied by the two servants who are to bind the child to a chair and hold him fast while the atrocity is being committed. The little prince, who has no mistrust of Hubert, but only a general dread of his uncle's malice, as yet divines no danger, and is full of sympathy and childlike tenderness. The passage is one of extraordinery grace :—

> " *Arthur.*   You are sad.
> *Hubert.* Indeed, I have been merrier.
> *Arth.*   Mercy on me
> Methinks, nobody should be sad but I :
>
> .   .   .   .
>
>   I would to Heaven,
> I were your son, so you would love me, Hubert.
> *Hub.* [*Aside.*] If I talk to him, with his innocent prate
> He will awake my mercy, which lies dead :
> Therefore I will be sudden, and despatch.
> *Arth.* Are you sick, Hubert? you look pale to-day.
> In sooth, I would you were a little sick,
> That I might sit all night, and watch with you :
> I warrant, I love you more than you do me."

Hubert gives him the royal mandate to read :—

> " *Hubert.* Can you not read it? is it not fair writ?
> *Arthur.* Too fairly, Hubert, for so foul effect.
> Must you with hot irons burn out both mine eyes?
> *Hub.* Young boy, I must.
> *Arth.*   And will you?
> *Hub.*   And I will.
> *Arth.* Have you the heart? When your head did but ache,
> I knit my handkerchief about your brows,
> (The best I had, a princess wrought it me,)
> And I did never ask it you again ;
> And with my hand at midnight held your head."

Hubert summons the executioners, and the child promises to sit still and offer no resistance if only he will send these "bloody men" away. One of the servants as he goes out speaks a word of pity, and Arthur is in despair at having "chid away his friend." In heart-breaking accents he begs mercy of Hubert until the iron has grown cold, and Hubert has not the heart to heat it afresh.

Arthur's entreaties to the rugged Hubert to spare his eyes, must have represented in Shakespeare's thought the prayers of his little Hamnet to be suffered still to see the light of day, or rather Shakespeare's own appeal to Death to spare the child— prayers and appeals which were all in vain.

It is, however, in the lamentations of Arthur's mother, Constance, when the child is carried away to prison (iii. 4), that we most clearly recognise the accents of Shakespeare's sorrow :—

> " *Pandulph.* Lady, you utter madness, and not sorrow.
> *Constance.* I am not mad : this hair I tear is mine.
>
> .   .   .   .

If I were mad, I should forget my son,
Or madly think, a babe of clouts were he.
I am not mad : too well, too well I feel
The different plague of each calamity."

She pours forth her anguish at the thought of his sufferings in prison :—

" Now will canker sorrow eat my bud,
And chase the native beauty from his cheek,
And he will look as hollow as a ghost,
As dim and meagre as an ague's fit,
And so he'll die.

.   .   .   .

Pandulph. You hold too heinous a respect of grief.
Constance. He talks to me, that never had a son.
K. Philip. You are as fond of grief as of your child.
Const. Grief fills the room up of my absent child,
Lies in his bed, walks up and down with me,
Puts on his pretty looks, repeats his words,
Remembers me of all his gracious parts,
Stuffs out his vacant garments with his form."

It seems as though Shakespeare's great heart had found an outlet for its own sorrows in transfusing them into the heart of Constance.

Shakespeare used as the basis of his *King John* an old play on the same subject published in 1591.[1] This play is quite artless and spiritless, but contains the whole action, outlines all the characters, and suggests almost all the principal scenes. The poet did not require to trouble himself with the invention of external traits. He could concentrate his whole effort upon vitalising, spiritualising, and deepening everything. Thus it happens that this play, though never one of his most popular (it seems to have been but seldom performed during his lifetime, and remained in manuscript until the appearance of the First Folio), nevertheless contains some of his finest character-studies and a multitude of pregnant, imaginative, and exquisitely worded speeches.

The old play was a mere Protestant tendency-drama directed against Catholic aggression, and full of the crude hatred and coarse ridicule of monks and nuns characteristic of the Reformation period. Shakespeare, with his usual tact, has suppressed the religious element, and retained only the national and political attack upon Roman Catholicism, so that the play had no slight actuality for the Elizabethan public. But he has also displaced

---

[1] The full title runs thus : " The Troublesome Raigne of *John*, King of *England*, with the discouerie of King Richard Cordelions Base sonne (vulgarly named The Bastard Fawconbridge) : also the death of King John at Swinstead Abbey. As it was (sundry times) publikely acted by the Queenes Maiesties Players, in the honorable Citie of London."

the centre of gravity of the old play. Everything in Shakespeare turns upon John's defective right to the throne: therein lies the motive for the atrocity he plans, which leads (although it is not carried out as he intended) to the barons' desertion of his cause.

Despite its great dramatic advantages over *Richard II.*, the play suffers from the same radical weakness, and in an even greater degree: the figure of the King is too unsympathetic to serve as the centre-point of a drama. His despicable infirmity of purpose, which makes him kneel to receive his crown at the hands of the same Papal legate whom he has shortly before defied in blusterous terms; his infamous scheme to assassinate an innocent child, and his repentance when he sees that its supposed execution has alienated the chief supporters of his throne—all this hideous baseness, unredeemed by any higher characteristics, leads the spectator rather to attach his interest to the subordinate characters, and thus the action is frittered away before his eyes. It lacks unity, because the King is powerless to hold it together.

He himself is depicted for all time in the masterly scene (iii. 3) where he seeks, without putting his thought into plain words, to make Hubert understand that he would fain have Arthur murdered:—

> "Or if that thou couldst see me without eyes,
> Hear me without thine ears, and make reply
> Without a tongue, using conceit alone,
> Without eyes, ears, and harmful sound of words :
> Then, in despite of brooded-watchful day,—
> I would into thy bosom pour my thoughts.
> But, ah! I will not :—yet I love thee well."

Hubert protests his fidelity and devotion. Even if he were to die for the deed, he would execute it for the King's sake. Then John's manner becomes hearty, almost affectionate. "Good Hubert, Hubert!" he says caressingly. He points to Arthur, bidding Hubert "throw his eye on yon young boy;" and then follows this masterly dialogue :—

> "I'll tell thee what, my friend,
> He is a very serpent in my way ;
> And wheresoe'er this foot of mine doth tread,
> He lies before me. Dost thou understand me?
> Thou art his keeper.
> *Hub.* And I'll keep him so,
> That he shall not offend your majesty.
> *K. John.* Death.
> *Hub.* My Lord.
> *K. John.* A grave.
> *Hub.* He shall not live.
> *K. John.* Enough.

> *I could be merry now.*   Hubert, I love thee;
> Well, I'll not say what I intend for thee:
> Remember.—Madam, fare you well:
> I'll send those powers o'er to your majesty.
>   *Elinor.* My blessing go with thee!"

The character that bears the weight of the piece, as an acting play, is the illegitimate son of Richard Cœur-de-Lion, Philip Faulconbridge.   He is John Bull himself in the guise of a mediæval knight, equipped with great strength and a racy English humour, not the wit of a Mercutio, a gay Italianising cavalier, but the irrepressible ebullitions of rude health and blunt gaiety befitting an English Hercules.   The scene in the first act, in which he appears along with his brother, who seeks to deprive him of his inheritance as a Faulconbridge on the ground of his alleged illegitimacy, and the subsequent scene with his mother, from whom he tries to wring the secret of his paternity, both appear in the old play; but in it everything that the Bastard says is in grim earnest—the embroidery of wit belongs to Shakespeare alone.   It is he who has placed in Faulconbridge's mouth such sayings as this:—

> " Madam, I was not old Sir Robert's son:
> Sir Robert might have eat his part in me
> Upon Good Friday, and ne'er broke his fast."

And it is quite in Shakespeare's spirit when the son, after her confession, thus consoles his mother:—

> " Madam, I would not wish a better father.
> Some sins do bear their privilege on earth,
> And so doth yours."

In later years, at a time when his outlook upon life was darkened, Shakespeare accounted for the villainy of Edmund, in *King Lear,* and for his aloofness from anything like normal humanity, on the ground of his irregular birth; in the Bastard of this play, on the contrary, his aim was to present a picture of all that health, vigour, and full-blooded vitality which popular belief attributes to a "love-child."

The antithesis to this national hero is Limoges, Archduke of Austria, in whom Shakespeare, following the old play, has mixed up two entirely distinct personalities: Vidomar, Viscount of Limoges, at the siege of one of whose castles Richard Cœur-de-Lion was killed, in 1199, and Leopold V., Archduke of Austria, who had kept Cœur-de-Lion in prison.   Though the latter, in fact, died five years before Richard, we here find him figuring as the dastardly murderer of the heroic monarch.   In memory of this deed he wears a lion's skin on his shoulders, and

thus brings down upon himself the indignant scorn of Constance
and Faulconbridge's taunting insults :—

> " *Constance.* Thou wear a lion's hide ! doff it for shame,
> And hang a calf's-skin on those recreant limbs.
> *Austria.* O, that a man should speak those words to me !
> *Bastard.* And hang a calf's-skin on those recreant limbs.
> *Aust.* Thou dar'st not say so, villain, for thy life.
> *Bast.* And hang a calf's-skin on those recreant limbs."

Every time the Archduke tries to get in a word of warning or
counsel, Faulconbridge silences him with this coarse sarcasm.

Faulconbridge is at first full of youthful insolence, the true
mediæval nobleman, who despises the burgess class simply as
such. When the inhabitants of Angiers refuse to open their
gates either to King John or to King Philip of France, who has
espoused the cause of Arthur, the Bastard is so indignant at this
peace-loving circumspection that he urges the kings to join their
forces against the unlucky town, and cry truce to their feud
until the ramparts are levelled to the earth. But in the course
of the action he ripens more and more, and displays ever greater
and more estimable qualities—humanity, right-mindedness, and a
fidelity to the King which does not interfere with generous freedom
of speech towards him.

His method of expression is always highly imaginative, more
so than that of the other male characters in the play. Even the
most abstract ideas he personifies. Thus he talks (iii. 1) of—

> " Old Time, the clock-setter, that bald sexton Time."

In the old play whole scenes are devoted to his execution of the
task here allotted him of visiting the monasteries of England and
lightening the abbots' bursting money-bags. Shakespeare has
suppressed these ebullitions of an anti-Catholic fervour, which he
did not share. On the other hand, he has endowed Faulconbridge
with genuine moral superiority. At first he is only a cheery,
fresh-natured, robust personality, who tramples upon all social
conventions, phrases, and affectations ; and indeed he preserves
to the last something of that contempt for " cockered silken
wantons " which Shakespeare afterwards elaborates so magnificently in Henry Percy. But there is real greatness in his attitude
when, at the close of the play, he addresses the vacillating John
in this manly strain (v. 1) :—

> " Let not the world see fear, and sad distrust,
> Govern the motion of a kingly eye :
> Be stirring as the time ; be fire with fire ;
> Threaten the threatener, and outface the brow
> Of bragging horror : so shall inferior eyes,
> That borrow their behaviours from the great,
> Grow great by your example, and put on
> The dauntless spirit of resolution."

K

Faulconbridge is in this play the spokesman of the patriotic spirit. But we realise how strong was Shakespeare's determination to make this string sound at all hazards, when we find that the first eulogy of England is placed in the mouth of England's enemy, Limoges, the slayer of Cœur-de-Lion, who speaks (ii. 1) of—

> "that pale, that white-fac'd shore,
> Whose foot spurns back the ocean's roaring tides,
> And coops from other lands her islanders,
> . . . that England, hedg'd in with the main,
> That water-walled bulwark, still secure
> And confident from foreign purposes."

How slight is the difference between the eulogistic style of the two mortal enemies, when Faulconbridge, who has in the meantime killed Limoges, ends the play with a speech, which is, however, only slightly adapted from the older text :—

> " This England never did, nor never shall,
> Lie at the proud foot of a conqueror.
>
> .   .   .   .
>
> Come the three corners of the world in arms,
> And we shall shock them.   Naught shall make us rue,
> If England to itself do rest but true."

Next to Faulconbridge, Constance is the character who bears the weight of the play ; and its weakness arises in great part from the fact that Shakespeare has killed her at the end of the third act.   So lightly is her death treated, that it is merely announced in passing by the mouth of a messenger.   She does not appear at all after her son Arthur is put out of the way, possibly because Shakespeare feared to lengthen the list of sorrowing and vengeful mothers already presented in his earlier histories.

He has treated this figure with a marked predilection, such as he usually manifests for those characters which, in one way or another, forcibly oppose every compromise with lax worldliness and euphemistic conventionality.   He has not only endowed her with the most passionate and enthusiastic motherly love, but with a wealth of feeling and of imagination which gives her words a certain poetic magnificence.   She wishes that "her tongue were in the thunder's mouth, Then with a passion would she shake the world " (iii. 4).   She is sublime in her grief for the loss of her son :—

> " I will instruct my sorrows to be proud,
> For grief is proud, and makes his owner stoop.
> To me, and to the state of my great grief,
> Let kings assemble ;
>
> .   .   .   .   .   .
>
> Here I and sorrows sit ;
> Here is my throne, bid kings come bow to it.
> [*Seats herself on the ground.*"

Yet Shakespeare is already preparing us, in the overstrained violence of these expressions, for her madness and death.

The third figure which fascinates the reader of *King John* is that of Arthur. All the scenes in which the child appears are contained in the old play of the same name, and, among the rest, the first scene of the second act, which seems to dispose of Fleay's conjecture that the first two hundred lines of the act were hastily inserted after Shakespeare had lost his son. Nevertheless almost all that is gracious and touching in the figure is due to the great reviser. The old text is at its best in the scene where Arthur meets his death by jumping from the walls of the castle. Shakespeare has here confined himself for the most part to free curtailment; in the old *King John*, his fatal fall does not prevent Arthur from pouring forth copious lamentations to his absent mother and prayers to "sweete Iesu." Shakespeare gives him only two lines to speak after his fall.

In this play, as in almost all the works of Shakespeare's younger years, the reader is perpetually amazed to find the finest poetical and rhetorical passages side by side with the most intolerable euphuistic affectations. And we cannot allege the excuse that these are legacies from the older play. On the contrary, there is nothing of the kind to be found in it; they are added by Shakespeare, evidently with the express purpose of displaying delicacy and profundity of thought. In the scenes before the walls of Angiers, he has on the whole kept close to the old drama, and has even followed faithfully the sense of all the more important speeches. For example, it is a citizen on the ramparts, who, in the old play, suggests the marriage between Blanch and the Dauphin; Shakespeare merely re-writes his speech, introducing into it these beautiful lines (ii. 2) :—

> " If lusty love should go in quest of beauty,
> Where should he find it fairer than in Blanch ?
> If zealous love should go in search of virtue,
> Where should he find it purer than in Blanch ?
> If love ambitious sought a match of birth,
> Whose veins bound richer blood than Lady Blanch ? "

The surprising thing is that the same hand which has just written these verses should forthwith lose itself in a tasteless tangle of affectations like this :—

> " Such as she is, in beauty, virtue, birth,
> Is the young Dauphin every way complete :
> If not complete of, say, he is not she ;
> And she again wants nothing, to name want,
> If want it be not, that she is not he : "

and this profound thought is further spun out with a profusion of images. Can we wonder that Voltaire and the French critics of the eighteenth century were offended by a style like this, even to the point of letting it blind them to the wealth of genius elsewhere manifested ?

Even the touching scene between Arthur and Hubert is disfigured by false cleverness of this sort. The little boy, kneeling to the man who threatens to sear out his eyes, introduces, in the midst of the most moving appeals, such far-fetched and contorted phrases as this (iv. 1) :—

> " The iron of itself, though heat red-hot,
> Approaching near these eyes, would drink my tears,
> And quench this fiery indignation
> Even in the matter of mine innocence ;
> Nay, after that, consume away in rust,
> But for containing fire to harm mine eye."

And again, when Hubert proposes to reheat the iron :—

> " An if you do, you will but make it blush,
> And glow with shame of your proceedings, Hubert."

The taste of the age must indeed have pressed strongly upon Shakespeare's spirit to prevent him from feeling the impossibility of these quibbles upon the lips of a child imploring in deadly fear that his eyes may be spared to him.

As regards their ethical point of view, there is no essential difference between the old play and Shakespeare's. The King's defeat and painful death is in both a punishment for his wrongdoing. There has only been, as already mentioned, a certain displacement of the centre of gravity. In the old play, the dying John stammers out an explicit confession that from the moment he surrendered to the Roman priest he has had no more happiness on earth ; for the Pope's curse is a blessing, and his blessing a curse. In Shakespeare the emphasis is laid, not upon the King's weakness in the religio-political struggle, but upon the wrong to Arthur. Faulconbridge gives utterance to the fundamental idea of the play when he says (iv. 3) :—

> " From forth this morsel of dead royalty,
> The life, the right, and truth of all this realm
> Is fled to heaven."

Shakespeare's political standpoint is precisely that of the earlier writer, and indeed, we may add, of his whole age.

The most important contrasts and events of the period he seeks to represent do not exist for him. He naïvely accepts the first kings of the House of Plantagenet, and the Norman princes in general, as English national heroes, and has evidently no suspicion of the deep gulf that separated the Normans from the Anglo-Saxons down to this very reign, when the two hostile

races, equally oppressed by the King's tyranny, began to fuse
into one people. What would Shakespeare have thought had he
known that Richard Cœur-de-Lion's favourite formula of denial
was "Do you take me for an Englishman?" while his pet oath,
and that of his Norman followers, was "May I become an Englishman if——," &c. ?

Nor does a single phrase, a single syllable, in the whole play,
refer to the event which, for all after-times, is inseparably associated with the memory of King John—the signing of the Magna
Charta. The reason of this is evidently, in the first place,
that Shakespeare kept close to the earlier drama, and, in the
second place, that he did not attribute to the event the importance it really possessed, did not understand that the Magna
Charta laid the foundation of popular liberty, by calling into existence a middle class which supported even the House of Tudor
in its struggle with an overweening oligarchy. But the chief
reason why the Magna Charta is not mentioned was, no doubt,
that Elizabeth did not care to be reminded of it. She was not
fond of any limitations of her royal prerogative, and did not care
to recall the defeats suffered by her predecessors in their struggles
with warlike and independent vassals. And the nation was willing
enough to humour her in this respect. People felt that they had
to thank her government for a great national revival, and therefore showed no eagerness either to vindicate popular rights against
her, or to see them vindicated in stage-history. It was not until
long after, under the Stuarts, that the English people began to
cultivate its constitution. The chronicle-writers of the period
touch very lightly upon the barons' victory over King John in the
struggle for the Great Charter; and Shakespeare thus followed
at once his own personal bias with regard to history, and the
current of his age.

XX

*"THE TAMING OF THE SHREW" AND "THE MERCHANT OF
VENICE"* — *SHAKESPEARE'S PREOCCUPATION WITH
THOUGHTS OF PROPERTY AND GAIN—HIS GROWING
PROSPERITY—HIS ADMISSION TO THE RANKS OF THE
"GENTRY"—HIS PURCHASE OF HOUSES AND LAND—
MONEY TRANSACTIONS AND LAWSUITS*

THE first plays in which we seem to find traces of Italian travel
are *The Taming of the Shrew* and *The Merchant of Venice*, the
former written at latest in 1596, the latter almost certainly in that
or the following year.

Enough has already been said of *The Taming of the Shrew*.
It is only a free and spirited reconstruction of an old piece of
scenic architecture, which Shakespeare demolished in order to
erect from its materials a spacious and airy hall. The old play
itself had been highly popular on the stage; it took new life under
Shakespeare's hands. His play is not much more than a farce,
but it possesses movement and fire, and the leading male character, the somewhat coarsely masculine Petruchio, stands in amusing
and typical contrast to the spoilt, headstrong, and passionate little
woman whom he masters.

The Merchant of Venice, Shakespeare's first important comedy,
is a piece of work of a very different order, and is elaborated to a
very different degree. There is far more of his own inmost nature
in it than in the light and facile farce.

No doubt he found in Marlowe's *Jew of Malta* the first, purely
literary, impulse towards *The Merchant of Venice*. In Marlowe's
play the curtain rises upon the chief character, Barabas, sitting in
his counting-house, with piles of gold before him, and revelling
in the thought of the treasures which it takes a soliloquy of
nearly fifty lines to enumerate—pearls like pebble-stones, opals,
sapphires, amethysts, jacinths, topazes, grass-green emeralds, beauteous rubies and sparkling diamonds. At the beginning of the play,
he is possessed of all the riches wherewith the Genie of the Lamp
endowed Aladdin, which have at one time or another sparkled in
the dreams of all poor poets.

Barabas is a Jew and usurer, like Shylock. Like Shylock, he
has a daughter who is in love with a poor Christian; and, like
him, he thirsts for revenge. But he is a monster, not a man.

When he has been misused by the Christians, and robbed of his whole fortune, he becomes a criminal fit only for a fairy-tale or for a madhouse: he uses his own daughter as an instrument for his revenge, and then poisons her along with all the nuns in whose cloister she has taken refuge.   Shakespeare was attracted by the idea of making a real man and a real Jew out of this intolerable demon in a Jew's skin.

But this slight impulse would scarcely have set Shakespeare's genius in motion had it found him engrossed in thoughts and images of an incongruous nature.   It took effect upon his mind because it was at that moment preoccupied with the ideas of acquisition, property, money-making, wealth.   He did not, like the Jew, who was in all countries legally incapable of acquiring real estate, dream of gold and jewels ; but, like the genuine country-born Englishman he was, he longed for land and houses, meadows and gardens, money that yielded sound yearly interest, and, finally, a corresponding advancement in rank and position.

We have seen with what indifference he treated his plays, how little he thought of winning fame by their publication.   All the editions of them which appeared in his lifetime were issued without his co-operation, and no doubt against his will, since the sale of the books did not bring him in a farthing, but, on the contrary, diminished his profits by diminishing the attendance at the theatre on which his livelihood depended.   Furthermore, when we see in his Sonnets how discontented he was with his position as an actor, and how humiliated he felt at the contempt in which the stage was held, we cannot doubt that the calling into which he had drifted in his needy youth was in his eyes simply and solely a means of making money.   It is true that actors like himself and Burbage were, in certain circles, welcomed and respected as men who rose above their calling ; but they were admitted on sufferance, they had not full rights of citizenship, they were not "gentlemen." There is extant a copy of verses by John Davies of Hereford, beginning, " *Players*, I love yee, and your *Qualitie*," with a marginal note citing as examples " W. S., R. B." [William Shakespeare, Richard Burbage] ; but they are clearly looked upon as exceptions :—

> " And though the *stage* doth staine pure gentle *bloud*,
> Yet generous yee are in *minde* and *moode*."

The calling of an actor, however, was a lucrative one.   Most of the leading players became well-to-do, and it seems clear that this was one of the reasons why they were evilly regarded.   In *The Return from Parnassus* (1606), Kemp assures two Cambridge students who apply to him and Burbage for instruction in acting, that there is no better calling in the world, from a financial point of view, than that of the player.   In a pamphlet of the same year, *Ratsey's Ghost*, the executed thief, with a satirical allusion to Shakespeare, advises a strolling player to buy property in the country when he is tired of play-acting, and by that means attain honour and dignity. In an epigram entitled *Theatrum Licentia* (in *Laquei Ridiculosi*, 1616), we read of the actor's calling :—

> " For here's the spring (saith he) whence pleasures flow
> And brings them damnable excessive gains."

The primary object of Shakespeare's aspirations was neither renown as a poet nor popularity as an actor, but worldly prosperity, and prosperity regarded specially as a means of social advancement. He had taken greatly to heart his father's decline in property and civic esteem ; from youth upwards he had been passionately bent on restoring the sunken name and fame of his family. He had now, at the age of only thirty-two, amassed a small capital, which he began to invest in the most advantageous way for the end he had in view—that of elevating himself above his calling.

His father had been afraid to cross the street lest he should be arrested for debt. He himself, as a youth, had been whipped and consigned to the lock-up at the command of the lord of the manor. The little town which had witnessed this disgrace should also witness the rehabilitation. The townspeople, who had heard of his equivocal fame as an actor and playwright, should see him in the character of a respected householder and landowner. At Stratford and elsewhere, those who had classed him with the proletariat should recognise in him a *gentleman*. According to a tradition which Rowe reports on the authority of Sir William Davenant, Lord Southampton is said to have laid the foundation of Shakespeare's prosperity by a gift of £1000. Though Bacon received more than this from Essex, the magnitude of the sum discredits the tradition—it is equivalent to something like £5000 in modern money. No doubt the young Earl gave the poet a present in acknowledgment of the dedication of his two poems ; for the poets of that time did not live on royalties, but on their dedications. But as the ordinary acknowledgment of a dedication was only £5, a gift of even £50 would have been reckoned princely. What is practically certain is, that Shakespeare was early in a position to become a shareholder in the theatre ; and he evidently had a special talent for putting the money he earned to profitable use. His firm determination to work his way up in the world, combined with the Englishman's inborn practicality, made him an excellent man of business ; and he soon develops such a decided talent for finance as only two other great national writers, probably, have ever possessed—to wit, Holberg and Voltaire.

It is from the year 1596 onwards that we find evidences of his growing prosperity. In this year his father, no doubt prompted and supplied with means by Shakespeare himself, makes application to the Heralds' College for a coat-of-arms, the sketch of which is preserved, dated October 1596. The conferring of a coat-of-arms implied formal admittance into the ranks of "the gentry." It was necessary before either father or son could append the word "gentleman" (*armiger*) to his name, as we find Shakespeare doing in legal documents after this date, and in his will. But Shakespeare himself was not in a position to apply for a coat-of-arms. That was out of the question—a player was far too mean a person to come within the cognisance of heraldry. He therefore adopted the shrewd device of furnishing his father with means for making the application on his own behalf.

According to the ideas and regulations of the time, indeed, not even Shakespeare senior had any real right to a coat-of-arms. But the Garter-King-at-Arms for the time being, Sir William Dethick, was an exceedingly compliant personage, probably not inaccessible to pecuniary arguments. He was sharply criticised in his own day, and indeed at last superseded, on account of the facility with which he provided applicants with armorial bearings, and we possess his defence in this very matter of the Shakespeare coat-of-arms. All sorts of small falsehoods were alleged; for instance, that John Shakespeare had, twenty years before, had "his auncient cote of arms assigned to him," and that he was then "Her Majestie's officer and baylefe," whereas his office had in fact been merely municipal. Nevertheless, there must have been some hitch in the negotiations, for in 1597 John Shakespeare is still described as *yeoman*, and not until 1599 did the definite assignment of the coat-of-arms take place, along with the permission (of which the son, however, did not avail himself) to impale the Shakespeare arms with those of the Arden family. The coat-of-arms is thus described :—"Gould on a bend sable a speare of the first, the poynt steeled, proper, and for creast or cognizance, a faulcon, his wings displayed, argent, standing on a wreathe of his coullors, supporting a speare gould steled as aforesaid." The motto runs (with a suspicion of irony), *Non sans droict.* Yet to what insignia had not *he* the right !

In the spring of 1597, William Shakespeare bought the mansion of New Place, the largest, and at one time the handsomest, house in Stratford, which had now fallen somewhat out of repair, and was therefore sold at the comparatively low price of £60. He thoroughly restored the house, attached two gardens to it, and soon extended his domain by new purchases of land, some of it arable ; for we see that during the corn - famine of 1598 (February), he appears on the register as owner of ten quarters of corn and malt—that is to say, the third largest stock in the town. The house stood opposite the Guild Chapel, the sound of whose bells must have been among his earliest memories.

At the same time he gives his father money to revive the lawsuit against John Lambert concerning the property of Asbies, mortgaged nineteen years before—that lawsuit whose unfavourable issue young Shakespeare had taken so much to heart, as we have seen, that he introduced a gibe at the Lambert family into the Induction to *The Taming of the Shrew*, now just completed.

A letter of January 24, 1597–8, written by a certain Abraham Sturley in Stratford to his brother-in-law, Richard Quiney, whose son afterwards married Shakespeare's youngest daughter, shows that the poet already passed for a man of substance, since one of his fellow-townsmen sends him a message recommending him, instead of buying land at Shottery, to lease part of the Stratford tithes. This would be advantageous both to him and to the town, for the purchase of tithes was generally a good investment, and the character of the purchaser was of importance to the town, since a portion of the sum raised went into the municipal treasury.[1]

It appears, however, that the purchase-money required was still beyond Shakespeare's means, for not until seven years later, in 1605, does he buy, for the considerable sum of £440, a moiety of the lease of the tithes of Stratford, Old Stratford, ·Bishopton, and Welcombe. These tithes originally belonged to the Church, but passed to the town in 1554, and from 1580 onwards were farmed by private persons. As might have been expected, the purchase of them involved Shakespeare in several lawsuits.

In a letter of 1598 or 1599, Adrian Quiney, of Stratford, writes to his son Richard, who looked after the interests of his fellow-townsmen in the capital: "Yff yow bargen with Wm. Sha. or receve money therfor, brynge youre money homme that yow maye." This Richard Quiney is the writer of the only extant letter addressed to Shakespeare (probably never despatched), in which he begs his "loveinge contreyman," in moving and pious terms, for a loan of £30, promising security and interest. Another letter from Sturley, dated November 4, 1598, mentions the news "that our countriman Mr. Wm. Shak. would procure us monei, which I will like of as I shall heare when, and wheare, and howe."

All these documents render it sufficiently apparent that Shakespeare did not share the loathing of interest which it was the fashion of his day to affect, and which Antonio, in *The Merchant of Venice*, flaunts in the face of Shylock. The taking of interest was at that time regarded as forbidden to a Christian, but was

---

[1] Sturley writes:—"This is one speciall remembrance from ur fathers motion. Itt semeth bi him that our countriman, Mr. Shaksper, is willinge to disburse some monei upon some od yarde land or other att Shotterie or neare about us; he thinketh it a veri fitt patterne to move him to deale in the matter of our tithes. Bi the instruccions u can geve him thereof, and bi the frendes he can make therefore, we thinke it a faire marke for him to shoote att, and not unpossible to hitt. It obtained would advance him in deede, and would do us muche good."

usual nevertheless; and Shakespeare seems to have charged the current rate, namely, ten per cent.

During the following years he continued to acquire still more land. In 1602 he buys, at Stratford, arable land of the value of no less than £320, and pays £60 for a house and a piece of ground. In 1610 he adds twenty acres to his property. In 1612, in partnership with three others, he buys a house and garden in London for £140.

And Shakespeare was a strict man of business. We find him proceeding by attorney against a poor devil named Philip Rogers of Stratford, who in the years 1603–4 had bought small quantities of malt from him to the total value of £1, 19s. 10d., and who had besides borrowed two shillings of him. Six shillings he had repaid; and Shakespeare now sets the law in motion to recover the balance of £1, 15s. 10d. In 1608–9 he again brings an action against a Stratford debtor. This time he gets a verdict for £6, with £1, 4s. of costs; and as the debtor has absconded, Shakespeare proceeds against his security.

All these details show, in the first place, how closely Shakespeare kept up his connection with Stratford during his residence in London. By the year 1599 he has succeeded in restoring the credit of his family. He has made his poor, debt-burdened father a gentleman with a coat-of-arms, and has himself become one of the largest and richest landowners in his native place. He continues steadily to increase his capital and his property at Stratford; and it is obviously a mere corollary to this whole course of action that he should, while still in the full vigour of manhood, leave London, the theatre, and literature behind him, to return to Stratford and pass his last years as a prosperous landowner.

We next observe Shakespeare's eagerness to rise above his calling as a player. From 1599 onwards, he had the satisfaction of being able to write himself down: *Wm. Shakespeare of Stratford-upon-Avon in the County of Warwick, gentleman.* But it must not, of course, be understood that he was now in a position of equality with men of genuinely noble birth. So little was this the case, that even in the "Epistle Dedicatorie" to the Folio of 1623, the two actors, his comrades, who issue the book, describe him as the "servant" of the Earls of Pembroke and Montgomery, whose "dignity" they know to be "greater than to descend to the reading of these trifles" They nevertheless inscribe the "trifles" to the "incomparable paire of brethren" out of gratitude for the great "indulgence" and "favour" which they had "used" to the deceased poet.

The chief interest, however, of these old contracts and business letters lies in the insight they give us into a region of Shakespeare's soul, the existence of which, in their absence, we should never have divined. We see that he may very well have been thinking of himself when he makes Hamlet (v. 1) say beside

Ophelia's open grave: "This fellow might be in's time a great buyer of land, with his statutes, his recognizances, his fines, his double vouchers, his recoveries: is this the fine of his fines, and the recovery of his recoveries, to have his fine pate full of fine dirt?"

And—to return to our point of departure—we see that when Shakespeare, in *The Merchant of Venice*, makes the whole play turn upon the different relations of different men to property, position, and wealth, the problem was one with which he was at the moment personally preoccupied.

XXI

WE learn from Ben Jonson's *Volpone* (iv. 1) that the traveller
who arrived in Venice first rented apartments, and then applied
to a Jew dealer for the furniture. If the traveller happened to be
a poet, he would thus have an opportunity, which he lacked in
England, of studying the Jewish character and manner of expression. Shakespeare seems to have availed himself of it. The
names of the Jews and Jewesses who appear in *The Merchant of
Venice* he has taken from the Old Testament. We find in Genesis
(x. 24) the name Salah (Hebrew Schelach ; at that time appearing
as the name of a Maronite from Lebanon: Scialac) out of which
Shakespeare has made Shylock ; and in Genesis (xi. 29) there
occurs the name Iscah (she who looks out, who spies), spelt
"Jeska" in the English translations of 1549 and 1551, out of
which he made his Jessica, the girl whom Shylock accuses of a
fondness for "clambering up to casements" and "thrusting her
head into the public street" to see the masquers pass.

Shakespeare's audiences were familiar with several versions
of the story of the Jew who relentlessly demanded the pound of
flesh pledged to him by his Christian debtor, and was at last sent
empty and baffled away, and even forced to become a Christian.
The story has been found in Buddhist legends (along with the
adventure of the Three Caskets, here interwoven with it), and
many believe that it came to Europe from India. It may, however, have migrated in just the opposite direction. Certain it is,
as one of Shakespeare's authorities points out, that the right to
take payment in the flesh of the insolvent debtor was admitted in
the Twelve Tables of ancient Rome. As a matter of fact, this
antique trait was quite international, and Shakespeare has only
transferred it from old and semi-barbarous times to the Venice of
his own day.

The story illustrates the transition from the unconditional en-
forcement of strict law to the more modern principle of equity.
Thus it afforded an opening for Portia's eloquent contrast between
justice and mercy, which the public understood as an assertion of

the superiority of Christian ethics to the Jewish insistence on the letter of the law.

One of the sources on which Shakespeare drew for the figure of Shylock, and especially for his speeches in the trial scene, is *The Orator* of Alexander Silvayn. The 95th Declamation of this work bears the title: "Of a Jew who would for his debt have a pound of the flesh of a Christian." Since an English translation of Silvayn's book by Anthony Munday appeared in 1596, and *The Merchant of Venice* is mentioned by Meres in 1598 as one of Shakespeare's works, there can scarcely be any doubt that the play was produced between these dates.

In *The Orator* both the Merchant and the Jew make speeches, and the invective against the Jew is interesting in so far as it gives a lively impression of the current accusations of the period against the Israelitish race :—

"But it is no marvaile if this race be so obstinat and cruell against us, for they doe it of set purpose to offend our God whom they have crucified: and wherefore? Because he was holie, as he is yet so reputed of this worthy Turkish nation : but what shall I say? Their own bible is full of their rebellion against God, against their Priests, Judges, and leaders. What did not the verie Patriarks themselves, from whom they have their beginning? They sold their brother. . . ." &c.

Shakespeare's chief authority, however, for the whole play was obviously the story of Gianetto, which occurs in the collection entitled *Il Pecorone*, by Ser Giovanni Fiorentino, published in Milan in 1558.

A young merchant named Gianetto comes with a richly laden ship to a harbour near the castle of Belmonte, where dwells a lovely young widow. She has many suitors, and is, indeed, prepared to surrender her hand and her fortune, but only on one condition, which no one has hitherto succeeded in fulfilling, and which is stated with mediæval simplicity and directness. She challenges the aspirant, at nightfall, to share her bed and make her his own ; but at the same time she gives him a sleeping-draught which plunges him in profound unconsciousness from the moment his head touches the pillow, so that at daybreak he has forfeited his ship and its cargo to the fair lady, and is sent on his way, despoiled and put to shame.

This misfortune happens to Gianetto ; but he is so deeply in love that he returns to Venice and induces his kind foster-father, Ansaldo, to fit out another ship for him. But his second visit to Belmonte ends no less disastrously, and in order to enable him to make a third attempt his foster-father is forced to borrow 10,000 ducats from a Jew, upon the conditions which we know. By following the advice of a kindly-disposed waiting-woman, the young man this time escapes the danger, becomes a happy bridegroom, and in his rapture forgets Ansaldo's obligation to the Jew.

He is not reminded of it until the very day when it falls due, and then his wife insists that he shall instantly start for Venice, taking with him a sum of 100,000 ducats. She herself presently follows, dressed as an advocate, and appears in Venice as a young lawyer of great reputation, from Bologna. The Jew rejects every proposition for the deliverance of Ansaldo, even the 100,000 ducats. Then the trial-scene proceeds, just as in Shakespeare; Gianetto's young wife delivers judgment, like Portia; the Jew receives not a stiver, and dares not shed a drop of Ansaldo's blood. When Gianetto, in his gratitude, offers the young advocate the whole 100,000 ducats, she, as in the play, demands nothing but the ring which Gianetto has received from his wife; and the tale ends with the same gay unravelling of the sportive complication, which gives Shakespeare the matter for his fifth act.

Being unable to make use of the condition imposed by the fair lady of Belmonte in *Il Pecorone*, Shakespeare cast about for another, and found it in the *Gesta Romanorum*, in the tale of the three caskets, of gold, silver, and lead. Here it is a young girl who makes the choice in order to win the Emperor's son. The inscription on the golden casket promises that whoever chooses that shall find what he deserves. The girl rejects this out of humility, and rightly, since it proves to contain dead men's bones. The inscription on the silver casket promises to whoever chooses it what his nature craves. The girl rejects that also; for, as she says naïvely, "My nature craves for fleshly delights." Finally, the leaden casket promises that whoever chooses it shall find what God has decreed for him; and it proves to be full of jewels.

In Shakespeare, Portia, in accordance with her father's will, makes her suitors choose between the three caskets (here furnished with other legends), of which the humblest contains her portrait.

It is not probable that Shakespeare made any use of an older play, now lost, of which Stephen Gosson, in his *School of Abuse* (1579), says that it represented "the greedinesse of worldly chusers, and the bloody mindes of usurers."

The great value of *The Merchant of Venice* lies in the depth and seriousness which Shakespeare has imparted to the vague outlines of character presented by the old stories, and in the ravishing moonlight melodies which bring the drama to a close.

In Antonio, the royal merchant, who, amid all his fortune and splendour, is a victim to melancholy and spleen induced by forebodings of coming disaster, Shakespeare has certainly expressed something of his own nature. Antonio's melancholy is closely related to that which, in the years immediately following, we shall find in Jaques in *As You Like It*, in the Duke in *Twelfth Night*, and in Hamlet. It forms a sort of mournful undercurrent to the joy of life which at this period is still dominant in Shakespeare's soul. It leads, after a certain time, to the substitution of

dreaming and brooding heroes for those men of action and resolution who, in the poet's brighter youth, had played the leading
parts in his dramas.   For the rest, despite the princely elevation
of his nature, Antonio is by no means faultless.   He has insulted
and baited Shylock in the most brutal fashion on account of his
faith and his blood.   We realise the ferocity and violence of the
mediæval prejudice against the Jews when we find a man of
Antonio's magnanimity so entirely a slave to it.   And when, with
a little more show of justice, he parades his loathing and contempt for Shylock's money-dealings, he strangely (as it seems to
us) overlooks the fact that the Jews have been carefully excluded
from all other means of livelihood, and have been systematically
allowed to scrape together gold in order that their hoards may
always be at hand when circumstances render it convenient to
plunder them.   Antonio's attitude towards Shylock cannot possibly be Shakespeare's own.   Shylock cannot understand Antonio,
and characterises him (iii. 3) in the words—

" This is the fool that lent out money gratis."

But Shakespeare himself did not belong to this class of fools.
He has endowed Antonio with an ideality which he had neither
the resolution nor the desire to emulate.   Such a man's conduct
towards Shylock explains the outcast's hatred and thirst for
revenge.
    Shakespeare has lavished peculiar and loving care upon the
figure of Portia.   Both in the circumstances in which she is
placed at the outset, and in the conjuncture to which Shylock's
bond gives rise, there is a touch of the fairy tale.   In so far, the
two sides of the action harmonise well with each other.   Now-a-
days, indeed, we are apt to find rather too much of the nursery
story in the preposterous will by which Portia is bound to marry
whoever divines the very simple answer to a riddle—to the effect
that a showy outside is not always to be trusted.   The fable of
the three caskets pleased Shakespeare so much as a means of
expressing and enforcing his hatred of all empty show that he
ignored the grotesque improbability of the method of selecting a
bridegroom.
    His thought seems to have been : Portia is not only nobly
born ; she is thoroughly genuine, and can therefore be won only
by a suitor who rejects the show for the substance.   This is suggested in Bassanio's long speech before making his choice (iii. 2).
If there is anything that Shakespeare hated with a hatred somewhat disproportionate to the triviality of the matter, a hatred
which finds expression in every stage of his career, it is the use
of rouge and false hair.   Therefore he insists upon the fact that
Portia's beauty owes nothing to art ; with others the case is
different :—

> " Look on beauty,
> And you shall see 'tis purchas'd by the weight;
>
> . . . . . .
>
> So are those crisped snaky golden locks,
> Which make such wanton gambols with the wind,
> Upon supposed fairness, often known
> To be the dowry of a second head,
> The skull that bred them, in the sepulchre."

And he deduces the moral :—

> " Thus ornament is but the guiled shore
> To a most dangerous sea."

Before the choice, Portia dares not openly avow her feelings towards Bassanio, but does so nevertheless by means of a graceful and sportive slip of the tongue :—

> " Beshrew your eyes,
> They have o'erlook'd me, and divided me :
> One half of me is yours, the other half yours,—
> Mine own, I would say ; but if mine, then yours,
> And so all yours ! "

Bassanio answers by begging permission to make instant choice between the caskets, since he lives upon the rack until his fate is sealed; whereupon Portia makes some remarks as to confessions on the rack, which seem to allude to an occurrence of a few years earlier, the barbarous execution of Elizabeth's Spanish doctor, Don Roderigo Lopez, in 1594, after two ruffians had been racked into making confessions which, no doubt falsely, incriminated him. Portia says jestingly—

> " Ay, but I fear, you speak upon the rack,
> Where men, enforced, do speak anything ; "

and Bassanio answers—

> " Promise me life, and I'll confess the truth."

When the choice has been made and has fallen as she hoped and desired, her attitude clearly expresses Shakespeare's ideal of womanhood at this period of his life. It is not Juliet's passionate self-abandonment, but the perfect surrender in tenderness of the wise and delicate woman. For her own sake she does not wish herself better than she is, but for him " she would be trebled twenty times herself." She knows that she—

> " Is an unlesson'd girl, unschool'd, unpractis'd :
> Happy in this, she is not yet so old
> But she may learn ; happier than this,
> She is not bred so dull but she can learn ;
> Happiest of all is, that her gentle spirit
> Commits itself to yours to be directed,
> As from her lord, her governor, her king."

L

In such humility does she love this weak spendthrift, whose sole motive in seeking her out was originally that of clearing off the debts in which his frivolity had involved him. It thus happens, quaintly enough, that what her father thought to prevent by his strange device, namely, that Portia should be won by a mercenary suitor, is the very thing that happens—though it is true that her personal charms throw his original motive into the background.

In spite of Portia's womanly self-surrender in love, there is something independent, almost masculine, in her character. She has the orphan heiress's habit and power of looking after herself, directing others, and acting on her own responsibility without seeking advice or taking account of convention. The poet has borrowed traits from the Italian novel in order to make her as prompt in counsel as she is magnanimous. How much money does Antonio owe? she asks. Three thousand ducats? Give the Jew six thousand, and tear up the bond.

Shakespeare has equipped her with the bright and victorious temperament with which he henceforth, for a certain time, endows nearly all the heroines of his comedies. To another of these ladies it is said, "Without question, you were born in a merry hour." She answers, "No, sure, my lord, my mother cried; but then there was a star danced, and under that I was born." All these young women were born under a star that danced. Even the most subdued of them overflows with the rapture of existence.

Portia's nature is health, its utterance joy. Radiant happiness is her element. She is descended from happiness, she has grown up in happiness, she is surrounded with all the means and conditions of happiness, and she distributes happiness with both hands. She is noble to the heart's core. She is no swan born in the duck-yard, but is in complete harmony with her surroundings and with herself.

Shylock's riches consist of gold and jewels, easy to conceal or to transport at a moment's notice, but also inviting to robbery and rapine. Antonio's riches consist in cargoes tossed on many seas, and exposed to danger from storms and from pirates. What Portia owns she owns in security: estates and palaces inherited from her fathers. There has needed, perhaps, as much as a century of direct preparation for the birth of such a creature. Her noble forefathers for generations back must have led free and stainless lives, favoured by destiny, prosperous and happy, in order to amass the riches which are her pedestal, to gain the respect which is her throne, to gather the household which forms her retinue, to decorate the palace in which she rules as a princess, and to endow her mind with the high faculty and culture befitting a reigning sovereign. She is healthy, though she is delicate; she is gay, although she is mentally a head taller than any of those around her; and she is young, although she is wise. She is of a fresher stock than the nervous women of to-day. She is borne aloft by an unfailing serenity of nature, which has never suffered any rude disturbance. It manifests itself in her gaiety under circumstances of painful uncertainty, in her self-control in overwhelming joy, and in her promptitude of action in an unforeseen and threatening conjuncture. She has inexhaustible resources in her soul, a profusion of ideas and inspirations, as great a superabundance of wit as of wealth. In contradistinction to her lover, she never makes a display of what is not her own to command. Hence her equilibrium and queenly repose. If we do not realise this radiant joy of life in the inmost chambers of her soul, we are apt, even from her first scene with Nerissa, to think her jesting forced and her wit far-fetched, and are almost ready to make the criticism that only a poor intelligence plays tricks with speech and fantasticates in words. But when we have looked into the depths of this well-spring of health, we understand how her thoughts gush forth, flashing and plashing, as freely and inevitably as the jets of a fountain rise into the air. She evokes and discards image after image, as one plucks and throws away flowers in a luxuriant garden. She delights to wreath and plait her words, as she wreaths and plaits her hair.

It harmonises with her whole nature when she says (i. 2): "The brain may devise laws for the blood; but a hot temper leaps o'er a cold decree: such a hare is madness, the youth, to skip o'er the meshes of good counsel, the cripple." Such phrases must be conceived as springing from a delight in laughter and sport for the sport's sake; otherwise they would be stiff and cumbrous. In the same way, such a sally as this (iv. 1)—

> "Your wife would give you little thanks for that,
> If she were by to hear you make the offer,"

must be taken as springing from a gleeful assurance of victory, else it might seem to show callous indifference to Antonio's apparently hopeless plight. There is an innate harmony in Portia's soul; but it is full-toned, complex, and woven of strongly contrasted elements, so that it requires some imagination to represent it to ourselves. There is something in the harmonious subtlety of her physiognomy which reminds us of Lionardo's female heads. Dignity and tenderness, the power to command and to obey, acuteness such as thrives in courts, and simple womanliness, an almost inflexible seriousness and an almost mischievous gaiety, are here cunningly commingled and combined.

How Shakespeare himself would have us regard her may be gathered from the enthusiasm with which he makes Jessica describe her to her lover (iii. 5). When one young woman so warmly eulogises another, we may safely assume that her merits are unimpeachable. "It is very meet," she says,

" The Lord Bassanio live an upright life,
For, having such a blessing in his lady,
He finds the joys of heaven here on earth ;
And, if on earth he do not mean it, then
In reason he should never come to heaven.
Why, if two gods should play some heavenly match,
And on the wager lay two earthly women,
And Portia one, there must be something else
Pawn'd with the other, for the poor rude world
Hath not her fellow."

The central figure of the play, however, in the eyes of modern readers and spectators, is of course Shylock, though there can be no doubt that he appeared to Shakespeare's contemporaries a comic personage, and, since he makes his final exit before the last act, by no means the protagonist. In the humaner view of a later age, Shylock appears as a half-pathetic creation, a scapegoat, a victim ; to the Elizabethan public, with his rapacity and his miserliness, his usury and his eagerness to dig for another the pit into which he himself falls, he seemed, not terrible, but ludicrous. They did not even take him seriously enough to feel any real uneasiness as to Antonio's fate, since they all knew beforehand the issue of the adventure. They laughed when he went to Bassanio's feast " in hate, to feed upon the prodigal Christian ; " they laughed when, in the scene with Tubal, he suffered himself to be bandied about between exultation over Antonio's misfortunes and rage over the prodigality of his runaway daughter; and they found him odious when he exclaimed, " I would my daughter were dead at my foot and the jewels in her ear ! " He was, simply as a Jew, a despised creature; he belonged to the race which had crucified God himself; and he was doubly despised as an extortionate usurer. For the rest, the English public— like the Norwegian public so lately as the first half of this century —had no acquaintance with Jews except in books and on the stage. From 1290 until the middle of the seventeenth century the Jews were entirely excluded from England. Every prejudice against them was free to flourish unchecked.

Did Shakespeare in a certain measure share these religious prejudices, as he seems to have shared the patriotic prejudices against the Maid of Orleans, if, indeed, he is responsible for the part she plays in *Henry VI.?* We may be sure that he was very slightly affected by them, if at all. Had he made a more undisguised effort to place himself at Shylock's standpoint, the censorship, on the one hand, would have intervened, while, on the other hand, the public would have been bewildered and alienated. It is quite in the spirit of the age that Shylock should suffer the punishment which befalls him. To pay him out for his stiff-necked vengefulness, he is mulcted not only of the sum he lent Antonio, but of half his fortune, and is finally, like Marlowe's

Jew of Malta, compelled to change his religion. The latter detail gives something of a shock to the modern reader. But the respect for personal conviction, when it conflicted with orthodoxy, did not exist in Shakespeare's time. It was not very long since Jews had been forced to choose between kissing the crucifix and mounting the faggots; and in Strasburg, in 1349, nine hundred of them had in one day chosen the latter alternative. It is strange to reflect, too, that just at the time when, on the English stage, one Mediterranean Jew was poisoning his daughter, and another whetting his knife to cut his debtor's flesh, thousands of heroic and enthusiastic Hebrews in Spain and Portugal, who, after the expulsion of the 300,000 at the beginning of the century, had secretly remained faithful to Judaism, were suffering themselves to be tortured, flayed, and burnt alive by the Inquisition, rather than forswear the religion of their race.

It is the high-minded Antonio himself who proposes that Shylock shall be forced to become a Christian. This is done for his good; for baptism opens to him the possibility of salvation after death; and his Christian antagonists, who, by dint of the most childish sophisms, have despoiled him of his goods and forced him to forswear his God, can still pose as representing the Christian principle of mercy, in opposition to one who has taken his stand upon the Jewish basis of formal law.

That Shakespeare himself, however, in nowise shared the fanatical belief that a Jew was of necessity damned, or could be saved by compulsory conversion, is rendered clear enough for the modern reader in the scene between Launcelot and Jessica (iii. 5), where Launcelot jestingly avers that Jessica is damned. There is only one hope for her, and that is, that her father may not be her father :—

"*Jessica.* That were a kind of bastard hope, indeed: so the sins of my mother should be visited upon me.

"*Launcelot.* Truly then I fear you are damned both by father and mother: thus when I shun Scylla, your father, I fall into Charybdis, your mother. Well, you are gone both ways.

"*Jes.* I shall be saved by my husband; he hath made me a Christian.

"*Laun.* Truly, the more to blame he: we were Christians enow before; e'en as many as could well live one by another. This making of Christians will raise the price of hogs: if we grow all to be pork-eaters, we shall not shortly have a rasher on the coals for money."

And Jessica repeats Launcelot's saying to Lorenzo :—

"He tells me flatly, there is no mercy for me in heaven, because I am a Jew's daughter: and he says, you are no good member of the commonwealth, for, in converting Jews to Christians, you raise the price of pork."

No believer would ever speak in this jesting tone of matters that must seem to him so momentous.

It is none the less astounding how much right in wrong, how much humanity in inhumanity, Shakespeare has succeeded in imparting to Shylock. The spectator sees clearly that, with the treatment he has suffered, he could not but become what he is. Shakespeare has rejected the notion of the atheistically-minded Marlowe, that the Jew hates Christianity and despises Christians as fiercer money-grubbers than himself. With his calm humanity, Shakespeare makes Shylock's hardness and cruelty result at once from his passionate nature and his abnormal position; so that, in spite of everything, he has come to appear in the eyes of later times as a sort of tragic symbol of the degradation and vengefulness of an oppressed race.

There is not in all Shakespeare a greater example of trenchant and incontrovertible eloquence than Shylock's famous speech (iii. 1):—

"I am a Jew. Hath not a Jew eyes? hath not a Jew hands, organs, dimensions, senses, affections, passions? fed with the same food, hurt with the same weapons, subject to the same diseases, healed by the same means, warmed and cooled by the same winter and summer, as a Christian is? If you prick us, do we not bleed? if you tickle us, do we not laugh? if you poison us, do we not die? and if you wrong us, shall we not revenge? If we are like you in the rest, we will resemble you in that. If a Jew wrong a Christian, what is his humility? revenge. If a Christian wrong a Jew, what should his sufferance be by Christian example? why, revenge. The villany you teach me, I will execute; and it shall go hard but I will better the instruction."

But what is most surprising, doubtless, is the instinct of genius with which Shakespeare has seized upon and reproduced racial characteristics, and emphasised what is peculiarly Jewish in Shylock's culture. While Marlowe, according to his custom, made his Barabas revel in mythological similes, Shakespeare indicates that Shylock's culture is founded entirely upon the Old Testament, and makes commerce his only point of contact with the civilisation of later times. All his parallels are drawn from the Patriarchs and the Prophets. With what unction he speaks when he justifies himself by the example of Jacob! His own race is always "our sacred nation," and he feels that "the curse has never fallen upon it" until his daughter fled with his treasures. Jewish, too, is Shylock's respect for, and obstinate insistence on, the letter of the law, his reliance upon statutory rights, which are, indeed, the only rights society allows him, and the partly instinctive, partly defiant restriction of his moral ideas to the principle of retribution. He is no wild animal; he is no heathen who simply gives the rein to his natural instincts; his hatred is not ungoverned; he restrains it within its legal rights, like a tiger in its cage. He is entirely lacking, indeed, in the freedom and serenity, the easy-going, light-hearted carelessness which characterises a ruling caste in its virtues and its vices, in its charities as in its prodigalities; but he has not a single twinge of conscience about anything that he does; his actions are in perfect harmony with his ideals.

Sundered from the regions, the social forms, the language, in which his spirit is at home, he has yet retained his Oriental character. Passion is the kernel of his nature. It is his passion that has enriched him; he is passionate in action, in calculation, in sensation, in hatred, in revenge, in everything. His vengefulness is many times greater than his rapacity. Avaricious though he be, money is nothing to him in comparison with revenge. It is not until he is exasperated by his daughter's robbery and flight that he takes such hard measures against Antonio, and refuses to accept three times the amount of the loan. His conception of honour may be unchivalrous enough, but, such as it is, his honour is not to be bought for money. His hatred of Antonio is far more intense than his love for his jewels; and it is this passionate hatred, not avarice, that makes him the monster he becomes.

From this Hebrew passionateness, which can be traced even in details of diction, arises, among other things, his loathing of sloth and idleness. To realise how essentially Jewish is this trait we need only refer to the so-called Proverbs of Solomon. Shylock dismisses Launcelot with the words, " Drones hive not with me." Oriental, rather than specially Jewish, are the images in which he gives his passion utterance, approaching, as they so often do, to the parable form. (See, for example, his appeal to Jacob's cunning, or the speech in vindication of his claim, which begins, " You have among you many a purchased slave.") Specially Jewish, on the other hand, is the way in which this ardent passion throughout employs its images and parables in the service of a curiously sober rationalism, so that a sharp and biting logic, which retorts every accusation with interest, is always the controlling force. This sober logic, moreover, never lacks dramatic impetus. Shylock's course of thought perpetually takes the form of question and answer, a subordinate but characteristic trait which appears in the style of the Old Testament, and reappears to this day in representations of primitive Jews. One can feel through his words that there is a chanting quality in his voice; his movements are rapid, his gestures large. Externally and internally, to the inmost fibre of his being, he is a type of his race in its degradation.

Shylock disappears with the end of the fourth act in order that no discord may mar the harmony of the concluding scenes. By means of his fifth act, Shakespeare dissipates any preponderance of pain and gloom in the general impression of the play.

This act is a moonlit landscape thrilled with music. It is

altogether given over to music and moonshine. It is an image of
Shakespeare's soul at that point of time. Everything is here reconciled, assuaged, silvered over, and borne aloft upon the wings
of music.

The speeches melt into each other like voices in part-singing:—

> " *Lorenzo.* The moon shines bright.—In such a night as this,
> When the sweet wind did gently kiss the trees,
> And they did make no noise, in such a night,
> Troilus, methinks, mounted the Trojan walls,
> And sigh'd his soul toward the Grecian tents,
> Where Cressid lay that night.
>   *Jessica.*   In such a night
> Did Thisbe fearfully o'ertrip the dew;
>
> . . . . . .
>
> *Lor.*   In such a night
> Stood Dido with a willow in her hand;"

and so on for four more speeches—the very poetry of moonlight
arranged in antiphonies.

The conclusion of *The Merchant of Venice* brings us to the
threshold of a term in Shakespeare's life instinct with high-
pitched gaiety and gladness. In this, his brightest period, he
fervently celebrates strength and wisdom in man, intellect and wit
in woman; and these most brilliant years of his life are also the
most musical. His poetry, his whole existence, seem now to be
given over to music, to harmony.

He had been early familiar with the art of music, and must
have heard much music in his youth.[1] Even in his earliest plays,
such as *The Two Gentlemen of Verona*, we find a considerable
insight into musical technique, as in the conversation between
Julia and Lucetta (i. 2). He must often have heard the Queen's
choir, and the choirs maintained by noble lords and ladies, like
that which Portia has in her palace. And he no doubt heard
much music performed in private. The English were in his day,
what they have never been since, a musical people. It was the
Puritans who cast out music from the daily life of England. The
spinet was the favourite instrument of the time. Spinets stood
in the barbers' shops, for the use of customers waiting their turn.
Elizabeth herself played on the spinet and the lute. In his
Sonnet cxxviii., addressed to the lady whom he caressingly
calls " my music," Shakespeare has described himself as standing
beside his mistress's spinet and envying the keys which could
kiss her fingers. In all probability he was personally acquainted
with John Dowland, the chief English musician of the time,
although the poem in which he is named, published as Shake-

---

[1] Förster: *Shakespeare und die Tonkunst, Shakespeare-Jahrbuch,* ii. 155; Karl
Elze: *William Shakespeare,* p. 474; Henrik Schück: *William Shakespere,* p. 313.

speare's in *The Passionate Pilgrim*, is not by him, but by Richard Barnfield.

In *The Taming of the Shrew* (iii. 1), written just before *The Merchant of Venice*, he had utilised his knowledge of singing and lute-playing in a scene of gay comedy. "The cause why music was ordained," says Lucentio—

> " Was it not to refresh the mind of man,
> After his studies, or his usual pain ? "

Its influence upon mental disease was also known to Shakespeare, and noted both in *King Lear* and in *The Tempest*. But here, in *The Merchant of Venice*, where music is wedded to moonlight, his praise of it takes a higher flight :—

> " How sweet the moonlight sleeps upon this bank !
> Here we will sit, and let the sounds of music
> Creep in our ears : soft stillness, and the night,
> Become the touches of sweet harmony."

And Shakespeare, who never mentions church music, which seems to have had no message for his soul, here makes the usually unimpassioned Lorenzo launch out into genuine Renaissance rhapsodies upon the music of the spheres :—

> " Sit, Jessica : look, how the floor of heaven
> Is thick inlaid with patines of bright gold.
> There 's not the smallest orb, which thou behold'st,
> But in his motion like an angel sings,
> Still quiring to the young-ey'd cherubins ;
> Such harmony is in immortal souls ;
> But, whilst this muddy vesture of decay
> Doth grossly close it in, we cannot hear it."

Sphere-harmony and soul-harmony, not bell-ringing or psalm-singing, are for him the highest music.

Shakespeare's love of music, so incomparably expressed in the last scenes of *The Merchant of Venice*, appears at other points in the play. Thus Portia says, when Bassanio is about to make his choice between the caskets (iii. 2) :—

> " Let music sound, while he doth make his choice ;
> Then, if he lose, he makes a swan-like end,
> Fading in music.
>
>   He may win ;
> And what is music then ? then music is
> Even as the flourish when true subjects bow
> To a new-crowned monarch."

It seems as though Shakespeare, in this play, had set himself to reveal for the first time how deeply his whole nature was penetrated with musical feeling. He places in the mouth of the frivolous Jessica these profound words, " I am never merry when I hear sweet music." And he makes Lorenzo answer, "The reason is, your spirits are attentive." The note of the trumpet, he says, will calm a wanton herd of "unhandled colts;" and Orpheus, as poets feign, drew trees and stones and floods to follow him :—

> " Since nought so stockish, hard, and full of rage,
> But music for the time doth change his nature.
> The man that hath no music in himself,
> Nor is not mov'd with concord of sweet sounds,
> Is fit for treasons, stratagems, and spoils ;
> The motions of his spirit are dull as night,
> And his affections dark as Erebus.
> Let no such man be trusted.—Mark the music."

This must not, of course, be taken too literally. But note the characters whom Shakespeare makes specially unmusical : in this play, Shylock, who loathes "the vile squeaking of the wry-necked fife ;" then Hotspur, the hero-barbarian ; Benedick, the would-be woman-hater; Cassius, the fanatic politician ; Othello, the half-civilised African ; and finally creatures like Caliban, who are nevertheless enthralled by music as though by a wizard's spell.

On the other hand, all his more delicate creations are musical. In the First Part of *Henry IV.* (iii. 1) we have Mortimer and his Welsh wife, who do not understand each other's speech :—

> " But I will never be a truant, love,
> Till I have learn'd thy language ; for thy tongue
> Makes Welsh as sweet as ditties highly penn'd,
> Sung by a fair queen in a summer's bower,
> With ravishing division, to her lute."

Musical, too, are the pathetic heroines, such as Ophelia and Desdemona, and characters like Jaques in *As You Like It*, and the Duke and Viola in *Twelfth Night*. The last-named comedy, indeed, is entirely interpenetrated with music. The keynote of musical passion is struck in the opening speech :—

> " If music be the food of love, play on ;
> Give me excess of it, that, surfeiting,
> The appetite may sicken, and so die.—
> That strain again ! it had a dying fall :
> O ! it came o'er my ear like the sweet south
> That breathes upon a bank of violets,
> Stealing and giving odour."

Here, too, Shakespeare's love of the folk-song finds expression, when he makes the Duke say (ii. 4) :—

"Now, good Cesario, but that piece of song,
That old and antique song, we heard last night;
Methought, it did relieve my passion much,
More than light airs, and recollected terms,
Of these most brisk and giddy-paced times:
Come; but one verse."

No less sensitive and devoted to music than the Duke in
Twelfth Night or Lorenzo in *The Merchant of Venice* must
their creator himself have been in the short and happy interval
in which, as yet unmastered by the melancholy latent in his as
in all deep natures, he felt his talents strengthening and unfolding, his life every day growing fuller and more significant,
his inmost soul quickening with creative impulse and instinct
with harmony. The rich concords which bring *The Merchant
of Venice* to a close symbolise, as it were, the feeling of inward
wealth and equipoise to which he had now attained.

XXII

*"EDWARD III." AND "ARDEN OF FEVERSHAM"—SHAKE-
SPEARE'S DICTION—THE FIRST PART OF "HENRY IV."
—FIRST INTRODUCTION OF HIS OWN EXPERIENCES OF
LIFE IN THE HISTORIC DRAMA—WHY THE SUBJECT
APPEALED TO HIM—TAVERN LIFE—SHAKESPEARE'S
CIRCLE—SIR JOHN FALSTAFF—FALSTAFF AND THE
GRACIOSO OF THE SPANISH DRAMA—RABELAIS AND
SHAKESPEARE—PANURGE AND FALSTAFF*

THERE is extant a historical play, dating from 1596, entitled
*The Raigne of King Edward third. As it hath bin sundrie
times plaied about the Citie of London,* which several English
students and critics, among them Halliwell-Phillips, have attributed in part to Shakespeare, arguing that the better scenes, at
least, must have been carefully retouched by him. Although
the drama, as a whole, is not much more Shakespearean in style
than many other Elizabethan plays, and although Swinburne, the
highest of all English authorities, has declared the piece to be
the work of an imitator of Marlowe, yet there is a good deal to
be said in favour of the hypothesis that Shakespeare had some
hand in *Edward III.* His touch may be recognised in several
passages ; and especially noteworthy are the following lines from
a speech of Warwick's :—

> " A spacious field of reasons could I urge
> Between his glory, daughter, and thy shame :
> That poison shows worst in a golden cup ;
> Dark night seems darker by the lightning flash ;
> *Lilies that fester smell far worse than weeds,*
> And every glory that inclines to sin,
> The shame is treble by the opposite."

The italicised verse reappears as the last line of Shakespeare's
Sonnet xciv. ; and as this Sonnet seems to refer (as we shall
afterwards see) to circumstances in Shakespeare's life which did
not arise until 1600, we cannot suppose that it was one of those
written at an earlier date and circulated in manuscript. The
probability is that Shakespeare simply reclaimed this line from a
speech contributed by him to another man's play.

It is natural that a foreign student should shrink from opposing his judgment to that of English critics, where English diction
and style are in question.   Nevertheless he is sometimes driven
into dissent with regard to the many Elizabethan plays which
now one critic, and now another, has attributed wholly or in
part to Shakespeare.   Take, for instance, *Arden of Feversham*,
certainly one of the most admirable plays of that rich period,
whose merit impresses one even when one reads it for the first
time in uncritical youth.   Swinburne writes of it (*Study of
Shakespeare*, p. 141):—

"I cannot but finally take heart to say, even in the absence of all
external or traditional testimony, that it seems to me not pardonable
merely nor permissible, but simply logical and reasonable, to set down
this poem, a young man's work on the face of it, as the possible work
of no man's youthful hand but Shakespeare's."

However small my authority in comparison with Swinburne's
upon such a question as this, I find it impossible to share his
view.   Highly as I esteem *Arden of Feversham*, I cannot believe
that Shakespeare wrote a single line of it.   It was not like him to
choose such a subject, and still less to treat it in such a fashion.
The play is a domestic tragedy, in which a wife, after repeated
attempts, murders her kind and forbearing husband, in order
freely to indulge her passion for a worthless paramour.   It is
a dramatisation of an actual case, the facts of which are closely
followed, but at the same time animated with great psychological
insight.   That Shakespeare had a distaste for such subjects is
proved by his consistent avoidance of them, except in this prob-
lematical instance; whereas if he had once succeeded so well
with such a theme, he would surely have repeated the experiment.
The chief point is, however, that only in a few places, in the
soliloquies, do we find the peculiar note of Shakespeare's style—
that wealth of imagination, that luxuriant lyrism, which plays
like sunlight over his speeches.   In *Arden of Feversham* the
style is a uniform drab.

Shakespeare's great characteristic is precisely the resilience
which he gives to every word and to every speech.   We take one
step on earth, and at the next we are soaring in air.   His verse
always tends towards a rich and stately melody, is never flat or
commonplace.   In the English historical plays, his diction sometimes verges upon the style of the ballad or romance.   There is
a continual undercurrent of emotion, of enthusiasm, or of pure
fantasy, which carries us away with it.   We are always far remote
from the humdrum monotony of everyday speech.   For everyday
speech is devoid of fantasy, and all Shakespeare's characters,
with the exception of those whose humour lies in their stupidity,
have a highly-coloured imagination.

We could find no better proof of this than the diction of the great work which he undertakes immediately after *The Merchant of Venice*—the First Part of *Henry IV.*

Harry Percy in this play is placed in opposition to the magniloquent, visionary, thaumaturgic Glendower, as the man of sober intelligence, who keeps to the common earth, and believes only in what his senses aver and his reason accepts. But there is nevertheless a spring within him which need only be touched in order to send him soaring into almost dithyrambic poetry. The King (i. 3) has called Mortimer a traitor; whereupon Percy protests that it was no sham warfare that Mortimer waged against Glendower:—

> " To prove that true,
> Needs no more but one tongue for all those wounds,
> Those mouthed wounds, which valiantly he took,
> When on the gentle Severn's sedgy bank,
> In single opposition, hand to hand,
> He did confound the best part of an hour
> In changing hardiment with great Glendower.
> Three times they breath'd, and three times did they drink,
> Upon agreement, of swift Severn's flood,
> Who then, affrighted with their bloody looks,
> Ran fearfully among the trembling reeds,
> And hid his crisp head in the hollow bank
> Blood-stained with these valiant combatants."

Thus Homer sings of the Scamander.

Worcester broaches to Percy an enterprise

> " As full of peril and adventurous spirit,
> As to o'er-walk a current, roaring loud,
> On the unsteadfast footing of a spear;"

whereon Percy bursts forth :—

> " Send danger from the east unto the west,
> So honour cross it from the north to south,
> And let them grapple:—O! the blood more stirs
> To rouse a lion than to start a hare."

Northumberland then says of him that " Imagination of some great exploit Drives him beyond the bounds of patience," and Percy answers :—

> " By Heaven, methinks, it were an easy leap
> To pluck bright honour from the pale-fac'd moon,
> Or dive into the bottom of the deep,
> Where fathom-line could never touch the ground,
> And pluck up drowned honour by the locks."

What a profusion of imagery is placed in the mouth of this despiser of rhetoric and music! From the comparatively weak metaphor of the speaking wounds up to actual myth-making! The river, affrighted by the bloody looks of the combatants, hides its crisp head in the reeds—a naiad fantasy in classic style. Danger, rushing from east to west, hurtles against Honour, crossing it from north to south—two northern Valkyries in full career. The wreath of honour is hung on the crescent moon—a metaphor from the tilting-yard, expressed in terms of fairy romance. Drowned Honour is to be plucked up by the locks from the bottom of the deep—having now become, by a daring personification, a damsel who has fallen into the sea and must be rescued. And all this in three short speeches!

Where this irrepressible vivacity of fancy is lacking, as in *Arden of Feversham*, Shakespeare's sign-manual is lacking along with it. Even when his style appears sober and measured, it is saturated with what may be called latent fantasy (as we speak of latent electricity), which at the smallest opportunity bursts its bounds, explodes, flashes forth before our eyes like the figures in a pyrotechnic set-piece, and fills our ears as with the music of a rushing, leaping waterfall.[1]

In 1598 appeared a Quarto with the following title: *The History of Henrie the Fovrth; With the battell at Shrewsburie, betweene the King and Lord Henry Percy, surnamed Henrie Hotspur of the North. With the hnmorous conceits of Sir John Falstaffe. At London. Printed by P. S. for Andrew Wise, dwelling in Paules Churchyard, at the signe of the Angell.* 1598. This was the First Part of Shakespeare's *Henry IV.*, which must have been written in 1597—the play in which Shakespeare first attains his great and overwhelming individuality. At the age of thirty-three, he stands for the first time at the summit of his artistic greatness. In wealth of character, of wit, of genius, this play has never been surpassed. Its dramatic structure is somewhat loose, though closer knit and technically stronger than that of the Second Part. But, as a poetical creation, it is one of the great masterpieces of the world's literature, at once heroic and burlesque, thrilling and side-splitting. And these contrasted elements are not, as in Victor Hugo's dramas, brought into hard-and-fast rhetorical antithesis, but move and mingle with all the freedom of life.

When it was written, the sixteenth century, that great period in the history of the human spirit, was drawing to its close; but no one had then conceived the cowardly idea of making the end of a century a sort of symbol of decadence in energy and vitality. Never had the waves of healthy self-confidence and productive power run higher in the English people or in Shakespeare's own mind. *Henry IV.*, and its sequel *Henry V.*, are written through-

---

[1] It was this characteristic of Shakespeare's style, at the period we are now considering, that so deeply influenced Goethe and the contemporaries of his youth, Lenz and Klinger (and, in Denmark, Hauch and Bredahl), determining the diction of their tragic dramas. Björnson shows traces of the same influence in his *Maria Stuart* and *Sigurd Slembe.*

out in a major key which we have not hitherto heard in Shakespeare, and which we shall not hear again.

Shakespeare finds the matter for these plays in Holinshed's Chronicle, and in an old, quite puerile play, *The Famous Victories of Henry the fifth, conteining the Honorable Battell of Agin-court*, in which the young Prince is represented as frequenting the company of roisterers and highway robbers. It was this, no doubt, that suggested to him the novel and daring idea of transferring direct to the stage, in historical guise, a series of scenes from the everyday life of the streets and taverns around him, and blending them with the dramatised chronicle of the Prince whom he regarded as the national hero of England. To this blending we owe the matchless freshness of the whole picture.

For the rest, Shakespeare found scarcely anything in the foolish old play, acted between 1580 and 1588, which could in any way serve his purpose. He took from it only the anecdote of the box on the ear given by the Prince of Wales to the Lord Chief-Justice, and a few names—the tavern in Eastcheap, Gadshill, Ned, and the name, not the character, of Sir John Oldcastle, as Falstaff was originally called.

Shakespeare felt himself attracted to the hero, the young Prince, by some of the most deep-rooted sympathies of his nature. We have seen how vividly and persistently the contrast between appearance and reality preoccupied him ; we saw it last in *The Merchant of Venice*. In proportion as he was irritated and repelled by people who try to pass for more than they are, by creatures of affectation and show, even by women who resort to artificial colours and false hair in quest of a beauty not their own, so his heart beat warmly for any one who had appearances against him, and concealed great qualities behind an unassuming and misinterpreted exterior. His whole life, indeed, was just such a paradox—his soul was replete with the greatest treasures, with rich humanity and inexhaustible genius, while externally he was little better than a light-minded mountebank, touting, with quips and quiddities, for the ha'pence of the mob. Now and then, as his Sonnets show, the pressure of this outward prejudice so weighed upon him that he came near to being ashamed of his position in life, and of the tinsel world in which his days were passed ; and then he felt with double force the inward need to assure himself how great may be the gulf between the apparent and the real worth of human character.

Moreover, this view of his material gave him an occasion, before tuning the heroic string of his lyre, to put in a word for the right of high-spirited youth to have its fling, and indirectly to protest against the hasty judgments of narrow-minded moralists and Puritans. He would here show that great ambitions and heroic energy could pass unscathed through the dangers even of exceedingly questionable diversions. This Prince of Wales was "merry England" and "martial England" in one and the same person.

For the young noblemen among the audience, again, nothing could be more attractive than to see this great King, in his youth, haunting such resorts as they themselves frequented, and yet, as the best of them also tried to do, preserving the consciousness of his high dignity, the hope of a great future, and the determination to achieve renown, even while associating with Falstaff and Bardolph, Dame Quickly and Doll Tearsheet.

These young English aristocrats, who in Shakespeare appear under the names of Mercutio and Benedick, Gratiano and Lorenzo, made pleasure their pursuit through the whole of the London day. Dressed in silk or ash-coloured velvet, and with gold lace on his cloak, the young man of fashion began by riding to St. Paul's and promenading half-a-dozen times up and down its middle aisle. He then "repaired to the Exchange, and talked pretty Euphuisms to the citizens' daughters," or looked in at the bookseller's to inspect the latest play-book or pamphlet against tobacco. Next he rode to the ordinary where he had appointed to meet his friends and dine. At dinner he discussed Drake's expedition to Portugal, or Essex's exploits at Cadiz, or told how he had yesterday broken a lance with Raleigh himself at the Tilt-yard. He would mingle snatches of Italian and Spanish with his talk, and let himself be persuaded, after dinner, to recite a sonnet of his own composition. At three he betook himself to the theatre, saw Burbage as Richard III., and applauded Kemp in his new jig; after which he would spend an hour at the bear-garden. Then to the barber's, to have his hair and beard trimmed, in preparation for the carouse of the evening at whichever tavern he and his friends had selected— the "Mitre," the "Falcon," the "Apollo," the "Boar's Head," the "Devil," or (most famous of all) the "Mermaid," where the literary club, the Syren, founded by none other than Sir Walter Raleigh himself, held its meetings.[1] In these places the young aristocrat rubbed shoulders with the leading players, such as Burbage and Kemp, and with the best-known men of letters, such as John Lyly, George Chapman, John Florio, Michael Drayton, Samuel Daniel, John Marston, Thomas Nash, Ben Jonson, William Shakespeare.

Thornbury has aptly remarked that the characteristic of the Elizabethan age was its sociability. People were always meeting at St. Paul's, the theatre, or the tavern. Family intercourse, on the other hand, was almost unknown; women, as in ancient Greece, played no prominent part in society. The men gathered at the tavern club to drink, talk, and enjoy themselves. The festive bowl circulated freely, even more so than in Denmark, which nevertheless passed for the toper's paradise. (Compare the utterances on this subject in *Hamlet*, i. 4, and *Othello*, ii. 3.)

---

[1] Thornbury : *Shakspere's England*, i. 104, *et seq.*

M

The taverns were, moreover, favourite places for the rendezvous of court gallants with citizens' wives; fast young men would bring their mistresses with them, and here, after supper, gambling went on merrily.

At the taverns, writers and poets met in good fellowship, and carried on wordy wars, battles of wit, sparkling with mirth and fantasy. They were like tennis-rallies of words, in which the great thing was to tire out your adversary; they were skirmishes in which the combatants poured into each other whole volleys of conceits. Beaumont has celebrated them in some verses to Ben Jonson, who, both as a great drinker and as an entertaining *magister bibendi*, was much admired and fêted:—

> "What things have we seen
> Done at the Mermaid! heard words that have been
> So nimble, and so full of subtile flame,
> As if that every one from whence they came
> Had meant to put his whole wit in a jest
> And had resolv'd to live a fool the rest
> Of his dull life."

In his comedy *Every Man out of His Humour* (v. 4), Ben Jonson has introduced either himself or Marston, under the name of Carlo Buffone, waiting alone for his friends at the "Mitre," and has placed these words in Carlo's mouth when the waiter, George, has brought him the wine he had ordered:—

> "*Carlo (drinks)*. Ay, marry, sir, here's purity; O George—I could bite off his nose for this now, sweet rogue, he has drawn nectar, the very soul of the grape! I'll wash my temples with some on't presently, and drink some half a score draughts; 'twill heat the brain, kindle my imagination, I shall talk nothing but crackers and fireworks to-night. So, sir! please you to be here, sir, and I here: so. (*Sets the two cups asunder, drinks with the one, and pledges with the other, speaking for each of the cups, and drinking alternately.*)"

Well known and often quoted is the passage in Fuller's *Worthies* as to the many wit-combats between Shakespeare and the learned Ben:—

> "Which two I behold like a *Spanish great Gallion* and an *English man of War*: Master *Johnson* (like the former) was built far higher in Learning; *Solid*, but *Slow* in his performances. *Shake-spear*, with the *English man of War*, lesser in *bulk*, but lighter in *sailing*, could turn with all tides, tack about, and take advantage of all winds, by the quickness of his Wit and Invention."

Although Fuller was not himself present at these symposia, yet his account of them bears the stamp of complete authenticity.

Among the members of the circle which Shakespeare in his youth frequented, there must, of course, have been types of every kind, from the genius down to the grotesque; and there were some, no doubt, in whom the genius and the grotesque, the wit and the butt, must have quaintly intermingled.   As every great household had at that time its *jester*, so every convivial circle had its clown or buffoon.   The jester was the terror of the kitchen—for he would steal a pudding the moment the cook's back was turned—and the delight of the dinner-table, where he would mimic voices, crack jokes, play pranks, and dissipate the spleen of the noble company.   The comic man of the tavern circle was both witty himself and the cause of wit in others.   He was always the butt of the others' merriment, yet he always held his own in the contest, and ended by getting the best of his tormentors.

   To Shakespeare's circle Chettle must doubtless have belonged, that Chettle who in bygone days had published Greene's *Groatsworth of Wit*, and afterwards made amends to Shakespeare for Greene's coarse attack upon him.   In Dekker's tract, *A Knights Conjuring*, dating from 1607, he figures among the poets in Elysium, where he is introduced in the following terms:—" In comes Chettle sweating and blowing, by reason of his fatnes; to welcome whom, because hee was of olde acquaintance, all rose vp, and fell presentlie on their knees, to drinck a health to all the louers of Hellicon."   Elze has conjectured, possibly with justice, that in this puffing and sweating old tun of flesh, who is so whimsically greeted with mock reverence by the whole gay company, we have the very model from whom Shakespeare drew his demigod, the immortal Sir John Falstaff, beyond comparison the gayest, most concrete, and most entertaining figure in European comedy.

   In his close-woven and unflagging mirthfulness, in the inexhaustible wealth of drollery concentrated in his person, Falstaff surpasses all that antiquity and the Middle Ages have produced in the way of comic character, and all that the stage of later times can show.

   There is in him something of the old Greek Silenus, swag-bellied and infinitely jovial, and something of the *Vidushakas* of the old Indian drama, half court-fool, half friend and comrade to the hero.   He unites in himself the two comic types of the old Roman comedy, Artotrogus and Pyrgopolinices, the parasite and the boastful soldier.   Like the Roman *scurra*, he leaves his patron to pay the reckoning, and in return entertains him with his jests, and, like the *Miles Gloriosus*, he is a braggart above all braggarts, a liar above all liars.   Yet he is in his single person richer and more entertaining than all the ancient Silenuses and court-fools and braggarts and parasites put together.

   In the century after he came into existence, Spain and France each developed its own theatre.   In France there is only one quaint and amusing person, Moron in Molière's *La Princesse d'Élide*, who bears some faint resemblance to Falstaff.   In Spain, where the great and delightful character of Sancho Panza affords the starting-point for the whole series of comic figures in the works of Calderon, the *Gracioso* stands in perpetual contrast to the hero, and here and there reminds us for a moment of Falstaff, but always only as an abstraction of one side or another of his nature, or because of some external similarity of situation. In *La Dama Duende* he is a drunkard and coward; in *La Gran Cenobia* he boasts fantastically, and, like Falstaff, becomes entangled in his lies. In *La Puente de Mantible* he actually becomes (as it appears from the scenes with the Chief Justice and Colevile that Falstaff also was) renowned and dreaded for his military valour; yet he is, like Falstaff, extremely ill at ease when there is any fighting to be done, often creeping into cover, hiding himself behind a bush, or climbing a tree. In *La Hija del Ayre* and *El Principe Constante* he uses precisely the device adopted by Falstaff and certain lower animals, of lying down and shamming death. Hernando in *Los Empeños de un Acaso* (like Molière's Moron) expresses sentiments very similar to those of Falstaff in his celebrated discourse upon honour. Falstaff's airs of protection, his bland fatherliness, we find in Fabio in *El Secreto a Voces*. Thus single characteristics, detached sides of Falstaff's character, have to do duty as complete personages. Calderon as a rule looks with fatherly benevolence upon his Gracioso. Yet he sometimes loses patience, as it were, with his buffoon's epicurean, unchristian, and unchivalrous view of life. In *La Vida es Sueño*, for instance, a cannon-ball kills poor Clarin, who has crept behind a bush during the battle; the moral being that the coward does not escape danger any more than the brave man. Calderon bestows on him a very solemn funeral speech, almost as moral as King Henry's parting words to Falstaff.

It is certain, of course, that neither Calderon nor Molière knew anything of Shakespeare or of Falstaff; and Shakespeare, for his part, was equally uninfluenced by any of his predecessors on the comic stage, when he conceived his fat knight.

Nevertheless there is among Shakespeare's predecessors a great writer, one of the greatest, with whom we cannot but compare him; to wit, Rabelais, the master spirit of the early Renaissance in France. He is, moreover, one of the few great writers with whom Shakespeare is known to have been acquainted. He alludes to him in *As You Like It* (iii. 2), where Celia says, when Rosalind asks her a dozen questions and bids her answer in one word: "You must borrow me Gargantua's mouth first: 'tis a word too great for any mouth of this age's size."

If we compare Falstaff with Panurge, we see that Rabelais stands to Shakespeare in the relation of a Titan to an Olympian god. Rabelais is gigantic, disproportioned, potent, but formless. Shakespeare is smaller and less excessive, poorer in ideas, though richer in fancies, and moulded with the utmost firmness of outline.

Rabelais died at the age of seventy, ten years before Shakespeare was born; there is between them all the difference between the morning and the noon of the Renaissance. Rabelais is a poet, philosopher, polemist, reformer, "even to the very fire exclusively," but always threatened with the stake. Shakespeare's coarseness compared with Rabelais's is as a manure-bed compared with the *Cloaca Maxima*. Burlesque uncleanness pours in floods from the Frenchman's pen.

His Panurge is larger than Falstaff, as Utgard-Loki is larger than Asa-Loki. Panurge, like Falstaff, is loquacious, witty, crafty, and utterly unscrupulous, a humorist who stops the mouths of all around him by unblushing effrontery. In war, Panurge is no more of a hero than Falstaff, but, like Falstaff, he stabs the foemen who have already fallen. He is superstitious, yet his buffoonery holds nothing sacred, and he steals from the church-plate. He is thoroughly selfish, sensual, and slothful, shameless, revengeful, and light-fingered, and as time goes on becomes ever a greater poltroon and braggart.

Pantagruel is the noble knight, a king's son, like Prince Henry. Like the Prince, he has one foible: he cannot resist the attractions of low company. When Panurge is witty, Pantagruel cannot deny himself the pleasure of laughing at his side-splitting drolleries.

But Panurge, unlike Falstaff, is a satire on the largest scale. In representing him as a notable economist or master of finance, who calls borrowing credit-creating, and has 63 methods of raising money and 214 methods of spending it, Rabelais made him an abstract and brief chronicle of the French court of his day. In giving him a yearly revenue from his barony of "6,789,106,789 royaulx en deniers certain," to say nothing of the fluctuating revenue of the locusts and periwinkles, "montant bon an mal an de 2,435,768 à 2,435,769 moutons à la grande laine," Rabelais was aiming his satire direct at the unblushing extortion which was at that time the glory and delight of the French feudal nobility.

Shakespeare does not venture so far in the direction of satire. He is only a poet, and as a poet stands simply on the defensive. The only power he can be said to attack is Puritanism (*Twelfth Night, Measure for Measure*, &c.), and that only in self-defence. His attacks, too, are exceedingly mild in comparison with those of the cavalier poets before the victory of Puritanism and after the reopening of the theatres. But Shakespeare was what Rabelais was not, an artist; and as an artist he was a very Prometheus in his power of creating human beings.

As an artist he has also the exuberant fertility which we find in Rabelais, even surpassing him in some respects. Max Müller has long ago remarked upon the wealth of his vocabulary. In this he seems to surpass all other writers. An Italian opera-libretto seldom contains more than 600 or 700 words. A well-educated modern Englishman, in social intercourse, will rarely use more than 3000 or 4000. It has been calculated that acute thinkers and great orators in England are masters of as many as 10,000 words. The Old Testament contains only 5642 words. Shakespeare has employed more than 15,000 words in his poems and plays; and in few of the latter do we find such overflowing fulness of expression as in *Henry IV.*

In the original form of the play, Falstaff's name, as already mentioned, was Sir John Oldcastle. A trace of this remains in the second scene of the first act (Part I.), where the Prince calls the fat knight "my old lad of the castle." In the second scene of the second act the line, "Away, good Ned, Falstaff sweats to death," is short of a syllable, because the dissyllable Falstaff has been substituted for the trisyllable Oldcastle. In the earliest Quarto of the Second Part, the contraction *Old.* has been left before one of Falstaff's speeches; and in Act ii. Sc. 2 of the same play, it is said of Falstaff that he was page to Thomas Mowbray, Duke of Norfolk, a position which the historic Oldcastle actually held. Oldcastle, however, was so far from being the boon companion depicted by Shakespeare that he was, at the instance of Henry V. himself, handed over to the Ecclesiastical Courts as an adherent of Wicklif's heresies, and roasted over a slow fire outside the walls of London on Christmas morning 1417. His descendants having protested against the degradation to which the name of their ancestor was subjected in the play, the fat knight was rechristened. Therefore, too, it is stated in the Epilogue to the Second Part that the author intends to produce a further continuation of the story, "where, for anything I know, Falstaff shall die of a sweat . . . *for Oldcastle died a martyr, and this is not the man.*"

Under the name of Falstaff he became, after the lapse of half a century, the most popular of Shakespeare's creations. Between 1642 and 1694 he is more frequently mentioned than any other of Shakespeare's characters. But it is noteworthy that in his own time, although popular enough, he was not alluded to nearly so often as Hamlet, who, up to 1642, is mentioned forty-five times to Falstaff's twenty; even *Venus and Adonis* and *Romeo and Juliet* are mentioned oftener than he, and *Lucrece* quite as often.[1] The element of low comedy in his figure made it, according to the notions of the day, obviously less distinguished, and people stood too near to Falstaff to appreciate him fully.

He was, as it were, the wine-god of merry England at the meeting of the centuries. Never before or since has England enjoyed so many sorts of beverages. There was ale, and all other kinds of strong and small beer, and apple-drink, and honey-drink, and strawberry-drink, and three sorts of mead (meath, metheglin,

[1] *Fresh Allusions to Shakespeare*, p. 372.

hydromel), and every drink was fragrant of flowers and spiced with herbs. In white meath alone there was infused rosemary and thyme, sweet-briar, pennyroyal, bays, water-cresses, agrimony, marsh-mallow, liverwort, maiden-hair, betony, eye-bright, scabious, ash-leaves, eringo roots, wild angelica, rib-wort, sennicle, Roman wormwood, tamarisk, mother thyme, saxifrage, philipendula; and strawberries and violet-leaves were often added. Cherry-wine and sack were mixed with gillyflower syrup.[1]

There were fifty-six varieties of French wine in use, and thirty-six of Spanish and Italian, to say nothing of the many home-made kinds. But among the foreign wines none was so famous as Falstaff's favourite sherris-sack. It took its name from Xeres in Spain, but differed from the modern sherry in being a sweet wine. It was the best of its kind, possessing a much finer bouquet than sack from Malaga or the Canary Islands (Jeppe paa Bjergets, "Canari-Sæk"),[2] although these were stronger and sweeter. Sweet as it was too, people were in the habit of putting sugar into it. The English taste has never been very delicate. Falstaff always put sugar into his wine. Hence his words when he is playing the Prince while the Prince impersonates the king (Pt. First, ii. 4):—"If sack and sugar be a fault, God help the wicked." He puts not only sugar but toast in his wine: "Go fetch me a quart of sack, put a toast in it" (*Merry Wives*, iii. 5). On the other hand, he does not like (as others did) to have it mulled with eggs: "Brew me a pottle of sack . . . simple of itself; I'll no pullet-sperm in my brewage" (*Merry Wives*, iii. 5). And no less did he resent its sophistication with lime, an ingredient which the vintners used to increase its strength and make it keep: "You rogue, here's lime in this sack, too. . . . A coward is worse than a cup of sack with lime in it" (I. *Henry IV.*, ii. 4). Falstaff is as great a wine-knower and wine-lover as Silenus himself. But he is infinitely more than that.

He is one of the brightest and wittiest spirits England has ever produced. He is one of the most glorious creations that ever sprang from a poet's brain. There is much rascality and much genius in him, but there is no trace of mediocrity. He is always superior to his surroundings, always resourceful, always witty, always at his ease, often put to shame, but, thanks to his inventive effrontery, never put out of countenance. He has fallen below his social position; he lives in the worst (though also in the best) society; he has neither soul, nor honour, nor moral sense; but he sins, robs, lies, and boasts, with such splendid exuberance, and is so far above any serious attempt at hypocrisy, that he seems unfailingly amiable whatever he may choose to do.

---

[1] Thornbury: *Shakspere's England*, i. 227; Nathan Drake, *Shakespeare and His Times*, ii. 131.

[2] Jeppe paa Bjerget, a Danish Abou Hassan or Christopher Sly, is the hero of one of Holberg's most admirable comedies.

Therefore he charms every one, although he is a butt for the wit of all. He perpetually surprises us by the wealth of his nature. He is old and youthful, corrupt and harmless, cowardly and daring, "a knave without malice, a liar without deceit; and a knight, a gentleman, and a soldier, without either dignity, decency, or honour."[1] The young Prince shows good taste in always and in spite of everything seeking out his company.

How witty he is in the brilliant scene where Shakespeare is daring enough to let him parody in advance the meeting between Prince Henry and his offended father! And with what sly humour does Shakespeare, through his mouth, poke fun at Lyly and Greene and the old play of King Cambyses! How delightful is Falstaff's unabashed self-mockery when he thus apostrophises the hapless merchants whom he is plundering :—

"Ah! whoreson caterpillars! bacon-fed knaves! they hate us youth : down with them ; fleece them. . . . Hang ye, gorbellied knaves. Are ye undone? No, ye fat chuffs; I would your store were here! On, bacons, on! What! ye knaves, young men must live."

And what humour there is in his habit of self-pitying regret that his youth and inexperience should have been led astray :—

"I'll be damned for never a king's son in Christendom. . . . I have forsworn his company hourly any time this two-and-twenty years, and yet I am bewitched with the rogue's company. . . . Company, villainous company, hath been the spoil of me."

But if he has not been led astray, neither is he the " abominable misleader of youth " whom Prince Henry, impersonating the King, makes him out to be. For to this character there belongs malicious intent, of which Falstaff is innocent enough. It is unmistakable, however, that while in the First Part of *Henry IV.* Shakespeare keeps Falstaff a purely comic figure, and dissipates in the ether of laughter whatever is base and unclean in his nature, the longer he works upon the character, and the more he feels the necessity of contrasting the moral strength of the Prince's nature with the worthlessness of his early surroundings, the more is he tempted to let Falstaff deteriorate. In the Second Part his wit becomes coarser, his conduct more indefensible, his cynicism less genial; while his relation to the hostess, whom he cozens and plunders, is wholly base. In the First Part of the play he takes a whole-hearted delight in himself, in his jollifications, his drolleries, his exploits on the highway, and his almost purposeless mendacity; in the Second Part he falls more and more under the suspicion of making capital out of the Prince, while he is found in

---

[1] Maurice Morgann : *An Essay on the Dramatic Character of Sir John Falstaff*, p. 150.

ever worse and worse company. The scheme of the whole, indeed, demands that there shall come a moment when the Prince, who has succeeded to the throne and its attendant responsibilities, shall put on a serious countenance and brandish the thunderbolts of retribution.

But here, in the First Part, Falstaff is still a demi-god, supreme alike in intellect and in wit. With this figure the popular drama which Shakespeare represented won its first decisive battle over the literary drama which followed in the footsteps of Seneca. We can actually hear the laughter of the "yard" and the gallery surging around his speeches like waves around a boat at sea. It was the old sketch of Parolles in *Love's Labour's Won* (see above, p. 49), which had here taken on a new amplitude of flesh and blood. There was much to delight the groundlings—Falstaff is so fat and yet so mercurial, so old and yet so youthful in all his tastes and vices. But there was far more to delight the spectators of higher culture, in his marvellous quickness of fence, which can parry every thrust, and in the readiness which never leaves him tongue-tied, or allows him to confess himself beaten. Yes, there was something for every class of spectators in this mountain of flesh, exuding wit at every pore, in this hero without shame or conscience, in this robber, poltroon, and liar, whose mendacity is quite poetic, Münchausenesque, in this cynic with the brazen forehead and a tongue as supple as a Toledo blade. His talk is like Bellman's after him :—

> "A dance of all the gods upon Olympus,
> With fauns and graces and the muses twined." [1]

The men of the Renaissance revelled in his wit, much as the men of the Middle Ages had enjoyed the popular legends of Reinecke Fuchs and his rogueries.

Falstaff reaches his highest point of wit and drollery in that typical soliloquy on honour, in which he indulges on the battle-field of Shrewsbury (I. *Henry IV.*, v. 1), a soliloquy which almost categorically sums him up, in contradistinction to the other leading personages. For all the characters here stand in a certain relation to the idea of honour—the King, to whom honour means dignity ; Hotspur, to whom it means the halo of renown ; the Prince, who loves it as the opposite of outward show ; and Falstaff, who, in his passionate appetite for the material good things of life, rises entirely superior to it and shows its nothingness :—

"Honour pricks me on. Yea, but how if honour prick me off when I come on? how then? Can honour set to a leg? No. Or an arm? No. Or take away the grief of a wound? No. Honour hath no skill in surgery then? No. What is honour? A word. What is that word

---

[1] From a poem by Tegnér on Bellman, the Swedish convivial lyrist.

honour? Air. A trim reckoning!—Who hath it? He that died o'
Wednesday. Doth he feel it? No. Doth he hear it? No. Is it in-
sensible then? Yea, to the dead. But will it not live with the living?
No. Why? Detraction will not suffer it.—Therefore, I'll none of it:
honour is a mere scutcheon ; and so ends my catechism."

Falstaff will be no slave to honour; he will rather do without
it altogether. He demonstrates in practice how a man can live
without it, and we do not miss it in him, so perfect is he in his
way.

XXIII

HENRY PERCY—THE MASTERY OF THE CHARACTER-DRAWING—HOTSPUR AND ACHILLES

IN contrast to Falstaff, Shakespeare has placed the man whom his ally Douglas expressly calls "the king of honour"—a figure as firmly moulded and as great as the Achilles of the Greeks or Donatello's Italian St. George—"the Hotspur of the North," an English national hero quite as much as the young Prince.

The chronicle and the ballad of Douglas and Percy gave Shakespeare no more than the name and the dates of a couple of battles. He seized upon the name Harry Percy, and although its bearer was not historically of the same age as Prince Henry, but as old as his father, the King, he docked him of a score of years, with the poetical design of opposing to the hero of the play a rival who should be his peer, and should at first seem to outshine him.

Percy is above everything and every one avid of honour. It is he who would have found it easy to pluck down honour from the moon or drag it up from the depths of the sea. But he is of an open, confiding, simple nature, with nothing of the diplomatist about him. He is hasty and impetuous; his spur is never cold until he is dead. Under the mistaken impression that women cannot keep their counsel, he is reticent towards his wife, in whom he might quite well confide, since she adores him, and calls him "the miracle of men." On the other hand, he suffers himself to be driven by the King's sour suspiciousness into foolhardy rebellion, and he is so simple-minded as to trust to his father and his uncle Worcester, one of whom deserts him in the hour of need, while the other plays a double game with him.

Shakespeare has thrown himself so passionately into the creation of this character that he has actually painted for us Hotspur's exterior, giving him a peculiar walk and manner of speech. The warmth of the poet's sympathy has rendered his hero irresistibly attractive, and made him, in his manliness, a pattern for the youth of the whole country.

Henry Percy enters (ii. 3) with a letter in his hand, and reads:—

"—'But, for mine own part, my lord, I could be well contented to be there, in respect of the love I bear your house.'—He could be contented,—why is he not then? In respect of the love he bears our house :—he shows in this, he loves his own barn better than he loves our house. Let me see some more. ' The purpose you undertake is dangerous; '—why, that's certain : 'tis dangerous to take a cold, to sleep, to drink ; but I tell you, my lord fool, out of this nettle, danger, we pluck this flower, safety. ' The purpose you undertake, is dangerous ; the friends you have named, uncertain ; the time itself unsorted, and your whole plot too light for the counterpoise of so great an opposition.' —Say you so, say you so? *I say unto you again, you are a shallow, cowardly hind, and you lie.* What a lack-brain is this ! By the Lord, our plot is as good a plot as ever was laid; our friends true and constant : a good plot, good friends, and full of expectation ; an excellent plot, very good friends. . . . O! I could divide myself and go to buffets, for moving such a dish of skimmed milk with so honourable an action. Hang him ! let him tell the King ; we are prepared. I will set forward to-night."

We can see him before our eyes, and hear his voice. He strides up and down the room as he reads, and we can hear in the rhythm of his speech that he has a peculiar gait of his own. Not for nothing is Henry Percy called Hotspur ; whether on foot or on horseback, his movements are equally impetuous. Therefore his wife says of him after his death (II. *Henry IV.,* ii. 3):—

> " He was, indeed, the glass
> Wherein the noble youth did dress themselves.
> *He had no legs, that practised not his gait."*

Everything is here consistent, the bodily movements and the tone of speech. We can hear in Hotspur's soliloquy how his sentences stumble over each other ; how, without giving himself time to articulate his words, he stammers from sheer impatience, and utters no phrase that does not bear the stamp of his choleric temperament :—

> " And speaking thick, which nature made his blemish,
> Became the accents of the valiant ;
> For those that could speak low, and tardily,
> Would turn their own perfection to abuse,
> To seem like him : so that, in speech, in gait,
> In diet, in affections of delight,
> In military rules, humours of blood,
> He was the mark and glass, copy and book,
> That fashion'd others."

Shakespeare found no hint of these external traits in the chronicle. He bodied forth Hotspur's idiosyncrasy with such ardour that everything, down to his outward habit, shaped itself accordantly. Hotspur speaks in impatient ejaculations ; he is absent and forgetful out of sheer passionateness. His characteristic impetuousness shows itself in such little traits as his inability to remember the names he wants to cite. When the rebels are portioning out the country between them, he starts up with an oath because he has forgotten his map. When he has something to relate, he is so absorbed in the gist of his matter, and so impatient to get at it, that the intermediate steps escape his memory (i. 3):—

> " Why, look you, I am whipp'd and scourg'd with rods,
> Nettled, and stung with pismires, when I hear
> Of this vile politician, Bolingbroke.
> *In Richard's time,—what do ye call the place?—*
> *A plague upon 't—it is in Glostershire:—*
> *'Twas where the madcap Duke his uncle kept,*
> *His uncle York,—*where I first bow'd my knee
> Unto this king of smiles, this Bolingbroke."

When another person speaks to him, he listens for a moment, but presently his thoughts are away on their own affairs; he forgets where he is and what is said to him; and when Lady Percy has finished her long and moving appeal (ii. 3) with the words—

> " Some heavy business hath my lord in hand,
> And I must know it, else he loves me not,"

all the reply vouchsafed her is :—

> " *Hotspur.* What, ho !
>
> *Enter Servant.*
> Is Gilliams with the packet gone ?
> *Serv.* He is, my lord, an hour ago.
> *Hot.* Hath Butler brought those horses from the sheriff?" &c.

Perpetually baulked of an answer, she at last cannot help coming out with this caressing menace, which gives us in one touch the whole relation between the pair of married lovers :—

> " In faith, I'll break thy little finger, Harry,
> An if thou wilt not tell me all things true."

And this absence of mind of Percy's is so far from being accidental or momentary that it is the very trait which Prince Henry seizes upon to characterise him (ii. 4):—

> " I am not yet of Percy's mind, the Hotspur of the North ; he that kills me some six or seven dozen of Scots at a breakfast, washes his hands, and says to his wife,—'Fie upon this quiet life! I want work.' 'O my sweet Harry,' says she, 'how many hast thou killed to-day?' 'Give my roan horse a drench,' says he, and answers, 'Some fourteen,' an hour after ; 'a trifle, a trifle.'"

Shakespeare has put forth all his poetic strength in giving to Percy's speeches, and especially to his descriptions, the most graphic definiteness of detail, and a naturalness which raises into a higher sphere the racy audacity of Faulconbridge. Hotspur sets about explaining (i. 3) how it happened that he refused to hand over his prisoners to the King, and begins his defence by describing the courtier who demanded them of him :—

> " When I was dry with rage and extreme toil,
> Breathless and faint, leaning upon my sword,
> Came there a certain lord, neat, trimly dress'd,
> Fresh as a bridegroom ; and his chin, new reap'd,
> Show'd like a stubble-land at harvest-home.
> He was perfumed like a milliner."

But he is not content with a general outline, or with relating what this personage said with regard to the prisoners ; he gives an example even of his talk :—

> " He made me mad,
> To see him shine so brisk, and smell so sweet,
> And talk so like a waiting-gentlewoman
> Of guns, and drums, and wounds, God save the mark !
> And telling me, the sovereign'st thing on earth
> Was parmacity for an inward bruise ;
> And that it was great pity, so it was,
> That villainous saltpetre should be digg'd
> Out of the bowels of the harmless earth."

Why this spermaceti ? Why this dwelling upon so trivial and ludicrous a detail ? Because it is a touch of reality and begets illusion. Precisely because we cannot at first see the reason why Percy should recall so trifling a circumstance, it seems impossible that the thing should be a mere invention. And from this insignificant word all the rest of the speech hangs as by a chain. If this be real, then all the rest is real, and Henry Percy stands before our eyes, covered with dust and blood, as on the field of Holmedon. We see the courtier at his side holding his nose as the bodies are carried past, and we hear him giving the young commander his medical advice and irritating him to the verge of frenzy.

With such solicitude, with such minute attention to tricks, flaws, whims, humours, and habits, all deduced from his temperament, from the rapid flow of his blood, from his build of body, and from his life on horseback and in the field, has Shakespeare executed this heroic character. Restless gait, stammering speech, forgetfulness, absence of mind, he overlooks nothing as being too trivial. Hotspur portrays himself in every phrase he utters, without ever saying a word directly about himself ; and behind his outward, superficial peculiarities, we see into the deeper and more significant characteristics from which they spring. These, too, are closely interwoven ; these, too, reveal themselves in his lightest words. We hear this same hero whom pride, sense of honour, spirit of independence, and intrepidity inspire with the sublimest utterances, at other times chatting, jesting, and even talking nonsense. The jests and nonsense are an integral part of the real human being; in them, too, one side of his nature reveals itself (iii. 1):—

"*Hotspur.* Come, Kate, I'll have your song too.
Lady Percy. Not mine, in good sooth.
Hot. Not yours, in good sooth ! 'Heart! you swear like a comfit-maker's wife. 'Not you, in good sooth;' and, 'As true as I live;' and, 'As God shall mend me;' and, 'As sure as day:'

> Swear me, Kate, like a lady as thou art,
> A good mouth-filling oath ; and leave 'in sooth,'
> And such protest of pepper-gingerbread,
> To velvet-guards, and Sunday-citizens."

In a classical tragedy, French, German, or Danish, the hero is too solemn to talk nonsense and too lifeless to jest.

In spite of his soaring energy and ambition, Hotspur is sober, rationalistic, sceptical. He scoffs at Glendower's belief in spirits and pretended power of conjuring them up (iii. 1). His is to the inmost fibre a truth-loving nature :—

"*Glend.* I can call spirits from the vasty deep.
Hot. Why, so can I, or so can any man ;
But will they come, when you do call for them?
Glend. Why, I can teach you, cousin, to command the devil.
Hot. And I can teach thee, coz, to shame the devil,
By telling truth : tell truth, and shame the devil."

There is a militant rationalism in these words which was rare, very rare, in Shakespeare's time, to say nothing of Hotspur's own.

He has also, no doubt, the defects of his qualities. He is contentious, quarrels the moment he is thwarted over the division of booty that has yet to be won, and then, having gained his point, gives up his share in the spoils. He is jealous in his ambition, cannot bear to hear any one else praised, and would like to see Harry of Monmouth poisoned with a pot of ale, so tired is he of hearing him spoken of. He judges hastily, according to appearances; he has the profoundest contempt for the Prince of Wales on account of the levity of his life, and does not divine what lies behind it. He of course lacks all æsthetic faculty. He is a bad speaker, and sentiment is as foreign to him as eloquence. He prefers his dog's howling to music, and declares that the turning of brass candlesticks does not set his teeth on edge so much as the rhyming of balladmongers.

Yet, with all his faults, he is the greatest figure of his time. Even the King, his enemy, becomes a poet when he speaks of him (iii. 2).:—

> " Thrice hath this Hotspur, Mars in swathing-clothes,
>   This infant warrior, in his enterprises
>   Discomfited great Douglas: ta'en him once,
>   Enlarged him, and made a friend of him."

The King longs daily that he could exchange his son for Northumberland's; Hotspur is worthier than Prince Henry to be heir to the throne of England.

From first to last, from top to toe, Hotspur is the hero of the feudal ages, indifferent to culture and polish, faithful to his brother-in-arms to the point of risking everything for his sake, caring neither for state, king, nor commons; a rebel, not for the sake of any political idea, but because independence is all in all to him; a proud, self-reliant, unscrupulous vassal, who, himself a sort of sub-king, has deposed one king, and wants to depose the usurper he has exalted, because he has not kept his promises. Clothed in renown, and ever more insatiate of military honour, he is proud from independence of spirit and truthful out of pride. He is a marvellous figure as Shakespeare has projected him, stammering, absent, turbulent, witty, now simple, now magniloquent. His hauberk clatters on his breast, his spurs jingle at his heel, wit flashes from his lips, while he moves and has his being in a golden nimbus of renown.

Individual as he is, Shakespeare has embodied in him the national type. From the crown of his head to the sole of his foot, Hotspur is an Englishman. He unites the national impetuosity and bravery with sound understanding; he is English in his ungallant but cordial relation to his wife; in the form of his chivalry, which is Northern, not Romanesque; in his Viking-like love of battle for battle's and honour's sake, apart from any sentimental desire for a fair lady's applause.

But Shakespeare's especial design was to present in him a master-type of manliness. He is so profoundly, so thoroughly a man that he forms the one counterpart in modern poetry to the Achilles of the Greeks. Achilles is the hero of antiquity, Henry Percy of the Middle Ages. The ambition of both is entirely personal and regardless of the common weal. For the rest, they are equally noble and high-spirited. The one point on which Hotspur is inferior to the Greek demigod is that of free naturalness. His soul has been cramped and hardened by being strapped into the harness of the feudal ages. Hero as he is, he is at the same time a soldier, obliged and accustomed to be over-bold, forced to restrict his whole activity to feuds and fights. He cannot weep like Achilles, and he would be ashamed of himself if he could. He cannot play the lyre like Achilles, and he would think himself bewitched if he could be brought to admit that music sounded sweeter in his ears than the baying of a dog or the mewing of a cat.[1] He compensates for these deficiencies by the unyielding, restless, untiring energy of his character, by the spirit of enterprise in his manly soul, and by his healthy and amply justified pride. It is in virtue of these qualities that he can, without shrinking, sustain comparison with a demigod.

So deep are the roots of Hotspur's character. Eccentric in externals, he is at bottom typical. The untamed and violent spirit of feudal nobility, the reckless and adventurous activity of the English race, the masculine nature itself in its uncompromising genuineness, all those vast and infinite forces which lie deep under the surface and determine the life of a whole period, a whole people, and one half of humanity, are at work in this character. Elaborated to infinitesimal detail, it yet includes the immensities into which thought must plunge if it would seek for the conditions and ideals of a historic epoch.

But in spite of all this, Henry Percy is by no means the hero of the play. He is only the foil to the hero, throwing into relief the young Prince's unpretentious nature, his careless sporting with rank and dignity, his light-hearted contempt for all conventional honour, all show and appearance. Every garland with which Hotspur wreathes his helm is destined in the end to deck the brows of Henry of Wales. The answer to Hotspur's question as to what has become of the madcap Prince of Wales and his comrades, shows what colours Shakespeare has held in reserve for the portraiture of his true hero. Even Vernon, an enemy of the Prince, thus depicts his setting forth on the campaign (iv. 1):—

> " All furnished, all in arms,
> All plum'd like estridges that wing the wind ;

---

[1] " And Achilles at last
Brake suddenly forth into weeping, and turned from his comrades aside,
And sat by the cold grey sea, looking forth o'er the harvestless tide."
Iliad, i. 348.

" So when to the tents and the ships of the Myrmidon host they had won,
They found him delighting his soul as rang to the sweep of his hand
His beautiful rich-wrought lyre with a silver cross-bar spanned,
Which he chose from the spoils of the war when he smote Eëtion's town.
Sweetly it rang as he sang old deeds of hero-renown."
Iliad, ix. 185.

So Greek and so musical is he who can yet give this answer to the dying Hector's appeal :—

" ' Knee me no knees, thou dog, neither prate of my parents to me !
Would God my spirit within me would leave my fury free
To carve the flesh of thee raw, and devour, for the deeds thou hast done.' "
Iliad, xxii. 345.

(Translated by Arthur S. Way.)

N

Bated like eagles having lately bath'd;
Glittering in golden coats, like images;
As full of spirit as the month of May,
And gorgeous as the sun at midsummer;
Wanton as youthful goats, wild as young bulls.
I saw young Harry, with his beaver on,
His cuisses on his thighs, gallantly arm'd,
Rise from the ground like feather'd Mercury,
And vaulted with such ease into his seat,
As if an angel dropp'd down from the clouds,
To turn and wind a fiery Pegasus,
And witch the world with noble horsemanship.ᴿ

XXIV

HENRY V. was, in the popular conception, the national hero of England. He was the man whose glorious victories had brought France under English rule. His name had a ring like that of Valdemar in Denmark, bringing with it memories of a time of widespread dominion, which the weakness of his successors had suffered to shrink again. As a matter of history, Henry had been a soldier almost from his boyhood, had been stationed on the Welsh borders from his sixteenth to his one-and-twentieth year, and had afterwards, in London, enjoyed the full confidence of his father and of the Parliament. But there was some hint in the old chronicles of his having, in his youth, frequented bad company and led a wild life which gave no foretaste of his coming greatness. This hint had been elaborated in the old and worthless play, *The Famous Victories;* and no more was needed to set Shakespeare's imagination to work, and render it productive. He revelled in the idea of representing the young Prince of Wales roistering among drunkards and demireps, only to rise all the more brilliantly and superbly into the irreproachable sovereign, the greatest soldier among England's kings, the humiliator of France, the victor of Agincourt.

No doubt Shakespeare's imagination here started from a basis of personal experience. As a young player and poet, he in all probability lived a Bohemian life in London, not, indeed, of debauchery, but full of such passions and dissipations as his vigorous temperament, his overflowing vitality, and his position beyond the pale of staid and respectable citizenship, would tend to throw in his way. The Sonnets, which speak so plainly of vehement and fateful emotions on his part, also hint at temptations which he did not resist. We read, for instance, in Sonnet cxix. :—

> " What potions have I drunk of Siren tears,
> Distill'd from limbecks foul as hell within,
> Applying fears to hopes, and hopes to fears,
> Still losing when I saw myself to win !

What wretched errors hath my heart committed,
Whilst it hath thought itself so blessed never !
How have mine eyes out of their spheres been fitted,
In the distraction of this madding fever !"

And again in Sonnet cxxix. :—

" The expense of spirit in a waste of shame
Is lust·in action ; and till action, lust
Is perjur'd, murderous, bloody, full of blame,
Savage, extreme, rude, cruel, not to trust ;
Enjoy'd no sooner but despised straight ;
Past reason hunted ; and no sooner had,
Past reason hated, as a swallow'd bait,
On purpose laid to make the taker mad :

All this the world well knows ; yet none knows well
To shun the heaven that leads men to this hell."

This is the philosophy of the morrow, of the reaction.   But
Shakespeare had also, no doubt, his hours of light-hearted enjoyment, when such moralising reflections were far enough from his
mind.   We have evidence of this in more than one anecdote.   In
the diary of John Manningham, of the Middle Temple, the following entry occurs, under the date March 13, 1602 :—

" Upon a tyme when Burbidge played Rich. 3, there was a Citizen
grone soe farr in liking with him, that before shee went from the play
shee appointed him to come that night vnto hir by the name of Ri: the 3.
Shakespeare ouerhearing their conclusion went before, [and] was inter-
tained . . . ere Burbidge came.   Then message being brought that
Rich. the 3ᵈ was at the dore, Shakespeare caused returne to be made
that William the Conquerour was before Rich. the 3. Shakespere's name
was William."

Aubrey, who, however, did not write until 1680, is the authority, supported by several others (Pope, Oldys, &c.), for the legend
that Shakespeare, on his yearly journeys from London to Stratford-on-Avon and back, by way of Oxford and Woodstock, used
to alight at the "Crown" tavern, kept by one Davenant in
Oxford, and there won the heart of his hostess, the buxom and
merry Mrs. Davenant, who "used much to delight in his pleasant
company."   According to this tradition, the young William
Davenant, afterwards a poet of note, commonly passed in Oxford for Shakespeare's son, and was said to bear some resemblance to him.   Sir William himself was not unwilling to have
it believed that he was "more than a poetic child only" of
Shakespeare's.[1]

[1] This tradition seems in no way improbable, and its probability is not diminished
by the fact that an anecdote connected with it has been shown by Halliwell-Phillips
to be an old Joe Miller, merely adapted to the case in point. "One day an old

Be this as it may, Shakespeare had certainly sufficient personal experience to enable him to sympathise with this princely
youth, who, despite the consciousness of his high aims, revels in
his freedom, shuns the court life and ceremonial which await him,
throws his dignity to the winds, riots in reckless high spirits,
boxes the ears of the Lord Chief-Justice, and has yet self-
command enough to suffer arrest without resistance, takes part
in a tourney with a common wench's glove in his helm—in
short, does everything that most conflicts with his people's sense
of propriety and his father's doctrines of prudence, but does it
without coarseness, with a certain innocence, and without ever
having to reproach himself with any actual self-degradation.
Henry IV. misunderstands his son as completely as Frederick
William of Prussia misunderstood the young Frederick the Great.

We see him, indeed, plunging into the most boyish and
thoughtless diversions, in company with topers, tavern-wenches,
and pot-boys; but we see, also, that he is magnanimous, and full
of profound admiration for Harry Percy, that admiration for a
rival of which Percy himself was incapable. And he rises, ere
long, above this world of triviality and make-believe to the true
height of his nature. His alert self-esteem, his immovable self-
confidence, can early be traced in minor touches. When Falstaff
asks him if "his blood does not thrill" to think of the alliance
between three such formidable foes as Percy, Douglas, and Glendower, he dismisses with a smile all idea of fear. A little later, he
plays upon his truncheon of command as upon a fife. He has the
great carelessness of the great natures; he does not even lose it
when he feels himself unjustly suspected. At bottom he is a good
brother, a good son, a great patriot; and he has the makings of
a great ruler. He lacks Hotspur's optimism (which sees some
advantage even in his father's desertion), nor has he his impetuous
pugnacity; yet we see outlined in him the daring, typically English conqueror, adventurer, and politician, unscrupulous, and, on
occasion, cruel, undismayed though the enemy outnumber him
tenfold—the prototype of the men who, a century and a half after
Shakespeare's death, achieved the conquest of India.

It is a pity that Shakespeare could find no other way of displaying his military superiority to Percy than simply to make him
a better swordsman and let him kill his rival in single combat.
This is a return to the Homeric conception of martial prowess.
It was by such traits as this that Shakespeare repelled Napoleon.
These things appeared to him childish. He found more "politics"
in Corneille.

With complete magnanimity, Prince Henry leaves to Falstaff

townsman, observing the boy running homeward almost out of breath, asked him
whither he was posting in that heat and hurry. He answered to see his *god*father
Shakespeare. 'There is a good boy,' said the other; 'but have a care that you don't
take *God's* name in vain'" (*Oldys*).

the honour of having slain Hotspur, that honour whose true nature forms the central theme of the whole play, although the idea is nowhere formulated in any individual speech. But after Henry Percy's death, Shakespeare, strangely enough, sometimes actually transfers to Henry Plantagenet his fallen rival's characteristics. He says, for example (*Henry V.*, iv. 3), "If it be a sin to covet honour, I am the most offending soul alive." He declares that he understands neither rhyme nor metre. He woos his bride as ungallantly as Hotspur talks to his Kate, and he answers the challenges of the French with a boastfulness that throws Hotspur's into the shade. In *Henry V.* Shakespeare strikes the key of pure panegyric. The play is a National Anthem in five acts.

We must remember that Shakespeare from the first could not treat this character with perfect freedom. There is a touch of reverence, of patriotic religion in his tone, even where he shows the Prince given over to wild and wanton frolics. At the close of the Second Part of *Henry IV.* he is already transformed by his sense of responsibility; and he develops, as Henry V., a sincerely religious frame of mind, based on personal humility and on the consciousness of his father's defective right to the throne, which no one could ever have divined in the light-hearted Prince Hal.

These later plays, however, are not to be compared with this First Part of *Henry IV.*, which in its day made so great and well-deserved a success. It presented life itself in all its fulness and variety, great typical creations and figures of racy reality, which, without standing in symmetrical antithesis or parallelism to each other, moved freely over the boards where a never-to-be-forgotten history was enacted. Here no fundamental idea held tyrannical sway, forcing every word that was spoken into formal relation to the whole; here nothing was abstract. No sooner has the rebellion been hatched in the royal palace than the second act opens with a scene in an inn-yard on the Dover road. It is just daybreak; some carriers cross the yard with their lanterns, going to the stable to saddle their horses; they hail each other, gossip, and tell each other how they have passed the night. Not a word do they say about Prince Henry or Falstaff; they talk of the price of oats, and of how "this house is turned upside down since Robin ostler died." Their speeches have nothing to do with the action; they merely sketch its locality and put the audience in tune for it; but seldom in poetry has so much been effected in so few words. The night sky, with Charles's Wain "over the new chimney," the flickering gleam of the lanterns in the dirty yard, the fresh air of the early dawn, the misty atmosphere, the mingled odour of damp peas and beans, of bacon and ginger, all comes straight home to our senses. The situation takes hold of us with all the irresistible force of reality.

Shakespeare must have written this drama with a feeling of almost infallible inspiration and triumphant ease. We understand in reading it what his contemporaries say of his manuscripts: he did not blot a single line.

The political developments arising from Henry IV.'s wrongful seizure of the throne of Richard II. afford the groundwork of the play.

The King, situated partly like Louis Philippe, partly like Napoleon III., does all he can to obliterate the memory of his usurpation. But he does not succeed. Why not? Shakespeare gives a twofold answer. First there is the natural, human reason: the relation of characters and circumstances. The King has risen by the "fell working" of his friends; he is afraid of falling again before their power. His position forces him to be mistrustful, and his mistrust repels every one from him, first Mortimer, then Percy, then, as nearly as possible, his own son. Secondly, we have the prescribed religious reason: that wrong avenges itself, that punishment follows upon the heels of guilt—in a word, the so-called principle of "poetic justice." If only to propitiate the censorship and the police, Shakespeare could not but do homage to this principle. It was bad enough that the theatres should be suffered to exist at all; if they so far forgot themselves as to show vice unpunished and virtue unrewarded, the playwright would have to be sternly brought to his senses.

The character of the King is a masterpiece. He is the shrewd, mistrustful, circumspect ruler, who has made his way to the throne by dint of smiles and pressures of the hand, has employed every artifice for making an impression, has first ingratiated himself with the populace by his affability, and has then been sparing of his personal presence. Hence those words of his which so deeply impressed Sören Kierkegaard,[1] who despised and acted in direct opposition to the principle they formulated (Pt. i. iii. 2):—

> " Had I so lavish of my presence been,
> So common-hackney'd in the eyes of men,
> So stale and cheap to vulgar company,
> Opinion, that did help me to the crown,
> Had still kept loyal to possession,
> And left me in reputeless banishment,
> A fellow of no mark, nor likelihood.
> By being seldom seen, I could not stir,
> But like a comet I was wonder'd at."

He thus illustrates, from the point of view of an old diplomatist,

---

[1] A Danish ethical and theological thinker, a Northern Pascal, said to have in some measure suggested to Ibsen the character of Brand.

the injury his son does himself by flaunting it among his disreputable associates.

Yet the son is not so unlike the father as the father believes. Shakespeare has made him, in his own way, adopt a scarcely less diplomatic policy: that of establishing a false opinion about himself, letting himself pass for a frivolous debauchee, in order to make all the deeper impression by his firmness and energy as soon as an opportunity offers of showing what is in him. Even in his first soliloquy (i. 2) he lays down this line of policy with a definiteness which is psychologically feeble:—

> " I know you all, and will awhile uphold
> The unyok'd humour of your idleness.
> Yet herein will I imitate the sun,
> Who doth permit the base contagious clouds
> To smother up his beauty from the world,
> That when he please again to be himself,
> Being wanted, he may be more wondered at."

This self-consciousness on Henry's part was to some extent imposed upon Shakespeare. Without it, he could scarcely have brought upon the stage, in such questionable company, a prince who had become a national hero. Yet if the Prince had acted with the cut-and-dried deliberation of purpose which he here attributes to himself, we should have to write him down an unmitigated charlatan.

Here, as in a former instance of psychological crudity— Richard III.'s description of himself as a villain—we must allow for Shakespeare's use of the soliloquy. He frequently regards it as an indispensable stage-convention, which does not really reveal the inmost thoughts of the speaker, but only serves to place the hearer at a certain point of view, and to give him information which he needs. Furthermore, such a soliloquy as this ought to be spoken with a good deal of sophistical self-justification on the Prince's part, or else, as the German actor, Josef Kainz, treats it, in a tone of gay raillery. Finally, it is to be regarded as a first hint—rather a broad one, it must be admitted—which Shakespeare gives us thus early in order to get rid of the improbability he found in the Chronicle, where the Prince is instantaneously and miraculously transformed through a single resolve. The soliloquy is introduced at this point to ensure the coherence of his character, lest the spectator should feel that the Prince's conversion to a totally different manner of life was mechanically tacked on and had no root in his inner nature. And it must have been one of the chief attractions of the theme for Shakespeare to show precisely this conversion. No doubt he enjoyed depicting his hero's gay and thoughtless life, at war with all the morality which is founded on mere social convention; but at least as great must have been the pleasure he took, as a man of ripe experience, in vindicating that morality which he now felt to be the determining factor in human life— the morality of voluntary self-reform and self-control, without which there can be no concentration of purpose or systematic activity. When the new-crowned king will no longer recognise Falstaff, when he repulses him with the words :—

> " How ill white hairs become a fool and jester. . . .
> Reply not to me with a fool-born jest ;
> Presume not that I am the thing I was,"

he speaks out of Shakespeare's own soul. Behind the words there glows a new-born warmth of feeling. The calm sense of justice of the island king makes haste to express itself, and · to refuse all further dallying with evil. He grants Falstaff a maintenance and banishes him from his presence. Shakespeare's hero is at this point a living embodiment of that earnestness and sense of responsibility which the poet, whom one of his greatest and ablest admirers (Taine) has represented as being devoid of moral feeling, held to be the indispensable condition of all high endeavour.

XXV

THE Second Part of *Henry IV.*, which must have been written
in 1598, since Justice Silence is mentioned in Ben Jonson's
Every Man out of his Humour, acted in 1599, abounds, no less
than the First Part, in poetic power, but is only a dramatised chronicle, not a drama.   In its serious scenes, the play
is more faithful to history than the First Part, and it is not
Shakespeare's fault that the historical characters are here of
less interest.   In the comic scenes, which are very amply developed, Shakespeare has achieved the feat of bringing Falstaff
a second time upon the stage without giving us the least sense
of anticlimax.   He is incomparable as ever in his scenes with
the Lord Chief-Justice and with the women of the tavern ; and
when he goes down into Gloucestershire in his character of
recruiting-officer, he is still at the height of his genius.   As
new comrades and foils to him, Shakespeare has here created
the two contemptible country Justices, Shallow and Silence.
Shallow is a masterpiece, a compact of mere stupidity, foolishness, boastfulness, rascality, and senility; yet he appears a
genius in comparison with the ineffable Silence.   Here, as in
the First Part, the poet evidently drew his comic types from the
life of his own day.   Another very amusing new personage, who,
like Falstaff, was much imitated by the minor dramatists of the
time, is Falstaff's Ancient, the braggart Pistol, whose talk is an
anthology of playhouse bombast.   This inept affectation not only
makes him a highly comic personage, but gives Shakespeare
an opportunity of girding at the robustious style of the earlier
tragic poets, which had become repulsive to him.   He parodies
Marlowe's *Tamburlaine* in Pistol's outburst (ii. 4):—

> "Shall packhorses,
> And hollow pamper'd jades of Asia,
> Which cannot go but thirty miles a-day,
> Compare with Cæsars and with Cannibals,
> And Trojan Greeks?"

The passage in *Tamburlaine* (Second Part, ii. 4) runs thus:—

> "Holla, ye pamper'd jades of Asia,
> What? can ye draw but twenty miles a day?"

He makes fun of Peele's *Turkish Mahomet and Hyren the fair Greek*, when Pistol, alluding to his sword, exclaims, "Have we not Hiren here?" And again it is George Peele who is aimed at when Pistol says to the hostess:—

> "Then feed and be fat, my fair Calipolis;
> Come, give's some sack."

In *The Battle of Alcazar* (see above, p. 31), Muley Mahomet brings his wife some flesh on the point of his sword and says—

> "Hold thee, Calipolis, feed and faint no more!"

But Falstaff himself is, and must ever remain, the chief attraction of the comic scenes. Never was the Fat Knight wittier than when he answers the Lord Chief-Justice, who has told him that his figure bears "all the characters of age" (i. 2):—

> "My Lord, I was born about three of the clock in the afternoon, with a white head, and something a round belly. For my voice, I have lost it with hollaing and singing of anthems. To approve my youth further, I will not: the truth is, I am only old in judgment and understanding; and he that will caper with me for a thousand marks, let him lend me the money, and have at him."

The play is a mere bundle of individual passages, but each of these passages is admirable. A great example is King Henry's soliloquy which opens the third act, the profoundly imaginative apostrophe to sleep:—

> "O thou dull god! why liest thou with the vile,
> In loathsome beds, and leav'st the kingly couch,
> A watch-case, or a common 'larum bell?
> Wilt thou upon the high and giddy mast
> Seal up the ship-boy's eyes, and rock his brains
> In cradle of the rude imperious surge,
> And in the visitation of the winds,
> Who take the ruffian billows by the top,
> Curling their monstrous heads, and hanging them
> With deaf'ning clamours in the slippery clouds,
> That with the hurly death itself awakes?
> Canst thou, O partial sleep! give thy repose
> To the wet sea-boy in an hour so rude;
> And in the calmest and most stillest night,
> With all appliances and means to boot,
> Deny it to a king? Then, happy low, lie down!
> Uneasy lies the head that wears a crown."

Throughout this Second Part, the King, besieged by cares and living in the shadow of death, is richer in thought and wisdom than ever before. What he says, and what is said to him, seems drawn by the poet from the very depths of his own experience, and addressed to men of the like experience and thought. Every word of that first scene of the third act is in the highest degree significant and admirable. It is here that the King turns to what we now call geology (see above, p. 95) for an image of the historical mutability of all things. When he mournfully reminds his attendants that Richard II., whom he displaced, prophesied a Nemesis to come from those who had helped him to the throne, and that this Nemesis has now over-taken him, Warwick answers with the profound and astonishingly modern reflection that history is apparently governed by laws, and that each man's life—

> " Figures the nature of the times deceas'd ;
> The which observ'd, a man may prophesy,
> With a near aim, of the main chance of things
> As yet not come to life."

To this the King returns the no less philosophical answer :—

> "Are these things, then, necessities ?
> Then let us meet them like necessities."

But it is at the close of the fourth act, where news of the total defeat of the rebels is brought to the dying King, that he utters what is perhaps his most profoundly pessimistic speech, complain-ing that Fortune never comes with both hands full, but "writes her fair words still in foulest letters," so that life is like a feast at which either the food or the appetite [or the guests] are always lacking.

From the moment of King Henry's death, Shakespeare con-centrates all his poetical strength upon the task of presenting in his great son the pattern and ideal of English kingship. In all the earlier Histories the King had grave defects ; Shakespeare now applies himself, with warm and undisguised enthusiasm, to the portrayal of a king without a flaw.

His *Henry V.* is a glorification of this national ideal. The five choruses which introduce the acts are patriotic pæans, Shake-speare's finest heroic lyrics ; and the play itself is an epic in dialogue, without any sort of dramatic structure, development, or conflict. It is an English ἐγκώμιον, a dramatic monument, as was the *Persæ* of Æschylus for ancient Athens. As a work of creative art, it cannot be compared with the two preceding Histories, to which it forms a supplement. Its theme is English patriotism, and its appeal is to England rather than to the world.

The allusion to Essex's command in Ireland in the prologue

to the fifth act gives us beyond a doubt the date of its first performance. Essex was in Ireland from the 15th of April 1599 to
the 28th of September in the following year. As we find the
play alluded to by other poets in 1600, it must in all probability
have been produced in 1599.

How strongly Shakespeare was impressed by the greatness
of his theme appears in his reiterated expressions of humility in
approaching it. He begins, like the epic poets of antiquity, with
an invocation of the Muse; he implores forgiveness, not only for
the imperfection of his scenic apparatus, but for the "flat unraised
spirits" in which he treats so mighty a theme. And in the prologue to the fourth act he returns to the subject of his unworthiness and the pitiful limitations of the stage. Throughout the
choruses, he has done his utmost, by dint of vivid imagery and
lyric impetus and splendour, to make up for the sacrifice of unity
and cohesion involved in his faithfulness to history. Shakespeare
was evidently unconscious of the naïveté of the lecture on the
Salic law, establishing Henry's claim to the crown of France,
with which the Archbishop opens the play; no doubt he thought
it absolutely imposed upon him.

For he here strives to make Henry an epitome of all the
virtues he himself most highly values. Even in the last act of
the Second Part of *Henry IV.* he had endowed him with traits
of irreproachable kingly magnanimity. Henry confirms in his
office the Chief-Justice, who, in the execution of his duty, had
arrested the Prince of Wales, addresses him with the deepest
respect, and even calls him "father." In reality this Chief-
Justice was dismissed at the King's accession. *Henry V.* com-
pletes the evolution of the royal butterfly from the larva and
chrysalis stages of the earlier plays. Henry is at once the
monarch who always thinks royally, and never forgets his pride
as the representative of the English people; the man with no
pose or arrogance, who bears himself simply, talks modestly, acts
energetically, and thinks piously; the soldier who endures priva-
tions like the meanest of his followers, is downright in his jesting
and his wooing, and enforces discipline with uncompromising
strictness, even as against his own old comrades; and finally,
the citizen who is accessible alike to small and great, and in
whom the youthful frolicsomeness of earlier days has become
the humourist's relish for a practical joke, like that which he
plays off upon Williams and Fluellen. Shakespeare shows him,
like a military Haroun Al Raschid, seeking personally to insinuate himself into the thoughts and feelings of his followers;
and—what is very unlike him—he manifests no disapproval
where the King sinks far below the ideal, as when he orders
the frightful massacre of all the French prisoners taken at
Agincourt. Shakespeare tries to pass the deed off as a measure
of necessity.

The reason of this is that the spirit which here prevails is not pure patriotism, but in many points a narrow Chauvinism. King Henry's two speeches before Harfleur (iii. 1 and iii. 3) are bombastic, savage, and threatening to the point of frothy bluster; and wherever Frenchmen and Englishmen are brought into contrast, the French, even if they at that time showed themselves inferior soldiers, are treated with obvious injustice. With his sharp eye for national, as for personal peculiarities, Shakespeare has of course seized upon certain weaknesses of the French character; but for the most part his Frenchmen are mere caricatures for the diversion of the gallery. Quite childish is the way in which he makes the Frenchmen mix fragments of French in their speeches. But it is consistent enough with the national and popular design of the play that not a little of it should seem to be addressed to the common, uneducated public—for instance, the scene in which the miserable blusterer Pistol makes prisoner a French nobleman whom he has succeeded in overawing, and that in which the young Princess Katherine of France takes lessons in English from one of her ladies-in-waiting. This passage (iii. 4) and the wooing scene between King Henry and the Princess (v. 2) are incidentally interesting as giving us a good idea of Shakespeare's acquaintance with French. No doubt he could read French, but he must have spoken it very imperfectly. He is perhaps not to blame for such blunders as *le possession* and *à les anges*. On the other hand, it was doubtless he who placed in the mouth of the Princess such comically impossible expressions as these when Henry has kissed her hand :—

"*Je ne veux point que vous abbaissez vostre grandeur, en baisant le main d'une vostre indigne serviteur.*"

And this :—

"*Les dames, et damoiselles, pour estre baisées devant leur nopces, ii n'est pas le costume de France.*"

According to his custom, and in order to preserve continuity of style with the foregoing plays, Shakespeare has interspersed *Henry V.* with comic figures and scenes. Falstaff himself does not appear, his death being announced at the beginning of the play ; but the members of his gang wander around, as living and ludicrous mementos of him, until they disappear one by one by way of the gallows, so that nothing may survive to recall the great king's frivolous youth. To console us for their loss, we are here introduced to a new circle of comic figures—soldiers from the different English-speaking countries which make up what we now call the United Kingdom. Each of them speaks his own dialect, in which resides much of the comic effect for English ears. We have a Welshman, a Scot, and an Irishman. The

Welshman is intrepid, phlegmatic, somewhat pedantic, but all fire and flame for discipline and righteousness; the Scot is immovable in his equilibrium, even-tempered, sturdy, and trustworthy; the Irishman is a true Celt, fiery, passionate, quarrelsome and apt at misunderstanding. Fluellen, the Welshman, with his comic phlegm and manly severity, is the most elaborate of these figures.

But in placing on the stage these representatives of the different English-speaking peoples, Shakespeare had another and deeper purpose than that of merely amusing his public with a medley of dialects. At that time the Scots were still the hereditary enemies of England, who always attacked her in the rear whenever she went to war, and the Irish were actually in open rebellion. Shakespeare evidently dreamed of a Greater England, as we nowadays speak of a Greater Britain. When he wrote this play, King James of Scotland was busily courting the favour of the English, and the question of the succession to the throne, when the old Queen should die, was not definitely settled. Shakespeare clearly desired that, with the coming of James, the old national hatred between the Scotch and the English should cease. Essex, in Ireland, was at this very time carrying out the policy which was to lead to his destruction—that, namely, of smoothing away hatred by means of leniency, and trying to come to an arrangement with the leader of the Catholic rebellion. Southampton was with him in Ireland as his Master of the Horse, and we cannot doubt that Shakespeare's heart was in the campaign. Bates in this play (iv. 1) probably expresses Shakespeare's own political ideas when he says—

" Be friends, you English fools, be friends: we have French [Spanish] quarrels enow, if you could tell how to reckon."

Henry V. is not one of Shakespeare's best plays, but it is one of his most amiable. He here shows himself not as the almost superhuman genius, but as the English patriot, whose enthusiasm is as beautiful as it is simple, and whose prejudices, even, are not unbecoming. The play not only points backward to the greatest period of England's past, but forward to King James, who, as the Protestant son of the Catholic Mary Stuart, was to put an end to religious persecutions, and who, as a Scotchman and a supporter of the Irish policy of Essex, was for the first time to show the world not only a sturdy England, but a powerful Great Britain.

XXVI

ELIZABETH AND FALSTAFF — THE MERRY WIVES OF WINDSOR — THE PROSAIC AND BOURGEOIS TONE OF THE PIECE—THE FAIRY SCENES

SHAKESPEARE must have written *The Merry Wives of Windsor* immediately after *Henry V.*, probably about Christmas 1599; for Sir Thomas Lucy, on whom the poet here takes his revenge, died in 1600, and it is improbable that Shakespeare would have cared to gird at him after his death. He almost certainly did not write the piece of his own motive, but at the suggestion of one whose wish was a command. There is the strongest internal evidence for the truth of the tradition which states that the play was written at the request of Queen Elizabeth. The first Quarto of 1602 has on its title-page the words, " As it hath been divers times acted by the right honourable my Lord Chamberlain's servants. Both before Her Majesty, and elsewhere." A century later (1702), John Dennis, who published an adaptation of the play, writes, " I know very well that it had pleased one of the greatest queens that ever was in the world. . . . This comedy was written at her command and by her direction, and she was so eager to see it acted, that she commanded it to be finished in fourteen days." A few years later (1709) Rowe writes, " She was so well pleased with that admirable character of Falstaff in the two parts of *Henry IV.*, that she commanded him to continue it for one play more and show him in love. This is said to be the occasion of his writing *The Merry Wives*. How well she was obeyed, the play itself is an admirable proof."

Old Queen Bess can scarcely have been a great judge of art, or she would not have conceived the extravagant notion of wanting to see Falstaff in love; she would have understood that if there was anything impossible to him it was this. She would also have realised that his figure was already a rounded whole and could not be reproduced. It is true that in the Epilogue to *Henry IV.* (which, however, is probably not by Shakespeare) a continuation of the history is promised, in which, "for anything I know, Falstaff shall die of a sweat, unless already he be killed with your hard opinions;" but no such continuation is to be found in *Henry V.*, evidently because Shakespeare felt that Falstaff had played out his part. Neither is *The Merry Wives* the promised continuation, for Falstaff does not die, and the action is conceived as an earlier episode in his life, though it is entirely removed from its historical setting and brought forward into the poet's own time, so unequivocally that there is even in the fifth act a direct mention of "our radiant queen" in Windsor Castle.

The poet must have set himself unwillingly to the fulfilment of the "radiant queen's" barbarous wish, and tried to make the best of a bad business. He was compelled entirely to ruin his inimitable Falstaff, and degrade the fat knight into an ordinary avaricious, wine-bibbing, amatory old fool. Along with him, he resuscitated the whole merry company from *Henry V.*, who had all come to an unpleasant end—Bardolph, Pistol, Nym, and Dame Quickly— making the men repeat themselves with a difference, endowing Pistol with the splendid phrase "The world's mine oyster, which I with sword will open," and giving to Dame Quickly softened and more commonplace lineaments. From the Second Part of *Henry IV.*, too, he introduces Justice Shallow, placing him in a less friendly relation to Falstaff, and giving him a highly comic nephew, Slender, who, in his vanity and pitifulness, is like a first sketch for Sir Andrew Aguecheek in *Twelfth Night.*

His task was now to entertain a queen and a court "with their hatred of ideas, their insensibility to beauty, their hard, efficient manners, and their demand for impropriety."[1] As it amused the London populace to see kings and princes upon the stage, so it entertained the Queen and her court to have a glimpse into the daily life of the middle classes, so remote from their own, to look into their rooms, and hear their chat with the doctor and the parson, to see a picture of the prosperity and contentment which flourished at Windsor right under the windows of the Queen's summer residence, and to witness the downright virtue and merry humour of the red-cheeked, buxom townswomen. Thus was the keynote of the piece determined. Thus it became more prosaic and bourgeois than any other play of Shakespeare's. *The Merry Wives* is indeed the only one of his works which is almost entirely written in prose, and the only one of his comedies in which, the scene being laid in England, he has taken as his subject the contemporary life of the English middle classes. It is not quite unlike the more farcical of Molière's comedies, which also were often written with an eye to royal and courtly audiences. All the more significant is the fact that Shakespeare has found it impossible to content himself with thus dwelling on the common earth, and has introduced at the close a fairy-dance and fairy-song, as though from the *Midsummer Night's Dream* itself, executed, it is true, by children and young girls dressed up as elves, but preserving throughout the air and style of genuine fairy scenes.

[1] Dowden: *Shakspere—his Mind and Art*, p. 370.

Shakespeare had just been trying his hand in *Henry V.* at writing the broken English spoken by a Welshman and by a Frenchman. He knew that at court, where people prided themselves on the purest pronunciation of their mother-tongue, he would find an audience exceedingly alive to the comic effects thus obtained, and he therefore, while he was in the vein, introduced into this hasty and occasional production two not unkindly caricatures—the Welsh priest, Sir Hugh Evans, in whom he perhaps immortalised one of his Stratford schoolmasters, and the French Doctor Caius, a thoroughly farcical eccentric, who pronounces everything awry.

The hurry with which Shakespeare wrote this comedy has led him into some confusion as to the process of time. In Act iii. 4, when Dame Quickly is sent to Falstaff to make a second appointment with him, it is the afternoon of the second day; in the following scene, when she comes to him, it is the morning of the third day. But this haste has also given the play an unusually dramatic swing and impetus; it is quite free from the episodes in which the poet is at other times apt to loiter.

Nevertheless Shakespeare has here woven together no fewer than three different actions—Falstaff's advances to the two Merry Wives, Mrs. Ford and Mrs. Page, and all the consequences of his ill-timed rendezvous; the rivalry between the foolish doctor, the imbecile Slender, and young Fenton for the hand of fair Anne Page; and finally, the burlesque duel between the Welsh priest and the French doctor, which is devised and set afoot by the jovial Windsor innkeeper.

Shakespeare has himself invented much more than usual of the complicated intrigue. But Falstaff's concealment in the buck-basket was suggested by a similar incident in Fiorentino's *Il Pecorone*, from which Shakespeare had already borrowed in the *Merchant of Venice;* and the idea of making Falstaff incessantly confide his designs and his rendezvous to the husband of the lady in question came from another Italian story by Straparola, which had been published some ten years earlier, under the title of *Two Lovers of Pisa*, in Tarlton's *News of Purgatory.*

The invention is not always very happy. For instance, it is a highly unpleasing and improbable touch that Ford, as Master Brook, should bribe Falstaff to procure him possession of the woman (his own wife) whom he affects to desire, and whom Falstaff also is pursuing. Ford's jealousy, moreover, is altogether too stupid and crude in its manifestations. But we have especially to deplore that the nature of the intrigue and the moral tendency to be impressed on the play should have made Falstaff, who used to be quickness and ingenuity personified, so preternaturally dense that his incessant defeats afford his opponents a very poor triumph.

He is ignorant of everything it would have been his interest to know, and he is perpetually committing afresh the same inconceivable blunders. It is foolish enough, in the first place, to write two identical love-letters to two women in the same little town, who, as he ought to know, are bosom friends. It is incredibly stupid of him to walk three times in succession straight into the coarse trap which they set for him; in doing so he betrays such a monstrous vanity that we find it impossible to recognise in him the ironical Falstaff of the Histories. It is inexpressibly guileless of him never to conceive the slightest suspicion of "Master Brook," who, being his only confidant, is therefore the only man who can have betrayed him to the husband. And finally, it is not only childish, but utterly inconsistent with the keen understanding of the earlier Falstaff, that he should believe in the supernatural nature of the beings who pinch him and burn him by night in the park.

On the other hand, the old high spirits and the old wit now and again flame forth in him, and a few of his speeches to Shallow, to Pistol, to Bardolph and others are exceedingly amusing. He shows a touch of his old self when, after having been soused in the water along with the foul linen, he protests that drowning is "a death that I abhor, for the water swells a man, and what a thing should I have been when I had been swelled!" And he has a highly humorous outburst in the last act (v. 5) when he declares, " I think the devil will not have me damned, lest the oil that is in me should set hell on fire." But what are these little flashes in comparison with the inexhaustible whimsicality of the true Falstaff!

The play is more consistently farcical than any earlier comedy of Shakespeare's, *The Taming of the Shrew* not excepted. The graceful and poetical passages are few. We have in Mr. and Mrs. Page a pleasant English middle-class couple; and though the young lovers, Fenton and Anne Page, have only one short scene together, they display in it some attractive qualities. Anne Page is an amiable middle-class girl of Shakespeare's day, one of the healthy and natural young women whom Wordsworth has celebrated in the nineteenth century. Fenton, who is said (though we cannot believe it) to have been at one time a comrade of Prince Hal and Poins, is certainly attached to her; but it is very characteristic that Shakespeare, with his keen sense for the value of money, sees nothing to object to in the fact that Fenton, as he frankly confesses, was first attracted to Anne by her wealth. This is the same trait which we found in another wooer, Bassanio, of a few years earlier.

Finally, there is real poetry in the short fairy scene of the last act. The poet here takes his revenge for the prose to which he has so long been condemned. It is full of the aromatic woodscents of Windsor Park by night. What is altogether most valuable in *The Merry Wives* is its strong smack of the English soil. The play appeals to us, in spite of the drawbacks inseparable from a work hastily written to order, because the poet has here for once remained faithful to his own age and his own country, and has given us a picture of the contemporary middle-class, in its sturdy and honest worth, which even the atmosphere of farce cannot quite obscure.

XXVII

*SHAKESPEARE'S MOST BRILLIANT PERIOD—THE FEMININE
TYPES BELONGING TO IT — WITTY AND HIGHBORN
YOUNG WOMEN—MUCH ADO ABOUT NOTHING—SLAVISH
FAITHFULNESS TO HIS SOURCES—BENEDICK AND BEA-
TRICE—SPIRITUAL DEVELOPMENT—THE LOW-COMEDY
FIGURES*

SHAKESPEARE now enters upon the stage in his career in which
his wit and brilliancy of spirit reach a perfection hitherto un-
attained. It seems as though these years of his life had been
bathed in sunshine. They certainly cannot have been years of
struggle, and still less of sorrow; there must have been a sort
of lull in his existence—a tranquil zone, as it were, in the troubled
waters of life. He seems for a short time to have revelled in his
own genius with a sort of pensive happiness, to have drunk
exhilarating draughts of his own inspiration. He heard the
nightingales warbling in the sacred grove of his spirit. His
whole nature burst into flower.

In the Republican Calendar one of the months was named
Floréal. There is such a flower-month in almost every human
life; and this is Shakespeare's.

He was doubtless in love at this time—as he had probably
been all his life through—but his love was not an overmastering
passion like Romeo's, nor did it depress him with that half-
despairing feeling of the unworthiness of its object which he
betrays in his Sonnets; nor, again, was it the airy ecstasy of
youthful imagination that ran riot in *A Midsummer Night's
Dream.* No, it was a happy love, which filled his head as well
as his heart, accompanied with joyous admiration for the wit and
vivacity of the beloved one, for her graciousness and distinction.
Her coquetry is gay, her heart is excellent, and her intelligence
so quick that she seems to be wit incarnate in the form of a
woman.

In his early years he had presented not a few unamiable,
mannish women in his comedies, and not a few ambitious, bloodthirsty, or corrupt women in his serious plays—figures such as
Adriana and the shrewish Katharine on the one hand, Tamora
and Margaret of Anjou on the other hand, who have all a stiff-
necked will, and a certain violence of manners. In the later years

213

of his ripe manhood he displays a preference for young women who are nothing but soul and tenderness, silent natures without wit or sparkle, figures such as Ophelia, Desdemona, and Cordelia.

Between these two strongly-marked groups we come upon a bevy of beautiful young women, who all have their heart in the right place, but whose chief attraction lies in their sparkling quickness of wit. They are often as lovable as the most faithful friend can be, and witty as Heinrich Heine himself, though with another sort of wit. We feel that Shakespeare must have admired with all his heart the models from whom he drew these women, and must have rejoiced in them as one brilliant mind rejoices in another. These types of delicate and aristocratic womanhood cannot possibly have had plebeian models.

In his first years in London, Shakespeare, as an underling in a company of players, can have had no opportunity of associating with other women than, firstly, those who sat for his Mistress Quickly and Doll Tearsheet; secondly, those passionate and daring women who make the first advances to actors and poets; and, thirdly, those who served as models for his "Merry Wives," with their sound bourgeois sense and not over delicate gaiety. But the ordinary citizen's wife or daughter of that day offered the poet no sort of spiritual sustenance. They were, as a rule, quite illiterate. Shakespeare's younger daughter could not even write her own name.

But he was presently discovered by men like Southampton and Pembroke, cordially received into their refined and thoroughly cultivated circle, and in all probability presented to the ladies of these noble families. Can we doubt that the tone of conversation among these aristocratic ladies must have enchanted him, that he must have rejoiced in the nobility and elegance of their manners, and that their playful freedom of speech must have afforded him an object for imitation and idealisation?

The great ladies of that date were exceedingly accomplished. They had been educated as highly as the men, spoke Italian, French, and Spanish fluently, and were not infrequently acquainted with Latin and Greek. Lady Pembroke, Sidney's sister, the mother of Shakespeare's patron, was regarded as the most intellectual woman of her time, and was equally celebrated as an author and as a patroness of authors. And these ladies were not oppressed by their knowledge or affected in their speech, but natural, rich in ideas as in acquirements, free in their wit, and sometimes in their morals; so that we can easily understand how a daring, high-bred, womanly intelligence should have been, for a series of years, the object which it most delighted Shakespeare to portray. He supplements this intellectual superiority, in varying measures, with independence, goodness of heart, pride, humility, tenderness, the joy of life; so that from the central conception there radiates a fan-like semicircle of different personalities. It was of such women that he had dreamt when he sketched his Rosaline in *Love's Labour's Lost*. Now he knew them, as he had already shown in Portia, the first of the group.

In spite of his latent melancholy, he is now highly-favoured and happy, this young man of thirty-five ; the sun of his career is in the sign of the Lion ; he feels himself strong enough to sport with the powers of life, and he now writes nothing but comedies. He does not take the trouble to invent them; he employs his old method of carving a play out of this or that mediocre romantic novel, or he revises inferior old pieces. As a rule, he goes thus to work : he retains without a qualm those traits in his fable which are fantastic, improbable, even repulsive to a more delicate taste—such points are always astonishingly unimportant in his eyes ; he sometimes transfers to his play undigested masses of the material before him, with no care for psychological plausibility ; but he seizes upon some leading situation in the novel, or upon some single character in the earlier play, and he animates this situation or this character, or (it may be) added characters of his own invention, with the whole fervour of his soul, until the speeches shine forth as in letters of fire, and sparkle with wit or glow with passion.

Thus, in *Much Ado about Nothing*, he retains a fable which offers almost insuperable difficulties to satisfactory poetical treatment, and nevertheless produces, partly outside of its framework, poetical values of the first order.

The play was entered in the Stationers' Register on the 4th of August 1600, and appeared in the same year under the title : *Much Adoe about Nothing. As it hath been sundrie times publikely acted by the Right Honourable the Lord Chamberlaine his Servants. Written by William Shakespeare.* It must thus have been written in 1599 or 1600; and we find, too, in its opening scene, certain allusions that accord with this date. Thus Leonato's speech, "A victory is twice itself when the achiever brings home full numbers," and Beatrice's "You had musty victual," are both thought to point to Essex's campaign in Ireland.

Shakespeare has taken the details of his plot from several Italian sources. From the first book of Ariosto's *Orlando Furioso* (the story of Ariodante and Genevra), which was translated in 1591, and had already provided the material for a play performed before the Queen in 1582, he borrowed the idea of a malevolent nobleman persuading a youthful lover that his lady is untrue to him, and suborning a waiting-woman to dress like her mistress, and receive a nocturnal visit by means of a ladder placed against her lady's window, so that the bridegroom, watching the scene from a distance, may accept it as proof of the calumny, and so break off the match. All the other details he took from a novel of Bandello's, the story of Timbreo of Cardona.

Timbreo is represented by Claudio; through the medium of a friend, he woos the daughter of Leonato, a nobleman of Messina. The intrigue which separates the young pair is woven by Girondo (in Shakespeare, Don John) just as in the play, but with a more adequate motive, since Girondo himself is in love with the lady. She faints when she is accused, is given out to be dead, and there is a sham funeral, as in the play. But in the story it is represented that the whole of Messina espouses her cause and believes in her innocence, while in the play Beatrice alone remains true to her young kinswoman. The truth is discovered and the engagement renewed, just as in Shakespeare.

Only for a much cruder habit of mind than that which prevails among people of culture in our days can this story provide the motive for a comedy. The very title indicates a point of view quite foreign to us. The implication is that since Hero was innocent, and the accusation a mere slander; since she was not really dead, and the sorrow for her loss was therefore groundless; and since she and Claudio are at last married, as they might have been at first—therefore the whole thing has been much ado about nothing, and resolves itself in a harmony which leaves no discord behind.

The ear of the modern reader is otherwise attuned. He recognises, indeed, that Shakespeare has taken no small pains to make this fable dramatically acceptable. He appreciates the fact that here again, in the person of Don John, the poet has depicted mere unmixed evil, and has disdained to supply a motive for his vile action in any single injury received, or desire unsatisfied. Don John is one of the sour, envious natures which suck poison from all sources, because they suffer from the perpetual sense of being unvalued and despised. He is, for the moment, constrained by the forbearance with which his victorious brother has treated him, but "if he had his mouth he would bite." And he does bite, like the cur and coward he is, and makes himself scarce when his villainy is about to be discovered. He is an ill-conditioned, base, and tiresome scoundrel; and, although he conscientiously does evil for evil's sake, we miss in him all the defiant and brilliantly sinister qualities which appear later on in Iago and in Edmund. There is little to object to in Don John's repulsive scoundrelism; at most we may say that it is a strange motive-power for a comedy. But to Claudio we cannot reconcile ourselves. He allows himself to be convinced, by the clumsiest stratagem, that his young bride, in reality as pure and tender as a flower, is a faithless creature, who deceives him the very day before her marriage. Instead of withdrawing in silence, he prefers, like the blockhead he is, to confront her in the church, before the altar, and in the hearing of every one overwhelm her with coarse speeches and low accusations; and he induces his patron, the Prince Don Pedro, and even the lady's own father, Leonato, to join him in heaping upon the unhappy bride their idiotic accusations. When, by the advice of the priest, her relatives have given her out as dead, and the worthy old Leonato has lied up hill and down dale about her hapless end, Claudio, who now learns too late that he has been duped, is at once taken into favour again. Leonato only demands of him—in accordance with the mediæval fable—that he shall declare himself willing to marry whatever woman he (Leonato) shall assign to him. This he promises, without a word or thought about Hero; whereupon she is placed in his arms. The original spectators, no doubt, found this solution satisfactory; a modern audience is exasperated by it, very much as Nora, in *A Doll's House*, is exasperated on finding that Helmer, after the danger has passed away, regards all that has happened in their souls as though it had never been, merely because the sky is clear again. If ever man was unworthy a woman's love, that man is Claudio. If ever marriage was odious and ill-omened, this is it. The old taleteller's invention has been too much even for Shakespeare's art.

When we moderns, however, think of *Much Ado about Nothing*, it is not this distasteful story that rises before our mind's eye. It is Benedick and Beatrice, and the intrigue in which they are involved. The light from these figures, and especially from that of Beatrice, irradiates the play, and we understand that Shakespeare was forced to make Claudio so contemptible, because by that means alone could the enchanting personality of Beatrice shine forth in its fullest splendour.

Beatrice is a great lady of the Renaissance in her early youth, overflowing with spirits and energy, brightly, defiantly virginal, inclined, in the wealth of her daring wit, to a somewhat aggressive raillery, and capable of unabashed freedom of speech, astounding to our modern taste, but permitted by their education to the foremost women of that age. Her behaviour to Benedick, whom she cannot help perpetually twitting and teasing, is as headstrong and refractory as Katharine's treatment of Petruchio.

Her diction is marvellous, glittering with unrestrained fantasy. For instance, after she has assured her uncle (ii. 1) that she "is on her knees every morning and evening" to be spared the infliction of a husband, since a man with a beard and a man without one would be equally intolerable to her, she proceeds—

"*Beatrice.* . . . Therefore I will even take sixpence in earnest of the bear-ward, and lead his apes into hell.

"*Leonato.* Well, then, go you into hell?

"*Beat.* No; but to the gate; and there will the devil meet me, like an old cuckold, with horns on his head, and say, 'Get you to heaven, Beatrice, get you to heaven; here's no place for you maids:' so deliver I up my apes, and away to Saint Peter for the heavens; he shows me where the bachelors sit, and there live we as merry as the day is long."

She holds that—

"Wooing, wedding, and repenting, is as a Scotch jig, a measure, and a cinque-pace: the first suit is hot and hasty, like a Scotch jig, and full as fantastical; the wedding, mannerly modest, as a measure, full of state and ancientry; and then comes repentance, and with his bad legs falls into the cinque-pace faster and faster, till he sink into his grave."

Therefore she exclaims with roguish irony—

"Good Lord, for alliance!—Thus goes every one to the world but I, and I am sun-burnt. I may sit in a corner, and cry heigh-ho for a husband!"

In her battles with Benedick she outdoes him in fantasy, both congruous and incongruous, or burlesque. Here, again, Shakespeare has evidently taken Lyly as his model, and has tried to reproduce the polished facets of his dialogue, while at the same time correcting its unnaturalness, and giving it fresh life. And Beatrice follows up her victory over Benedick, even when he is no longer her interlocutor, with a freedom which is now-a-days unthinkable in a young girl:—

"*D. Pedro.* You have put him down, lady; you have put him down.

"*Beat.* So I would not he should do me, my lord, lest I should prove the mother of fools."

But this unbridled whimsicality conceals the energetic virtues of a firm and noble character. When her poor cousin is falsely accused and cruelly put to shame; when those who should have been her natural protectors fall away from her, and even outside spectators like Benedick waver and lean to the accuser's side; then it is Beatrice alone who, unaffected even for an instant by the slander, indignantly and passionately takes up her cause, and shows herself faithful, high-minded, right-thinking, far-seeing, superior to them all—a pearl of a woman.

By her side Shakespeare has placed Benedick, a Mercutio redivivus; a youth who is the reverse of amatory, opposed to a maiden who is the reverse of tender. He abhors betrothal and marriage quite as vehemently as she, and is, from the man's point of view, no less scornful of all sentimentality than she, from the woman's; so that he and she, from the first, stand on a warlike footing with each other. In virtue of a profound and masterly psychological observation, Shakespeare presently makes these two fall suddenly in love with each other, over head and ears, for no better reason than that their friends persuade Benedick that Beatrice is secretly pining for love of him, and Beatrice that Benedick is mortally enamoured of her, accompanying this information with high-flown eulogies of both. Their thoughts were already occupied with each other; and now the amatory fancy flames forth in both of them all the more strongly, because it has so long been banked down. And here, where everything was of his own invention and he could move quite freely, Shakespeare has with delicate ingenuity brought the pair together, not by means of empty words, but in a common cause, Beatrice's first advance to Benedick taking place in the form of an appeal to him for chivalrous intervention in behalf of her innocent cousin.

The reversal in the mutual relations of Benedick and Beatrice is, moreover, highly interesting in so far as it is probably the first instance of anything like careful character-development which we have as yet encountered in any single play of Shakespeare's. In the earlier comedies there was nothing of the kind, and the chronicle-plays afforded no opportunity for it. The characters had simply to be brought into harmony with the given historical events, and in every case Shakespeare held firmly to the character-scheme once laid down. Neither *Richard III.* nor *Henry V.* presents any spiritual history; both kings, in the plays which take their names from them, are one and the same from first to last. Enough has already been said of Henry's change of front with respect to Falstaff in *Henry IV.;* we need only remark further that here the old play of *The Famous Victories*[1] unmistakably pointed the way to Shakespeare. But this melting of all that is hard and frozen in the natures of Benedick and Beatrice is without a parallel in any earlier work, and is quite plainly executed *con amore.* And the real substance of the play lies not in the plot from which it takes its name, but in the relation between these two characters, freely invented by Shakespeare.

Some other characters Shakespeare has added, and they are among the most admirable of his comic creations: the peace-officer Dogberry, and his subordinate Verges. Dogberry is a country constable, simple as a child, and vain as a peacock—a well-meaning, timid, honest, good-natured blockhead. To show that, in those days, such functionaries were almost as helpless in real life as they are here represented, Henrik Schück has cited a letter from Elizabeth's Prime Minister, Lord Burghley,

[1] In this play the king says :—

> " Ah, Tom, your former life greeves me,
> And makes me to abandon and abolish your company for ever,
> And therefore not upon pain of death to approach my presence
> By ten miles' space, then if I heare well of you,
> It may be I will do somewhat for you."

In Shakespeare :—

> " Till then I banish thee on pain of death
> As I have done the rest of my misleaders,
> Not to come near our person by ten mile.
> For competence of life I will allow you."

in which he relates how, in 1586, on a journey from London into the country, he found at the gate of every town ten or twelve persons armed with long poles. On inquiring, he learned that they were stationed there to seize three young men, unknown. Asked what description they had received of the malefactors, they replied that one of them was said to have a crooked nose. "And have you no other mark to recognise them by?" "No," was the answer. Moreover, they always stood so openly in a body, that no criminal could fail to give them a wide berth.

Dogberry is still less formidable than this detective force. Here are the wise and wary instructions which he gives to his watchmen :—

"*Dogberry.* If you meet a thief, you may suspect him, by virtue of your office, to be no true man; and, for such kind of men, the less you meddle or make with them, why, the more is for your honesty.

"2 *Watch.* If we know him to be a thief, shall we not lay hands on him?

"*Dogb.* Truly, by your office you may; but, I think, they that touch pitch will be defiled. The most peaceable way for you, if you do take a thief, is, to let him show himself what he is, and steal out of your company."

XXVIII

NEVER had Shakespeare produced with such rapidity and ease as in this bright and happy interval of two or three years. It is positively astounding to note all that he accomplished in the year 1600, when he stood, not exactly at the height of his poetical power, for that steadily increased, but at the height of his poetical serenity. Among the exquisite comedies he now writes, *As You Like It* is one of the most exquisite.

The play was entered in the Stationers' Register, along with *Much Ado About Nothing*, on the 4th of August 1600, and must in all probability have been written in that year. Meres does not mention it, in 1598, in his list of Shakespeare's plays; it contains (as already noted, page 36) a quotation from Marlowe's *Hero and Leander*, published in 1598—

> "Who ever lov'd, that lov'd not at first sight?"

a quotation, by the way, which sums up the matter of the comedy; and we find in Celia's words (i. 2), "Since the little wit that fools have was silenced," an allusion to the public and judicial burning of satirical publications which took place on the 1st of June 1599. As there does not seem to be room in the year 1599 for more works than we have already assigned to it, *As You Like It* must be taken as dating from the first half of the following year.

As usual, Shakespeare took from another poet the whole material of this enchanting comedy. His contemporary, Thomas Lodge (who, after leaving Oxford, became first a player and playwright in London, then a lawyer, then a doctor and writer on medical subjects, until he died of the plague in the year 1625), had in 1590 published a pastoral romance, with many poems interspersed, entitled *Euphues golden Legacie, found after his death in his Cell at Silexedra,*[1] which he had written, as he sets forth in his Dedication to Lord Hunsdon, "to beguile the time" on a voyage to the Canary Islands. The style is laboured and exceedingly diffuse, a true pastoral style; but Lodge had that

---

[1] Reprinted in Haziitt's Shakespeare's Library, ed. 1875, part i. vol. ii.

221

gift of mere external invention in which Shakespeare, with all his powers, was so deficient. All the different stories which the play contains or touches upon are found in Lodge, and likewise all the characters, with the exception of Jaques, Touchstone, and Audrey. Very remarkable to the attentive reader is Shakespeare's uniform passivity with regard to what he found in his sources, and his unwillingness to reject or alter anything, combined as it is with the most intense intellectual activity at the points upon which he concentrates his strength.

We find in *As You Like It*, as in Lodge, a wicked Duke who has expelled his virtuous brother, the lawful ruler, from his domains. The banished Duke, with his adherents, has taken refuge in the Forest of Arden, where they live as free a life as Robin Hood and his merry men, and where they are presently sought out by the Duke's daughter Rosalind and her cousin Celia, the daughter of the usurper, who will not let her banished friend wander forth alone. In the circle of nobility subordinate to the princes, there is also a wicked brother, Oliver, who seeks the life of his virtuous younger brother, Orlando, a hero as modest and amiable as he is brave. He and Rosalind fall in love with each other the moment they meet, and she makes sport with him throughout the play, disguised as a boy. These scenes should probably be acted as though he half recognised her. At last all ends happily. The wicked Duke most conveniently repents; the wicked brother is all of a sudden converted (quite without rhyme or reason) when Orlando, whom he has persecuted, kills a lioness—a lioness in the Forest of Arden!—which is about to spring upon him as he lies asleep. And the caitiff is rewarded (no less unreasonably), either for his villainy or for his conversion, with the hand of the lovely Celia.

This whole story is perfectly unimportant; Shakespeare, that is to say, evidently cared very little about it. We have here no attempt at a reproduction of reality, but one long festival of gaiety and wit, a soulful wit that vibrates into feeling.

First and foremost, the play typifies Shakespeare's longing, the longing of this great spirit, to get away from the unnatural city life, away from the false and ungrateful city folk, intent on business and on gain, away from flattery and falsehood and deceit, out into the country, where simple manners still endure, where it is easier to realise the dream of full freedom, and where the scent of the woods is so sweet. There the babble of the brooks has a subtler eloquence than any that is heard in cities; there the trees and even the stones say more to the wanderer's heart than the houses and streets of the capital; there he finds " good in everything."

The roving spirit has reawakened in his breast—the spirit which in bygone days sent him wandering with his gun through Charlcote Park—and out yonder in the lap of Nature, but in a

remoter, richer Nature than that which he has known, he dreams
of a communion between the best and ablest men, the fairest and
most delicate women, in ideal fantastic surroundings, far from the
ugly clamours of a public career, and the oppression of everyday
cares. A life of hunting and song, and simple repasts in the
open air, accompanied with witty talk; and at the same time a
life full to the brim with the dreamy happiness of love. And
with this life, the creation of his roving spirit, his gaiety and
his longing for Nature, he animates a fantastic Forest of Arden.

But with this he is not content. He dreams out the dream,
and feels that even such an ideal and untrammelled life could not
satisfy that strange and unaccountable spirit lurking in the inmost
depths of his nature, which turns everything into food for melancholy and satire. From this rib, then, taken from his own side,
he creates the figure of Jaques, unknown to the romance, and sets
him wandering through his pastoral comedy, lonely, retiring, self-
absorbed, a misanthrope from excess of tenderness, sensitiveness,
and imagination.

Jaques is like the first light and brilliant pencil-sketch for
Hamlet. Taine, and others after him, have tried to draw a
parallel between Jaques and Alceste—of all Molière's creations,
no doubt, the one who contains most of his own nature. But
there is no real analogy between them. In Jaques everything
wears the shimmering hues of wit and fantasy, in Alceste everything is bitter earnest. Indignation is the mainspring of Alceste's
misanthropy. He is disgusted at the falsehood around him, and
outraged to see that the scoundrel with whom he is at law,
although despised by every one, is nevertheless everywhere
received with open arms. He declines to remain in bad company,
even in the hearts of his friends; therefore he withdraws from
them. He loathes two classes of people :

> " Les uns parcequ'ils sont méchants et malfaisants,
> Et les autres pour être aux méchants complaisants."

These are the accents of Timon of Athens, who hated the
wicked for their wickedness, and other men for not hating the
wicked.

It is, then, in Shakespeare's Timon, of many years later, that
we can alone find an instructive parallel to Alceste. Alceste's
nature is keenly logical, classically French; it consists of sheer
uncompromising sincerity and pride, without sensibility and
without melancholy.

The melancholy of Jaques is a poetic dreaminess. He is
described to us (ii. 1) before we see him. The banished Duke
has just been blessing the adversity which drove him out into the
forest, where he is exempt from the dangers of the envious court.
He is on the point of setting forth to hunt, when he learns that

the melancholy Jaques repines at the cruelty of the chase, and calls him in that respect as great a usurper as the brother who drove him from his dukedom. The courtiers have found him stretched beneath an oak, and dissolved in pity for a poor wounded stag which stood beside the brook, and "heaved forth such groans That their discharge did stretch his leathern coat Almost to bursting." Jaques, they continue, "moralised this spectacle into a thousand similes:"—

> "Then, being there alone,
> Left and abandon'd of his velvet friends;
> ''Tis right,' quoth he; 'thus misery doth part
> The flux of company.' Anon, a careless herd,
> Full of the pasture, jumps along by him,
> And never stays to greet him. 'Ay,' quoth Jaques,
> 'Sweep on, you fat and greasy citizens;
> 'Tis just the fashion: wherefore do you look
> Upon that poor and broken bankrupt there?"

His bitterness springs from a too tender sensibility, a sensibility like that of Sakya Mouni before him, who made tenderness to animals part of his religion, and like that of Shelley after him, who, in his pantheism, realised the kinship between his own soul and that of the brute creation.

Thus we are prepared for his entrance. He introduces himself into the Duke's circle (ii. 7) with a glorification of the fool's motley. He has encountered Touchstone in the forest, and is enraptured with him. The motley fool lay basking in the sun, and when Jaques said to him, "Good morrow, fool!" he answered, "Call me not fool till heaven have sent me fortune." Then this sapient fool drew a dial from his pocket, and said very wisely—

> "'It is ten o'clock:
> Thus may we see,' quoth he, 'how the world wags:
> 'Tis but an hour ago since it was nine,
> And after one hour more 'twill be eleven;
> And so from hour to hour we ripe and ripe,
> And then from hour to hour we rot and rot,
> And thereby hangs a tale.'"

"O noble fool!" Jaques exclaims with enthusiasm. "A worthy fool! Motley's the only wear."

In moods of humorous melancholy, it must have seemed to Shakespeare as though he himself were one of these jesters, who had the privilege of uttering truths to great people and on the stage, if only they did not blurt them out directly, but disguised them under a mask of folly. It was in a similar mood that Heinrich Heine, centuries later, addressed to the German people these words: "Ich bin dein Kunz von der Rosen, dein Narr."

Therefore it is that Shakespeare makes Jaques exclaim—

> " O, that I were a fool!
> I am ambitious for a motley coat."

When the Duke answers, " Thou shalt have one," he declares that it is the one thing he wants, and that the others must "weed their judgments " of the opinion that he is wise :—

> " I must have liberty
> Withal, as large a charter as the wind,
> To blow on whom I please; for so fools have:
> And they that are most galled with my folly,
> They most must laugh.
>   .   .   .   .
> Invest me in my motley : give me leave
> To speak my mind, and I will through and through
> Cleanse the foul body of the infected world,
> If they will patiently receive my medicine."

It is Shakespeare's own mood that we hear in these words. The voice is his. The utterance is far too large for Jaques : he is only a mouthpiece for the poet. Or let us say that his figure dilates in such passages as this, and we see in him a Hamlet *avant la lettre*.

When the Duke, in answer to this outburst, denies Jaques' right to chide and satirise others, since he has himself been "a libertine, As sensual as the brutish sting itself," the poet evidently defends himself in the reply which he places in the mouth of the melancholy philosopher :—

> " Why, who cries out on pride,
> That can therein tax any private party ?
> Doth it not flow as hugely as the sea,
> Till that the weary very means do ebb ?
> What woman in the city do I name,
> When that I say, the city-woman bears
> The cost of princes on unworthy shoulders ?
> Who can come in, and say that I mean her,
> When such a one as she, such is her neighbour ? "

This exactly anticipates Holberg's self-defence in the character of Philemon in *The Fortunate Shipwreck*. The poet is evidently rebutting a common prejudice against his art. And as he makes Jaques an advocate for the freedom which poetry must claim, so also he employs him as a champion of the actor's mis-judged calling, in placing in his mouth the magnificent speech on the Seven Ages of Man. Alluding, no doubt, to the motto of *Totus Mundus Agit Histrionem*, inscribed under the Hercules as Atlas, which was the sign of the Globe Theatre, this speech opens with the words :—

P

> " All the world's a stage,
> And all the men and women merely players;
> They have their exits and their entrances;
> And one man in his time plays many parts."

Ben Jonson is said to have inquired, in an epigram against the motto of the Globe Theatre, where the spectators were to be found if all the men and women were players? And an epigram attributed to Shakespeare gives the simple answer that all are players and audience at one and the same time. Jaques' survey of the life of man is admirably concise and impressive. The last line—

> " Sans teeth, sans eyes, sans taste, sans everything "—

with its half French equivalent for " without," is imitated from the *Henriade* of the French poet Garnier, which was not translated, and which Shakespeare must consequently have read in the original.

This same Jaques, who gives evidence of so wide an outlook over human life, is in daily intercourse, as we have said, nervously misanthropic and formidably witty. He is sick of polite society, pines for solitude, takes leave of a pleasant companion with the words: " I thank you for your company; but, good faith, I had as lief have been myself alone." Yet we must not take his melancholy and his misanthropy too seriously. His melancholy is a comedy-melancholy, his misanthropy is only the humourist's craving to give free vent to his satirical inspirations.

And there is, as aforesaid, only a certain part of Shakespeare's inmost nature in this Jaques, a Shakespeare of the future, a Hamlet in germ, but not that Shakespeare who now bathes in the sunlight and lives in uninterrupted prosperity, in growing favour with the many, and borne aloft by the admiration and goodwill of the few. We must seek for this Shakespeare in the interspersed songs, in the drollery of the fool, in the lovers' rhapsodies, in the enchanting babble of the ladies. He is, like Providence, everywhere and nowhere.

When Celia says (i. 2), " Let us sit and mock the good housewife, Fortune, from her wheel, that her gifts may henceforth be bestowed equally," she strikes, as though with a tuning-fork, the keynote of the comedy. The sluice is opened for that torrent of jocund wit, shimmering with all the rainbows of fancy, which is now to rush seething and swirling along.

The Fool is essential to the scheme: for the Fool's stupidity is the grindstone of wit, and the Fool's wit is the touchstone of character. Hence his name.

The ways of the real world, however, are not forgotten. The good make enemies by their very goodness, and the words of the old servant Adam (Shakespeare's own part) to his young master Orlando (ii. 3), sound sadly enough :—

"Your praise is come too swiftly home before you.
Know you not, master, to some kind of men
Their graces serve them but as enemies?
No more do yours : your virtues, gentle master,
Are sanctified, and holy traitors to you.
O, what a world is this, when what is comely
Envenoms him that bears it ! "

But soon the poet's eye is opened to a more consolatory life-philosophy, combined with an unequivocal contempt for school-philosophy. There seems to be a scoffing allusion to a book of the time, which was full of the platitudes of celebrated philosophers, in Touchstone's speech to William (v. 1), "The heathen philosopher, when he had desire to eat a grape, would open his lips when he put it into his mouth, meaning thereby that grapes were made to eat and lips to open;" but no doubt there also lurks in this speech a certain lack of respect for even the much-belauded wisdom of tradition. The relativity of all things, at that time a new idea, is expounded with lofty humour by the Fool in his answer to the question what he thinks of this pastoral life (iii. 2) :—

"Truly, shepherd, in respect of itself it is a good life, but in respect that it is a shepherd's life, it is naught. In respect that it is solitary, I like it very well; but in respect that it is private, it .is a very vile life. Now, in respect it is in the fields, it pleaseth me well; but in respect it is not in the court, it is tedious. As it is a spare life, look you, it fits my humour well; but as there is no more plenty in it, it goes much against my stomach. Hast any philosophy in thee, shepherd?"

The shepherd's answer makes direct sport of philosophy, in the style of Molière's gibe, when he accounts for the narcotic effect of opium by explaining that the drug possesses a certain *facultas dormitativa* :—

"*Corin.* No more, but that I know, the more one sickens, the worse at ease he is; and that he that wants money, means, and content, is without three good friends; that the property of rain is to wet, and fire to burn; that good pasture makes fat sheep, and that a great cause of the night is lack of the sun. . . .
"*Touchstone.* Such a one is a natural philosopher."

This sort of philosophy leads up, as it were, to Rosalind's sweet gaiety and heavenly kindness.

The two cousins, Rosalind and Celia, seem at first glance like variations of the two cousins, Beatrice and Hero, in the play Shakespeare has just finished. Rosalind and Beatrice in particular are akin in their victorious wit. Yet the difference between them is very great; Shakespeare never repeats himself. The wit of Beatrice is aggressive and challenging; we see, as it were, the gleam of a rapier in it. Rosalind's wit is gaiety without a sting; the gleam in it is of "that sweet radiance" which Oehlenschläger attributed to Freia; her sportive nature masks the depth of her love. Beatrice can be brought to love because she is a woman, and stands in no respect apart from her sex; but she is not of an amatory nature. Rosalind is seized with a passion for Orlando the instant she sets eyes on him. From the moment of Beatrice's first appearance she is defiant and combative, in the highest of spirits. We are introduced to Rosalind as a poor bird with a drooping wing; her father is banished, she is bereft of her birth-right, and is living on sufferance as companion to the usurper's daughter, being, indeed, half a prisoner in the palace, where till lately she reigned as princess. It is not until she has donned the doublet and hose, appears in the likeness of a page, and wanders at her own sweet will in the open air and the greenwood, that she recovers her radiant humour, and roguish merriment flows from her lips like the trilling of a bird.

Nor is the man she loves, like Benedick, an overweening gallant with a sharp tongue and an unabashed bearing. This youth, though brave as a hero and strong as an athlete, is a child in inexperience, and so bashful in the presence of the woman who instantly captivates him, that it is she who is the first to betray her sympathy for him, and has even to take the chain from her own neck and hang it around his before he can so much as muster up courage to hope for her love. So, too, we find him passing his time in hanging poems to her upon the trees, and carving the name of Rosalind in their bark. She amuses herself, in her page's attire, by making herself his con-fidant, and pretending, as it were in jest, to be his Rosalind. She cannot bring herself to confess her passion, although she can think and talk (to Celia) of no one but him, and although his delay of a few minutes in keeping tryst with her sets her beside herself with impatience. She is as sensitive as she is intelligent, in this differing from Portia, to whom, in other respects, she bears some resemblance, though she lacks her persuasive eloquence, and is, on the whole, more tender, more virginal. She faints when Oliver, to excuse Orlando's delay, brings her a handker-chief stained with his blood; yet has sufficient self-mastery to say with a smile the moment she recovers, "I pray you tell your brother how well I counterfeited." She is quite at her ease in her male attire, like Viola and Imogen after her. The fact that female parts were played by youths had, of course, something to do with the frequency of these disguises.

Here is a specimen of her wit (iii. 2). Orlando has evaded the page's question what o'clock it is, alleging that there are no clocks in the forest.

"*Rosalind.* Then, there is no true lover in the forest; else sighing every minute, and groaning every hour, would detect the lazy foot of Time as well as a clock.

"*Orlando.* And why not the swift foot of Time? had not that been as proper?

"*Ros.* By no means, sir. Time travels in divers paces with divers persons. I'll tell you, who Time ambles withal, who Time trots withal, who Time gallops withal, and who he stands still withal.

"*Orl.* I pr'ythee, who doth he trot withal?

"*Ros.* Marry, he trots hard with a young maid, between the contract of her marriage, and the day it is solemnised: if the interim be but a se'nnight, Time's pace is so hard that it seems the length of seven years.

"*Orl.* Who ambles Time withal?

"*Ros.* With a priest that lacks Latin, and a rich man that hath not the gout; for the one sleeps easily, because he cannot study; and the other lives merrily, because he feels no pain. . . .

"*Orl.* Who doth he gallop withal?

"*Ros.* With a thief to the gallows; for though he go as softly as foot can fall, he thinks himself too soon there.

"*Orl.* Who stays it still withal?

"*Ros.* With lawyers in the vacation; for they sleep between term and term, and then they perceive not how Time moves."

She is unrivalled in vivacity and inventiveness. In every answer she discovers gunpowder anew, and she knows how to use it to boot. She explains that she had an old uncle who warned her against love and women, and, from the vantage-ground of her doublet and hose, she declares—

"I thank God, I am not a woman, to be touched with so many giddy offences, as he hath generally taxed their whole sex withal.

"*Orl.* Can you remember any of the principal evils that he laid to the charge of women?

"*Ros.* There were none principal: they were all like one another, as half-pence are; every one fault seeming monstrous, till its fellow fault came to match it.

"*Orl.* I pr'ythee, recount some of them.

"*Ros.* No; I will not cast away my physic but on those that are sick. There is a man haunts the forest, that abuses our young plants with carving Rosalind on their barks; hangs odes upon hawthorns, and elegies on brambles; all, forsooth, deifying the name of Rosalind: if I could meet that fancy-monger, I would give him some good counsel, for he seems to have the quotidian of love upon him."

Orlando admits that he is the culprit, and they are to meet daily that she may exorcise his passion. She bids him woo her in jest, as though she were indeed Rosalind, and answers (iv. 1):—

"*Ros.* Well, in her person, I say—I will not have you.

"*Orl.* Then, in mine own person, I die.

"*Ros.* No, 'faith, die by attorney. The poor world is almost six thousand years old, and in all this time there was not any man died in his own person, *videlicet*, in a love-cause. Troilus had his brains dashed out with a Grecian club; yet he did what he could to die before, and he is one of the patterns of love. Leander, he would have lived many a fair year, though Hero had turned nun, if it had not been for a hot midsummer night; for, good youth, he went but forth to wash him in the Hellespont, and, being taken with the cramp, was drowned, and the foolish chroniclers of that age found it was—Hero of Sestos. But these are all lies: men have died from time to time, and worms have eaten them, but not for love."

What Rosalind says of women in general applies to herself in particular: you will never find her without an answer until you find her without a tongue. And there is always a bright and merry fantasy in her answers. She is literally radiant with youth, imagination, and the joy of loving so passionately and being so passionately beloved. And it is marvellous how thoroughly feminine is her wit. Too many of the witty women in books written by men have a man's intelligence. Rosalind's wit is tempered by feeling.

She has no monopoly of wit in this Arcadia of Arden. Every one in the play is witty, even the so-called simpletons. It is a festival of wit. At some points Shakespeare seems to have followed no stricter principle than the simple one of making each interlocutor outbid the other in wit (see, for example, the conversation between Touchstone and the country wench whom he befools). The result is that the piece is bathed in a sunshiny humour. And amid all the gay and airy wit-skirmishes, amid the cooing love-duets of all the happy youths and maidens, the poet intersperses the melancholy solos of his Jaques :—

" I have neither the scholar's melancholy, which is emulation ; nor the musician's, which is fantastical ; nor the courtier's, which is proud ; nor the soldier's, which is ambitious ; nor the lawyer's, which is politic ; nor the lady's, which is nice ; nor the lover's, which is all these ; but it is a melancholy of mine own, compounded of many simples, extracted from many objects."

This is the melancholy which haunts the thinker and the great creative artist; but in Shakespeare it as yet modulated with ease into the most engaging and delightful merriment.

XXIX

CONSUMMATE SPIRITUAL HARMONY—TWELFTH NIGHT—
JIBES AT PURITANISM—THE LANGUISHING CHARAC-
TERS—VIOLA'S INSINUATING GRACE—FAREWELL TO
MIRTH

IF the reader would picture to himself Shakespeare's mood during
this short space of time at the end of the old century and beginning of the new, let him recall some morning when he has awakened
with the sensation of complete physical well-being, not only
feeling no definite or indefinite pain or uneasiness, but with a
positive consciousness of happy activity in all his organs: when
he drew his breath lightly, his head was clear and free, his heart
beat peacefully: when the mere act of living was a delight: when
the soul dwelt on happy moments in the past and dreamed of joys
to come. Recall such a moment, and then conceive it intensified
an hundredfold—conceive your memory, imagination, observation,
acuteness, and power of expression a hundred times multiplied—
and you may divine Shakespeare's prevailing mood in those days,
when the brighter and happier sides of his nature were turned to
the sun.

There are days when the sun seems to have put on a new
and festal splendour, when the air is like a caress to the cheek,
and when the glamour of the moonlight seems doubly sweet;
days when men appear manlier and wittier, women fairer and
more delicate than usual, and when those who are disagreeable
and even odious to us appear, not formidable, but ludicrous—so
that we feel ourselves exalted above the level of our daily life,
emancipated and happy. Such days Shakespeare was now passing
through.

It is at this period, too, that he makes sport of his adversaries
the Puritans without bitterness, with exquisite humour. Even
in *As You Like It* (iii. 2), we find a little allusion to them, where
Rosalind says, " O most gentle Jupiter!—what tedious homily of
love have you wearied your parishioners withal, and never cried,
'Have patience, good people!'" In his next play, the typical,
solemn, and self-righteous Puritan is held up to ridicule in the
Don-Quixote-like personage of the moralising and pompous Malvolio, who is launched upon a billowy sea of burlesque situations.
Of course the poet goes to work with the greatest circumspection.

Sir Toby has made some inquiry about Malvolio, to which Maria answers (ii. 3):—

"*Maria.* Marry, sir, sometimes he is a kind of Puritan.

"*Sir Andrew.* O! if I thought that, I'd beat him like a dog.

"*Sir Toby.* What, for being a Puritan? thy exquisite reason, dear knight?

"*Sir And.* I have no exquisite reason for't, but I have reason good enough.

"*Mar.* The devil a Puritan that he is, or anything constantly but a time-pleaser; an affectioned ass, that cons state without book, and utters it by great swarths."

Not otherwise does Molière expressly insist that Tartuffe is not a clergyman, and Holberg that Jacob von Tyboe is not an officer.

A forged letter, purporting to be written by his noble mistress, is made to fall into Malvolio's hands, in which she begs for his love, and instructs him, as a sign of his affection towards her, always to smile, and to wear cross-gartered yellow stockings. He "smiles his face into more lines than are in the new map [of 1598] with the augmentation of the Indies;" he wears his preposterous garters in the most preposterous fashion. The conspirators pretend to think him mad, and treat him accordingly. The Clown comes to visit him disguised in the cassock of Sir Topas the curate. "Well," says the mock priest (not without intention on the poet's part), when Maria gives him the gown, "I'll put it on, and I will dissemble myself in't; and I would I were the first that ever dissembled in such a gown."

It is to Malvolio, too, that the merry and mellow Sir Toby, amid the applause of the Clown, addresses the taunt:—

"*Sir Toby.* Dost thou think, because thou art virtuous, there shall be no more cakes and ale?

"*Clown.* Yes, by Saint Anne; and ginger shall be hot i' the mouth too."

In these words, which were one day to serve as a motto to Byron's *Don Juan*, there lies a gay and daring declaration of rights.

Twelfth Night, or What you Will, must have been written in 1601, for in the above-mentioned diary kept by John Manningham, of the Middle Temple, we find this entry, under the date February 2, 1602: "At our feast wee had a play called Twelve Night, or what you will, much like the commedy of errores, or Menechmi in Plautus, but most like and neere to that in Italian called *Inganni*. A good practise in it to make the steward beleeve his lady widdowe was in love with him," &c. That the play cannot have been written much earlier is proved by the fact that the song, "Farewell, dear heart, since I must needs be gone," which is sung by Sir Toby and the Clown (ii. 3), first appeared in a song-book (*The Booke of Ayres*) published by Robert Jones,

London, 1601. Shakespeare has altered its wording very slightly. In all probability *Twelfth Night* was one of the four plays which were performed before the court at Whitehall by the Lord Chamberlain's company at Christmastide, 1601–2, and no doubt it was acted for the first time on the evening from which it takes its name.

Among several Italian plays which bore the name of *Gl' Inganni* there is one by Curzio Gonzaga, published in Venice in 1592, in which a sister dresses herself as her brother and takes the name of Cesare—in Shakespeare, Cesario—and another, published in Venice in 1537, the action of which bears a general resemblance to that of *Twelfth Night*. In this play, too, passing mention is made of one "Malevolti," who may have suggested to Shakespeare the name Malvolio.

The matter of the play is found in a novel of Bandello's, translated in Belleforest's *Histoires Tragiques ;* and also in Barnabe Rich's translation of Cinthio's *Hecatomithi*, published in 1581, which Shakespeare appears to have used. The whole comic part of the action, and the characters of Malvolio, Sir Toby, Sir Andrew Aguecheek, and the Clown, are of Shakespeare's own invention.

There occurs in Ben Jonson's *Every Man out of his Humour* a speech which seems very like an allusion to *Twelfth Night ;* but as Jonson's play is of earlier date, the speech, if the allusion be not fanciful, must have been inserted later.[1]

As was to be expected, *Twelfth Night* became exceedingly popular. The learned Leonard Digges, the translator of Claudian, enumerating in his verses, "Upon Master William Shakespeare" (1640), the poet's most popular characters, mentions only three from the comedies, and these from *Much Ado* and *Twelfth Night*. He says :—

> "Let but *Beatrice*
> And *Benedicke* be seene, loe in a trice
> The Cockpit, Galleries, Boxes, all are full
> To hear *Malvoglio*, that crosse garter'd Gull."

Twelfth Night is perhaps the most graceful and harmonious comedy Shakespeare ever wrote. It is certainly that in which all the notes the poet strikes, the note of seriousness and of raillery, of passion, of tenderness, and of laughter, blend in the richest and fullest concord. It is like a symphony in which no strain can be dispensed with, or like a picture veiled in a golden haze, into which all the colours resolve themselves. The play does not overflow with wit and gaiety like its predecessor ; we feel that Shakespeare's joy of life has culminated and is about to pass over

---

[1] There is some (ironic) discussion of a possible criticism that might be brought against a playwright : "That the argument of his comedy might have been of some other nature, as of a duke to be in love with a countess, and that countess to be in love with the duke's son, and the son to love the lady's waiting-maid ; some such cross woning, with a clown to their servingman. . . ."

into melancholy; but there is far more unity in it than in *As You Like It*, and it is a great deal more dramatic.

A. W. Schlegel long ago made the penetrating observation that, in the opening speech of the comedy, Shakespeare reminds us how the same word, "fancy," was applied in his day both to love and to fancy in the modern sense of the term; whence the critic argued, not without ingenuity, that love, regarded as an affair of the imagination rather than of the heart, is the fundamental theme running through all the variations of the play. Others have since sought to prove that capricious fantasy is the fundamental trait in the physiognomy of all the characters. Tieck has compared the play to a great iridescent butterfly, fluttering through pure blue air, and soaring in its golden glory from the many-coloured flowers into the sunshine.

Twelfth Night, in Shakespeare's time, brought the Christmas festivities of the upper classes to an end; among the common people they usually lasted until Candlemas. On Twelfth Night all sorts of sports took place. The one who chanced to find a bean baked into a cake was hailed as the Bean King, chose himself a Bean Queen, introduced a reign of unbridled frivolity, and issued whimsical commands, which had to be punctually obeyed. Ulrici has sought to discover in this an indication that the play represents a sort of lottery, in which Sebastian, the Duke, and Maria chance to win the great prize. The bibulous Sir Toby, however, can scarcely be regarded as a particularly desirable prize for Maria; and the second title of the play, *What you Will*, indicates that Shakespeare did not lay any stress upon the *Twelfth Night*.

This comedy is connected by certain filaments with its predecessor, *As You Like It*. The passion which Viola, in her male attire, awakens in Olivia, reminds us of that with which Rosalind inspires Phebe. But the motive is quite differently handled. While Rosalind gaily and unfeelingly repudiates Phebe's burning love, Viola is full of tender compassion for the lady whom her disguise has led astray. In the admirably worked-up confusion between Viola and her twin brother Sebastian, an effect from the *Comedy of Errors* is repeated; but the different circumstances and method of treatment make this motive also practically new.

With a careful and even affectionate hand, Shakespeare has elaborated each one of the many characters in the play.

The amiable and gentle Duke languishes, sentimental and fancy-sick, in hopeless enamourment. He is devoted to the fair Countess Olivia, who will have nothing to say to him, and whom he none the less besieges with his suit. An ardent lover of music, he turns to it for consolation; and among the songs sung to him by the Clown and others, there occurs the delicate little poem, of wonderful rhythmic beauty, "Come away, come away, death." It exactly expresses the soft and melting mood in which his days pass, lapped in a nerveless melancholy. To the melody abiding in it we may apply the lovely words spoken by Viola of the melody which preludes it :—

> " It gives a very echo to the seat
> Where love is throned."

In his fruitless passion, the Duke has become nervous and excitable, inclined to violent self-contradictions. In one and the lame scene (ii. 4) he first says that man's love is

> " More giddy and unfirm,
> More longing, wavering, sooner lost and worn "

than woman's; and then, a little further on, he says of his own love—

> " There is no woman's sides
> Can bide the beating of so strong a passion
> As love doth give my heart; no woman's heart
> So big to hold so much : they lack retention."

The Countess Olivia forms a pendant to the Duke; she, like him, is full of yearning melancholy. With an ostentatious exaggeration of sisterly love, she has vowed to pass seven whole years veiled like a nun, consecrating her whole life to sorrow for her dead brother. Yet we find in her speeches no trace of this devouring sorrow; she jests with her household, and rules it ably and well, until, at the first sight of the disguised Viola, she flames out into passion, and, careless of the traditional reserve of her sex, takes the most daring steps to win the supposed youth. She is conceived as an unbalanced character, who passes at a bound from exaggerated hatred for all worldly things to total forgetfulness of her never-to-be-forgotten sorrow. Yet she is not comic like Phebe; for Shakespeare has indicated that it is the Sebastian type, foreshadowed in the disguised Viola, which is irresistible to her; and Sebastian, we see, at once requites the love which his sister had to reject. Her utterance of her passion, moreover, is always poetically beautiful.

Yet while she is sighing in vain for Viola, she necessarily appears as though seized with a mild erotic madness, similar to that of the Duke : and the folly of each is parodied in a witty and delightful fashion by Malvolio's entirely ludicrous love for his mistress, and vain confidence that she returns it. Olivia feels and says this herself, where she exclaims (iii. 4)—

> " Go call him hither.—I am as mad as he
> If sad and merry madness equal be."

Malvolio's figure is drawn in very few strokes, but with incomparable certainty of touch. He is unforgetable in his turkey-like pomposity, and the heartless practical joke which is played off upon him is developed with the richest comic effect. The inimitable love-letter, which Maria indites to him in a handwriting like that of the Countess, brings to light all the lurking vanity in his nature, and makes his self-esteem, which was patent enough before, assume the most extravagant forms. The scene in which he approaches Olivia, and triumphantly quotes the expressions in the letter, "yellow stockings," and "cross-gartered," while every word confirms her in the belief that he is mad, is one of the most effective on the comic stage. Still more irresistible is the scene (iv. 2) in which Malvolio is imprisoned as a madman in a dark room, while the Clown outside now assumes the voice of the Curate, and seeks to exorcise the devil in him, and again, in his own voice, converses with the supposed Curate, sings songs, and promises Malvolio to carry messages for him. We have here a comic *jeu de théâtre* of the first order.

In harmony with the general tone of the play, the Clown is less witty and more musical than Touchstone in *As You Like It*. He is keenly alive to the dignity of his calling: "Foolery, sir, does walk about the orb like the sun: it shines everywhere." He has many delightful sayings, as for example, "Many a good hanging prevents a bad marriage," or the following demonstration (v. 1) that one is the better for one's foes, and the worse for one's friends :—

"Marry, sir, my friends praise me, and make an ass of me; now, my foes tell me plainly I am an ass: so that by my foes, sir, I profit in the knowledge of myself, and by my friends I am abused: so that, conclusions to be as kisses, if your four negatives make your two affirmatives, why then, the worse for my friends, and the better for my foes."

Shakespeare even departs from his usual practice, and, as though to guard against any misunderstanding on the part of his public, makes Viola expound quite dogmatically that it "craves a kind of wit" to play the fool (iii. 1):—

"He must observe their mood on whom he jests,
The quality of persons, and the time,
And, like the haggard, check at every feather
That comes before his eye. This is a practice
As full of labour as a wise man's art."

The Clown forms a sort of connecting-link between the serious characters and the exclusively comic figures of the play—the pair of knights, Sir Toby Belch and Sir Andrew Aguecheek, who are entirely of Shakespeare's own invention. They are sharply contrasted. Sir Toby, sanguine, red-nosed, burly, a practical joker, always ready for "a hair of the dog that bit him," a figure after the style of Bellman;[1] Sir Andrew, pale as though with the

---

[1] See *ante*, p. 185.

ague, with thin, smooth, straw-coloured hair, a wretched little nincompoop, who values himself on his dancing and fencing, quarrelsome and chicken-hearted, boastful and timid in the same breath, and grotesque in his every movement. He is a mere echo and shadow of the heroes of his admiration, born to be the sport of his associates, their puppet, and their butt; and while he is so brainless as to think it possible he may win the love of the beautiful Olivia, he has at the same time an inward suspicion of his own stupidity which now and then comes in refreshingly: "Methinks sometimes I have no more wit than a Christian or an ordinary man has; but I am a great eater of beef, and, I believe, that does harm to my wit" (i. 3). He does not understand the simplest phrase he hears, and is such a mere reflex and parrot that "I too" is, as it were, the watchword of his existence. Shakespeare has immortalised him once for all in his reply when Sir Toby boasts that Maria adores him (ii. 3), "I was adored once too." Sir Toby sums him up in the phrase:

"For Andrew, if he were opened, and you find so much blood in his liver as will clog the foot of a flea, I'll eat the rest of the anatomy."

The central character in *Twelfth Night* is Viola, of whom her brother does not say a word too much when, thinking that she has been drowned, he exclaims, "She bore a mind that envy could not but call fair."

Shipwrecked on the coast of Illyria, her first wish is to enter the service of the young Countess; but learning that Olivia is inaccessible, she determines to dress as a page (a eunuch) and approach the young unmarried Duke, of whom she has heard her father speak with warmth. He at once makes the deepest impression upon her heart, but being ignorant of her sex, does not dream of what is passing within her; so that she is perpetually placed in the painful position of being employed as a messenger from the man she loves to another woman. She gives utterance to her love in carefully disguised and touching words (ii. 4) :—

" My father had a daughter lov'd a man,
    As it might be, perhaps, were I a woman,
    I should your lordship.
        Duke.   And what's her history?
        Vio. A blank, my lord. She never told her love,—
    But let concealment, like a worm i' the bud,
    Feed on her damask cheek: she pin'd in thought:
    And, with a green and yellow melancholy,
    She sat like Patience on a monument,
    Smiling at grief."

But the passion which possesses her makes her a more eloquent messenger of love than she designs to be. To Olivia's question as to what she would do if she loved her as her master does, she answers (i. 5):—

> Make me a willow cabin at your gate,
> And call upon my soul within the house;
> Write loyal cantons of contemned love,
> And sing them loud even in the dead of night;
> Holla your name to the reverberate hills,
> And make the babbling gossip of the air
> Cry out, Olivia! O! you should not rest
> Between the elements of air and earth,
> But you should pity me."

In short, if she were a man, she would display all the energy which the Duke lacks. No wonder that, against her own will, she awakens Olivia's love. She herself, as a woman, is condemned to passivity; her love is wordless, deep, and patient. In spite of her sound understanding, she is a creature of emotion. It is a very characteristic touch when, in the scene (iii. 5) where Antonio, taking her for Sebastian, recalls the services he has rendered, and begs for assistance in his need, she exclaims that there is nothing, not even "lying vainness, babbling drunkenness, or any taint of vice," that she hates so much as ingratitude. However bright her intelligence, her soul from first to last outshines it. Her incognito, which does not bring her joy as it does to Rosalind, but only trouble and sorrow, conceals the most delicate womanliness. She never, like Rosalind or Beatrice, utters an audacious or wanton word. Her heart-winning charm more than makes up for the high spirits and sparkling humour of the earlier heroines. She is healthful and beautiful, like these her somewhat elder sisters; and she has also their humorous eloquence, as she proves in her first scene with Olivia. Yet there rests upon her lovely figure a tinge of melancholy. She is an impersonation of that "farewell to mirth" which an able English critic discerns in this last comedy of Shakespeare's brightest years.[1]

---

[1] " It is in some sort a farewell to mirth, and the mirth is of the finest quality, an incomparable ending. Shakespeare has done greater things, but he has never done anything more delightful."—*Arthur Symons.*

XXX

*THE REVOLUTION IN SHAKESPEARE'S SOUL—THE GROW-
ING MELANCHOLY OF THE FOLLOWING PERIOD—
PESSIMISM, MISANTHROPY*

FOR the time is now approaching when mirth, and even the
joy of life, are extinguished in his soul. Heavy clouds have
massed themselves on his mental horizon—their nature we can
only divine—and gnawing sorrows and disappointments have
beset him. We see his melancholy growing and extending; we
observe its changing expressions, without knowing its causes.
This only we know, that the stage which he contemplates with
his mind's eye, like the material stage on which he works, is
now hung with black. A veil of melancholy descends over
both.

He no longer writes comedies, but sends a train of gloomy
tragedies across the boards which so lately echoed to the laughter
of Beatrice and Rosalind.

From this point, for a certain period, all his impressions of
life and humanity become ever more and more painful. We can
see in his Sonnets how even in earlier and happier years a restless
passionateness had been constantly at war with the serenity of his
soul, and we can note how, at this time also, he was subject to
accesses of stormy and vehement unrest. As time goes on, we
can discern in the series of his dramas how not only what he
saw in public and political life, but also his private experience,
began to inspire him, partly with a burning compassion for
humanity, partly with a horror of mankind as a breed of noxious
wild animals, partly, too, with loathing for the stupidity, falsity,
and baseness of his fellow-creatures. These feelings gradually
crystallise into a large and lofty contempt for humanity, until,
after a space of eight years, another revolution occurs in his
prevailing mood. The extinguished sun glows forth afresh, the
black heaven has become blue again, and the kindly interest in
everything human has returned. He attains peace at last in a
sublime and melancholy clearness of vision. Bright moods,
sunny dreams from the days of his youth, return upon him,
bringing with them, if not laughter, at least smiles. High-
spirited gaiety has for ever vanished; but his imagination, feeling itself less constrained than of old by the laws of reality,

moves lightly and at ease, though a deep earnestness now underlies it, and much experience of life.

But this inward emancipation from the burthen of earthly life
does not occur, as we have said, until about eight years after the
point which we have now reached.

For a little time longer the strong and genial joy of life is still
dominant in his mind. Then it begins to darken, and, after a
short tropical twilight, there is night in his soul and in all his
works.

In the tragedy of *Julius Cæsar* there still reigns only a manly
seriousness. The theme seems to have attracted him on account
of the analogy between the conspiracy against Cæsar and the
conspiracy against Elizabeth. Despite the foolish precipitancy
of their action, the leaders of this conspiracy, men like Essex
and his comrade Southampton, had Shakespeare's full personal
sympathy; and he transferred some of that sympathy to Brutus
and Cassius. He created Brutus under the deeply-imprinted conviction that unpractical magnanimity, like that of his noble friends,
is unfitted to play an effective part in the drama of history, and
that errors of policy revenge themselves at least as sternly as
moral delinquencies.

In *Hamlet* Shakespeare's growing melancholy and bitterness
take the upper hand. For the hero, as for the poet, youth's bright
outlook upon life has been overclouded. Hamlet's belief and trust
in mankind have gone to wreck. Under the disguise of apparent
madness, the melancholy life-lore which Shakespeare, at his fortieth
year, had stored up within him, here finds expression in words of
spiritual profundity such as had not yet been thought or uttered
in Northern Europe.

We catch a glimpse at this point of one of the subsidiary causes
of Shakespeare's melancholy. As actor and playwright he stands
in a more and more strained relation to the continually growing
Free Church movement of the age, to Puritanism, which he comes
to regard as nothing but narrow-mindedness and hypocrisy. It
was the deadly enemy of his calling; it secured, even in his lifetime, the prohibition of theatrical performances in the provinces,
a prohibition which after his death was extended to the capital.
From *Twelfth Night* onwards, an unremitting war against Puritanism, conceived as hypocrisy, is carried on through *Hamlet*,
through the revised version of *All's Well that Ends Well*, and
through *Measure for Measure*, in which his wrath rises to a
tempestuous pitch, and creates a figure to which Molière's Tartuffe can alone supply a parallel.

What struck him so forcibly in these years was the pitifulness
of earthly life, exposed as it is to disasters, not allotted by destiny,
but brought about by a conjunction of stupidity with malevolence.

It is especially the power of malevolence that now looms large
before his eyes. We see this in Hamlet's astonishment that it is

possible for a man "to smile and smile and be a villain." Still more strongly is it apparent in *Measure for Measure* (v. 1):—

> " Make not impossible
> That which but seems unlike. 'Tis not impossible,
> But one, the wicked'st caitiff on the ground,
> May seem as shy, as grave, as just, as absolute,
> As Angelo ; even so may Angelo,
> In all his dressings, characts, titles, forms,
> Be an arch-villain."

It is this line of thought that leads to the conception of Iago, Goneril, and Regan, and to the wild outbursts of Timon of Athens.

Macbeth is Shakespeare's first attempt, after *Hamlet*, to explain the tragedy of life as a product of brutality and wickedness in conjunction—that is, of brutality multiplied and raised to the highest power by wickedness. Lady Macbeth poisons her husband's mind. Wickedness instils drops of venom into brutality, which, in its inward essence, may be either weakness, or brave savagery, or stupidity of manifold kinds. Whereupon brutality falls a-raving, and becomes terrible to itself and others.

The same formula expresses the relation between Othello and Iago.

Othello was a monograph. *Lear* is a world-picture. Shakespeare turns from *Othello* to *Lear* in virtue of the artist's need to supplement himself, to follow up every creation with its counterpart or foil.

Lear is the greatest problem Shakespeare had yet proposed to himself, all the agonies and horrors of the world compressed into five short acts. The impression of *Lear* may be summed up in the words : a world-catastrophe. Shakespeare is no longer minded to depict anything else. What is echoing in his ears, what is filling his mind, is the crash of a ruining world.

This becomes even clearer in his next play, *Antony and Cleopatra*. This subject enabled him to set new words to the music within him. In the history of Mark Antony he saw the deep downfall of the old world-republic—the might of Rome, austere and rigorous, collapsing at the touch of Eastern luxury.

By the time Shakespeare had written *Antony and Cleopatra*, his melancholy had deepened into pessimism. Contempt becomes his abiding mood, an all-embracing scorn for mankind, which impregnates every drop of blood in his veins, but a potent and creative scorn, which hurls forth thunderbolt after thunderbolt. *Troilus and Cressida* strikes at the relation of the sexes, *Coriolanus* at political life; until all that, in these years, Shakespeare has endured and experienced, thought and suffered, is concentrated into the one great despairing figure of Timon of Athens, "misanthropos," whose savage rhetoric is like a dark secretion of clotted blood and gall, drawn off to assuage pain.

Q

BOOK SECOND

I

INTRODUCTION—THE ENGLAND OF ELIZABETH IN SHAKESPEARE'S YOUTH

EVERYTHING had flourished in the England of Elizabeth while Shakespeare was young. The sense of belonging to a people which, with great memories and achievements behind it, was now making a decisive and irresistible new departure—the consciousness of living in an age when the glorious culture of antiquity was being resuscitated, and when great personalities were vindicating for England a lofty and assured position, alike in the practical and in the intellectual departments of life—these feelings mingled in his breast with the vernal glow of youth itself. He saw the star of his fatherland ascending, with his own star in its train.

It seemed to him as though men and women had in that day richer abilities, a more daring spirit, and fuller powers of enjoyment than they had possessed in former times. They had more fire in their blood, more insatiable longings, a keener appetite for adventure, than the men and women of the past. They knew how to rule with courage and wisdom, like the Queen and Lord Burghley; how to live nobly and fight gloriously, to love with passion and sing with enthusiasm, like the beautiful hero of the younger generation, Sir Philip Sidney, who found an early Achilles-death. They were bent on enjoying existence with all their senses, comprehending it with all their powers, revelling in wealth and splendour, in beauty and wit; or they set forth to voyage round the world, to see its marvels, conquer its treasures, give their names to new countries, and display the flag of England on unknown seas.

Statesmanship and generalship were represented among them by the men who, in these years, had humbled Spain, rescued Holland, held Scotland in awe. They were sound and vigorous natures. Although they all had the literary proclivities of the Renaissance, they were before everything practical men, keen observers of the signs of the times, firm and wary in adversity, in prosperity prudent and temperate.

Shakespeare had seen Spenser's faithful friend, Sir Walter Raleigh, next to himself and Francis Bacon the most brilliant and interesting Englishman of his day, after covering himself with renown as a soldier, a viking, and a discoverer, win the favour of Elizabeth as a courtier, and the admiration of the people as a hero and poet.   Shakespeare no doubt laid to heart these lines in his elegy on Sidney :—

> " England doth hold thy limbs, that bred the same ;
> Flanders thy valour, where it last was tried ;
> The camp thy sorrow, where thy body died :
> Thy friends thy want ; the world thy virtues' fame."

For Raleigh, too, was a poet, as well as an orator and historian. " We picture him to ourselves," says Macaulay, " sometimes reviewing the Queen's guard, sometimes giving chase to a Spanish galleon, then answering the chiefs of the country party in the House of Commons, then again murmuring one of his sweet love-songs too near the ears of her Highness's maids of honour, and soon after poring over the Talmud, or collating Polybius with Livy." [1]

And Shakespeare had seen the young Robert Devereux, Earl of Essex, who in 1577, when only ten years old, had made a sensation at court by wearing his hat in the Queen's presence and denying her request for a kiss ; at the age of eighteen win renown for himself as a cavalry general under Leicester in the Netherlands, and at the age of twenty depose Raleigh from the highest place in Elizabeth's favour.   He played " cards or one game or another with her . . . till birds' sing in the morning." She shut herself up with him in the daytime, while the Venetian and French ambassadors, who had already learnt to wait at locked doors in the time of his step-father, Leicester, jested with each other in the anteroom as to whether mounting guard in this fashion ought to be called *tener la mula* or *tenir la chandelle*. And Essex demanded that Raleigh should be sacrificed to his youthful devotion.   As captain of the guard, Raleigh had to stand at the door with a drawn sword, in his brown and orange uniform, while the handsome youth whispered to the spinster Queen of fifty-four things which set her heart beating.   He made all the mischief he could between her and Raleigh.   She assured him that he had no reason to " disdain " a man like that. But Essex asked her—so he himself writes—" Whether he could have comfort to give himself over to the service of a mistress that was in awe of such a man ; " " and," he continues, " I think he, standing at the door, might very well hear the worst I spoke of him."

[1] Macaulay, *Essays*—" Burleigh and his Times."

This impetuosity characterised Essex throughout his career; but he soon developed great qualities, of which his first appearances gave no promise; and when Shakespeare made his acquaintance, probably in the year 1590, his personality must have been extremely winning. Himself a poet, he no doubt knew how to value *A Midsummer Night's Dream*, and its author. In all probability, Shakespeare even at this time found a protector in the young nobleman, and afterwards made acquaintance through him with his kinsman Southampton, six years younger than himself. Essex had already distinguished himself as a soldier. In May 1589 he had been the first Englishman to wade ashore upon the coast of Portugal, and in the lines before Lisbon he had challenged any of the Spanish garrison to single combat in honour of his queen and mistress. In July 1591 he joined the standard of Henry of Navarre with an auxiliary force of 4000 men; he shared all the hardships of the common soldiers; during the siege of Rouen he challenged the leader of the enemy's forces to single combat; and then by his incapacity he dissipated all the results of the campaign. His army melted away to almost nothing.

He was at home during the following years, when Shakespeare probably came to know him well, and to appreciate his chivalrous nature, his courage and talent, his love of poetry and science, and his helpfulness towards men of ability, such as Francis Bacon and others. He therefore, no doubt, followed with more than the ordinary patriotic interest the expedition of the English fleet to Cadiz in 1596, in which the two old antagonists, Raleigh and Essex, were to fight side by side. Raleigh here won a brilliant victory over the great galleons of the Spanish fleet, burning them all except two, which he captured; while on the following day, when a severe wound in the leg prevented Raleigh from taking part in the action, Essex, at the head of his troops, stormed and sacked the town of Cadiz. In his despatches to Elizabeth, Raleigh praised Essex for this exploit. He became the hero of the day; his name was in every mouth, and he was even eulogised from the pulpit of St. Paul's.

It was indeed a great age. England's world-wide power was founded at the expense of defeated and humiliated Spain; England's world-wide commerce and industry came into existence. Before Elizabeth came to the throne, Antwerp had been the metropolis of commerce; during her reign, London took that position. The London Exchange was opened in 1571; and twenty years later, English merchants all the world over had appropriated to themselves the commerce which had formerly been almost entirely in the hands of the Hanseatic Towns. London urchins hung about the wharves of the Thames, listening to the marvels related by seamen who had made the voyage round the Cape of Good Hope to Hindostan.   Sunburnt, scarred, and bearded men haunted the taverns; they had crossed the ocean, lived in the Bermuda Islands, and brought negroes and Red Indians and great monkeys home with them.   They told tales of the golden Eldorado, and of real and imaginary perils in distant quarters of the globe.

This peaceful development of commerce and industry had taken place simultaneously with the development of naval and military power.   And the scientific and poetical culture of England advanced with equal strides.   While mariners had brought home tidings of many an unknown shore, scholars also had made voyages of discovery in Greek and Roman letters; and while they praised and translated authors unheard of before, dilettanti brought forward and interpreted Italian and Spanish poets who served as models of invention and delicacy.   The world, which had hitherto been a little place, had suddenly grown vast; the horizon, which had been narrow, widened out all of a sudden, and every mind was filled with hopes for the days to come.

It had been a vernal season, and it was a vernal mood that had uttered itself in the songs of the many poets.   In our days, when the English language is read by hundreds of millions, the poets of England may be quickly counted.   In those days the country possessed something like three hundred lyric and dramatic poets, who, with potent productivity, wrote for a reading public no larger than that of Denmark to-day; for of the six millions of the population, four millions could not read.   But the talent for writing verses was as widespread among the Englishmen of that time as the talent for playing the piano among German ladies of to-day.   The power of action and the gift of song did not exclude each other.

But the blossoming springtide had been short, as springtide always is.

II

ELIZABETH'S OLD AGE

AT the dawn of the new century the national mood had already altered.

Elizabeth herself was no longer the same. There had always been a dark side to her nature, but it had passed almost unnoticed in the splendour which national prosperity, distinguished men, great achievements and fortunate events had shed around her person. Now things were changed.

She had always been excessively vain; but her coquettish pretences to youth and beauty reached their height after her sixtieth year. We have seen how, when she was sixty, Raleigh, from his prison, addressed a letter to Sir Robert Cecil, intended for her eyes, in which he sought to regain her favour by comparing her to Venus and Diana. When she was sixty-seven, Essex's sister, in a supplication for her brother's life, wrote of that brother's devotion to "her beauties," which did not merit so hard a punishment, and of her "excellent beauties and perfections," which "ought to feel more compassion." In the same year the Queen took part, masked, in a dance at Lord Herbert's marriage; and she always looked for expressions of flattering astonishment at the youthfulness of her appearance.

When she was sixty-eight, Lord Mountjoy wrote to her of her "faire eyes," and begged permission to "fill his eyes with their onely deere and desired object." This was the style which every one had to adopt who should have the least prospect of gaining, preserving, or regaining her favour.

In 1601 Lord Pembroke, then twenty-one years old, writes to Cecil (or, in other words, to Elizabeth, in her sixty-eighth year) imploring permission once more to approach the Queen, "whose incomparable beauty was the onely sonne of my little world."

When Sir Roger Aston, about this time, was despatched with letters from James of Scotland to the Queen, he was not allowed to deliver them in person, but was introduced into an ante-chamber from which, through open door-curtains, he could see Elizabeth dancing alone to the music of a little violin,—the object being that he should tell his master how youthful she still was, and how small the likelihood of his succeeding to her crown for many a long day.[1] One can readily understand, then, how she stormed with wrath when Bishop Rudd, so early as 1596, quoted in a sermon Kohélet's verses as to the pains of age, with unmistakable reference to her.

She was bent on being flattered without ceasing and obeyed without demur. In her lust of rule, she knew no greater pleasure than when one of her favourites made a suggestion opposed to one of hers, and then abandoned it. Leicester had employed this means of confirming himself in her favour, and had bequeathed it to his successors. So strong was her craving to enjoy incessantly the sensation of her autocracy, that she would intrigue to set her courtiers up in arms against each other, and would favour first one group and then the other, taking pleasure in their feuds and cabals. In her later years her court was one of the most corrupt in the world. The only means of prospering in it were those set forth in Roger Ascham's distich :

> "Cog, lie, flatter and face
> Four ways in court, to win men grace."

The two main parties were those of Cecil and Essex. Whoever gained the favour of one of these great lords, be his merits what they might, was opposed by the other party with every weapon in their power.

In some respects, however, Elizabeth in her later years had made progress in the art of government. So weak had been her faith in the warlike capabilities of her country, and so potent, on the other hand, her avarice, that she had neglected to make preparation for the war with Spain, and had left her gallant seamen inadequately equipped ; but after the victory over the Spanish Armada she ungrudgingly devoted all the resources of her treasury to the war, which survived her and extended well into the following century. This war had forced Elizabeth to take a side in the internal religious dissensions of the country. She was the head of the Church, regarded ecclesiastical affairs as subject to her personal control, and, so far as she was able, would suffer no discussion of religious questions in the House of Commons. Like her contemporary Henri Quatre of France, she was in her heart entirely indifferent to religion, had a certain general belief in God, but thought all dogmas mere cobwebs of the brain, and held one rite neither better nor worse than another. They both regarded religious differences exclusively from the political point of view. Henry ended by becoming a Catholic and assuring his former co-religionists freedom of conscience. Elizabeth was of necessity a Protestant, but tolerance was an unknown doctrine in England. It was an established

---

[1] Arthur Weldon : *The Court and Character of King James*, 1650 ; quoted by Drake, ii. 149.

principle that every subject must accept the religion of the State.

Authoritarian to her inmost fibre, Elizabeth had a strong bent towards Catholicism. The circumstances of her life had placed her in opposition to the Papal power, but she was fond of describing herself to foreign ambassadors as a Catholic in all points except subjection to the Pope. She did not even make any secret of her contempt for Protestantism, whose head she was, and whose support she could not for a moment dispense with. She felt it a humiliation to be regarded as a co-religionist of the French, Scotch, or Dutch heretics. She looked down upon the Anglican Bishops whom she had herself appointed, and they, in their worldliness, deserved her scorn. But still deeper was her detestation of all sectarianism within the limits of her Church, and especially of Puritanism in all its forms. If she did not in the first years of her reign indulge in open persecution of the Puritans, it was only because she was as yet dependent on their support; but as soon as she felt herself firmly seated on her throne, she established, in spite of the stiff-necked opposition of Parliament, the jurisdiction of the Bishops on all matters of ecclesiastical politics, and suffered Puritan writers to be condemned to death or life-long imprisonment for free but quite innocent expressions of opinion regarding the relation of the State to religion.

Her greatness had mainly reposed upon the insight she had shown in the choice of her counsellors and commanders. But the most distinguished of those who had shed glory on her throne died one after the other in the last decade of the century. The first to die was Walsingham, one of her most disinterested servants, whom she had repaid with black ingratitude. He had done her great and loyal services, and had saved her life at the time of the last conspiracy, which led to the execution of Mary Stuart. Then she lost such notable members of her Council as Lord Hunsdon and Sir Francis Knowles; then Lord Burghley himself, the true ruler of England during her reign; and finally, Sir Francis Drake, the great naval hero of the war with Spain. She felt herself lonely and deserted. She no longer took any pleasure in the position of power to which England had attained under her rule. In spite of all she could do to conceal it, she began to feel the oppression of age, and to see how little real affection those men felt for her who were always posing in the light of adorers. She was the last of her line, and the thought of her successor was so intolerable to her, that she deferred his final nomination until she lay on her death-bed. But it availed her nothing; she knew very well that her ministers and courtiers, during the last years of her life, were in constant and secret communication with James of Scotland. They would kneel in the dust as she passed with exclamations of enchantment at her youthful appearance, and then rise, brush the dust from their knees, and write to James that the Queen looked ghastly and could not possibly last long.   They did all they possibly could to conceal from her their Scotch intrigues; but she divined what went on behind her back, even if she did not realise the extent to which it was carried, or know definitely which of her most trusted servants were shrinking from nothing that could assure them the favour of James.   For example, she did not suspect Robert Cecil of the double game he was carrying on, at the very time when he was doing his best to drive Essex to desperation and secure his punishment for an act of disobedience scarcely more heinous in the Queen's eyes than his own underhand dealings.   But she felt herself isolated in the midst of a crowd of courtiers impatiently awaiting the new era that was to dawn after her death.   She realised that the men who still flattered her had never been attached to her for her own sake, and she specially resented the fact that they no longer seemed even to fear her.

One result of this deep dejection was that she gave her tyrannical tendencies a freer course than before, and became less and less inclined to forbearance or mercy towards those who had once been dear to her but had fallen into disgrace.

She had always taken it very ill when one of her favourites showed any inclination towards matrimony, and they had therefore always been forced to marry secretly, though that did not in the end save them from her displeasure.   Now her despotism rose to such a pitch that she wanted to control the marriages even of those courtiers who had never enjoyed her favour.

One of the things which Shakespeare doubtless took most to heart at the end of the old century and beginning of the new was the hard fate which overtook his distinguished and highly valued patron Southampton.   This nobleman had fallen in love with Essex's cousin, the Lady Elizabeth Vernon.   The Queen forbade him to marry her, but he would not relinquish his bride. He was hot-headed and high-spirited.   Young as he was, he had boarded and taken a Spanish ship of war in the course of the expedition commanded by his friend Essex.   Once, in the palace itself, when Southampton, Raleigh, and another courtier had been laughing and making a noise over a game of primero, the captain of the guard, Ambrose Willoughby, called them to order because the Queen had gone early to bed; whereupon Southampton struck this high official in the face and actually had a bout of fisticuffs with him.   Such being his character, we cannot wonder that he contracted a private marriage in spite of the prohibition (August 1598).   Elizabeth sent him to pass his honeymoon in the Tower, and thenceforth viewed him with high disfavour.

His close relationship to Essex led to a new outburst of the

Queen's displeasure. When Essex took command of the army in Ireland in 1599, he appointed Southampton his General of Horse; but simply out of resentment for Southampton's disobedience in the matter of his marriage, the Queen forced Essex to rescind the appointment.

One must bear in mind, among other things, this attitude of the Queen towards Shakespeare's first patron in order to understand the evident coolness of his feeling towards Elizabeth. He did not, for example, join in the threnodies of the other English poets on her death, and even after Chettle had expressly urged him,[1] refrained from writing a single line in her praise. He probably read her character much as Froude did in our own day.

Froude admits that she was "supremely brave," and was turned aside from her purposes by no care for her own life, though she was "perpetually a mark for assassination." He admits, too, that she lived simply, worked hard, and ruled her household with economy. "But her vanity was as insatiable as it was commonplace. . . . Her entire nature was saturated with artifice. Except when speaking some round untruths, Elizabeth never could be simple. Her letters and her speeches were as fantastic as her dress, and her meaning as involved as her policy. She was unnatural even in her prayers, and she carried her affectations into the presence of the Almighty. . . . Obligations of honour were not only occasionally forgotten by her, but she did not seem to understand what honour meant."[2]

At the point we have now reached in Shakespeare's life, the event occurred which, of all external circumstances of his time, seems to have made the deepest impression upon his mind: the ill-starred rebellion of Essex and Southampton, the execution of the former, and the latter's condemnation to imprisonment for life.

---

[1] "Nor doth the silver-tongued *Melicert*
　　Drop from his honied muse one sable teare
　　To mourne her death that graced his desert,
　　And to his laies opend her Royall eare.
　　　　Shepheard, remember our *Elizabeth*,
　　　　And sing her Rape, done by that *Tarquin*, Death."

[2] Froude: *History of England*, vol. xii. Conclusion.

III

ELIZABETH, ESSEX, AND BACON

IN order rightly to understand these events a short retrospect is necessary.

We have seen how Essex in 1587 ousted Raleigh from the Queen's favour. From the very first he united with the insinuating tone of the adorer the domineering attitude of the established favourite. This was new to her, and for a considerable time obviously impressed more than it irritated her.

Here is an instance, from the early days of their relationship. Essex's sister, Penelope, had, against her will, been married to Lord Rich. She was adored by Sir Philip Sidney, who sang of her as his Stella, and their mutual passion was an open secret. The Maiden Queen, who was always very strict as to the moral purity of those around her, during a visit which she paid with Essex to the Earl of Warwick at North Hall in 1587, took offence at the presence of Lady Rich, and insisted that she should leave the house. Essex declared that the Queen subjected him and his sister to this insult "only to please that knave Raleigh," and left the house at midnight along with Lady Rich. He wanted to join the army in the Netherlands, but the Queen, finding that she could not do without him, had him brought back again.

At the time of the Armada, therefore, the Queen kept him at court, much against his own will. Nor would he have been allowed to take part in the war of 1589 if he had not secretly made his escape from England, leaving behind him a letter to the Queen and Council to the effect that "he would return alive at no one's bidding." An angry letter from Elizabeth forced him, however, to come back after he had distinguished himself before Lisbon. They were then reconciled, but the practical-minded Queen immediately demanded of him the repayment of a sum of £3000 which she had lent him, so that he was forced to sell his mansion of Keyston. He received in return "the farm of sweet wines," a very lucrative monopoly, the withdrawal of which many years afterwards led to the boiling over of his discontent.

We have seen how his secret marriage in 1590 enraged the Queen, who at once vented her wrath upon his bride. Presently, however, he was once more in favour, and in the middle of the French campaign of 1591, Elizabeth recalled him to England for a week, which was passed in all sorts of festivities. She wept when he returned to the army, and laid upon him an injunction, to which he paid very little heed, that he must on no account incur any personal danger.

During the subsequent four years which Essex passed in England, occupied with his plans of ambition, it became clear to him that Burghley's son, Sir Robert Cecil, was the chief obstacle to his advancement. All of those, therefore, who for one reason or another hated the house of Cecil, cast in their lot with Essex. Thus it happened that Cecil's cousin, Francis Bacon, who had in vain besought first the father and then the son for some profitable office, became a close personal adherent of Essex. It was necessary to make choice of one party or the other if you were to hope for any preferment. In the years 1593 and 1594, accordingly, we find Essex again and again importuning Elizabeth for offices for Bacon. She had no very great confidence in Bacon, and bore him a grudge, moreover, because he had incautiously spoken in Parliament against a Government measure; so that Essex, to his great annoyance and disgust, met with a refusal to all his applications. As a consolation to his client, he made him a present of land to the value of not less than £1800. That was the price for which Bacon sold the property; Essex had believed it to be worth more.[1] This gift, we see, was nearly twice as large as that which Southampton is reported to have made to Shakespeare (see above, p. 152).

Henceforward Bacon is to be regarded as an attentive and officious adherent of Essex, while Essex makes it a point of honour to obtain for him every recognition, preferment, and advantage. Again and again Bacon places his pen at the disposal of Essex. There are extant three long letters from Essex to his young cousin Lord Rutland, dated 1596, giving him excellent advice as to how to reap most profit from his first Continental tour, on which he was then setting out. In many passages of these letters we recognise Bacon's ideas, and in some his style, his acknowledged writings containing almost identical parallels. The probability is that in these, as in many subsequent instances, Bacon supplied Essex with the ideas and the first draft of the letters. Well knowing that the Queen's dissatisfaction with Essex arose chiefly from his desire for military glory and the popularity which follows in its train— well knowing, too, that Essex's enemies at court were always representing this ambition to the Queen as a hindrance to the peace with Spain, which nevertheless must one day be concluded —Bacon thought it a good move for his protector to display un-

[1] James Spedding : *Letters and Life of Francis Bacon*, i. 371.

equivocally his care for the occupations of peace, the acquisition of useful knowledge, and other unmilitary advantages, in letters which, although private, were likely enough to come into her Majesty's hands.

Francis Bacon's brother, Anthony, about the same time attached himself closely (and more faithfully) to Essex. Through him the Earl established communications with all the foreign courts, so that for a time his knowledge of European affairs rivalled that of the Foreign Ministry itself.

The zeal which Essex had displayed in unravelling Doctor Roderigo Lopez's suspected plot against Elizabeth (see above, p. 161) had placed him very high in her renewed favour. His heroic exploits at Cadiz ought to have strengthened his position; but his adversary, Robert Cecil, had during his absence acquired new power, and the rapacious Elizabeth complained of the smallness of the booty (it amounted to £13,000). As a matter of fact, Essex alone had wanted to follow up the advantage gained, and to seize the Indian fleet, which was allowed to escape: he had been out-voted in the council of war.

In order to overcome this new resentment on the Queen's part, Bacon, who regarded his fate as bound up in that of the Earl, wrote a letter to Essex (dated October 4, 1596), full of good advice with respect to the attitude he ought to adopt towards Elizabeth, especially in order to disabuse her mind of the idea that his disposition was ungovernable—advice which Bacon himself, with his courtier temperament, might easily enough have followed, but which was too hard for the downright Essex, who had no sooner made humble submission than his pride again brought arrogant expressions to his lips.

At the close of the year 1596 Bacon's protector was accused by his client's mother, Lady Bacon, of misconduct with one of the ladies of the court. He denied the charge, but confessed to "similar errors."

In 1597 Essex, who had been longing for a new command, undertook an expedition to the Azores with twenty ships and 6000 men—an enterprise which, largely owing to his inexperience and unfortunate leadership, was entirely unsuccessful. On his return he was very coldly received by the Queen, especially on the ground that towards the end of the expedition he had behaved ill to Raleigh, his colleague in command. In order to make his peace with Elizabeth, he sent her insinuating letters; but he was mortally offended when the eminent services of the old Lord Howard were rewarded by the appointment of Lord High Admiral. As the victor of Cadiz, he regarded himself as the one possible man for this distinction, which gave Howard precedence over him. He bemoaned his fate, however, to such purpose that he soon after secured the appointment of Earl Marshal of England, which in turn gave him precedence over

Howard. He received a very valuable present—worth £7000—and for the first and last time induced the Queen to grant an audience to his mother, Lady Lettice, whose marriage with Leicester, twenty-three years before, was not yet forgiven, although in 1589, at the age of forty-nine, she had married a third husband, Sir Christopher Blount.

But Essex was not long at peace with the Queen and Court. In 1598 he was accused of illicit relations with no fewer than four ladies of the court (Elizabeth Southwell, Elizabeth Brydges, Mrs. Russell, and Lady Mary Howard), and the charge seems to have been well founded. At the same time violent dissensions broke out as to whether an attempt should or should not be made to bring the war with Spain to a close. Essex carried the day, and it was continued. It was at this time that he wrote a pamphlet defending himself warmly from the charge of desiring war at any price. It was not published until 1602, under the title: *An apology of the Earle of Essex against those which jealously and maliciously tax him to be the hinderer of the peace and quiet of his country.*

To the Queen's birthday of this year (November 17, 1598) belongs an anecdote which shows what ingenuity Essex displayed in annoying his rival. As was the custom of the day, the leading courtiers tilted at the ring in honour of her Majesty, and each knight was required to appear in some disguise. It was known, however, that Sir Walter Raleigh would ride in his own uniform of orange-tawny medley, trimmed with black budge of lamb's wool. Essex, to vex him, came to the lists with a body-guard of two thousand retainers all dressed in orange-tawny, so that Raleigh and his men seemed only an insignificant division of Essex's splendid retinue.[1]

No later than June or July 1598 there occurred a new scene between Essex and the Queen in the Council, the most unpleasant and grotesque passage which had yet taken place between them. The occasion was trifling, being nothing more than the choice of an official to be despatched to Ireland. Essex was in the habit of permitting himself every liberty towards Elizabeth; and it was now, or soon after, that, as Raleigh relates, he told her "that her conditions were as crooked as her carcase." Certain it is that, on this occasion, he turned his back to her with an expression of contempt. She retorted by giving him a box on the ear and bidding him "Go and be hanged." He laid his hand upon his sword-hilt, declared that he would not have suffered such an insult from Henry the Eighth himself, and held aloof from the court for months.

Not till October was Essex forgiven, and even then with no heartiness or sincerity. The Irish rebellion, however, had to be put down, so a truce was called to all trivial quarrels. O'Neil,

[1] Gosse: *Raleigh*, p. 311.

Earl of Tyrone, had got together an army, as he had often done before, and the whole island was in revolt. Public opinion, for no sufficient reason, pointed to Essex as the only man who could deal with the rebels. He, on his part, was by no means eager to accept the mission. It was of the utmost importance for every courtier, and especially for the head of a party, not to be out of the Queen's sight more than was imperatively necessary. There was every reason to fear that his enemies of the opposite party would avail themselves of his absence in order so to blacken him in the eyes of his omnipotent mistress that he would never regain her favour. Elizabeth, at this juncture, like Louis XIV. in the following century, was monarch and constitution in one. Her displeasure meant ruin, her favour was the only source of prosperity. Therefore Essex did all he could to secure permission to return from the front whenever he pleased, in order to report personally to the Queen; and it was therefore that, in the following year, when he was forbidden to leave his post, he threw caution to the winds, and defied the prohibition. He knew that he was lost unless he could speak to Elizabeth face to face.

In March 1599 Essex took the command of the English troops; he was to suppress the rebellion and grant Tyrone his life only on condition of his complete surrender. But instead of carrying out his orders, which were to attack the rebels in their stronghold, Ulster, Essex remained for long inactive, and at last marched into Munster. One of his subordinate officers, Sir Henry Harington, suffered a disgraceful defeat, partly through his own incompetence, partly through the cowardice of his officers and men. He was tried by court-martial in Dublin, and he himself, and every tenth man of his command, were shot. The summer slipped away, and in its course the 16,000 men with whom Essex had come to Ireland were reduced by sickness and desertion to a quarter of their original number. Under these circumstances, Essex again deferred his march upon Ulster, so that the Queen, who was excessively displeased, expressly forbade him to return from Ireland without her permission.

When at last, in the beginning of September 1599, he confronted with his shrunken forces Tyrone's unbreathed army, which had taken up a strong position to await the coming of the English, he abandoned his plan of attack, invited Tyrone to a parley, had half an hour's conversation with him on the 6th of September, and concluded a fourteen weeks' armistice, to be renewed every six weeks until the 1st of May. According to his own account, he promised Tyrone that this treaty should not be placed in writing, lest it should fall into the hands of the Spaniards and be used against him.

This was certainly not what Elizabeth had expected of the Irish campaign, which had opened with such a flourish of trumpets, and we cannot wonder that her anger was fierce and deep-seated. No sooner had she received the intelligence, than she forbade the conclusion of any treaty whatsoever.

Convinced that his enemies now had the entire ear of the Queen, Essex sought safety in once more disobeying Elizabeth's express command. With a train of only six followers, which in the indictment against him afterwards grew into a body of 200 picked men, he crossed to England to attempt his own justification, rode direct to Nonsuch Palace, where Elizabeth then was, forced all the doors, and, travel-stained as he was, threw himself on his knees before the Queen, whom he surprised in her bed-chamber, with her hair undressed, at ten o'clock in the morning of the 28th of September.

It is a strong proof of the power which his personality still retained over Elizabeth, that at the first moment she felt nothing but pleasure in seeing him. As soon as he had changed his clothes, he was admitted to an audience, which lasted an hour and a half. As yet all seemed well. He dined at the Queen's table and told her about Ireland and its people. But in the evening he was "commanded to keep his chamber" until the lords of the Council should have spoken with him; and a few days later he was confined to York House, with his friend the Lord Keeper, however, for his gaoler.

He presently fell ill, when it appeared that the Queen had by no means forgotten her former tenderness for him. In the middle of December she sent eight physicians to consult as to his case. They despaired of his life, but he recovered.

While matters thus looked very black for Essex, his nearest friends also were, of course, in disgrace. In a letter from Rowland Whyte to Sir Robert Sidney (dated October 11, 1599), we find the following significant statement: "My Lord *Southhampton*, and Lord *Rutland* come not to the court; the one doth but very seldome; they pass away the Tyme in *London* merely in going to Plaies euery day." [1] Southampton had married a cousin of Essex, and Rutland a daughter of Lady Essex by her first marriage with Sir Philip Sidney; so that both were in the same boat with their more distinguished kinsman.

On the 5th of June 1600, Essex was brought to trial—not before the Star Chamber, but, by particular favour, before a special court, consisting of four earls, two barons, and four judges, which assembled at the Lord Keeper's residence, York House, the general public being excluded. The procedure was mainly dictated by the Queen's wish to justify the arrest of Essex in the face of public opinion, which idolised him and regarded him as a martyr.

---

[1] A. Collins: *Letters and Memorials of State*, ii. 132.

IV

THE FATE OF ESSEX AND SOUTHAMPTON

THE indictment did not press too severely upon Essex, did not as yet seek to discover treasonable motives for his inactivity in Ireland, but simply dwelt upon his disobedience to the Queen's commands, and the dangerous and dishonourable agreement with Tyrone. Francis Bacon had not been allotted any part in the proceedings; but on his writing to the Queen and expressing his desire to serve her in this conjuncture, he was assigned the quite subordinate task of calling Essex to account for his indiscretion in accepting the dedication, in unbefitting terms, of a political pamphlet written by a certain Dr. Hayward. Bacon exceeded his instructions by dwelling at length on certain passionate expressions in a letter from Essex to the Lord Keeper, in which he had spoken of the hardness of the Queen's heart and compared her princely wrath to a tempest. A man who was less nervously anxious to retain the Queen's favour would have declined this commission on the ground of his close relations with Essex; Bacon begged for it, went farther than it required him to go, and is scarcely to be believed when he afterwards, in his *Apology*, represents himself as actuated by the wish ultimately to be of service to Essex with the Queen. Still, he evidently had not ceased to regard a reconciliation between Elizabeth and Essex as the most probable result, and he may perhaps have done his best in private conversations to soften the Queen's resentment.

The sentence passed by the Lord Keeper was the not very severe one that Essex should, in the meantime, be deprived of all his offices, and remain a prisoner in Essex House "till it shall please her Majesty to release both this and all the rest."

Bacon, who still did not think Essex irretrievably lost, now tried, in a carefully worded letter to him, to explain his attitude, and at once received from his magnanimous friend a forgiveness which was scarcely deserved. Bacon declared that, next to the interests of the Queen and the country, those of Essex always lay nearest his heart; and he now composed two documents: first, a very judicious letter, which Essex was partly to re-write and then to send to the Queen, and next a fictitious letter, a masterpiece of diplomacy, purporting to have been written by his brother, Anthony Bacon, Essex's faithful adherent, to Essex himself. This letter, and Essex's reply to it, which prove to admiration Bacon's talent for reproducing the styles of two such different men, were to be copied by them respectively, and to be brought to the knowledge of the Queen, on whom they would no doubt produce the desired impression. With Machiavellian subtlety, these letters are carefully framed so as to place Francis Bacon himself in the light which should most appeal to the Queen: Essex is represented as regarding him as entirely won over to her side, and Anthony expresses the hope that she will show him the favour he has deserved "for that he hath done and suffered."

Bacon did not succeed in inducing Elizabeth to restore Essex to his former position in her favour. In August, a couple of months after the date of the sentence, he was placed at full liberty; but access to Elizabeth's person was denied him, and he was bidden to regard himself as still in disgrace. The consequence was that few now came about him except the members of his own family. Add to this, that he was over head and ears in debt, and that his monopoly of sweet wines, which had been his chief source of income, and on the renewal of which his financial rescue depended, ran out in the following month.

He wavered between fear and hope, and was for ever "shifting from sorrow and repentance to rage and rebellion so suddenly, as well proveth him devoid of good reason as of right mind." At one moment he is appealing to the Queen with the deepest humility in flattering letters, and at the next he is speaking of her—so his friend Sir John Harington reports—as "became no man who had *mens sana in corpore sano.*"

Then came the catastrophe. His sources of income were cut off, and his hope of the Queen's relenting was broken. He was convinced—without reason, as it appears—that his enemies at court, who had deprived him of his wealth, had now laid a plot to deprive him of his life as well. He imagined, too, that Sir Robert Cecil was weaving intrigues to bring about the nomination of the Infanta of Spain as Elizabeth's successor; and in his desperation he began to nurse the illusion that it was as necessary for the welfare of the state as for his own that he should gain forcible access to the Queen and secure the banishment from court of her present advisers. In his dread of being once more placed under arrest, and this time sent to the Tower, he determined, in February 1601, to carry out a plan he had been hatching, for taking the court by storm.

Southampton had at this time allowed the malcontents to make his residence, Drury House, their meeting-place for discussing the situation. Here the general plan was laid that they should seize upon Whitehall and that Essex should force his way into the Queen's presence; the time was to depend upon the arrival of the Scotch envoy. On the 5th of February, four or five of the Earl's

friends presented themselves at the Globe Theatre, and promised
the players eleven shillings more than they usually received if,
on the 7th, they would perform the play of the deposition and
death of King Richard II. (see above, p. 125). In the meantime, Essex had, in the beginning of February, assembled his
adherents in his own residence, Essex House, and this induced
the Government, which had heard with uneasiness of so large a
concourse of people, to summon Essex before the Council. He
received the summons on the 7th of February 1601, excused
himself on the ground of indisposition, and at once called his
friends together. On the same evening three hundred men were
gathered at his house, although no real plan had as yet been
determined upon. He informed them that his life was threatened
by Cobham and Raleigh. On the morning of the 8th of February, the Lord Keeper with three other noblemen, commissioned
by the Queen to inquire into what was going on, appeared at
Essex House, and demanded to see the Earl. They told him
that any complaints he might have to make to the Queen should
receive attention, but that in the first place he must order his
adherents to disperse.

Essex made only confused replies: his life was threatened, he
was to be murdered in his bed, he had been treacherously dealt
with, and so forth. In the meantime shouts arose from the crowd
of his retainers, "Away, my lord; they abuse you, they betray
you, they undo you; you lose time!" Essex led the noblemen
into his house amid cries from his armed friends of "Kill them,
kill them!" and "Shut them up! Keep them as pledges, cast
the great seal out at the window!" He had them locked up in
his library as prisoners or hostages. Then he came out again,
and, amid cries of "To Court! to Court!" his party rushed through
the gates. At the last moment, Essex learned that the Court was
prepared, the watch was doubled, and every access to Whitehall
was barred. They were therefore forced to attempt, in the first
place, to stir up an insurrection in the city. But in order to pass
through the streets horses were needed; they were sent for, but
there was delay in procuring them. So impatient was every
one by this time, that instead of awaiting their arrival, several
hundred men, headed by Essex, Southampton, Rutland, Blount,
and other gentlemen, but without any real leader or effective
plan of action, set off for the city. Essex nowhere made any
speech to the populace, but merely shouted, as though beside himself, that an attempt had been made to murder him. A good many
people, indeed, appeared to join him, but none of them were
armed, and they were in reality no more than onlookers. In the
meantime, the Government despatched high officials on horseback to different quarters of the town to proclaim Essex a traitor;
whereupon many of his following deserted him. Troops, too,
were despatched against him, so that he, with the remainder of

his band, with difficulty made their way by water back to Essex House, which was immediately besieged and fired upon. In the evening Essex and Southampton opened negotiations, and about ten o'clock surrendered with their little force, on the understanding that they should be courteously treated and accorded an honourable trial. The prisoners were taken to the Tower.

Francis Bacon now again plays a part, and this time a decisive one, in Essex's history. There was no need for him to take any share in the trial; and even if his office had imposed it upon him, he ought in common decency to have refrained. He was neither Attorney-General nor Solicitor, but only one of the "Learned Counsel." The very fact of his close friendship with Essex, however, made the Government anxious that he should appear in the case. He was at once advocate and witness, and was not summoned as one of the learned counsel, but expressly as "friend to the accused."

On the 19th February, Essex and Southampton were brought before a court consisting of twenty-five peers and nine judges. Already, on the 17th, Thomas Leigh, a captain in Essex's Irish army, for trying to gain access to the palace on the 8th February, had been beheaded in the Tower. Now that Essex's cause was irreparably lost, Bacon had no other thought than to make himself useful to the party in power and prove his devotion to the Queen. The purport of his first speech against Essex was to prove that the plan of exciting an insurrection in the city, which was in reality an inspiration of the moment, had been the result of three months' deliberation. He represented as false and hypocritical Essex's assurance that he was driven to action by dread of the machinations of powerful enemies. He compared Essex to Cain, the first murderer, who also sought excuses for his deed, and to Pisistratus, who wounded himself and ran through the streets of Athens, crying that an attempt had been made upon his life. The Earl of Essex, he said, in reality had no enemies.

Essex rejoined that he could "call forth Mr. Bacon against Mr. Bacon." Bacon, "being a daily courtier," had promised to plead his cause with the Queen. He had with great address composed a letter to her, to be signed by Essex. He had also written another letter in his brother Anthony's name, and an answer to it from Essex, both of which he was to show to the Queen; and in these "he laid down the grounds of my discontent, and the reasons I pretend against mine enemies, pleading as orderly for me as I could do myself."

This rejoinder told sensibly against Bacon, and drove him in his reply to launch against his benefactor a new and much more malignant and dangerous comparison. He likened him to a renowned contemporary, also a nobleman and a rebel, the Duke of Guise: "It was not the company you carried with you, but the assistance you hoped for in the City which you trusted unto.

The Duke of Guise thrust himself into the streets of Paris on the day of the Barricados in his doublet and hose, attended only with eight gentlemen, and found that help in the city which (thanks be to God) you failed of here. And what followed ? The King was forced to put himself into a pilgrim's weeds, and in that disguise to steal away to scape their fury."

In view of Essex's persistent denial that he had aspired to the throne or sought to do the Queen any injury, this parallel was a terrible one for him.

Both he and Southampton were found guilty and condemned to death.

The trial of Shakespeare's protector, Southampton, and his signed confession, have a special interest for us. In a private letter from John Chamberlain, dated the 24th February, we read: "The Earl of Southampton spake very well (but methought somewhat too much, as well as the other), and as a man that would fain live, pleaded hard to acquit himself; but all in vain, for it could not be: whereupon he descended to entreaty and moved great commiseration, and though he were generally well liked, yet methought he was somewhat too low and submiss, and seemed too loath to die before a proud enemy."

Southampton, in his own confession, admits that immediately after his arrival in Ireland, he became aware of Essex's letter to King James of Scotland, urging that, for his own sake, he ought not to permit the government of England to remain in the hands of his and Essex's common enemies, proposing that he should, at a fitting opportunity, assemble an army, and promising that Essex, in so far as his duty to her Majesty permitted, should support the King with his Irish troops. James replied evasively, and nothing came of the plan, in which Southampton soon regretted that he had taken share. After losing his post in Ireland, he went to the Netherlands, and had no other desire than to regain the favour of the Queen, when Essex, his kinsman and friend, summoned him to London and requested his support in the plan he had formed for seeking access to her Majesty. With a heavy heart, he had consented, and engaged in the enterprise, not from any treachery or disrespect towards her Majesty, but solely on account of his affection for Essex. He repents and abhors his action, and promises on his knees to consecrate to the Queen's service every day that remains to him, if she will but spare his life.

Southampton impresses us as a man of fiery but yielding character, entirely under the influence of a stronger personality ; but he is never betrayed into a single unworthy word with respect to his kinsman and friend, whose cause he of course knew to be hopeless. His sentence was commuted to imprisonment for life.

Essex himself, at the end, endured with less resolution **the** cruel ordeal to which he was subjected. Finding himself condemned to death, and knowing that many of his closest friends had confessed to the Drury House discussions and designs, he lost all balance during the last days of his life, entirely forgot his dignity, and overwhelmed those around him, his sister, his friends, his secretary, and himself, with a torrent of reproaches.

In the meantime his enemies were not idle. Even Raleigh, on whose proud nature one is sorry to find such a stain, impelled, of course, not only by their old enmity, but by Essex's recent assertions that he was plotting against his life, wrote to Cecil, in his uneasiness lest Essex should be pardoned, and urged him "not to relent," but to see that the sentence was carried out.

Elizabeth had first signed the death-warrant, and then recalled it. On the 24th February she signed it a second time, and on the 25th February 1601, Essex's head was severed by three blows of the axe.

The populace could not be persuaded of their favourite's guilt. They loathed his executioner, and detested those men who, like Bacon and Raleigh, had, by their malice, contributed to his downfall.

In order to justify itself, the Government issued an official *Declaration touching the Treasons of the late Earl of Essex and his complices*, in the composition of which Bacon bore a large part. It is very untrustworthy. James Spedding, indeed, one of Bacon's best biographers, has tried to reconcile it with the facts; but he has not succeeded in explaining away the damnatory circumstance that everything is omitted which tended at the trial to establish Essex's intention to use no violence, and to prove how entirely unpremeditated was the attempt to raise an insurrection in the city. Where passages of this nature occur in the records, all of which are preserved, we find the letters *om.* (meaning, of course, "to be omitted") written in the margin, sometimes in Bacon's hand, sometimes in that of the Attorney-General, Coke.[1]

Bacon, with his brilliant intellectual equipment and his consciousness of his great powers, is not to be set down as simply a bad man. But his heart was cold, and he had no greatness of soul. He was absorbed, to a quite unworthy degree, in the pursuit of worldly prosperity. Always deeply in debt, he coveted above everything fine houses and gardens, massive plate, great revenues, and, as essential preliminaries, high offices and employments, titles and distinctions, which he might well have left to men of meaner worth. He passed half his life in the character of an office-seeker, met with one humiliating refusal after another, and returned humble thanks for the gracious denial. Once and once

---

[1] Compare *Dictionary of National Biography*, Robert Devereux; Spedding, *Letters and Life of Francis Bacon*, ii. 190–374; Edwin Abbott, *Francis Bacon, an Account of his Life and Works*, pp. 53–82; Macaulay, *Lord Bacon;* Gosse, *Raleigh*.

only, in his early days in Parliament, did he display some independence and rectitude; but when he saw that it gave offence in the highest places, he repented as bitterly as though he had been guilty of a sin against all political morality, and besought her Majesty's forgiveness in terms that might have befitted a detected thief. With the likebaseness and pusillanimity he now turned against Essex. He had often cited the maxim, which even Cicero criticised in the *De Amicitia :* " Love as if you should hereafter hate, and hate as if you should hereafter love." He had never loved Essex otherwise. His excuse, if there can be any, for seeking advancement at all costs, must be found in the fact that he had the highest conception of his own value to science, and thought that it would be to the honour and advantage of learning that he, its high-priest, should be highly placed.

If we examine Essex's portrait, with its regular beauty, its air of distinction and gentleness, the high forehead, the curly hair, and the carefully combed long light beard, we can readily understand that such a man, surrounded by a halo of adventurous renown, must become the idol of the populace, and that the military incompetence which he had twice displayed should not greatly affect the high esteem in which the people held him. He was in reality as little of a statesman as of a general; he was simply a free-speaking, passionate man, innocent of diplomacy, a brave soldier without an idea of tactics. He misunderstood his influence over Elizabeth, and did not realise that the Queen, while she felt the charm of his personality, contemned his political counsels. There was a good deal of the poet in his composition ; he wrote pretty sonnets, was a patron of writers no less than of fighters, showed himself generous to profusion towards his friends and clients, and found, perhaps, his sincerest and most convinced admirers among the authors and poets of the day. Innumerable are the books which are dedicated to him.

There is no doubt that after his melancholy death, a marked decline was apparent in the Queen's courage and spirits. The legend, however, that it was the fact of his execution which she took so much to heart, is scarcely to be believed, and the story about Essex's ring, which was conveyed to her too late, is unquestionably a fable. It is certain, on the other hand— for the Duc de Biron, the envoy of Henri IV., had no motive for telling a falsehood—that on the 12th September 1601, after a conversation about Essex in which she jested over her departed favourite, Elizabeth opened a box and took out of it Essex's skull, which she showed to Biron. Ten months later, this favourite of the French king — whose name Shakespeare had borrowed for the hero of his first comedy—met with the very fate of Essex, and for a similar crime.

Bacon, no doubt, mourned Essex's disappearance even less than did the Queen. After Elizabeth's death, however. when the friends of Essex stood in the highest favour with the new King, he was shameless enough to send a letter to Southampton (who, though not yet released from the Tower, was already regarded as a power in the land), in which, after having expressed his fear of being met with distrust, he concludes thus: "It is as true as a thing that God knoweth, that this great change hath wrought in me no other change towards your Lordship than this, that I may safely be now that which I was truly before."

The circumstances of Essex's condemnation were of course not known in the London of those days so minutely as we now know them. But we see, as already indicated, that public opinion turned vehemently against Bacon, regarding and despising him as the traitor to his lord who, more than any one else, had brought about his unhappy end. We see that Raleigh, in spite of his greatness, now became one of the most unpopular men in England; and we observe that, notwithstanding all that was done to disparage him in the general regard, Essex's memory continued to be idolised by the great mass of the people.

If we now inquire in what relation Shakespeare stood to these events which so absorbed the English people, it seems more than probable that he, who had so recently been so intimately associated with Southampton, and cannot therefore have been very far from Essex, followed the accused with his sympathy, felt a lively resentment towards their enemies, and took their fate much to heart. And when we observe that just at this juncture a revolution occurs in Shakespeare's hitherto cheerful habit of mind, and that he begins to take ever gloomier views of human nature and of life, we cannot but recognise the probability that grief for the fate which had overtaken Essex, Southampton, and their fellows, was one of the sources of his growing melancholy.

V

THE DEDICATION OF THE SONNETS

WE naturally looked for one source of Shakespeare's henceforth deepening melancholy in outward events, in the political drama which reached its crisis and catastrophe in 1601; but it is still more imperative that we should look into his private and personal experiences for the ultimate cause of the revolution in his soul. We must inquire what light his works throw upon his private circumstances and state of mind at this period.

Now, we find among Shakespeare's works one which, more than any other, seems to enable us to look into his inmost soul— I mean his Sonnets. It is to these that we must mainly address ourselves for the information we require. Public events can, indeed, cast a certain measure of light or shadow over a man's inward world of thought and feeling; but they are never the efficient factors in determining the happiness or melancholy of his fundamental mood. If he has personal reasons for feeling that fate is against him, utmost serenity in the political atmosphere will not dissipate his gloom; and, conversely, if a deep joy abides within him, and he has personal reasons for feeling himself favoured by fortune, then public discontent will be powerless to disturb the harmony of his soul. But his depression will, of course, be doubly severe if public events and private experiences combine to cast a gloom over his mind.

Shakespeare's "sugred Sonnets" are first mentioned in the well-known passage in Meres's *Palladis Tamia* (1598), where they are spoken of as passing from hand to hand "among his private friends." In the following year the two important Sonnets now numbered cxxxviii. and cxliv. were printed (with readings subsequently revised) in a collection of poems named *The Passionate Pilgrim*, dishonestly published, and falsely attributed to Shakespeare, by a bookseller named Jaggard. The first of them especially is very interesting in this older form. For, although technically inferior to the later version, the words here flow more naturally, and have all the freshness of the first sketch. For the next ten years we find no mention of Sonnets by Shakespeare, until, in 1609, a bookseller named Thomas Thorpe issued a quarto entitled *Shakespeares Sonnets. Neuer before Imprinted*—an edition which the poet himself certainly cannot have revised for the press, but which may possibly have been printed from an authentic manuscript.

To this first edition is prefixed a dedication, written by the bookseller in the most contorted style, which has given rise to theories and conjectures without number. It runs as follows :—

TO . THE . ONLIE . BEGETTER . OF
THESE . INSVING . SONNETS .
MR . W . H . ALL . HAPPINESSE .
AND . THAT . ETERNITIE .
PROMISED .
BY .
OVR . EVER-LIVING . POET .
WISHETH .
THE . WELL-WISHING .
ADVENTVRER . IN .
SETTING .
FORTH .
T . T .

The meaning of the signature is clear enough, since "A booke called Shakespeare's Sonnets" was entered in the Stationers' Register on May 20, 1609, under the name of Thomas Thorpe. On the other hand, in the eighteenth and throughout the nineteenth century there has been no end to the discussion as to what was meant by "onlie begetter" (only producer, or only procurer, or only inspirer ?); and numberless have been the attempts to identify the " Mr. W. H." who is so designated.   While the far-fetched expression "begetter" has been subjected to equally far-fetched interpretations, the most impossible guesses have been hazarded as to the initials W. H., and the most incredible conjectures put forward as to the person to whom the Sonnets were addressed.

Strange as it may seem, it is nevertheless the fact, that during the first eighty years of the eighteenth century the Sonnets were taken as being all addressed to a woman, all written in honour of Shakespeare's mistress.   It was not till 1780 that Malone and his circle pointed out that more than one hundred of the poems were addressed to a man.   This view of the matter, however, did not even then command general assent, and so late as 1797 Chalmers seriously maintained that all the Sonnets were addressed to Queen Elizabeth, who was also, he believed, the inspirer of Spenser's famous *Amoretti*, in reality addressed to the lady who afterwards became his wife.   Not until the beginning of the nineteenth century did people in general understand, what Shakespeare's contemporaries can never have doubted, that the first hundred and twenty-six Sonnets were inspired by a young man.

It now followed almost of necessity that this young man should be identified with the "Mr. W. H." who is described as the "onlie begetter" of the poems.   The second group, indeed, is addressed to a woman ; but the first group is much the larger, and follows immediately upon the dedication.

Some have taken the word "begetter" to signify the man who procured the manuscript for the bookseller, and have conjectured that the initials are those of William Hathaway, a brother-in-law of Shakespeare's (Neil, Elze). Dr. Farmer last century advanced the claims of William Hart, the poet's nephew, who, as was afterwards discovered, was not born until 1600. The mere fact that, by a whim or oversight of which there are many other examples in the first edition, the word "hues," in Sonnet xx., is printed in italics with a capital, and spelt *Hews*, led Tyrwhitt to assume the existence of an otherwise unknown Mr. William Hughes, to whom he supposed the Sonnets to have been addressed. People have even been found to maintain foolishly that "Mr. W. H." referred to Shakespeare himself, some taking the "H." to be a mere misprint for "S.," others holding that the initials meant "Mr. William Himself" (Barnstorff).

Serious and competent critics for a long time inclined to the opinion that the "W. H." was a transposition of "H. W.," and represented none other than Henry Wriothesley, Earl of Southampton, whose close relation to the poet had long been known, and to whom his two narrative poems had been dedicated. This theory was held by Drake and Gervinus. But so early as 1832, Boaden advanced some objections to this view. He urged that Southampton never possessed the personal beauty incessantly dwelt upon in these poems. Finally, the Sonnets fit neither his age, nor his character, nor his history, full of movement, activity, and adverse fortune, to which no smallest allusion appears.

There is not the slightest doubt that these poems are addressed to a patron of rank; but our knowledge of the history of Shakespeare is so inconsiderable, that with regard to his patrons at the court, we have nothing to judge from but the dedications of *Venus* and of *Lucrece* to Southampton, and the dedication of the First Folio to Lords Pembroke and Montgomery, in which reference is made to the favour they had always shown these plays and their author, while he was alive. Bright and Boaden had already, in 1819 and 1832 respectively, advanced the opinion that Pembroke was the hero of the Sonnets. This view was shared by almost every one (Charles Armitage, Brown Hallan, Massey, Henry Brown, Minto, W. M. Rossetti), and towards the end of the nineteenth century this opinion could be considered as having established itself, since it was concurred in by the chief Shakespeare students (Dowden), and seemed to have obtained its final confirmation in the penetrating criticisms of Thomas Tyler (1890). All the above-mentioned authors agree about the fact, that there is only one person whose age, history, appearance, virtues, and vices accord in every respect with those of the young man to whom the Sonnets are addressed, just as his initials agree with those of the "Mr. W. H." to whom they are dedicated, and that is the young William Herbert, who in 1601 became Earl of Pembroke. Born on April 8, 1580, he came to London in the autumn of 1597 or spring of 1598, and very soon, in all probability, made the acquaintance of Shakespeare, whose patron, as the first folio edition of the dramas prove, he remained until the poet's death.

The way by which we arrive at William Herbert is this: The Sonnets cxxxv. and cxxxvi. as well as cxliii. contain plays on the word *will*, and the name *Will;* obscure as they are, they show that the friend whom the Sonnets glorify had the same Christian name as Shakespeare. This was true of Pembroke, but not of Southampton, whose Christian name was Henry. Shakespeare's Sonnets are not isolated poems. Though we are not certain whether the order of the Sonnets in the original edition is the sequence chosen by the poet himself, still it is evident that they stand in an intimate relation to each other, a thought or motive suggested in one being developed more at length in the next or one of the subsequent Sonnets. The grouping does not seem to be arbitrary; at any rate, it is so far careful that all attempts to alter it have only rendered the poems more obscure. The first seventeen Sonnets, for example, form a closely interwoven group; in all of them, the friend is exhorted not to die unmarried, but to leave the world an heir to his beauty, which must otherwise fade and perish with him. Sonnets c.–cxxvi., which are inseparably connected, turn on the reunion of two friends after a coldness or misunderstanding has for a time severed them. Finally, Sonnets cxxvii.–clii. are all addressed, not to a friend, but to a mistress, the Dark Lady whose relation to the two friends has already formed the subject of earlier Sonnets.

Sonnet cxliv.—one of the most interesting, inasmuch as it depicts in straightforward terms the poet's situation between friend and mistress—had already appeared, as above mentioned, in *The Passionate Pilgrim* (1599). It characterises the friend as the poet's " better angel," the mistress as his "worser spirit," and expresses the painful suspicion that the friend is entangled in the Dark Lady's toils—

"I guess one angel in another's hell";

so that both at once are lost to him, he through her and she through him.

But precisely the same theme is treated in Sonnet xl., which turns on the fact that the friend has robbed Shakespeare of his "love." These two Sonnets must thus be of the same date; and from Sonnet xxxiii., which relates to the same circumstances, we see that the friendship had existed only a very short time when it was overshadowed by the intrigue between the friend and the mistress:—

"But out, alack! he was but one hour mine."

At what time, then, did the friendship begin ? The date may be determined with some confidence, even apart from the question as to who the friend was. We know that Shakespeare must have written sonnets before 1598, since Meres published in that year his often-quoted words about the "sugred Sonnets"; but we cannot possibly determine which Sonnets these were, or whether we possess them at all, since those which passed from hand to hand "among his private friends" may very possibly have disappeared. If they are included in our collection, we may take them to be those in which we find frequent parallels to lines in *Venus and Adonis* and the early plays, though these coincidences are by no means sufficient, as some of the German critics[1] would have us believe, finally to establish the date of the Sonnets in which they occur. However, they vary greatly in quality, and may have been written at different periods. The first group, with its reiterated appeal (seventeen times repeated) to the friend, to leave the world a living copy of his beauty, is unquestionably the least valuable. The personal feelings of the poet do not come much into play here, and though these poems may have been addressed to William Herbert in 1598, it is not impossible, taking into account the many analogies in thought and mode of expression to be found in them and in *Venus and Adonis* and *Romeo and Juliet*, that they were produced several years before, and in this case, addressed to Southampton. Thomas Tyler believed he had satisfactorily established the date of one important group by showing that a passage in Meres's book had influenced the conception and expression of one of Shakespeare's Sonnets. It cannot reasonably be doubted that Shakespeare saw *Palladis Tamia ;* the author perhaps sent him a copy; and in any case he could not but have read with interest the warm and sincere commendation there bestowed upon himself. Now there occurs in Meres's book a passage in which, after quoting Ovid's

> " Jamque opus exegi, quod nec Jovis ira, nec ignis,
> Nec poterit ferrum, nec edax abolere vetustas,"

and Horace's

> " Exegi momentum aere perennius,"

the critic goes on to apply these words to his contemporaries, Sir Philip Sidney, Spenser, Daniel, Drayton, Shakespeare, and Warner, and then winds up with a Latin eulogy of the same writers, composed by himself, partly in prose and partly in verse. But on reading attentively Shakespeare's Sonnet lv., whose resemblance to the well-known lines of Horace and Ovid must have struck every reader, we find several expressions from this passage

---

[1] Hermann Conrad in *Preussische Jahrbücher*, February 1895. Hermann Isaac in *Jahrbuch der Deutschen Shakespeare-Gesellschaft*, vol. xix. p. 176.

in *Palladis Tamia*, and even from the lines written by Meres himself, reappearing in it. The Sonnet must thus have been written at earliest at the end of 1598—Meres's book was entered in the Stationers' Register in September—and possibly not till the beginning of 1599. Since, then, the following Sonnet (lvi.), which must date from about the same time, speaks of the friendship as newly formed—

> " Let this sad interim like the ocean be
> Which parts the shores, where *two contracted new*
> Come daily to the banks "—

we may confidently assign to the year 1598 the first contract of amity between the poet and his friend. However, all this is by no means conclusive. Shakespeare may have known Horace from other sources than Meres, and the quotation from Ovid, together with the expressions used by Meres, he certainly had encountered in Golding's translation of the *Metamorphoses*, with which he was familiar.

The historical allusions in Sonnets c.–cxxvi., which form a continuous poem, are not, indeed, by any means clear or easy to interpret; but Sonnet civ. dates the whole group definitely enough, in the statement that three years have elapsed since the first meeting of the friends:—

> " Three winters cold
> Have from the forests shook three summers' pride;
> Three beauteous springs to yellow autumn turn'd
> In process of the seasons have I seen;
> Three April perfumes in three hot Junes burn'd,
> Since first I saw you fresh, which yet are green."

Thus we must assign this important group to the year 1601; and this being so, it must also appear probable that the line—

> "The mortal moon hath her eclipse endured "—

alludes to the fact that Elizabeth (for whom, in the mode of the day, the moon was the accepted symbol) had come unharmed through the dangers of Essex's rebellion—the more so as the beautiful lines—

> " Now with the drops of this most balmy time
> My love looks fresh "—

show that the poem was written in the spring. It would be unreasonable to infer from this allusion any ill-will on the poet's part towards Essex and his comrades. Still less can we follow Tyler, when, by the aid of a complex scaffolding of hypotheses built up, in German rather than in English fashion, around Sonnets cxxiv. and cxxv., he laboriously works up to the air-drawn conjecture that Shakespeare is here expressing himself offensively towards his former patron Southampton, now a prisoner in the Tower, and even that Southampton is aimed at in the line about those "who have lived for crime." Equally baseless, of course, is the corollary which would find in Sonnet cxxv. Shakespeare's defence against an accusation of faithlessness towards the man to whom he had written, seven years earlier, in the dedication of *Lucrece*, " The love I dedicate Your Lordship is without end." It is absurd to construct a whole repulsive and fantastic romance on the basis of a single obscure phrase.

Turning now from the poems to the person to whom we believe them to have been addressed, this is what we learn of him :—

William Herbert, son of Henry Herbert and his third wife, the celebrated Mary Sidney, had for his tutor as a boy the poet Samuel Daniel; entered at Oxford in 1593, where he remained for two years; received permission in April, 1597, when he was seventeen years old, to live in London, but, as we gather from letters of the period, does not seem to have come up to town until the spring of 1598.

In August, 1597, negotiations were conducted by letter between his parents and Lord Burghley, with a view to his marriage with Burghley's grand-daughter, Bridget Vere, a daughter of the Earl of Oxford. It is true that she was only thirteen, but William Herbert was quite prepared to enter upon the engagement. He was to travel abroad before the marriage. Although his mother, the Countess of Pembroke, perhaps divining her son's too inflammable nature, and therefore wanting to see him married betimes, was much in favour of this project, and although the Earl of Oxford was pleased with the young man, and praised his " many good partes," difficulties arose of which we have no record, and the plan came to nothing.

In London, young Herbert lived at Baynard's Castle, close to the Blackfriars Theatre, and may thus have been brought in contact with the players. It is more probable, however, that so brilliant a woman as " Sidney's sister, Pembroke's mother," should have aroused his interest in Shakespeare ; and in that case the poet, in all probability, made the acquaintance of this distinguished and discerning patroness of arts and artists as early as 1598. Herbert's father, who died soon afterwards, was already an invalid.

It appears that in August, 1599, Herbert " followed the camp " at the annual musters, attending her Majesty with two hundred horse, and " swaggering it among the men of war."

He is from the first described as a bad courtier. Rowland Whyte writes of him at this time : " He was much blamed for his cold and weeke Maner of pursuing her Majesties favour, having had soe good steps to lead him unto it. There is want of Spirit and Courage laid to his charge, and that he is a melancholy young man." We may gather from this what fiery devotion every hand-

some and well-born young man was expected to pay to the elderly
Queen. Soon after, however, it appears from a letter from his
father to Elizabeth, that she must have expressed herself highly
satisfied with the young man, and we also learn that he was
" exceedingly beloued at Court of all Men." He appears to have
been very handsome, and to have possessed all the fascination
which so often belongs to an amiable *mauvais sujet*. Clarendon
says of him, in the first book of his *History of the Rebellion*,
that " he was immoderately given up to women," and that " he
indulged himself in pleasures of all kind, almost in all excesses."
Clarendon remarks, however, what is of particular interest for us,
that the young Pembroke possessed a good deal of self-control :
" He retained such a power and jurisdiction over his very appetite,
that he was not so much transported with beauty and outward
allurements as with those advantages of the mind as manifested
an extraordinary wit, and spirit, and knowledge, and administered
great pleasure in the conversation. To these he sacrificed himself, his precious time, and much of his fortune."

In November, 1599, Herbert had an hour's private audience
with Elizabeth. Whyte, who relates this, remarks that he now
stands high in the Queen's favour, " but he greatly wants advise."
He passed the rest of the winter in the country, suffering from an
illness which seems to have taken the form of ague, with incessant
headaches.

Tyler is inclined, not without reason, to assign Sonnets xc.-
xcvi. to this period. Shakespeare's complaints of his friend's
" desertion " may refer to his life at Court ; the expressions in
Sonnet xci. as to horses, hawks, and hounds, perhaps point to the
young man's absorption in sport. The following Sonnets dwell
unequivocally upon discreditable rumours as to the friend's life
and conduct. Here appears the above-quoted (p. 172) line :—

> " Lilies that fester smell far worse than weeds."

Here occurs the couplet :—

> " How like Eve's apple doth thy beauty grow,
> If thy sweet virtue answer not thy show ! "

And, in spite of all the loving forbearance which the poet manifests
towards his friend, he seems to imply that the ugly rumours were
not unfounded :—

> " How sweet and lovely dost thou make the shame,
> Which, like a canker in the fragrant rose,
> Doth spot the beauty of thy budding name !
> O, in what sweets dost thou thy sins enclose !
> That tongue that tells the story of thy days,
> (Making lascivious comments on thy sport,)
> Cannot dispraise but in a kind of praise ·
> Naming thy name blesses an ill report."

There was an improvement in the health of Herbert's father during the year 1600, yet Lord and Lady Pembroke were absent from London all summer, remaining at their country seat, Wilton. In the month of May, Herbert, accompanied by Sir Charles Danvers, went to Gravesend to pay his respects to Lady Rich and Lady Southampton. This visit proves clearly that there was not, as Tyler's above-mentioned interpretation of certain Sonnets would lead us to assume, any coolness between Herbert and the houses of Essex and Southampton. It is also worth noting that his companion on this excursion was so intimately associated with the chiefs of the malcontent party, that in the following year he had to pay with his life for his share in the rebellion.

In the accounts of a splendid and very much talked-of wedding, between a Lord Herbert and one of the Queen's ladies, which took place at Blackfriars in June, 1600, we for the first time come upon William Herbert's name in company with that of a young lady in whose life he played a disastrous part, and whom Tyler considers to be the heroine of Shakespeare's Sonnets. The bride, Mrs. Anne Russell, was conducted to church by William Herbert and Lord Cobham. After supper there was a masque, in which eight splendidly dressed ladies executed a new and unusual dance. Among these are mentioned Mrs. Fitton, and two of the ladies-in-waiting whose names had shortly before been coupled with that of Essex (Mrs. Southwell and Mrs. Bess Russell). Each had "a skirt of Cloth of Siluer, a Mantell of Carnacion Taffete cast vnder the Arme, and their Haire loose about their Shoulders, curiously knotted and interlaced." The leader of this double quadrille was Mrs. Fitton. She approached the Queen and "woed her to dawnce; her Majestie asked what she was; '*Affection*,' she said. '*Affection!*' said the Queen, '*affection* is false.' Yet her Majestie rose and dawnced."

Later in the year Whyte remarks in his letters that Herbert shows no "disposition to marry"; and we find him in September and October, 1600, vigorously training at Greenwich for a Court tournament.

On January 19, 1601, his father's death made William Herbert Earl of Pembroke. Very soon afterwards (the matter is mentioned in a letter from Robert Cecil so early as February 5) he got into deep disgrace over a love affair. He had for some time carried on a secret intrigue with the aforesaid Mary Fitton, a maid-of-honour who stood high in the Queen's good graces; and the secret now came to light. "Mistress Fitton," writes Cecil, "is proved with child, and the Earl of Pembroke, being examined, confesseth a fact, but utterly renounceth all marriage. I fear they will both dwell in the Tower awhile, for the Queen hath vowed to send them thither." In another contemporary letter it is stated that "in that tyme when that Mres Fytton was in great fauor . . . and duringe the time yt the Earle of

S

Pembrooke fauord her, she would put off her head tire and tucke vp her clothes and take a large white cloake, and march as though she had bene a man to meete the said Earle out of the Courte."

Mary Fitton gave birth to a still-born son ; Pembroke lay for a month in the Fleet Prison, and was banished from Court. He shortly afterwards applied through Cecil for leave to travel abroad. The Queen's displeasure, he says, is "a hell" to him; he hopes the Queen will not carry her resentment so far as to bind him to the country which has now become "hateful to him of all others." The permission to travel seems to have been given and then revoked. In the middle of June he writes that imploring letter to Cecil in which the reference to "her whose Incomparable beauty was the onely sonne of my little world," was designed to touch Elizabeth's hard heart; for Pembroke, it is plain, had now realised that what had offended her Majesty was not so much his intrigue with Mary Fitton, as the fact of his having overlooked her own much higher perfections. But the compliments came too late. Elizabeth, as we have already seen in the case of Essex, knew how to make the objects of her resentment suffer in that most sensitive point—the pocket. The "patent of the Forest of Dean," which had been held by the late Lord Pembroke, expired with him, and the son expected, according to use and wont, to have it renewed in his favour; but it was assigned to Pembroke's rival, Sir Edward Winter, and not until seven years later, under James, did Pembroke recover it.

Pembroke continued in disgrace, his renewed applications for permission to travel were persistently refused, and he was ordered to regard himself as banished from Court, and to "keep house in the country." Tyler looks upon this overshadowing of Pembroke's fortunes in 1601 as an explanation of the temporary breaking-off of his relations with Shakespeare in London, indicated by the "Envoi" with which Sonnet cxxvi. ends the series addressed to the Friend.

The close and affectionate relation between them was no doubt revived under James. This appears clearly enough from the Dedication of the First Folio. Let us now cast a rapid glance over the remainder of Pembroke's career.

His father's death placed him in possession of a large fortune, but the irregularity of his life left him seldom free from money embarrassments. In 1604 he married Lady Mary, the seventh daughter of Lord Talbot, and the marriage was celebrated with a tournament. His wife brought him a large property, but it was thought at the time that he paid very dearly for it in having to take her into the bargain. The marriage was far from happy.

Pembroke shared the love of literature which had distinguished his mother and his uncle, Sir Philip Sidney. According to Aubrey, he was "the greatest Mæcenas to learned men of any peer of his time or since." Among his "learned" friends were the poets Donne, and Daniel, and Massinger, who was the son of his father's steward. Ben Jonson composed an eulogistic epigram in his honour, as well he might, for every New Year Pembroke sent Ben £20 to buy books with. Inigo Jones is said to have visited Italy at his expense, and was frequently employed by him. Davison's *Poetical Rhapsody* and numerous other books are dedicated to him. Chapman, who was among his intimates, inscribed a sonnet to him at the close of his translation of the *Iliad*. This fact is of particular interest to us, because Chapman —probably the rival poet who paid court to Pembroke—won his goodwill and admiration, and thereby aroused jealousy and melancholy self-criticism in Shakespeare's breast, as we read in Sonnets lxxviii.-lxxxvi.[1]

It is especially on Sonnet lxxxvi. that Minto bases his identification of the rival poet with Chapman. The very opening line, referring to the " proud full sail of his great verse," suggests at once the fourteen-syllable measure in which Chapman translated the *Iliad*. Chapman was full of a passionate enthusiasm for the art of poetry, which he lost no opportunity of glorifying; and he laid claim to supernatural inspiration. In the Dedication to his poem *The Shadow of the Night* (1594), he speaks with severe contempt of the presumption of those who " think Skill so mightily pierced with their loves that she should prostitutely show them her secrets, when she will scarcely be looked upon by others but with invocation, fasting, watching—yea, not without having drops of their souls, *like a heavenly familiar*." Hence Shakespeare's lines—

"Was it his spirit, by spirits taught to write
Above a mortal pitch that struck me dead?"

and the expression—

" He, nor that affable familiar ghost
Which nightly gulls him with intelligence."

After the accession of James, Pembroke immediately took a high position at the new Court. Before the year 1603 was out, he was a Knight of the Garter, and had entertained the King at Wilton. He rose from one high post to another, until in 1615 he became Lord Chamberlain; but he continued to the last the dissipated life of his youth. He devoted large sums of money to the exploration and colonisation of America. Places were named after him in the Bermudas and Virginia. In 1614, moreover, he became a member of the East India Company.

He opposed the Spanish Alliance, and was no friend to the King's foreign policy. He is thought to have instigated in some measure the attack on the Mexico fleet for which Raleigh paid

---

[1] I do not find that Mr. G. A. Leigh has succeeded in identifying the rival poet with Tasso (*Westminster Review*, February 1897).

so dear. He was an opponent of Bacon as Lord Chancellor, and in 1621 advocated an inquiry into the charges of corruption which were brought against him; but afterwards, like Southampton, displayed great moderation, and spoke strongly against the proposal to deprive Bacon of his peerage.

He stood by the King's deathbed in March, 1625, had a serious illness in 1626, and died in April, 1630, "of an apoplexy after a full and cheerful supper." Donne in 1660 published some poems of his among a collection by several other hands.

VI

THE "DARK LADY" OF THE SONNETS

IN speaking of *Love's Labour's Lost*, I remarked that it was not difficult to distinguish the original text of the comedy from the portions added and altered during the revision of 1598; and I cited (p. 38) several instances in which the distinction was clear. Especial emphasis was laid on the fact that Biron's (or, as the context shows, Biron-Shakespeare's) rapturous panegyrics of love in the fourth act belong to the later date.

At another place (p. 83) it was pointed out that the two Rosalines of *Love's Labour's Lost* (end of the third act) and of *Romeo and Juliet* (ii. 4) were in all probability drawn from the same model, since she is in both places described as a blonde with black eyes. In the original text of *Love's Labour's Lost* (Act iii.) she is expressly called—

> "A whitely wanton with a velvet brow,
> With two pitch balls stuck in her face for eyes."

All the more surprising must it seem that during the revision the poet quite obviously had before his eyes another model, repeatedly described as "black," whose dark complexion indeed, so uncommon and un-English that it was apt to be thought ugly, is insisted upon as strongly as that of the "Dark Lady" in the Sonnets. Immediately before Biron bursts forth into his great hymn to Eros, in which Shakespeare so clearly makes him his mouthpiece, the King banters him as to the murky hue of the object of his adoration :—

> "*King.* By heaven, thy love is black as ebony.
> *Biron.* Is ebony like her? O wood divine!
> O wife of such wood were felicity.
> O! who can give an oath? where is a book?

> That I may swear beauty doth beauty lack,
> If that she learn not of her eye to look:
> No face is fair, that is not full so black.
>   *King.* O paradox ! Black is the badge of hell,
> The hue of dungeons, and the scowl of night;
> And beauty's crest becomes the heavens well."

Biron's answer to this is highly remarkable; for it is exactly what Shakespeare himself says, in Sonnet cxxvii., to the advantage of his dark beauty :—

> " *Biron.* Devils soonest tempt, resembling spirits of light.
> O ! if in black my lady's brows be deck'd.
> It mourns, that painting, and usurping hair,
> Should ravish doters with a false aspect ;
> And therefore is she born to make black fair.
> Her favour turns the fashion of the days ;
> For native blood is counted painting now,
> And therefore red, that would avoid dispraise,
> Paints itself black, to imitate her brow."

The Sonnet runs thus :—

> " In the old age black was not counted fair
> Or if it were, it bore not beauty's name ;
> But now is black beauty's successive heir,
> And beauty slander'd with a bastard shame ;
> For since each hand hath put on nature's power,
> Fairing the foul with art's false borrow'd face,
> Sweet beauty hath no name, no holy bower,
> But is profan'd, if not lives in disgrace.
> Therefore my mistress' eyes are raven black ;
> Her eyes so suited, and they mourners seem
> At such, who, not born fair, no beauty lack,
> Slandering creation with a false esteem :
>   Yet so they mourn, becoming of their woe,
>   That every tongue says, beauty should look so."

It appears, then, that the dark beauty in *Love's Labour's Lost* must also have had a living model ; and when we observe that the revision, as the title-page tells us, took place when the comedy was to be presented before her Highness at Christmas, 1597, and further, that the dark Rosaline in the play is maid-of-honour to a princess who is called, in words strongly suggesting a passing compliment to the Queen, "a gracious moon"—we can scarcely avoid the conclusion that the beautiful brunette must have been one of the Queen's ladies, and that the whole end of the fourth act was addressed to her over the heads of the uninitiated spectators. Who she was we know not ; no contemporary has mentioned her name. But assuming Pembroke to be the hero of the Sonnets, Tyler has put forward a plausible hypothesis as to her identity ; for it is known with tolerable certainty which of the Queen's ladies brought Pembroke into disgrace. Was then the lady who enthralled Pembroke the black-eyed brunette whom Shakespeare, in his own words, loved to " distraction " and to " madding fever " ?

On the monument of Mary Fitton's mother in Gawsworth Church, in Cheshire, a highly coloured bust of Mary Fitton herself[1] led Tyler to assert that she must have been a marked brunette. It is true that the bust cannot give us a very accurate idea of her appearance in the year 1600, since it was executed in 1626, when she was forty-eight; but the complexion is dark, the high-piled hair and the large eyes black. That it does not suggest a beautiful original is a point in favour of its identity with the Dark Lady as described in Sonnet cxli. :—

> " In faith, I do not love thee with mine eyes,
>   For they in thee a thousand errors note;
>   But 'tis my heart that loves what they despise,
>   Who in despite of view is pleas'd to dote,
>   Nor are mine ears with thy tongue's tune delighted;
>   Nor tender feeling to base touches prone,
>   Nor taste, nor smell, desire to be invited
>   To any sensual feast with thee alone:
>   But my five wits nor my five senses can
>   Dissuade one foolish heart from serving thee,
>   Who leaves unsway'd the likeness of a man,
>   Thy proud heart's slave and vassal wretch to be:
>   Only my plague thus far I count my gain,
>   That she that makes me sin awards me pain."

The Rev. W. A. Harrison discovered a family tree from which it appeared that Mary Fitton, christened June 24, 1578, became a maid-of-honour to Elizabeth in 1595, at the age of seventeen. Thus she was nineteen years old when, at the Court festivities of 1597, Shakespeare's company acted *Love's Labour's Lost*, with the panegyric of the dark beauty, Rosaline. She would have made the acquaintance of the poet and player, then thirty-three years old, at earlier Court entertainments. It is probable that it was she, with her high position and daring spirit, who made the first advances ?

That the Dark Lady did not live with Shakespeare appears clearly enough in the Sonnets—for instance, in Sonnet cxliv. ("but being both from me"). It may be gathered from Sonnet cli., with the expressions "triumphant prize," "proud of this pride," that she was greatly his superior in rank and station, so that her conquest for some time filled him with a sense of triumph. Tyler even believes, that there is an actual allusion to her name in Sonnet cli., which, as a whole, abounds in such daring equivoques as would be impossible in modern poetry.

---

[1] Reproduced in Tyler's *Shakespeare's Sonnets.*

It was thought surprising that in Sonnet clii., in which Shakespeare calls himself forsworn because he loves his lady although married to another, he also states expressly that she too is married, calling her "twice forsworn," since she has not only broken her "bed-vow," but broken her "new faith" to Shakespeare himself. It seemed difficult to reconcile this with the fact that Mrs. Fitton ("Mistress" in those days being applicable to unmarried no less than to married women) was always called by her father's name. She was married in 1607 to a certain William Polwheele, with whom she appears to have had a love-intrigue before the wedding. After the death of her husband she was married a second time to John Lougher.

However, it must now be pointed out that a work, published in 1897, which for the first time gave a trustworthy account of Mary Fitton's life, has rendered it excessively improbable that she should be identical with the Dark Lady of the Sonnets. The title of the work is : *Gossip from a Muniment-Room, being Passages in the lives of Anne and Mary Fitton*, 1574–1618 ; it is published by Lady Newdigate-Newdegate, who is married to a descendant of the elder sister, Anne Fitton, and it contains many interesting letters to this lady, with other communications from the family-archives. Here it is proved—in spite of Tyler's attempted contradiction—that the two well-preserved portraits of Mary Fitton at Arbury show that she was not dark at all, but had a light complexion, brown hair, and grey eyes.

From Mary Fitton herself there is only a brief note contained in the collection, but her name is often mentioned in the letters. They prove, that at the beginning of her career as maid-of-honour to the Queen, she had an admirer in the elderly court-functionary, Sir William Knollys, inspector of the household, who later, under King James, became a very potent personality as Lord Knollys ; and it was evidently arranged between them that they would marry as soon as Sir William should become a widower. Their relations were not severed until the Pembroke scandal came out. Sir William married another lady after the death of his wife. This relation appeared to support the belief that Mary Fitton was Shakespeare's lady, as far as it gave a clue to the expression *thy bed vow broke*, and in so far as Knollys' Christian name William seemed to explain the two first lines in Sonnet cxxxv. : You have your will (or William) and William (or will) a second time and William (or will) into the bargain. It had long been admitted that the two last of these *Wills* referred to Pembroke and Shakespeare. And it was suggested that a third Will was hidden in the first. In 1881 Dowden wrote : "As we know that the lady had a husband, it may be possible that he too bore the name of William." As against the unmistakable evidence of the portraits, however, it is impossible to attribute any weight to this circumstance. Moreover, the name of Shakespeare is never mentioned in the recently-published papers of the Fitton family. Of course the silence in itself is not conclusive. Mary Fitton may have known Shakespeare intimately without her relatives being aware of the fact. Besides, we know, from the dedication, which the clown of the Shakespearian troupe, the well known William Kemp, in 1600, addressed to her in his little book "Nine Daies Wonder," that she had certain relations with the company. This dedication runs as follows : *Mistress Anne (supposed to be Mary) Fitton, Mayde of Honour of the most sacred Mayde Royal Queene Elisabeth.* But I confess, that Mary's grey eyes decide the matter for me.

However, even if it be unreasonable to identify Mary Fitton with the Dark Lady of the Sonnets, after the publication of the Fitton family papers, this does not exclude the possibility that Pembroke may have been Shakespeare's rival. If Essex, as above mentioned, was obliged to acknowledge that he had had intrigues with four of the ladies of the court at the same time, Pembroke may well have had intimate relations with two of them at once.

The Dark Lady must have been a woman in the extremest sense of the word, a daughter of Eve, alluring, ensnaring, greedy of conquest, mendacious and faithless, born to deal out rapture and torment with both hands, the very woman to set in vibration every chord in a poet's soul.

There can be no reasonable doubt that in the early days of his relation with the well-born mistress, Shakespeare felt himself a favourite of fortune, intoxicated with love and happiness, exalted above his station, honoured and enriched. She must at first have been to him what Maria Fiammetta, the natural daughter of a king, was to Boccaccio. She must have brought a breath from a Higher world, an aroma of aristocratic womanhood, into his life. He must have admired her wit, her presence of mind and her daring, her capricious fancy and her quickness of retort. He must have studied, enjoyed, and adored in her—and that in the closest intimacy—the well-bred ease, the sportive coquetry, the security, elegance, and gaiety of the emancipated lady. Who can tell how much of her personality has been transferred to his brilliant young Beatrices and Rosalinds ?

First and foremost he must have owed to her the rapture of feeling his vitality intensified—a main element in the happiness which, in the first years of their communion, finds expression in the sparkling love-comedies we have just reviewed. Let it not be objected that the Sonnets do not dwell upon this happiness. The Sonnets date from the period of storm and stress, when he had ascertained what at first, no doubt, he had but vaguely suspected, that his mistress had ensnared his friend ; and in composing them he no doubt antedated many of the passionate and distracted moods which overwhelmed him at the crisis, when he not only realised the fact of their intrigue, but saw it dragged to the light of day.   He then felt as though, doubly betrayed, he had irrevocably lost them both.   Thus the picture of his mistress drawn in the Sonnets shows her, not as she appeared to him in earlier years, but as he saw her during this later period.

Yet he also depicts moments, and even hours, when his whole nature must have been lapped in tenderness and harmony.   The scene, tor instance, so melodiously portrayed in Sonnet cxxviii. is steeped in an atmosphere of happy love—the scene in which, seated at the virginals, the lady, whom the poet addresses as " my music," lets her delicate aristocratic fingers wander over the keys, enchanting with their concord the listener who longs to press her fingers and her lips to his.   He envies the keys that "kiss the tender inward of her hand," and concludes :—

> " Since saucy jacks so happy are in this,
>   Give them thy fingers, me thy lips to kiss."

It is only natural, however, that the morbidly passionate, complaining, and accusing Sonnets should be in the majority.

Again and again he reverts to her faithlessness and laxity of conduct.   In Sonnet cxxxvii. he speaks of his love as " anchored in the bay where all men ride."   Sonnet cxxxviii. begins :—

> "When my love swears that she is made of truth,
>   I do believe her, though I know she lies."

And in Sonnet clii. he reproaches himself with having sworn a host of false oaths in swearing to her good qualities :—

> " But why of two oaths' breach do I accuse thee,
>   When I break twenty ?   I am perjur'd most ;
>   For all my vows are oaths but to misuse thee,
>   And all my honest faith in thee is lost :
>   For I have sworn deep oaths of thy deep kindness,
>   Oaths of thy love, thy truth, thy constancy ;
>   And, to enlighten thee, gave eyes to blindness,
>   Or made them swear against the thing they see."

In Sonnet cxxxix. he depicts her as carrying her thirst for admiration to such a pitch of wantonness, that even in his presence she could not refrain from coquetting on every hand :—

> " Tell me thou lov'st elsewhere ; but in my sight,
>   Dear heart, forbear to glance thine eye aside :
>   What need'st thou wound with cunning, when thy might
>   Is more than my o'erpress'd defence can 'bide ? "

She cruelly abuses her witchery over him.   She is as tyrannical, he says in Sonnet cxxxi., " as those whose beauties proudly make them cruel," well knowing that to his " dear-doting heart " she is "the finest and most precious jewel."   There is actual magic in the power she exerts over him. He does not understand it himself, and exclaims in Sonnet cl. :—

> " Whence hast thou this becoming of things ill,
>   That in the very refuse of thy deeds
>   There is such strength and warrantise of skill,
>   That in my mind thy worst all best exceeds ? "

No French poet of the eighteen-thirties, not even Musset himself, has given more passionate utterance than Shakespeare to the fever and agony and distraction of love. See, for instance, Sonnet cxlvii. :—

> " My love is as a fever, longing still
>   For that which longer nurseth the disease :
>   Feeding on that which doth preserve the ill,
>   The uncertain-sickly appetite to please.
>   My reason, the physician to my love,
>   Angry that his prescriptions are not kept,
>   Hath left me, and I desperate now approve
>   Desire is death, which physic did except.
>   Past cure I am, now reason is past care,
>   And frantic-mad with evermore unrest :
>   My thoughts and my discourse as madmen's are,
>   At random from the truth vainly express'd ;
>   For I have sworn thee fair, and thought thee bright,
>   Who art as black as hell, as dark as night."

He depicts himself as a lover frenzied with passion. His eyes are dimmed with vigils and with tears. He no longer understands either himself or the world : " If that is fair whereon his false eyes dote, What means the world to say it is not so ? " If it is not fair, then his love proves that a lover's eye is less trustworthy than that of the indifferent world (Sonnet cxlviii.).

And yet he well knows the seat of the witchery by which she holds him in thrall. It lies in the glow and expression of her exquisite " raven black " eyes (Sonnets cxxvii. and cxxxix.). He loves her soulful eyes, which, knowing the torments her disdain inflicts upon him—

> " Have put on black, and loving mourners be,
>   Looking with pretty ruth upon my pain."
>   —Sonnet cxxxii.

Young as she is, her nature is all compounded of passion and will ; she is ungovernable in her caprices, born for conquest and for self-surrender.

While we can guess that towards Shakespeare she made the first advances, we know that she did so in the case of his friend. In more than one sonnet she is expressly spoken of as " wooing him."[1]   In Sonnet cxliii. Shakespeare uses an image which, in all its homeliness, is exceedingly graphic :—

> " Lo ! as a careful housewife runs to catch
> One of her feather'd creatures broke away,
> Sets down her babe, and makes all swift despatch
> In pursuit of the thing she would have stay ;
> Whilst her neglected child holds her in chase,
> Cries to catch her whose busy care is bent
> To follow that which flies before her face,
> Not prizing her poor infant's discontent :
> So runn'st thou after that which flies from thee,
> Whilst I, thy babe, chase thee afar behind ;
> But if thou catch thy hope, turn back to me,
> And play the mother's part, kiss me, be kind :
>   So will I pray that thou may'st have thy *Will*,
>   If thou turn back, and my loud crying still."

The tenderness of feeling here apparent is characteristic of the poet's whole attitude of mind in this dual relation.   Even when he cannot acquit his friend of all guilt, even when he mournfully upbraids him with having robbed the poor man of his ewe lamb, his chief concern is always lest any estrangement should arise between his friend and himself.   See, for instance, the exquisitely melodious Sonnet xl. :—

> " Take all my loves, my love, yea, take them all :
> What hast thou then more than thou hadst before ?
> No love, my love, that thou mayst true love call :
> All mine was thine before thou hadst this more.
>
> .   .   .   .
>
> I do forgive thy robbery, gentle thief,
> Although thou steal thee all my poverty."

The same tone of sentiment runs through the moving Sonnet xlii., which begins :—

> "That thou hast her, it is not all my grief,
> And yet it may be said, I loved her dearly ;
> That she hath thee, is of my wailing chief,
> A loss in love that touches me more nearly."

It closes with this somewhat vapid conceit :—

> " But here's the joy : my friend and I are one ;
> Sweet flattery ! then she loves but me alone."

All these expressions, taken together, point not only to the enormous value which Shakespeare attached to his young protector's friendship, but also to the sensual and spiritual attraction

[1] "And when a woman *woos*, what woman's son will sourly leave her ?" (Sonnet xli.).   " *Wooing* his purity with her foul pride " (Sonnet cxliv.).

which, in spite of everything, his fickle mistress continued to possess for him.

It is not impossible that a passage in Ben Jonson's *Bartholomew Fair* (1614) may contain a satirical allusion to the relation portrayed in the Sonnets (published in 1609). In Act v. sc. 3 there is presented a puppet-show setting forth "The ancient modern history of Hero and Leander, otherwise called the Touchstone of true Love, with as true a trial of Friendship between Damon and Pythias, two faithful friends o' the Bankside." Hero is "a wench o' the Bankside," and Leander swims across the Thames to her. Damon and Pythias meet at her lodging, and abuse each other most violently when they find that they have but one love, only to finish up as the best friends in the world.[1]

[1] "*Damon.* Whore-master in thy face ;
Thou hast lain with her thyself, I'll prove it in this place.
  "*Leatherhead.* They are whore-masters both, sir, that's a plain case.
  "*Pythias.* Thou liest like a rogue.
  "*Leatherhead.* Do I lie like a rogue?
  "*Pythias.* A pimp and a scab.
  "*Leatherhead.* A pimp and a scab !
I say, between you *you have both but one drab.*
  "*Pythias and Damon.* Come, now we'll go together to breakfast to Hero.
  "*Leatherhead.* Thus, gentles, you perceive without any denial
'Twixt Damon and Pythias here friendship's true trial."

VII

PLATONISM — SHAKESPEARE'S AND MICHAEL ANGELO'S SONNETS—THE TECHNIQUE OF THE SONNETS

THE fact that the person to whom Shakespeare's Sonnets are dedicated is simply entitled "Mr. W. H." long served to divert attention from William Herbert, as it was thought that it would have been an impossible impertinence thus to address a noble-man like the Earl of Pembroke, without his title. It is ima-ginable that this form of address was adopted precisely in order that Pembroke might not be exhibited to the great public as the hero of the conflict darkly adumbrated in the Sonnets. They were not, indeed, written quite without an eye to publication, as is proved by the poet's promises that they are to immortalise the memory of his friend's beauty. But it was not Shakespeare him-self who gave them to the press, and bookseller Thorpe must have known very well that Lord Pembroke would not care to see himself unequivocally designated as the lover of the Dark Lady and the poet's favoured rival, especially as that dramatic episode of his youth ended in a manner which it can scarcely have been pleasant to recall.

A weighty work, *A Life of Shakespeare*, published in the year 1898, by Mr. Sidney Lee, has, however, thoroughly shaken the theories of those who held Pembroke to be the person to whom the Sonnets were dedicated, and the youth who inspired so many of them. Mr. Lee, who—rather arbitrarily—declines to attach any importance to the mention of Pembroke's name, and the appeal to his relations with Shakespeare in the folio edition, takes it for granted that Southampton was the one literary patron to whom Shakespeare expressed his gratitude, and he concludes that he alone is the hero of the Sonnets. As Mr. Lee supposes that most of them were written between the spring of 1593 and the autumn of 1594, Southampton would have been young enough to be mentioned as in the poems. As to the dedication of the Sonnets, Sidney Lee declares that it would have been an impossible breach of decorum to designate a man of such high rank and importance as Pembroke was in the year 1609 as "Mr. W. H." In his youthful days, even before he had a right to the title, he was always called Lord Herbert. In 1616 Thorpe dedicated a book to him in these respectful, nay servile terms : To the right honourable William, Earle of Pembroke, Lord Chamberlaine to his Majestie, one of his most honorable Privie Counsell, and Knight of the Garter, etc.

Sidney Lee interprets the word *begetter* as procurer merely, and thinks that Thorpe, in the dedication, simply meant to express his gratitude to a man who had procured one of the manuscripts of the Sonnets, then circulating, and had given it to him. And as a dedication of the poems of the Jesuit Robert Southwell (of 1606), was signed with the letters W. H., indicating another pirate-editor, William Hall, Sidney Lee concludes that it was the latter, who three years later had laid hold of the manuscript of the Sonnets for Thorpe, and that Thorpe had accordingly placed his enterprise under his patronage. In a domain where all is obscure it is difficult to uphold a definite opinion in the face of an opponent so much more learned than myself. Yet I cannot but feel that there is in the wording of the dedication something quite incompatible with the idea that Thorpe addresses himself to a friend and colleague, and Sidney Lee meets this objection only with the remark that Thorpe was notably careless in the use of language. Besides, it is suggestive, that in the three existing dedications by Thorpe, other than that to W. H., the first is addressed to Florio, the two others to the Earl of Pembroke, consequently to real protectors of rank, while the one, which he nine years before addressed to the editor, Edward Blount, who published the manuscript of Marlowe's translation of Lucan for him, is drawn up in a very different and much more intimate way. It is addressed to his "kind and true friend," and gives the friend in question a few hints " as to how to fit himself" for this unaccustomed part of patron. The distance from this to the dedication of the Sonnets is great.

What Sidney Lee attempts to prove by his researches and conjectures is, that the man, who figures in the Sonnets as the protector of the poet, was Southampton, and not Pembroke. The name of the youth is not of the first importance, nor does it signify greatly whether the woman celebrated and attacked in the Sonnets bore the name of Mary Fitton or another. However, the main point is, that in common with a number of previous authors, who have thoroughly studied the contemporaneous literature of Europe, and more especially the sonnet-poetry of Italy, France and England, such as Delius and Elze in Germany, and Henrik Schück in Sweden, Lee, relying on the numerous traits that these poems share with other sonnet-cycles of their period, stamps the whole argument of the text as fiction, and denies their autobiographical character. Scarcely any writer before him has so boldly endeavoured to limit Shakespeare's originality in the domain of sonnet-poetry.

In the first place Lee points out, that the whole body of sixteenth-century sonnets was so dependent firstly on Petrarch, then on such French writers as Ronsard, du Bellay and Desportes, that even the finest of them, the sonnets of Spenser, Sidney, Watson, Lodge, Drayton and Daniel may be characterised as imitative studies, if not simply as a mosaic of plagiarisms. Hereupon he tries to show Shakespeare's dependence on his predecessors. Shakespeare picked up, without scruple, ideas and expressions from the sonnets published by Daniel, Drayton, Watson, Barnabe Barnes, Constable and Sidney; he did this as deliberately and imperturbably as in his comedies he manipulated dramas and novels by contemporary and older poets. To Drayton especially is Shakespeare indebted. As all the Englishmen imitated the Frenchmen, Shakespeare has a false air of having been directly influenced by Ronsard, de Baif and Desportes, though he scarcely knew these poets in their own language.

The Danish translator of the Sonnets, Adolf Hansen, had already pointed out numerous impersonal traits. Some of the poorer Sonnets with their forced and complicated metaphors so obviously bear the impress of the spirit of the age, that it is quite impossible to regard them as characteristic of Shakespeare, and some few Sonnets are such complete imitations, that they cannot be accepted as confessions. Sonnets xviii. and xix. work out the same idea as Daniel's *Delia*, and Sonnets lv. and lxxxi. treat the very same subject as the sixty-ninth Sonnet in Spenser's *Amoretti*. Finally the story of the friends, one of whom deprives the other of his mistress, is to be found in Lyly's *Euphues*.

Sidney Lee maintains that when in Sonnets xxiv. and cxxii. Shakespeare propounds that the image of his friend is engraved in the depths of his heart, or that his brain is a better memorandum-book, as to the friend, than the book with which the latter has presented him, he is merely struggling with conceits of Ronsard's. When in Sonnets xliv. and xlv. he speaks about man as compounded of the elements, earth, air, fire and water, he appropriates motives from Spenser and Barnes. Sonnets xlvi. and xlvii., on the debate of the eye and the heart, are written in terms borrowed from the twentieth Sonnet in Watson's *Tears of Fancy*. Where he proclaims his assurance of the immortality of his verse, and the consequent eternity of his friend's fame, he does not speak from conviction, he only treats a motive, which, following the example of Pindar, Horace and Ovid, the Frenchmen Desportes and Ronsard, and after them such English sonneteers as Spenser, Drayton and Daniel had played upon. Not even when he writes that his lady is beautiful, though dark, and consequently unlovely, is he original; for Sidney had already used a similar phrase. And when he changes his mind, and in the dark eyes and dark complexion of his lady professes to read the blackness of her soul, he is even less original, for at that period the sonnet of invective was the standard variant of the sonnet of amorous eulogy. Nothing is more common than to find the sonneteer grossly abusing his mistress. Ronsard called his a tigress, a murderess, a Medusa; Barnabe Barnes describes his as a tyrant, a Gorgon, a rock; the transition from tenderness to reproach was so frequent, that it was even parodied by Gabriel Harvey. Following many other critics Sidney Lee finally points out that no weight can be attached to the fact, that in Sonnets xxii., lxii., lxxiii., and cxxxviii., Shakespeare speaks of himself as old, for this, too, was a standing conceit of the sonnet-poets of that time. Daniel in *Delia* (23) when he was only twenty-nine speaks as if his life were finished. Richard Barnfield, only twenty years old, invites the boy Ganymedes to contemplate his silver hair, his wrinkled skin, the deep furrows of his face, all this in imitation of Petrarch.

Lee admits, however, that the group of Sonnets, most interesting to the reader, the most mature as to ideas and style, cannot be considered to date from the poet's thirtieth year; he even thinks that Shakespeare continued to write Sonnets until 1603, and propounds—regardless of the wording of the poem—that Sonnet cvii. was written in that year, on the occasion of the death of Queen Elizabeth. That the word "moon" here means Elizabeth is obvious. But that the expression

"The mortal moon hath her eclipse endured"

can mean the final eclipse of the moon is incredible. That the moon has passed through her eclipse, means, I take it, that she is shining brightly again, and thus the interpretation put forth above, of a hint at the frustrated conspiracy of Essex, is far more reasonable. But then this Sonnet, as well as those kindred to it in spirit and tone, point, not to the year 1603, but to 1601.

Yet here details are of minor importance. We take our stand on a fundamental conception of poetic production. All art, even that of the greater artists, begins with imitation ; no poet avoids influences, and up to the present time no poet has hesitated to appropriate from predecessors all that might be of use to him. Even nowadays, when the appreciation of the duty of originality is so infinitely stronger than in the sixteenth, seventeenth, and eighteenth centuries, it is easy to point out appropriations of foreign thoughts and turns of phrase among excellent poets, and it would be possible to enumerate a great variety of common traits among the lyrical poets of Europe. The range of subjects fit for lyrical poetry is not so very great, to be sure. As men, lyrists have after all many emotions and conditions in common. In the mode of expression alone—especially when ideas have to be expressed in an identical form of fourteen lines—is it possible for the poet to manifest his true originality.

No intelligent critic would think of looking to lyrical poems as to biographical sources, in the rough meaning of the term. The poetical is rarely identical with the personal *ego.* But on the other hand it cannot be too strongly insisted upon that books (I mean great, inspired books, such as are read for hundreds of years) are never engendered by other books, but by life. Nobody, who has a drop of artist's blood in his veins, can imagine that a poet of the rank of Shakespeare can have written sonnets by the score only as exercises or metrical experiments, without any bearing on his life, its passions and its crises. The formula for good epic poetry is surely this: that it must always be founded on real life, even if rarely or never an exact copy of it. Lyrical poetry, in which the poet speaks in his own name, and especially of himself, must necessarily, if first-rate, be rooted in what the poet has felt so strongly that it has made him break into song.

The learned critics of Shakespeare's Sonnets regard them merely as metrical *tours de force*, penned in cold blood on subjects prescribed by fashion and convention. They look upon fancy as upon a spider, which spins chimera in all sorts of typical and artificial figures out of itself. It seems more natural to look upon it as a plant, extracting nourishment from the only soil in which it could thrive, namely, the observations and experiences of the poet.

The great modern poets, whose lives lie open before us, have betrayed to us how fancy springs out of impressions of real life, transforming them and making them unrecognisable by its mysterious workings. In several cases we are able to discern the dispersed elements, which in due time crystallise in the poem. Discerning criticism has opened our eyes to the intermixture of these elements in the magic caldron of fancy, while inferior criticism goes astray in a trivial search after possible models. In spite of German scholars and their exertions, we know nothing about whom Goethe had in his mind when he painted Clärchen, nor is this fact of any importance; but this is certain, that the whole poetical life-work of Goethe is founded upon experience. When Max Klinger one evening returned home from having seen a performance of Goethe's *Faust*, he said: What most impressed me was that it was the life of Goethe.

As, knowing the life and experiences of the great modern poet, we are now generally able to trace how these are worked upon and transformed in his works, it is reasonable to suppose that in olden times poets were moved by the same causes, and acted in the same way, at least those of them who have been efficient. When we know of the adventures and emotions of the modern poet, and are able to trace them in the production of his free fancy; when it is possible, where they are unknown to us, to evolve the hidden personality of the poet, and—as every capable critic has experienced—to have our conjectures finally borne out by facts revealed by the contemporary author, then we cannot feel it to be impossible, that in the case of an older poet, we might also be successful in determining when he speaks earnestly from his heart, and in tracing his feelings and experiences through his

T

works, especially when these are lyrical, and their mode of expression passionate and emotional.

Any one who holds fast to the by no means fantastic theory, that there *is* a certain connection between the life and the works of Shakespeare, will be but little moved by successive attempts to deny the Sonnets any autobiographical value, because of the conventional traits and frequent imitations to be pointed out in them.

The modern reader who takes up the Sonnets with no special knowledge of the Renaissance, its tone of feeling, its relation to Greek antiquity, its conventions and its poetic style, finds nothing in them more surprising than the language of love in which the poet addresses his young friend, the positively erotic passion for a masculine personality which here finds utterance. The friend is currently addressed as "my love." Sometimes it is stated in so many words that in the eyes of his admirer the friend combines the charms of man and woman; for instance, in Sonnet xx. :—

> "A woman's face, with Nature's own hand painted,
> Hast thou, the master mistress of my passion."

This Sonnet ends with a playful lament that the friend had not been born of the opposite sex; yet such is the warmth of expression in other Sonnets that one very well understands how the critics of last century supposed them to be addressed to a woman.[1]

This tone, however, is a characteristic fashion of the age. And here, again, it has been insisted that love for a beautiful youth, which the study of Plato had presented to the men of the Renaissance in its most attractive light, was a standing theme among English poets of that age, who, moreover, as in Shakespeare's case, were wont to praise the beauty of their friend above that of their mistress. The woman, as in this case, often enters as a disturbing element into the relation. It was an accepted part of the convention that the poet as above noted should represent himself as withered and wrinkled, whatever his real age might be; Shakespeare does so again and again, though he was at most thirty-seven. Finally, it was quite in accordance with use and wont that the fair youth should be exhorted to marry, so that his beauty might not die with him. Shakespeare had already placed such exhortations in the mouth of the Goddess of Love in *Venus and Adonis*.

All this is true, and yet there is no reasonable ground for doubting that the Sonnets stand in pretty close relation to actual facts.

---

[1] For instance, in Sonnet xxiii. :—

> "O let my books be then the eloquence
> And dumb presagers of my speaking breast,
> Who plead for love, and look for recompense."

And in Sonnet xxvi. :—

> "Lord of my love, to whom in vassalage
> Thy merit hath my duty strongly knit."

The age, indeed, determines the tone, the colouring, of the expressions in which friendship clothes itself. In Germany and Denmark, at the end of the eighteenth century, friendship was a sentimental enthusiasm, just as in England and Italy during the sixteenth century it took the form of platonic love. We can clearly discern, however, that the different methods of expression answered to corresponding shades of difference in the emotion itself. The men of the Renaissance gave themselves up to an adoration of friendship and of their friend which is now unknown, except in circles where a perverted sexuality prevails. Montaigne's friendship for Estienne de la Boëtie, and Languet's passionate tenderness for the youthful Philip Sidney, are cases in point. The observations concerning friendship in Sir Thomas Browne's *Religio Medici*, 1642 (pp. 98, 99), accord entirely with that of Shakespeare: " I love my friend more than myself, and yet I think that I do not love him enough. In a few months my manifold doubled passion will make me believe that I have not at all loved him before. When I am away from him, I am dead, until I meet him again. When I am together with him, I am not content, but always long for a closer connection with him. United souls are not contented, but wish for being truly identical with each other ; and this being impossible, their yearnings are endless and must increase without any possibility of being gratified." But the most remarkable example of a frenzied friendship in Renaissance culture and poetry is undoubtedly to be found in Michael Angelo's letters and sonnets.

Michael Angelo's relation to Messer Tommaso de' Cavalieri presents the most interesting parallel to the attitude which Shakespeare adopted towards William Herbert (?). We find the same expressions of passionate love from the older to the younger man ; but here it is still more unquestionably certain that we have not to do with mere poetical figures of speech, since the letters are not a whit less ardent and enthusiastic than the sonnets. The expressions in the sonnets are sometimes so warm that Michael Angelo's nephew, in his edition of them, altered the word *Signiore* into *Signora*, and these poems, like Shakespeare's, were for some time supposed to have been addressed to a woman.[1]

On January 1, 1533, Michael Angelo, then fifty-seven years old, writes from Florence to Tommaso de' Cavalieri, a youth of noble Roman family, who afterwards became his favourite pupil : " If I do not possess the art of navigating the sea of your potent genius, that genius will nevertheless excuse me, and neither despise my inequality, nor demand of me that which I have it not in me to give ; since that which stands alone in everything can in nothing find its counterpart. Wherefore your lordship, *the only light in our age vouchsafed to this world*, having no equal or peer, cannot find satisfaction in the work of any other hand. If, there-

[1] Ludwig von Scheffler : *Michel Angelo. Eine Renaissancestudie*, 1892.

fore, this or that in the works which I hope and promise to execute should happen to please you, I should call that work, not good, but fortunate. And if I should ever feel assured that—as has been reported to me—I have given your lordship satisfaction in one thing or another, I will make a gift to you of my present and of all that the future may bring me; and it will be a great pain to me to be unable to recall the past, in order to serve you so much the longer, instead of having only the future, which cannot be long, since I am all too old. There is nothing more left for me to say. Read my heart and not my letter, for my pen cannot approach the expression of my good will." [1]

Cavalieri writes to Michael Angelo that he regards himself as born anew since he has come to know the Master; who replies, " I for my part should regard myself as not born, born dead, or, deserted by heaven and earth, if your letters had not brought me the persuasion that your lordship accepts with favour certain of my works." And in a letter of the following summer to Sebastian del Piombo, he sends a greeting to Messer Tommaso, with the words: " I believe *I should instantly fall down dead* if he were no longer in my thoughts." [2]

Michael Angelo plays upon his friend's surname as Shakespeare plays upon his friend's Christian name. These are the last lines of the thirty-first sonnet :—

> " Se vint' e pres' i' debb' esser beato,
> Meraviglia non è se, nud' e solo,
> Resto prigion d'un *Cavalier* armato."

> " If only chains and bands can make me blest,
> No marvel if alone and bare I go
> An armed knight's captive and slave confessed."
>
> (*J. A. Symonds.*)

In other sonnets the tone is no less passionate than Shakespeare's—take, for example, the twenty-second :—

> " More tenderly perchance than is my due,
> Your spirit sees into my heart, where rise
> The flames of holy worship, nor denies
> The grace reserved for those who humbly sue.
> Oh blessèd day when you at last are mine !
> Let time stand still, and let noon's chariot stay ;
> Fixed be that moment on the dial of heaven !
> That I may clasp and keep, by grace divine—

---

[1] " E se io non àrò l'arte del navicare per l'onde del mare del vostro valoroso ingegno, quello mi scuserà, nè si sdegnierà del mio disaguagliarsigli, nè desiderrà da me quello che in me non è : perchè chi è solo in ogni cosa, in cosa alcuna non può aver compagni. Però la vostra Signoria, luce del secol nostro unica al mondo, non puo sodisfarsi di opera d'alcuno altro, non avendo pari nè simile à sè," &c.

[2] " E io non nato, o vero nato morto mi reputerei, e direi in disgrazia, del cielo e della terra, se per la vostra non avessi visto e creduto vostra Signoria accettare volentieri alcune delle opere mie." "Avete data la copia de' sopradetti Madrigali a messer Tomaso . . . che se m'uscissi della mente, credo che súbito cascherei morto."

Clasp in these yearning arms and keep for aye
My heart's loved lord to me desertless given." [1]

(J. A. Symonds.)

In comparison with Cavalieri, Michael Angelo could with justice call himself old. Some critics, on the other hand, have seen in the fact that Shakespeare was not really old at the time when the Sonnets were written, a proof of their conventional and unreal character. But this is to overlook the relativity of the term. As compared with a youth of eighteen, Shakespeare was in effect old, with his sixteen additional years and all his experience of life. And if we are right in assigning Sonnets lxiii. and lxxiii. to the year 1600 or 1601, Shakespeare had then reached the age of thirty-seven, an age at which, as Tyler has very aptly pointed out, Byron in his swan-song uses expressions about himself which might have been copied from Shakespeare's seventy-third Sonnet. Shakespeare says :—

"That time of year thou mayst in me behold
When *yellow leaves*, or none, or few, do hang
Upon those boughs which shake against the cold
Bare ruin'd choirs, where late the sweet birds sang."

Byron thus expresses himself :—

" My days are in *the yellow leaf,*[2]
The flowers and fruits of love are gone,
The worm, the canker and the grief
Are mine alone."

In Shakespeare we read :—

" In me thou seest *the glowing of such fire*
That on the ashes of his youth doth lie
As the *death-bed* whereon it must expire,
Consum'd with that which it was nourished by."

Byron's words are :—

" *The fire that on my bosom preys*
Is lone as some volcanic isle ;
No torch is kindled at its blaze—
A funeral pile."

Thus both poets liken themselves, at this comparatively early age, to the wintry woods with their yellowing leaves, and without blossom, fruit, or the song of birds ; and both compare the fire

---

[1] " Accio ch' i' abbi, e non già per mie merto,
Il desiato mio dolce signiore
Per sempre nell' indegnie e pronte braccia."

[2] This line, however, is obviously suggested by the famous passage in *Macbeth* (Act v.)—

" My way of life
Is fall'n into the sere, the yellow leaf."

which still glows in their soul to a solitary flame which finds no nourishment from without. The ashes of my youth become its death-bed, says Shakespeare. They are a funeral pile, says Byron.

Nor is it possible to conclude, as Schück does, from the conventional style of the first seventeen Sonnets—for instance, from their almost verbal identity with a passage in Sidney's *Arcadia*—that they are quite devoid of relation to the poet's own life.

In short, the elements of temporary fashion and convention which appear in the Sonnets in no way prove that they were not genuine expressions of the poet's actual feelings.

They lay bare to us a side of his character which does not appear in the plays. We see in him an emotional nature with a passionate bent towards self-surrender in love and idolatry, and with a corresponding, though less excessive, yearning to be loved.

We learn from the Sonnets to what a degree Shakespeare was oppressed and tormented by his sense of the contempt in which the actor's calling was held. The scorn of ancient Rome for the mountebank, the horror of ancient Judea for one who disguised himself in the garments of the other sex, and finally the age-old hatred of Christianity for theatres and all the temptations that follow in their train—all these habits of thought had been handed down from generation to generation, and, as Puritanism grew in strength and gained the upper hand, had begotten a contemptuous tone of public opinion under which so sensitive a nature as Shakespeare's could not but suffer keenly. He was not regarded as a poet who now and then acted, but as an actor who now and then wrote plays. It was a pain to him to feel that he belonged to a caste which had no civic status. Hence his complaint, in Sonnet xxix., of being "in disgrace with fortune and men's eyes." Hence, in Sonnet xxxvi., his assurance to his friend that he will not obtrude on others the fact of their friendship :—

> "I may not evermore acknowledge thee,
> Lest my bewailèd guilt should do thee shame:
> Nor thou with public kindness honour me,
> Unless thou take that honour from thy name :
> But do not so ; I love thee in such sort,
> As, thou being mine, mine is thy good report."

The bitter complaint in Sonnet lxxii. seems rather to refer to the writer's situation as a dramatist :—

> "For I am shamed by that which I bring forth,
> And so should you, to love things nothing worth."

The melancholy which fills Sonnet cx. is occasioned by the writer's profession and his nature as a poet and artist :—

> "Alas ! 'tis true, I have gone here and there,
> And made myself a motley to the view ;

Gor'd mine own thoughts, sold cheap what is most dear,
Made old offences of affections new :
Most true it is, that I have look'd on truth
Askance and strangely; but, by all above,
These blenches gave my heart another youth,
And worse essays prov'd thee my best of love."

Hence, finally, his reproach to Fortune, in Sonnet cxi., that she did not "better for his life provide Than public means which public manners breeds":—

" Thence comes it that my name receives a brand;
And almost thence my nature is subdu'd
To what it works in, like the dyer's hand."

We must bear in mind this continual writhing under the prejudice against his calling and his art, and this indignation at the injustice of the attitude adopted towards them by a great part of the middle classes, if we would understand the high pressure of Shakespeare's feelings towards the noble youth who had approached him full of the art-loving traditions of the aristocracy, and the burning enthusiasm of the young for intellectual superiority. This young Lord, with his beauty and his personal charm, must have come to him like a very angel of light, a messenger from a higher world than that in which his lot was cast. He was a living witness to the fact that Shakespeare was not condemned to seek the applause of the multitude alone, but could win the favour of the noblest in the land, and was not excluded from a deep and almost passionate friendship which placed him on an equal footing with the bearer of an ancient name. The young nobleman's great beauty no doubt made a deep impression upon the beauty-lover in Shakespeare's soul. It is very probable, too, that the young aristocrat, according to the fashion of the times, made the poet his debtor for more solid benefactions than mere friendship ; and Shakespeare must thus have found doubly painful the situation in which he was placed by the intrigue between his mistress and his friend.[1]

In any case, the affection with which the young Lord inspired Shakespeare—the passionate attachment, leading even to jealousy of other poets admired by the young nobleman—had not only a vividness, but an erotic fervour such as we never find in our own age manifested between man and man. Note such an expression as this in Sonnet cx. :—

"Then give me welcome, next my heaven the best,
Even to thy pure and most most loving breast."

---

[1] Several passages in the Sonnets suggest that Pembroke must have conferred substantial gifts upon Shakespeare—for example, that expression "wealth" in Sonnet xxxvii., "your bounty" in Sonnet liii., and "your own dear-purchased right" in Sonnet cxvii.

This exactly corresponds to Michael Angelo's recently-quoted desire to "clasp in his yearning arms his heart's loved lord." Or observe such a line as this in Sonnet lxxv. :—

> "So are you to my thoughts as food to life."

We have here an exact counterpart to the following expressions in a letter from Michael Angelo to Cavalieri, dated July, 1533 : " I would far rather forget the food on which I live, which wretchedly sustains the body alone, than your name, which sustains both body and soul, filling both with such happiness that I can feel neither care nor fear of death while I have it in my memory."[1]

The passionate fervour of this friendship on the Platonic model is accompanied in Shakespeare, as in Michael Angelo, by a submissiveness on the part of the elder friend towards the younger, which, in these two supreme geniuses, affects the modern reader painfully. Each had put off every shred of pride in relation to his idolised young friend. How strange it seems to find Shakespeare calling himself his young protector's "slave," and assuring him that his time, more precious than that of any other man then living, is of no value, so that his friend may let him wait or summon him to his side as his caprice and fancy dictate. In Sonnet lviii. he speaks of "that God who made me first your slave." Sonnet lvii. runs thus :—

> " Being *your slave*, what should I do but tend
> Upon the hours and times of your desire ?
> I have no precious time at all to spend,
> Nor services to do, till you require.
> Nor dare I chide the world-without-end hour,
> Whilst I, my sovereign, watch the clock for you,
> Nor think the bitterness of absence sour,
> When you have bid your servant once adieu ;
> Nor dare I question with my jealous thought,
> Where you may be, or your affairs suppose ;
> But, like a sad slave, stay and think of nought,
> Save, where you are how happy you make those."

Just as Michael Angelo spoke to Cavalieri of his works as though they were scarcely worth his friend's notice, so does Shakespeare sometimes speak of his verses. In Sonnet xxxii. he begs his friends to " re-survey " them when he is dead :—

> " And though they be outstripp'd by every pen,
> Reserve them for my love, not for their rhyme,
> Exceeded by the height of happier men."

This humility becomes quite despicable when a breach is threatened between the friends. Shakespeare then repeatedly

---

[1] " Anzi posso prima dimenticare il cibo di ch'io vivo, che nutrisce solo il corpo infelicemente, che il nome vostro, che nutrisce il corpo e l'anima, riempiendo l'uno e l'altro di tanta dolcezza, che nè noia nè timor di morte, mentre la memoria mi vi serba, posso sentire."

promises so to blacken himself that his friend shall reap, not shame, but honour, from his faithlessness. In Sonnet lxxxviii. :—

> " With mine own weakness being best acquainted,
> Upon thy part I can set down a story
> Of faults concealed wherein I am attainted,
> That thou, in losing me, shalt win much glory."

Sonnet lxxxix. is still more strongly worded :—

> " Thou canst not, love, disgrace me half so ill,
> To set a form upon desirèd change,
> As I'll myself disgrace : knowing thy will,
> I will acquaintance strangle, and look strange ;
> Be absent from thy walks ; and in my tongue
> Thy sweet-belovèd name no more shall dwell,
> Lest I (too much profane) should do it wrong,
> And haply of our old acquaintance tell.
>   For thee, against myself I'll vow debate,
>   For I must ne'er love him whom thou dost hate."

We are positively surprised when, in a single passage, in Sonnet lxii., we come upon a forcible expression of self-love ; but it does not extend beyond the first half of the Sonnet ; in the second half this self-love is already regarded as a sin, and Shakespeare humbly effaces himself before his friend. All the more gladly does the reader welcome the few Sonnets (lv. and lxxxi.) in which the poet confidently predicts the immortality of these his utterances. It is true that Shakespeare is here greatly influenced by antiquity and by the fashion of his age ; and it is simply as records of his friend's beauty and amiability that his verses are to be preserved through all ages to come. But no poet without a sound and vigorous self-confidence could have written either these lines in Sonnet lv. :—

> " Not marble, nor the gilded monuments
> Of princes shall outlive this powerful rhyme "—

or these others in Sonnet lxxxi. :—

> " Your monument shall be my gentle verse,
> Which eyes not yet created shall o'erread ;
> And tongues to be your being shall rehearse,
> When all the breathers of this world are dead."

Yet, as we see, the first and last thought is always that of the friend, his beauty, worth, and fame. And as he will live in the future, so he has lived in the past. Shakespeare cannot conceive existence without him. In Sonnets which have no direct connection with each other (lix., cvi., cxxiii.) he returns again and again to that strange thought of a perpetual cycle or recurrence of events, which runs through the whole of the world's history, from the Pythagoreans and Kohélet to Friedrich Nietzsche. In

view of such high-pitched idolatry, we can well understand that
the friend's faithlessness, or, if you will, the mistress's conquest
of the friend, must have made a deep impression upon Shakespeare's sensitive soul. The crisis left its mark upon him for
many a long day.

And at the same time another and purely personal mortification
was added to his troubles. It appears that Shakespeare's name
was just then involved in a degrading scandal of one sort or
another. He says so expressly in Sonnet cxii. :—

> "Your love and pity doth the impression fill
> Which vulgar scandal stamped upon my brow."

He here avers that he cares very little "to know his shames or
praises" from the tongues of others, and that his friend's judgment is all in all to him ; but in Sonnet cxxi., where he goes more
closely into the matter, he confesses that some "frailty" in him
has given rise to these malignant rumours, and we see that for
this frailty his "sportive blood" was to blame. He does not deny
the accusation, but asks—

> "Why should others' false adulterate eyes
> Give salutation to my sportive blood?
> Or on my frailties why are frailer spies,
> Which in their wills count bad what I think good?"

The details of this scandal are unknown to us. We can only
conclude that it referred to Shakespeare's alleged relation to some
woman, or implication in some amorous adventure. In discussing
this point, Tyler has aptly cited two passages in contemporary
writings, though of course without absolutely proving that they
have any bearing on the matter. The first is the above-quoted
anecdote in John Manningham's Diary for March 13, 1601 (New
Style, 1602), as to Shakespeare's forestalling Burbage in the
graces of a citizen's wife, and announcing himself as "William
the Conqueror"—an anecdote which seems to have been widely
current at the time, and no doubt arose from more or less recent
events. The second passage occurs in *The Returne from Per-
nassus*, dating from December 1601, in which (iv. 3) Burbage
and Kemp are introduced, and these words are placed in the
mouth of Kemp: "O that *Ben Ionson* is a pestilent fellow, he
brought vp *Horace* giuing the Poets a pill, but our fellow *Shakespeare* hath giuen him a purge that made him beray his credit."
The allusion is evidently to the feud between Ben Jonson on the
one hand and Marston and Dekker on the other, which culminated
in 1601 with the appearance of Ben Jonson's *Poetaster*, in which
Horace serves as the Poet's mouthpiece. Dekker and Marston
retorted in the same year with *Satiromastix or the Untrussing
of the Humorous Poet.* As Shakespeare took no direct part in
this quarrel, we can only conjecture what is meant by the above

allusion. Mr. Richard Simpson has suggested that King William Rufus, in whose reign the action of *Satiromastix* takes place, and who "presides over the untrussing of the humorous poet," may be intended for William Shakespeare. Rufus, in the play, is by no means a model of chastity, and carries off Walter Terrill's bride very much as "William the Conqueror" in Manningham's anecdote carries off "Richard the Third's" mistress. Simpson thinks it probable that the spectators would have little difficulty in recognising the William the Conqueror of the anecdote in the William Rufus of the play, whose nickname, indeed, might be taken as referring to Shakespeare's complexion. If we accept this interpretation, we find in *Satiromastix* a further proof of the notoriety of the anecdote. Whether it be this scandal or another of the same kind to which the Sonnets refer, Shakespeare seems to have taken greatly to heart the besmirching of his name.

It remains that we should glance at the form of the Sonnets and say a word as to their poetic value.

As regards the form, the first and most obvious remark is that, in spite of their name, these poems are not in reality sonnets at all, and have, indeed, nothing in common with the sonnet except their fourteen lines. In the structure of his so-called Sonnets Shakespeare simply followed the tradition and convention of his country.

Sir Thomas Wyatt, the leading figure in the earlier English school of lyrists, travelled in Italy in the year 1527, familiarised himself with the forms and style of Italian poetry, and introduced the sonnet into English literature. A somewhat younger poet, Henry, Earl of Surrey, soon followed in his footsteps; he, too, travelled in Italy, and cultivated the same poetic models. Not until after the death of both poets were their sonnets published in the collection known as *Tottel's Miscellany* (1557). Neither of the poets succeeded in keeping to the Petrarchan model—an octave and a sestett. Wyatt, it is true, usually preserves the octave, but breaks up the sestett and finishes with a couplet. Surrey departs still more widely from his model's strict and difficult form: his "Sonnet" consists, like Shakespeare's after him, of three quatrains and a couplet, the rhymes of which are in nowise interwoven. Sidney, again, preserved the octave, but broke up the sestett. Spenser attempted a new rhyme-scheme, interweaving the second and third quatrain, but keeping to the final couplet. Daniel, who is Shakespeare's immediate predecessor and master, returns to Surrey's really formless form. The chief defect in Shakespeare's Sonnets as a metrical whole consists in the appended couplet, which hardly ever keeps up to the level of the beginning, hardly ever presents any picture to the eye, but is, as a rule, merely reflective, and often brings the burst of feeling which animates the poem to a feeble, or at any rate more rhetorical than poetic, issue.

In actual poetic value the Sonnets are extremely unequal. The first group as we have already pointed out (p. 270) stands lowest in the scale, necessarily expressing but little of the poet's personal feeling.

The last two Sonnets in the collection (cliii. and cliv.), dealing with a conventional theme borrowed from the antique, are likewise entirely impersonal. W. Hertzberg, having been put on the track by Herr von Friesen, in 1878 discovered the Greek original of these two Sonnets in the ninth book of the Palatine Anthology.[1] The poem which Shakespeare has adapted, and in Sonnet cliv. almost translated, was written by the Byzantine scholar Marianus, probably in the fifth century after Christ; it was published in Latin, among other epigrams, at Basle in 1529, was retranslated several times before the end of the sixteenth century, and must have become known to Shakespeare in one or other of these different forms.

Next in order stand the Sonnets of merely conventional inspiration, those in which the eye and heart go to law with each other, or in which the poet plays upon his own name and his friend's. These cannot possibly claim any high poetic value.

But the poems thus set apart form but a small minority of the collection. In all the others the waves of feeling run high, and it may be said in general that the deeper the sentiment and the stronger the emotion they express, the more admirable is their force of diction and their marvellous melody. There are Sonnets whose musical quality is unsurpassed by any of the songs introduced into the plays, or even by the most famous and beautiful speeches in the plays themselves. The free and lax form he had adopted was of evident advantage to Shakespeare. The triple and quadruple rhymes, which in Italian involve scarcely any difficulty or constraint, would have proved very hampering in English. As a matter of fact, Shakespeare has been able to follow out every inspiration unimpeded by the shackles of an elaborate rhyme-scheme, and has achieved a rare combination of terseness and harmony in the expression of sorrow, melancholy, anguish, and resignation. Nothing could be more melodious than the opening of Sonnet xl., quoted above, or these lines from Sonnet lxxxvi. :—

> "Was it the proud full sail of his great verse,
> Bound for the prize of all-too-precious you,
> That did my ripe thoughts in my brain inhearse,
> Making their tomb the womb wherein they grew?"

And how moving is the earnestness of Sonnet cxvi., on faith in love :—

> "Let me not to the marriage of true minds
> Admit impediments. Love is not love

---

[1] *Jahrbuch der deutschen Shakespeare-Gesellschaft*, Band xiii. S. 158.

Which alters when it alteration finds,
Or bends with the remover to remove :
O, no ! it is an ever-fixèd mark,
That looks on tempests, and is never shaken ;
It is the star to every wandering bark,
. Whose worth's unknown, although his height be taken."

Shakespeare's Sonnets are for the general reader the most inaccessible of his works, but they are also the most difficult to tear oneself away from.   " With this key Shakespeare unlocked his heart," says Wordsworth ; and some people are repelled from them by the *Menschliches*, or, as they think, *Allzumenschliches*, which is there revealed.   In any case they think Shakespeare belittled by his candour.   Browning, for example, thus retorts upon Wordsworth :—

" ' With this same key
Shakespeare unlocked his heart.'   Once more
Did Shakespeare ?   If so, the less Shakespeare he."

The reader who can reconcile himself to the fact that great geniuses are not necessarily models of correctness will pass a very different judgment.   He will follow with eager interest the experiences which rent and harrowed Shakespeare's soul.   He will rejoice in the insight afforded by these poems, which the crowd ignores, into the tempestuous emotional life of one of the greatest of men.   Here, and here alone, we see Shakespeare himself, as distinct from his poetical creations, loving, admiring, longing, yearning, adoring, disappointed, humiliated, tortured. Here alone does he enter the confessional.   Here more than anywhere else can we, who at a distance of three centuries do homage to the poet's art, feel ourselves in intimate communion, not only with the poet, but with the man.

VIII

JULIUS CÆSAR—ITS FUNDAMENTAL DEFECT

IT is afternoon, a little before three o'clock. Whole fleets of wherries are crossing the Thames, picking their way among the swans and the other boats, to land their passengers on the south bank of the river. Skiff after skiff puts forth from the Black-friars stair, full of theatre-goers who have delayed a little too long over their dinner and are afraid of being too late; for the flag waving over the Globe Theatre announces that there is a play to-day. The bills upon the street-posts have informed the public that Shakespeare's *Julius Cæsar* is to be presented, and the play draws a full house. People pay their sixpences and enter; the balconies and the pit are filled. Distinguished and specially favoured spectators take their seats on the stage behind the curtain. Then sound the first, the second, and the third trumpet-blasts, the curtain parts in the middle, and reveals a stage entirely hung with black.

Enter the tribunes Flavius and Marullus; they scold the rabble and drive them home because they are loafing about on a week-day without their working-clothes and tools—in contravention of a London police regulation which the public finds so natural that they (and the poet) can conceive it as in force in ancient Rome. At first the audience is somewhat restless. The groundlings talk in undertones as they light their pipes. But the Second Citizen speaks the name of Cæsar. There are cries of "Hush! hush!" and the progress of the play is followed with eager attention.

It was received with applause, and soon became very popular. Of this we have contemporary evidence. Leonard Digges, in the poem quoted above (p. 233), vaunts its scenic attractiveness at the expense of Ben Jonson's Roman plays :—

> " So have I seene, when Cesar would appeare,
> And on the Stage at halfe-sword parley were
> *Brutus* and *Cassius:* oh how the Audience
> Were ravish'd, with what new wonder they went thence,
> When some new day they would not brooke a line
> Of tedious (though well laboured) *Catiline.*"

The learned rejoiced in the breath of air from ancient Rome which met them in these scenes, and the populace was entertained and fascinated by the striking events and heroic characters of the drama. A quatrain in John Weever's *Mirror of Martyrs, or The Life and Death of Sir Iohn Oldcastle · Knight, Lord Cobham*, tells how

> " The many-headed multitude were drawne
> By *Brutus* speech, that *Cæsar* was ambitious,
> When eloquent *Mark Antonie* had showne
> His vertues, who but *Brutus* then was vicious ? "

There were, indeed, numerous plays on the subject of Julius Cæsar—they are mentioned in Gosson's *Schoole of Abuse*, 1579, in *The Third Blast of Retraite from Plaies*, 1580, in Henslow's Diary, 1594 and 1602, in *The Mirrour of Policie*, 1598, &c.— but Weever's words do not apply to any of those which have come down to us. It can therefore scarcely be doubted that they refer to Shakespeare's drama; and as the poem appeared in 1601, it affords us almost decisive evidence as to the date of *Julius Cæsar*. In all probability, it was in the same year that the play was written and produced. Weever, indeed, says in his dedication that his poem was " some two yeares agoe made fit for print;' but even if this be true, the lines above quoted may quite well have been inserted later. There are several reasons for believing that *Julius Cæsar* can scarcely have been produced earlier than 1601. The years 1599 and 1600 are already so full of work that we can scarcely assign to them this great tragedy as well; and internal evidence indicates that the play must have been written about the same time as *Hamlet*, to which its style offers so many striking resemblances.

The immediate success of the play is proved by this fact, among others, that it at once called forth a rival production on the same theme. Henslow notes in his diary that in May 1602, on behalf of Lord Nottingham's company, he paid five pounds for a drama called *Cæsar's Fall* to the poets Munday, Drayton, Webster, Middleton, and another. It was evidently written to order. And as *Julius Cæsar*, in its novelty, was unusually successful, so, too, we find it still reckoned one of Shakespeare's greatest and profoundest plays, unlike the English " Histories " in standing alone and self-sufficient, characteristically composed, forming a rounded whole in spite of its apparent scission at the death of Cæsar, and exhibiting a remarkable insight into Roman character and the life of antiquity.

What attracted Shakespeare to this theme ? And, first and foremost, what *is* the theme ? The play is called *Julius Cæsar*, but it was obviously not Cæsar himself that attracted Shakespeare. The true hero of the piece is Brutus; he it is who has aroused the poet's fullest interest. We must explain to ourselves the why and wherefore.

The answer is to be found in the point of time at which the

play was written. It was that eventful year when Shakespeare's earliest friends among the great, Essex and Southampton, had set on foot their foolhardy conspiracy against Elizabeth, and when their attempted insurrection had ended in the death of the one, the imprisonment of the other. He had seen how proud and nobly-disposed characters might easily be seduced into political error, and tempted to rebellion, on the plea of independence. It is true that there was little enough resemblance of detail between the mere palace-revolution designed by Essex, which should free him from his subjection to the Queen's incalculable caprices, and the attempt of the Roman patricians to liberate an aristo-cratic republic, by assassination, from the yoke of a newly-founded despotism. The point of resemblance lay in the mere fact of the imprudent and ill-starred attempt to effect a subversion of public order.

Add to this the fact that Shakespeare, in the present stage of his career, displays a certain preference for characters who, in spite of noble qualities, have fortune against them and are unable to bring their projects to a successful issue. While he himself was still fighting for his position, Henry V., the man of practical genius, the born victor and conqueror, had been his ideal ; now that he stood on firm ground, and was soon to reach the height of his reputation, he seems to have turned with a sort of melancholy predilection to characters like Brutus and Hamlet, who, in spite of the highest endowments, proved unequal to the tasks proposed to them.[1] They appealed to him as profound dreamers and high-minded idealists. He found something of their nature, too, in his own.

A good score of years earlier, in 1579, North's version of Plutarch's parallel biographies had been published, not translated from the original, but from the French translation of Amyot. In this book Shakespeare found his material.

His method of using this material differs considerably from his treatment of his other authorities. From a chronicler like Holinshed he, as a rule, takes nothing but the course of events, the outline of the leading personages and such anecdotes as suit his purpose. From novelists like Bandello or Cinthio he takes the main lines of the action, but relies almost entirely on his own invention for the characters and the dialogue. From the earlier plays, which he adapts or re-casts, such as *The Taming of a Shrew, King John, The Famous Victories* of Henry V., and *King Leir* (the original *Hamlet* is unfortunately not preserved), he transfers into his own work every scene and speech that is worth anything ; but in the cases in which we can make the comparison, there is little enough that he finds available. Here, on the other hand, we find a curious and instructive example of his method of

---

[1] Compare Dowden, *Shakspere*, p. 280.

work when he most faithful₊ followed his original.   We realise
that the more developed the ᵣt and the more competent the
psychology of the writer before im, the more closely did Shakespeare tread in his footsteps.

Here for the first time he fouₗ himself in touch with a wholly
civilised spirit—not seldom childlik in his antique simplicity, but
still no mean artist.   Jean Paul, witₕ some exaggeration, yet not
quite extravagantly, has called Plutarch the biographical Shakespeare of world-history.

The whole drama of *Julius Cæsar* may be read in Plutarch.
Shakespeare had before him three Lives—those of Cæsar, Brutus,
and Mark Antony.   Read them consecutively, and you find in
them every detail of *Julius Cæsar*.

Let us take some examples from the first act of the play.   It
begins with the tribunes' jealousy of the favour in which Cæsar
stands with the common people ; and everything down to the
minutest trait is taken from Plutarch.   The same with what follows : Mark Antony's repeated offer of the crown to Cæsar at the
feast of the Lupercal, and his unwilling refusal of it.   So too with
Cæsar's suspicions of Cassius ; Cæsar's speech on his second
entrance—

> " Let me have men about me that are fat,
> Sleek-headed men, and such as sleep o' nights :
> Yond Cassius has a lean and hungry look ;
> He thinks too much ; such men are dangerous,"—

occurs word for word in Plutarch ; the anecdote, indeed, made
such an impression on him that he has repeated it three times in
different Lives.   We find, furthermore, in the Greek historian,
how Cassius gradually involves Brutus in the conspiracy ; how
papers exhorting Brutus to action are thrown into his house ; the
deliberations as to whether Antony is to die along with Cæsar,
and Brutus's mistaken judgment of Antony's character ; Portia's
complaint at being excluded from her husband's confidence ; the
proof of courage which she gives by plunging a knife into her
thigh ; all the omens and prodigies that precede the murder ; the
sacrificial ox without a heart ; the fiery warriors fighting in the
clouds ; Calphurnia's warning dream ; Cæsar's determination not
to go to the Senate on the Ides of March ; Decius [Decimus]
Brutus's endeavour to change his purpose ; the fruitless efforts of
Artemidorus to restrain him from facing the danger, &c., &c.   It
is all in Plutarch, point for point.

Here and there we find small and subtle divergences from the
original, which may be traced now to Shakespeare's temperament,
now to his view of life, and again to his design in the play.
Plutarch, for example, has not Shakespeare's contempt for the
populace, and does not make them so senselessly fickle.   Then,
again, he gives no hint for Brutus's soliloquy before taking the

U

final resolution (II. 1). For the rest, wherever it is possible, Shakespeare employs the very words of North's translation. Nay, more, he accepts the characters, such as Brutus, Portia, Cassius, just as they stand in Plutarch. His Brutus is absolutely the same as Plutarch's; his Cassius is a man of somewhat deeper character.

In dealing with the great figure of Cæsar, which gives the play its name, Shakespeare follows faithfully the detached, anecdotic indications of Plutarch; but he, strangely enough, seems altogether to miss the remarkable impression we receive from Plutarch of Cæsar's character, which, for the rest, the Greek historian himself was not in a position fully to understand. We must not forget the fact, of which Shakespeare of course knew nothing, that Plutarch, who was born a century after Cæsar's death, at a time when the independence of Greece was only a memory, and the once glorious Hellas was part of a Roman province, wrote his comparative biographies to remind haughty Rome that Greece had a great man to oppose to each of her greatest sons. Plutarch was saturated with the thought that conquered Greece was Rome's lord and master in every department of the intellectual life. He delivered Greek lectures in Rome and could not speak Latin, while every Roman spoke Greek to him and understood it as well as his native tongue. Significantly enough, Roman literature and poetry do not exist for Plutarch, though he incessantly cites Greek authors and poets. He never mentions Virgil or Ovid. He wrote about his great Romans as an enlightened and unprejudiced Pole might in our days write about great Russians. He, in whose eyes the old republics shone transfigured, was not specially fitted to appreciate Cæsar's greatness.

Shakespeare, having so arranged his drama that Brutus should be its tragic hero, had to concentrate his art on placing him in the foreground, and making him fill the scene. The difficulty was not to let his lack of political insight (in the case of Antony), or of practical sense (in his quarrel with Cassius), detract from the impression of his superiority. He had to be the centre and pivot of everything, and therefore Cæsar was diminished and belittled to such a degree, unfortunately, that this matchless genius in war and statesmanship has become a miserable caricature.

We find in other places clear indications that Shakespeare knew very well what this man was and was worth. Edward's young son, in *Richard III.*, speaks with enthusiasm of Cæsar as that conqueror whom death has not conquered; Horatio, in the almost contemporary *Hamlet*, speaks of "mightiest Julius" and his death; and Cleopatra, in *Antony and Cleopatra*, is proud of having been the mistress of Cæsar. It is true that in *As You Like It* the playful Rosalind uses the expression, "Cæsar's thrasonical brag," with reference to the famous *Veni, vidi, vici*, but in an entirely jocose context and acceptation.

But here! here Cæsar has become in effect no little of a braggart, and is compounded, on the whole, of anything but attractive characteristics. He produces the impression of an invalid. His liability to the " falling sickness " is emphasised. He is deaf of one ear. He has no longer his old strength. He faints when the crown is offered to him. He envies Cassius because he is a stronger swimmer. He is as superstitious as an old woman. He rejoices in flattery, talks pompously and arrogantly, boasts of his firmness and is for ever wavering. He acts incautiously and unintelligently, and does not realise what threatens him, while every one else sees it clearly.

Shakespeare dared not, says Gervinus, arouse too great interest in Cæsar; he had to throw into relief everything about him that could account for the conspiracy ; and, moreover, he had Plutarch's distinct statement that Cæsar's character had greatly deteriorated shortly before his death. Hudson practically agrees with this, holding that Shakespeare wished to present Cæsar as he appeared in the eyes of the conspirators, so that "they too might have fair and equal judgment at our hands;" admitting, for the rest, that "Cæsar was literally too great to be seen by them," and that "Cæsar is far from being himself in these scenes ; hardly one of the speeches put in his mouth can be regarded as historically characteristic." Thus Hudson arrives at the astonishing result that "there is an undertone of irony at work in the ordering and tempering of this composition," explaining that, "when such a shallow idealist as Brutus is made to overtop and outshine the greatest practical genius the world ever saw," we are bound to assume that the intention is ironical.

This is the emptiest cobweb-spinning. There is no trace of irony in the representation of Brutus. Nor can we fall back upon the argument that Cæsar, after his death, becomes the chief personage of the drama, and as a corpse, as a memory, as a spirit, strikes down his murderers. How can so small a man cast so great a shadow! Shakespeare, of course, intended to show Cæsar as triumphing after his death. He has changed Brutus's evil genius, which appears to him in the camp and at Philippi, into Cæsar's ghost; but this ghost is not sufficient to rehabilitate Cæsar in our estimation.

Nor is it true that Cæsar's greatness would have impaired the unity of the piece. Its poetic value, on the contrary, suffers from his pettiness. The play might have been immeasurably richer and deeper than it is, had Shakespeare been inspired by a feeling of Cæsar's greatness.

Elsewhere in Shakespeare one marvels at what he has made out of poor and meagre material. Here, history was so enormously rich, that his poetry has become poor and meagre in comparison with it.

Just as Shakespeare (if the portions of the first part of

Henry VI. which deal with La Pucelle are by him) represented
Jeanne d'Arc with no sense for the lofty and simple poetry that
breathed around her figure—national prejudice and old superstition blinding him—so he approached the characterisation of Cæsar
with far too light a heart, and with imperfect knowledge and care.
As he had made Jeanne d'Arc a witch, so he makes Cæsar a
braggart.   Cæsar !

If, like the schoolboys of later generations, he had been given
Cæsar's *Gallic War* to read in his childhood, this would not
have been possible to him.   Is it conceivable that, in what he had
heard about the Commentaries, he had naïvely seized upon and
misinterpreted the fact that Cæsar always speaks of himself in the
third person, and calls himself by his name ?

Let us compare for a moment this posing self-worshipper of
Shakespeare's with the picture of Cæsar which the poet might
easily have formed from his Plutarch alone, thus explaining
Cæsar's rise to the height of autocracy on which he stands at the
beginning of the play, and at the same time the gradual piling up
of the hatred to which he succumbed.   On the very second page
of the life of Cæsar he must have read the anecdote of how Cæsar,
when quite a young man, on his way back from Bithynia, was
taken prisoner by Cilician pirates.   They demanded a ransom of
twenty talents (about £4000). He answered that they clearly did
not know who their prisoner was, promised them fifty talents, sent
his attendants to different towns to raise this sum, and remained
with only a friend and two servants among these notoriously
bloodthirsty bandits.   He displayed the greatest contempt for
them, and freely ordered them about; he made them keep perfectly quiet when he wanted to sleep ; for the thirty-eight days
he remained among them he treated them as a prince might his
bodyguard.   He went through his gymnastic exercises, and wrote
poems and orations in the fullest security.   He often assured them
that he would certainly have them hanged, or rather crucified.
When the ransom arrived from Miletus, the first use he made of
his liberty was to fit out some ships, attack the pirates, take them
all prisoners, and seize upon their booty.   Then he carried them
before the Prætor of Asia, Junius, whose business it was to
punish them.   Junius, out of avarice, replied that he would take
time to reflect what should be done with the prisoners ; whereupon
Cæsar returned to Pergamos, where he had left them in prison,
and kept his word by having them all crucified.

What has become of this masterfulness, this grace, and this
iron will, in Shakespeare's Cæsar ?

> " I fear him not :
> Yet if my name were liable to fear,
> I do not know the man I should avoid
> So soon as that spare Cassius.

.   .   .   .

I rather tell thee what is to be fear'd
Than what I fear, for always I am Cæsar."

It is well that he himself makes haste to say so, otherwise one
would scarcely believe it. And does one believe it, after all ?

As Shakespeare conceives the situation, the Republic which
Cæsar overthrew might have continued to exist but for him, and
it was a criminal act on his part to destroy it.

But the old aristocratic Republic had already fallen to pieces
when Cæsar welded its fragments into a new monarchy. Sheer
lawlessness reigned in Rome. The populace was such as even
the rabble of our own great cities can give no conception of: not
the brainless mob, for the most part tame, only now and then
going wild through mere stupidity, which in Shakespeare listens to
the orations over Cæsar's body and tears Cinna to pieces ; but a
populace whose innumerable hordes consisted mainly of slaves,
together with the thousands of foreigners from all the three conti-
nents, Phrygians from Asia, Negroes from Africa, Iberians and
Celts from Spain and France, who flocked together in the capital
of the world. To the immense bands of house-slaves and field-
slaves, there were added thousands of runaway slaves who had
committed theft or murder at home, lived by robbery on the way,
and now lay hid in the purlieus of the city. But besides foreigners
with no means of support and slaves without bread, there were
swarms of freedmen, entirely corrupted by their servile condition,
for whom freedom, whether combined with helpless poverty or
with new-made riches, meant only the freedom to do harm. Then
there were troops of gladiators, as indifferent to the lives of others
as to their own, and entirely at the beck and call of whoever
would pay them. It was from ruffians of this class that a man
like Clodius had recruited the armed gangs who surrounded him,
divided like regular soldiers into decuries and centuries under
duly appointed commanders. These bands fought battles in the
Forum with other bands of gladiators or of herdsmen from the
wild regions of Picenum or Lombardy, whom the Senate imported for its own protection. There was practically no street
police or fire-brigade. When public disasters happened, such
as floods or conflagrations, people regarded them as portents
and consulted the augurs. The magistrates were no longer
obeyed ; consuls and tribunes were attacked, and sometimes even
killed. In the Senate the orators covered each other with abuse,
in the Forum they spat in each other's faces. Regular battles
took place on the Campus Martius at every election, and no man
of position ever appeared in the streets without a bodyguard of
gladiators and slaves. " If we try to conceive to ourselves,"
wrote Mommsen in 1857, "a London with the slave population
of New Orleans, with the police of Constantinople, with the
non-industrial character of the modern Rome, and agitated by

politics after the fashion of the Paris of 1848, we shall acquire an approximate idea of the republican glory, the departure of which Cicero and his associates in their sulky letters deplore."[1]

Compare with this picture Shakespeare's conception of an ambitious Cæsar striving to introduce monarchy into a well-ordered republican state!

What enchanted every one, even his enemies, who came in contact with Cæsar, was his good-breeding, his politeness, the charm of his personality. These characteristics made a doubly strong impression upon those who, like Cicero, were accustomed to the arrogance and coarseness of Pompey, the so-called Great. However busy he might be, Cæsar had always time to think of his friends and to jest with them. His letters are gay and amiable. In Shakespeare, when he is not familiar, he is pompous.

For the space of twenty-five years, Cæsar, as a politician, had by every means in his power opposed the aristocratic party in Rome. He had early resolved to make himself, without the employment of force, the master of the then known world, assured as he was that the Republic would fall to pieces of its own accord. Not until his prætorship in Spain had he displayed ability as a soldier and administrator outside the every-day round of political life. Then suddenly, when everything seems to be prospering with him, he breaks away from it all, leaves Rome, and passes into Gaul. At the age of forty-four, he enters upon his military career, and becomes perhaps the greatest commander known to history, an unrivalled conqueror and organiser, revealing, in middle life, a whole host of unsuspected and admirable qualities. Shakespeare conveys no idea of the wealth and many-sidedness of his gifts. He makes him belaud himself with unceasing solemnity (II. 2):—

> " Cæsar shall forth : the things that threaten'd me
> Ne'er look'd but on my back ; when they shall see
> The face of Cæsar, they are vanishèd."

Cæsar had nothing of the stolid pomposity and severity which Shakespeare attributes to him. He united the rapid decision of the general with the man of the world's elegance and lofty indifference to trifles. He liked his soldiers to wear glittering weapons and to adorn themselves. "What does it matter," he said, "though they use perfumes ? They fight none the worse for that." And soldiers who under other leaders did not surpass the average became invincible under him.

He, who in Rome had been the glass of fashion, was so careless of his comfort in the field that he often slept under the open sky, and ate rancid oil without so much as a grimace; but richly-decked tables always stood in his tents, and all the golden

---

[1] Mommsen, *History of Rome*, translated by W. P. Dickson, ed. 1894, vol. v. p. 371. Gaston Boissier, *Cicéron et ses Amis*, p. 224.

youth, for whom Gaul was at that time what America became in the days of the first discoverers, made their way from Rome to his camp. It was the most wonderful camp ever seen, crowded with men of elegance and learning, young writers and poets, wits and thinkers, who, in the midst of the greatest and most imminent dangers, busied themselves with literature, and sent regular reports of their meetings and conversations to Cicero, the acknowledged arbiter of the literary world of Rome. During the brief space of Cæsar's expedition into Britain, he writes two letters to Cicero. Their relation, in its different phases, in some ways reminds us of the relation between Frederick the Great and Voltaire. What a paltry picture does Shakespeare draw of Cicero as a mere pedant !—

" *Cassius.* Did Cicero say anything ?
" *Casca.* Ay, he spoke Greek.
" *Cassius.* To what effect ?
" *Casca.* Nay, an I tell you that, I'll ne'er look you in the face again : but those that understood him smiled at one another, and shook their heads ; but, for mine own part, it was Greek to me."

Amid labours of every sort, his life always in danger, incessantly fighting with warlike enemies, whom he beats in battle after battle, Cæsar writes his grammatical works and his Commentaries. His dedication to Cicero of his work *De Analogia* is a homage to literature no less than to him : "You have discovered all the treasures of eloquence and been the first to employ them. . . . You have achieved the crown of all honours, a triumph the greatest generals may envy ; for it is a nobler thing to remove the barriers of the intellectual life than to extend the boundaries of the Empire." These are the words of the man who has just beaten the Helvetii, conquered France and Belgium, made the first expedition into Britain, and so effectually repelled the German hordes that they were for long innocuous to the Rome which they had threatened with destruction.

How little does this Cæsar resemble the pompous and high-flown puppet of Shakespeare :—

" Danger knows full well
That Cæsar is more dangerous than he.
We are two lions litter'd in one day,
And I the elder and more terrible."

Cæsar could be cruel at times. In his wars, he never shrank from taking such revenges as should strike terror into his enemies. He had the whole senate of the Veneti beheaded. He cut the right hand off every one who had borne arms against him at Uxellodunum. He kept the gallant Vercingetorix five years in prison, only to exhibit him in chains at his triumph and then to have him executed.

Yet, where severity was unnecessary, he was tolerance and mildness itself. Cicero, during the civil war, went over to the camp of Pompey, and after the defeat of that party sought and received forgiveness. When he afterwards wrote a book in honour of Cæsar's mortal enemy Cato, who killed himself so as not to have to obey the dictator, and thereby became the hero of all the republicans, Cæsar wrote to Cicero: "In reading your book, I feel as though I myself had become more eloquent." And yet in his eyes Cato was only an uncultured personage and a fanatic for an obsolete order of things. When a slave, out of tenderness for his master, refused to hand Cato his sword wherewith to kill himself, Cato gave him such a furious blow in the face that his hand was dyed with blood. Such a trait must have spoiled for Cæsar the impressiveness of this suicide.

Cæsar was not content with forgiving almost all who had borne arms against him at Pharsalia; he gave many of them, and among the rest Brutus and Cassius, an ample share of his power. He tried to protect Brutus before the battle and heaped honours upon him after it. Again and again Brutus came forward in opposition to Cæsar, and even, in his conscientious quixotism, took part against him with Pompey, although Pompey had had his father assassinated. Cæsar forgave him this and everything else; he was never tired of forgiving him. He had, it appears, transferred to Brutus the love of his youth for Brutus's mother Servilia, Cato's sister, who had been passionately and faithfully devoted to Cæsar. Voltaire, in his *Mort de César*, makes Cæsar hand to Brutus a letter just received from the dying Servilia, in which she begs Cæsar to watch well over their son. Plutarch relates that on one occasion, at the time of Catiline's conspiracy, a letter was brought to Cæsar in the Senate. Cato, seeing him rise and go apart to read it, gave open utterance to the suspicion that 'it was a missive from the conspirators. Cæsar laughingly handed him the letter, which contained declarations of love from his sister; whereupon Cato, enraged, burst out with the epithet "Drunkard!"—the direst term of abuse a Roman could employ. (Ben Jonson has introduced this anecdote in his *Catiline*, v. 6.)

Brutus inherited his uncle Cato's hatred for Cæsar. A certain brutality was united with a noble stoicism in these two last Roman republicans of the time of the Republic's downfall. The rawness of antique Rome survived in Cato's nature, and Brutus, in his conduct towards the towns of the Asiatic provinces, was nothing but a bloodthirsty usurer, who, in the name of a man of straw (Scaptius) extorted from them his exorbitant interests with threats of fire and sword. He had lent to the inhabitants of the town of Salamis a sum of money at 48 per cent. On their failure to pay, he kept their Senate so closely besieged by a squadron of cavalry that five senators died of starvation. Shakespeare, in his ignorance, attributes no such vices to Brutus, but makes him simple and great, at Cæsar's expense.

Cæsar as opposed to Cato—and afterwards as opposed to Brutus—is the many-sided genius who loves life and action and power, in contradistinction to the narrow Puritan who hates such emancipated spirits, partly on principle, partly from instinct.

What a strange misunderstanding that Shakespeare—himself a lover of beauty, intent on a life of activity, enjoyment, and satisfied ambition, who always stood to Puritanism in the same hostile relation in which Cæsar stood—should out of ignorance take the side of Puritanism in this case, and so disqualify himself from extracting from the rich mine of Cæsar's character all the gold contained in it. In Shakespeare's Cæsar we find nothing of the magnanimity and sincerity of the real man. He never assumed a hypocritical reverence towards the past, not even on questions of grammar. He grasped at power and seized it, but did not, as in Shakespeare, pretend to reject it. Shakespeare has let him keep the pride which he in fact displayed, but has made it unbeautiful, and eked it out with hypocrisy.

This further trait, too, in Cæsar's character Shakespeare has failed to understand. When at last, after having conquered on every side, in Africa as in Asia, in Spain as in Egypt, he held in his hands the sovereign power which had been the object of his twenty years' struggle, it had lost its attraction for him. Knowing that he was misunderstood and hated by those whose respect he prized the most, he found himself compelled to make use of men whom he despised, and contempt for humanity took possession of his mind. He saw nothing around him but greed and treachery. Power had lost all its sweetness for him, life itself was no longer worth living, worth preserving. Hence his answer when he was besought to take measures against his would-be assassins: "Rather die once than tremble always!" and he went to the Senate on the 15th of March without arms and without a guard. In the tragedy, the motives which ultimately lure him thither are the hope of a title and a crown, and the fear of being esteemed a coward.

Those foolish persons who attribute Shakespeare's works to Francis Bacon argue, amongst other things, that such an insight into Roman antiquity as is manifested in *Julius Cæsar* could be attained by no one who did not possess Bacon's learning. On the contrary, this play is obviously written by a man whose learning was in no sense on a level with his genius, so that its faults, no less than its merits, afford a proof, however superfluous, that Shakespeare himself was the author of Shakespeare's works. Bunglers in criticism never realise to what an extent genius can supply the place of book-learning, and how vastly greater is its importance. But, on the other hand, one is bound to declare unequivocally that there are certain domains in which no amount of genius can compensate for reconstructive insight and study of recorded fact, and where even the greatest genius falls short when it tries to create out of its own head, or upon a scanty basis of knowledge.

Such a domain is that of historical drama, when it deals with periods and personalities in regard to which recorded fact surpasses all possible imagination. Where history is stranger and more poetic than any poetry, more tragic than any antique tragedy, there the poet requires many-sided insight in order to rise to the occasion. It was because of Shakespeare's lack of historical and classical culture that the incomparable grandeur of the figure of Cæsar left him unmoved. He depressed and debased that figure to make room for the development of the central character in his drama—to wit, Marcus Brutus, whom, following Plutarch's idealising example, he depicted as a stoic of almost flawless nobility.

IX

JULIUS CÆSAR—THE MERITS OF THE DRAMA—
BRUTUS

NONE but a naïve republican like Swinburne can believe that it was by reason of any republican enthusiasm in Shakespeare's soul that Brutus became the leading character. He had assuredly no systematic political conviction, and manifests at other times the most loyal and monarchical habit of mind.

Brutus was already in Plutarch the protagonist of the Cæsar tragedy, and Shakespeare followed the course of history as represented by Plutarch, under the deep impression that an impolitic revolt, like that of Essex and his companions, can by no means stem the current of the time, and that practical errors revenge themselves quite as severely as moral sins—nay, much more so. The psychologist was now awakened in him, and he found it a fascinating task to analyse and present a man who finds a mission imposed upon him for which he is by nature unfitted. It is no longer outward conflicts like that in *Romeo and Juliet* between the lovers and their surroundings, or in *Richard III.*, between Richard and the world at large, that fascinate him in this new stage of his development, but the inner processes and crises of the spiritual life.

Brutus has lived among his books and fed his mind upon Platonic philosophy; therefore he is more occupied with the abstract political idea of republican freedom, and the abstract moral conception of the shame of enduring a despotism, than with the actual political facts before his eyes, or the meaning of the changes which are going on around him. This man is vehemently urged by Cassius to place himself at the head of a conspiracy against his fatherly benefactor and friend. The demand throws his whole nature into a ferment, disturbs its harmony, and brings it for ever out of equilibrium.

On Hamlet also, who is at the same time springing to life in Shakespeare's mind, the spirit of his murdered father imposes the duty of becoming an assassin, and the claim acts as a stimulus, a spur to his intellectual faculties, but as a solvent to his character; so close is the resemblance between the situation of Brutus, with his conflicting duties, and the inward strife which we are soon to find in Hamlet.

Brutus is at war with himself, and therefore forgets to show others attention and the outward signs of friendship. His comrades summon him to action, but he hears no answering summons from within. As Hamlet breaks out into the well known words :—

> " The time is out of joint :—O, cursed spite
> That ever I was born to set it right ! "

so also Brutus shrinks with horror from his task. He says (I. 2):—

> " Brutus had rather be a villager
> Than to repute himself a son of Rome
> Under these hard conditions as this time
> Is like to lay upon us."

His noble nature is racked by these doubts and uncertainties.

From the moment Cassius has spoken to him, he is sleepless. The rugged Macbeth becomes sleepless after he has killed the King—"Macbeth has murdered sleep." Brutus, with his delicate, reflective nature, bent on obeying only the dictates of duty, is calm after the murder, but sleepless before it. His preoccupation with the idea has altered his whole manner of being; his wife does not know him again. She tells how he can neither converse nor sleep, but strides up and down with his arms folded, sighing and lost in thought, does not answer her questions, and, when she repeats them, waves her off with rough impatience.

It is not only his gratitude to Cæsar that keeps Brutus in torment ; it is especially his uncertainty as to what Cæsar's intentions really are. Brutus sees him, indeed, idolised by the people and endowed with supreme power ; but as yet Cæsar has never abused it. He concurs with Cassius's view that when Cæsar declined the crown he in reality hankered after it ; but, after all, they have nothing to go upon but his supposed desire :—

> " To speak truth of Cæsar,
> I have not known when his affections sway'd
> More than his reason. But 'tis a common proof
> That lowliness is young ambition's ladder."

If Cæsar is to be slain, then, it is not for what he has done, but for what he may do in the future. Is it permissible to commit a murder upon such grounds ?

In Hamlet we find this variant of the difficulty : Is it certain that the king murdered Hamlet's father ? May not the ghost have been a hallucination, or the devil himself ?

Brutus feels the weakness of his basis of action the more clearly the more he leans towards the murder as a political duty. And Shakespeare has not hesitated to attribute to him, highminded as he is, that doctrine of expediency, so questionable in the eyes of many, which declares that a necessary end sanctifies impure means. Two separate times, once when he is by himself, and once in addressing the conspirators, he recommends political hypocrisy as judicious and serviceable. In the soliloquy he says (II. 1):—

> " And, since the quarrel
> Will bear no colour for the thing he is,
> Fashion it thus : that what he is, augmented,
> Would run to these and these extremities."

To the conspirators his words are :—

> " And let our hearts, as subtle masters do,
> Stir up their servants to an act of rage,
> And after seem to chide 'em."

That is to say, the murder is to be carried out with as much decency as possible, and the murderers are afterwards to pretend that they deplore it.

As soon as the murder is resolved upon, however, Brutus, assured of the purity of his motives, stands proud and almost unconcerned in the midst of the conspirators. Far too unconcerned, indeed ; for though he has not shrunk in principle from the doctrine that one cannot will the end without willing the means, he yet shrinks, upright and unpractical as he is, from employing means which seem to him either too base or too unscrupulous. He will not even suffer the conspirators to be bound by oath : " Swear priests and cowards and men cautelous." They are to trust each other without the assurance of an oath, and to keep their secret unsworn. And when it is proposed that Antony shall be killed along with Cæsar, a necessary step, to which, as a politician, he was bound to consent, he rejects it, in Shakespeare as in Plutarch, out of humanity : " Our course will seem too bloody, Caius Cassius." He feels that his will is as clear as day, and suffers at the thought of employing the methods of night and darkness :

> " O Conspiracy !
> Sham'st thou to show thy dangerous brow by night,
> When evils are most free ? O, then, by day
> Where wilt thou find a cavern dark enough
> To mask thy monstrous visage ? "

Brutus is anxious that a cause which is to be furthered by assassination should achieve success without secrecy and without violence. Goethe has said : " Only the man of reflection has a conscience." The man of action cannot have one while he is acting. To plunge into action is to place oneself at the mercy of one's nature and of external powers. One acts rightly or wrongly, but always upon instinct—often stupidly, sometimes, it may be, brilliantly, never with full consciousness. Action implies the inconsiderateness of instinct, or egoism, or genius ; Brutus, on the other hand, is bent on acting with every consideration.

Kreyssig, and after him Dowden, have called Brutus a Girondin, in opposition to his brother-in-law, Cassius, a sort of Jacobin in antique dress. The comparison is just only in regard to the lesser or greater inclination to the employment of violent means; it halts when we reflect that Brutus lives in the rarefied air of abstractions, face to face with ideas and principles, while Cassius lives in the world of facts; for the Jacobins were quite as stiff-necked theorists as any Girondin. Brutus, in Shakespeare, is a strict moralist, excessively cautious lest any stain should mar the purity of his character, while Cassius does not in the least aspire to moral flawlessness. He is frankly envious of Cæsar, and openly avows that he hates him; yet he is not base; for envy and hatred are in his case swallowed up by political passion, strenuous and consistent. And, unlike Brutus, he is a good observer, looking right through men's words and actions into their souls. But as Brutus is the man whose name, birth, and position as Cæsar's intimate friend, point him out to be the head of the conspiracy, he is always able to enforce his impolitic and short-sighted will.

When we find that Hamlet, who is so full of doubts, never for a moment doubts his right to kill the king, we must remember that Shakespeare had just exhausted this theme in his characterisation of Brutus.

Brutus is the ideal whom Shakespeare, like all men of the better sort, cherished in his soul—the man whose pride it is before everything to keep his hands clean and his mind high and free, even at the cost of failure in his undertakings and the wreck of his tranquillity and of his fortunes.

He does not care to impose an oath upon the others; he is too proud. If they want to betray him, let them! These others, it is true, may be moved by their hatred of the great man, and eager to quench their malice in his blood; he, for his part, admires him, and will sacrifice, not butcher him. The others fear the consequences of suffering Antony to address the people; but Brutus has explained to the people his reasons for the murder, so Antony may now eulogise Cæsar as much as he pleases. Did not Cæsar deserve eulogy? Does not he himself desire that Cæsar shall lie honoured, though punished, in his grave? He is too proud to keep a watch upon Antony, who has approached him in friendly fashion, though at the same time in the character of Cæsar's friend; therefore he leaves the Forum before Antony begins his speech. Such moods are familiar to many. Many another has acted in this apparently unwise way, proudly reckless of consequences, moved by the dislike of the magnanimous man for all that savours of base cautiousness. Many a one, for example, has told the truth where it was stupid to do so, or has let slip an opportunity of revenge because he despised his enemy too much to seek compensation for his injuries, though he thereby neglected to render him innocuous for the future. An intense realisation of the necessity for confidence, or, on the other hand, of the untrustworthiness of friends and the contemptibleness of enemies, may easily lead one to despise every measure of prudence.

It was upon the basis of an intense feeling of this nature that Shakespeare created Brutus. With the addition of humour and a touch of genius he would be Hamlet, and he becomes Hamlet. With the addition of despairing bitterness and misanthropy he would be Timon, and he becomes Timon. Here he is the man of uncompromising character and principle, who is too proud to be prudent and too bad an observer to be practical; and this man is so situated that not only the life and death of another and of himself, but the welfare of the State, and even, as it appears, that of the whole civilised world, depend upon the resolution at which he arrives.

At Brutus's side Shakespeare places the figure which forms his female counterpart, the kindred spirit who has become one with him, his cousin and wife, Cato's daughter married to Cato's disciple. He has here, and here alone, given us a picture of the ideal marriage as he conceived it.

In the scene between Brutus and Portia the poet takes up afresh a motive which he has handled once before—the anxious wife beseeching her husband to initiate her into his great designs. It first appears in *Henry IV.*, Part I., where Lady Percy implores her Harry to let her share his counsels. (See above, p. 189.) The description which she gives of Hotspur's manner and conduct exactly corresponds to Portia's description of the transformation which has taken place in Brutus. Both husbands, indeed, are nursing a similar project. But Lady Percy learns nothing. Her Harry no doubt loves her, loves her now and then, between two skirmishes, briskly and gaily; but there is no sentiment in his love for her, and he never dreams of any spiritual communion between them.

When Portia, in this case, begs her husband to tell her what is weighing on his mind, he at first, indeed, replies with evasions about his health; but on her vehemently declaring that she feels herself degraded by this lack of confidence (Shakespeare has but slightly softened the antique frankness of the words which Plutarch places in her mouth), Brutus answers her with warmth and beauty. And when (again as in Plutarch) she tells of the proof she has given of her steadfastness by thrusting a knife into her thigh and never complaining of the "voluntary wound," he bursts forth with the words which Plutarch places in his mouth:—

> " O ye gods,
> Render me worthy of this noble wife,"

and promises to tell her everything.

Neither Shakespeare nor Plutarch, however, regards his facile communicativeness as a mark of prudence. For it is not Portia's fault that it does not betray everything. When it comes to the point, she can neither hold her tongue nor control herself. She betrays her anxiety and uneasiness to the boy Lucius, and herself exclaims :—

> " I have a man's mind, but a woman's might.
> How hard it is for women to keep counsel ! "

This reflection is obviously not Portia's, but an utterance of Shakespeare's own philosophy of life, which he has not cared to keep to himself. In Plutarch she even falls down as though dead, and the news of her death surprises Brutus just before the time appointed for the murder of Cæsar, so that he needs all his self-control to save himself from breaking down.

From the character with which Shakespeare has thus endowed Brutus spring the two great scenes which carry the play.

The first is the marvellously-constructed scene, the turning-point of the tragedy, in which Antony, speaking with Brutus's consent over the body of Cæsar, stirs up the Romans against the murderers of the great imperator.

Even Brutus's own speech Shakespeare has moulded with the rarest art. Plutarch relates that when Brutus wrote Greek he cultivated a " compendious " and laconic style, of which the historian adduces a string of examples. He wrote to the Samians : " Your councels be long, your doings be slow ; consider the end." And in another epistle : " The Xanthians, despising my good wil, haue made a graue of dispaire ; and the Patareians, that put themselves into my protection, have lost no iot of their liberty : and therefore whilst you haue libertie, either chuse the iudgement of the Patareians or the fortune of the Xanthians." See now, what Shakespeare has made out of these indications :—

" Romans, countrymen, and lovers ! hear me for my cause, and be silent, that you may hear : believe me for mine honour, and have respect to mine honour, that you may believe. . . . If there be any in this assembly, any dear friend of Cæsar's, to him I say, that Brutus' love to Cæsar was no less than his. If, then, that friend demand, why Brutus rose against Cæsar, this is my answer :—Not that I loved Cæsar less, but that I loved Rome more."

And so on, in this style of laconic antithesis. Shakespeare has made a deliberate effort to assign to Brutus the diction he had cultivated, and, with his inspired faculty of divination, has, as it were, reanimated it :—

" As Cæsar loved me, I weep for him ; as he was fortunate, I rejoice at it ; as he was valiant, I honour him : but, as he was ambitious, I slew him."

With ingenious and yet noble art the speech culminates in
the question, " Who is here so vile that will not love his country !
If any, speak ; for him have I offended." And when the crowd
answers, "None, Brutus, none," he chimes in with the serene
assurance, " Then none have I offended."

The still more admirable oration of Antony is in the first
place remarkable for the calculated difference of style which it
displays. Here we have no antitheses, no literary eloquence ;
but a vernacular eloquence of the most powerful demagogic type.
Antony takes up the thread just where Brutus has dropped it,
expressly assures his hearers at the outset that this is to be a
speech over Cæsar's bier, but not to his glory, and emphasises
to the point of monotony the fact that Brutus and the other
conspirators are all, all honourable men. Then the eloquence
gradually works up, subtle and potent in its adroit crescendo,
and yet in truth exalted by something which is not subtlety :
glowing enthusiasm for Cæsar, scathing indignation against his
assassins. The contempt and anger are at first masked, out of
consideration for the mood of the populace, which has for the
moment been won over by Brutus ; then the mask is raised a
little, then a little more and a little more, until, with a wild
gesture, it is torn off and thrown aside.

Here again Shakespeare has utilised in a masterly fashion
the hints he found in Plutarch, scanty as they were :—

" Afterwards, when Cæsar's body was brought into the market-place,
Antonius, making his funeral oration in praise of the dead, according
to the auncient custome of Rome, and perceiuing that his words moued
the common people to compassion : he framed his eloquence to make
their harts yerne the more."

Mark what Shakespeare has made of this :—

" Friends, Romans, countrymen, lend me your ears :
  I come to bury Cæsar, not to praise him.
  The evil that men do lives after them,
  The good is oft interred with their bones ;
  So let it be with Cæsar. The noble Brutus
  Hath told you, Cæsar was ambitious :
  If it were so, it was a grievous fault,
  And grievously hath Cæsar answered it.
  Here, under leave of Brutus and the rest,
  (For Brutus is an honourable man,
  So are they all, all honourable men),
  Come I to speak in Cæsar's funeral.
  He was my friend, faithful and just to me :
  But Brutus says he was ambitious ;
  And Brutus is an honourable man."

Then Antony goes on to insinuate doubts as to Cæsar's
ambition, and tells how he rejected the kingly diadem, rejected

it three times. Was this ambition ? Thereupon he suggests that Cæsar, after all, was once beloved, and that there is no reason why he should not be mourned. Then with a sudden outburst :—

> " O judgment ! thou art fled to brutish beasts,
> And men have lost their reason !—Bear with me ;
> My heart is in the coffin there with Cæsar,
> And I must pause till it come back to me."

Next comes an appeal to their pity for this greatest of men, whose word but yesterday might have stood against the world, and who now lies so low that the poorest will not do him reverence. It would be wrong to make his speech inflammatory, a wrong towards Brutus and Cassius "who—as you know—are honourable men" (mark the jibe in the parenthetic phrase); no, he will rather do wrong to the dead and to himself. But here he holds a parchment—he assuredly will not read it—but if the people came to know its contents they would kiss dead Cæsar's wounds, and dip their handkerchiefs in his sacred blood. And then, when cries for the reading of the will mingle with curses upon the murderers, he stubbornly refuses to read it. Instead of doing so, he displays to them Cæsar's cloak with all the rents in it.

What Plutarch says here is :—

> " To conclude his Oration, he unfolded before the whole assembly the bloudy garments of the dead, thrust through in many places with their swords, and called the malefactors cruell and cursed murtherers."

Out of these few words Shakespeare has made this miracle of invective :—

> " You all do know this mantle ! I remember
> The first time ever Cæsar put it on :
> 'Twas on a summer's evening, in his tent,
> That day he overcame the Nervii.
> Look ! in this place ran Cassius' dagger through :
> See, what a rent the envious Casca made :
> Through this, the well-beloved Brutus stabb'd ;
> And, as he pluck'd his cursed steel away,
> Mark how the blood of Cæsar followed it,
> As rushing out of doors, to be resolv'd
> If Brutus so unkindly knock'd, or no ;
> For Brutus, as you know, was Cæsar's angel.
> Judge, O you gods, how dearly Cæsar lov'd him !
> This was the most unkindest cut of all ;
> For when the noble Cæsar saw him stab,
> Ingratitude, more strong than traitors' arms,
> Quite vanquish'd him : then burst his mighty heart ;
> And, in his mantle muffling up his face,

Even at the base of Pompey's statua,
Which all the while ran blood, great Cæsar fell.
O, what a fall was there, my countrymen !
Then I, and you, and all of us fell down,
Whilst bloody treason flourish'd over us.
O ! now you weep ; and, I perceive, you feel
The dint of pity : these are gracious drops.
Kind souls ! what, weep you, when you but behold
Our Cæsar's vesture wounded ?   Look you here,
Here is himself, marr'd, as you see, with traitors."

He uncovers Cæsar's body; and not till then does he read
the will, overwhelming the populace with gifts and benefactions.
This climax is of Shakespeare's own invention.

No wonder that even Voltaire was so struck with the beauty
of this scene, that for its sake he translated the first three acts
of the play. At the end of his own *Mort de César*, too, he
introduced a feeble imitation of the scene ; and he had it in his
mind when, in his *Discours sur la Tragédie*, dedicated to Bolingbroke, he expressed so much enthusiasm and envy for the freedom
of the English stage.

In the last two acts, Brutus is overtaken by the recoil of his
deed. He consented to the murder out of noble, disinterested
and patriotic motives ; nevertheless he is struck down by its
consequences, and pays for it with his happiness and his life.
The declining action of the last two acts is—as is usual with
Shakespeare—less effective and fascinating than the rising action
which fills the first three; but it has one significant, profound,
and brilliantly constructed and executed scene—the quarrel and
reconciliation between Brutus and Cassius in the fourth act,
which leads up to the appearance of Cæsar's ghost.

This scene is significant because it gives a many-sided picture
of the two leading characters—the sternly upright Brutus, who
is shocked at the means employed by Cassius to raise the money
without which their campaign cannot be carried on, and Cassius,
a politician entirely indifferent to moral scruples, but equally
unconcerned as to his own personal advantage. The scene is
profound because it presents to us the necessary consequences
of the law-defying, rebellious act: cruelty, unscrupulous policy,
and lax tolerance of dishonourable conduct in subordinates, when
the bonds of authority and discipline have once been burst.
The scene is brilliantly constructed because, with its quick play
of passion and its rising discord, which at last passes over into
a cordial and even tender reconciliation, it is dramatic in the
highest sense of the word.

The fact that Brutus was in Shakespeare's own mind the
true hero of the tragedy appears in the clearest light when we
find him ending the play with the eulogy which Plutarch, in

his life of Brutus, places in the mouth of Antony; I mean the famous words :—

> " This was the noblest Roman of them all :
> All the conspirators, save only he,
> Did that they did in envy of great Cæsar ;
> He only, in a general honest thought
> And common good to all, made one of them.
> His life was gentle ; and the elements
> So mixed in him that Nature might stand up,
> And say to all the world, ' This was a man ! ' "

The resemblance between these words and a celebrated speech of Hamlet's is unmistakable. Everywhere in *Julius Cæsar* we feel the proximity of *Hamlet*. The fact that Hamlet hesitates so long before attacking the King, finds so many reasons to hold his hand, is torn with doubts as to the act and its consequences, and insists on considering everything even while he upbraids himself for considering so long—all this is partly due, no doubt, to the circumstance that Shakespeare comes to him directly from Brutus. His Hamlet has, so to speak, just seen what happened to Brutus, and the example is not encouraging, either with respect to action in general, or with respect to the murder of a step-father in particular.

It is not difficult to conceive that Shakespeare may at this period have been subject to moments of scepticism, in which he could scarcely understand how any one could make up his mind to act, to assume responsibility, to set in motion the rolling stone which is the type of every action. If we once begin to brood over the incalculable consequences of an action and all that circumstance may make of it, all action on a great scale becomes impossible. Therefore it is that very few old men understand their youth ; they dare not and could not act again as, in their recklessness of consequences, they acted then. Brutus forms the transition to Hamlet, and Hamlet no doubt grew up in Shakespeare's mind during the working out of *Julius Cæsar*.

The stages of transition are perhaps these : the conspirators, in egging Brutus on to the murder, are always reminding him of the elder Brutus, who pretended madness and drove out the Tarquins. This may have led Shakespeare to dwell upon his character as drawn by Livy, which had always been exceedingly popular. But Brutus the elder is an antique Hamlet ; and the very name of Hamlet, as he found it in the older play and in Saxo, seems always to have haunted Shakespeare. It was the name he had given to the little boy whom he lost so early.

X

BEN JONSON AND HIS ROMAN PLAYS

IN precisely the same year as Shakespeare, his famous brother-poet, Ben Jonson, made his first attempt at a dramatic presentation of Roman antiquity. His play, *The Poetaster*, was written and acted in 1601. Its purpose is the literary annihilation of two playwrights, Marston and Dekker, with whom the author was at feud; but its action takes place in the time of Augustus; and Jonson, in spite of his satire on contemporaries, no doubt wanted to utilise his thorough knowledge of ancient literature in giving a true picture of Roman manners. As Shakespeare's *Julius Cæsar* was followed by two other tragedies of antique Rome, *Antony and Cleopatra* and *Coriolanus*, so Ben Jonson also wrote two other plays on Roman themes, the tragedies of *Sejanus* and *Catiline*. It is instructive to compare his method of treatment with Shakespeare's; but a general comparison of the two creative spirits must precede this comparison of artistic processes in a single limited field.

Ben Jonson was nine years younger than Shakespeare, born in 1573, a month after the death of his father, the son of a clergyman whose forefathers had belonged to "the gentry." He was a child of the town, while Shakespeare was a child of the country; and the fact is not without significance, though town and country were not then so clearly opposed to each other as they are now. When Ben was two years old, his mother married a worthy master-bricklayer, who did what he could to procure his stepson a good education, so that, after passing some years at a small private school, he was sent to Westminster. Here the learned William Camden, his teacher, introduced him to the two classical literatures, and seems, moreover, to have exercised a not altogether fortunate influence upon his subsequent literary habits; for it was Camden who taught him first to write out in prose whatever he wanted to express in verse. Thus the foundation was laid at school, not only of his double ambition to shine as a scholar and a poet, or rather as a scholar-poet, but also of his heavy and rhetorically emphatic verse.

In spite of his worship of learning, his dislike to all handi-craft, and his unfitness for practical work, he was forced by poverty to break off his studies in order to enter the employment of his bricklayer stepfather—a fact which, in his subsequent literary feuds, always procured him the nickname of "the bricklayer." He could not long endure this occupation, went as a soldier to the Netherlands, killed one of the enemy in single combat, under the eyes of both camps, returned to London and married—almost as early as Shakespeare—at the age of only nineteen. Twenty-six years later, in his conversations with Drummond, he called his wife "a shrew, yet honest." He seems to have been an affectionate father, but had the misfortune to survive his children.

He was strong and massive in body, racy and coarse, full of self-esteem and combative instincts, saturated with the conviction of the scholar's high rank and the poet's exalted vocation, full of contempt for ignorance, frivolity, and lowness, classic in his tastes, with a bent towards careful structure and leisurely development of thought in all that he wrote, and yet a true poet in so far as he was not only irregular in his life and quite incapable of saving any of the money he now and then earned, but was, moreover, subject to hallucinations: once saw Carthaginians and Romans fighting on his great toe, and, on another occasion, had a vision of his son with a bloody cross on his brow, which was supposed to forbode his death.

Like Shakespeare, he sought to make his bread by entering the theatre and appearing as an actor. To him, as to Shakespeare, old pieces of the repertory were entrusted to be rewritten, expanded, and furbished up. Thus as late as 1601-2 he made a number of very able additions, in the style of the old play, to that *Spanish Tragedy* of Kyd's, which must in many ways have been in Shakespeare's mind during the composition of *Hamlet*.

He did this work on the commission of Henslow, for whose company, which competed with Shakespeare's, he worked regularly from 1597 onwards. He collaborated with Dekker in a tragedy, and had a hand in other plays; in short, he made himself useful to the theatre as best he could, but did not, like Shakespeare, acquire a share in the enterprise, and thus never became a man of substance. He was to the end of his life forced to rely for his income upon the liberality of royal and noble patrons.

The end of 1598 is doubly significant in Ben Jonson's life. In September he killed in a duel another of Henslow's actors, a certain Gabriel Spencer (who seems to have challenged him), and was therefore branded on the thumb with the letter T (Tyburn). A couple of months later, this occurrence having evidently led to a break in his connection with Henslow's company, his first original play, *Every Man in his Humour*, was acted by the Lord Chamberlain's men. According to a tradition preserved by Rowe, and apparently trustworthy, the play had already been refused, when Shakespeare happened to see it and procured its acceptance.

It met with the success it deserved, and henceforward the author's name was famous.

Even in the first edition of this play he makes Young Knowell speak with warm enthusiasm of poetry, of the dignity of the sacred art of invention, and express that hatred for every profanation of the Muses which appears so frequently in later works, finding, perhaps, its most vehement utterance in *The Poetaster*, where the young Ovid eulogises his art in opposition to the scorn of his father and others. From the first, too, he made no concealment of his strong sense of being at once a high-priest of art, and, in virtue of his learning, an Aristarchus of taste. He not only scorned all attempts to tickle the public ear, but, with the firm and superior attitude of a teacher, he again and again imprinted on spectators and readers what Goethe has expressed in the well-known words: " Ich schreibe nicht, Euch zu gefallen ; Ihr sollt was lernen." Again and again he claimed for his own person the sanctity and inviolability of art, and attacked his inferior rivals unsparingly, with ferocious rather than witty satire. His prologues and epilogues are devoted to a self-acclamation which was entirely foreign to Shakespeare's nature. Asper in *Every Man out of his Humour* (1599), Crites in *Cynthia's Revels* (1600), and Horace in *The Poetaster* (1601), are so many pieces of self-idolising self-portraiture.

All who, in his judgment, degrade art are made to pay the penalty in scathing caricatures. In *The Poetaster*, for example, his taskmaster, Henslow, is presented under the name of Histrio as a depraved slave-dealer, and his colleagues Marston and Dekker are held up to ridicule under Roman names, as intrusive and despicable scribblers. Their attacks upon the admirable poet Horace, whose name and personality the extremely dissimilar Ben Jonson has arrogated to himself, spring from contemptible motives, and receive a disgraceful punishment.

This whole warfare must not be taken too seriously. The worthy Ben could be at the same time an indignant moralist and a genial boon-companion. We presently find him taking service afresh with the very Henslow whom he has just treated with such withering contempt; and though his attack of 1601 had been met by a most malicious retort in Marston and Dekker's *Satiromastix*, he, three years afterwards, accepts the dedication of Marston's *Malcontent*, and in 1605 collaborates with this lately-lampooned colleague and with Chapman in the comedy of *Eastward Ho!* One could not but think of the German proverb, " Pack schlägt sich, Pack verträgt sich," were it not that Jonson's action at this juncture reveals him in anything but a vulgar light. Marston and Chapman having been thrown into prison for certain gibes at the Scotch in this play, which had come to the notice of the King, and being reported to be in danger of having their noses and ears cut off, Ben Jonson, of his own free will, claimed his share in the responsibility and joined them in prison. At a supper which, after their liberation, he gave to all his friends, his mother clinked glasses with him, and at the same time showed him a paper, the contents of which she had intended to mix with his drink in prison if he had been sentenced to mutilation. She added that she herself would not have survived him, but would have taken her share of the poison. She must have been a mother worthy of such a son.

While Ben lay in durance on account of his duel, he had been converted to Catholicism by a priest who attended him—a conversion at which his adversaries did not fail to jeer. He does not seem, however, to have embraced the Catholic dogma with any great fervour, for twelve years later he once more changes his religion and returns to the Protestant Church. Equally characteristic of Ben and of the Renaissance is his own statement, preserved for us by Drummond, that at his first communion after his reconciliation with Protestantism, in token of his sincere return to the doctrine which gave laymen as well as priests access to the chalice, he drained at one draught the whole of the consecrated wine.

Not without humour, moreover—to use Jonson's own favourite word—is his story of the way in which Raleigh's son, to whom he acted as governor during a tour in France (while Raleigh himself was in the Tower), took a malicious pleasure in making his mentor dead drunk, having him wheeled in a wheelbarrow through the streets of Paris, and showing him off to the mob at every street corner. Ben's strong insistence on his spiritual dignity was not infrequently counterbalanced by an extreme carelessness of his personal dignity.

With all his weaknesses, however, he was a sturdy, energetic, and high-minded man, a commanding, independent, and very comprehensive intelligence; and from 1598, when he makes his first appearance on Shakespeare's horizon, throughout the rest of his life, he was, so far as we can see, the man of all his contemporaries whose name was oftenest mentioned along with Shakespeare's. In after days, especially outside England, the name of Ben Jonson has come to sound small enough in comparison with the name of solitary greatness with which it was once bracketed; but at that time, although Jonson was never so popular as Shakespeare, they were commonly regarded in literary circles as the dramatic twin-brethren of the age. For us it is still more interesting to remember that Ben Jonson was one of the few with whom we know that Shakespeare was on terms of constant familiarity, and, moreover, that he brought to this intercourse a set of definite artistic principles, widely different from Shakespeare's own. Though his society may have been somewhat fatiguing, it must nevertheless have been both instructive and stimulating to Shakespeare, since Ben was greatly his superior in historical and linguistic knowledge, while as a poet he pursued a totally different ideal.

Ben Jonson was a great dramatic intelligence. He never, like the other poets of his time, took this or that novel and dramatised it as it stood, regardless of its more or less incoherent structure, its more or less flagrant defiance of topographical, geographical, or historical reality. With architectural solidity—was he not the step-son of a master-builder?—he built up his dramatic plan out of his own head, and, being a man of great learning, he did his best to avoid all incongruities of local colour. If he is now and then negligent in this respect —if the characters in *Volpone* now and then talk as if they were in London, not in Venice, and those in *The Poetaster* as if they were in England, not in Rome—it is because of his satiric purpose, and not at all by reason of the indifference to such considerations which characterises all other dramatists of the time, Shakespeare not the least.

The fundamental contrast between them can be most shortly expressed in the statement that Ben Jonson accepted the view of human nature set forth in the classic comedies and the Latin tragedies. He does not represent it as many-sided, with inward developments and inconsistencies, but fixes character in typical forms, with one dominant trait thrown into high relief. He portrays, for example, the crafty parasite, or the eccentric who cannot endure noise, or the braggart captain, or the depraved anarchist (Catiline), or the stern man of honour (Cato)—and all these personalities are neither more nor less than the labels imply, and act up to their description always and in all circumstances. The pencil with which he draws is hard, but he wields it with such power that his best outlines subsist through the centuries, unforgettable, despite their occasional oddity of design, in virtue of the indignation with which wickedness and meanness are branded, and the racy merriment with which the caricatures are sketched, the farces worked out.

Some of Molière's farces may now and then remind us of Jonson's, but, as regards the pitiless intensity of the satire, we shall find no counterpart to his *Volpone* until we come in our own times to Gogol's *Revisor*.

The Graces stood by Shakespeare's cradle, not by Jonson's; and yet this heavy-armed warrior has now and then attained to grace as well—has now and then given a holiday to his sound systematic intelligence and his solidly-constructed logic, and, like a true poet of the Renaissance, soared into the rarer atmosphere of pure fantasy.

He shows himself very much at home in the allegorical masques which were performed at court festivals; and in the pastoral play *The Sad Shepherd,* which seems to have been written upon his death-bed, he proved that even in the purely romantic style he could challenge comparison with the best writers of his day. Yet it is not in this sphere that he displays his true originality. It is in his keen and faithful observation of the conditions and manners of his time, which Shakespeare left on one side, or depicted only incidentally and indirectly. The London of Elizabeth lives again in Jonson's plays; both the lower and higher circles, but especially the lower: the haunters of taverns and theatres, the men of the riverside and the markets, rogues and vagabonds, poets and players, watermen and jugglers, bear-leaders and hucksters, rich city dames, Puritan fanatics and country squires, English oddities of every class and kind, each speaking his own language, dialect, or jargon. Shakespeare never kept so close to the life of the day.

It is especially Jonson's scholarship that must have made his society full of instruction for Shakespeare. Ben's acquirements were encyclopædic, and his acquaintance with the authors of antiquity was singularly complete and accurate. It has often been remarked that he was not content with an exhaustive knowledge of the leading writers of Greece and Rome. He knows not only the great historians, poets, and orators, such as Tacitus and Sallust, Horace, Virgil, Ovid, and Cicero, but sophists, grammarians, and scholiasts, men like Athenæus, Libanius, Philostratus, Strabo, Photius. He is familiar with fragments of Æolic lyrists and Roman epic poets, of Greek tragedies and Roman inscriptions; and, what is still more remarkable, he manages to make use of all his knowledge. Whatever in the ancients he found beautiful or profound or stimulating, that he wove into his work. Dryden says of him in his "Essay of Dramatic Poesy":—

"The greatest man of the last age (Ben Jonson) was willing to give place to the ancients in all things: he was not only a professed imitator of Horace, but a learned plagiary of all the others; you track him everywhere in their snow. If Horace, Lucan, Petronius Arbiter, Seneca, and Juvenal had their own from him, there are few serious thoughts which are new in him. . . . But he has done his robberies so openly, that one may see he fears not to be taxed by any law. He invades authors like a monarch; and what would be theft in other poets is only victory in him."

Certain it is that an uncommon learning and an extraordinary memory supplied him with an immense store of small touches, poetical and rhetorical details, which he could not refrain from incorporating in his plays.

Yet his mass of learning was not of a merely verbal or rhetorical nature; he knew things as well as words. Whatever subject he treats of, be it alchemy, or witchcraft, or cosmetics in the time of Tiberius, he handles it with competence and has its whole literature at his fingers' ends. He thus becomes universal like Shakespeare, but in a different way. Shakespeare knows, firstly, all that cannot be learnt from books, and in the second place, whatever can be gleaned by genius from a casual utterance, an intelligent hint, a conversation with a man of high acquirements. Besides this, he knows the literature which was at that time within the reach of a quick-witted and studious man without special scholarship. Ben Jonson, on the other hand, is a scholar by profession. He has learnt from books all that the books of his day—for the most part, of course, the not too numerous survivals of the classic literatures—could teach a man who made scholarship his glory. He not only possesses knowledge, but he knows whence he has acquired it; he can cite his authorities by chapter and paragraph, and he sometimes garnishes his plays with so many learned references that they bristle with notes like an academic thesis.

Colossal, coarse-grained, vigorous, and always ready for the fray, with his gigantic burden of learning, he has been compared by Taine to one of those war-elephants of antiquity which bore on their backs a whole fortress, with garrison, armoury, and munitions, and under the weight of this panoply could yet move as quickly as a fleet-footed horse.

It must have been intensely interesting for their comrades at the Mermaid to listen to the discussions between Jonson and Shakespeare, to follow two such remarkable minds, so differently organised and equipped, when they debated, in jest or earnest, this or that historic problem, this or that moot point in æsthetics; and no less interesting is it for us, in our days, to compare their almost contemporaneous dramatic treatment of Roman antiquity. We might here expect Shakespeare to have the worst of it, since he, according to Jonson's well-known phrase, had "small Latine and less Greek;" while Ben was as much at home in ancient Rome as in the London of his day, and, with his altogether masculine talent, could claim a certain kinship with the Roman spirit.

And yet even here Shakespeare stands high above Jonson, who, with all his learning and industry, lacks his great contemporary's sense for the fundamental element in human nature, to which the terms good and bad do not apply, and has, besides, very few of those unforeseen inspirations of genius which constitute Shakespeare's strength, and make up for all the gaps in his knowledge. Jonson, moreover, could not modulate into the minor key, and is thus unable to depict the inmost subtleties of feminine character.

None the less would it be unjust to make Jonson, as the Germans are apt to do, nothing but a foil to Shakespeare. We must, in mere equity, bring out the points at which he attains to real greatness.

Although the scene of *The Poetaster* is laid in Rome in the days of Augustus, the play eludes comparison with Shakespeare's Roman dramas in so far as its costume is partly a mere travesty under which Ben Jonson defends himself against his contemporaries Marston and Dekker, who also figure, of course, in a Roman disguise. Even here, however, he has done his best to give an accurate picture of antique Roman manners, and has applied to the task all his learning, with rather too little aid, perhaps, from his fancy. His comic figures, for instance, the intrusive Crispinus and the foolish singer Hermogenes, are taken bodily from Horace's Satires (Book i. Satires 3 and 9); but both these pleasant caricatures are executed with vigour and life.

Ben Jonson has in this play woven together three different actions, one only of which has a symbolic meaning outside the frame of the picture. In the first place, he presents Ovid's struggle for leave to follow his poetic vocation, his suspected love-affair with Augustus's daughter, Julia, and his banishment from the court when Augustus discovers the intrigue between the young poet and his child. In the second place, he introduces us into the house of the rich bourgeois Albius, who has been ill-advised enough to marry one of the emancipated great ladies of the period, Chloe by name, and who, by her help, obtains admission to court society. Chloe's house is a meeting-place for all the love-poets of the period, Tibullus, Propertius, Ovid, Cornelius Gallus, and the ladies who favour them ; and Jonson has succeeded very fairly in suggesting the free tone of conversation prevalent in those circles, which was doubtless reproduced in many circles of London life during the Renaissance. Finally, we have a representation — Jonson's chief object in writing the play — of the conspiracy of the bad and envious poets against Horace, which culminates in a formal impeachment. The Emperor himself, and the famous poets of his court, form a sort of tribunal before which the case is tried. Horace is acquitted on every count, and the accusers are sentenced to a punishment entirely in the spirit of the Aristophanic comedy—so foreign to Shakespeare—Crispinus being forced to take a pill of hellebore, which makes him vomit up all the affected or merely novel words he has used, which appear to Ben Jonson ridiculous. Some of them—for example the first two, " retrograde " and " reciprocal "—have nevertheless survived in modern English. In spite of its allegorical character, the episode is not deficient in an almost too pungent realism.

The most Roman of all these scenes are doubtless those in which the gallantry between the young men and the ladies, and the snobbery which forces its way into Augustus's court, are freely represented. Less Roman, by reason of their too palpable tendency, are the scenes in which Augustus appears in the circle of his court poets. No serious attempt is made to portray the

Emperor's character, and the speeches placed in the mouths of the poets are very clearly designed simply for the glorification of poetry in general, and Ben Jonson in particular.

The sins of which his enemies were always accusing him were "self-love, arrogancy, impudence, and railing," together with "filching by translation." As he explains in the defensive dialogue which he appended to his play, it was his purpose—

> " To show that Virgil, Horace, and the rest
> Of those great master-spirits, did not want
> Detractors then, or practisers against them."

He makes foolish persons find injurious allusions to themselves, and even insults to the Emperor, in entirely innocent poems of Horace's, and shows how the Emperor orders them to be whipped as backbiters. Horace's literary relation to the Greeks, be it noted, was not unlike that of Ben Jonson himself to the Latin writers.

A special interest attaches for us to the passage in the fifth act, where, immediately before Virgil's entrance, the different poets, at the suggestion of the Emperor, express their judgment of his genius, and where Horace, after warmly protesting against the common belief that one poet is necessarily envious of another, joins in the general eulogy of his great rival. There is this remarkable circumstance about the encomiums on Virgil, here placed in the mouths of Gallus, Tibullus, and Horace, that while some of them are appropriate enough to the real Virgil (else all verisimilitude would have been sacrificed), others seem unmistakably to point away from Virgil towards one or other famous contemporary of Jonson's own. Look for a moment at these speeches (v. 1):—

> " *Tibullus.* That which he hath writ
> Is with such judgment labour'd, and distill'd
> Through all the needful uses of our lives,
> That could a man remember but his lines,
> He should not touch at any serious point,
> But he might breathe his spirit out of him.
> *Augustus.* You mean, he might repeat part of his works
> As fit for any conference he can use?
> *Tibullus.* True, royal Cæsar.
> *Horace.* His learning savours not the school-like gloss
> That most consists in echoing words and terms,
> And soonest wins a man an empty name;
> Nor any long or far-fetch'd circumstance
> Wrapp'd in the curious generalties of arts,
> But a direct and analytic sum
> Of all the worth and first effects of arts.
> And for his poesy, 'tis so ramm'd with life,
> That it shall gather strength of life, with being,
> And live hereafter more admired than now."

Can we conceive that Ben Jonson had not Shakespeare in his eye as he wrote these speeches, which apply better to him than to any one else ? It is true that a Shakespeare scholar of such authority as the late C. M. Ingleby, the compiler of *Shakespeare's Centurie of Prayse*, has declared against this theory, together with Nicholson and Furnivall. But none of them has brought forward any conclusive argument to prevent us from following Ben Jonson's admirer, Gifford, and his impartial critic, John Addington Symonds, in accepting these speeches as allusions to Shakespeare. It is useless to be for ever citing the passage in *The Return from Parnassus*, as to the " purge " Shakespeare has given Ben Jonson, in proof that there was an open feud between them, when, in fact, there is no evidence whatever of any hostility on Shakespeare's part ; and the very stress laid on the assertion that Horace, as a poet, is innocent of envy towards a famous and popular colleague, makes it unreasonable to take the eulogies as applying solely to the real Virgil, whom they fit so imperfectly. Of course it by no means follows that we are to conceive every word of these eulogies as unreservedly applied to Shakespeare ; the speeches seem to have been purposely left somewhat vague, so that they might at once point to the ancient poet and suggest the modern. But out of the mists of the characterisation certain definite contours stand forth ; and the physiognomy which they form, the picture of the great teacher in all earthly affairs, rich, not in book-learning, but in the wisdom of life, whose poetry is so vital that it will live through the ages with an ever-intenser life—this portrait we know and recognise as that of the genius with the great, calm eyes under the lofty brow.

Ben Jonson's *Sejanus*, which dates from 1603, only two years after *The Poetaster*, is a historical tragedy of the time of Tiberius, in which the poet, without any reference to contemporary personalities, sets forth to depict the life and customs of the imperial court. It is as an archæologist and moralist, however, that he depicts them, and his method is thus very different from Shakespeare's. He not only displays a close acquaintance with the life of the period, but penetrates through the outward forms to its spirit. He is animated, indeed, by a purely moral indignation against the turbulent and corrupt protagonist of his tragedy, but his wrath does not prevent him from giving a careful delineation of the figure of Sejanus in relation to its surroundings, by means of thoughtfully-designed and even imaginative individual scenes. Jonson does not, like Shakespeare, display from within the character of this unscrupulous and audacious man, but he shows the circumstances which have produced it, and its modes of action.

The difference between Jonson's and Shakespeare's method is not that Jonson pedantically avoids the anachronisms which swarm in *Julius Cæsar*. In both plays, for instance, watches are spoken of.[1] But Ben, on occasion, can paint a scene of Roman life with as much accuracy as we find in a picture by Alma Tadema or a novel by Flaubert. For example, when he depicts an act of worship and sacrifice in the Sacellum or private chapel of Sejanus's house (v. 4), every detail of the ceremonial is correct. After the Herald (Præco) has uttered the formula, "Be all profane far hence," and horn and flute players have performed their liturgical music, the priest (Flamen) exhorts all to appear with "pure hands, pure vestments, and pure minds;" his acolytes intone the complementary responses; and while the trumpets are again sounded, he takes honey from the altar with his finger, tastes it, and gives it to the others to taste; goes through the same process with the milk in an earthen vessel; and then sprinkles milk over the altar, "kindleth his gums," and goes with the censer round the altar, upon which he ultimately places it, dropping "branches of poppy" upon the smouldering incense. In justification of these traits, Jonson gives no fewer than thirteen footnotes, in which passages are cited from a very wide range of Latin authors. Kalisch has counted the notes appended to this play, and finds 291 in all. The ceremonial is here employed to introduce a scene in which "great Mother Fortune," to whom the libation is made, averts her face from Sejanus, and thereby portends his fall; whereupon, in an access of fury, he overturns her statue and altar.

Another scene, constructed with quite as much learning, and far more able and remarkable, is that which opens the second Act. Livia's physician, Eudemus, has been suborned by Sejanus to procure him a meeting with the princess, and, moreover, to concoct a potent poison for her husband. In the act of assisting his mistress to rouge her cheek, and recommending her an effective "dentrifice" and a "prepared pomatum to smooth the skin," he answers her casual questions as to who is to present the poisoned cup to Drusus and induce him to drink it. Here, again, Ben Jonson's mastery of detail displays itself. Eudemus's remark, for example, that the "ceruse" on Livia's cheeks has faded in the sun, is supported by a reference to an epigram of Martial, from which it appears that this cosmetic was injured by heat. But here all these details are merged in the potent general impression produced by the dispassionate and business-like calmness with which the impending murder is arranged in the intervals of a disquisition upon those devices of the toilet which are to enchain the contriver of the crime.

Ben Jonson possesses the undaunted insight and the vigorous pessimism which render it possible to represent Roman depravity and wild-beast-like ferocity under the first Emperors without extenuation and without declamation. He cannot, indeed, dispense with a sort of chorus of honourable Romans, but they express themselves, as a rule, pithily and without prolixity; and he has

---

[1] "Observe him as his watch observes his clock."—*Sejanus*, i. I.

enough sense of art and of history never to let his ruffians and courtesans repent.

Now and then he even attains to a Shakespearian level. The scene in which Sejanus approaches Eudemus first with jesting talk, and then, with wily insinuations, worms himself into his acquaintance and makes him his creature, while Eudemus, with crafty servility, shows that he can take a half-spoken hint, and, without for a moment committing himself, offers his services as pander and assassin—this passage is in no way inferior to the scene in Shakespeare's *King John* in which the King suggests to Hubert the murder of Arthur.

The most remarkable scene, however, is that (v. 10) in which the Senate is assembled in the Temple of Apollo to hear messages from Tiberius in his retreat at Capri. The first letter confers upon Sejanus "the tribunitial dignity and power," with expressions of esteem, and the Senate loudly acclaims the favourite. Then the second letter is read. It is expressed in a strangely contorted style, begins with some general remarks on public policy, hypocritical in tone, then turns, like the first, to Sejanus, and, to the astonishment of all, dwells with emphasis upon his low origin and the rare honours to which he has been preferred. Already the hearers are alarmed; but the impression is obliterated by new sentences of flattery. Then unfavourable opinions and judgments regarding the favourite are cited and dwelt upon with a certain complacency; then they are refuted with some vehemence; finally, they are brought forward again, and this time in a manner unmistakably hostile to Sejanus. Immediately the senators who have swarmed around him withdraw from his neighbourhood, leaving him in the centre of an empty space; and the reading continues until Laco enters with the guards who are to arrest the hitherto all-powerful favourite and lead him away. We can find no parallel to this reading of the letter and the vacillations it produces among the cringing senators, save in Antony's speech over the body of Cæsar and the consequent revulsion in the attitude and temper of the Roman mob. Shakespeare's scene is more vividly projected, and shines with the poet's humour; Jonson's scene is elaborated with grim energy, and worked out with the moralist's bitterness. But in the dramatic movement of the moralist's scene, no less than of the poet's, antique Rome lives again.

Jonson's *Catiline*, written some time later, appeared in 1611, and was dedicated to Pembroke. Although executed on the same principles, it is on the whole inferior to *Sejanus;* but it is better fitted for comparison with *Julius Cæsar* in so far as its action belongs to the same period, and Cæsar himself appears in it. The second act of the tragedy is in its way a masterpiece. As soon as Jonson enters upon the political action proper, he transcribes endless speeches from Cicero, and becomes intolerably tedious; but so long as he keeps to the representation of manners, and seeks, as in his comedies, to paint a quite unemotional picture of the period, he shows himself at his best.

This second act takes place at the house of Fulvia, the lady who, according to Sallust, betrayed to Cicero the conspirators' secret. The whole picture produces an entirely convincing effect. She first repels with unfeeling coldness an intrusive friend and protector, Catiline's fellow-conspirator, Curius; but when he at last turns away in anger, telling her that she will repent her conduct when she finds herself excluded from participation in an immense booty which will fall to the share of others, she calls him back, full of curiosity and interest, becomes suddenly friendly, and even caressing, and wrings from him his secret, instantly recognising, however, that Cicero will pay for it without stint, and that this money is considerably safer than the sum which might fall to her share in a general revolution. Her visit to Cicero, with his craftily friendly interrogatory, first of her, and then of her lover Curius, whom he summons and converts into one of his spies, deserves the highest praise. These scenes contain the concentrated essence of Sallust's *Catiline* and of Cicero's Orations and Letters. The Cicero of this play rises high above the Cicero to whom Shakespeare has assigned a few speeches. Cæsar, on the other hand, comes off no better at Ben Jonson's hands than at Shakespeare's. The poet was obviously determined to show a certain independence of judgment in the way in which he has treated Sallust's representation both of Cæsar and of Cicero. Sallust, whom Jonson nevertheless follows in the main, is hostile to Cicero and defends Cæsar. The worthy Ben, on the other hand, was, as a man of letters, a sworn admirer of Cicero, while in Cæsar he sees only a cold, crafty personage, who sought to make use of Catiline for his own ends, and therefore joined forces with him, but repudiated him when things went wrong, and was so influential that Cicero dared not attack him when he rooted out the conspiracy. Thus the great Caius Julius did not touch Jonson's manly heart any more than Shakespeare's. He appears throughout in an extremely unsympathetic light, and no speech, no word of his, portends his coming greatness.

Of this greatness Jonson had probably no deep realisation. It is surprising enough to note that the scholars and poets of the Renaissance, in so far as they took sides in the old strife between Cæsar and Pompey, were all on Pompey's side. Even in the seventeenth century, in France, under a despotism more absolute than Cæsar's, the men who were familiar with antique history, and who, for the rest, vied with each other in loyalty and king-worship, were unanimously opposed to Cæsar. Strange as it may seem, it is not until our century, with its hostility to despotism and its continuous advance in the direction of democracy, that Cæsar's genius has been fully appreciated, and the benefits his life conferred on humanity have been thoroughly understood.

The personal relation between Ben Jonson and Shakespeare is not to this day quite clearly ascertained. It was for long regarded as distinctly hostile, no one doubting that Jonson, during his great rival's lifetime, cherished an obstinate jealousy towards him. More recently, Jonson's admirers have argued with warmth that cruel injustice has been done him in this respect. So far as we can now judge, it appears that Jonson honestly recognised and admired Shakespeare's great qualities, but at the same time felt a displeasure he never could quite conquer at seeing him so much more popular as a dramatist, and—as was only natural—regarded his own tendencies in art as truer and better justified.

In the preface to *Sejanus* (edition of 1605) Jonson uses an expression which, as the piece was acted by Shakespeare's company, and Shakespeare himself appeared in it, was long interpreted as referring to him. Jonson writes:—

"Lastly, I would inform you that this book, in all numbers, is not the same with that which was acted on the public stage, wherein a second pen had good share ; in place of which, I have rather chosen to put weaker, and, no doubt, less pleasing, of mine own, than to defraud so happy a genius of his right by my loathed usurpation."

The words "so happy a genius," in particular, together with the other circumstances, have directed the thoughts of commentators to Shakespeare. Mr. Brinsley Nicholson, however (in the *Academy*, Nov. 14th, 1874), has shown it to be far more probable that the person alluded to is not Shakespeare, but a very inferior poet, Samuel Sheppard. The marked politeness of Jonson's expressions may be due to his having inflicted on his collaborator a considerable disappointment, almost an insult, by omitting his portion of the work, and at the same time excluding his name from the title-page. It seems, at any rate, that Samuel Sheppard felt wounded by this proceeding, since, more than forty years later, he claimed for himself the honour of having collaborated in *Sejanus*, in a verse which is ostensibly a panegyric on Jonson.[1] Symonds, so late as 1888, nevertheless maintains in his *Ben Jonson* that the preface most probably refers to Shakespeare ; but he

---

[1] He says of Jonson in *The Times Displayed in Six Sestyads :—*

"So His, that Divine Plautus equalled,
Whose Commick vain Menander nere could hit,
Whose tragic sceans shal be with wonder Read
By after ages, for unto his wit
My selfe gave personal ayd, *I* dictated
To him when as *Sejanus* fall he writ,
And yet on earth some foolish sots there bee
That dare make Randolph his Rival in degree."

does not refute or even mention Nicholson's carefully-marshalled argument.

It is not, however, of great importance to decide whether a compliment in one of Jonson's prefaces is or is not addressed to Shakespeare, since we have ample evidence in the warm eulogy and mild criticism in his *Discoveries*, and in the enthusiastic poem prefixed to the First Folio, that the crusty Ben (who, moreover, is said to have been Shakespeare's boon companion on his last convivial evening) regarded him with the warmest feelings, at least towards the close of his life and after his death.

This does not exclude the probability that Jonson's radically different literary ideals may have led him to make incidental and sometimes rather tart allusions to what appeared to him weak or mistaken in Shakespeare's work.

There is no foundation for the theory which has sometimes been advanced, that the passage in *The Poetaster* ridiculing Crispinus's coat of arms is an allusion to Shakespeare. It is beyond all doubt that the figure of Crispinus was exclusively intended for Marston; he himself, at any rate, did not for a moment doubt it. For the rest, Jonson's ascertained or conjectured side-glances at Shakespeare are these:—

In the prologue to *Every Man in his Humour*, which can scarcely have been spoken when the play was performed by the Lord Chamberlain's company, not only is realistic art proclaimed the true art, in opposition to the romanticism which prevailed on the Shakespearian stage, but a quite definite attack is made on those who

> " With three rusty swords,
> And help of some few foot and half-foot words,
> Fight over York and Lancaster's long jars."

And this is followed by a really biting criticism of the works of other playwrights, concluding—

> " There's hope left then,
> You, that have so graced monsters, may like men."

The possible jibe at *Twelfth Night* in *Every Man out of his Humour* (iii. 1) has already been mentioned (*ante*, p. 233). That, too, must be of late insertion, and is at worst extremely innocent.

Much has been made of the passage in *Volpone* (iii. 2) where Lady Politick Would-be, speaking of Guarini's *Pastor Fido*, says:—

> " All our English writers
> Will deign to steal out of this author, mainly:
> Almost as much as from Montagnié."

This has been interpreted as an accusation of plagiarism, some pointing it at the well-known passage in *The Tempest*, where

Shakespeare has annexed some lines from Montaigne's Essays; others at *Hamlet*, which has throughout many points of contact with the French philosopher. But *The Tempest* was undoubtedly written long after *Volpone*, and the relation of *Hamlet* to Montaigne is such as to render it scarcely conceivable that an accusation of plagiarism could be founded upon it. Here again Jonson seems to have been groundlessly suspected of malice.

Jacob Feis (*Shakespeare and Montaigne*, p. 183) would fain see in Nano's song about the hermaphrodite Androgyno a shameless attack upon Shakespeare, simply because the names Pythagoras and Euphorbus appear in it (*Volpone*, i. 1), as they do in the well-known passage in Meres; but this accusation is entirely fantastic. Equally unreasonable is it of Feis to discover an obscene besmirching of the figure of Ophelia in that passage of Jonson, Marston, and Chapman's *Eastward Ho!* (iii. 2) where there occur some passing allusions to *Hamlet*.

There remain, then, in reality, only one or two passages in *Bartholomew Fair*, dating from 1614. We have already seen (*ante*, p. 285) that there may possibly be a satirical allusion to the Sonnets in the introduced puppet-play, *The Touchstone of True Love*. The Induction contains an unquestionable jibe, both at *The Tempest* and *The Winter's Tale*, whose airy poetry the downright Ben was unable to appreciate.[1] Neither Caliban nor the element of enchantment in *The Tempest* appealed to him, and in *The Winter's Tale*, as in *Pericles*, it offended his classic taste and his Aristotelian theories that the action should extend over a score of years, so that we see infants in one act reappear in the next as grown-up young women.

But these trifling intolerances and impertinences must not tempt us to forget that it was Ben Jonson who wrote of Shakespeare those great and passionate lines :—

> " Triumph, my Britain ! thou hast one to show
> To whom all scenes of Europe homage owe.
> He was not of an age, but for all time ! "

---

[1] " If there be never a servant-monster in the fair, who can help it, he says, nor a nest of antiques ? He is loth to make Nature afraid in his plays, like those that beget tales, tempests, and such-like drolleries."

XI

HAMLET: ITS ANTECEDENTS IN FICTION, HISTORY, AND DRAMA

MANY and various emotions crowded upon Shakespeare's mind in the year 1601. In its early months Essex and Southampton were condemned. At exactly the same time there occurs the crisis in the relations of Pembroke and Shakespeare with the Dark Lady. Finally, in the early autumn, Shakespeare suffered a loss which he must have felt deeply. The Stratford register of burials for 1601 contains this line—

Septemb. 8. *Mr. Johannes Shakespeare.*

He lost his father, his earliest friend and guardian, whose honour and reputation lay so near to his heart. The father probably lived with his son's family in the handsome New Place, which Shakespeare had bought four years before. He had doubtless brought up the two girls Susannah and Judith ; he had doubtless sat by the death-bed of the little Hamnet. Now he was no more. All the years of his youth, spent at his father's side, revived in Shakespeare's mind, memories flocked in upon him, the fundamental relation between son and father preoccupied his thoughts, and he fell to brooding over filial love and filial reverence.

In the same year *Hamlet* began to take shape in Shakespeare's imagination.

Hamlet has given the name of Denmark a world-wide renown. Of all Danish men, there is only one who can be called famous on the largest scale ; only one with whom the thoughts of men are for ever busied in Europe, America, Australia, aye, even in Asia and Africa, wherever European culture has made its way ; and this one never existed, at any rate in the form in which he has become known to the world. Denmark has produced several men of note—Tycho Brahe, Thorvaldsen, and Hans Christian Andersen—but none of them has attained a hundredth part of Hamlet's fame. The *Hamlet* literature is comparable in extent to the literature of one of the smaller European peoples—the Slovaks, for instance.

As it is interesting to follow with the eye the process by which a block of marble slowly assumes human form, so it is interesting to observe how the *Hamlet* theme gradually acquires its Shakespearian character.

The legend first appears in Saxo Grammaticus. Fengo murders his brave brother Horvendil, and marries his widow Gerutha (Gertrude). Horvendil's son, Amleth, determines to disarm Fengo's malevolence by feigning madness. In order to test whether he is really mad, a beautiful girl is thrown in his way, who is to note whether, in his passion for her, he still maintains the appearance of madness. But a foster-brother and friend of Amleth's reveals the plot to him; the girl, too, has an old affection for him; and nothing is discovered. Here lie the germs of Ophelia and Horatio.

With regard to Amleth's mad talk, it is explained that, having a conscientious objection to lying, he so contorted his sayings that, though he always said what he meant, people could not discover whether he meant what he said, or himself understood it—an account of the matter which applies quite as well to the dark sayings of the Shakespearian Hamlet as to the naïve riddling of the Jutish Amleth.

Polonius, too, is here already indicated—especially the scene in which he plays eavesdropper to Hamlet's conversation with his mother. One of the King's friends (*præsumtione quam solertia abundantior*) proposes that some one shall conceal himself in the Queen's chamber. Amleth runs his sword through him and throws the dismembered body to the pigs, as Hamlet in the play drags the body out with him. Then ensues Amleth's speech of reproach to his mother, of which not a little is retained even in Shakespeare:—

"Think'st thou, woman, that these hypocritical tears can cleanse thee of shame, thee, who like a wanton hast cast thyself into the arms of the vilest of nithings, hast incestuously embraced thy husband's murderer, and basely flatterest and fawnest upon the man who has made thy son fatherless! What manner of creature doest thou resemble? Not a woman, but a dumb beast who couples at random."

Fengo resolves to send Amleth to meet his death in England, and despatches him thither with two attendants, to whom Shakespeare, as we know, has given the names of Rosencrantz and Guildenstern—the names of two Danish noblemen whose signatures have been found in close juxtaposition (with the date 1577) in an album which probably belonged to a Duke of Würtemberg. They were colleagues in the Council of Regency during the minority of Christian IV. These attendants (according to Saxo) had rune-staves with them, on which Amleth altered the runes, as in the play he re-writes the letters.

One more little touch is, as it were, led up to in Saxo: the exchange of the swords. Amleth, on his return, finds the King's men assembled at his own funeral feast. He goes around with a drawn sword, and on trying its edge against his nails he once or twice cuts himself with it. Therefore they nail his sword fast into its sheath. When Amleth has set fire to the hall and rushes into Fengo's chamber to murder him, he takes the King's sword from its hook and replaces it with his own, which the King in vain attempts to draw before he dies.

Now that Hamlet, more than any other Dane, has made the name of his fatherland world-famous, it impresses us strangely to read this utterance of Saxo's: " Imperishable shall be the memory of the steadfast youth who armed himself against false-hood with folly, and with it marvellously cloaked the splendour of heaven-radiant wisdom. . . . He left history in doubt as to whether his heroism or his wisdom was the greater."

The Hamlet of the tragedy, with reference to his mother's too hasty marriage, says, " Frailty, thy name is woman ! " Saxo re-marked with reference to Amleth's widow, who was in too great a hurry to marry again : " Thus it is with all the promises of women : they are scattered like chaff before the wind and pass away like waves of the sea. Who then will trust to a woman's heart, which changes as flowers shed their leaves, as seasons change, and as new events wipe out the traces of those that went before ? "

In Saxo's eyes, Amleth represented not only wisdom, but bodily strength. While the Hamlet of Shakespeare expressly emphasises the fact that he is anything but Herculean (" My father's brother, but no more like my father than I to Hercules "), Saxo expressly compares his hero to the Club-Bearer whose name is a synonym for strength : " And the fame of men shall tell of him that, if it had been given him to live his life fortunately to the end, his excellent dispositions would have displayed them-selves in deeds greater than those of Hercules, and would have adorned his brows with the demigod's wreath." It sounds almost as though Shakespeare's Hamlet entered a protest against these words of Saxo.

In the year 1559 the legend was reproduced in French in Belleforest's *Histoires Tragiques*, and seems in this form to have reached England, where it furnished material for the older *Hamlet* drama, now lost, but to which we find frequent allusions. It cannot be proved that this play was founded upon Pavier's English translation of Belleforest, or even that Shakespeare had Pavier before him ; for the oldest edition of the translation which has come down to us (reprinted in Collier's *Shakespeare's Library*, ed. 1875, pt. I. vol. ii. p. 224) dates from 1608, and contains certain details (such as the eavesdropper's concealment behind the arras, and Hamlet's exclamation of " A rat ! a rat ! " before he kills Polonius) of which there is no trace in Belleforest, and which may quite as well have been taken from Shakespeare's tragedy, as borrowed by him from an unknown older edition of the novel.

The earliest known allusion to the old *Hamlet* drama is the phrase of Thomas Nash, dating from 1589, quoted above (p. 91). In 1594 the Lord Chamberlain's men (Shakespeare's company), acting together with the Lord Admiral's men at the Newington Butts theatre under the management of Henslow and others, performed a *Hamlet* with reference to which Henslow notes in his account-book for June 9th: " Rd. at hamlet . . . viii s." This play must have been the old one, for Henslow would otherwise have added the letters *ne* (new), and the receipts would have been much greater. His share, as we see, was only eight shillings, whereas it was sometimes as much as nine pounds.

The chief interest of this older play seems to have centred in a figure added by the dramatist—the Ghost of the murdered King, which cried " Hamlet, revenge!" This cry is frequently quoted. It first appears in 1596 in Thomas Lodge's *Wits Miserie*, where it is said of the author that he " looks as pale as the visard of ye ghost, which cried so miserably at ye theator like an oister-wife, *Hamlet, revenge.*" It next occurs in Dekker's *Satiromastix*, 1602, where Tucca says, " My name's *Hamlet, revenge!*" In 1605 we find it in Thomas Smith's *Voiage and Entertainement in Rushia;* and it is last found in 1620 in Samuel Rowland's *Night Raven*, where, however, it seems to be an inaccurate quotation from the *Hamlet* we know.

Shakespeare's play was entered in the Stationers' Register on the 26th of July 1602, under the title " A booke called ' *the Revenge of Hamlett Prince [of] Denmarke' as yt was latelie Acted by the Lord Chamberleyne his servantes.*"

That it made an instant success on the stage is almost proved by the fact that so early as the 7th of July the opposition manager Henslow pays Chettle twenty shillings for " The Danish Tragedy," evidently a furbishing up of the old play.

The publication of Shakespeare's *Hamlet*, however, did not take place till 1603. Then appeared the First Quarto, indubitably a pirated edition, either founded entirely on shorthand notes, or on shorthand notes eked out by aid of the actors' parts, and completed, in certain passages, from memory. Although this edition certainly contains a debased and corrupt text, it is impossible to attribute to the misunderstandings or oversights of a copyist or stenographer all its divergences from the carefully-printed quarto of the following year, which is practically identical with the First Folio text. The differences are so great as to exclude such a theory. We have evidently before us Shakespeare's first sketch of the play, although in a very defective form ; and, as far as we can see, this first sketch keeps considerably closer than the definitive text to the old *Hamlet* drama, on which Shakespeare

based his play. Here and there, though with considerable uncertainty, we can even trace scenes from the old play among
Shakespeare's, and touches of its style mingling with his. It is
very significant, also, that there are more rhymes in the First than
in the Second Quarto.

The most remarkable feature in the 1603 edition is a scene
between Horatio and the Queen in which he tells her of the
King's frustrated scheme for having Hamlet murdered in England.
The object of this scene is to absolve the Queen from complicity
in the King's crime; a purpose which can also be traced in
other passages of this first edition, and which seems to be a
survival from the older drama. So far as we can gather, Horatio
appears to have played an altogether more prominent part in the
old play; Hamlet's madness appears to have been wilder; and
Polonius probably bore the name of Corambis, which is prefixed
to his speeches in the edition of 1603. Finally, as we have
seen, Shakespeare took the important character of the Ghost,
not indicated in either the legend or the novel, from this earlier
Hamlet tragedy. The theory that it is the original of the German
tragedy, *Der bestrafte Brudermord*, published by Cohn, from a
manuscript of 1710, is unsupported by evidence.

Looking backward through the dramatic literature of England,
we find that the author of the old *Hamlet* drama in all probability
sought inspiration in his turn in Kyd's *Spanish Tragedy*. It
appears from allusions in Jonson's *Cynthia's Revels* and *Bartholomew Fair* that this play must have been written about 1584.
It was one of the most popular plays of its day with the theatre-
going public. So late as 1632, Prynne in his *Histriomastix*
speaks of a woman who, on her death-bed, instead of seeking the
consolations of religion, cried out: "Hieronimo, Hieronimo! O
let me see Hieronimo acted!"

The tragedy opens, after the fashion of its models in Seneca,
with the apparition of the murdered man's ghost, and his demand
for vengeance. Thus the Ghost in Shakespeare's *Hamlet* is
lineally descended from the spirit of Tantalus in Seneca's *Thyestes*,
and from the spirit of Thyestes in Seneca's *Agamemnon*. Hieronimo, who has been driven mad by sorrow for the loss of his son,
speaking to the villain of the piece, gives half-ironical, half-crazy
expression to the anguish that is torturing him :—

> " *Lorenzo.* Why so, Hieronimo? use me.
> *Hieronimo.* Who? you my lord?
>   I reserve your favour for a greater honour :
>   This is a very toy, my lord, a toy.
> *Lor.* All's one, Hieronimo, acquaint me with it.
> *Hier.* I' faith, my lord, 'tis an idle thing . . .
>   The murder of a son, or so—
>   A thing of nothing, my lord!"

These phrases foreshadow Hamlet's speeches to the King. But Hieronimo is really mad, although he speaks of his madness much as Hamlet does, or rather denies it point-blank—

> "Villain, thou liest, and thou dost naught
> But tell me I am mad: thou liest, I am not mad.
> I know thee to be Pedro, and he Jaques;
> I'll prove it to thee; and were I mad, how could I?"

Here and there, especially in Ben Jonson's additions, we come across speeches which lie very close to passages in Hamlet. A painter, who also has lost his son, says to Hieronimo: "Ay, sir, no man did hold a son so dear;" whereupon he answers—

> "What, not as thine? That is a lie,
> As massy as the earth: I had a son,
> Whose least unvalued hair did weigh
> A thousand of thy sons; and he was murdered."

Thus Hamlet cries to Laertes:—

> "I lov'd Ophelia: forty thousand brothers
> Could not, with all their quantity of love,
> Make up my sum."

Hieronimo, like Hamlet, again and again postpones his vengeance:—

> "All times fit not for revenge.
> Thus, therefore, will I rest me in unrest,
> Dissembling quiet in unquietness:
> Not seeming that I know their villainies,
> That my simplicity may make them think
> That ignorantly I will let all slip."

At last he determines to have a play acted, as a means to his revenge. The play is Kyd's own *Solyman and Perseda*, and in the course of it the guilty personages, who play the chief parts, are slaughtered, not in make-believe, but in reality.

Crude and naïve though everything still is in *The Spanish Tragedy*, which resembles *Titus Andronicus* in style rather than any other of Shakespeare's works, it evidently, through the medium of the earlier *Hamlet* play, contributed a good deal to the foundations of Shakespeare's *Hamlet*.

Before going more deeply into the contents of this great work, and especially before trying to bring it into relation to Shakespeare's personality, we have yet to see what suggestions or impulses the poet may have found in contemporary history.

We have already remarked upon the impression which the Essex family tragedy must have made upon Shakespeare in his early youth, before he had even left Stratford. All England was talking of the scandal: how the Earl of Leicester, who was commonly suspected of having had Lord Essex poisoned, immediately after his death had married his widow, Lady Lettice, whose lover no one doubted that he had been during her husband's lifetime. There is much in the character of King Claudius to suggest that Shakespeare has here taken Leicester as his model. The two have in common ambition, sensuality, an ingratiating conciliatory manner, astute dissimulation, and complete unscrupulousness. On the other hand, it is quite unreasonable to suppose, with Hermann Conrad,[1] that Shakespeare had Essex in his eye in drawing Hamlet himself.

Almost as near to Shakespeare's own day as the Essex-Leicester catastrophe had been the similar events in the Royal Family of Scotland. Mary Stuart's second husband, Lord Darnley, who bore the title of King of Scotland, had been murdered in 1567 by her lover, the daring and unscrupulous Bothwell, whom the Queen almost immediately afterwards married. Her contemporaries had no doubt whatever of Mary's complicity in the assassination, and her son James saw in his mother and his stepfather his father's murderers. The leaders of the Scottish rebellion displayed before the captive Queen a banner bearing a representation of Darnley's corpse, with her son kneeling beside it and calling to Heaven for vengeance. Darnley, like the murdered King in *Hamlet*, was an unusually handsome, Bothwell an unusually repulsive, man.

James was brought up by his mother's enemies, and during her lifetime, and after her death, was perpetually wavering between her adherents, who had defended her legal rights, and her adversaries, who had driven her from the country and placed James himself upon the throne. He made one or two efforts, indeed, to soften Elizabeth's feelings towards his mother, but refrained from all attempt to avenge her death. His character was irresolute. He was learned and—what Hamlet is very far from being—a superstitious pedant; but, like Hamlet, he was a lover of the arts and sciences, and was especially interested in the art of acting. Between 1599 and 1601 he entertained in Scotland a portion of the company to which Shakespeare belonged; but it is uncertain whether Shakespeare himself ever visited Scotland. There is little doubt, on the other hand, that when, after Elizabeth's death in 1603, James made his entrance into London, Shakespeare, richly habited in a uniform of red cloth, walked in his train along with Burbage and a few others of the leading players. Their company was henceforth known as "His Majesty's Servants."

Although there is in all this no lack of parallels to Hamlet's circumstances, it is, of course, as ridiculous to take James as to take Essex for the actual model of Hamlet. Nothing could at that time have been stupider or more tactless than to remind the heir-presumptive to the throne, or the new King, of the deplorable

[1] *Preuss. Jahrbücher*, February 1895.

circumstances of his early history. This does not exclude the supposition, however, that contemporary history supplied Shakespeare with certain outward elements, which, in the moment of conception, contributed to the picture bodied forth by the creative energy of his genius.

From this point of view, too, we must regard the piles of material which well-meaning students bring to light, in the artless belief that they have discovered the very stones of which Shakespeare constructed his dramatic edifice. People do not distinguish between the possibility that the poet may have unconsciously received a suggestion here and there for details of his work, and the theory that he deliberately intended an imaginative reproduction of definite historic events. No work of imagination assuredly, and least of all such a work as *Hamlet*, comes into existence in the way these theorists assume. It springs from within, has its origin in an overmastering sensation in the poet's soul, and then, in the process of growth, assimilates certain impressions from without.

XII

"HAMLET"—MONTAIGNE AND GIORDANO BRUNO— ANTECEDENTS IN ETHNOGRAPHY

ALONG with motives from novel, drama, and history, impressions of a philosophical and quasi-scientific order went to the making of *Hamlet*. Of all Shakespeare's plays, this is the profoundest and most contemplative; a philosophic atmosphere breathes around it. Naturally enough, then, criticism has set about inquiring to what influences we may ascribe these broodings over life and death and the mysteries of existence.

Several students, such as Tschischwitz and König, have tried to make out that Giordano Bruno exercised a preponderating influence upon Shakespeare.[1] Passages suggesting a cycle in nature, such as Hamlet's satirical outburst to the King about the dead Polonius (iv. 3), have directed their thoughts to the Italian philosopher. In some cases they have found or imagined a definite identity between sayings of Hamlet's and of Bruno's— for instance, on determinism. Bruno has a passage in which he emphasises the necessity by which everything is brought about: "Whatever may be my preordained eventide, when the change shall take place, I await the day, I, who dwell in the night; but they await the night who dwell in the daylight. All that is, is either here or there, near or far off, now or after, soon or late." In the same spirit Hamlet says (v. 2): "There is a special providence in the fall of a sparrow. If it be now, 'tis not to come; if it be not to come, it will be now; if it be not now, yet it will come: the readiness is all." Bruno says: "Nothing is absolutely imperfect or evil; it only seems so in relation to something else, and what is bad for one is good for another." In *Hamlet* (ii. 2), "There is nothing either good or bad, but thinking makes it so."

When once attention had been directed to Giordano Bruno, not only his philosophical and more popular writings, but even his plays were ransacked in search of passages that might have influenced Shakespeare. Certain parallels and points of resemblance were indeed discovered, very slight and trivial in themselves, but which theorists would not believe to be for-

[1] Tschischwitz: *Shakespeare-Forschungen*; König: *Shakespeare-Jahrbuch*, xi.

tuitous, since it was known that Giordano Bruno had passed some time in England in Shakespeare's day, and had frequented the society of the most distinguished men. As soon as the matter was closely investigated, however, the probability of any direct influence vanished almost to nothing.

Giordano Bruno remained on English ground from 1583 to 1585. Coming from France, where he had instructed Henri III. in the Lullian art, a mechanical, mnemotechnic method for the solution of all possible scientific problems, he brought with him a letter of recommendation to Mauvissière, the French Ambassador, in whose house he was received as a friend of the family during the whole of his stay in London. He made the acquaintance of many leading men of the time, such as Walsingham, Leicester, Burghley, Sir Philip Sidney and his literary circle, but soon went on to Oxford in order to lecture there and disseminate the doctrines which lay nearest his heart. These were the Copernican system in opposition to the Ptolemaic, which still held the field at Oxford, and the theory that the same principle of life is diffused through everything—atoms and organisms, plants, animals, human beings, and the universe at large. He quarrelled with the Oxford scholars, and held them up to ridicule and contempt in his dialogue *La Cena de le Ceneri*, published soon after, in which he speaks in the most disparaging terms of the coarseness of English manners. The dirtiness of the London streets, for example, and the habit of letting one goblet go round the table, from which every one drank, aroused his dislike and scorn scarcely less than the rejection of Copernicus by the pedants of the University.

At the very earliest, Shakespeare cannot have come to London until the year of Bruno's departure from England, and can therefore scarcely have met him. The philosopher exercised no influence upon the spiritual life of the day in England. Not even Sir Philip Sidney was attracted by his doctrine, and his name does not once occur in Greville's Life of Sidney, although Greville had seen much of Bruno. Brunnhofer, who has studied the question, points out, as showing how little trace Bruno left behind him in England, that there is not in the Bodleian a single contemporary manuscript or document of any kind which throws the least light upon Bruno's stay in London or Oxford.[1] It has been maintained, nevertheless, that Shakespeare must have read his philosophic writings in Italian. It is, of course, possible; but there is nothing in *Hamlet* to prove it—nothing that cannot be fully accounted for without assuming that he had the slightest acquaintance with them.

The only expression in Shakespeare which, probably by accident, has an entirely pantheistic ring is "The prophetic soul of the wide world" in Sonnet cvii.; the only passages containing an idea, not certainly identical, but comparable with Bruno's doctrine

---

[1] Brunnhofer : *Giordano Bruno's Weltanschauung und Verhängniss.*

of the metamorphosis of natural forms are the cyclical Sonnets lix., cvi., cxxiii. If Giordano Bruno really had anything to do with these passages, it must be because Shakespeare had heard some talk about the great Italian's doctrine, which may just at that time have been recalled to the recollection of his English acquaintances by his death at the stake in Rome, on February 17, 1600. If Shakespeare had studied his writings, he would, among other things, have obtained some glimmering of the Copernican system, of which he knows nothing. On the other hand, it is quite conceivable that he may have picked up in conversation an approximate and incomplete conception of Bruno's philosophy, and that this conception may have given birth to the above-mentioned philosophical reveries. All the passages in *Hamlet* which have been attributed to the influence of Bruno really stand in much closer relation to writers under whose literary and philosophical influence we know beyond a doubt that Shakespeare fell.

There is preserved in the British Museum a copy of Florio's translation of Montaigne's Essays, folio, London, 1603, with Shakespeare's name written on the fly-leaf. The signature is, I believe, a forgery; but that Shakespeare had read Montaigne is clear beyond all doubt.

There are many evidences of the influence exerted by Montaigne's Essays on English readers of that date. It was only natural that the book should vividly impress the greatest men of the age; for there were not at that time many such books as Montaigne's—none, perhaps, containing so living a revelation, not merely of an author, but of a human being, natural, many-sided, full of ability, rich in contradictions.

Outside of *Hamlet*, we trace Montaigne quite clearly in one passage in Shakespeare, who must have had the Essays lying on his table while he was writing *The Tempest*. Gonzalo says (ii. 1)—

> " I' the commonwealth I would by contraries
> Execute all things, for no kind of traffic
> Would I admit; no name of magistrate;
> Letters should not be known; riches, poverty,
> And use of service, none; contract, succession,
> Bourn, bound of land, tilth, vineyard, none;
> No use of metal, corn, or wine, or oil:
> No occupation, all men idle, all;
> And women too."

We find this speech almost word for word in Montaigne (Book i. chap. 30): " It is a nation that hath no kind of traffike, no knowledge of letters, no intelligence of numbers, no name of magistrate, nor of politike superioritie; no vse of service, of riches or of povertie; no contracts, no successions, no partitions, no occupation but idle . . . no manuring of lands, no vse of wine, corn or metal."

Since it is thus proved beyond a doubt that Shakespeare was acquainted with Montaigne's Essays, it is not improbable that the resemblance between passages in that book and passages in *Hamlet* are due to something more than chance. When such passages occur in the First Quarto (1603), we must assume either that Shakespeare knew the French original, or that—as is likely enough—he may have had an opportunity of reading Florio's translation before it was published. It happened not infrequently in those days that a book was handed round in manuscript among the author's private friends five or six years before it was given to the public. Florio's close connection with the household of Southampton renders it almost certain that Shakespeare must have been acquainted with him; and his translation had been entered in the Stationers' Register as ready for publication so early as 1599.

Florio was born in 1545, of Italian parents, who, as Waldenses, had been forced to leave their country. He had become to all intents and purposes an Englishman, had studied and given lessons in Italian at Oxford, had been some years in the service of the Earl of Southampton, and was married to a sister of the poet Samuel Daniel. He dedicated each separate book of his translation of Montaigne to two noble ladies. Among them we find Elizabeth, Countess of Rutland, Sidney's daughter; Lady Penelope Rich, Essex's sister; and Lady Elizabeth Grey, renowned for her beauty and learning. Each of these ladies was celebrated in a sonnet.

Every one remembers those incomparably-worded passages in *Hamlet* where the great brooder over life and death has expressed, in terms at once harsh and moving, his sense of the ruthlessness of the destructive forces of Nature, or what might be called the cynicism of the order of things. Take for instance the following (v. 1):—

"Why may not imagination trace the noble dust of Alexander, till he find it stopping a bung-hole? . . . As thus: Alexander died, Alexander was buried, Alexander returneth into dust; the dust is earth; of earth we make loam; and why of that loam, whereto he was converted, might they not stop a beer-barrel?

> Imperious Cæsar, dead, and turn'd to clay,
> Might stop a hole to keep the wind away:
> O that that earth which kept the world in awe
> Should patch a wall to expel the winter's flaw!"

Hamlet's grisly jest upon the worms who are eating Polonius is a variation on the same theme (iv. 3):—

"*Ham.* A man may fish with the worm that hath eat of a king; and eat of the fish that hath fed of that worm.

"*King.* What dost thou mean by this?

" *Ham.* Nothing, but to show you how a king may go a progress through the guts of a beggar."

An attempt has been made to attribute these passages to the influence of Giordano Bruno; but, as Robert Beyersdorff has strikingly demonstrated,[1] this theory assumes that Bruno's doctrine was an atomistic materialism, whereas it was, in fact, pantheism, a perpetual insistence upon the unity of God and Nature. The very atoms, in Bruno, partake of spirit and life; it is not their mechanical conjunction that produces life; no, they are monads. While cynicism is the keynote of these utterances of Hamlet, enthusiasm is the keynote of Bruno's. Three passages from Bruno's writings (*De la Causa* and *La Cena de le Ceneri*) have been cited as coinciding with Hamlet's words as to the transformations of matter. But in the first Bruno is speaking of the transformation of natural forms, and of the emanation of all forms from the universal soul; in the second, he is insisting that in all compound bodies there live numerous individuals who remain immortal after the dissolution of the bodies; in the third, he treats of the globe as a vast organism, which, just like animals and men, is renewed by the transformation of matter. The whole resemblance, then, between these passages and Hamlet's bitter outburst is that they treat of transformations of form and matter in Nature. In spirit they are radically different. Bruno maintains that even what seems to belong entirely to the world of matter is permeated with soul; Hamlet, on the contrary, asserts the wretchedness and transitoriness of human existence.[2]

But precisely in these points Hamlet comes very near to Montaigne, who has many expressions like those above quoted, and speaks of Sulla very much as Hamlet speaks of Alexander and Cæsar.

On a close comparison of Shakespeare's expressions with Montaigne's, their similarity is very striking. Hamlet, for example, says that Polonius is at supper, not where he eats but where he is eaten. "A certain convocation of politic worms are e'en at him. Your worm is your only emperor for diet: we fat all creatures else to fat us, and we fat ourselves for maggots: your fat king,

---

[1] *Giordano Bruno und Shakespeare*, Oldenburg, 1889, p. 26.

[2] A comic analogy to Bruno's doctrine may be found in the following lines of Hotspur's (*Henry IV.*, Pt. I. iii. 1):—

> "Diseased nature oftentimes breaks forth
> In strange eruptions : oft the teeming earth
> Is with a kind of colic pinch'd and vex'd
> By the imprisoning of unruly wind
> Within her womb ; which, for enlargement striving,
> Shakes the old beldam Earth, and topples down
> Steeples and moss-grown towers."

But no one will seriously attribute this passage to the philosophical influence of Giordano Bruno. Hotspur was quite capable of hitting upon this image without any suggestion from Nola or Naples.

and your lean beggar, is but variable service; two dishes, but to one table: that's the end."

Compare Montaigne, Book ii. chap. 12:—

"He [man] need not a Whale, an Elephant, nor a Crocodile, nor any such other wilde beast, of which one alone is of power to defeat a great number of men: seely lice are able to make Silla give over his Dictatorship: The heart and life of a mighty and triumphant Emperor, is but the break-fast of a seely little Worm."

We have seen that an attempt has been made to trace to Bruno Hamlet's utterance as to the relativity of all concepts. In reality it may rather be traced to Montaigne. Hamlet, having remarked (ii. 2) that "Denmark is a prison," Rosencrantz replies, "We think not so, my lord;" whereupon Hamlet rejoins, "Why, then 'tis none to you; for there is nothing either good or bad, but thinking makes it so."[1] The passage in Montaigne is almost identical (Book i. chap. 40):—

"If that which we call evill and torment, be neither torment nor evill, but that our fancie only gives it that qualitie, it is in us to change it."

We have seen that an attempt has been made to trace Hamlet's saying about death, "If it be now, 'tis not to come," &c. to Bruno's words in the dedication of his *Candelajo:* "Tutto quel ch'è o è qua o è là, o vicino o lunghi, o adesso o poi, o presso o tardi." But the same course of thought which leads Hamlet to the conclusion, "The readiness is all," is found, with the same conclusion, in the nineteenth chapter of Montaigne's first book: "That to Philosophie, is to learne how to die"—a chapter which has inspired a great many of Hamlet's graveyard cogitations.[2] Montaigne says of death:—

"Let us not forget how many waies our joyes or our feastings be subject unto death, and by how many hold-fasts shee threatens us and them. . . . It is uncertaine where death looks for us; let us expect her everie where. . . . I am ever prepared about that which I may be. . . . A man should ever be ready booted to take his journey. . . . What matter is it when it commeth, since it is unavoidable?"

Furthermore, we find striking points of resemblance between the celebrated soliloquy, "To be or not to be," and the passage in Montaigne (Book iii. chap. 12) where he reproduces the substance of Socrates' Apology. Socrates, as we know, suggests several different possibilities: death is either an "amendment" of our condition or the annihilation of our being; but even in the latter case it is an "amendment" to enter upon a long and peaceful

---

[1] This speech first occurs in the First Folio.
[2] This was first pointed out (about 1860) by Otto Ludwig. See his *Shakespeare-Studien*, p. 373. The relation between Shakespeare and Montaigne is dwelt upon in an ill-arranged book by G. F. Stedefeld: *Hamlet, ein Tendenz-Drama* (1871).

night; for there is nothing better in life than a deep, calm, dreamless sleep. Shakespeare seems to have had no belief in an actual amelioration of our condition at death; Hamlet does not even mention it as a possible contingency; whereas the poet makes him dwell upon the thought of an endless sleep, and on the possibility of horrible dreams. Now and then we seem to find traces in *Hamlet* of Plato's monologue, in the vesture given to it by Montaigne. In the French text there is mention of the joy of being free in another life from having to do with unjust and corrupt judges; Hamlet speaks of freeing himself from "The oppressor's wrong, the proud man's contumely." Some lines added in the edition of 1604 remind us forcibly of a passage in Florio's translation. Florio reproduces Montaigne's "Si c'est un anéantissement de notre être" by the phrase, "If it be a consummation of one's being." Hamlet, using a word which occurs in only two other places in Shakespeare, says, "A consummation devoutly to be wished."

Many other small coincidences can be pointed out in the use of names and turns of phrase, which do not, however, actually prove anything. Where Montaigne is describing the anarchic condition of public affairs, his words are rendered in Florio by the curiously poetic expression, "All is out of frame." This bears a certain resemblance to the phrase which Hamlet, already in the 1603 edition, employs to describe the disorganisation which has followed his father's death, "The time is out of joint." The coincidence may be fortuitous, but as one among many other points of resemblance it supports the conjecture that Shakespeare had read the translation before it was published.[1]

For the rest, Rushton, in *Shakespeare's Euphuism* (1871), and after him Beyersdorff, have pointed out not a few parallels to *Hamlet* in Lyly's *Euphues*, precisely at the points where critics have sought to trace the much more improbable influence of Bruno. Beyersdorff sometimes goes too far in trying to find in *Euphues* the origin of ideas which it would be an insult to suppose that Shakespeare needed to borrow from such a source. But sometimes there is a real analogy. It has been alleged that the King must have borrowed from Bruno's philosophy the topics of consolation whereby (i. 2) he seeks to convince Hamlet of the unreasonableness of "obstinate condolement" over his father's death. As a matter of fact, the letter of Euphues to Ferardo on his daughter's death contains precisely the same arguments:—
"Knowest thou not, Ferardo, that lyfe is the gifte of God, deathe the due of Nature, as we receive the one as a benefitte, so must we abide the other of necessitie," &c.

It has been suggested that where Hamlet (ii. 2) speaks of "the satirical rogue" who, in the book he is reading, makes merry over

[1] Compare Jacob Feis, *Shakespeare and Montaigne*, pp. 64–130. Beyersdorff *Giordano Bruno und Shakespeare*, p. 27 *et seq.*

the decrepitude of old age, Shakespeare must have been alluding to a passage in Bruno's *Spaccio*, where old men are described as those who have "snow on their head and furrows in their brow." But if we insist on identifying the "satirical rogue" with any actual author (a quite unreasonable proceeding), Lyly at once presents himself as answering to the description. Again and again in *Euphues*, where old men give good advice to the young, they appear with "hoary haire and watry eyes." And Euphues repulses, quite in the manner of Hamlet, an old gentleman whose moralising he regards as nothing more than the envy of decrepit age for lusty youth, and whose intellect seems to him as tottering as his legs.

Finally, an attempt has been made to refer Hamlet's harsh sayings to Ophelia, and his contemptuous utterances about women in general ("Frailty, thy name is woman," &c.), to a dialogue of Bruno's (*De la Causa IV.*) in which the pedant Pollinnio appears as a woman-hater. But the resemblance seems trifling enough when we find that in this case woman is attacked in sound theological fashion as the source of original sin and the cause of all our woe. Many expressions in *Euphues* lie infinitely nearer to Hamlet's. "What means your lordship?" Ophelia asks (iii. 1), and Hamlet replies, "That if you be honest and fair, your honesty should admit no discourse to your beauty." Compare in *Euphues* Ferardo's words to Lucilla: "For oftentimes thy mother woulde saye, that thou haddest more beautie then was convenient for one that shoulde bee honeste," and his exclamation, "O Lucilla, Lucilla, woulde thou wert lesse fayre!" Again, Hamlet rails against women's weakness, crying, "Wise men know well enough what monsters you make of them;" and we find in *Euphues* exactly similar outbursts: "I perceive they be rather woe vnto men, by their falsehood, gelousie, inconstancie. . . . I see they will be corasiues (corrosives)."[1] Beyersdorff, moreover, is no doubt right in suggesting that the artificial style of *Euphues* is apparent in such speeches as this of Hamlet's: "For the power of beauty will sooner transform honesty from what it is to a bawd than the force of honesty can translate beauty into his likeness."

In *Hamlet* and elsewhere in Shakespeare we come across traces of a sort of atomistic-materialistic philosophy. In the last scene of *Julius Cæsar*, Antony actually employs with regard to Brutus the expression, "The elements so *mix'd* in him." In *Measure for Measure* (iii. 1) the Duke says to Claudio—

> "Thou art not thyself;
> For thou exist'st on many a thousand grains
> That issue out of dust."

---

[1] Beyersdorff, *op. cit.*, p. 33. John Lyly, *Evphves: The Anatomy of Wit*, ed. Landmann, pp. 72, 75.

Hamlet says (i. 2)—

> " O that this too too solid flesh would melt,
> Thaw, and dissolve itself into a dew ; "

and to Horatio (iii. 2)—

> " Bless'd are those
> Whose blood and judgment are so well *co-mingled.*"

It has already been pointed out how far this atomism, if we can so regard it, differs from Bruno's idealistic monadism. But in all probability we have here only the expressions of the dominant belief of Shakespeare's time, that all differences of temperament depended upon the mixture of the juices or "humours." Shakespeare is on this point, as on many others, more popular and less book-learned, more naïve and less metaphysical, than book-learned commentators are willing to allow.

Writers like Montaigne and Lyly were no doubt constantly in Shakespeare's hands while *Hamlet* was taking shape within him. But it would be absurd to suppose that he consulted them especially with *Hamlet* in view. He did consult authorities with regard to Hamlet, but they were men, not books, and men, moreover, with whom he was in daily intercourse. Hamlet being a Dane and his destiny being acted out in distant Denmark—a name not yet so familiar in England as it was soon to be, when, with the new King, a Danish princess came to the throne— Shakespeare would naturally seize whatever opportunities lay in his way of gathering intelligence as to the manners and customs of this little-known country.

In the year 1585 a troupe of English players had appeared in the courtyard of the Town-Hall of Elsinore. If we are justified in assuming this troupe to have been the same which we find in the following year established at the Danish Court, it numbered among its members three persons who, at the time when Shakespeare was turning over in his mind the idea of *Hamlet*, belonged to his company of actors, and probably to his most intimate circle : namely, William Kemp, George Bryan, and Thomas Pope. The first of these, the celebrated clown, belonged to Shakespeare's company from 1594 till March 1602, when he went over for six months to Henslow's company ; the other two also joined Shakespeare's company as early as 1594. It was evidently from these comrades of his, and perhaps also from other English actors who, under the management of Thomas Sackville, had performed at Copenhagen in 1596 at the coronation of Christian IV., that Shakespeare gathered information on several matters relating to Denmark.

First and foremost, he picked up some Danish names, which we find, indeed, mutilated by the printers in the different texts of *Hamlet*, but which are easily recognisable. The *Rossencraft* of the First Quarto has become *Rosencraus* in the second, and *Rosincrane* in the Folio; it is clearly enough the name of the ancient Danish family of *Rosenkrans*. Thus, too, we find in the three editions the name *Gilderstone, Guyldensterne,* and *Guildensterne,* in which we recognise the Danish *Gyldenstierne;* while the names given to the ambassador, *Voltemar, Voltemand, Valtemand, Voltumand,* are so many corruptions of the Danish *Valdemar*. The name *Gertrude,* too, Shakespeare must have learned from his comrades as a Danish name; he has substituted it for the *Geruth* of the novel. In the Second Quarto it is misprinted *Gertrad*.

It is evidently in consequence of what he had learnt from his comrades that Shakespeare has transferred the action of *Hamlet* from Jutland to Elsinore, which they had visited and no doubt described to him. That is how he comes to know of the Castle at Elsinore (finished about a score of years earlier), though he does not mention the name of Kronborg.

The scene in which Polonius listens behind the arras, and in which Hamlet, in reproaching the Queen, points to the portraits of the late and of the present King, has even been regarded as proving that Shakespeare knew something of the interior of the Castle. On the stage, Hamlet is often made to wear a miniature portrait of his father round his neck, and to hold it up before his mother; but the words of the play prove incontestably that Shakespeare imagined life-sized pictures hanging on the wall. Now we find a contemporary description of a "great chamber" at Kronborg, written by an English traveller, in which occurs this passage: "It is hanged with Tapistary of fresh coloured silke without gold, wherein all the Danish kings are exprest in antique habits, according to their severall times, with their armes and inscriptions, containing all their conquests and victories."[1] It is possible, then, though not very probable, that Shakespeare may have heard of the arrangement of this room. When Polonius wanted to play the eavesdropper, it was a matter of course that he should get behind the arras; and it was easy to imagine that portraits of the kings would hang on the walls of a royal castle, without the least knowledge that this was actually the case at Kronborg.

It is probable, on the other hand, that Shakespeare made Hamlet study at Wittenberg because he knew that many Danes went to this University, which, being Lutheran, was not frequented by Englishmen. And it is quite certain that when, in the first and fifth acts, he makes trumpet-blasts and the firing of cannon accompany the healths which are drunk, he must have known that this was a specially Danish custom, and have tried to give his play local colour by introducing it. While Hamlet and his

---

[1] *New Shakspere Society's Transactions,* 1874, p. 513. Compare Schück, "Englische Komödianten in Skandinavien," *Skandinavisches Archiv.*

friends (i. 4) are awaiting the appearance of the Ghost, trumpets and cannon are heard "within." "What does this mean, my lord?" Horatio asks; and Hamlet answers—

> "The king doth wake to-night, and takes his rouse,
> Keeps wassail, and the swaggering up-spring reels;
> And as he drains his draughts of Rhenish down,
> The kettle-drum and trumpet thus bray out
> The triumph of his pledge."

Similarly, in the last scene of the play, the King says—

> "Give me the cups;
> And let the kettle to the trumpet speak,
> The trumpet to the cannoneer without,
> The cannons to the heavens, the heavens to earth,
> 'Now the king drinks to Hamlet!'"

Shakespeare must even have been eager to display his knowledge of the intemperate habits of the Danes, and the strange usages resulting therefrom, for, as Schück has ingeniously remarked, in order to bring in this piece of information, he has made Horatio, himself a Dane, ask Hamlet whether it is the custom of the country to celebrate every toàst with this noise of trumpets and of ordnance. In answer to this question Hamlet speaks of the custom as though he were addressing a foreigner, and makes the profound remark that a single blemish will often mar a nation's good report, no less than an individual's, and that its character

> "Shall in the general censure take corruption
> From that particular fault."

It is evident that Denmark "took corruption" from its drinking usages in the "censure" of the better sort of Englishmen. In a notebook kept by "Maister William Segar, Garter King at Armes," we read under the date July 14, 1603—

"That afternoone the King [of Denmark] went aboord the English ship [which was lying off Elsinore], and had a banket prepared for him vpon the vpper decks, which were hung with an Awning of cloaths of Tissue; every health reported sixe, eight, or ten shot of great Ordinance, so that during the king's abode, the ship discharged 160 shot."

Of the same king's "solemne feast to the [English] embassadour," Segar writes:—

"It were superfluous to tell you of all superfluities that were vsed; and it would make a man sick to heare of their drunken healths: vse hath brought it into a fashion, and fashion made it a habit, which ill beseemes our nation to imitate."[1]

---

[1] *New Shakspere Society's Transactions*, 1874, p. 512.

The King here spoken of is Christian IV., then twenty-six years of age. When he, three years afterwards, visited England, it seems as though the Court, which had previously been very sober, justified the fears of the worthy diarist by catching the infection of Danish intemperance. Noble ladies as well as gentlemen took to over-indulgence in wine. The Rev. H. Harington, in his *Nugæ Antiquæ* (edit. 1779, ii. 126), prints a letter from Sir John Harington to Mr. Secretary Barlow, giving a very humorous description of the festivities in which the Danish King took part. One day after dinner, he relates, "the representation of Solomon his temple and the coming of the Queen of Sheba was made." But alas! the lady who played the Queen, and who was to bring "precious gifts to both their Majesties, forgetting the steppes arising to the canopy, overset her caskets into his Danish Majesties lap, and fell at his feet, though I rather think it was in his face. Much was the hurry and confusion; cloths and napkins were at hand to make all clean. His Majesty then got up, and would dance with the Queen of Sheba; but he fell down and humbled himself before her, and was carried to an inner chamber, and laid on a bed of state; which was not a little defiled with the presents of the Queen which had been bestowed upon his garments; such as wine, cream, jelly, beverage, cakes, spices and other good matters." The entertainment proceeded, but most of the "presenters fell down, wine did so occupy their upper chambers." Now there entered in gorgeous array Faith, Hope, and Charity. Hope "did assay" to speak, but could not manage it, and withdrew, stammering excuses to the King; Faith staggered after her; Charity alone succeeded in kneeling at the King's feet, and when she returned to her sisters, she found them lying very sick in the lower hall. Then Victory made her entrance in bright armour, but did not triumph long, having to be led away a "silly captive" and left to sleep upon the ante-chamber stairs. Last of all came Peace, who "much contrary to her semblance, most rudely made war with her olive branch upon" those who tried, from motives of propriety, to get her out of the way.

Shakespeare, then, conceived intemperance in drinking, and glorification of drunkenness as a polite and admirable accomplishment, to be a Danish national vice. It is clear enough, however, that no more here than elsewhere was it his main purpose to depict a foreign people. It was not national peculiarities that interested him, but the characteristics common to humanity; and he did not need to search outside of England for the prototypes of his Polonius, his Horatio, his Ophelia, and his Hamlet.

XIII

THE PERSONAL ELEMENT IN HAMLET

IN trying to bring together, as we have done, a mass of historical, dramatic, and fictional material, fragments of philosophy, and ethnographical details, which Shakespeare utilised during his work upon *Hamlet*, or which may, without his knowing it, have hovered in his memory, we do not, of course, mean to imply that the initial impulse to the work came to him from without. The piecing together of external impressions, as we have already remarked, has never produced a work of immortal poetry. In approaching the theme, Shakespeare obeyed a fundamental instinct in his nature; and as he worked it out, everything that stood in relation to it rushed together in his mind. He might have said with Goethe: "After long labour in piling up fuel and straw, I have often tried in vain to warm myself . . . until at last the spark catches all of a sudden, and the whole is wrapped in flame."

It is this flame which shines forth from *Hamlet*, shooting up so high and glowing so red that to this day it fascinates all eyes.

Hamlet assumes madness in order to lull the suspicions of the man who has murdered his father and wrongfully usurped his throne; but under this mask of madness he gives evidence of rare intelligence, deep feeling, peculiar subtlety, mordant satire, exalted irony, and penetrating knowledge of human nature.

Here lay the point of attraction for Shakespeare. The indirect form of expression had always allured him; it was the favourite method of his clowns and humourists. Touchstone employs it, and it enters largely into the immortal wit of Falstaff. We have seen how Jaques, in *As You Like It*, envied those whose privilege it was to speak the truth under the disguise of folly; we remember his sigh of longing for "as large a charter as the wind to blow on whom he pleased." He it was who declared motley the only wear; and in his melancholy and longing Shakespeare disguised his own, exclaiming through his mouth—

> "Invest me in my motley; give me leave
> To speak my mind, and I will through and through
> Cleanse the foul body of th' infected world."

In *Hamlet* Shakespeare put this motley coat on his own shoulders; he seized the opportunity of making Hamlet, in the guise of apparent madness, speak sharp and bitter truths in a way that would not soon be forgotten. The task was a grateful one; for earnestness cuts the deeper the more it sounds like jest or triviality; and wisdom appears doubly wise when it is thrown out lightly under the mask of folly, instead of pedantically asserting itself as the fruit of reflection and experience. Difficult for any one else, to Shakespeare the enterprise was merely alluring: it was, in fact, to do what no other poet had as yet succeeded in doing— to draw a genius. Shakespeare had not far to go for his model, and genius would seem doubly effective when it wore the mask of madness, now speaking through that mouthpiece, and again unmasking itself in impassioned monologues.

It cost Shakespeare no effort to transform himself into Hamlet. On the contrary, in giving expression to Hamlet's spiritual life he was enabled quite naturally to pour forth all that during the recent years had filled his heart and seethed in his brain. He could let this creation drink his inmost heart's blood; he could transfer to it the throbbing of his own pulses. Behind its forehead he could hide his melancholy; on its tongue he could lay his wit; its eyes he could cause to glow and lighten with flashes of his own spirit.

It is true that Hamlet's outward fortunes were different enough from his. He had not lost his father by assassination; his mother had not degraded herself. But all these details were only outward signs and symbols. He had lived through all of Hamlet's experience—all. Hamlet's father had been murdered and his place usurped by his brother; that is to say, the being whom he most reverenced and to whom he owed most had been overpowered by malice and treachery, instantly forgotten and shamelessly supplanted. How often had not Shakespeare himself seen worthlessness strike greatness down and usurp its place! Hamlet's mother had married her husband's murderer; in other words, that which he had long honoured and loved and held sacred, sacred as is a mother to her son, that on which he could not endure to see any stain, had all of a sudden shown itself impure, besmirched, frivolous, perhaps criminal. What a terrible impression must it have made upon Shakespeare himself when he first discovered the unworthiness of that which he had held in highest reverence, and when he first saw and realised that his ideal had fallen from its pedestal into the mire.

The experience which shook Hamlet's nature was no other than that which every nobly-disposed youth, on first seeing the world as it is, concentrates in the words: "Alas! life is not what I thought it was." The father's murder, the mother's possible complicity, and her indecent haste in entering upon a new wedlock, were only symptoms in the young man's eyes of the worthlessness of human nature and the injustice of life—only the individual instances from which, by instinctive generalisation, he inferred the dire disillusions and terrible possibilities of existence —only the chance occasion for the sudden vanishing of that rosy light in which everything had hitherto been steeped for him, and in the absence of which the earth seemed to him a sterile promontory, and the heavens a pestilent congregation of vapours.

Just such a crisis, bringing with it the "loss of all his mirth," Shakespeare himself had recently undergone. He had lost in the previous year the protectors of his youth. The woman he loved, and to whom he had looked up as to a being of a rarer, loftier order, had all of a sudden proved to be a heartless, faithless wanton. The friend he loved, worshipped, and adored had conspired against him with this woman, laughed at him in her arms, betrayed his confidence, and treated him with coldness and distance. Even the prospect of winning the poet's wreath had been overcast for him. Truly he too had seen his illusions vanish and his vision of the world fall to ruins.

In his first consternation he had been submissive, had stood defenceless, had spoken words without a sting, had been all mildness and melancholy. But this was not his whole, nor his inmost, nature. In his heart of hearts he knew himself a power—a power! He was incomparably armed, quick and keen of fence, full of wit and indignation, the master of them all, and infinitely greater than his fate. Burrow as they might, "it should go hard but he would delve one yard below their mines." He had suffered many a humiliation; but the revenge which was denied him in real life he could now take incognito through Hamlet's bitter and scathing invectives.

He had seen high-born gentlemen play a princely part in the society of artists, players, men whom public opinion undervalued and contemned. Now he himself would be the high-born gentleman, would show how the truly princely spirit bore itself towards the poor artists, and give utterance to his own thoughts about art, and his conception of its value and significance.

He merged himself in Hamlet; he felt as Hamlet did; he now and then so mingled their identities that, in placing his own weightiest thoughts in Hamlet's mouth, as in the famous "To be or not to be" soliloquy, he made him think, not as a prince, but as a subject, with all the passionate bitterness of one who sees brutality and stupidity lording it in high places. Thus it was that he made Hamlet say—

> " For who would bear the whips and scorns of time,
> *The oppressor's wrong, the proud man's contumely,*
> The pangs of despis'd love, *the law's delay,*
> *The insolence of office, and the spurns*
> *That patient merit of the unworthy takes,*

When he himself might his quietus make
With a bare bodkin ? ”

Every one can see that this is felt and thought from below
upwards, not from above downwards, and that the words are
improbable, almost impossible, in the mouth of the Prince. But
they embody feelings and thoughts to which Shakespeare had
recently given expression in his own name in Sonnet lxvi. :—

" Tir'd with all these, for restful death I cry ;—
As, to behold desert a beggar born,
And needy nothing trimm'd in jollity,
And purest faith unhappily forsworn,
And gilded honour shamefully misplac'd,
And maiden virtue rudely strumpeted,
And right perfection wrongfully disgrac'd,
And strength by limping sway disabled,
And art made tongue-tied by authority,
And folly (doctor-like) controlling skill,
And simple truth miscall'd simplicity,
And captive good attending captain ill :
Tir'd with all these, from these would I be gone,
Save that, to die, I leave my love alone.”

The bright view of life which had prevailed in his youth
was overclouded; he saw the strength of malignity, the power
of stupidity, unworthiness exalted, true desert elbowed aside.
Existence turned its seamy side towards him. Through what
experiences had he not come ! How often, in the year that had
just passed, must he have exclaimed, like Hamlet in his first
soliloquy, " Frailty, thy name is woman !" and how much cause
had he had to say, " Let her not walk i' the sun: conception is
a blessing; but not as your daughter may conceive." So far had
it gone with him that, finding everything "weary, stale, flat, and
unprofitable," he thought it monstrous that such an existence
should be handed on from generation to generation, and that ever
new hordes of miserable creatures should come into existence:
"Get thee to a nunnery ! Why wouldst thou be a breeder of
sinners ? "

The glimpse of high life which he had seen, his relations with
the Court, and the gossip from Whitehall and Greenwich which
circulated through the town, had proved to him the truth of the
couplet—

"Cog, lie, flatter, and face
Four ways in Court to win men grace."

Sheer criminals such as Leicester and Claudius flourished and
waxed fat at Court.

What did men do at Court but truckle to the great ? What
throve except wordy morality, mutual espionage, artificial wit,

double-tongued falsity, inveterate lack of principle, perpetual hypocrisy? What were these great ones but flatterers and lip-servers, always ready to turn their coats according to the wind? And so Polonius and Osrick, Rosencrantz and Guildenstern, took shape in his imagination. They knew how to bow and cringe; they were masters of elegant phrases; they were members of the great guild of time-servers. "To be honest as this world goes, is to be one man picked out of ten thousand."

And the Danish Court was only a picture in little of all Denmark—that Denmark in whose state there was something rotten, and which was to Hamlet a prison. "Then is the world one?" says Rosencrantz; and Hamlet does not recoil from the conclusion: "A goodly one," he replies, "in which there are many confines, wards, and dungeons." The Court-world of *Hamlet* was but an image of the world at large.

But if this is how matters stand, if a pure and princely nature is thus placed in the world and thus surrounded, we are necessarily confronted with the great and unanswerable questions: "How comes it?" and "Why is it?" The problem of the relation of good and evil in this world, an unsolved riddle, involves further problems as to the government of the world, as to a righteous Providence, as to the relation between the world and a God. And thought—Shakespeare's no less than Hamlet's—beats at the locked door of the mystery.

XIV

THE PSYCHOLOGY OF HAMLET

THOUGH there are in *Hamlet* more direct utterances of the poet's inmost spiritual life than in any of his earlier works, he has none the less succeeded in thoroughly disengaging his hero's figure, and making it an independent entity. What he gave him of his own nature was its unfathomable depth; for the rest, he retained the situation and the circumstances much as he found them in his authorities. It cannot be denied that he thus involved himself in difficulties which he by no means entirely overcame. The old legend, with its harsh outlines, its mediæval order of ideas, its heathen groundwork under a varnish of dogmatic Catholicism, its assumption of vengeance as the unquestionable right, or rather duty, of the individual, did not very readily harmonise with the rich life of thoughts, dreams, and feelings which Shakespeare imparted to his hero. There arose a certain discrepancy between the central figure and his surroundings. A Prince who is the intellectual peer of Shakespeare himself, who knows and declares that "no traveller returns" from beyond the grave, yet sees and holds converse with a ghost. A royal youth of the Renaissance, who has gone through a foreign university, whose chief bent is towards philosophic brooding, who writes verses, who cultivates music, elocution, and rapier-fencing, and proves himself an expert in dramatic criticism, is at the same time pre-occupied with thoughts of personal and bloody vengeance. Now and then, in the course of the drama, a rift seems to open between the shell of the action and its kernel.

But Shakespeare, with his consummate instinct, managed to find an advantage precisely in this discrepancy, and to turn it to account. His Hamlet believes in the ghost and—doubts. He accepts the summons to the deed of vengeance and—delays. Much of the originality of the figure, and of the drama as a whole, springs almost inevitably from this discrepancy between the mediæval character of the fable and its Renaissance hero, who is so deep and many-sided that he has almost a modern air.

The figure of Hamlet, as it at last shaped itself in Shakespeare's imagination and came to life in his drama, is one of the very few immortal figures of art and poetry, which, like Cervantes' Don Quixote, exactly its contemporary, and Goethe's Faust of two centuries later, present to generation after generation problems to brood over and enigmas to solve. If we compare the two great figures of Hamlet (1604) and Don Quixote (1605), we find Hamlet undoubtedly the more enigmatic and absorbing of the two. Don Quixote belongs to the past. He embodies the naïve spirit of chivalry which, having outlived its age, gives offence on all hands in a time of prosaic rationalism, and makes itself a laughing-stock through its importunate enthusiasms. He has the firm, easily-comprehensible contours of a caricature. Hamlet belongs to the future, to the modern age. He embodies the lofty and reflective spirit, standing isolated, with its severely exalted ideals, in corrupt or worthless surroundings, forced to conceal its inmost nature, yet everywhere arousing hostility. He has the unfathomable spirit and ever-changing physiognomy of genius. Goethe, in his celebrated exposition of Hamlet (*Wilhelm Meister*, Book iv. chap. 13), maintains that in this case a great deed is imposed upon a soul which is not strong enough for it :—

"There is an oak-tree planted in a costly jar, which should have borne only pleasant flowers in its bosom ; the roots expand, the jar is shivered. A lovely, pure, noble, and most moral nature, without the strength of nerve which forms a hero, sinks beneath a burden which it cannot bear and must not cast away."

This interpretation is brilliant and thoughtful, but not entirely just. One can trace in it the spirit of the period of humanity, transforming in its own image a figure belonging to the Renaissance. Hamlet cannot really be called, without qualification, "lovely, pure, noble and most moral"—he who says to Ophelia the penetratingly true, unforgettable words, " I am myself indifferent honest ; but yet I could accuse me of such things, that it were better my mother had not borne me." The light of such a saying as this takes the colour out of Goethe's adjectives. It is true that Hamlet goes on to ascribe to himself evil qualities of which he is quite innocent ; but he was doubtless sincere in the general tenor of his speech, to which all men of the better sort will subscribe. Hamlet is no model of virtue. He is not simply pure, noble, moral, &c., but is, or becomes, other things as well— wild, bitter, harsh, now tender, now coarse, wrought up to the verge of madness, callous, cruel. No doubt he is too weak for his task, or rather wholly unsuited to it ; but he is by no means devoid of physical strength or power of action. He is no child of the period of humanity, moral and pure, but a child of the Renaissance, with its impulsive energy, its irrepressible fulness of life and its undaunted habit of looking death in the eyes.

Shakespeare at first conceived Hamlet as a youth. In the First Quarto he is quite young, probably nineteen. It accords with this age that he should be a student at Wittenberg ; young men at that time began and ended their university course much earlier than in our days. It accords with this age that his mother should address him as " boy " (" How now, boy ! " iii. 4—a phrase which is deleted in the next edition), and that the word " young " should be continually prefixed to his name, not merely to distinguish him from his father. The King, too, in the early edition (not in that of 1604) currently addresses him as " son Hamlet ; " and finally his mother is still young enough to arouse—or at least to enable Claudius plausibly to pretend—the passion which has such terrible results. Hamlet's speech to his mother—

> " At your age
> The hey-day of the blood is tame, it's humble,
> And waits upon the judgment,"

does not occur in the 1603 edition. The decisive proof, however, of the fact that Hamlet at first appeared in Shakespeare's eyes much younger (eleven years, to be precise) than he afterwards made him, is to be found in the graveyard scene (v. 1). In the older edition, the First Gravedigger says that the skull of the jester Yorick has lain a dozen years in the earth ; in the edition of 1604 this is changed to twenty-three years. Here, too, it is explicitly indicated that Hamlet, who as a child knew Yorick, is now thirty years old ; for the Gravedigger first states that he took to his trade on the very day on which Prince Hamlet was born, and a little later adds : " I have been sexton here, man and boy, thirty years." It accords with this that the Player-King now mentions thirty years as the time that has elapsed since his marriage with the Queen, and that Ophelia (iii. 1) speaks of Hamlet as the " unmatch'd form of blown [*i.e.* mature] youth."

The process of thought in Shakespeare's mind is evident. At first it seemed to him as if the circumstances of the case demanded that Hamlet should be a youth ; for thus the overwhelming effect produced upon him by his mother's prompt forgetfulness of his father and hasty marriage seemed most intelligible. He had been living far from the great world, in quiet Wittenberg, never doubting that life was in fact as harmonious as it is apt to appear in the eyes of a young prince. He believed in the realisation of ideals here on earth, imagined that intellectual nobility and fine feelings ruled the world, that justice reigned in public, faith and honour in private, life. He admired his great father, honoured his beautiful mother, passionately loved the charming Ophelia, thought nobly of humankind, and especially of women. From the moment he loses his father, and is forced to change his opinion of his mother, this serene view of life is darkened. If his mother has been able to forget his father and marry this man, what is woman worth ? and what is life worth ? At the very outset, then, when he has not even heard of his father's ghost, much less seen or held converse with it, sheer despair speaks in his monologue :

> " O that this too too solid flesh would melt,
> Thaw, and resolve itself into a dew :
> Or that the Everlasting had not fix'd
> His canon 'gainst self-slaughter ! "

Hence, also, his naïve surprise that one may smile and smile and yet be a villain. He regards what has happened as a typical occurrence, a specimen of what the world really is. Hence his words to Rosencrantz and Guildenstern: " I have of late—but wherefore I know not—lost all my mirth." And those others: "What a piece of work is a man! how noble in reason! how infinite in faculty! . . . in action, how like an angel! in apprehension, how like a god! the beauty of the world!" These words express his first bright view of life. But that has vanished, and the world is no longer anything to him but a "foul and pestilent congregation of vapours." And man! What is this "quintessence of dust" to him? He has no pleasure in man or woman.

Hence arise his thoughts of suicide. The finer a young man's character, the stronger is his desire, on entering life, to see his ideals consummated in persons and circumstances. Hamlet suddenly realises that everything is entirely different from what he had imagined, and feels as if he must die because he cannot set it right.

He finds it very difficult to believe that the world is so bad; therefore he is always seeking for new proofs of it; therefore, for instance, he plans the performance of the play. His joy whenever he tears the mask from baseness is simply the joy of realisation, with deep sorrow in the background—abstract satisfaction produced by the feeling that at last he understands the worthlessness of the world. His divination was just—events confirm it. There is no cold-hearted pessimism here. Hamlet's fire is never quenched; his wound never heals. Laertes' poisoned blade gives the quietus to a still tortured soul.[1]

All this, though we can quite well imagine it of a man of thirty, is more natural, more what we should expect, in one of nineteen. But as Shakespeare worked on at his drama, and came to deposit in Hamlet's mind, as in a treasury, more and more of his own life-wisdom, of his own experience, and of his own keen and virile wit, he saw that early youth was too slight a framework to support this intellectual weight, and gave Hamlet the age of ripening manhood.[2]

[1] See Hermann Türck : *Das psychologische Problem in der Hamlet-Tragödie.* 1890.
[2] See E. Sullivan: "On Hamlet's Age." *New Shakspere Society's Transactions.* 1880–86.

Hamlet's faith and trust in humankind are shattered before the Ghost appears to him. From the moment when his father's spirit communicates to him a far more appalling insight into the facts of the situation, his whole inner man is in wild revolt.

This is the cause of the leave-taking, the silent leave-taking, from Ophelia, whom in letters he had called his soul's idol. His ideal of womanhood no longer exists. Ophelia now belongs to those " trivial fond records " which the sense of his great mission impels him to efface from the tablets of his memory. There is no room in his soul for his task and for her, passive and obedient to her father as she is. Confide in her he cannot; she has shown how unequal she is to the exigencies of the situation by refusing to receive his letters and visits. She actually hands over his last letter to her father, which means that it will be shown and read at court. At last, she even consents to play the spy upon him. He no longer believes or can believe in any woman.

He intends to proceed at once to action, but too many thoughts crowd in upon him. He broods over that horror which the Ghost has revealed to him, and over the world in which such a thing could happen; he doubts whether the apparition was really his father, or perhaps a deceptive, malignant spirit; and, lastly, he has doubts of himself, of his ability to upraise and restore what has been overthrown, of his fitness for the vocation of avenger and judge. His doubt as to the trustworthiness of the Ghost leads to the performance of the play within the play, which proves the King's guilt. His feeling of his own unfitness for his task leads to continued procrastination.

During the course of the play it is sufficiently proved that he is not, in the main, incapable of action. He does not hesitate to stab the eavesdropper behind the arras; without wavering and without pity he sends Rosencrantz and Guildenstern to certain death; he boards a hostile ship; and, never having lost sight of his purpose, he takes vengeance before he dies. But it is clear, none the less, that he has a great inward obstacle to overcome before he proceeds to the decisive act. Reflection hinders him; his "resolution is sicklied o'er with the pale cast of thought," as he says in his soliloquy.

He has become to the popular mind the great type of the procrastinator and dreamer; and far on into this century, hundreds of individuals, and even whole races, have seen themselves reflected in him as in a mirror.

We must not forget, however, that this dramatic curiosity— a hero who does not act—was, to a certain extent, demanded by the technique of this particular drama. If Hamlet had killed the King directly after receiving the Ghost's revelation, the play would have come to an end with the first act. It was, therefore, absolutely necessary that delays should arise.

Shakespeare is misunderstood when Hamlet is taken for that entirely modern product—a mind diseased by morbid reflection, without capacity for action. It is nothing less than a freak of ironic fate that *he* should have become a sort of symbol of reflective sloth, this man who has gunpowder in every nerve, and all the dynamite of genius in his nature.

It was undeniably and indubitably Shakespeare's intention to give distinctness to Hamlet's character by contrasting it with youthful energy of action, unhesitatingly pursuing its aim.

While Hamlet is letting himself be shipped off to England, the young Norwegian prince, Fortinbras, arrives with his soldiers, ready to risk his life for a patch of ground that "hath in it no profit but the name. To pay five ducats, five, I would not farm it." Hamlet says to himself (iv. 4) :

> " How all occasions do inform against me,
> And spur my dull revenge ! . . .
> . . . I do not know
> Why yet I live to say, ' This thing's to do.' "

And he despairs when he contrasts himself with Fortinbras, the delicate and tender prince, who, at the head of his brave troops, dares death and danger " even for an egg-shell " :

> " Rightly to be great
> Is not to stir without great argument,
> But greatly to find quarrel in a straw
> When honour 's at the stake."

But with Hamlet it is a question of more than "honour," a conception belonging to a sphere far below his. It is natural that he should feel ashamed at the sight of Fortinbras marching off to the sound of drum and trumpet at the head of his forces—he, who has not carried out, or even laid, any plan ; who, after having by means of the play satisfied himself of the King's guilt, and at the same time betrayed his own state of mind, is now writhing under the consciousness of impotence. But the sole cause of this impotence is the paralysing grasp laid on all his faculties by his new realisation of what life is, and the broodings born of this realisation. Even his mission of vengeance sinks into the background of his mind. Everything is at strife within him—his duty to his father, his duty to his mother, reverence, horror of crime, hatred, pity, fear of action, and fear of inaction. He feels, even if he does not expressly say so, how little is gained by getting rid of a single noxious animal. He himself is already so much more than what he was at first—the youth chosen to execute a vendetta. He has become the great sufferer, who jeers and mocks, and rebukes the world that racks him. He is the cry of humanity, horror-struck at its own visage.

There is no "general meaning" on the surface of *Hamlet*, Lucidity was not the ideal Shakespeare had before him while he was producing this tragedy, as it had been when he was composing *Richard III*. Here there are plenty of riddles and self-contradictions; but not a little of the attraction of the play depends on this very obscurity.

We all know that kind of well-written book which is blameless in form, obvious in intention, and in which the characters stand out sharply defined. We read it with pleasure; but when we have read it, we are done with it. There is nothing to be read between the lines, no gulf between this passage and that, no mystic twilight anywhere in it, no shadows in which we can dream. And, again, there are other books whose fundamental idea is capable of many interpretations, and affords matter for much dispute, but whose significance lies less in what they say to us than in what they lead us to imagine, to divine. They have the peculiar faculty of setting thoughts and feelings in motion; more thoughts than they themselves contain, and perhaps of a quite different character. *Hamlet* is such a book. As a piece of psychological development, it lacks the lucidity of classical art; the hero's soul has all the untranspicuousness and complexity of a real soul; but one generation after another has thrown its imagination into the problem, and has deposited in Hamlet's soul the sum of its experience.

To Hamlet life is half reality, half a dream. He sometimes resembles a somnambulist, though he is often as wakeful as a spy. He has so much presence of mind that he is never at a loss for the aptest retort, and, along with it, such absence of mind that he lets go his fixed determination in order to follow up some train of thought or thread some dream-labyrinth. He appals, amuses, captivates, perplexes, disquiets us. Few characters in fiction have so disquieted the world. Although he is incessantly talking, he is solitary by nature. He typifies, indeed, that solitude of soul which cannot impart itself.

"His name," says Victor Hugo, "is as the name on a woodcut of Albert Dürer's: *Melancholia*. The bat flits over Hamlet's head; at his feet sit Knowledge, with globe and compass, and Love, with an hour-glass; while behind him, on the horizon, rests a giant sun, which only serves to make the sky above him darker." But from another point of view Hamlet's nature is that of the hurricane—a thing of wrath and fury, and tempestuous scorn, strong enough to sweep the whole world clean.

There is in him no less indignation than melancholy; in fact, his melancholy is a result of his indignation. Sufferers and thinkers have found in him a brother. Hence the extraordinary popularity of the character, in spite of its being the reverse of obvious.

Audiences and readers feel with Hamlet and understand him;

for all the better-disposed among us make the discovery, when we go forth into life as grown-up men and women, that it is not what we had imagined it to be, but a thousandfold more terrible. Something is rotten in the state of Denmark. Denmark is a prison, and the world is full of such dungeons. A spectral voice says to us: "Horrible things have happened; horrible things are happening every day. Be it your task to repair the evil, to rearrange the course of things. The world is out of joint; it is for you to set it right." But our arms fall powerless by our sides. Evil is too strong, too cunning for us.

In *Hamlet*, the first philosophical drama of the modern era, we meet for the first time the typical modern character, with its intense feeling of the strife between the ideal and the actual world, with its keen sense of the chasm between power and aspiration, and with that complexity of nature which shows itself in wit without mirth, cruelty combined with sensitiveness, frenzied impatience at war with inveterate procrastination.

XV

HAMLET AS A DRAMA

LET us now look at *Hamlet* as a drama; and, to get the full impression of Shakespeare's greatness, let us first recall its purely theatrical, materially visible side, that which dwells in the memory simply as pantomime.[1]

The night-watch on the platform before the Castle of Elsinore, and the appearance of the Ghost to the soldiers and officers there. Then, in contrast to the splendidly-attired courtiers, the black-robed figure of the Prince, standing apart, a living image of grief, his countenance bespeaking both soul and intellect, but with an expression which seems to say that henceforth joy and he are strangers. Next, his meeting with his father's spirit; the oath upon the sword, with the constant change of place. Then his wild behaviour when, to hide his excitement, he feigns madness. Then the play within the play; the sword-thrust through the arras; the beautiful Ophelia with flowers and straw in her hair; Hamlet with Yorick's skull in his hand; the struggle with Laertes in Ophelia's grave, that grotesque but most significant episode. According to the custom of the time, a dumb show foretold the poisoning in the play, and this fight in the grave is the dumb show which foretells the mortal combat that is soon to take place: both are presently to be swallowed up by the grave in which they stand. Then follows the fencing-scene, during the course of which the Queen dies by the poison which the King destined for Hamlet, and Laertes by the stroke of the poisoned sword also prepared for the Prince, who, with a last great effort, kills the King, and then sinks down poisoned. This wholesale "havock" arranged by the poet, a fourfold lying-in-state, has its gloom broken by the triumphal march of young Fortinbras, which, in its turn, soon changes to a funeral measure. The whole is as effective to the eye as it is great and beautiful.

And now add to this ocular picturesqueness of the play the fascination which it owes to the sympathy Shakespeare has made us feel for its principal character, the impression he has given us of the agonies of a strong and sensitive spirit surrounded by corruption and depravity. Hamlet was by nature candid, en-

---

[1] K. Werder: *Vorlesungen über Hamlet*, p. 3 *et seq.*

thusiastic, trustful, loving; the guile of others forces him to take
refuge in guile; the wickedness of others drives him to distrust
and hate; and the crime committed against his murdered father
calls upon him from the underworld for vengeance.

His indignation at the infamy around him is heartrending,
his contempt for it is stimulating.

By nature he is a thinker. He thinks not only when he is
contemplating and planning a course of action, but also from a
passionate longing for comprehension in the abstract. Though he
is merely making use of the players to unmask the murderer, he
gives them apt and profound advice with regard to the practice of
their art. When Rosencrantz and Guildenstern question him as
to the reason of his melancholy, he expounds to them in words
of deep significance his rooted distaste for life.

The feeling produced in him by any strong impression never
finds vent in straightforward, laconic words. His speeches never
take the direct, the shortest way to express his thoughts. They
consist of ingenious, far-fetched similes and witty conceits, apparently remote from the matter in hand. Sarcastic and enigma-
tical phrases conceal his emotions. This dissimulation is forced
upon him by the very strength of his feelings: in order not to
betray himself, not to give way to the pain he is suffering, he
must smother it in fantastic and boisterous ejaculations. Thus
he shouts after having seen the apparition: "Hillo, ho, ho, boy!
come, bird, come!" Thus he apostrophises the Ghost: "Well
said, old mole! canst work i' the earth so fast?" And therefore, after the play has made the King betray himself, he cries:
"Ah, ha! Come, some music! come, the recorders!" His
feigned madness is only an intentional exaggeration of this
tendency.

The horrible secret that has been discovered to him has upset
his equilibrium. The show of madness enables him to find solace
in expressing indirectly what it tortures him to talk of directly,
and at the same time his seeming lunacy diverts attention from
the real reason of his deep melancholy. He does not altogether
dissemble when he talks so wildly; given his surroundings, these
fantastic and daring sarcasms are a natural enough mode of utterance for the wild agitation produced by the horror that has
entered into his life; "though this be madness, yet there is
method in 't." But the almost frenzied excitement into which he
is so often thrown by the action of others subsides at intervals,
when he feels the need for mental concentration—a craving which
he satisfies in the solitary reflections forming his monologues.

When his passions are roused, he has difficulty in controlling
them. It is nervous over-excitement that finds vent when he bids
Ophelia get her to a nunnery, and it is in a fit of nervous frenzy
that he stabs Polonius. But his passion generally strikes inwards.
Constrained as he is, or thinks himself, to employ dissimulation

and cunning, he is in a fever of impatience, and is for ever reviling and scoffing at himself for his inaction, as though it were due to indifference or cowardice.

Distrust, that new element in his character, makes him cautious; he cannot act on impulse, nor even speak. "There's ne'er a villain dwelling in all Denmark," he begins; "so great as the King" should be the continuation; but fear of being betrayed by his comrades takes possession of him, and he ends with, "but he's an arrant knave."

He is by nature open-hearted and warm, as we see him with Horatio; he speaks to the sentinel on the platform as to a comrade; he is cordial, at first, to old acquaintances like Rosencrantz and Guildenstern; and he is frank, amiable, kind without condescension, to the troupe of travelling players. But reticence has been suddenly forced upon him by the bitterest, most agonising experiences; no sooner has he put on a mask, so as not to be instantly found out, than he feels that he is being spied upon; even his friends and the woman he loves are on the side of his opponents; and though he believes his life to be threatened, he feels that he must keep silent and wait.

His mask is often enough only of gauze; if only for the sake of the spectators, Shakespeare had to make the madness transparent, that it might not pall.

Read the witty repartees of Hamlet to Polonius (ii. 2), beginning with, "What do you read, my lord?" "Words, words, words." In reality there is no trace of madness in all these keen-edged sayings, till Hamlet at last, in order to annul their effect, concludes with the words, "For yourself, sir, should be old as I am, if, like a crab, you could go backward."

Or take the long conversation (iii. 2) between Hamlet and Rosencrantz and Guildenstern about the pipe he has sent for, and asks them to play on. The whole is a parable as simple and direct as any in the New Testament. And he points the moral with triumphant logic in poetic form—

"Why, look you now, how unworthy a thing you would make of me! You would play upon me; you would seem to know my stops; you would pluck out the heart of my mystery; you would sound me from my lowest notes to the top of my compass: and there is much music, excellent music in this little organ; yet cannot you make it speak. 'Sblood, do you think I am easier to be played on than a pipe? Call me what instrument you will, though you can fret me, yet you cannot play upon me."

It is in order to account for such contemptuous and witty outbursts that Hamlet says: "I am but mad north-north-west: when the wind is southerly I know a hawk from a handsaw."

To outward difficulties are added inward hindrances, which he cannot overcome. He reproaches himself passionately for this, as we have seen. But these self-reproaches of Hamlet's do not represent Shakespeare's view of his character or judgment of his action. They express the impatience of his nature, his longing for reparation, his eagerness for the triumph of the right; they do not imply his guilt.

The old doctrine of tragic guilt and punishment, which assumes that the death at the end of a tragedy must always be in some way deserved, is nothing but antiquated scholasticism, theology masking as æsthetics; and it may be regarded as an instance of scientific progress that this view of the matter, which was heretical only a generation since, is now very generally accepted. Very different was the case when the author of these lines, in his earliest published work, entered a protest against such an intrusion of traditional morality into a sphere from which it ought simply to be banished.[1]

Some critics have summarily disposed of the question of Hamlet's possible guilt by the assertion that his madness was not only assumed, but real. Brinsley Nicholson, for instance, in his essay " Was Hamlet Mad ? " (*New Shakspere Society's Transactions*, 1880–86), insists on his morbid melancholy; his strange and incoherent talk after the apparition of the Ghost; his lack of any sense of responsibility for the deaths of Polonius, Rosencrantz, and Guildenstern, of which he was either the direct or indirect cause; his fear of sending King Claudius to heaven by killing him while he is praying; his brutality towards Ophelia; his constant suspiciousness, &c., &c. But to see symptoms of real insanity in all this is not only a crudity of interpretation, but a misconception of Shakespeare's evident meaning. It is true that Hamlet does not dissemble as systematically and coldly as Edgar in the subsequent *King Lear;* but that is no reason why his state of mental exaltation should be mistaken for derangement. He makes use of insanity; he is not in its power.

Not that it proves really serviceable to him or facilitates his task of vengeance; on the contrary, it impedes his action by tempting him from the straight path into witty digressions and deviations. It is meant to hide his secret; but after the performance of the play the King knows it, and, though he keeps it up, the feigned madness is useless. It is because his secret is betrayed that Hamlet now, in obedience to the Ghost's command, endeavours to awaken his mother's sense of shame and to detach her from the King. But having run Polonius through the body, in the belief that he is killing his stepfather, he is put under guards and sent away, and has still farther to postpone his revenge.

While many critics of this century, especially Germans, such as Kreyssig, have contemned Hamlet as a " witty weakling," one German writer has passionately denied that Shakespeare intended

---

[1] Georg Brandes: *Æsthetiske Studier.* Essay " On the Concept : Tragic Fate."

to represent him as morbidly reflective. This critic, with much enthusiasm, with fierce onslaughts upon many of his countrymen, but with a conception of the play which debases its whole idea and belittles its significance, has tried to prove that the hindrances Hamlet had to contend with were purely external. I refer to the lectures on Hamlet delivered by the old Hegelian, Karl Werder, in the University of Berlin between 1859 and 1872.[1] Their train of thought, in itself not unreasonable, may be rendered thus :—

What is demanded of Hamlet ? That he should kill the King immediately after the Ghost has revealed his father's fate ? Good. But how, after this assassination, is he to justify his deed to the court and the people, and ascend the throne ? He can produce no proof whatever of the truth of his accusation. A ghost has told him; that is all his evidence. He himself is not the hereditary supreme judge of the land, deprived of his throne by a usurper. The Queen is "jointress to this warlike state." Denmark is an elective monarchy—and it is not till the very end of the play that Hamlet speaks of the King as having "popp'd in between the election and my hopes." In the eyes of all the characters in the play, the existing state of the government is quite normal. And is he to overturn it with a dagger-thrust ? Will the Danish people believe his tale of the apparition and the murder ? And suppose that, instead of having recourse to the dagger, he comes forward with a public accusation, can there be any doubt that such a king and such a court will speedily make away with him ? For where in this court are the elder Hamlet's adherents ? We see none of them. It seems as though the old hero-king had taken them all with him to the grave. What has become of his generals and of his council ? Did they die before him ? Or was he solitary in his greatness ? Certain it is that Hamlet has no friend but Horatio, and finds no supporters at the court.

As matters stand, the truth can be brought to light only by the royal criminal's betraying himself. Hence Hamlet's perfectly logical, most ingenious device for forcing him to do so. Hamlet's object is not to take a purely material revenge for the crime, but to reinstate right and justice in Denmark, to be judge and avenger in one. And this he cannot be if he simply kills the king offhand.

All this is acute, and in part correct; only it misstates the theme of the play. Had Shakespeare had this outward difficulty in mind, he would have made Hamlet expound, or at least allude to it. As a matter of fact, Hamlet does nothing of the sort. On the contrary, he upbraids himself for his inaction and sloth, thereby indicating clearly enough that the great fundamental difficulty is an inward one, and that the real scene of the tragedy lies in the hero's soul.

[1] Karl Werder: *Vorlesungen über Shakespeare's Hamlet,* 1875.

Hamlet himself is comparatively planless, but, as Goethe has profoundly remarked, the play is not therefore without a plan. And where Hamlet is most hesitating, where he tries to palliate his planlessness, there the plan speaks loudest and clearest. Where, for example, Hamlet comes upon the King at his prayers, and will not kill him, because he is not to die "in the purging of his soul" but revelling in sinful debauch, we hear Shakespeare's general idea in the words which, in the mouth of the hero, sound like an evasion. Shakespeare, not Hamlet, reserves the King for the death which in fact overtakes him just as he has poisoned Laertes's blade, seasoned "a chalice" for Hamlet, out of cowardice allowed the Queen to drain it, and been the efficient cause of both Laertes's and Hamlet's fatal wounds. Hamlet thus actually attains his declared object in allowing the King to live.

XVI

HAMLET AND OPHELIA

THERE is nothing more profoundly conceived in this play than the Prince's relation to Ophelia. Hamlet is genius in love—genius with its great demands and its highly unconventional conduct. He does not love like Romeo, with a love that takes entire possession of his mind. He has felt himself drawn to Ophelia while his father was still in life, has sent her letters and gifts, and thinks of her with an infinite tenderness; but she has not it in her to be his friend and confidant. "Her whole essence," we read in Goethe, "is ripe, sweet sensuousness." This is saying too much; it is only the songs she sings in her madness, "in the innocence of madness," as Goethe himself strikingly says, that indicate an undercurrent of sensual desire or sensual reminiscence; her attitude towards the Prince is decorous, almost to severity. Their relations to each other have been close—how close the play does not tell.

There is nothing at all conclusive in the fact that Hamlet's manner to Ophelia is extremely free, not only in the affecting scene in which he orders her to a nunnery, but still more in their conversation during the play, when his jesting speeches, as he asks to be allowed to lay his head in her lap, are more than equivocal, and in one case unequivocally loose. We have already seen (p. 48) that this is no evidence against Ophelia's inexperience. Helena in *All's Well that Ends Well* is chastity itself, yet Parolles's conversation with her is extremely—to our way of thinking impossibly—coarse. In the year 1602, speeches like Hamlet's could be made without offence by a young prince to a virtuous maid of honour.

Whilst English Shakespearians have come forward as Ophelia's champions, several German critics (among others Tieck, Von Friesen, and Flathe) have had no doubt that her relations with Hamlet were of the most intimate. Shakespeare has intentionally left this undecided, and it is difficult to see why his readers should not do the same.

Hamlet draws away from Ophelia from the moment when he feels himself the appointed minister of a sacred revenge. In deep grief he bids her farewell without a word, grasps her wrist, holds it at arm's length from him, "peruses" her face as if he would draw it—then shakes her arm gently, nods his head thrice, and departs with a "piteous" sigh.

If after this he shows himself hard, almost cruel, to her, it is because she was weak and tried to deceive him. She is a soft, yielding creature, with no power of resistance; a loving soul, but without the passion which gives strength. She resembles Desdemona in the unwisdom with which she acts towards her lover, but falls far short of her in warmth and resoluteness of affection. She does not in the least understand Hamlet's grief over his mother's conduct. She observes his depression without divining its cause. When, after seeing the Ghost, he approaches her in speechless agitation, she never guesses that anything terrible has happened to him; and, in spite of her compassion for his morbid state, she consents without demur to decoy him into talking to her, while her father and the King spy upon their meeting. It is then that he breaks out into all those famous speeches: "Are you honest? Are you fair?" &c.; the secret meaning of them being: You are like my mother! You too could have acted as she did!

Hamlet has not a thought for Ophelia in his excitement after the killing of Polonius; but Shakespeare gives us indirectly to understand that grief on her account overtook him afterwards— "he weeps for what is done." Later he seems to forget her, and therefore his anger at her brother's lamentations as she is placed in her grave, and his own frenzied attempt to outdo the "emphasis" of Laertes's grief, seem strange to us. But from his words we understand that she has been the solace of his life, though she could not be its stay. She on her side has been very fond of him, has loved him with unobtrusive tenderness. It is with pain she has heard him speak of his love for her as a thing of the past ("I did love you once"); with deep grief she has seen what she takes to be the eclipse of his bright spirit in madness ("Oh, what a noble mind is here o'er-thrown!"); and at last the death of her father by Hamlet's hand deprives her of her own reason. At one blow she has lost both father and lover. In her madness she does not speak Hamlet's name, nor show any trace of sorrow that it is he who has murdered her father. Forgetfulness of this cruellest blow mitigates her calamity; her hard fate condemns her to solitude; and this solitude is peopled and alleviated by madness.

In depicting the relation between Faust and Gretchen, Goethe appropriated and reproduced many features of the relation between Hamlet and Ophelia. In both cases we have the tragic love-tie between genius and tender girlhood. Faust kills Gretchen's mother as Hamlet kills Ophelia's father. In *Faust* also there is a duel between the hero and his mistress's brother, in which the brother is killed. And in both cases the young girl in her misery goes mad. It is clear that Goethe actually had Ophelia in his thoughts, for he makes his Mephistopheles sing a song to Gretchen which is a direct imitation, almost a translation, of Ophelia's song about Saint Valentine's Day.[1]   There is, however, a more delicate poetry in Ophelia's madness than in Gretchen's. Gretchen's intensifies the tragic impression of the young girl's ruin ; Ophelia's alleviates both her own and the spectator's suffering.

Hamlet and Faust represent the genius of the Renaissance and the genius of modern times ; though Hamlet, in virtue of his creator's marvellous power of rising above his time, covers the whole period between him and us, and has a range of significance to which we, on the threshold of the twentieth century, can foresee no limit.

Faust is probably the highest poetic expression of modern humanity—striving, investigating, enjoying, and mastering at last both itself and the world.   He changes gradually under his creator's hands into a great symbol ; but in the second half of his life a superabundance of allegoric traits veils his individual humanity.   It did not lie in Shakespeare's way to embody a being whose efforts, like Faust's, were directed towards experience, knowledge, perception of truth in general.   Even when Shakespeare rises highest, he keeps nearer the earth.

But none the less dear to us art thou, O Hamlet! and none the less valued and understood by the men of to-day.   We love thee like a brother.   Thy melancholy is ours, thy wrath is ours, thy contemptuous wit avenges us on those who fill the earth with their empty noise and are its masters.   We know the depth of thy suffering when wrong and hypocrisy triumph, and oh! thy still deeper suffering on feeling that that nerve in thee is severed which should lead from thought to victorious action.   To us, too, the voices of the mighty dead have spoken from the under-world.

---

[1] OPHELIA.

" To-morrow is Saint Valentine's day,
    All in the morning betime,
And I a maid at your window,
    To be your Valentine.
Then up he rose, and donn'd his clothes
    And dupp'd the chamber-door ;
Let in the maid, that out a maid
    Never departed more."

MEPHISTOFELES.

' Was machst Du mir
    Vor Liebchens Thür
    Kathrinchen, hier
Bei frühem Tagesblicke ?
Lass, lass es sein !
    Er lässt dich ein
    Als Mädchen ein
    Als Mädchen nicht zurücke."

We, too, have seen our mother wrap the purple robe of power round the murderer of "the majesty of buried Denmark." We, too, have been betrayed by the friends of our youth ; for us, too, have swords been dipped in poison. How well do we know that graveyard mood in which disgust and sorrow for all earthly things seize upon the soul. The breath from open graves has set us, too, dreaming with a skull in our hands !

XVII

HAMLET'S INFLUENCE ON LATER TIMES

IF we to-day can feel with Hamlet, it is certainly no wonder that the play was immensely popular in its own day. It is easy to understand its charm for the cultivated youth of the period ; but it would be surprising, if we did not realise the alertness of the Renaissance and its wonderful receptivity for the highest culture, to find that *Hamlet* was in as great favour with the lower ranks of society as with the higher. A remarkable proof of this tragedy's and of Shakespeare's popularity in the years immediately following its appearance, is afforded by some memoranda in a log-book kept by a certain Captain Keeling, of the ship *Dragon*, which, in September 1607, lay off Sierra Leone in company with another English vessel, the *Hector* (Captain Hawkins), both bound for India. · They run as follows :—

"September 5 [At "Serra Leona"]. I sent the interpreter, according to his desier, abord the Hector, whear he brooke fast, and after came abord mee, wher we gave the tragedie of Hamlett.

"[Sept.] 30. Captain Hawkins dined with me, wher my companions acted Kinge Richard the Second.

"31. I invited Captain Hawkins to a ffishe dinner, and had Hamlet acted abord me: wch I permitt to keepe my people from idlenes and unlawfull games, or sleepe."

Who could have imagined that *Hamlet*, three years after its publication, would be so well known and so dear to English sailors that they could act it for their own amusement at a moment's notice ! Could there be a stronger proof of its universal popularity ? It is a true picture of the culture of the Renaissance, this tragedy of the prince of Denmark acted by common English sailors off the west coast of Africa. It is a pity that Shakespeare himself, in all human probability, never knew of it.

Hamlet's ever-increasing significance as time rolls on is proportionate to his significance in his own day. A great deal in the poetry of the nineteenth century owes its origin to him. Goethe interpreted and remodelled him in *Wilhelm Meister*, and this remodelled Hamlet resembles Faust. The trio, Faust, Gretchen, Valentin, in Goethe's drama answers to the trio, Hamlet, Ophelia, Laertes. Faust transplanted into English soil produced Byron's Manfred, a true though far-off descendant of the Danish Prince. In Germany, again, the Byronic development assumed a new and Hamlet-like (or rather Yorick-like) form in Heine's bitter and fantastic wit, in his hatreds and caprices and intellectual superiority. Börne is the first to interpret Hamlet as the German of his day, always moving in a circle and never able to act. But he feels the mystery of the play, and says aptly and beautifully, " Over the picture hangs a veil of gauze. We want to lift it to examine the painting more closely, but find that the veil itself is painted."

In France, the men of Alfred de Musset's generation, whom he has portrayed in his *Confessions d'un Enfant du Siècle*, remind us in many ways of Hamlet—nervous, inflammable as gunpowder, broken-winged, with no sphere of action commensurate with their desires, and with no power of action in the sphere which lay open to them. And Lorenzaccio, perhaps Musset's finest male character, is the French Hamlet—practised in dissimulation, procrastinating, witty, gentle to women yet wounding them with cruel words, morbidly desirous to atone for the emptiness of his evil life by one great deed, and acting too late, uselessly, desperately.

Hamlet, who centuries before had been young England, and was to Musset, for a time, young France, became in the 'forties, as Börne had foretold, the accepted type of Germany. " Hamlet is Germany," sang Freiligrath.[1]

Kindred political conditions determined that the figure of Hamlet should at the same period, and twenty years later to a still greater extent, dominate Russian literature. Its influence can be traced from Pushkin and Gogol to Gontscharoff and Tolstoi, and it actually pervades the whole life-work of Turgueneff. But in this case Hamlet's vocation of vengeance is overlooked; the whole stress is laid on the general discrepancy between reflection and power of action.

In the development of Polish literature, too, during this century, there came a time when the poets were inclined to say: "We are Hamlet; Hamlet is Poland." We find marked traits of

---

[1] "Deutschland ist Hamlet! Ernst und stumm
In seinen Thoren jede Nacht
Geht die begrabne Freiheit um,
Und winkt den Männern auf der Wacht.
Da steht die Hohe, blank bewehrt,
Und sagt dem Zaudrer, der noch zweifelt:
'Sei mir ein Rächer, zieh dein Schwert!
Man hat mir Gift in's Ohr geträufelt.'"

his character towards the middle of the century in all the imaginative spirits of Poland: in Mickiewicz, in Slowacki, in Krasinski. From their youth they had stood in his position. Their world was out of joint, and was to be set right by their weak arms. High-born and noble-minded, they feel, like Hamlet, all the inward fire and outward impotence of their youth; the conditions that surround them are to them one great horror; they are disposed at one and the same time to dreaming and to action, to over-much reflection and to recklessness.

Like Hamlet, they have seen their mother, the land that gave them birth, profaned by passing under the power of a royal robber and murderer. The court to which at times they are offered access strikes them with terror, as the court of Claudius struck terror to the Danish Prince, as the court in Krasinski's *Temptation* (a symbolic representation of the court of St. Petersburg) strikes terror to the young hero of the poem. These kinsmen of Hamlet are, like him, cruel to their Ophelia, and forsake her when she loves them best; like him, they allow themselves to be sent far away to foreign lands; and when they speak they dissemble like him—clothe their meaning in similes and allegories. What Hamlet says of himself applies to them: "Yet have I something in me dangerous." Their peculiarly Polish characteristic is that what enervates and impedes them is not their reflective but their poetic bias. Reflection is what ruins the German of this type; wild dissipation the Frenchman; indolence, self-mockery, and self-despair the Russian; but it is imagination that leads the Pole astray and tempts him to live apart from real life.

The Hamlet character presents a multitude of different aspects. Hamlet is the doubter; he is the man whom over-scrupulousness or over-deliberation condemns to inactivity; he is the creature of pure intelligence, who sometimes acts nervously, and is sometimes too nervous to act at all; and, lastly, he is the avenger, the man who dissembles that his revenge may be the more effectual. Each of these aspects is developed by the poets of Poland. There is a touch of Hamlet in several of Mickiewicz's creations—in Wallenrod, in Gustave, in Conrad, in Robak. Gustave speaks the language of philosophic aberration; Conrad is possessed by the spirit of philosophic brooding; Wallenrod and Robak dissemble or disguise themselves for the sake of revenge, and the latter, like Hamlet, kills the father of the woman he loves. In Slowacki's work the Hamlet-type takes a much more prominent place. His Kordjan is a Hamlet who follows his vocation of avenger, but has not the strength for it. The Polish tendency to fantasticating interposes between him and his projected tyrannicide. And while Slowacki gives us the radical Hamlet type, so we find the corresponding conservative Hamlet in Krasinski. The hero of Krasinski's *Undivine Comedy* has more than one trait in

2 B

common with the Prince of Denmark. He has Hamlet's sensitiveness and power of imagination. He is addicted to monologues and cultivates the drama. He has an extremely tender conscience, but can commit most cruel actions. He is punished for the excessive irritability of his character by the insanity of his wife, very much as Hamlet, by his feigned madness, leads to the real madness of Ophelia. But this Hamlet is consumed by a more modern doubt than that which besets his Renaissance prototype. Hamlet doubts whether the spirit on whose behest he is acting is more than an empty phantasm. When Count Henry shuts himself up in "the castle of the Holy Trinity," he is not sure that the Holy Trinity itself is more than a figment of the brain.

In other words: nearly two centuries and a half after the figure of Hamlet was conceived in Shakespeare's imagination, we find it living in English and French literature, and reappearing as a dominant type in German and two Slavonic languages. And now, three hundred years after his creation, Hamlet is still the confidant and friend of sad and thoughtful souls in every land. There is something unique in this. With such piercing vision has Shakespeare searched out the depths of his own, and at the same time of all human, nature, and so boldly and surely has he depicted the outward semblance of what he saw, that, centuries later, men of every country and of every race have felt their own being moulded like wax in his hand, and have seen themselves in his poetry as in a mirror.

XVIII

HAMLET AS A CRITIC

ALONG with so much else, *Hamlet* gives us what we should scarcely have expected—an insight into Shakespeare's own ideas of his art as poet and actor, and into the condition and relations of his theatre in the years 1602–3.

If we read attentively the Prince's words to the players, we see clearly why it is always the sweetness, the mellifluousness of Shakespeare's art that his contemporaries emphasise. To us he may seem audacious, harrowingly pathetic, a transgressor of all bounds; in comparison with contemporary artists—not only with the specially violent and bombastic writers, like the youthful Marlowe, but with all of them—he is self-controlled, temperate, delicate, beauty-loving as Raphael himself. Hamlet says to the players—

"Speak the speech, I pray you, as I pronounced it to you, trippingly on the tongue; but if you mouth it, as many of your players do, I had as lief the town-crier spoke my lines. Nor do not saw the air too much with your hand, thus; but use all gently: for in the very torrent, tempest, and (as I may say) the whirlwind of passion, you must acquire and beget a temperance that may give it smoothness. O! it offends me to the soul to hear a robustious periwig-pated fellow tear a passion to tatters, to very rags, to split the ears of the groundlings, who, for the most part, are capable of nothing but inexplicable dumb-shows, and noise: I would have such a fellow whipped for o'er-doing Termagant; it out-herods Herod: pray you, avoid it.

"1 *Play.* I warrant your honour.

"*Ham.* Be not too tame neither, but let your own discretion be your tutor."

Here ought logically to follow a warning against the dangers of excessive softness and sweetness. But it does not come. He continues—

" Suit the action to the word, the word to the action, with this special observance, that you o'erstep not the modesty of nature; *for anything so overdone is from the purpose of playing, whose end, both at the first and now, was, and is, to hold, as 't were, the mirror up to nature; to show virtue her own feature, scorn her own image, and the very age and body of the time, his form and pressure.* Now, this overdone, or come tardy off, though it make the unskilful laugh, cannot but make the judicious grieve ; the censure of the which one must, in your allowance, o'erweigh a whole theatre of others. O ! there be players, that I have seen play,—and heard others praise, and that highly,—not to speak it profanely, that, neither having the accent of Christians, nor the gait of Christian, pagan, nor man, have so strutted and bellowed, that I have thought that some of nature's journeymen had made men, and not made them well, they imitated humanity so abominably.

" 1 *Play.* I hope we have reformed that indifferently with us.

" *Ham.* O ! reform it altogether."

Thus, although it appears to be Hamlet's wish to caution equally against too much wildness and too much tameness, his warning against tameness is of the briefest, and he almost immediately resumes his homily against exaggeration, bellowing, what we should now call ranting declamation. It is not the danger of tameness, but of violence, that is uppermost in Shakespeare's mind.

As already pointed out, it is not merely his own general effort as a dramatist which Shakespeare here formulates ; he lays down a regular definition of dramatic art and its aim. It is noteworthy that this definition is identical with that which Cervantes, almost at the same time, places into the mouth of the priest in *Don Quixote.* " Comedy," he says, " should be as Tullius enjoins, a mirror of human life, a pattern of manners, a presentation of the truth."

Shakespeare and Cervantes, who shed lustre on the same age and died within a few days of each other, never heard of each other's existence; but, led by the spirit of their time, both borrowed from Cicero their fundamental conception of dramatic art. Cervantes says so openly ; Shakespeare, who did not wish his Hamlet to pose as a scholar, indicates it in the words, "Whose end, both *at the first* and now, *was,* and is."

And as Shakespeare here, by the mouth of Hamlet, has expressed his own idea of his art's unalterable nature and aim, he has also for once given vent to his passing artistic anxieties, his dissatisfaction with the position of his theatre at the moment. We have already (p. 106) noticed the poet's complaint of the harm done to his company at this time by the rivalry of the troupe of choir-boys from St. Paul's Cathedral playing at the Blackfriars Theatre. It is in Hamlet's dialogue with Rosencrantz that this complaint occurs. There is a bitterness about the wording of it, as though the company had for the time been totally worsted. This was no doubt largely due to the circumstance that its most popular member, its clown, the famous Kemp, had just left it (in 1602), and gone over to Henslow's troupe. Kemp had from the beginning played all the chief low-comedy parts in Shakespeare's dramas—Peter and Balthasar in *Romeo and Juliet*, Shallow in *Henry IV.*, Lancelot in *The Merchant of Venice*, Dogberry in

Much Ado About Nothing, Touchstone in *As You Like It*. Now that he had gone over to the enemy, his loss was deeply felt.

The above-mentioned little book, dedicated to Mary Fitton, gives us a most interesting glimpse into the English life of that age.

The most important duty of the clown was not to appear in the play itself, but to sing and dance his jig at the end of it, even after a tragedy, in order to soften the painful impression. The common spectator never went home without having seen this afterpiece, which must have resembled the comic "turns" of our variety-shows. Kemp's jig of *The Kitchen-Stuff Woman*, for instance, was a screaming farrago of rude verses, some spoken, others sung, of good and bad witticisms, of extravagant acting and dancing. It is of such a performance that Hamlet is thinking when he says of Polonius: "He's for a jig, or a tale of bawdry, or he sleeps."

As the acknowledged master of his time in the art of comic dancing, Kemp was immoderately loved and admired. He paid professional visits to all the German and Italian courts, and was even summoned to dance his Morrice Dance before the Emperor Rudolf himself at Augsburg. It was in his youth that he undertook the nine days' dance from London to Norwich which he describes in his book.

He started at seven o'clock in the morning from in front of the Lord Mayor's house, and half London was astir to see the beginning of the great exploit. His suite consisted of his "taberer," his servant, and an "overseer" or umpire to see that everything was performed according to promise. The journey was almost as trying to the "taberer" as to Kemp, for he had his drum hanging over his left arm and held his flageolet in his left hand while he beat the drum with his right. Kemp himself, on this occasion, contributed nothing to the music except the sound of the bells which were attached to his gaiters.

He reached Romford on the first day, but was so exhausted that he had to rest for two days. The people of Stratford-Langton, between London and Romford, had got up a bear-baiting show in his honour, knowing "how well he loved the sport"; but the crowd which had gathered to see him was so great that he himself only succeeded in hearing the bear roar and the dogs howl. On the second day he strained his hip, but cured the strain by dancing. At Burntwood such a crowd had gathered to see him that he could scarcely make his way to the tavern. There, as he relates, two cut-purses were caught in the act, who had followed with the crowd from London. They declared that they had laid a wager upon the dance, but Kemp recognised one of them as a noted thief whom he had seen tied to a post in the theatre. Next day he reached Chelmsford, but here the crowd which had accompanied him from London had dwindled away to a couple of hundred people.

In Norwich the city waits received him in the open market-place with an official concert in the presence of thousands. He was the guest of the town and entertained at its expense, received handsome presents from the mayor, and was admitted to the Guild of Merchant Venturers, being thereby assured a share in their yearly income, to the amount of forty shillings. The very buskins in which he had performed his dance were nailed to the wall in the Norwich Guild Hall and preserved in perpetual memory of the exploit.

So popular an artist as this must of course have felt himself at least Shakespeare's equal. He certainly assumed the right to address one of her Majesty's Maids-of-Honour with no slight familiarity. The tone in which he dedicates this catchpenny performance to Mrs. Fitton offers a remarkable contrast to the profoundly respectful tone in which professional authors couch their dedications to their noble patrons or patronesses :—

" In the waine of my little wit I am forst to desire your protection, else every Ballad-singer will proclaime me bankrupt of honesty. . . . To shew my duety to your honourable selfe, whose favours (among other bountifull friends) make me (dispight this sad world) iudge my hert Corke and my heeles feathers, so that me thinkes I could fly to Rome (at least hop to Rome, as the old Prouerb is) with a Morter on my head."

His description of the *Nine Daies Wonder*, with its arrogant dedication, has shown us how conceited he must have been. Hamlet lets us see that he had frequently annoyed Shakespeare by the irrepressible freedom of his "gags" and interpolations. From the text of the plays of an earlier period which have come down to us, we can understand that the clowns were in those days as free to do what they pleased with their parts as the Italian actors in the *Commedia dell' Arte*. Shakespeare's rich and perfect art left no room for such improvisations. Now that Kemp was gone, the poet sent the following shaft after him from the lips of Hamlet :—

" And let those that play your clowns speak no more than is set down for them : for there be of them that will themselves laugh, to set on some quantity of barren spectators to laugh too : though, in the meantime, some necessary question of the play be then to be considered : that's villainous, and shows a most pitiful ambition in the fool that uses it."

This reproof is, however, as the reader sees, couched in quite general terms; wherefore it was allowed to stand when Kemp returned to the company. But a far sharper and much more personal attack, which appears in the edition of 1603, was expunged in the following editions (and consequently from our text of the play), as being no longer in place after the return of the wanderer. It speaks of a clown whose witticisms are so popular that they are noted down by the gentlemen who frequent the theatre. A whole series of extremely poor specimens of his burlesque sallies is given—mere circus-clown drolleries—and then Hamlet disposes of the wretched buffoon by remarking that he "cannot make a jest unless by chance, as a blind man catcheth a hare."

It is notorious that an artist will more easily forgive an attack on himself than warm praise of a rival in the same line. There can be very little doubt that Shakespeare, in making Hamlet praise the dead Yorick, had in view the lamented Tarlton, Kemp's amiable and famous predecessor. If there had been no purpose to serve by making the skull that of a jester, it might quite as well have belonged to some old servant of Hamlet's. But if Shakespeare, in his first years of theatrical life, had known Tarlton personally, and Kemp's objectionable behaviour vividly recalled by contrast his predecessor's charming whimsicality, it was natural enough that he should combine with the attack on Kemp a warm eulogy of the great jester.[1]

Tarlton was buried on the 3rd of September 1588. This date accords with the statement in the first quarto that Yorick has lain in the earth for a dozen years. Not till we have these facts before us can we fully understand the following strong outburst of feeling:—

"Alas, poor Yorick!—I knew him, Horatio: a fellow of infinite jest, of most excellent fancy: he hath borne me on his back a thousand times; and now, how abhorred in my imagination it is! my gorge rises at it. Here hung those lips that I have kissed I know not how oft. Where be your gibes now? your gambols? your songs? your flashes of merriment that were wont to set the table on a roar?"

Alas, poor Yorick! Hamlet's heartfelt lament will keep his memory alive when his Owlglass jests recorded in print are utterly forgotten.[2] His fooling was equally admired by the populace, the court, and the theatrical public. He is said to have told Elizabeth more truths than all her chaplains, and cured her melancholy better than all her physicians.

Shakespeare, in *Hamlet*, has not only spoken his mind freely on theatrical matters; he has also eulogised the distinguished actor after his death, and given a great example of the courteous and becoming treatment of able actors during their lives. His Prince of Denmark stands far above the vulgar prejudice against them. And, lastly, Shakespeare has glorified that dramatic art which was the business and pleasure of his life, by making the play the effective means of bringing the truth to light and furthering the ends of justice. The acting of the drama of

---

[1] Compare *New Shakspere Society's Transactions*, 1880–86, p. 60.
[2] *Tarlton's Jests and News out of Purgatory*. Edited by J. O. Halliwell. London, 1844.

Gonzago's death is the hinge on which the tragedy turns. From the moment when the King betrays himself by stopping the performance, Hamlet knows all that he wants to know.

When James ascended the throne, *Hamlet* received, as it were, a new actuality, from the fact that his queen, Anne, was a Danish princess. At the splendid festival held on the occasion of the triumphal procession of King James, Queen Anne, and Prince Henry Frederick, from the Tower through the city, "the Danish March" was brilliantly performed, out of compliment to the Queen, by a band consisting of nine trumpeters and a kettledrum, stationed on a scaffolding at the side of St. Mildred's Church. How this march went we do not know; but there can be little doubt that from that time it was played in the second scene of the fifth act of *Hamlet*, where music of trumpets and drums is prescribed, and where, in our days, at the Théâtre-Français, they naïvely play, "Kong Christian stod ved höjen Mast." [1]

[1] The Danish national song of to-day, written by Ewald, and the music composed by Hartmann, 1778.

XIX

ALL'S WELL THAT ENDS WELL—ATTACKS ON
PURITANISM

THE fortunes of the company having declined by reason of the competition complained of in *Hamlet*, it became necessary to intersperse a few comedies among the sombre tragedies on which alone Shakespeare's mind was now bent.

Comedies, therefore, had to be produced. But the disposition of mind in which Shakespeare had created *A Midsummer Night's Dream* had long deserted him; and infinitely remote, though so near in point of time, was the mood in which he had produced *As You Like It*.

Still the thing had to be done. He took one of his old sketches in hand again, the play called *Love's Labour's Won*, which has already been noticed (p. 47). Its original form we do not exactly know; all we can do is to pick out the rhymed and youthfully frivolous passages as having doubtless belonged to the earlier play, to whose title there is probably a reference in Helena's words in the concluding scene :—

> "This is done.
> Will you be mine, now you are doubly won?"

It is clear that Shakespeare in his young days took hold of the subject with the purpose of making a comedy out of it. But now it did not turn out a comedy; the time was past when Shakespeare's chief strength lay in his humour. We could quite well imagine his subsequent tragedies to have been written by his Hamlet, if Hamlet had had life before him; and in the same way we could imagine this and the following play, *Measure for Measure*, to have been written by his Jaques.

We find many indications in *All's Well that Ends Well*— most, as was natural, in the first two acts—of Shakespeare's having come straight from *Hamlet*. In the very first scene, the Countess chides Helena for the immoderate grief with which she mourns her father: it is wrong to let oneself be so overwhelmed. Just so the King speaks to Hamlet of the "obstinate condolement" to which he gives himself up. The Countess's advice to her son, when he is setting off for France, reminds us strongly of the advice Polonius gives to Laertes in exactly the same situation. She says, for instance :—

> "Thy blood and virtue
> Contend for empire in thee ; and thy goodness
> Share with thy birthright !   Love all, trust a few,
> Do wrong to none : be able for thine enemy
> Rather in power than use, and keep thy friend
> Under thy own life's key : be check'd for silence,
> But never tax'd for speech."

Compare with these injunctions those of Polonius :—

> "Give thy thoughts no tongue,
> Nor any unproportion'd thought his act.
> Be thou familiar, but by no means vulgar.
> The friends thou hast, and their adoption tried,
> Grapple them to thy soul with hoops of steel ;
> But do not dull thy palm with entertainment
> Of each new-hatch'd, unfledg'd comrade.   Beware
> Of entrance to a quarrel ; but, being in,
> Bear't that the opposed may beware of thee.
> Give every man thine ear, but few thy voice."

Notice also in this comedy the numerous sallies against court life and courtiers, which are quite in the spirit of *Hamlet*. The scene in which Polonius changes his opinion according as Hamlet thinks the cloud like a camel, a weasel, or a whale, and that in which Osric, who "did comply with his dug before he sucked it," reels off his elegant speeches, seem actually to be commented on in general terms when the Clown (ii. 2) thus discourses about the court :—

"Truly, madam, if God have lent a man any manners, he may easily put it off at court : he that cannot make a leg, put off's cap, kiss his hand, and say nothing, has neither leg, hands, lip, nor cap ; and, indeed, such a fellow, to say precisely, were not for the court."

Now and again, too, we come upon expressions which recall well-known speeches of Hamlet's.   For instance, when Helena (ii. 3) says to the First Lord :

> "Thanks, sir ; all the rest is mute,"

we are reminded of Hamlet's ever-memorable last words :

> "The rest is silence."

Among other more external touches, which likewise point clearly to the period 1602–1603, may be mentioned the many subtle, cautious sallies against Puritanism which are interwoven in the play.   They express the bitter contempt for demonstrative piety which filled Shakespeare's mind just at that time.

Hamlet itself had treated of a hypocrite on the largest scale. Notice, too, the stinging reference to existing conditions in Act iii. Scene 2 :—

"*Hamlet.* Look you, how cheerfully my mother looks, and my father died within's two hours.

"*Ophelia.* Nay, 'tis twice two months, my lord.

"*Ham.* So long? Nay, then, let the devil wear black, for I'll have a suit of sables. O heavens! die two months ago, and not forgotten yet? Then there's hope a great man's memory may outlive his life half a year; *but by'r lady, he must build churches then,* or else shall he suffer not thinking on, with the hobby-horse; whose epitaph is, 'For, O! for, O! the hobby-horse is forgot.'"

In *All's Well that Ends Well* Shakespeare has his sanctimonious enemies constantly in mind. He makes the Clown jeer at the fanatics in both the Protestant and the Catholic camp. They may be of different faiths, but they are alike in being unlucky husbands. The Clown says (i. 3) :—

"Young Charbon the Puritan, and old Poysam the Papist, how soe'er their hearts are severed in religion, their heads are both one; they may joll horns together, like any deer i' the herd."

A little farther on he continues :—

"Though honesty be no Puritan, yet it will do no hurt; it will wear the surplice of humility over the black gown of a big heart."

When Lafeu (ii. 3) is talking to Parolles of the marvellous cure of the King of France which Helena has undertaken, he has a hit at those who will find matter in it for a pious treatise :—

"*Lafeu.* I may truly say, it is a novelty to the world.

"*Parolles.* It is, indeed : if you will have it in showing, you shall read it in—what do you call there?—

"*Laf.* A showing of a heavenly effect in an earthly actor."

Shakespeare clearly took a mischievous pleasure in imitating the title of a Puritanic work of edification.

This polemical tendency, which extends from *Hamlet* through *All's Well that Ends Well* to *Measure for Measure*, in the form of an increasingly marked opposition to the growing religious strictness and sectarianism of the day, with its accompaniment of hypocrisy, proves plainly that Shakespeare at this time shared the animosity of the Government towards both Puritanism and Catholicism.

Though there is little true mirth to be found in *All's Well that Ends Well*, the piece reminds us in various ways of some of Shakespeare's real comedies. The story resembles in several details that of *The Merchant of Venice*. Portia in disguise persuades the unwilling Bassanio to give up his ring to her; and

Helena, in the darkness of night mistaken for another, coaxes Bertram out of the ring which he had made up his mind she should never obtain from him. In the closing scenes, both Bertram and Bassanio are minus their rings; both are wretched because they have not got them; and in both cases the knot is unravelled by their wives being found in possession of them. There is a more essential relation—that of direct contrast—between the story of *All's Well that Ends Well* and that of *The Taming of the Shrew*. The earlier comedy sets forth in playful fashion how a man by means of the attributes of his sex —physical superiority, boldness, and coolness—helped out by imperiousness, bluster, noise, and violence, wins the devotion of a passionately recalcitrant young woman. *All's Well that Ends Well* shows us how a woman, by means of the attributes of her sex—gentleness, goodness of heart, cunning, and finesse—conquers a vehemently recalcitrant man. And in both cases the pair are married before the action proper of the play begins.

Seeing that Shakespeare in *The Taming of the Shrew* followed the older play on the same subject, and that he took the story of *All's Well that Ends Well* from Boccaccio's Gilette of Narbonne, a translation of which appeared as early as 1566 in Paynter's *Palace of Pleasure*, this contrast cannot be said to have been devised by the poet. But it is evident that one of the chief attractions of the latter subject for Shakespeare was the opportunity it offered him of delineating that rare phenomenon: a woman wooing a man and yet possessing and retaining all the charm of her sex. Shakespeare has worked out the figure of Helena with the tenderest partiality. Pity and admiration in concert seem to have guided his pen. We feel in his portraiture a deep compassion for the pangs of despised love—the compassion of one who himself has suffered—and over the whole figure of Helena he has shed a Raphael-like beauty. She wins all, charms all, wherever she goes—old and young, women and men—all except Bertram, the one in whom her life is bound up. The King and the old Lafeu are equally captivated by her, equally impressed by her excellences. Bertram's mother prizes her as if she were her daughter; more highly, indeed, than she prizes her own obstinate son. The Italian widow becomes so devoted to her that she follows her to a foreign country in order to vouch for her statement and win her back her husband.

She ventures all that she may gain her well-beloved, and in the pursuit of her aim shows an inventive capacity not common among women. For the real object of her journey to cure the King is, as she frankly confesses, to be near Bertram. As in the tale, she obtains the King's promise that she may, if she is successful in curing him, choose herself a husband among the lords of his court; but in Boccaccio it is the King who, in answer to her question as to the reward, gives her this promise of his

own accord; in the play it is she who first states her wish.   So
possessed is she by her passion for one who does not give her a
thought or a look.   But when he rejects her (unlike Gilette in the
tale), she has no desire to attain her object by compulsion; she
simply says to the King with noble resignation—

> " 'That you are well restored, my lord,
>   I'm glad; let the rest go."

She offers no objection when Bertram, immediately after the
wedding, announces his departure, alleging pretexts which she
does not choose to see through; she suffers without a murmur
when, at the moment of parting, he refuses her a kiss.   When
she has learnt the whole truth, she can at first utter nothing
but short ejaculations (iii. 2): "My lord is gone, for ever gone."
"This is a dreadful sentence!"   " 'Tis bitter!"—and presently
she leaves her home, that she may be no hindrance to his returning
to it.   Predisposed though she is to self-confidence and pride, no
one could possibly love more tenderly and humbly.

All the most beautiful passages of her part show by the
structure of the verse and the absence of rhyme that they belong
to the poet's riper period.   Note, for example, the lines (i. 1) in
which Helena tells how the remembrance of her dead father has
been effaced in her mind by the picture of Bertram :—

> " My imagination
> Carries no favour in 't but Bertram's.
> I am undone : there is no living, none,
> If Bertram be away.   It were all one
> That I should love a bright particular star,
> And think to wed it; he is so above me :
> In his bright radiance and collateral light
> Must I be comforted, not in his sphere.
> The ambition in my love thus plagues itself:
> The hind that would be mated by the lion
> Must die for love.   'Twas pretty, though a plague,
> To see him every hour : to sit and draw
> His arched brows, his hawking eye, his curls,
> In our heart's table ; heart too capable
> Of every line and trick of his sweet favour:
> But now he's gone, and my idolatrous fancy
> Must sanctify his relics."

If we compare the style of this passage with that which prevails in Helena's rhymed speeches, with their euphuistic word-
plays and antitheses, the difference is very striking, and we feel
what a distance Shakespeare has traversed since the days of his
apprenticeship.   Here we find no glitter of wit, but the utterance
of a heart that loves simply and deeply.

Though the play as a whole was evidently not one of those
which Shakespeare cared most about, and though he has allowed

things to stand in it which preclude the possibility of a satisfactory and harmonious end, yet he has evidently concentrated
his whole poetic strength on the development and perfection of
Helena's most winning character.   These are the terms (i. 3) in
which, speaking to Bertram's mother, she makes confession of
her love :—

> " Be not offended, for it hurts not him,
> That he is lov'd of me.   I follow him not
> By any token of presumptuous suit ;
> Nor would I have him till I do deserve him,
> Yet never know how that desert should be.
> I know I love in vain, strive against hope ;
> Yet, in this captious and intenible sieve
> I still pour in the waters of my love,
> And lack not to lose still.   Thus, Indian-like,
> Religious in mine error, I adore
> The sun, that looks upon his worshipper,
> But knows of him no more."

There is something in her nature which anticipates the charm,
earnestness, and boundless devotion with which Shakespeare
afterwards endows Imogen.   When Bertram goes off to the war,
simply to escape acknowledging her and living with her as his
wife, she exclaims (iii. 2)—

> "Poor lord ! is't I
> That chase thee from thy country, and expose
> Those tender limbs of thine to the event
> Of the none-sparing war? . . .
> O you leaden messengers,
> That ride upon the violent speed of fire,
> Fly with false aim ; move the still-'pearing air,
> That sings with piercing, do not touch my lord !
> Whoever shoots at him, I set him there ;
> Whoever charges on his forward breast,
> I am the caitiff that do hold him to it."

In this there is a fervour and a glow that we do not find in the
earlier comedies.   When one reads these verses, one understands
how it is that Coleridge calls Helena, " Shakespeare's loveliest
character."

Pity that this deep passion should have been inspired by so
unworthy an object.   It undoubtedly lessens the interest of the
play that Shakespeare should not have given Bertram some more
estimable qualities along with the all too youthful and unchivalrous ones which he possesses.   The poet has here been guilty of
a certain negligence, which shows that it was only to parts of the
play that he gave his whole mind.   Bertram is right enough in
refusing to have a wife thrust upon him against his will, simply
because the King has a debt of gratitude to pay.   But this first

motive for refusing gives place to one with which we have less sympathy: to wit, pride of rank, which makes him look down on Helena as being of inferior birth, though king, courtiers, and his own mother consider her fit to rank with the best. Even this, however, need not lower Bertram irretrievably in our esteem; but he adds to it traits of unmanliness, even of baseness. For instance, he enjoins Helena, through Parolles, to invent some explanation of his sudden departure which will make the King believe it to have been a necessity; and then he leaves her, not, as he falsely declares, for two days, but for ever. His readiness to marry a daughter of Lafeu the moment the report of Helena's death has reached him is a very extraordinary preparation for the reunion of the couple at the end of the play, and reminds us unpleasantly of the exactly similar incident in *Much Ado About Nothing* (p. 217). But, worst of all, and an indisputable dramatic mistake, is his entangling himself, just before the final reconciliation, in a web of mean lies with reference to the Italian girl to whom he had laid siege in Tuscany.

It was to make Helena's position more secure, and to avoid any suspicion of the adventuress about her, that Shakespeare invented the character of the Countess, that motherly friend whose affection sets a seal on all her merits. In the same way Parolles was invented with the purpose of making Bertram less guilty. Bertram is to be considered as ensnared by this old "fool, notorious liar, and coward" (as Helena at once calls him), who figures in the play as his evil genius.

Parolles in *Love's Labour's Won* was doubtless a gay and purely farcical figure—the first slight sketch for Falstaff. Coming after Falstaff, he necessarily seems a weak repetition; but this is no fault of the poet's. Still, it is very plain that in the re-writing Shakespeare's attempt at gaiety missed fire. His frame of mind was too serious; the view of the subject from the moral standpoint displaces and excludes pure pleasure in its comicality. Parolles, who has Falstaff's vices without a gleam of his genius, brings anything but unmixed merriment in his train. The poet is at pains to impress on us the lesson we ought to learn from Parolles's self-stultification, and the shame that attends on his misdeeds. Thus the Second Lord (iv. 3), speaking of the rascality he displays in his outpourings when he is blindfolded, says—

"I will never trust a man again for keeping his sword clean, nor believe he can have everything in him by wearing his apparel neatly."

And Parolles himself says when his effrontery is crushed (iv. 3)—

"If my heart were great,
'Twould burst at this. Captain I'll be no more;
But I will eat and drink, and sleep as soft
As captain shall: simply the thing I am

Shall make me live.   *Who knows himself a braggart,*
Let him fear this ; for it will come to pass
That every braggart shall be found an ass."

The other comic figure, the Clown, witty as he is, has not
the serene gaiety of the earlier comedies. He speaks here and
there, as already noted (p. 49), in the youthfully whimsical style
of the earliest comedies ; but as a humoristic house-fool he does
not rank with such a sylvan fool as Touchstone, a creation of a
few years earlier, nor with the musical court-fool in *Twelfth
Night.*

A single passage in *All's Well that Ends Well* has always
struck me as having a certain personal note. It is one of those
which were quite evidently added at the time of the re-writing.
The King is speaking of Bertram's deceased father, and quotes
his words (i. 2)—

" ' Let me not live,'—
Thus his good melancholy oft began,
On the catastrophe and heel of pastime,
When it was out,—' Let me not live,' quoth he,
' After my flame lacks oil, to be the snuff
Of younger spirits, whose apprehensive senses
All but new things disdain.' . . .
                    This he wish'd :
I, after him, do after him wish too."

A courtier objects to this despondent utterance—

" You are lov'd, sir ;
They that least lend it you shall lack you first."

Whereupon the King replies with proud humility—

"I fill a place, I know 't."

These words could not have been written save by a mature
man, who has seen impatient youth pressing forward to take his
place, and who has felt the sting of its criticism. The disposition
of mind which here betrays itself foretells that overpowering
sense of the injustice of men and of things which is soon to take
possession of Shakespeare's soul.

XX

MEASURE FOR MEASURE—ANGELO AND TARTUFFE

A COVERT polemical intention could be vaguely divined here and there in *All's Well that Ends Well*. It contained, as we have seen, some incidental mockery of the increasing Puritanism of the time, with its accompaniment of self-righteousness, moral intolerance, and unctuous hypocrisy. The bent of thought which gave birth to these sallies reappears still more clearly in the choice of the theme treated in *Measure for Measure*.

The plot of *All's Well that Ends Well* turns on the incident, familiar in every literature, of one woman passing herself off for another at a nocturnal rendezvous, without the substitution being detected by the man—an incident so fruitful in dramatic situations, that even its gross improbability has never deterred poets from making use of it.

A standing variation of this theme, also to be found in the most diverse literatures, is as follows:—A man is condemned to death. His mistress, his wife, or his sister implores the judge to pardon him. The judge promises, on condition that she shall pass a night with him, to let the prisoner go free, but afterwards has him executed all the same.

This subject has been treated over and over again from mediæval times down to our own days, its latest appearances, probably, being in Paul Heyse's novel, *Der Kinder Sünde der Väter Fluch*, and in Victorien Sardou's play *La Tosca*. In Shakespeare's time it appeared in the form of an Italian novella in Giraldi Cinthio's *Hecatommithi* (1565), on which an English dramatist, George Whetstone, founded his play, *The Right Excellent and Famous History of Promos and Cassandra* (1578), and also a prose story in his *Heptameron of Civil Discourses*, published in 1582. Whetstone's utterly lifeless and characterless comedy is the immediate source from which Shakespeare derived the outlines of the story. He is indebted to Whetstone for nothing else.

What attracted Shakespeare to this unpleasant subject was clearly his indignation at the growing Pharisaism in matters of sexual morality which was one outcome of the steady growth of Puritanism among the middle classes. It was a consequence of his position as an actor and theatrical manager that he saw only the ugliest side of Puritanism—the one it turned towards him.

2 C

Its estimable sides well deserved a poet's sympathy. Small wonder, indeed, that independent and pious men should seek the salvation of their souls without the bounds of the Anglican State Church, with its Thirty-Nine Articles, to which all clergymen and state officials were bound to swear, and to which all citizens must make submission. It was a punishable offence to use any other ritual than the official one, or even to refuse to go to church. The Puritans, who dreamed of leading the Christian Church back to its original purity, and who had returned home after their banishment during the reign of Mary with the ideal of a demo-cratic Church before their eyes, could not possibly approve of a State Church subject to the crown, or of such an institution as Episcopacy. Some of them looked to Scottish Presbyterianism as a worthy model, and desired to see Church government by laymen, the elders of the congregation, introduced into England, in place of the spiritual aristocracy of the bishops. Others went still farther, denied the necessity of one common form of worship for all, and desired to have the Church broken up into independent congregations, in which any believer might officiate as priest. We have here the germs of the great party division in Cromwell's time into Presbyterians and Independents.

So far as we can see, Shakespeare took no interest whatever in any of these ecclesiastical or religious movements. He came into contact with Puritanism only in its narrow and fanatical hatred of his art, and in its severely intolerant condemnation and punishment of moral, and especially of sexual, frailties. All he saw was its Pharisaic aspect, and its often enough only simulated virtue.

It was his indignation at this hypocritical virtue that led him to write *Measure for Measure.* He treated the subject as he did, because the interests of the theatre demanded that the woof of comedy should be interwoven with the severe and sombre warp of tragedy. But what a comedy! Dark, tragic, heavy as the poet's mood—a tragi-comedy, in which the unusually broad and realistic comic scenes, with their pictures of the dregs of society, cannot relieve the painfulness of the theme, or disguise the positively criminal nature of the action. One feels throughout, even in the comic episodes, that Shakespeare's burning wrath at the moral hypocrisy of self-righteousness underlies the whole structure like a volcano, which every moment shoots up its flames through the superficial form of comedy and the interludes of obligatory merriment.

And yet it is not really against hypocrisy that his attack is aimed. At this stage of his development he is far too great a psychologist to depict a ready-made, finished hypocrite. No, he shows us how weak even the strictest Pharisee will prove, if only he happens to come across the temptation which really tempts him; and how such a man's desire, if it meets with opposition, reveals in him quite another being—a villain, a brute beast—who allows himself actions worse a hundredfold than those which, in the calm superiority of a spotless conscience, he has hitherto punished in others with the utmost severity.

It is not a type of Shakespeare's opponents that he here unmasks and brands—it is a man in many ways above the average type, as he saw it. The chief character in *Measure for Measure* is the judge of public morality, the hard and stern *Censor morum*, who in his moral fanaticism believes that he can root out vice by persecuting its tools, and imagines that he can purify and reform society by punishing every transgression, however natural and comparatively harmless, as a capital crime. The play shows us how this man, as soon as a purely sensual passion takes possession of him, does not hesitate to commit, under the mask of piety, a crime against real morality so revolting and so monstrous that no expression of loathing and contempt would be too severe for it, and scarcely any punishment too rigorous.

From its nature such a drama ought to end by appeasing in some satisfactory manner the craving for justice awakened in the spectator. But comedy was what Shakespeare's company wanted ; and besides, it would have been unwise, and perhaps even dangerous, to carry to extremities this question of the punishment of moral hypocrisy. So the knot in the play was summarily loosed, without any great expenditure of pathos, by the provident care and timely intervention of a wise and invisibly omnipresent prince, an occidental Haroun-al-Raschid. Fastidious in his choice of means this prince was not. With an ingenuity which is profoundly unsatisfactory to any one of the least delicacy of feeling, he substitutes a lovable girl, whom the iniquitous judge had at one time promised to marry, for the beautiful young woman who is the object of his bestial desire.

The Duke, wishing to test his servants, gives out that he is leaving Vienna on a long journey. He intrusts the regency during his absence to Angelo, an official of high standing and reputation.

No sooner does Angelo come into power than he begins a regular crusade against licentiousness and all laxity in the domain of morals. In the first place, he decrees that all houses of ill-fame in the city of Vienna are to be pulled down. In the older drama by Whetstone, which Shakespeare used as a foundation for his play, there was a whole troop of disreputable personages, procuresses, prostitutes, bullies, improper characters of every description. Shakespeare retains part of this company ; he has a single procuress, Mistress Overdone, who reminds us slightly of Doll Tearsheet, a single bully, that very amusing personage, Pompey ; and he adds to them an extremely entertaining character, the utterly dissolute but witty tattler and liar, Lucio.

But the chief alteration he makes in the subject-matter of

the play is that the Duke, disguised as a friar, is witness from the beginning of Angelo's abuse of his power as ruler and judge. Among other advantages resulting from this modification, we must reckon the fact that the spectators are thus reassured in advance as to the final issue. On the Duke's disguise, moreover, depends most of the comic effect arising out of the character of Lucio, who is constantly repeating to him the most absurd slanders about himself, as if he had them from the best authority. Further, the Duke's concealed presence is essential to the other great change made in the story, namely, that Isabella is not really required to sacrifice herself for her brother, her place being filled, as in *All's Well that Ends Well*, by a woman who has old claims on the man concerned. In this manner the too revoltingly painful part of the subject is avoided.

Shakespeare has imagined one of the men who were the bitterest enemies of his art and his calling invested with absolute power, and using it to proceed against immorality with cruel rigour. The first step is his attack on common prostitution, which he persuades himself he can exterminate. This vain imagination is repeatedly ridiculed. "What shall become of me?" says Mistress Overdone. "Come; fear not you: good counsellors lack no clients." In the Act ii. sc. 1 we read :—

"*Escalus.* How would you live, Pompey? by being a bawd? What do you think of the trade, Pompey? is it a lawful trade?

"*Pompey.* If the law would allow it, sir.

"*Escal.* But the law will not allow it, Pompey; nor it shall not be allowed in Vienna.

"*Pomp.* Does your worship mean to geld and splay all the youth of the city.

"*Escal.* No, Pompey.

"*Pomp.* Truly, sir, in my poor opinion, they will to't then."

And Lucio (iii. 2) also ridicules Angelo's severity as fruitless :—

"*Lucio.* A little more lenity to lechery would do no harm in him : something too crabbed that way, friar.

"*Duke.* It is too general a vice, and severity must cure it.

"*Lucio.* Yes, in good sooth, the vice is of a great kindred : it is well allied ; but it is impossible to extirp it quite, friar, till eating and drinking be put down. They say, this Angelo was not made by man and woman, after this downright way of creation : is it true, think you?"

But besides taking strict proceedings against actual debauchery, Angelo revives an old law which has long been in disuse—according to the Duke for fourteen, according to Claudio for nineteen years—making death the punishment of all sexual commerce without marriage ; and by this law young Claudio is condemned to death for his relation to Juliet.

It was an innocent relation.   He says (i. 3) :—

> " She is fast my wife
> Save that we do the denunciation lack
> Of outward order : this we came not to,
> Only for propagation of a dower
> Remaining in the coffer of her friends."

But this avails nothing.   An example is to be made.   It is in vain that even the highly respectable Provost feels compassion for him, and says (ii. 2) :—

> " All sects, all ages smack of this vice, and he
> To die for it ! "

The young men of the town cannot explain this insane severity in any other way than by the supposition that Lord Angelo is a man with " snow-broth " in his veins in place of blood.

It soon appears, however, that he is not the man of ice he is taken to be.

Escalus, an old, honourable nobleman, bids him bear in mind that though his own virtue be of the straitest, it has, perhaps, never been tempted; had it been exposed to temptations, it might not have stood the test better than that of others.   Angelo answers haughtily that to be tempted is one thing, to fall another.   But now comes Claudio's sister, Isabella, young, charming, and intelligent, and beseeches him to spare her brother's life (ii. 2) :—

> " Good, good my lord, bethink you :
> Who is it that hath died for this offence ?
> There 's many have committed it."

He is inexorable.   She shows the unreason of punishing so stringently the errors of love :

> " *Isab.* Could great men thunder
> As Jove himself does, Jove would ne'er be quiet,
> For every pelting, petty officer
> Would use his heaven for thunder ; nothing but thunder.—
> Merciful heaven !
> Thou rather with thy sharp and sulphurous bolt
> Splitt'st the unwedgeable and gnarled oak,
> Than the soft myrtle."

And she continues in such a strain, that we cannot but hear the poet's voice through hers :—

> " But man, proud man !
> Drest in a little brief authority,
> Most ignorant of what he 's most assur'd,
> His glassy essence,—like an angry ape,
> Plays such fantastic tricks before high heaven
> As make the angels weep ; who, with our spleens,
> Would all themselves laugh mortal."

And she appeals to his own self-knowledge :—

> "Go to your bosom ;
> Knock there, and ask your heart what it doth know
> That's like my brother's fault."

He invites her to come again the next day; and hardly is she gone when, in a monologue, he reveals his hateful passion, and even hints at his still more hateful purpose of forcing her to gratify it in payment for her brother's release.

He makes her his proposal.   She is appalled; she now sees, like Hamlet, what life can be, what undreamt-of horrors can happen, to what a pitch villainy can be carried, even on the judgment-seat :—

> "O, 'tis the cunning livery of hell,
> The damned'st body to invest and cover
> In princely guards !   Dost thou think, Claudio ?—
> If I would yield him my virginity,
> Thou mightst be freed."

She cannot even denounce him, for, as he himself points out to her, no one will believe her; his stainless name, his strict life and high rank, will stifle the accusation if she dares to make it. Feeling himself safe, he is doubly audacious.   Thus, when, at the conclusion of the play (v. 3), she lays her indictment before the reinstated Duke, Angelo says brazenly, "My lord, her wits, I fear me, are not firm."   Then follows, as if in continuation of Isabella's just-quoted speech, the fiery protest springing from the poet's intensest conviction :—

> "Make not impossible
> That which but seems unlike.   'Tis not impossible,
> But one, the wicked'st caitiff on the ground,
> May seem as shy, as grave, as just, as absolute,
> As Angelo."

(See p. 241.)
But the protest has no immediate result.   Isabella is, for the time being, sent to prison for slandering a man of unblemished honour.   And the irony is kept up to the last.   The Duke, in his character as a friar, has learnt bitter lessons ; amongst others, that there is hardly enough honesty in the world to hold society together.   But when he himself, in his disguise, relates what he has witnessed, his own faithful servants are on the point of sending him also to prison.   In his role of Haroun-al-Raschid, he has seen and realised that law is made to serve as a screen for might.   Thus he says—

> "My business in this state
> Made me a looker-on here in Vienna,
> Where I have seen corruption boil and bubble
> Till it o'er-run the stew : laws for all faults,
> But faults so countenanc'd, that the strong statutes

Stand like the forfeits in a barber's shop,
As much in mock as mark.
Escal. Slander to the state! Away with him to prison."

As a play, *Measure for Measure* rests entirely on three scenes: the one in which Angelo is tempted by Isabella's beauty; that in which he makes the shameless proposal that she shall give her honour in exchange for her brother's life; and, thirdly, that most dramatic one in which Claudio, after first hearing with fortitude and indignation what his sister has to tell him of Angelo's baseness, breaks down, and, like Kleist's Prince of Homburg two centuries later, begins meanly to beg for his life. Round these principal scenes are grouped the many excellent and vigorously realistic comic passages, treated in a spirit which afterwards revived in Hogarth and Thackeray; and other scenes designed solely to retard the dramatic wheel a little, which, therefore, jar upon us as conventional. It is, for example, an entirely unjustifiable experiment which the Duke tries on Isabella in the fourth act, when he falsely assures her that her brother's head has already been cut off and sent to Angelo. This is introduced solely for the sake of an effect at the end.

In this very unequally elaborated play, it is evident that Shakespeare cared only for the main point—the blow he was striking at hypocrisy. And it is probable that he here ventured as far as he by any means dared. It is a giant stride from the stingless satire on Puritanism in the character of Malvolio to this representation of a Puritan like Angelo. Probably for this very reason, Shakespeare has tried in every way to shield himself. The subject is treated entirely as a comedy. There is a threat of executing first Claudio, then the humorous scoundrel Barnardine, whose head is to be delivered instead of Claudio's; Barnardine is actually brought on the scene directly before execution, and the spectators sit in suspense; but all ends well at last, and the head of a man already dead is sent to Angelo. A noble maiden is threatened with dishonour; but another woman, Mariana, who was worthy of a better fate, keeps tryst with Angelo in her stead, and this danger is over. Finally, threats of retribution close round Angelo, the villain, himself; but after all he escapes unpunished, being merely obliged to marry the amiable girl whom he had at an earlier period deserted. In this way the play's terrible impeachment of hypocrisy is most carefully glozed over, and along with it the pessimism which animates the whole.

For it is remarkable how deeply pessimistic is the spirit of this play. When the Duke is exhorting Claudio (iii. 1) not to fear his inevitable fate, he goes farther in his depreciation of human life than Hamlet himself when his mood is blackest:—

"Reason thus with life:—
If I do lose thee, I do lose a thing

That none but fools would keep; a breath thou art,
Servile to all the skyey influences,
That do this habitation, where thou keep'st,
Hourly afflict.   Merely, thou art death's fool;
For him thou labour'st by thy flight to shun,
And yet runn'st toward him still.

  .   .   .   .   .   .

Happy thou art not;
For what thou hast not, still thou striv'st to get,
And what thou hast, forgett'st.   Thou art not certain;
For thy complexion shifts to strange effects,
After the moon.   If thou art rich, thou'rt poor;
For, like an ass, whose back with ingots bows,
Thou bear'st thy heavy riches but a journey,
And death unloads thee.   Friends hast thou none;
For thine own bowels, which do call thee sire,
The mere effusion of thy proper loins,
Do curse the gout, serpigo, and the rheum,
For ending thee no sooner.   Thou hast nor youth, nor age,
But, as it were, an after-dinner's sleep,
Dreaming on both; for all thy blessed youth
Becomes as aged, and doth beg the alms
Of palsied eld: and when thou art old and rich,
Thou hast neither heat, affection, limb, nor beauty
To make thy riches pleasant.   What's yet in this,
That bears the name of life?   Yet in this life
Lie hid more thousand deaths; yet death we fear,
That makes these odds all even."

Note with what art and care everything is here assembled that can confound and abash the normal instinct that makes for life.   Here for the first time Shakespeare anticipates Schopenhauer.

It is clear that in this play the poet was earnestly bent on proving his own standpoint to be the moral one.   In hardly any other play do we find such persistent emphasis laid, with small regard for consistency of character, upon the general moral.

For example, could there be a more direct utterance than the Duke's monologue at the end of Act iii. :—

"He who the sword of heaven will bear
  Should be as holy as severe;
Pattern in himself to know,
  Grace to stand, and virtue go;
More nor less to others paying,
  Than by self-offences weighing.
Shame to him whose cruel striking
Kills for faults of his own liking!
Twice treble shame on Angelo,
To weed my vice, and let his grow!"

Similarly, and in a like spirit, the moral pointer comes into play wherever there is an opportunity of showing how apt princes and rulers are to be misjudged, and how recklessly they are disparaged and slandered.

Thus the Duke says towards the close of Act iii. :—

> "No might nor greatness in mortality
> Can censure scape : black-wounding calumny
> The whitest virtue strikes. What king so strong
> Can tie the gall up in the slanderous tongue?"

And later (iv. 1), again :—

> "O place and greatness! millions of false eyes
> Are stuck upon thee. Volumes of report
> Run with these false and most contrarious quests
> Upon thy doings."

It is quite remarkable how this dwelling on baseless criticism by subjects is accompanied by a constant tendency to invoke the protection of the sovereign, or, in other words, of James I., who had just ascended the throne, and who, with his long-accumulated bitterness against Scottish Presbyterianism, was already showing himself hostile to English Puritanism. Hence the politic insistence, at the close, upon a point quite irrelevant to the matter of the play: all other sins being declared pardonable, save only slander or criticism of the sovereign. Lucio alone, who, to the great entertainment of the spectators, has told lies about the Duke, and, though only in jest, has spoken ill of him, is to be mercilessly punished. To the last moment it seems as if he were to be first whipped, then hanged. And even after this sentence is commuted in order that the tone of comedy may be preserved, and he is commanded instead to marry a prostitute, it is expressly insisted that whipping and hanging ought by rights to have been his punishment. "Slandering a prince deserves it," says the Duke, at the beginning of the final speech.

This attitude of Shakespeare's presents an exact parallel to that of Molière in the concluding scene of *Tartuffe*, sixty years later. The prince, in accordance with James of Scotland's theories of princely duty, appears as the universally vigilant guardian of his people; he alone chastises the hypocrite, whose lust of power and audacity distinguish him from the rest. The appeal to the prince in *Measure for Measure* answers exactly to the great Deus-ex-machinâ speech in *Tartuffe*, which relieves the leading characters from the nightmare that has oppressed them :—

> "Nous vivons sous un prince, ennemi de la fraude,
> Un prince dont les yeux se font jour dans les cœurs
> Et que ne peut tromper tout l'art des imposteurs."

In the seventeenth century kings were still the protectors of art and artists against moral and religious fanaticism.

XXI

*ACCESSION ·OF JAMES AND ANNE — RALEIGH'S FATE —
SHAKESPEARE'S COMPANY BECOME HIS MAJESTY'S
SERVANTS—SCOTCH INFLUENCE.*

IN *Measure for Measure* it is not only the monarchical tone of
the play, but some quite definite points, that mark it out as having been produced at the time of James's accession to the throne
in 1603. In the very first scene there is an allusion to the new
king's nervous dislike of crowds. This peculiarity, which caused
much surprise on the occasion of his entrance into England, is
here placed in a flattering light. The Duke says:—

> " I'll privily away : I love the people,
>   But do not like to stage me to their eyes.
>   Though it do well, I do not relish well
>   Their loud applause and Aves vehement,
>   Nor do I think the man of safe discretion
>   That does affect it."

It is also with unmistakable reference to James's antipathy
for a throng that Angelo, in Act ii. sc. 4, describes the crowding of the people round a beloved sovereign as an inadmissible
intrusion :—

> "So play the foolish throngs with one that swoons,
>   Come all to help him, and so stop the air
>   By which he should revive : and even so
>   The general, subject to a well-wish'd king,
>   Quit their own part, and in obsequious fondness
>   Crowd to his presence, where their untaught love
>   Must needs appear offence."

Elizabeth had breathed her last on the 24th of March 1603.
On her deathbed, when she could no longer speak, she had made
the shape of a crown above her head with her hands, to signify
that she chose as her successor one who was already a king.
Her ministers had long been in secret negotiation with James VI.
of Scotland, and had promised him the succession, in spite of a
provision in Henry VIII.'s will which excluded his elder sister's
Scottish descendants from the throne. This had to be set aside ;
for there was not in the younger line any personage of sufficient

distinction to be at all eligible. There was obvious advantage, too, in uniting the crowns of England and Scotland on one head; too long had the neighbour kingdoms wasted each other's energies in mutual feuds. All parties in the nation agreed with the ministers in looking to James as Elizabeth's natural successor. The Protestants felt confidence in him as a Protestant; the Catholics looked for better treatment from the son of the Catholic martyr-queen; the Puritans hoped that he, as a new and peace-loving king, would sanction such alterations in the statutory form of worship as should enable them to take part in it without injury to their souls. Great expectations greeted him.

Hardly was the breath out of Queen Elizabeth's body when Sir Robert Carey, a gentleman on whom she had conferred many benefits, but who, in his anxiety to ensure the new King's favour, had post-horses standing ready at every station, galloped off to be the first to bring the news to James in Edinburgh. On the way he was thrown from his horse, which kicked him on the head; but in spite of this he reached Holyrood on the evening of the 26th of March, just after the King had gone to bed. He was hurriedly conducted into the bed-chamber, where he knelt and greeted James by the title of King of England, Scotland, France, and Ireland. "Hee gave mee his hand to kisse," writes Carey, "and bade me welcome." He also promised Carey a place as Gentleman of the Bed-Chamber, and various other things, in reward for his zeal; but forgot all these promises as soon as he stood on English ground.

In London all preparations had been carefully made. A proclamation of James as King had been drawn up by Cecil during Elizabeth's lifetime, and sent to Scotland for James's sanction. This the Prime Minister read, a few hours after the Queen's death, to an assembly of the Privy Council and chief nobility, and a great crowd of the people, amidst universal approbation. Three heralds with a trumpeter repeated the proclamation in the Tower, "whereof as well prysoners as others rejoyced, namely, the Earle of Southampton, in whom all signes of great gladnesse appeared." Not without reason; for almost the first order James gave was that a courier should convey to Southampton the King's desire that he should at once join him and accompany him on his progress through England to London, where he was to receive the oath of allegiance and to be crowned.

On the 5th of April 1603, James I. of Great Britain left Edinburgh to take possession of his new kingdom. His royal progress was a very slow one, for every nobleman and gentleman whose house he passed invited him to enter; he accepted all invitations, spent day after day in festivities, and rewarded hospitality by distributing knighthoods in unheard-of and excessive numbers. One of his actions was unequivocally censured. At Newark "was taken a cutpurse doing the deed," and James had him hanged without trial or judgment. The displeasure shown made it plain to him that he could not thus assume superiority to the laws of England. In Scotland there had been a general demand for a strong monarchy, which could hold the nobles and the clergy in check; in England the day for this was over, and the new King's successors learned to their cost the futility of trying to carry on the traditions of despotism on English soil.

James himself was received with the naïve, disinterested joy with which the mass of the people are apt to greet a new monarch, of whose real qualities nothing is yet known, and with the less disinterested flatteries by which every one who came into contact with the King sought personal favour in his eyes.

There was nothing kingly or even winning in King James's exterior. Strange that the handsome Henry Darnley and the beautiful Mary Stuart should have had such an insignificant and ungainly son! He was something over middle height, indeed, but his figure was awkward, his head lumpish, and his eyes projecting. His language was the broadest Scotch, and when he opened his mouth it was rather to spit out the words than to speak; he hustled them out so that they stumbled over each other. He talked, ate, and dressed like a peasant, and, in spite of his apparently decorous life, was addicted to the broadest improprieties of talk, even in the presence of ladies. He walked like one who has no command over his limbs, and he could never keep still, even in a room, but was always pacing up and down with clumsy, sprawling movements. His muscles were developed by riding and hunting, but his whole appearance was wanting in dignity.

The shock inflicted on his mother during her pregnancy, by Rizzio's assassination, probably accounts for his dread of the sight of drawn steel. The terrorism in which he was brought up had increased his natural timidity. While he was yet but a youth, the French ambassador, Fontenay, summed up his description of him thus: "In one word, he is an old young man."

Now, in the thirty-sixth year of his age, he was a learned personage, full of prejudices, wanting neither in shrewdness nor in wit, but with two absorbing passions—the one for conversation on theological and ecclesiastical matters, and the other for hunting expeditions, to which he sometimes gave up so much as six consecutive days. He had not Elizabeth's political instinct; she had chosen her councillors among men of the most different parties; he admitted to his council none but those whose opinions agreed with his own. But his vanity was quite equal to hers. He had the pedant's boastfulness; he was fond of bragging, for instance, that he could do more work in one hour than others in a day; and he was especially proud of his learning. Some Shakespeare students have, as already observed, seen in him the prototype of Hamlet. He was certainly no Hamlet, but rather what Alfred Stern somewhere calls him—a Polonius on the throne. We have a description by Sir John Harington of an audience James gave him in 1604. The King "enquyrede muche of lernynge" in such a way as to remind him of "his examiner at Cambridge aforetyme," quoted scraps of Aristotle which he hardly understood himself, and made Harington read aloud part of a canto of Ariosto. Then he asked him what he "thoughte pure witte was made of," and whom it best became, and thereupon inquired whether he did not think a king ought to be "the beste clerke" in his country. Farther, "His Majestie did much presse for my opinion touchinge the power of Satane in matter of witchcraft, and . . . why the Devil did worke more with anciente women than others." This question Sir John boldly and wittily answered by reminding him of the preference for "walking in dry places" ascribed in Scripture to the Devil. James then told of the apparition of "a bloodie heade dancinge in the aire," which had been seen in Scotland before his mother's death, and concluded: "Now, sir, you have seen my wisdome in some sorte, and I have pried into yours. I praye you, do me justice in your reporte, and, in good season, I will not fail to add to your understandinge, in suche pointes as I may find you lacke amendmente." Perhaps only one European sovereign since James has so plumed himself on his own omniscience.

James's relations with England during Elizabeth's reign had not been invariably friendly. Nourishing a lively ill-will to the Presbyterian clergy, who were always trying to interfere in matters of state, he had in 1584, at the age of eighteen, appealed to the Pope for assistance for himself and his imprisoned mother. But the very next year, in consideration of the payment of a pension of £4000 a year, he concluded a treaty with Elizabeth. When this was ratified in 1586, his mother disinherited him and nominated Philip II. her successor. At the very time when the trial of Mary Stuart was going on, James made application to have his title as heir to the throne of England acknowledged. This unworthy, unchivalrous proceeding made it impossible for him in any way to interfere with the carrying out of whatever sentence the English Government chose to pronounce in his mother's case. Nevertheless her execution naturally affected him painfully, and it was his resentment that made him hasten on his long-planned marriage with the Danish princess Anne, daughter of Frederick II.—an alliance which he knew to be disagreeable to Elizabeth. He gained a political advantage by it, Denmark waiving her claim to the Orkney Islands.

His bride, born at Skanderborg towards the close of 1574, was at the time of her marriage not fifteen years old—a pretty, fair-skinned, golden-haired girl. Daughter of a Lutheran father and the Lutheran Sophia of Mecklenburg, she had been brought up in Lutheran orthodoxy. She had received some instruction in chemistry from Tycho Brahe; but her education, on the whole, had been rather that of a spoilt child. Great ideas had been instilled into her of what it meant to belong to the royal house of Denmark, so that she agreed with her future husband in a conviction of the importance of kingly state. Other features of her character were good-humour, inborn wit, and a superficial gaiety which sometimes went to unguarded lengths. Her behaviour, only three years after her marriage, gave rise to a scandal—public opinion (doubtless unjustly) making James accessory to the assassination of the Earl of Murray, whom it was supposed that he had good reasons for wishing out of the way.

The difficulties which beset Anne's voyage from Denmark to Scotland in 1589 are well known. A storm, for raising which many Danish "witches" and no fewer than two hundred luckless Scottish crones had to suffer at the stake, drove the bride to Oslo in Norway. The impatient bridegroom then undertook the one romantic adventure of his life and set off in search of her. He found her at Oslo, was married there, and spent the winter in Denmark.

As Queen of Scotland, Anne already showed herself possessed by the same mania for building which characterised her brother, Christian IV. As Queen of England she aroused dissatisfaction by her constant coquetting with Roman Catholicism. By her own wish, the Pope sent her gifts of all sorts of Catholic gimcracks; they were taken from her, and the bearer was consigned to the Tower. She showed a certain amiable independence in the sympathy and good-will which she displayed towards Sir Walter Raleigh, whom her husband imprisoned in the Tower; but on the whole she was an insignificant woman, pleasure-loving and pomp-loving (consequently a patroness of those poets who, like Ben Jonson, wrote masques for court festivals), and, in contrast to the economical Elizabeth, so extravagant that she was always in debt. Very soon after her arrival in England, she owed enormous sums to jewellers and other merchants.

The new King soon disappointed the hopes which Puritans and Catholics had cherished as to his tolerance. Even during the course of his journey from Edinburgh to London numerous petitions for the better treatment of Dissenters had been handed to him, and he seemed to give good promises to both parties. But as early as January 1604, on the occasion of a conference he summoned at Hampton Court, there was a rupture between him and the Puritans—the very mention of the word "Presbyter" making him furious. The formula, "No bishop, no king," though not invented by him, expressed his principles. And when the House of Commons favoured measures of a Puritan tendency, he retaliated by proroguing Parliament, after rebuking the House in undignified and boastful terms. He complained in this speech that whereas in Scotland he had been regarded "not only as a king but as a counsellor," in England, on the contrary, there was "nothing but curiosity from morning to evening to find fault with his propositions." "There all things warranted that came from me. Here all things suspected," &c. &c. The Puritan clergy, who refused to accept the Anglican ritual, were driven from their livings.

The Catholics fared still worse. James had at first intended to lighten the heavy penalties to which they were subject, but the discovery of Catholic conspiracies led him to change his mind. The Catholic priests and the pupils of the Jesuit schools were banished. After the discovery of Guy Fawkes's great Gunpowder Plot in 1605, the position of the Catholics naturally became as bad as possible.

One of the most marked traits in James's political character was his eagerness to bring about and preserve peace with Spain. While yet on the way to London, he ordered a cessation of all hostilities, and by 1604 he had concluded peace. One of the reasons for his at once assuming a hostile attitude towards Raleigh was that he was well acquainted with Raleigh's hatred of Spain and disinclination to peace with that country; and Raleigh increased the King's displeasure during the following months by constantly urging upon him a war policy. But there were other and less impersonal reasons for the King's hostility. Raleigh had been Elizabeth's favourite, and had in 1601 presented to her a state-paper drawn up by himself on "The Dangers of a Spanish Faction in Scotland," the rumoured contents of which had so alarmed James that he offered Elizabeth the assistance of three thousand Scottish troops against Spain. Raleigh had been an opponent of Essex, who had sought support from James and attached himself to his fortunes. And what was worse, he had an enemy, though he scarcely knew it, in the person of a man who had opposed Essex much more strongly than he, but who had, even before the Queen's death, assured James of his absolute devotion. This was Robert Cecil, who feared Raleigh's ambition and ability.

Raleigh was in the West of England when the Queen died, and could not at once join in the great rush northwards to meet King James, which emptied London of all its nobility. By the time he started, with a large retinue, to wait on the King, he had already received a kind of command not to do so, in the shape of one of the orders dispensing the recipient from attendance on the King, which James had sent in blank to Cecil, to be filled in with the names of those whom Cecil thought he should keep at a distance. James received Raleigh ungraciously, and at once told him, with a bad pun on his name, that he had been prejudiced against him: "On my soul, man, I have heard but *rawly* of thee." A few weeks later he was deprived (though not without compensation) of the office of Captain of the Guard, which was given to a

Scotchman, Sir Thomas Erskine; and within the same month he was ordered immediately to give up to the Bishop of Durham the town palace of that See, which he had occupied, and on which he had spent great sums of money.

At last, one day in July 1603, as he was standing ready to ride out with the King, he was arrested and imprisoned on a charge of high treason. This was the beginning of a long series of base proceedings against this eminent man, who had deserved so well of his country. He was a prisoner in the Tower for thirteen years, and the persecution ended only with the judicial murder which was committed when, in 1618, after making the most beautiful speech ever heard from the scaffold, he laid his head on the block with incomparable courage and calm dignity.

It is difficult for us to-day to understand how a man of Raleigh's worth could at that time be the best-hated man in England. For us he is simply, as Gardiner has expressed it, "the man who had more genius than all the Privy Council put together;" or, as Gosse has called him, "the figure which takes the same place in the field of action which Shakespeare takes in that of imagination and Bacon in that of thought." But that he was generally hated at the time of his imprisonment is certain.

Many disliked him as the enemy of Essex. It was said that in Essex's last hours Raleigh had jeered at him. Raleigh himself wrote in 1618 :—

"It is said I was a persecutor of my Lord of Essex; that I puffed out tobacco in disdain when he was on the scaffold. But I take God to witness I shed tears for him when he died. I confess I was of a contrary faction, but I knew he was a noble gentleman. Those that set me up against him [evidently Cecil] did afterwards set themselves against me."

But what mattered the falseness of the accusation if it was believed? And there were other, much less reasonable, grounds of hatred. From one of Raleigh's letters, written in the last days of Queen Elizabeth, we learn that the tavern-keepers throughout the country held him responsible for a tax imposed on them, which was in fact due solely to the Queen's rapacity. In this letter he prays Cecil to prevail on Elizabeth to remit the tax, for, says he: "I cannot live, nor show my face out of my doors, without it, nor dare ride through the towns where these taverners dwell." It seems as if his very greatness had marked him out for universal hatred; and, being conscious of his worth, he would not stoop to a truckling policy.

There was much that was popularly winning about the tall, vigorous, rather large-boned Raleigh, with his bright complexion and his open expression; but, like a true son of the Renaissance, he challenged dislike by his pride and magnificence. His dress was always splendid, and he loved, like a Persian Shah or Indian

Rajah of our day, to cover himself, down to his shoes, with the most precious jewels. When he was arrested in 1603, he had gems to the value of £4000 (about £20,000 in modern money) on his breast, and when he was thrown into prison for the last time in 1618, his pockets were found full of jewels and golden ornaments which he had hastily stripped off his dress.

He was worshipped by those who had served under him; they valued his qualities of heart as well as his energy and intellect. But the crowd, whom he treated with disdain, and the courtiers and statesmen with whom he had competed for Elizabeth's favour, saw nothing in him but matchless effrontery and unscrupulousness. In spite of the favour he enjoyed, his rivals prevented his ever attaining any of the highest posts. On those naval expeditions in which he most distinguished himself, his place was always second in command. He was baulked even in the desire which he cherished during Elizabeth's later years for a place in the Privy Council.

He was now over fifty, and aged before his time. His untrustworthy friend, Lord Cobham, was suspected of complicity in Watson's Catholic plot; and this suspicion extended to Raleigh, who was thought to have been a party to intrigues for the dethronement of James in favour of his kinswoman, Arabella Stuart. He was tried for high treason; and as the law then stood in England, any man accused of such a crime was as good as lost, however innocent he might be. "A century later," says Mr. Gardiner, "Raleigh might well have smiled at the evidence which was brought against him." Then the law was as cruel as it was unjust. The accused was considered guilty until he proved his innocence; no advocate was allowed to plead his cause; unprepared, at a moment's notice, he had to refute charges which had been carefully accumulated and marshalled against him during a long period. That a man should be suspected of such an enormity as desiring to bring Spanish armies on to the free soil of England was enough to deprive him at once of all sympathy. Little wonder that Raleigh, a few days after his indictment, tried to commit suicide. His famous letter to his wife, written before the attempt, gives consummate expression to a great man's despair in face of a destiny which he does not fear, yet cannot master.

While this tragedy was being enacted in the Tower, London was making magnificent preparations for the state entrance of King James and Queen Anne into their new capital. Seven beautiful triumphal arches were erected; "England's Cæsar," as Henry Petowe in his coronation ode with some little exaggeration entitled James, was exalted and glorified by the poets of the day with as great enthusiasm as though his exploits had already rivalled those of "mightiest Julius."

Henry Chettle wrote *The Shepheard's Spring Song for the*

Entertainment of King James, our most potent Sovereign; Samuel Daniel, *A Panegyrike Congratulatorie to the King's Majestie;* Michael Drayton, *To the Majestie of King James, a Gratulatorie Poem.* The actor Thomas Greene composed *A Poet's Vision and a Prince's Glorie. Dedicated to the high and mightie Prince James, King of England, Scotland, France and Ireland;* and scores of other poets lifted up their voices in song. Daniel wrote a masque which was acted at Hampton Court; Dekker, a description of the King's "Triumphant Passage," with poetic dialogues; Ben Jonson, a similar description; and Drayton, a *Pæan Triumphall.* Ben Jonson also produced a masque called *Penates,* and another entitled *The Masque of Blackness;* while a host of lesser lights wrote poems in the same style. The unobtrusive, mildly flattering allusions to James, which we have found and shall presently find in Shakespeare's plays of this period, produce an exceedingly feeble, almost imperceptible effect amid this storm of adulation. To have omitted them altogether, or to have made them in the slightest degree less deferential, would have been gratuitously and indefensibly churlish, in view of the favour which James had made haste to extend to Shakespeare's company.

It is most interesting to-day to read the programme of the royal procession from the Tower to Whitehall in 1604, in which all the dignitaries of the realm took part, and all the privileged classes, court, nobility, clergy, royal guard, were fully represented.

In the middle of the enormous procession rides the King under a canopy. Immediately before him, the dukes, marquises, eldest sons of dukes, earls, &c. &c. Immediately behind him comes the Queen, and after her all the first ladies of the kingdom—duchesses, marchionesses, countesses, viscountesses, &c. Among the ladies mentioned by name is Lady Rich, with the note, "by especiall comandement." At the foot of the page, another note runs thus: "To go as a daughter to Henry Bourchier, Earl of Essex." James desired to honour in her the memory of her ill-fated brother. Among the lawyers in the procession Sir Francis Bacon has a place of honour; he is described as "the King's Counsell at Lawe." Bacon's learning and obsequious pliancy, James's pedantry and monarchical arrogance, quickly brought these two together. But among "His Majesty's Servants," at the very head of the procession, immediately after the heralds and the Prince's and Queen's men-in-waiting, William Shakespeare was no doubt to be seen, dressed in a suit of red cloth, which the court accounts show to have been provided for him.

James was a great lover of the play, but Scotland had neither drama nor actors of her own. Not long before this, in 1599, he had vigorously opposed the resolution of his Presbyterian Council to forbid performances by English actors.

As early as May 17, 1603, he had granted the patent *Pro Laurentio Fletcher et Willielmo Shakespeare et aliis*, which promoted the Lord Chamberlain's company to be the King's own actors.

The fact that Lawrence Fletcher is named first gives us a clue to the reasons for this proceeding on the part of the King. In the records of the Town Council of Aberdeen for October 1601, there is an entry to the effect that, by special recommendation of the King, a gratuity was paid to a company of players for their performances in the town, and that the freedom of the city was conferred on one of these actors, Lawrence Fletcher. There can be hardly any doubt that Charles Knight, in spite of Elze's objections in his *Essays on Shakespeare*, is correct in his opinion that this Fletcher was an Englishman, and that he was closely connected with Shakespeare; for the actor Augustine Philipps, who, in 1605, bequeaths thirty shillings in gold to his "fellowe" William Shakespeare, likewise bequeaths twenty shillings to his "fellowe" Lawrence Fletcher.

James arrived in London on the 7th of May 1603, removed to Greenwich on account of the plague on the 13th, and, as already mentioned, dated the patent from there on the 17th. It can scarcely be supposed that, in so short a space of time, the Lord Chamberlain's men should not only have played before James, but so powerfully impressed him that he at once advanced them to be his own company. He must evidently have known them before; perhaps he already, as King of Scotland, had some of them in his service. This supposition is supported by the fact that, as we have seen, some members of Shakespeare's company were in Aberdeen in the autumn of 1601. It is even probable that Shakespeare himself was in Scotland with his comrades. In *Macbeth*, he has altered the meadow-land, which Holinshed represents as lying around Inverness, into the heath which is really characteristic of the district; and the whole play, with its numerous allusions to Scottish affairs, bears the impress of having been conceived on Scottish soil. Possibly Shakespeare's thoughts were hovering round the Scottish tragedy while he passed along in the procession with the royal arms on his red dress.[1]

[1] S. R. Gardiner: *History of England*, vol. i. Thomas Milner: *The History of England*. Alfred Stern: *Geschichte der Revolution in England*. Gosse: *Raleigh*. J. Nicols: *The Progresses, Processions, and Magnificent Festivities of King James the First*, vol. i. Disraeli: *An Inquiry into the Literary and Political Character of James the First*. *Dictionary of National Biography*: *James, Anne*. Nathan Drake: *Shakespeare and his Times*.

XXII

MACBETH—MACBETH AND HAMLET—DIFFICULTIES ARISING FROM THE STATE OF THE TEXT

DOWDEN somewhere remarks that if Shakespeare had died at the age of forty, posterity would have said that this was certainly a great loss, but would have found comfort in the thought that *Hamlet* marked the zenith of his productive power—he could hardly have written another such masterpiece.

And now follow in rapid succession *Macbeth, Othello, King Lear, Antony and Cleopatra,* and the rest. *Hamlet* was not the conclusion of a career; *Hamlet* was the spring-board from which Shakespeare leaped forth into a whole new world of mystery and awe. Dowden has happily compared the tragic figures that glide one after the other across his field of vision between 1604 and 1610 with the bloody and threatening apparitions that pass before Macbeth in the witches' cavern.

The natural tendency of his youth had been to see good everywhere. He had even felt, with his King Henry, that "there is some soul of goodness in things evil." Now, when the misery of life, the problem of evil, presented itself to his inward eye, it was especially the potency of wickedness that impressed him as strange and terrible. We have seen him brooding over it in *Hamlet* and *Measure for Measure.* He had of course recognised it before, and represented it on the grandest scale; but in *Richard III.* the main emphasis is still laid on outward history; Richard is the same man from his first appearance to his last. What now fascinates Shakespeare is to show how the man into whose veins evil has injected some drops of its poison, becomes bloated, gangrened, foredoomed to self-destruction or annihilation, like Macbeth, Othello, Lear. Lady Macbeth's ambition, Iago's malice, the daughters' ingratitude, lead, step by step, to irresistible, ever-increasing calamity.

It is my conviction that *Macbeth* was the first of these subjects which Shakespeare took in hand. All we know with certainty, indeed, is that the play was acted at the Globe Theatre in 1610. Dr. Simon Forman, in his *Booke of Plaies and Notes thereon,* gave a detailed account of a performance of it at which he was present on the 20th of April of this year. But in the comedy of

The Puritan, dating from 1607, we find an unmistakable allusion to Banquo's ghost; and the lines in the play itself (iv. 1)—

> "And some I see
> That twofold balls and treble sceptres carry,"

—a reference to the union of England and Scotland, and their conjunction with Ireland under James—would have had little effect unless spoken from the stage shortly after the event. As James was proclaimed King of Great Britain and Ireland on the 20th of October 1604, we may conclude that *Macbeth* was not produced later than 1604–1605.

At James's accession a breath of Scottish air blew over England; we feel it in *Macbeth.* The scene of the tragedy is laid in the country from which the new king came, and most true to nature is the reproduction in this dark drama of Scotland's forests and heaths and castles, her passions and her poetry.

There is much to indicate that an unbroken train of thought led Shakespeare from *Hamlet* to *Macbeth.* The personality of Macbeth is a sort of counterpart to that of Hamlet. The Danish prince's nature is passionate, but refined and thoughtful. Before the deed of vengeance which is imposed upon him he is restless, self-reproachful, and self-tormenting; but he never betrays the slightest remorse for a murder once committed, though he kills four persons before he stabs the King. The Scottish thane is the rough, blunt soldier, the man of action. He takes little time for deliberation before he strikes; but immediately after the murder he is attacked by hallucinations both of sight and hearing, and is hounded on, wild and vacillating and frenzied, from crime to crime. He stifles his self-reproaches and falls at last, after defending himself with the hopeless fury of the "bear tied to the stake."

Hamlet says :—

> "And thus the native hue of resolution
> Is sicklied o'er with the pale cast of thought."

Macbeth, on the contrary, declares (iv. 1)—

> "From this moment
> The very firstlings of my heart shall be
> The firstlings of my hand."

They stand at opposite poles—Hamlet, the dreamer; Macbeth, the captain, "Bellona's bridegroom." Hamlet has a superabundance of culture and of intellectual power. His strength is of the kind that wears a mask; he is a master in the art of dissimulation. Macbeth is unsophisticated to the point of clumsiness, betraying himself when he tries to deceive. His wife has to beg him not to show a troubled countenance, but to "sleek o'er his rugged looks."

Hamlet is the born aristocrat: very proud, keenly alive to his worth, very self-critical—too self-critical to be ambitious in the common acceptation of the word. To Macbeth, on the contrary, a sounding title is honour, and a wreath on the head, a crown on the brow, greatness. When the Witches on the heath, and another witch, his wife in the castle, have held up before his eyes the glory of the crown and the power of the sceptre, he has found his great goal—a tangible prize in this life, for which he is willing to risk his welfare in "the life to come." Whilst Hamlet, with his hereditary right, hardly gives a thought to the throne of which he has been robbed, Macbeth murders his king, his benefactor, his guest, that he may plunder him and his sons of a chair with a purple canopy.

And yet there is a certain resemblance between Macbeth and Hamlet. One feels that the two tragedies must have been written close upon each other. In his first monologue (i. 7) Macbeth stands hesitating with Hamlet-like misgivings:—

> " If it were done, when 't is done, then 't were well
> It were done quickly: if the assassination
> Could trammel up the consequence, and catch
> With his surcease success; that but this blow
> Might be the be-all and the end-all here,
> But here, upon this bank and shoal of time,—
> We'd jump the life to come.—But in these cases
> We still have judgment here."

Hamlet says: Were we sure that there is no future life, we should seek death. Macbeth thinks: Did we not know that judgment would come upon us here, we should care little about the life to come. There is a kinship in these contradictory reflections. But Macbeth is not hindered by his cogitations. He pricks the sides of his intent, as he says, with the spur of ambition, well knowing that it will o'erleap itself and fall. He cannot resist when he is goaded onward by a being superior to himself, a woman.

Like Hamlet, he has imagination, but of a more timorous and visionary cast. It is through no peculiar faculty in Hamlet that he sees his father's ghost; others had seen it before him and see it with him. Macbeth constantly sees apparitions that no one else sees, and hears voices that are inaudible to others.

When he has resolved on the king's death he sees a dagger in the air:—

> " Is this a dagger which I see before me,
> The handle toward my hand? Come, let me clutch thee :—
> I have thee not, and yet I see thee still.
> Art thou not, fatal vision, sensible
> To feeling, as to sight? or art thou but

A dagger of the mind, a false creation,
Proceeding from the heat-oppressed brain ? "

Directly after the murder he has an illusion of hearing :—

" Methought I heard a voice cry, 'Sleep no more !
Macbeth does murder sleep.' "

And, very significantly, Macbeth hears this same voice give
him the different titles which are his pride :—

" Still it cried, 'Sleep no more ! ' to all the house :
'Glamis hath murder'd sleep, and therefore Cawdor
Shall sleep no more, Macbeth shall sleep no more ! ' "

Yet another parallel shows the kinship between the Danish
and the Scottish tragedy. It is in these dramas alone that the
dead leave their graves and reappear on the scene of life ; in them
alone a breath from the spirit-world reaches the atmosphere of the
living. There is no trace of the supernatural either in *Othello* or
in *King Lear*.

No more here than in *Hamlet* are we to understand by the
introduction of supernatural elements that an independently-
working superhuman power actively interferes in human life ;
these elements are transparent symbols. Nevertheless the supernatural beings that make their appearance are not to be taken as
mere illusions; they are distinctly conceived as having a real
existence outside the sphere of hallucination. As in *Hamlet*, the
Ghost is not seen by the prince alone, so in *Macbeth* it is not
only Macbeth himself who sees the Witches ; they even appear
with their queen, Hecate, when there is no one to see them
except the spectators of the play.

It must not be forgotten that this whole spirit- and witch-
world meant something quite different to Shakespeare's contemporaries from what it means to us. We cannot even be
absolutely certain that Shakespeare himself did not believe in
the possible existence of such beings. Great poets have seldom
been consistent in their incredulity—even Holberg believed that
he had seen a ghost. But Shakespeare's own attitude of mind
matters less than that of the public for whom he wrote.

In the beginning of the seventeenth century the English people
still believed in a great variety of evil spirits, who disturbed the
order of nature, produced storms by land and sea, foreboded
calamities and death, disseminated plague and famine. They were
for the most part pictured as old, wrinkled women, who brewed
all kinds of frightful enormities in hellish cauldrons ; and when
such beldams were thought to have been detected, the law took
vengeance on them with fire and sword. In a sermon preached
in 1588, Bishop Jewel appealed to Elizabeth to take strong

measures against wizards and witches. Some years later, one Mrs. Dyer was accused of witchcraft for no other reason than that toothache had for some nights prevented the Queen from sleeping. In the small town of St. Osees in Essex alone, seventy or eighty witches were burnt. In a book called "The Discoverie of Witchcraft," published in 1584, Reginald Scott refuted the doctrine of sorcery and magic with wonderful clearness and liberal-mindedness; but his voice was lost in the chorus of the superstitious. King James himself was one of the most prominent champions of superstition. He was present in person at the trial by torture of two hundred witches who were burnt for occasioning the storm which prevented his bride's crossing to Scotland. Many of them confessed to having ridden through the air on broomsticks or invisible chariots drawn by snails, and admitted that they were able to make themselves invisible—an art of which they, strangely enough, did not avail themselves to escape the law. In 1597 James himself produced in his *Dæmonologie* a kind of handbook or text-book of witchcraft in all its developments, and in 1598 he caused no fewer than 600 old women to be burnt. In the Parliament of 1604 a bill against sorcery was brought in by the Government and passed.

Shakespeare produced wonderful effects in *Hamlet* by drawing on this faith in spirits; the apparition on the castle platform is sublime in its way, though the speech of the Ghost is far too long. Now, in *Macbeth*, with the Witches' meeting, he strikes the keynote of the drama at the very outset, as surely as with a tuning-fork; and wherever the Witches reappear the same note recurs. But still more admirable, both psychologically and scenically, is the scene in which Macbeth sees Banquo's ghost sitting in his own seat at the banquet-table. The words run thus:—

> "*Rosse.*   Please it your highness
> To grace us with your royal company?
> *Macbeth.* The table's full.
> *Lennox.*   Here is a place reserv'd, sir.
> *Macb.* Where?
> *Len.* Here, my good lord. What is't that moves your highness?
> *Macb.* Which of you have done this?
> *Lords.*   What, my good lord?
> *Macb.* Thou canst not say I did it: never shake
> Thy gory locks at me."

The grandeur, depth, and extraordinary dramatic and theatrical effect of this passage are almost unequalled in the history of the drama.

The same may be said of well-nigh the whole outline of this tragedy—from a dramatic and theatrical point of view it is beyond all praise. The Witches on the heath, the scene before the murder of Duncan, the sleep-walking of Lady Macbeth—so potent is the effect of these and other episodes that they are burnt for ever on the spectator's memory.

No wonder that *Macbeth* has become in later times Shakespeare's most popular tragedy—his typical one, appreciated even by those who, except in this instance, have not been able to value him as he deserves. Not one of his other dramas is so simple in composition as this, no other keeps like this to a single plane. There is no desultoriness or halting in the action as in *Hamlet*, no double action as in *King Lear*. All is quite simple and according to rule: the snowball is set rolling and becomes the avalanche. And although there are gaps in it on account of the defective text, and although there may here and there be ambiguities—in the character of Lady Macbeth, for instance— yet there is nothing enigmatic, there are no riddles to perplex us. Nothing lies concealed between the lines; all is grand and clear—grandeur and clearness itself.

And yet I confess that this play seems to me one of Shakespeare's less interesting efforts; not from the artistic, but from the purely human point of view. It is a rich, highly moral melodrama; but only at occasional points in it do I feel the beating of Shakespeare's heart.

My comparative coolness of feeling towards *Macbeth* may possibly be due in a considerable degree to the shamefully mutilated form in which this tragedy has been handed down to us. Who knows what it may have been when it came from Shakespeare's own hand! The text we possess, which was not printed till long after the poet's death, is clipped, pruned, and compressed for acting purposes. We can feel distinctly where the gaps occur, but that is of no avail.

The abnormal shortness of the play is in itself an indication of what has happened. In spite of its wealth of incident, it is distinctly Shakespeare's shortest work. There are 3924 lines in *Hamlet*, 3599 in *Richard III.*, &c., &c., while in *Macbeth* there are only 1993.

It is plain, moreover, that the structure of the piece has been tampered with. The dialogue between Malcolm and Macduff (iv. 3), which, strictly speaking, must be called superfluous from the dramatic point of view, is so long as to form about an eighth part of the whole tragedy. It may be presumed that the other scenes originally stood in some sort of proportion to this; for there is no other instance in Shakespeare's work of a similar disproportion.

In certain places omissions are distinctly felt. Lady Macbeth (i. 5) proposes to her husband that he shall murder Duncan. He gives no answer to this. In the next scene the King arrives. In the next again, Macbeth's deliberations as to whether or not he is to commit the murder are all over, and he is only thinking how it can be done with impunity. When he wavers, and says to his wife, "I dare do all that may become a man; who dares do more is none," her answer shows how much is wanting here:—

> "When you durst do it, then you were a man;
> And, to be more than what you were, you would
> Be so much more the man. Nor time nor place
> Did then adhere, and yet you would make both."

We spectators or readers know nothing of all this. There has not even been time for the shortest conversation between husband and wife.

Shakespeare took the material for his tragedy from the same source on which he drew for all his English histories—Holinshed's Chronicle to wit. In this case Holinshed, at no time a trustworthy historian, simply reproduced a passage of Hector Boece's *Scotorum Historiæ*. Macdonwald's rebellion and Sweno's Viking invasion are fables; Banquo and Fleance, as founders of the race of Stuart, are inventions of the chroniclers. There was a blood-feud between the house of Duncan and the house of Macbeth. Lady Macbeth, whose real name was Gruoch, was the granddaughter of a king who had been killed by Malcolm II., Duncan's grandfather. Her first husband had been burnt in his castle with fifty friends. Her only brother was killed by Malcolm's order. Macbeth's father also, Finlegh or Finley, had been killed in a contest with Malcolm. Therefore they both had the right to a blood-revenge on Duncan. Nor did Macbeth sin against the laws of hospitality in taking Duncan's life. He attacked and killed him in the open field. It is further to be observed that by the Scottish laws of succession he had a better right to the throne than Duncan. After having seized the throne he ruled firmly and justly. There is a quite adequate psychological basis for the real facts of the year 1040, though it is much simpler than that underlying the imaginary events of Holinshed's Chronicle, which form the subject of the tragedy.

Shakespeare on the whole follows Holinshed with great exactitude, but diverges from him in one or two particulars. According to the Chronicle, Banquo was accessory to the murder of Duncan; Shakespeare alters this in order to give King James a progenitor of unblemished reputation. Instead of using the account of the murder which is given in the Chronicle, Shakespeare takes and applies to Duncan's case all the particulars of the murder of King Duffe, Lady Macbeth's grandfather, as committed by the captain of the castle of Forres, who "being the more kindled in wrath by the words of his wife, determined to follow her advice in the execution of so heinous an act." It is hardly necessary to remark that the finest parts of the drama, such as the appearance of Banquo's ghost and Lady Macbeth's sleep-walking scene, are due to Shakespeare alone.

Some sensation was made in the year 1778 by the discovery

ot the manuscript of *The Witch*, a play by Shakespeare's contemporary Middleton, containing in their entirety two songs which are only indicated in *Macbeth* by the quotation of their first lines. These are "Come away, come away" (iii. 5), and "Black spirits, &c." (iv. 1). A very idle dispute arose as to whether Shakespeare had here made use of Middleton or Middleton of Shakespeare. The latter is certainly the more probable assumption, if we must assume either to have borrowed from the other. It is likely enough, however, that single lines of the lesser poet have here and there been interpolated in the witch scenes of Shakespeare's text as contained in the Folio edition.

Shakespeare has employed in the treatment of this subject a style that suits it—vehement to violence, compressed to congestion—figures treading upon each other's heels, while general philosophic reflections occur but rarely. It is a style eminently fitted to express and to awaken terror; its tone is not altered, but only softened, even in the painfully touching conversation between Lady Macduff and her little son. It is sustained throughout with only one break—the excellent burlesque monologue of the Porter.

The play centres entirely round the two chief characters, Macbeth and Lady Macbeth; in their minds the essential action takes place. The other personages are only outlined.

The Witches' song, with which the tragedy opens, ends with that admirable line, in which ugliness and beauty are confounded:—

> " Fair is foul, and foul is fair."

And it is significant that Macbeth, who has not heard this refrain, recalls it in his very first speech :—

> "So foul and fair a day I have not seen."

It seems as if these words were ringing in his ears ; and this foreshadows the mysterious bond between him and the Witches. Many of these delicate consonances and contrasts may be noted in the speeches of this tragedy.

After Lady Macbeth, who is introduced to the spectator already perfected in wickedness, has said to herself (i. 5)—

> " The raven himself is hoarse,
> That croaks the fatal entrance of Duncan
> Under my battlements,"

the next scene opens serenely with the charming pictures of the following dialogue :—

> " *Duncan.* This castle hath a pleasant seat ; the air
> Nimbly and sweetly recommends itself
> Unto our gentle senses.

Banquo.   This guest of summer,
The temple-haunting martlet, does approve,
By his lov'd mansionry, that the heaven's breath
Smells wooingly here: no jutty, frieze,
Buttress, nor coign of vantage, but this bird
Hath made his pendent bed and procreant cradle:
Where they most breed and haunt, I have observ'd
The air is delicate."

Then the poet immediately plunges anew into the study of this
lean, slight, hard woman, consumed by lust of power and splendour.   Though by no means the impassive murderess she fain
would be, she yet goads her husband, by the force of her far
stronger will, to commit the crime which she declares he has
promised her :—

"I have given suck, and know
How tender 'tis to love the babe that milks me:
I would, while it was smiling in my face,
Have pluck'd my nipple from its boneless gums,
And dash'd the brains out, had I so sworn as you
Have done to this."

So coarsely callous is she!   And yet she is less hardened than
she would make herself out to be ; for when, just after this, she has
laid the daggers ready for her husband, she says :—

" Had he not resembled
My father as he slept, I had done 't."

The absolutely masterly, thrilling scene between husband and
wife after the murder, is followed, in horrible, humoristic contrast,
by the fantastic interlude of the Porter.   He conceives himself to
be keeping watch at hell-gate, and admitting, amongst others, an
equivocating Jesuit, with his casuistry and *reservatio mentalis ;*
and his soliloquy is followed by a dialogue with Macduff on the
influence of drink upon erotic inclination and capacity.   It is
well known that Schiller, in accordance with classical prejudices,
omitted the monologue in his translation, and replaced it by a
pious morning-song.   What seems more remarkable is that an
English poet like Coleridge should have found its effect disturbing and considered it spurious.   Without exactly ranking with
Shakespeare's best low-comedy interludes, it affords a highly
effective contrast to what goes before and what follows, and is
really an invaluable and indispensable ingredient in the tragedy.
A short break in the action was required at this point, to give
Macbeth and his wife time to dress themselves in their night-
clothes ; and what interruption could be more effective than the
knocking at the castle gate, which makes them both thrill with
terror, and gives occasion to the Porter episode ?
Another of the gems of the play is the scene (iv. 2) between

Lady Macduff and her wise little son, before the murderers come
and kill them both. All the witty child's sayings are interesting, and the mother's bitterly pessimistic speeches are not only
wonderfully characteristic of her, but also of the poet's own present frame of mind :—

> "Whither should I fly?
> I have done no harm. But I remember now
> I am in this earthly world, where, to do harm,
> Is often laudâble ; to do good, sometime,
> Accounted dangerous folly : why then, alas !
> Do I put up that womanly defence,
> To say I have done no harm ? "

Equally despairing is Macduff's ejaculation when he learns of
the slaughter in his home : " Did heaven look on, and would not
take their part ? " The beginning of this lengthy scene (iv. 3), with
its endless dialogue between Malcolm and Macduff, which Shakespeare has transcribed literally from his Holinshed, is weak and
flagging. It presents hardly any point of interest except the far-
fetched account of King Edward the Confessor's power of curing
the king's evil, evidently dragged in for the sake of paying King
James a compliment which the poet knew he would value, in the
lines—

> " 'Tis spoken,
> To the succeeding royalty he leaves
> The healing benediction."

But the close of the scene is admirable, when Rosse breaks the
news to Macduff of the attack on his castle and the massacre
of his family :—

> " *Macd.* My children too ?
> *Rosse.*   Wife, children, servants, all
> That could be found.
> *Macd.*   And I must be from thence !
> My wife kill'd too ?
> *Rosse.*   I have said.
> *Mal.*   Be comforted :
> Let's make us medicines of our great revenge,
> To cure this deadly grief.
> *Macd.* He has no children.—All my pretty ones ?
> Did you say, all ?—O hell-kite !—All ?
> What, all my pretty chickens, and their dam,
> At one fell swoop ?
> *Mal.* Dispute it like a man.
> *Macd.*   I shall do so ;
> But I must also feel it as a man :
> I cannot but remember such things were,
> That were most precious to me.—*Did Heaven look on,*
> *And would not take their part ?* "

The voice of revolt makes itself heard in these words, the same voice that sounds later through the despairing philosophy of *King Lear:* "As flies to wanton boys, are we to the gods: They kill us for their sport." But immediately afterwards Macduff falls back on the traditional sentiment :—

> " Sinful Macduff!
> They are all struck for thee. Naught that I am,
> Not for their own demerits, but for mine,
> Fell slaughter on their souls."

Among these horror-stricken speeches there is one in particular that gives matter for reflection—Macduff's cry, " He has no children." At the close of the third part of *Henry VI.* there is a similar exclamation of quite different import. There, when King Edward, Gloucester, and Clarence have stabbed Margaret of Anjou's son before her eyes, she says :—

> "You have no children, butchers! if you had,
> The thought of them would have stirr'd up remorse."

Many interpreters have attributed the same sense to Macduff's cry of agony; but their mistake is plain; for the context undeniably shows that the one thought of the now childless father is the impossibility of an adequate revenge.

But there is another noticeable point about this speech, " He has no children," which is, that elsewhere we are led to believe that he has children. Lady Macbeth says, " I have given suck, and know how tender 'tis to love the babe that milks me ;" and we have neither learned that these children are dead nor that they were born of an earlier marriage. Shakespeare never mentions the former marriage of the historical Lady Macbeth. Furthermore, not only does she talk of children, but Macbeth himself seems to allude to sons. He says (iii. 1) :—

> " Upon my head they plac'd a fruitless crown,
> And put a barren sceptre in my gripe,
> Thence to be wrench'd with an unlineal hand,
> No son of mine succeeding. If't be so,
> For Banquo's issue have I filed my mind."

If he had no children of his own, the last line is meaningless. Had Shakespeare forgotten these earlier speeches when he wrote that ejaculation of Macduff's? It is improbable; and, in any case, they must have been constantly brought to his mind again at rehearsals and performances of the play. We have here one of the difficulties which would be solved if we were in possession of a complete and authentic text.

The crown which the Witches promised to Macbeth soon becomes his fixed idea. He murders his king—and sleep. He slays, and sees the slain for ever before him. All that stand

between him and his ambition are cut down, and afterwards raise
their bloody heads as bodeful visions on his path. He turns
Scotland into one great charnel-house. His mind is "full of
scorpions;" he is sick with the smell of all the blood he has
shed. At last life and death become indifferent to him. When,
on the day of battle, the tidings of his wife's death are brought to
him, he speaks those profound words in which Shakespeare has
embodied a whole melancholy life-philosophy:—

> " She should have died hereafter :
> There would have been a time for such a word.—
> To-morrow, and to-morrow, and to-morrow,
> Creeps in this petty pace from day to day,
> To the last syllable of recorded time ;
> And all our yesterdays have lighted fools
> The way to dusty death. Out, out, brief candle !
> Life's but a walking shadow ; a poor player,
> That struts and frets his hour upon the stage,
> And then is heard no more : it is a tale
> Told by an idiot, full of sound and fury,
> Signifying nothing."

This is the final result arrived at by Macbeth, the man who
staked all to win power and glory. Without any underlining on
the part of the poet, a speech like this embodies an absolute
moral lesson. We feel its value all the more strongly, as Shakespeare's study of humanity in other parts of this play does not
seem to have been totally unbiassed, but rather influenced by the
moral impression which he desired to produce on the audience.
The drama is even a little marred by the constant insistence on
the *fabula docet*, the recurrent insinuation that "such is the
consequence of grasping at power by the aid of crime." Macbeth,
not by nature a bad man, might in the drama, as in real life, have
tried to reconcile the people to that crime, which, after all, he had
reluctantly committed, by making use of his power to rule well.
The moral purport of the play excludes this possibility. The
ice-cold, stony Lady Macbeth might be conceived as taking the
consequences of her counsel and action as calmly as the high-
born Locustas of the Renaissance, Catherine de' Medici, or the
Countess of Somerset. But in this case we should have missed
the moral lesson conveyed by her ruin, and, what would have
been worse, the incomparable sleep-walking scene, which—
whether it be perfectly motived or not—shows us in the most
admirable manner how the sting of an evil conscience, even
though it may be blunted by day, is sharpened again at night,
and robs the guilty one of sleep and health.

In dealing with the plays immediately preceding *Macbeth*, we
observed that Shakespeare at this period frequently gives a
formal exposition of the moral to be drawn from his scenes.

Possibly there is some connection between this tendency of his and the steadily-growing animosity of public opinion to the stage. In the year 1606, an edict was issued absolutely prohibiting the utterance of the name of God on the profane boards of the theatre. Not even a harmless oath was to be permitted. In view of the state of feeling which produced such an Act of Parliament, it must have been of vital importance to the tragic poet to prove as clearly as possible the strictly moral character of his works.

XXIII

OTHELLO—THE CHARACTER AND SIGNIFICANCE OF IAGO

WHEN we consider how *Macbeth* explains life's tragedy as the result of a union of brutality and malignity, or rather of brutality envenomed by malignity, we feel that the step from this to *Othello* is not a long one. But in *Macbeth* the treatment of life's tragedy as a whole, of wickedness as a factor in human affairs, lacks firmness, and is not in the great style.

In a very much grander and firmer style do we find the same subject treated in *Othello*.

Othello is, in the popular conception, simply the tragedy of jealousy, as *Macbeth* is simply the tragedy of ambition. Naïve readers and critics fancy in their innocence that Shakespeare, at a certain period of his life, determined to study one or two interesting and dangerous passions, and to put us on our guard against them. Following out this intention, he wrote a play on ambition and its dangers, and another of the same kind on jealousy and all the evils that attend it. But that is not how things happen in the inner life of a creative spirit. A poet does not write exercises on a given subject. His activity is not the result of determination or choice. A nerve in him is touched, vibrates, and reacts.

What Shakespeare here attempts to realise is neither jealousy nor credulity, but simply and solely the tragedy of life; whence does it arise? what are its causes? what its laws?

He was deeply impressed with the power and significance of evil. *Othello* is much less a study of jealousy than a new and more powerful study of wickedness in its might. The umbilical cord that connects the master with his work leads, not to the character of Othello, but to that of Iago.

Simple-minded critics have been of opinion that Shakespeare constructed Iago on the lines of the historic Richard III.—that is to say, found him in literature, in the pages of a chronicler.

Believe me, Shakespeare met Iago in his own life, saw portions and aspects of him on every hand throughout his manhood, encountered him piecemeal, as it were, on his daily path, till one fine day, when he thoroughly felt and understood what malignant cleverness and baseness can effect, he melted down all these fragments, and out of them cast this figure.

Iago—there is more of the grand manner in this figure than in the whole of *Macbeth*. Iago—there is more depth, more penetrating knowledge of human nature in this one character than in the whole of *Macbeth*. Iago is the very embodiment of the grand manner.

He is not the principle of evil, not an old-fashioned, stupid devil; nor a Miltonic devil, who loves independence and has invented firearms; nor a Goethe's Mephistopheles, who talks cynicism, makes himself indispensable, and is generally in the right. Neither has he the magnificently foolhardy wickedness of a Cæsar Borgia, who lives his life in open defiance and reckless atrocity.

Iago has no other aim than his own advantage. It is the circumstance that not he, but Cassio, has been appointed second in command to Othello, which first sets his craft to work on subtle combinations. He coveted this post, and he will stick at nothing in order to win it. In the meantime, he takes advantage of every opportunity of profit that offers itself; he does not hesitate to fool Roderigo out of his money and his jewels. He is always masked in falsehood and hypocrisy; and the mask he has chosen is the most impenetrable one, that of rough outspokenness, the straightforward, honest bluntness of the soldier who does not care what others think or say of him. He never flatters Othello or Desdemona, or even Roderigo. He is the free-spoken, honest friend.

He does not seek his own advantage without side-glances at others. He is mischievousness personified. He does evil for the pleasure of hurting, and takes active delight in the adversity and anguish of others. He is that eternal envy which merit or success in others never fails to irritate—not the petty envy which is content with coveting another's honours or possessions, or with holding itself more deserving of another's good fortune. No; he is an ideal personification. He is blear-eyed rancour itself, figuring as a great power—nay, as *the* motive force—in human life. He embodies the detestation for others' excellences which shows itself in obstinate disbelief, suspicion, or contempt; the instinct of hatred for all that is open, beautiful, bright, good, and great.

Shakespeare not only knew that such wickedness exists; he seized it and set his stamp on it, to his eternal honour as a psychologist.

Every one has heard it said that this tragedy is magnificent in so far as the true and beautiful characters of Othello and Desdemona are concerned; but Iago—who knows him?—what motive underlies his conduct?—what can explain such wickedness? If only he had even been frankly in love with Desdemona and therefore hated Othello, or had had some other incentive of a like nature!

Yes, if he had been the ordinary amorous villain and slanderer, everything would undoubtedly have been much simpler; but, at the same time, everything would have sunk into banality, and Shakespeare would here have been unequal to himself.

No, no! precisely in this lack of apparent motive lies the profundity and greatness of the thing. Shakespeare understood this. Iago in his monologues is incessantly giving himself reasons for his hatred. Elsewhere, in reading Shakespeare's monologues, we learn what the person really is; he reveals himself directly to us; even a villain like Richard III. is quite honest in his monologues. Not so Iago. This demi-devil is always trying to give himself reason for his malignity, is always half fooling himself by dwelling on half motives, in which he partly believes, but disbelieves in the main. Coleridge has aptly designated this action of his mind: "The motive-hunting of a motiveless malignity." Again and again he expounds to himself that he believes Othello has been too familiar with his wife, and that he will avenge the dishonour. He now and then adds, to account for his hatred of Cassio, that he suspects him too of tampering with Emilia.[1] He even thinks it worth while to allege, as a secondary motive, that he himself is enamoured of Desdemona. His words are (ii. 1):—

> "Now, I do love her too;
> Not out of absolute lust, (though, peradventure,
> I stand accountant for as great a sin,)
> But partly led to diet my revenge,
> For that I do suspect the lusty Moor
> Hath leap'd into my seat."

These are half-sincere attempts at self-understanding, sophistical self-justifications. Yellow-green, venomous envy has always a motive in its own eyes, and tries to make its malignity towards the better man pass muster as a desire for righteous vengeance. But Iago, who, a few lines before, has himself said of Othello that he is "of a constant, loving, noble nature," is a thousand times too clever to believe that he has been wronged by him. The Moor is, to his eyes, transparent as glass.

---

[1] He says (i. 3):—

> "I hate the Moor,
> And it is thought abroad, that 'twixt my sheets
> 'Has done my office. I know not if 't be true;
> But I for mere suspicion in that kind
> Will do as if for surety."

He adds (ii. 7):—

> "I'll have our Michael Cassio on the hip,
> Abuse him to the Moor in the rank garb,
> For I fear Cassio with my night-cap too."

An ordinary human capacity for love or hatred springing from a definite cause would degrade and detract from Iago's supremacy in evil. In the end, he is sentenced to torture, because he will not vouchsafe a word of explanation or enlightenment. Hard and, in his way, proud as he is, he will certainly keep his lips tightly closed under the torture; but even if he wanted to speak, it would not be in his power to give any real explanation. He has slowly, steadily poisoned Othello's nature. We watch the working of the venom on the simple-hearted man, and we see how the very success of the poisoning process brutalises and intoxicates Iago more and more. But to ask whence the poison came into Iago's soul would be a foolish question, and one to which he himself could give no answer. The serpent is poisonous by nature; it gives forth poison as the silkworm does its thread and the violet its fragrance.

Towards the close of the tragedy (iv. 2) there occurs one of its profoundest passages, which shows us how Shakespeare must have dwelt upon and studied the potency of evil during these years. After Emilia has witnessed the breaking out of Othello's mad rage against Desdemona, she says—

> "*Emil.* I will be hang'd, if some eternal villain,
> Some busy and insinuating rogue,
> Some cogging, cozening slave, to get some office,
> Have not devis'd this slander; I'll be hang'd else.
> *Iago.* Fie! there is no such man: it is impossible.
> *Des.* If any such there be, Heaven pardon him!
> *Emil.* A halter pardon him, and hell gnaw his bones!"

All three characters stand out in clear relief in these short speeches. But Iago's is the most significant. His "Fie! there is no such man; it is impossible," expresses the thought under shelter of which he has lived and is living: other people do not believe that such a being exists.

Here we meet once more in Shakespeare the astonishment of Hamlet at the paradox of evil, and once more, too, the indirect appeal to the reader which formed the burden, as it were, of *Hamlet* and *Measure for Measure*, the now thrice-repeated, "Say not, think not, that this is impossible!" The belief in the impossibility of utter turpitude is the very condition of existence of such a king as Claudius, such a magistrate as Angelo, such an officer as Iago. Hence Shakespeare's "Verily I say unto you, this highest degree of wickedness is possible in the world."

It is one of the two factors in life's tragedy. Stupidity is the other. On these two foundations rests the great mass of all this world's misery.

XXIV

OTHELLO—THE THEME AND ITS TREATMENT—
A MONOGRAPH IN THE GREAT STYLE

A MANUSCRIPT preserved in the Record Office, of doubtful date, but probably copied from an authentic document, contains the following entry :—

The plaiers	1605	The Poets wch
By the Kings	Hallamas Day being the	mayd the plaies
Maties plaiers	first of November A play	
	in the Banketing house	Shaxberd.
	att withall called the	
	Moore of Venis.	

Thus *Othello* was probably produced in the autumn of 1605. After this we have no proof of its performance till four and a half years later, when we hear of it again in the journal of Prince Ludwig Friedrich of Würtemberg, written by his secretary, Hans Wurmsser. The entry for the 30th of April 1610 runs thus :—

"Lundi, 30. S. E[minence] alla au Globe, lieu ordinaire ou l'on Joue les Commedies, y fut representé l'histoire du More de Venise."

In face of these data it matters nothing that there should appear in *Othello*, as we have it, a line that must have been written in or after 1611. The tragedy was printed for the first time in a quarto edition in 1622, for the second time in the Folio of 1623. The Folio text contains an additional 160 lines (proving that another manuscript has been made use of), and all oaths and mentions of the name of God are omitted. It is not only possible, but certain, that this line must have been a late interpolation. Its entire discordance with its position in the play shows this clearly enough, and seems to me to render it doubtful whether it is by Shakespeare at all.

In the scene where Othello bids Desdemona give him her hand, and loses himself in reflections upon it (iii. 4), he makes this speech :—

> " A liberal hand : the hearts of old gave hands ;
> But our new heraldry is hands, not hearts."

Here there is an allusion, which could only be understood by contemporaries, to the title of Baronet, created and sold by James, which gave its possessors the right of bearing in their coat-of-arms a bloody hand on a field argent. Most naturally Desdemona replies to this irrelevant remark: "I cannot speak of this."

In Cinthio's Italian collection of tales, where he had found the plot of *Measure for Measure*, Shakespeare at the same time (in Decade 3, Novella 7) came upon the material for *Othello*. The story in the *Hecatommitti* runs as follows: A young Venetian lady named Disdemona falls in love with a Moor, a military commander—"not from feminine desire," but because of his great qualities—and marries him in spite of the opposition of her relatives. They live in Venice in complete happiness; "no word ever passed between them that was not loving." When the Moor is ordered to Cyprus to take command there, his one anxiety is about his wife; he is equally unwilling to expose her to the dangers of the sea voyage and to leave her alone. She settles the question by declaring that she will rather follow him anywhere, into any danger, than live in safety apart from him; whereupon he rapturously kisses her, with the ejaculation: "May God long preserve you so loving, my dearest wife!" Thus the perfect initial harmony between the pair which Shakespeare depicts is suggested by his original.

The Ensign undermines their happiness. He is described as remarkably handsome, but "as wicked by nature as any man that ever lived in the world." He was dear to the Moor, "who had no idea of his baseness." For although he was an arrant coward, he managed by means of proud and blusterous talk, aided by his fine appearance, so to conceal his cowardice that he passed for a Hector or Achilles. His wife, whom he had taken with him to Cyprus, was a fair and virtuous young woman, much beloved by Disdemona, who spent the greater part of the day in her company. The Lieutenant (*il capo di squadra*) came much to the Moor's house, and often supped with him and his wife.

The wicked Ensign is passionately in love with Disdemona, but all his attempts to win her love are entirely unsuccessful, as she has not a thought for any one but the Moor. The Ensign, however, imagines that the reason for her rejection of him must be that she is in love with the Lieutenant, and therefore determines to rid himself of this rival, while his love for Disdemona is changed into the bitterest hatred. From this time forward, his object is not only to bring about the death of the Lieutenant, but to prevent the Moor from finding the pleasure in Disdemona's love which is denied to himself. He goes to work as in the drama, though of course with some differences of detail. In the novel, for example, the Ensign steals Disdemona's handkerchief whilst she is visiting his wife, and playing with their little girl.

Disdemona's death-scene is more horrible in the tale than in the tragedy. By command of the Moor, the Ensign hides himself in a room adjoining Othello's and Disdemona's bedchamber. He makes a noise, and Disdemona rises to see what it is; whereupon the Ensign gives her a violent blow on the head with a stocking filled with sand. She calls to her husband for help, but he answers by accusing her of infidelity; she in vain protests her innocence, and dies at the third blow of the stocking. The murder is concealed, but the Moor now begins to hate his Ensign, and dismisses him. The Ensign is so exasperated by this, that he lets the Lieutenant know who is responsible for the night assault that has just been made upon him. The Lieutenant accuses the Moor before the council, and Othello is put to torture. He refuses to confess, and is sent into banishment. The wicked Ensign, who has brought a false accusation of murder against one of his comrades, is himself in turn accused by the innocent man, and subjected to torture until he dies.

To the characters in the novel, Shakespeare has added two, Brabantio and Roderigo. Only one of the names he uses is found in the original. Disdemona, which seems made to designate the victim of an evil destiny, Shakespeare has changed into the sweeter-sounding Desdemona. The other names are of Shakespeare's own choosing. Most of them are Italian (Othello itself is a Venetian noble name of the sixteenth century); others, such as Iago and Roderigo, are Spanish.

With his customary adherence to his original, Shakespeare, like Cinthio, calls his protagonist a Moor; but it is quite unreasonable to suppose from this that he thought of him as a negro. It was, of course, inconceivable that a negro should attain the rank of general and admiral in the service of the Venetian Republic; and Iago's mention of Mauritania as the country to which Othello intends to retire, shows plainly enough that the "Moor" ought to be represented as an Arab. It is no argument against this that men who hate and envy him apply to him epithets that would befit a negro. Thus Roderigo in the first scene of the play calls him "thick-lips," and Iago, speaking to Brabantio, calls him "an old black ram." But a little later Iago compares him with "a Barbary horse"—that is to say, an Arab from North Africa. It is always animosity and hate that exaggerate the darkness of his hue, as when Brabantio talks of his "sooty bosom." That Othello calls himself *black* only means that he is dark. In this very play Iago says of dark women:

> "If she be *black*, and thereto have a wit,
> She'll find a white that shall her *blackness* fit."

And we have seen how, in the Sonnets and in *Love's Labour's Lost*, "black" is constantly employed in the sense of dark-complexioned. As a Moor, Othello has a complexion sufficiently swarthy to form a striking contrast to the white and even blonde Desdemona, and there is also a sufficiently marked race-contrast between him, as a Semite, and the Aryan girl. It is quite conceivable, too, that a Christianised Moor should reach a high position in the army and fleet of the Republic.

It ought further to be noted that the whole tradition of the Venetian "Moor" has possibly arisen from a confusion of words. Rawdon Browne, in 1875, suggested the theory that Giraldi had founded his tale on the simple misunderstanding of a name. In the history of Venice we read of an eminent patrician, Christoforo Moro by name, who in 1498 was Podestà of Ravenna, and afterwards held similar office in Faenza, Ferrara, and the Romagna; then became Governor of Cyprus; in 1508 commanded fourteen ships; and later still was Proveditore of the army. When this man was returning from Cyprus to Venice in 1508, his wife (the third), who is said to have belonged to the family of Barbarigo (note the resemblance to Brabantio), died on the voyage, and there seems to have been some mystery connected with her death. In 1515 he took as his fourth wife a young girl, who is said to have been nicknamed *Demonio bianco*—the white demon. From this the name Desdemona may have been derived, in the same way as Moor from Moro.

The additions which Shakespeare made to the story as he found it in Cinthio—Desdemona's abduction, the hurried and secret marriage, the accusation, to us so strange, but in those days so natural and common, of the girl's heart having been won by witchcraft—these all occur in the history of Venetian families of the period.

Be this as it may, when Shakespeare proceeds to the treatment of the subject, he arranges all the conditions and circumstances, so that they present the most favourable field for Iago's operations, and he so fashions Othello as to render him more susceptible than any other man would be to the poison which Iago (like Lucianus in the play-scene in *Hamlet*) drops into his ear. Then he lets us trace the growth of the passion from its first germ, through every stage of its development, until it blasts and shatters the victim's whole character.

Othello's is an inartificial soul, a simple, straightforward, soldier nature. He has no worldly wisdom, for he has lived his whole life in camps:

> "And little of this great world can I speak,
> More than pertains to feats of broil and battle."

A good and true man himself, he believes in goodness in others, especially in those who make a show of outspokenness, bluffness, undaunted determination to blame where blame is due—like Iago, who characteristically says of himself to Desdemona:

> "For I am nothing if not critical."

And Othello not only believes in Iago's honesty, but is inclined to take him for his guide, as being far superior to himself in knowledge of men and of the world.

Again, Othello belongs to the noble natures that are never preoccupied with the thought of their own worth. He is devoid of vanity. He has never said to himself that such exploits, such heroic deeds, as have won him his renown, must make a far deeper impression on the fancy of a young girl of Desdemona's disposition than the smooth face and pleasant manners of a Cassio. He is so little impressed with the idea of his greatness that it almost at once appears quite natural to him that he should be scorned.

Othello is the man of despised race, with the fiery African temperament. In comparison with Desdemona he is old—more of an age with her father than with herself. He tells himself that he has neither youth nor good looks to keep her love with, not even affinity of race to build upon. Iago exasperates Brabantio by crying:

> " Even now, now, very now, an old black ram
> Is tupping your white ewe."

Othello's race has a reputation for low sensuality, therefore Roderigo can inflame the rage of Desdemona's father by such expressions as "gross clasps of a lascivious Moor."

That she should feel attracted by him must have seemed to outsiders like madness or the effect of sorcery. For, far from being of an inviting, forward, or coquettish nature, Desdemona is represented as more than ordinarily reserved and modest. Her father calls her (i. 3):

> " A maiden never bold ;
> Of spirit so still and quiet, that her motion
> Blush'd at herself."

She has been brought up as a tenderly-nurtured patrician child in rich, happy Venice. The gilded youth of the city have fluttered around her daily, but she has shown favour to none of them. Therefore, her father says (i. 2):

> " For I'll refer me to all things of sense,
> If she in chains of magic were not bound,
> Whether a maid so tender, fair, and happy,
> So opposite to marriage, that she shunn'd
> The wealthy curled darlings of our nation,
> Would ever have, to incur a general mock,
> Run from her guardage to the sooty bosom
> Of such a thing as thou."

Shakespeare, who knew everything about Italy, knew that the Venetian youth of that period had their hair curled, and wore a lock down on the forehead.

Othello, on his part, at once feels himself strongly drawn to

Desdemona. And it is not merely the fair, delicate girl in her that allures him. Had he not loved her, her only, with burning passion, he would never have married her ; for he has the fear of marriage that belongs to his wild, freedom-loving nature, and he in no wise considers himself honoured and exalted by this connection with a patrician family. He is descended from the princes of his country (i. 2):

> " I fetch my life and being
> From men of royal siege ; "

And he has shrunk from binding himself:

> " But that I love the gentle Desdemona,
> I would not my unhoused free condition
> Put into circumscription and confine
> For the sea's worth."

Truly there is magic in it—not the gross and common sorcery which the others believe in and suppose to have been employed— not the "foul charms" and "drugs or minerals that weaken motion," to which her father alludes—but the sweet, alluring magic by which a man and a woman are mysteriously enchained.

Othello's speech of self-vindication in the council chamber, in which he explains to the Duke how he came to win Desdemona's sympathy and tenderness, has been universally admired.

Having gained her father's favour, he was often asked by him to tell the story of his life, of its dangers and adventures. He told of sufferings and hardships, of hairbreadth 'scapes from death, of imprisonment by cruel enemies, of far-off strange countries he had journeyed through. (The fantastic catalogue, it may be noted, is taken from the fabulous books of travel of the day.) Desdemona loved to listen, but was often called away by household cares, always returning when these were despatched to follow his story with a greedy ear. He "found means" to draw from her a request to tell her his history, not in fragments, but entire. He consented, and often her eyes were filled with tears when she heard of the distresses of his youth. With innocent candour she bade him at last, if ever he had a friend that loved her, to teach him how to tell her Othello's story— " and that would woo her."

In other words, she is not won through the eye, though we must take Othello to have been a stately figure, but through the ear—" I saw Othello's visage in his mind." She becomes his through her sympathy with him in all he has suffered and achieved :—

> " She lov'd me for the dangers I had pass'd,
> And I lov'd her that she did pity them.
> This only is the witchcraft I have us'd.
>   *Duke.* I think, this tale would win my daughter too."

Such, then, is the relation in which the poet has decreed that these two shall stand to each other. This is no love between two of the same age and the same race, whom only family enmity keeps apart, as in *Romeo and Juliet*. Still less is it a union of hearts like that of Brutus and Portia, where the perfect harmony is the result of tenderest friendship in combination with closest kinship, added to the fact that the wife's father is her husband's hero and ideal. No, in direct contrast to this last, it is a union which rests on the attraction of opposites, and which has everything against it—difference of race, difference of age, and the strange, exotic aspect of the man, with the lack of self-confidence which it awakens in him.

Iago expounds to Roderigo how impossible it is that this alliance should last. Desdemona fell in love with the Moor because he bragged to her and told her fantastical lies; does any one believe that love can be kept alive by prating? To inflame the blood anew, "sympathy in years, manners, and beauties" is required, "all which the Moor is defective in."

The Moor himself is at first troubled by none of these reflections. And why not? Because Othello is not jealous.

This sounds paradoxical, yet it is the plain truth. Othello not jealous! It is as though one were to say water is not wet or fire does not burn. But Othello's is no jealous nature; jealous men and women think very differently and act very differently. He is unsuspicious, confiding, and in so far stupid—there lies the misfortune; but jealous, in the proper sense of the word, he is not. When Iago is preparing to insinuate his calumnies of Desdemona, he begins hypocritically (iii. 3):

> "O beware, my lord, of jealousy;
> It is the green-eyed monster. . . . "

Othello answers:
> "'Tis not to make me jealous,
> To say—my wife is fair, feeds well, loves company,
> Is free of speech, sings, plays, and dances well;
> Where virtue is, these are more virtuous:
> Nor from mine own weak merits will I draw
> The smallest fear, or doubt of her revolt;
> For she had eyes, and chose me."

Thus not even his exceptional position causes him any uneasiness, so long as things take their natural course. But there is no escaping the steady pursuit of which he, all unwitting, is the object. He becomes as suspicious towards Desdemona as he is credulous towards Iago—"Brave Iago!" "Honest Iago!" Brabantio's malison recurs to his mind—"She has deceived her father, and may thee;" and close on it crowd Iago's reasons:

> "Haply, for I am black,
> And have not those soft parts of conversation

> That chamberers have; or, for I am declin'd
> Into the vale of years;—yet that's not much."

And the torment seizes him of feeling that one human being is a sealed book to the other—that it is impossible to control passion and appetite in a woman, though the law may have given her into one's hand—until at last he feels as if he were stretched on the rack, and Iago can exult in the thought that not all the drowsy syrups of the world can procure him the untroubled sleep of yesterday. Then follows the mournful farewell to all his previous life, and on this sadness once more follows doubt, and despair at the doubt :—

> "I think my wife be honest and think she is not;
> I think that thou art just and think thou art not,"

—until all his thoughts are centred in the craving for revenge and blood.

Not naturally jealous, he has become so through the working of the base but devilishly subtle slander which he is too simple to penetrate and spurn.

In these masterly scenes (the third and fourth of the third act) there are more reminiscences of other poets than we find elsewhere in Shakespeare within such narrow compass; and they are of interest as showing us what he knew, and what his mind was dwelling upon in those days.

In Berni's *Orlando Innamorato* (Canto 51, Stanza 1), we come upon Iago's declaration :—

> "Who steals my purse, steals trash; 'tis something, nothing;
> 'Twas mine, 'tis his, and has been slave to thousands;
> But he that filches from me my good name,
> Robs me of that which not enriches him,
> And makes me poor indeed."

The passage in Berni runs thus :—

> "Chi ruba un corno, un cavallo, un anello,
> E simil cose, ha qualche discrezione,
> E potrebbe chiamarsi ladroncello;
> Ma quel che ruba la riputazione
> E de l'altrui fatiche si fa bello
> Si può chiamare assassino e ladrone."

A reminiscence also lies hidden in Othello's exquisite farewell a soldier's life :—

> "O now for ever
> Farewell the tranquil mind! farewell content!
> Farewell the plumed troops, and the big wars,
> That make ambition virtue! O, farewell!
> Farewell the neighing steed, and the shrill trump,
> The spirit-stirring drum, the ear-piercing fife,

The royal banner, and all quality,
Pride, pomp, and circumstance of glorious war ! "

It is clear that there must have lurked in Shakespeare's mind a reminiscence of an apostrophe contained in the old play, *A Pleasant Comedie called Common Conditions*, which he must, doubtless, have seen as a youth in Stratford. In it the hero says :—

" But farewell now, my coursers brave, attrapped to the ground.
Farewell, adieu, all pleasures eke, with comely hawk and hound !
Farewell, ye nobles all ! Farewell, each martial knight !
Farewell, ye famous ladies all, in whom I did delight ! "

The study of Ariosto in Italian has also left its trace. It is where Othello, talking of the handkerchief, says :—

" A sibyl, that had number'd in the world
The sun to course two hundred compasses,
In her prophetic fury sew'd the work."

In *Orlando Furioso* (Canto 46, Stanza 80) we read :—

" Una donzella della terra d'Ilia,
Ch'avea *il furor profetico* congiunto
Con studio di gran tempo, e con vigilia
Lo fece di sua man di tutto punto."

The agreement here cannot possibly be accidental. And what makes it still more certain that Shakespeare had the Italian text before him is that the words *prophetic fury*, which are the same in *Othello* as in the Italian, are not to be found in Harington's English translation, the only one then in existence. He must thus, whilst writing *Othello*, have been interested in Orlando, and had Berni's and Ariosto's poems lying on his table.

Desdemona's innocent simplicity in these scenes rivals the boundless and actually tragic simplicity of Othello. In the first place, she is convinced that the Moor, whom she sees wrought up to the verge of madness, cannot possibly suspect her, and is unassailable by jealousy.

" *Emilia.*   Is he not jealous ?
Desdemona. Who ? he ! I think the sun where he was born
Drew all such humours from him."

So she acts with foolish indiscretion, continuing to tease Othello about Cassio's reinstatement, although she ought to feel that it is her harping on this topic that enrages him.

Then follow Iago's still more monstrous lies : the confession he pretends to have heard Cassio make in his sleep ; the story that she has presented the precious handkerchief to Cassio ; and the pretence that Desdemona is the subject of the words which Othello, from his hiding-place, hears Cassio let fall as to his relations with the courtesan, Bianca. To hear his wife, his beloved, thus derided, stings the Moor to frenzy.

It is such a consistently sustained imposture that there is, perhaps, only one at all comparable to it in history—the intrigue of the diamond necklace, in which Cardinal de Rohan was as utterly duped and ruined as Othello is here.

And now Othello has reached the stage at which he can no longer think coherently, or speak except in ejaculations (iv. 1) :—

> " *Iago.* Lie with her.
> " *Othello.* With her?
> " *Iago.* With her, on her, what you will.
> " *Othello.* Lie with her ! lie on her !—We say, lie on her when they belie her. Lie with her ! that's fulsome.—Handkerchief,—confessions, —handkerchief.—To confess, and be hanged for his labour.—First, to be hanged, and then to confess. . . . It is not words, that shakes me thus.—Pish !—Noses, ears, and lips.—Is it possible ?—Confess !— Handkerchief !—O devil ! "

With the mind's eye he sees them in each other's arms.[1] He is seized with an epileptic fit and falls.

This is not a representation of spontaneous but of artificially induced jealousy; in other words, of credulity poisoned by malignity. Hence the moral which Shakespeare, through the mouth of Iago, bids the audience take home with them:

> " Thus credulous fools are caught ;
> And many worthy and chaste dames even thus,
> All guiltless, meet reproach."

It is not Othello's jealousy, but his credulity that is the prime cause of the disaster; and even so must Desdemona's noble simplicity bear its share in the blame. Between them they render possible the complete success of a man like Iago.

When Othello bursts into tears before Desdemona's eyes, without her suspecting the reason (iv. 2), he says most touchingly that he could have borne affliction and shame, poverty and captivity—could even have endured to be made the butt of mockery and scorn—but that he cannot bear to see her whom he worshipped the object of his own contempt. He does not suffer most from jealousy, but from seeing " the fountain from the which his

---

[1] The development of this passage exactly corresponds to Spinoza's classic definition of jealousy, written seventy years later. See *Ethices, Pars III., Propositio XXXV., Scholium:* " Præterea hoc odium erga rem amatam majus erit pro ratione Lætitiæ, qua Zelotypus ex reciproco rei amatæ Amore solebat affici, et etiam pro ratione affectus, qua erga illum, quem sibi rem amatam jungere imaginatur, affectus erat. Nam si eum oderat, eo ipso rem amatam odio habebit, quia ipsam id, quod ipse odio habet, Lætitia afficere imaginatur ; et etiam ex eo, quod rei amatæ imaginem imagini ejus, quem odit, jungere cogitur, quæ ratio plerumque locum habet in Amore erga fœminam ; qui enim imaginatur mulierem, quam amat, alteri sese prostituere, non solum ex eo, quod ipsius appetitus coercetur, contristabitur, sed etiam quia rei amatæ maginem pudendis et excrementis alterius jungere cogitur, eandem aversatur."

current runs" a dried-up swamp, or "a cistern for foul toads to knot and gender in." This is pure, deep sorrow at seeing his idol sullied, not mean frenzy at the idol's preferring another worshipper.

And with that grace which is an attribute of perfect strength, Shakespeare has introduced as a contrast, directly before the terrible catastrophe, Desdemona's delicate little ditty of the willow-tree—of the maiden who weeps because her lover is untrue to her, but who loves him none the less. Desdemona is deeply touching when she pleads with her cruel lord for but a few moments' respite, but she is great in the instant of death, when she expires with the sublime lie, the one lie of her life, upon her lips, designed to shield her murderer from his punishment.

Ophelia, Desdemona, Cordelia—what a trefoil! Each has her characteristic features, but they resemble one another like sisters; they all present the type which Shakespeare at this point loves and most affects. Had they a model? Had they perhaps one and the same model? Had he about this time encountered a young and charming woman, living, as it were, under a cloud of sorrow, injustice, misunderstanding, who was all heart and tenderness, without any claims to intellect or wit? We may suspect this, but we know nothing of it.

The figure of Desdemona is one of the most charming Shakespeare has drawn. She is more womanly than other women, as the noble Othello is more manly than other men. So that after all there is a very good reason for the attraction between them; the most womanly of women feels herself drawn to the manliest of men.

The subordinate figures are worked out with hardly less skill than the principal characters of the tragedy. Emilia especially is inimitable—good-hearted, honest, and not exactly light, but still sufficiently the daughter of Eve to be unable to understand Desdemona's naïve and innocent chastity.

At the end of Act iv. (in the bedroom scene) Desdemona asks Emilia if she believes that there really are women who do what Othello accuses her of. Emilia answers in the affirmative. Then her mistress asks again: "Would'st thou do such a deed for all the world?" and receives the jesting answer, "The world is a huge thing; 'tis a great price for a small vice:

" Marry, I would not do such a thing for a joint-ring, nor for measures of lawn, nor for gowns, petticoats, nor caps, nor any petty exhibition; but, for the whole world! . . . Why, the wrong is but a wrong i' the world; and, having the world for your labour, 'tis a wrong in your own world, and you might quickly make it right."

In passages like this a mildly playful note is struck in the very midst of the horror. And according to his habit and the custom of the times, Shakespeare also introduces, by means of the Clown, one or two deliberately comic passages; but the Clown's merriment is subdued, as Shakespeare's merriment at this period always is.

The composition of *Othello* is closely akin to that of *Macbeth*. In these two tragedies alone there are no episodes; the action moves onward uninterrupted and undissipated. But the beautiful proportion of all its parts and articulations gives *Othello* the advantage over the mutilated *Macbeth* which we possess. Here the crescendo of the tragedy is executed with absolute *maestria;* the passion rises with a positively musical effect; Iago's devilish plan is realised step by step with consummate certainty; all details are knit together into one firm and well-nigh inextricable knot; and the carelessness with which Shakespeare has treated the necessary lapse of time between the different stages of the action, has, by compressing the events of months and years into a few days, heightened the effect of strict and firm cohesion which the play produces.

There are some inaccuracies in the text as we have it. At the close of the play there is a passage, to account for which we must almost assume that part of a vitiated text, adapted to some special performance, has been interpolated. In the full rush of the catastrophe, when only Othello's last speeches are wanting, Lodovico volunteers some information as to what has happened, which is not only superfluous for the spectator, but quite out of the general style and tone of the play:

> "*Lodovico.* Sir, you shall understand what hath befall'n,
> Which, as I think, you know not. Here is a letter,
> Found in the pocket of the slain Roderigo;
> And here another: the one of them imports
> The death of Cassio to be undertook
> By Roderigo.
> *Othello.* O villain!
> *Cassio.* Most heathenish and most gross!
> *Lod.* Now, here's another discontented paper,
> Found in his pocket too," &c., &c.

These speeches, and yet a third, are all aimed at making Othello understand how shamefully he has been deceived; but they are nerveless and feeble and detract from the effect of the scene. This passage ought to be expunged; it is not Shakespeare's, and it forms a little stain on his flawless work of art.

For flawless it is. I not only find several of Shakespeare's greatest qualities united in this work, but I see hardly a fault in it.

It is the only one of Shakespeare's tragedies which does not treat of national events, but is a family tragedy,—what was later known as *tragédie domestique* or *bourgeoise*. But the treatment is anything but bourgeois; the style is of the very grandest. One gets the best idea of the distance between it and the *tragédie bourgeoise* of later times on comparing with it Schiller's *Kabale und Liebe*, which is in many ways an imitation of *Othello*.

We see here a great man who is at the same time a great child ; a noble though impetuous nature, as unsuspicious as it is unworldly. We see a young woman, all gentleness and nobility of heart, who lives only for him she has chosen, and who dies with solicitude for her murderer on her lips. And we see these two elect natures ruined by the simplicity which makes them an easy prey to wickedness.

A great work *Othello* undoubtedly is, but it is a monograph. It lacks the breadth which Shakespeare's plays as a rule possess. It is a sharply limited study of a single and very special form of passion, the growth of suspicion in the mind of a lover with African blood and temperament—a great example of the power of wickedness over unsuspecting nobility. Taken all in all, this is a restricted subject, which becomes monumental only by the grandeur of its treatment.

No other drama of Shakespeare's had been so much of a monograph. He assuredly felt this, and with the impulse of the great artist to make his new work a complement and contrast to the immediately preceding one, he now sought and found the subject for that one of his tragedies which is least of all a monograph, which grew into nothing less than the universal tragedy— all the great woes of human life concentrated in one mighty symbol.

He turned from *Othello* to *Lear*.

XXV

KING LEAR—THE FEELING UNDERLYING IT—THE CHRONICLE — SIDNEY'S ARCADIA AND THE OLD PLAY

IN *King Lear*, Shakespeare's vision sounded the abyss of horror to its very depths, and his spirit showed neither fear, nor giddiness, nor faintness at the sight.

On the threshold of this work, a feeling of awe comes over one, as on the threshold of the Sistine Chapel, with its ceiling-frescoes by Michael Angelo—only that the suffering here is far more intense, the wail wilder, the harmonies of beauty more definitely shattered by the discords of despair.

Othello was a noble piece of chamber-music—simple and easily apprehended, powerfully affecting though it be. This work, on the other hand, is the symphony of an enormous orchestra—all earth's instruments sound in it, and every instrument.has many stops.

King Lear is the greatest task Shakespeare ever set himself, the most extensive and the most imposing—all the suffering and horror that can arise from the relation between a father and his children, expressed in five acts of moderate length.

No modern mind has dared to face such a subject; nor could any one have grappled with it. Shakespeare did so without even a trace of effort, by virtue of the overpowering mastery which he now, in the meridian of his genius, had attained over the whole of human life. He handles his theme with the easy vigour that belongs to spiritual health, though we have here scene upon scene of such intense pathos that we seem to hear the sobs of suffering humanity accompanying the action, much as one hears by the sea-shore the steady plash and sob of the waves.

Under what conditions did Shakespeare take hold of this subject? The drama tells plainly enough. He stood at the turning-point of human life; he had lived about forty-two years; ten years of life still lay before him, but of these certainly not more than seven were intellectually productive. He now brought that which makes life worse than death face to face with that which makes life worth living—the very breath of our lungs and Cordelia-like solace of our suffering—and swept them both forward to a catastrophe that appals us like the ruin of a world.

In what frame of mind did Shakespeare set himself to this work ? What was seething in his brain, what was moaning in his breast, at the time he chanced upon this subject ? The drama tells plainly enough. Of all the different forms of cruelty, coarseness, and baseness with which life had brought him into contact, of all the vices and infamies that embitter the existence of the nobler sort of men, one vice now seemed to him the worst—stood out before him as the most abominable and revolting of all—one of which he himself, no doubt, had again and again been the victim—to wit, ingratitude. He saw no baseness more widespread or more indulgently regarded.

Who can doubt that he, immoderately enriched by nature, he whose very existence was, like that of Shelley's cloud, a constant giving, an eternal beneficence, a perpetual bringing of "fresh showers to the thirsting flowers"—who can doubt that such a giver on the grandest scale must again and again have been rewarded with the blackest ingratitude ? We see, for instance, how *Hamlet*, so far his greatest work, was received with instant attack, with what Swinburne has aptly called "the jeers, howls, hoots and hisses of which a careful ear may catch some far, faint echo even yet—the fearful and furtive yelp from beneath of the masked and writhing poeticule."[1] His life passed in the theatre. We can very well guess, where we do not know, how comrades to whom he gave example and assistance ; stage poets, who envied while they admired him ; actors whom he trained and who found in him a spiritual father ; the older men whom he aided, the young men whom he befriended—how all these would now fall away from him, now fall upon him ; and each new instance of ingratitude was a shock to his spiritual life. For years he kept silence, suppressed his indignation, locked it up in his own breast. But he hated and despised ingratitude above all vices, because it at once impoverished and belittled his soul.

His was certainly not one of those artist natures that are free-handed with money when they have it, and confer benefits with good-natured carelessness. He was a competent, energetic business man, who spared and saved in order to gain an independence and restore the fallen fortunes of his family. But none the less he was evidently a good comrade in practical, a benefactor in intellectual, life. And he felt that ingratitude impoverished and degraded him, by making it hard for him to be helpful again, and to give forth with both hands out of the royal treasure of his nature, when he had been disappointed and deceived so often, even by those for whom he had done most and in whom he believed most. He felt that if there were

---

[1] Swinburne : *A Study of Shakespeare*, p. 164.

any baseness which could drive its victim to despair, to madness, it was the vice of black ingratitude.

In such a frame of mind he finds, one day, when he is as usual turning over the leaves of his Holinshed, the story of King Lear, the great giver. In the same temper he reads the old play on the subject, dating from 1593-4, and entitled *Chronicle History of King Leir*. Here he found what he needed, the half-worked clay out of which he could model figures and groups. Here, in this superficially dramatised chronicle of appalling ingratitude, was the very theme for him to develop. So he took it to his heart and brooded over it till it quickened and came to life.

We can determine without difficulty the period during which Shakespeare was working at *King Lear*. Were it not clear from other reasons that the play cannot have been written before 1603, we should know it from the fact that in this year was published Harsnet's *Declaration of Popish Impostures*, from which he took the names of some of the fiends mentioned by Edgar (iii. 4). And it cannot have been produced later than 1606, for on the 26th December of that year it was acted before King James. This we know from its being entered in the Stationers' Register on the 26th of November 1607, with the addition "as yt was played before the kinges maiestie at Whitehall vppon Sainct Stephens night at Christmas last." But we can get still nearer than this to the time of its composition. When Gloucester (i. 2) speaks of "these late eclipses," he is doubtless alluding to the eclipse of the sun in October 1605. And the immediately following remarks about "machinations, hollowness, treachery, and all ruinous disorders" prevailing at the time, refer in all probability to the great Gunpowder Plot of November 1605.

Thus it was towards the end of 1605 that Shakespeare began to work at *King Lear*.

The story was old and well known. It was told for the first time in Latin by Geoffrey of Monmouth in his *Historia Britonum*, for the first time in English by Layamon in his *Brut* about 1205. It came originally from Wales and bears a distinctly Celtic impress, which Shakespeare, with his fine feeling for all national peculiarities, has succeeded in retaining and intensifying.

He found all the main features of the story in Holinshed. According to this authority, Leir, son of Baldud, rules in Britain "at what time Joash reigned as yet in Juda." His three daughters are named Gonorilla, Regan, and Cordeilla. He asks them how great is their love for him, and they answer as in the tragedy. Cordeilla, repudiated and disinherited, marries one of the princes of Gaul. When the two elder daughters have shamefully ill-treated Leir, he flees to Cordeilla. She and her husband raise an army, sail to England, defeat the armies of the two sisters, and reinstate Leir on his throne. He reigns for two more years;

then Cordeilla succeeds to the throne—and this happens "in the yeere of the world 3155, before the bylding of Rome 54, Uzia then reigning in Juda and Jeroboam over Israell." She rules the kingdom for five years. Then her husband dies, and her sisters' sons rise in rebellion against her, lay waste a great part of the country, take her prisoner, and keep her strictly guarded. This so enrages Cordeilla, who is of a masculine spirit, that she takes her own life.

The material Shakespeare found in this tradition did not suffice him. The thoughts and imaginings which the story set astir within him led him to seek for a supplement to the action in the tale of Gloucester and his sons, which he took from Sir Philip Sidney's *Arcadia*, a book not yet twenty years old. With the story of the great giver, who is recompensed with ingratitude by his wicked daughters after he has banished his good daughter, he entwined the story of the righteous duke, who, deceived by slander, repudiates his good son, and is hurled by the bad one into the depths of misery, until at last his eyes are torn out of his head.

According to Sidney, some princes are overtaken by a storm in the kingdom of Galacia. They take refuge in a cave, where they find an old blind man and a youth, whom the old man in vain entreats to lead him to the top of a rock, from which he may throw himself down, and thus put an end to his life. The old man had formerly been Prince of Paphlagonia, but the "hard-hearted ungratefulness" of his illegitimate son had deprived him not only of his kingdom but of his eyesight. This bastard had previously had a fatal influence over his father. By his permission the Prince had given orders to his servants to take his legitimate son out into a wood and there kill him. The young man, however, escaped, went into foreign military service, and distinguished himself; but when he heard of the evils that had befallen his father, he hastened back to be a support to his hapless age, and is now heaping coals of fire upon his head. The old man begs the foreign princes to make his story known, that it may bring honour to the pious son,—the only reward he can expect.

The old drama of *King Leir* had kept strictly to Holinshed's chronicle. It is instructive reading for any one who is trying to mete out the compass of Shakespeare's genius. A childish work, in which the rough outlines of the principal action, as we know them from Shakespeare, are superficially reproduced, it compares with Shakespeare's tragedy as the melody of Schiller's "An die Freude," played with one finger, compares with Beethoven's Ninth Symphony. And even this comparison does rather too much honour to the old drama, in which the melody is barely suggested.

XXVI

KING LEAR—THE TRAGEDY OF A WORLD-CATASTROPHE

I IMAGINE that Shakespeare must, as a rule, have worked early in the morning. The division of the day at that time would necessitate this. But it can scarcely have been in bright morning hours, scarcely in the daytime, that he conceived *King Lear*. No; it must have been on a night of storm and terror, one of those nights when a man, sitting at his desk at home, thinks of the wretches who are wandering in houseless poverty through the darkness, the blustering wind, and the soaking rain—when the rushing of the storm over the house-tops and its howling in the chimneys sound in his ears like shrieks of agony, the wail of all the misery of earth.

For in *King Lear*, and *King Lear* alone, we feel that what we in our day know by the awkward name of the social problem, in other words, the problem of extreme wretchedness and want, existed already for Shakespeare. On such a night he says with Lear (iii. 4) :—

> " Poor naked wretches, wheresoe'er you are,
> That bide the pelting of this pitiless storm,
> How shall your houseless heads and unfed sides,
> Your loop'd and window'd raggedness, defend you
> From seasons such as these ? "

And he makes the King add :—

> " O ! I have ta'en
> Too little care of this. Take physic, pomp ;
> Expose thyself to feel what wretches feel,
> That thou may'st shake the superflux to them,
> And show the heavens more just."

On such a night was *Lear* conceived. Shakespeare, sitting at his writing-table, heard the voices of the King, the Fool, Edgar, and Kent on the heath, interwoven with each other, contrapuntally answering each to each, as in a fugue ; and it was for the sake of the general effect, in all its sublimity, that he wrote large portions of the tragedy which, in themselves, cannot have interested him. The whole introduction, for instance, deficient as it is in any reasonable motive for the King's behaviour, he took, with his usual sovereign indifference in unessential matters, from the old play.

With Shakespeare we always find that each work is connected with the preceding one, as ring is linked with ring in a chain. In the story of Gloucester the theme of *Othello* is taken up again and varied. The trusting Gloucester is spiritually poisoned by Edmund, exactly as Othello's mind is poisoned by Iago's lies. Edmund calumniates his brother Edgar, shows forged letters from him, wounds himself in a make-believe defence of his father's life against him—in short, upsets Gloucester's balance just as Iago did Othello's. And he employs the very same means as Schiller's Franz Moor employs, two centuries later, to blacken his brother Karl in their old father's estimation. *Die Räuber* is a sort of imitation of this part of *King Lear;* even the father's final blindness is copied.

Shakespeare moves all this away back into primeval times, into the grey days of heathendom ; and he welds the two originally independent stories together with such incomparable artistic dexterity that their interaction serves to bring out more forcibly the fundamental idea and feeling of the play. He skilfully contrives that Gloucester's compassion for Lear shall provide Edmund with means to bring about his father's utter ruin, and he ingeniously invents the double passion of Regan and Goneril for Edmund, which leads the two sisters to destroy each other. He fills the tame little play of the earlier writer with horrors such as he had not presented since his youthful days in *Titus Andronicus*, not even shrinking from the tearing out of Gloster's eyes on the stage. He means to show pitilessly what life is. "You see how this world goes," says Lear in the play.

Shakespeare has nowhere else shown evil and good in such immediate opposition — bad and good human beings in such direct conflict with each other; and nowhere else has he so deliberately shunned the customary and conventional issue of the struggle—the triumph of the good. In the catastrophe, blind and callous Fate blots out the good and the bad together.

Everything centres in the protagonist, poor, old, stupid, great Lear, king every inch of him, and every inch human. Lear's is a passionate nature, irritably nervous, all too ready to act on the first impulse. At heart he is so lovable that he arouses the unalterable devotion of the best among those who surround him ; and he is so framed to command and so accustomed to rule, that he misses every moment that power which, in an access of caprice, he has renounced. For a brief space at the beginning of the play the old man stands erect ; then he begins to bend. And the weaker he grows the heavier load is heaped upon him, till at last, overburdened, he sinks. He wanders off, groping his way, with his crushing fate upon his back. Then the light of his mind is extinguished ; madness seizes him

And Shakespeare takes this theme of madness and sets it for three voices—divides it between Edgar, who is mad to serve a purpose, but speaks the language of real insanity; the Fool, who is mad by profession, and masks the soundest practical wisdom under the appearance of insanity; and the King, who is bewildered and infected by Edgar's insane talk—the King, who is mad with misery and suffering.

As already remarked, it is evident from the indifference with which Shakespeare takes up the old material to make a beginning and set the play going, that all he really cared about was the essential pathos of the theme, the deep seriousness of the fundamental emotion. The opening scenes are of course incredible. It is only in fairy-tales that a king divides the provinces of his kingdom among his daughters, on the principle that she gets the largest share who can assure him that she loves him most; and only a childish audience could find it conceivable that old Gloucester should instantly believe the most improbable calumnies against a son whose fine character he knew. Shakespeare's individuality does not make itself felt in such parts as these; but it certainly does in the view of life, its course and character, which bursts upon Lear when he goes mad, and which manifests itself here and there all through the play. And Shakespeare's intellect has now attained such mastery, every passion is rendered with such irresistible power, that the play, in spite of its fantastic, unreal basis, produces an effect of absolute *truth*.

"*Lear.* A man may see how this world goes with no eyes. Look with thine ears: see how yond justice rails upon yond simple thief. Hark, in thine ear: change places; and, handy-dandy, which is the justice, which is the thief?—Thou hast seen a farmer's dog bark at a beggar?

"*Gloster.* Ay, sir.

"*Lear.* And the creature run from the cur? There thou might'st behold the great image of authority: a dog's obey'd in office."

And then follow outbursts to the effect that the punisher is generally worse than the punished; the beadle flogs the loose woman, but the rascally beadle is as lustful as she. The idea here answers to that in *Measure for Measure:* the beadle should flog himself, not the woman. And then come complaints that the rich are exempt from punishment: dress Sin in armour of gold-plate, and the lance of Justice will shiver against it. Finally, he concentrates his indictment of life in the words:—

"When we are born, we cry that we are come
To this great stage of fools."

We hear a refrain from *Hamlet* running through all this. But Hamlet's criticism of life is here taken up by many voices; it sounds louder, and awakens echo upon echo.

The Fool, the best of Shakespeare's Fools, made more conspicuous by coming after the insignificant Clown in *Othello*, is such an echo—mordantly witty, marvellously ingenious. He is the protest of sound common-sense against the foolishness of which Lear has been guilty, but a protest that is pure humour; he never complains, least of all on his own account. Yet all his foolery produces a tragic effect. And the words spoken by one of the knights, "Since my young lady's going into France, sir, the fool hath much pined away," atone for all his sharp speeches to Lear. Amongst Shakespeare's other master-strokes in this play must be reckoned that of exalting the traditional clown, the buffoon, into so high a sphere that he becomes a tragic element of the first order.

In no other play of Shakespeare's has the Fool so many proverbial words of wisdom. Indeed, the whole piece teems with such words: Lear's "'Ay' and 'no,' too, was no good divinity;" Edgar's "Ripeness is all;" Kent's "To be acknowledged, madam, is o'erpaid."

Whilst the elder daughters have inherited and over-developed Lear's bad qualities, Cordelia has fallen heir to his goodness of heart; but he has also transmitted to her a certain obstinacy and pride, but for which the conflict would not have arisen. His first question to her, and her answer to it, are equally wanting in tact. But as the action proceeds, we find that her obstinacy has melted away; her whole being is goodness and charm.

How touching is the passage where Cordelia finds her brainsick sire, and tends him until, by aid of the healing art, and sleep, and music, he slowly regains his health. Everything is beautiful here, from the first kiss to the last word. Lear is borne sleeping on to the stage. The doctor orders music to sound, and Cordelia says (iv. 7):—

> " *Cor.* O my dear father! Restoration hang
> Thy medicine on my lips, and let this kiss
> Repair those violent harms, that my two sisters
> Have in thy reverence made!
> *Kent.* Kind and dear princess!
> *Cor.* Had you not been their father, these white flakes
> Had challeng'd pity of them. Was this a face
> To be oppos'd against the warring winds?
>
> .   .   .   .
>
> Mine enemy's dog,
> Though he had bit me, should have stood that night
> Against my fire."

He awakes, and Cordelia says to him:—

> " *Cor.* How does my royal lord? How fares your majesty?
> *Lear.* You do me wrong to take me out o' the grave.
> Thou art a soul in bliss; but I am bound

Upon a wheel of fire, that mine own tears
Do scald like molten lead."

Then he comes to himself, asks where he has been, and where he is; is surprised that it is " fair daylight;" remembers what he has suffered :—

" *Cor.*   O look upon me, sir,
And hold your hands in benediction o'er me.—
No, sir, you must not kneel."

Notice this last line. It has its history. In the old drama of *King Leir* this kneeling was made a more prominent feature. There the King and his faithful Perillus (so Kent was called in the old play) are wandering about, perishing with hunger and thirst, when they fall in with the King of Gaul and Cordelia, who are spying out the land disguised as peasants. The daughter recognises her father, and gives the starving man food and drink; then, when he is satisfied, he tells her his story in deep anguish of spirit :—

" *Leir.* O no men's children are vnkind but mine.
Cordella. Condemne not all, because of others crime,
But looke, deare father, looke, behold and see
Thy louing daughter speaketh vnto thee.
                                                      (*She kneeles*).
Leir. O, stand thou vp, it is my part to kneele,
And aske forgiueness for my former faults.
                                                      (*He kneeles*)."

The scene is beautiful, and there is true filial feeling in it, but it would be impossible on the stage, where two persons kneeling to each other cannot but produce a comic effect. The incident, indeed, actually occurs in some of Molière's and Holberg's comedies. Shakespeare understood how to preserve and utilise this (with all other traits of any value in his predecessor's work) in such a manner that only its delicacy remains, while its external awkwardness disappears. Lear says to Cordelia, when they have fallen into the hands of their enemies :—

" Come, let's away to prison :
We two alone will sing like birds i' the cage :
*When thou dost ask me blessing, I'll kneel down
And ask of thee forgiveness.* So we'll live,
And pray, and sing, and tell old tales, and laugh
At gilded butterflies, and hear poor rogues
Talk of court news."

The old play ends naïvely and innocently with the triumph of the good. The King of Gaul and Cordelia conduct Leir home again, tell the wicked daughters sharp truths to their faces, and thereupon totally rout their armies. Leir thanks and rewards all who have been faithful to him, and passes the remainder of his days in agreeable leisure under the care of his daughter and son-in-law.

Shakespeare does not take such a bright view of life. According to him, Cordelia's army is defeated, and the old King and his daughter are thrown into prison. But no past and no present adversity can crush Lear's spirit now. In spite of everything, in spite of the loss of power, of self-reliance, and for a time of reason, in spite of defeat in the decisive battle, he is as happy as an old man can be. He has his lost daughter again. Age had already isolated him. In the peace that a prison affords he will live not much more lonely than great age is of necessity, shut in with the object, now the sole object, of his love. It seems for a moment as though Shakespeare would say: "Happy is that man, even though he may be in prison, who in the last years of his life has the darling of his heart beside him."

But this is not the conclusion to which Shakespeare leads us. Edmund commands that Cordelia shall be hanged in prison, and the murderer executes his order.

The tragedy does not culminate till Lear enters with Cordelia dead in his arms. After a wild outburst of grief, he asks for a looking-glass to see if she still breathes, and in the pause that ensues Kent says :—

> "Is this the promised end?"

And Edgar :—

> "Or image of that horror?"

Lear is given a feather. He utters a cry of joy—it moves—she is alive! Then he sees that he has been mistaken. Curses follow, and after them this exquisite touch of characterisation :—

> "Her voice was ever soft,
> Gentle, and low, an excellent thing in woman."

Then the disguised Kent makes himself known, and Lear learns that the two criminal daughters are dead. But his capacity for receiving new impressions is almost gone. He can feel nothing but Cordelia's death : "And my poor fool is hang'd! No, no, no life!" He faints and dies.

> "*Kent.* Vex not his ghost: O let him pass! He hates him
> That would upon the rack of this tough world
> Stretch him out longer."

That this old man should lose his youngest daughter—this is the catastrophe which Shakespeare has made so great that it is with reason Kent asks: "Is this the promised end? Is this the end of the world?" In the loss of this daughter he loses all; and the abyss that opens seems wide enough and deep enough to engulph a world.

The loss of a Cordelia—that is the great catastrophe. We all lose, or live under the dread of losing, our Cordelia. The loss of the dearest and the best, of that which alone makes life worth living—that is the tragedy of life. Hence the question: Is this the end of the world? Yes, it is. Each of us has only his world, and lives with the threat of its destruction hanging over him. And in the year 1606 Shakespeare was in no mood to write other than dramas on the doom of worlds.

For the end of all things seems to have come when we see the ruin of the moral world—when he who is noble and trustful like Lear is rewarded with ingratitude and hate; when he who is honest and brave like Kent is punished with dishonour; when he who is merciful like Gloucester, taking the suffering and injured under his roof, has the loss of his eyes for his reward; when he who is noble and faithful like Edgar must wander about in the semblance of a maniac, with a rag round his loins; when, finally, she who is the living emblem of womanly dignity and of filial tenderness towards an old father who has become as it were her child—when she meets her death before his eyes at the hands of assassins! What avails it that the guilty slaughter and poison each other afterwards? None the less is this the titanic tragedy of human life; there rings forth from it a chorus of passionate, jeering, wildly yearning, and desperately wailing voices.

Sitting by his fire at night, Shakespeare heard them in the roar of the storm against the window-pane, in the howling of the wind in the chimneys—heard all these terrible voices contrapuntally inwoven one with another as in a fugue, and heard in them the torture-shriek of suffering humanity.

XXVII

ANTONY AND CLEOPATRA—WHAT ATTRACTED
SHAKESPEARE TO THE SUBJECT

IF it is the last titanic tragedy of human life that has now been written, what is there more to add? There is nothing left to write. Shakespeare may lay down his pen.

So it would seem to us. But what is the actual course of events? what do we see? That for years to come, work follows work in uninterrupted succession. It is with Shakespeare as with all other great, prolific geniuses; time and again we think, "Now he has done his best, now he has reached his zenith, now he has touched the limit of his power, exhausted his treasury, made his crowning effort, his highest bid,"—when behold! he takes up a new work the day after he has let go the old; takes it up as if nothing had happened, unexhausted, unwearied by the tremendous task he has accomplished, fresh as if he had just arisen from repose, indefatigable as though he were only now setting forth with his name and fame yet to be won.

King Lear makes a sensation among Shakespeare's impressionable audience; crowds flock to the theatre to see it; the book is quickly sold out—two quarto editions in 1608; all minds are occupied with it; they have not nearly exhausted its treasures of profundity, of wit, of practical wisdom, of poetry—Shakespeare alone no longer gives a moment's thought to it; he has left it behind and is deep in his next work.

A world-catastrophe! He has no mind now to write of anything else. What is sounding in his ears, what is filling his thoughts, is the crash of a world falling to ruin.

For this music he seeks out a new text. He has not far to seek; he has found it already. Since the time when he wrote *Julius Cæsar*, Plutarch has never been out of his hands. In his first Roman drama he depicted the fall of the world-republic; but in that world, as a whole, fresh, strong forces were still at work. Cæsar's spirit dominated it. We heard more of his greatness than we saw of it; but we could infer his true significance from the effects of his disappearance from the scene. And the republic still lived in spirits proud like Brutus, or strong like Cassius, and did not expire with them. By Brutus's side stood Cato's daughter, delicate but steadfast, the tenderest and bravest of wives. In short, there were still many sound elements in the body politic. The republic fell by historical necessity, but there was no decadence of mind, no degeneracy, no ruin.

But Shakespeare read on in his Plutarch and came to the life of Marcus Antonius. This he read first out of curiosity, then with attention, then with eager emotion. For here, here was the real downfall of the Roman world. Not till now did he hear the final, fatal crash of the old world-republic. The might of Rome, stern and austere, shivered at the touch of Eastern voluptuousness. Everything sank, everything fell—character and will, dominions and principalities, men and women. Everything was worm-eaten, serpent-bitten, poisoned by sensuality—everything tottered and collapsed. Defeat in Asia, defeat in Europe, defeat in Africa, on the Egyptian coast; then self-abandonment and suicide.

Again a poisoning-story like that of *Macbeth*. In Macbeth's case the virus was ambition, in Antony's it was sensuality. But the story of Antony, with its far-reaching effects, was a very much weightier and more interesting subject than the story of the little barbarian Scottish king. Macbeth was spiritually poisoned by his wife, a woman ambitious to bloodthirstiness, an abnormal woman, more masculine than her husband, almost a virago. She speaks of dashing out the brains of babes as of one of those venial offences which one may commit on an emergency rather than break one's word, and she undertakes without a tremor to smear the faces of the murdered King's servants with his blood. What is Lady Macbeth to us? What's Hecuba to us? And what was this Hecuba now to Shakespeare!

In a very different and more personal way did he feel himself attracted by Cleopatra. She poisons slowly, half-involuntarily, and in wholly feminine fashion, the faculty of rule, the generalship, the courage, the greatness of Antony, ruler of half the world—and her, Cleopatra, he, Shakespeare, knew. He knew her as we all know her, the woman of women, quintessentiated Eve, or rather Eve and the serpent in one—" My serpent of old Nile," as Antony calls her. Cleopatra—the name meant beauty and fascination—it meant alluring sensuality combined with finished culture—it meant ruthless squandering of human life and happiness and the noblest powers. Here, indeed, was the woman who could intoxicate and undo a man, even the greatest; uplift him to such happiness as he had never known before, and then plunge him into perdition, and along with him that half of the world which it was his to rule.

Who knows! If he himself, William Shakespeare, had met her, who knows if he would have escaped with his life? And had he not met her? Was it not she whom in bygone days he had met and loved, and by whom he had been beloved and betrayed? It moved him strongly to find Cleopatra described as so dark, so tawny. His thoughts dwelt upon this. He too had stood in close relation to a dark, ensnaring woman—one whom in bitter moments he had been tempted to call a gipsy; "a right gipsy," as Cleopatra is called in this play, by those who are afraid of her or angry with her. She of whom he never thought without emotion, his black enchantress, his life's angel and fiend, whom he had hated and adored at the same time, whom he had despised even while he sued for her favour—what was she but a new incarnation of that dangerous, ensnaring serpent of the Nile! And how nearly had his whole inner world collapsed like a soap-bubble in his association with, and separation from, her! That would indeed have been the ruin of a world! How he had revelled and writhed, exulted and complained in those days! played ducks and drakes with his life, squandered his days and nights! Now he was a maturer man, a gentleman, a landed proprietor and tithe-farmer; but in him still lived the artist-Bohemian, fitted to mate with the gipsy queen.

Three times in Shakespeare (*Romeo and Juliet*, ii. 4, and *Antony and Cleopatra*, i. 1, and iv. 12) Cleopatra is slightingly called *gipsy*, probably from the word's resemblance in sound to *Egyptian*. But there was a certain significance in this word-play; for the high-mindedness of the princess and the fickleness of the gipsy were mysteriously combined in her nature. And how well he knew this combination! The model for the great Egyptian queen stood living before his eyes. With the same palette which he had used not many years before to sketch the "dark lady" of the Sonnets he could now paint this monumental historical portrait.

This figure charmed him, attracted him strongly. He came fresh from Cordelia. He had built up that whole titanic tragedy of *King Lear* as a pedestal for her. And what is Cordelia? The ideal which one's imagination reads on a young girl's white brow, and which the young girl herself hardly understands, much less realises. She was the ray of white light—the great, clear symbol of the purity and nobility of heart which were expressed in her very name. He believed in her; he had looked into her innocent eyes, whose expression inspired him with the idea of her character; he had chanced upon that obstinate, almost ungracious truthfulness in young women, which seems to augur a treasure of real feeling behind it; but he had not known or associated with Cordelia in daily life.

Cleopatra, on the contrary, O Cleopatra! He passed in succession before his eyes the most feminine, and therefore the most dangerous, women he had known since he gained a footing in London, and he gave her the grace of the one, the caprices of the other, the teasing humour of a third, a fourth's instability; but deep in his heart he was thinking of one only, who had been to him all women in one, a mistress in the art of love and of awakening love, inciting to it as no other incited, and faithlessly betraying as no other betrayed—true and false, daring and frail, actress and lover without peer!

There were several earlier English dramas on the subject of Antony and Cleopatra, but only one or two of them are worth mentioning. There was Daniel's *Cleopatra* of 1594, founded partly on Plutarch's Lives of Antonius and Pompeius, partly on a French book called the "History of the Three Triumvirates." Then there was a play entitled *The Tragedie of Antonie*, translated from the French by the Countess of Pembroke, the mother of Shakespeare's friend, in the year 1595. Shakespeare does not seem to have been indebted to either of these works, nor to any of the numerous Italian plays on the subject. He had none of them before him when he sat down to write his drama, which appears to have been acted for the first time shortly before the 20th of May 1608, on which day it is entered in the Stationers' Register as "a booke called *Anthony and Cleopatra*," by Edward Blount, one of the publishers who afterwards brought out the First Folio. It is probable, therefore, that the play was written during the course of the year 1607.

The only source, probably, from which Shakespeare drew, and from which he drew largely, was the Life cf Marcus Antonius, in North's translation of Plutarch. It was on the basis of what he read there that he planned and executed his work, even where, as in the first act, he writes without in every point adhering to Plutarch. The farther the drama progresses the more closely does he keep to Plutarch's narrative, ingeniously and carefully making use of every touch, great or small, that appears to him characteristic. It is evident, indeed, that several traits are included merely because they are true, or rather because Shakespeare thinks they are true. At times he introduces quite unnecessary personages, like Dolabella, simply because he will not put into the mouth of another the message which Plutarch assigns to him; and it is very seldom that he permits himself even the most trifling alteration.

Shakespeare ennobled the character of Antony to a certain extent. Plutarch depicts him as a Hercules in stature, and inclined to ape the demigod by certain affectations of dress; a hearty, rough soldier, given to praising himself and making game of others, but capable, too, of enduring banter as well as praise. His inclination to prodigality and luxurious living made him rapacious, but he was ignorant of most of the infamies that were committed in his name. There was no craft in his nature, but he was brutal, recklessly profligate, and devoid of all sense of decency. A popular, light-hearted, free-handed general, who sat far too many hours at table—indifferent whether it were with his own soldiers or with princes—who showed himself drunken on the public street, and would "sleepe out his drunkennesse" in the light of day, degraded himself by the lowest debauchery, exhausted whole treasuries on his journeys, travelled with priceless gold and silver plate for his table, had chariots drawn by lions, gave away tens of thousands of pounds in a single gift; but in defeat and misfortune rose to his full height as the inspiriting leader who uncomplainingly renounced all his own comforts and kept up the courage of his men. Calamity always raised him above himself—a sufficient proof that, in spite of everything, he was not without a strain of greatness. There was something of the stage-king in him, something of the Murat, a touch of Skobeloff, and a suggestion of the mediæval knight. What could be less antique than his twice challenging Octavius to single combat? And in the end, when misfortune overwhelmed him, and those on whom he had showered benefits ungratefully forsook him, there was something in him that recalled Timon of Athens nursing his melancholy and his bitterness. He himself recognised the affinity.

Women, according to Plutarch, were Antony's bane. After a youth in which many women had had a share, he married Fulvia, the widow of the notorious tribune, Clodius. She acquired the mastery over him, and bent him to all her wishes, so that from her hand he passed into Cleopatra's, ready broken-in to feminine dominion.

According to Plutarch, moreover, Antony was endowed with a considerable flexibility of character. He was fond of disguising himself, of playing practical jokes. Once, for instance, on returning from a campaign, he, dressed as a slave, delivered to his wife, Fulvia, a letter telling of his own death, and then suddenly embraced her as she stood terror-struck. This was only one of many manifestations of his power of self-metamorphosis. Sometimes he would seem nerveless, sometimes iron-nerved; sometimes effeminate, sometimes brave to foolhardiness; now avid of honour, now devoid of honour; now revengeful, now magnanimous. This undulant diversity and changeableness in Antony fascinated Shakespeare. Yet he did not accept the character exactly as he found it in Plutarch. He threw into relief the brighter sides of it, building upon the foundation of Antony's inborn magnificence, the superb prodigality of his nature, his kingly generosity, and that reckless determination to enjoy the passing moment, which is a not uncommon attribute both of great rulers and great artists.

There was a crevice in this antique figure through which Shakespeare's soul could creep in. He had no difficulty in imagining himself into Antony's moods; he was able to play him just as, in his capacity of actor, he could play a part that was quite in his line. Antony possessed that power of metamorphosis which is the essence of the artist nature. He was at one and the

2 G

same time a master in the art of dissimulation—see his funeral oration in *Julius Cæsar*, and in this play the manner in which he takes Octavia to wife—and an open, honest character; he was in a way faithful, felt closely bound to his mistress and to his comrades-in-arms, and was yet alarmingly unstable. In other words, his was an artist-nature.

Among his many contradictory qualities two stood out pre-eminent: the bent towards action and the bent towards enjoyment. Octavius says in the play that these two propensities are equally strong in him, and this is perhaps just about the truth. If, with his immense bodily strength, he had been still more voluptuously inclined, he would have become what in later history Augustus the Strong became, and Cleopatra would have been his Aurora von Königsmarck. If energy had been more strongly developed in him, then generalship and love of drink and dissipation would have combined in him much as they did in Alexander the Great, and Antony in Alexandria would have presented a parallel to Alexander in Babylon. The scales hung evenly balanced for a long time, until Antony met his fate in Cleopatra.

Shakespeare has endowed them both with extreme personal beauty, though neither of them is young. Antony's followers see in him a Mars, in her a Venus. Even the gruff Enobarbus (ii. 2) declares that when he saw her for the first time, she "o'erpictured that Venus where we see the fancy outwork nature." She is the enchantress whom, according to Antony, "everything becomes" —chiding, laughing, weeping, as well as repose. She is "a wonderful piece of work." Antony can never leave her, for, as Enobarbus says (ii. 2 ; compare Sonnet lvi.) :—

> " Age cannot wither her, nor custom stale
> Her infinite variety. Other women cloy
> The appetites they feed, but she makes hungry
> Where most she satisfies ; for vilest things
> Become themselves in her."

What matters it that Shakespeare pictures her to himself dark as an African (she was in reality of the purest Greek blood), or that she, with some exaggeration, calls herself old ? She can afford to jest on the subject of her complexion as on that of her age :—

> "Think on me
> That am with Phœbus amorous pinches black,
> And wrinkled deep in time."

She is what Antony calls her when he (viii. 2) exclaims in ecstasy, " O thou day o' the world ! "

In person and carriage Antony is as if created for her. It is not only Cleopatra's passion that speaks when she says of Antony (v. 2):—

> " I dream'd there was an Emperor Antony . . .
> His face was as the heavens . . ."

And to the beauty of his face answers that of his voice :—

> " Propertied
> As all the tunèd spheres, and that to friends ;
> But when he meant to quail and shake the orb,
> He was as rattling thunder."

She prizes his rich, generous nature :—

> " For his bounty,
> There was no winter in't ; and autumn 'twas,
> That grew the more by reaping :
>
> .　　.　　.　　.　　.　　.
>
> In his livery
> Walk'd crowns and crownets ; realms and islands were
> As plates dropped from his pocket."

And just as Enobarbus maintained that Cleopatra was more beautiful than that pictured Venus in which imagination had surpassed nature, Cleopatra, in her exaltation after Antony's death, maintains that his glorious humanity surpassed what fancy can invent :—

> " *Cleopatra.* Think you there was or might be such a man
> As this I dreamt of ?
> *Dolabella.* Gentle madam, no.
> *Cleopatra.* You lie, up to the hearing of the gods.
> But, if there be, or ever were, one such,
> It's past the size of dreaming : nature wants stuff
> To vie strange forms with fancy ; yet, to imagine
> An Antony, were nature's piece 'gainst fancy,
> Condemning shadows quite."

Not of an Antony should we speak thus now-a-days, but of a Napoleon in the world of action, of a Michael Angelo, a Beethoven, or a Shakespeare in the world of art.

But the figure of Antony had to be one which made such a transfiguration possible in order that it might be worthy to stand by the side of hers who is the queen of beauty, the very genius of love.

Pascal says in his *Pensées :* " Si le nez de Cléopâtre eût été plus court, toute la face de la terre aurait changé." But her nose was, as the old coins show us, exactly what it ought to have been ; and in Shakespeare we feel that she is not only beauty itself, but charm, except in one single scene, where the news of Antony's marriage throws her into a paroxysm of unbeautiful rage. Her charm is of the sense-intoxicating kind, and she has, by study and art, developed those powers of attraction which she possessed from the outset, till she has become inexhaustible in inventiveness and variety. She is the woman who has passed from hand to hand, from her husband and brother to Pompey, from Pompey to the great Cæsar, from Cæsar to countless others. She is the courtesan by temperament, but none the less does she possess the genius for a single, undivided love. She, like Antony, is complex, and being a woman, she is more so than he. *Vir duplex, femina triplex.*

From the beginning and almost to the end of the tragedy she plays the part of the great coquette. What she says and does is for long only the outcome of the coquette's desire and power to captivate by incalculable caprices. She asks where Antony is, and sends for him (i. 2). He comes. She exclaims: "We will not look upon him," and goes. Presently his absence irks her, and again she sends a messenger to remind him of her and keep him in play (i. 3):—

> "If you find him sad,
> Say I am dancing; if in mirth, report
> That I am sudden sick . . ."

He learns of his wife's death. She would have been beside herself if he had shown grief, but he speaks with coldness of the loss, and she attacks him because of this:—

> "Where be the sacred vials thou shouldst fill
> With sorrowful water? Now I see, I see
> In Fulvia's death how mine received shall be."

This incalculability, this capriciousness of hers extends to the smallest matters. She invites Mardian to play a game of billiards with her (an amusing anachronism), and, finding him ready, she turns him off with: "I'll none now."

But all this mutability does not exclude in her the most real, most passionate love for Antony. The best proof of its strength is the way in which she speaks of him when he is absent (i. 5):—

> "O Charmian!
> Where think'st thou he is now? Stands he, or sits he?
> Or does he walk? or is he on his horse?
> O happy horse, to bear the weight of Antony!
> Do bravely, horse, for wott'st thou whom thou mov'st?
> The demi-Atlas of this earth, the arm
> And burgonet of men."

So it is but the truth she is speaking when she tells with what immovable certainty and trust, with what absolute assurance for the future, love filled both her and Antony when they saw each other for the first time (i. 3):—

> "No going then;
> Eternity was in our lips and eyes,
> Bliss in our brows' bent; none our parts so poor,
> But was a race of heaven."

Nor is it irony when Enobarbus, in reply to Antony's complaint (i. 2), "She is cunning past man's thought," makes answer, "Alack, sir, no; her passions are made of nothing but the finest part of pure love." This is literally true—only that the love is not pure in the sense of being sublimated or unegoistic, but in the sense of being quintessential erotic emotion, chemically free from all the other elements usually combined with it.

And outward circumstances harmonise with the character and vehemence of this passion. He lays the kingdoms of the East at her feet; with reckless prodigality, she lavishes the wealth of Africa on the festivals she holds in his honour.

XXVIII

THE DARK LADY AS A MODEL—THE FALL OF THE REPUBLIC A WORLD-CATASTROPHE

ASSUMING that it was Shakespeare's design in *Antony and Cleopatra*, as in *King Lear*, to evoke the conception of a world-catastrophe, we see that he could not in this play, as in *Macbeth* or *Othello*, focus the entire action around the leading characters alone. He could not even make the other characters completely subordinate to them; that would have rendered it impossible for him to give the impression of majestic breadth, of an action embracing half of the then known world, which he wanted for the sake of the concluding effect.

He required in the group of figures surrounding Octavius Cæsar, and in the groups round Lepidus, Ventidius, and Sextus Pompeius, a counterpoise to Antony's group. He required the placid beauty and Roman rectitude of Octavia as a contrast to the volatile, intoxicating Egyptian. He required Enobarbus to serve as a sort of chorus and introduce an occasional touch of irony amid the high-flown passion of the play. In short, he required a throng of personages, and (in order to make us feel that the action was not taking place in some narrow precinct in a corner of Europe, but upon the stage of the world) he required a constant coming and going, sending and receiving of messengers, whose communications are awaited with anxiety, heard with bated breath, and not infrequently alter at one blow the situation of the chief characters.

The ambition which characterised Antony's past is what determines his relation to this great world; the love which has now taken such entire possession of him determines his relation to the Egyptian queen, and the consequent loss of all that his ambition had won for him. Whilst in a tragedy like Goethe's *Clavigo*, ambition plays the part of the tempter, and love is conceived as the good, the legitimate power, here it is love that is reprehensible, ambition that is proclaimed to be the great man's vocation and duty.

Thus Antony says (i. 2):

> " These strong Egyptian fetters I must break,
> Or lose myself in dotage."

We saw that one element of Shakespeare's artist-nature was of use to him in his modelling of the figure of Antony. He himself had ultimately broken his fetters, or rather life had broken them for him; but as he wrote this great drama, he lived through again those years in which he himself had felt and spoken as he now made Antony feel and speak:

> " A thousand groans, but thinking on thy face,
> One on another's neck, do witness bear,
> Thy black is fairest in my judgment's place."
>
> —(*Sonnet* cxxxi.)

Day after day that woman now stood before him as his model who had been his life's Cleopatra—she to whom he had written of " lust in action ":

> " Mad in pursuit, and in possession so ;
> Had, having, and in quest to have, extreme ;
> A bliss in proof,—and prov'd, a very woe."
>
> —(*Sonnet* cxxix.)

He had seen in her an irresistible and degrading Delilah, the Delilah whom De Vigny centuries later anathematised in a famous couplet.[1] He had bewailed, as Antony does now, that his beloved had belonged to many:

> " If eyes, corrupt by over-partial looks,
> Be anchor'd in the bay where all men ride,
>
> .   .   .   .   .   .
>
> Why should my heart think that a several plot
> Which my heart knows the wide world's common place ? "
>
> —(*Sonnet* cxxxvii.)

He had, like Antony, suffered agonies from the coquetry she would lavish on any one she wanted to win. He had then burst forth in complaint, as Antony in the drama breaks out into frenzy :

> " Tell me thou lov'st elsewhere ; but in my sight,
> Dear heart, forbear to glance thine eye aside :
> What need'st thou wound with cunning, when thy might
> Is more than my o'er-pressed defence can 'bide ? "
>
> —(*Sonnet* cxxxix.)

Now he no longer upbraided her; now he crowned her with a queenly diadem, and placed her, living, breathing, and in the largest sense true to nature, on that stage which was his world.

As in *Othello* he had made the lover-hero about as old as he was himself at the time he wrote the play, so now it interested him to represent this stately and splendid lover who was no

---

[1] " Toujours ce compagnon dont le cœur n'est pas sûr,
La Femme—enfant malade et douze fois impur."

longer young. In the Sonnets he had already dwelt upon his age. He says, for instance, in Sonnet cxxxviii.:

> " When my love swears that she is made of truth,
> I do believe her, though I know she lies,
> That she might think me some untutor'd youth,'
> Unlearned in the world's false subtleties.
> Thus vainly thinking that she thinks me young,
> Although she knows my days are past the best,
> Simply I credit her false-speaking tongue."

When Antony and Cleopatra perished with each other, she was in her thirty-ninth, he in his fifty-fourth year. She was thus almost three times as old as Juliet, he more than double the age of Romeo. This correspondence with his own age pleases Shakespeare's fancy, and the fact that time has had no power to sear or wither this pair seems to hold them still farther aloof from the ordinary lot of humanity. The traces years have left upon the two have only given them a deeper beauty. All that they themselves in sadness, or others in spite, say to the contrary, signifies nothing. The contrast between their age in years and that which their beauty and passion make for them merely enhances and adds piquancy to the situation. It is in sheer malice that Pompey exclaims (ii. 1):

> " But all the charms of love,
> Salt Cleopatra, soften thy *waned* lip ! "

This means no more than her own description of herself as "wrinkled." And it is on purpose to give the idea of Antony's age, of which in Plutarch there is no indication, that Shakespeare makes him dwell on the mixed colour of his own hair. He says (iii. 9):

> " My very hairs do mutiny; for the white
> Reprove the brown for rashness, and they them
> For fear and doting."

In the moment of despair he uses the expression (iii. 11): "To the boy Cæsar send this grizzled head." And again, after the last victory, he recurs to the idea in a tone of triumph. Exultingly he addresses Cleopatra (iv. 8):

> " What, girl ! though grey
> Do something mingle with our younger brown, yet ha' we
> A brain that nourishes our nerves, and can
> Get goal for goal of youth."

With a sure hand Shakespeare has depicted in Antony the mature man's fear of letting a moment pass unutilised: the vehement desire to enjoy before the hour strikes when all enjoyment must cease. Thus Antony says in one of his first speeches (i. 1):

"Now, for the love of Love and her soft hours. . . .
There's not a minute of our lives should stretch
Without some pleasure now."

Then he feels the necessity of breaking his bonds. He makes
Fulvia's death serve his purpose of gaining Cleopatra's consent
to his departure; but even then he is not free. In order to bring
out the contrast between Octavius the statesman and Antony the
lover, Shakespeare emphasises the fact that Octavius has reports
of the political situation brought to him every hour, whilst Antony
receives no other daily communication than the regularly arriving
letters from Cleopatra which foment the longing that draws him
back to Egypt.

As a means of allaying the storm and gaining peace to love
his queen at leisure, he agrees to marry his opponent's sister,
knowing that, when it suits him, he will neglect and repudiate her.
Then vengeance overtakes him for having so contemptuously
thrown away the empire over more than a third of the civilised
world—vengeance for having said as he embraced Cleopatra
(i. 1):

"Let Rome in Tiber melt, and the wide arch
Of the ranged empire fall! Here is my space."

Rome melts through his fingers. Rome proclaims him a foe to
her empire, and declares war against him. And he loses his
power, his renown, his whole position, in the defeat which he so
contemptibly brings upon himself at Actium. In Cleopatra flight
was excusable. Her flight in the drama (which follows Plutarch
and tradition) is due to cowardice; in reality it was prompted
by tactical, judicious motives. But Antony was in honour bound
to stay. He follows her in the tragedy (as in reality) from brainless, contemptible incapacity to remain when she has gone; leaving
an army of 112,000 men and a fleet of 450 ships in the lurch,
without leader or commander. Nine days did his troops await
his return, rejecting every proposal of the enemy, incapable of
believing in the desertion and flight of the general they admired
and trusted. When at last they could no longer resist the conviction that he had sunk his soldier's honour in shame, they went
over to Octavius.

After this everything turns on the mutual relation of Antony
and Cleopatra, and Shakespeare has admirably depicted its
ecstasies and its revulsions. Never before had they loved each
other so wildly and so rapturously. Now it is not only he who
openly calls her "Thou day o' the world!" She answers him
with the cry, "Lord of lords! O infinite virtue!" (iv. 8).

Yet never before has their mutual distrust been so deep.
She, who was at no time really great except in the arts of love
and coquetry, has always felt distrustful of him, and yet never
distrustful enough; for though she was prepared for a great deal,

his marriage with Octavia overwhelmed her. He, knowing her past, knowing how often she has thrown herself away, and understanding her temperament, believes her false to him even when she is innocent, even when, as with Desdemona, only the vaguest of appearances are against her. In the end we see Antony develop into an Othello.

Here and there we come upon something in his character which seems to indicate that Shakespeare had been lately occupied with Macbeth. Cleopatra stimulates Antony's voluptuousness, his sensuality, as Lady Macbeth spurred on her husband's ambition ; and Antony fights his last battle with Macbeth's Berserk fury, facing with savage bravery what he knows to be invincibly superior force. But in his emotional life after the disaster of Actium it is Othello whom he more nearly resembles. He causes Octavius's messenger, Thyreus, to be whipped, simply because Cleopatra at parting has allowed him to kiss her hand. When some of her ships take to flight, he immediately believes in an alliance between her and the enemy, and heaps the coarsest invectives upon her, almost worse than those with which Othello overwhelms Desdemona. And in his monologue (iv. 10) he raves groundlessly like Othello :

> "Betray'd I am.
> O this false soul of Egypt ! this grave charm,—
> Whose eye beck'd forth my wars, and call'd them home,
> Whose bosom was my crownet, my chief end,—
> Like a right gipsy, hath, at fast and loose,
> Beguil'd me to the very heart of loss."

They both, though faithless to the rest of the world, meant to be true to each other, but in the hour of trial they place no trust in each other's faithfulness. And all these strong emotions have shaken Antony's judgment. The braver he becomes in his misfortune, the more incapable is he of seeing things as they really are. Enobarbus closes the third act most felicitously with the words :

> " I see still
> A diminution in our captain's brain
> Restores his heart : when valour preys on reason
> It eats the sword it fights with."

To tranquillise Antony's jealous frenzy, Cleopatra, who always finds readiest aid in a lie, sends him the false tidings of her death. In grief over her loss, he falls on his sword and mortally wounds himself. He is carried to her, and dies. She bursts forth :

> " Noblest of men, woo't die ?
> Hast thou no care of me ? shall I abide
> In this dull world, which in thy absence is
> No better than a sty ?—O ! see, my women,
> The crown o' the earth doth melt."

In Shakespeare, however, her first thought is not of dying herself. She endeavours to come to a compromise with Octavius,
hands over to him an inventory of her treasures, and tries to trick
him out of the larger half. It is only when she has ascertained
that nothing, neither admiration for her beauty nor pity for her
misfortunes, moves his cold sagacity, and that he is determined
to exhibit her humiliation to the populace of Rome as one of the
spectacles of his triumph, that she lets "the worm of Nilus" give
her her death.

In these passages the poet has placed Cleopatra's behaviour
in a much more unfavourable light than the Greek historian,
whom he follows as far as details are concerned; and he has
evidently done so wittingly and purposely, in order to complete
his home-thrust at the type of woman whose dangerousness he
has embodied in her. In Plutarch all these negotiations with
Octavius were a feint to deceive the vigilance with which he
thought to prevent her from killing herself. Suicide is her one
thought, and he has baulked her in her first attempt. She pretends to cling to her treasures only to delude him into the belief
that she still clings to life, and her heroic imposture is successful.
Shakespeare, for whom she is ever the quintessence of the she-
animal in woman, disparages her intentionally by suppressing the
historical explanation of her behaviour.[1]

The English critic, Arthur Symons, writes: "*Antony and
Cleopatra* is the most wonderful, I think, of all Shakespeare's
plays, and it is so mainly because the figure of Cleopatra is
the most wonderful of Shakespeare's women. And not of
Shakespeare's women only, but perhaps the most wonderful of
women."

This is carrying enthusiasm almost too far. But thus much
is true: the great attraction of this masterpiece lies in the unique
figure of Cleopatra, elaborated as it is with all Shakespeare's
human experience and artistic enthusiasm. But the greatness
of the world-historic drama proceeds from the genius with which
he has entwined the private relations of the two lovers with the
course of history and the fate of empires. Just as Antony's ruin
results from his connection with Cleopatra, so does the fall of the
Roman Republic result from the contact of the simple hardihood
of the West with the luxury of the East. Antony is Rome,
Cleopatra is the Orient. When he perishes, a prey to the voluptuousness of the East, it seems as though Roman greatness and
the Roman Republic expired with him.

Not Cæsar's ambition, not Cæsar's assassination, but this
crumbling to pieces of Roman greatness fourteen years later

---

[1] Goethe has a marked imitation of Shakespeare's Cleopatra in the Adelheid
of *Götz von Berlichingen*. And he has placed Weislingen between Adelheid and
Maria as Antony stands between Cleopatra and Octavia—bound to the former and
marrying the latter.

brings home to us the ultimate fall of the old world-republic, and impresses us with that sense of *universal annihilation* which in this play, as in *King Lear*, Shakespeare aims at begetting.

This is no tragedy of a domestic, limited nature like the conclusion of *Othello;* there is no young Fortinbras here, as in *Hamlet*, giving the promise of brighter and better times to come; the victory of Octavius brings glory to no one and promises nothing. No; the final picture is that which Shakespeare was bent on painting from the moment he felt himself attracted by this great theme—the picture of a world-catastrophe.

BOOK THIRD

I

DISCORD AND SCORN

OUT of tune—out of tune!

Out of tune the instrument whereon so many enthralling melodies had been played—glad and gay, plaintive or resentful, full of love and full of sorrow. Out of tune the mind which had felt so keenly, thought so deeply, spoken so temperately, and stood so firmly "midst passion's whirlpool, storm, and whirlwind." His life's philosophy has become a disgust of life, his melancholy seeks the darkest side of all things, his mirth is grown to bitter scorn, and his wit is without shame.

There was a time when all before his eyes was green—vernally green, life's own lush, unfaded colour. This was followed by a period of gloom, during which he watched the shadows of life spread over the bright and beautiful, blotting out their colours. Now it is black, and worse than black; he sees the base mire cover the earth with its filth, and heeds how it fills the air with its stench.

Shakespeare had come to the end of his first great circumnavigation of life and human nature: an immense disillusionment was the result. Expectation and disappointment, yearning and content, life's gladness and holiday-making, battle mood and triumph, inspired wrath and desperate vehemence—all that once had thrilled him is now fused and lost in contempt.

Disdain has become a persistent mood, and scorn of mankind flows with the blood in his veins. Scorn for princes and people; for heroes, who are but fellow-brawlers and braggarts after all; and for artists, who are but flatterers and parasites seeking possible patrons. Scorn for old age, in whose venerableness he sees only the unction or hypocrisy of an old twaddler. Scorn for youth, wherein he sees but profligacy, slackness, and gullibility, while all enthusiasts are impostors, and all idealists fools. Men are either coarse and unprincipled, or so weakly sentimental as to be under a woman's thumb; and woman's distinguishing qualities are feebleness, voluptuousness, fickleness, and falsehood;

a fool he who trusts himself to them or lets his actions depend upon them.

This mood has been growing on Shakespeare for some time. We have felt it grow. It shows first in *Hamlet*, but is harmless as yet in comparison with the scathing bitterness of later times. There is a breath, a whisper, in the "Frailty, thy name is Woman!" addressed to Hamlet's mother. Ophelia is rather futile than specially weak; she is never false, still less faithless. Even the inconstant Queen Gertrude can scarcely be called false.

There was malignity and temper in that challenge of moral hypocrisy, *Measure for Measure*, and enough earnestness to overpower the comic, although not sufficient bitterness to make the peaceful conclusion impossible. The tragedy of *Macbeth* was brought to a consoling end; the powers of good triumphed at the last. There was only one malign character in *Othello*, evil indeed, but solitary. Othello, Desdemona, Emilia, &c., are all good at heart. There is no bitterness in *Lear*, no scorn of mankind, but sympathy and a wonderful compassion pervading and dominating all. Shakespeare has divided his own Ego among the characters of this play, in order to share with them the miseries and suffering of life on this earth; he has not gathered himself up to judge and despise.

It is from thenceforward that the undertone of contempt first begins to be felt. A period of some years follows, in which his being narrows and concentrates itself upon an abhorrence of human nature, accompanied, so far as we can judge, by a correspondingly enormous self-esteem. It is as though he had for a moment felt such a scorn for his surroundings of court and people, friends and rivals, men and women, as had nearly driven him wild.

We see the germs of it in *Antony and Cleopatra*. What a fool is this Antony, who puts his reputation and a world-wide dominion in jeopardy in order to be near a cold-blooded coquette, who has passed from hand to hand, and whose caprice puts on all the colours of the rainbow. We find it in full bloom in *Troilus and Cressida*. What a simpleton this Troilus, who, credulous as a child, devotes himself body and soul to a Cressida; a typical classic she, treachery in woman's form, as false and flighty as foam upon the waves, whose fickleness has become a by-word.

Shakespeare has now reached that point of departure where man feels the need of stripping woman of the glamour with which romantic naïveté and sensual attraction have surrounded her, and finds a gratification in seeing merely the sex in her. Sympathy with love, and a conception of woman as an object worthy of love, goes the way of all other sympathies and illusions at this stage. "All is vanity," says Kohelet, and Shakespeare with him. As in all artist souls, there was in his a peculiar blending of enthusiast and cynic. He has now parted with enthusiasm for a time, and cynicism is paramount.

Such an all-pervading change in the disposition and temper of a great personality was not without its reasons, possibly its one first cause. We can trace its workings without divining its origin, but we may seek to orient ourselves with regard to its conditions. Leverier came to the conclusion in 1846 that the disturbances in the path of Uranus were caused by something behind the planet which neither he nor anybody else had ever seen. He indicated its probable position, and three weeks afterwards Galle found Neptune on the very spot. Unfortunately, Shakespeare's history is so very obscure, and such fruitless search in every direction has been made after fresh documents, that we have no great hope of finding any new light.

We can but glance around the horizon of his life, and note how English circumstances and conditions grouped themselves about him. Material for cheering or depressing reflections can be found at all times, but the mind is not always equally prone to assimilate the cheering or depressing. Certain it is that Shakespeare has now elected to seek out and dwell upon the ugly and sorrowful, the unclean and the repulsive. His melancholy finds its nourishment therein, and his bitterness has learned to suck poison from every noxious plant which borders his path through life. His contempt of mankind and his weariness of existence swell and grow with each experience, and in the events and conditions of those years there was surely matter enough for abhorrence, rancour, and scorn.

II

THE COURT—THE KING'S FAVOURITES
AND RALEIGH

UNDER the circumstances Shakespeare could do nothing but
keep as close to King and Court as possible, even though the
King's dreary, and the Court's profligate qualities grew year by
year. James aspired to a comparison with Solomon for wisdom;
he certainly resembled him in prodigality, and Henry III. of
France in his susceptibility to manly beauty. His passion for
his various favourites recalls that of Edward II. for Gaveston in
Marlowe's drama. He was, says a chronicle of the time, as
susceptible as any schoolgirl to handsome features and well-
formed limbs in a man. The parallels his contemporaries drew
between him and his predecessor on this score did not work out
to his advantage. Elizabeth, they said, who was unmarried,
loved only individuals of the opposite sex, all eminent men,
whom, even then, she never allowed to rule her. James, on the
contrary, was married, and yet entertained a passion for one
mignon after another, giving the most exalted positions in the
country to these men, who were worthless and arrogant, and by
whom he was entirely led. In our day Swinburne has characterised James as combining with "northern virulence and pedantry . . . a savour of the worst qualities of the worst Italians
of the worst period of Italian decadence." Was he, in truth, of
Scotch descent on both sides? His exterior recalled little of his
mother's charms, and still less those of the handsome Darnley.
His contemporaries doubted. They neither believed that Darnley's jealousy was groundless, nor the modern embellishment that
the Italian singer and private secretary's ugly face made any tender
feeling on Mary Stuart's side quite impossible. The Scottish
Solomon was invariably alluded to by the outspoken, jest-loving
Henry IV. of France as " Solomon, the son of David " (Rizzio).

The general enthusiasm which greeted King James on his
accession speedily gave way to a very decided unpopularity.
Again and again, upon a score of different points, did he offend
English national pride, sense of justice, and decency.

The lively Queen, who romped through the court festivities,
and spent her days in dressing herself out for masquerades, had

her favourites, much as the King had his. At one time, indeed, the same family served them both. The Queen set her affection on the elder brother, the Earl of Pembroke, and the King bestowed his upon the younger, whom he made Earl of Montgomery and Knight of the Garter. Whether he did not find the harmony of disposition for which he had looked, or whether the impression Montgomery made upon him was displaced by another and stronger, certain it is that no later than 1603 he was already violently infatuated with a youth of twenty, who afterwards became the most powerful man in Great Britain.

This was a young Scot, Robert Carr, who first attracted the King's attention by breaking his leg in a tourney at which James was present. He had as a lad been one of the King's pages at home in Scotland, had since pursued his fortunes in France, and was now in service with Lord Hay. The King gave special orders that he should be nursed at the castle, sent his own doctor to him, visited him frequently during his illness, and made him Knight and Gentleman of the Bedchamber as soon as he was convalescent. He kept him constantly about his person, and even took the trouble to teach him Latin. Step by step the young man was advanced until he stood among the foremost ranks of the country.

It was his nationality which specially offended the people, for Scottish adventurers swarmed about the King, and the Scots were still regarded as stranger-folk in England. The new title of Great Britain had also caused great discontent. Was the glorious name of England no longer to distinguish them? Scotch moneys were made current on English soil, and English ships were compelled to carry the cross of St. Andrew, with that of St. George upon their flags. Englishmen found themselves slighted, and were fearful that the Scot would creep into English lordships and English ladies' beds, as a contemporary writing expresses it. The conflicts in Parliament concerning the extension of national privileges to the Scotch were incessant. Bacon undertook the King's cause, and discreet and biblical objections were made that things would fall out as they did with Lot and Abraham. Families combined together, or were set at variance among themselves; and it grew to a case of, "Go you to the right? I go to the left."

In 1607 James observed that he intended to "give England the labour and the sweat, Scotland the fruit and the sweet;" and it was a notorious fact, that where his passions were concerned, the Scotch were persistently preferred to the English.

James, having meanwhile found it necessary to provide his favourite with estates, procured them in the following manner. When Raleigh came to grief, he had secured the revenues of his estate, Sherborne, to Lady Raleigh, and his son as heir to it after his death. A few months later the King's lawyers discovered a technical error in the deed of conveyance which rendered it invalid. Raleigh wrote from his prison to Salisbury, entreating the King not to deprive his family of their subsistence for the sake of a copyist's blunder. The King made many promises, and assured Raleigh that a new and correct deed should be drawn up. The imprisoned hero had begun, at about this time, to entertain renewed hope of freedom, for he believed that Christian IV., then on a visit to England, 1606, would intercede for him. But when Lady Raleigh, under this impression, threw herself on her knees before James at Hampton Court, the King passed her by without a word. From the year 1607 the King had resolved upon seizing Sherborne for his favourite. In 1608 Raleigh was required to prove right and title thereunto, and he possessed only the faulty document. At Christmastide, taking her two little sons by the hand, Lady Raleigh cast herself a second time before James, and implored him for a new and accurate deed. The only reply she obtained was a broad Scotch, "I maun hae the lond—I maun hae it for Carr." It is said that the high-spirited woman lost all patience upon this, and springing to her feet called upon God to punish the despoiler of her property. Raleigh, on the 2nd of January 1609, tried the more politic method of writing to Carr, entreating him not to aspire to the possession of Sherborne. He received no answer, and upon the 10th of the same month the estate was handed over to the favourite as a gift. It is to be regretted that Raleigh, who had never concealed his opinion of the King's favourites, should have lowered himself by writing to Carr as "one whom I know not, but by honourable fame."

Lady Raleigh accepted a sum of money in compensation, which bore no relation to the real value of Sherborne, and Raleigh was left in the Tower. It is a highly characteristic feature that he remained there year after year until he succeeded (in 1616) in arousing his kingly gaoler's cupidity afresh. In the hope of his finding the anticipated gold-mines in Guiana his prison doors were opened for a while (1616–17), and his failure to discover them was made a pretext for his execution.[1]

---

[1] "Sir Walter Raleigh was freed out of the Tower the last week, and goes up and down, seeing sights and places built or bettered since his imprisonment."—Letter from John Chamberlain to Sir Dudley Carleton, 27th March 1616 ("The Court and Times of James the First").

Gardiner's "History of England," ii. 43; Gosse, "Raleigh," 172.

III

THE KING'S THEOLOGY AND IMPECUNIOSITY—HIS DISPUTES WITH THE HOUSE OF COMMONS

THE King's interest in parsons and theological discussions was not a whit inferior to his passion for his favourites. He constantly gave public expression to a superstition which diverted even contemporary culture. It is jestingly alluded to in a letter from Sir Edward Hoby to Sir Thomas Edmondes, dated Nov. 19, 1605. "His Majesty in his speech observed one principal point, that most of all his best fortunes had happened unto him upon the Tuesday; and particularly he repeated his deliverance from Gowry [the brothers Ruthven] and this [Gunpowder Plot], in which he noted precisely that both fell upon the fifth day of the month: and therefore concluded that he made choice that the next sitting of Parliament might begin upon a Tuesday." If James supported the claims of the clergy, it was less on religious grounds than because his own kingly power was thereby strengthened, and he disseminated, to the best of his ability, the doctrine that all questions must finally be referred to his personal wisdom and insight. Relations between the temporal and the spiritual jurisdictions were already strained. The secular judges frequently objected that the Spiritual Court entered into certain lawsuits before making sure that the case appertained to them. The clergy resisted, asserting that the two courts were independent of one another, and that their spiritual prerogatives emanated direct from the Crown. In 1605 the Archbishop of Canterbury complained of the secular judges to the King, and they, in their turn, appealed to Parliament. Fuller, a member of Parliament, and one of the principal advocates of the Puritan party, defended two of the accused who had been shamefully mishandled by the Spiritual Court (the High Commission), and he denied this "Popish authority," as he called it, any right to impose fines or inflict imprisonment. For these reckless utterances he was sent to gaol, and kept there until he retracted. The question of the supremacy of temporal jurisdiction over the spiritual began to ferment in the public mind. The King held by the latter, because it exercised an authority which Parliament was powerless to control, while Lord Chief Justice Coke stood by the former. On the latter giving vent, however, to the opinion, in the King's presence, that the sovereign was bound to respect the law of the land, and to remember that spiritual jurisdiction was extraneous, James clenched angry fists in his face, and would have struck him, had not Coke, alarmed, fallen on his knees and entreated pardon.

The King's ardent orthodoxy prompted him next to appear as a theological polemist. A certain professor of theology at Leyden, Conrad Vorstius by name, had, according to James's ideas, been guilty of heresy. It was of so slight a nature that, in spite of the rigid orthodoxy of the greater part of the Dutch theologians, it had raised no protest in Holland, since statesmen, nobles, and merchants were all agreed upon tolerance in matters of religion. James, however, made such a vindictive assault upon them, that, for fear of forfeiting their English alliance, they were compelled to give Vorstius his dismissal.

At the precise moment of James's full polemical heat against Vorstius, two unlucky Englishmen, Edward Wrightman and Bartholomew Legate, were convicted of holding heretical opinions. The latter admitted that he was an Aryan, and had not prayed to Jesus for many years. James was fire and flame. Elizabeth had burnt two heretics. Why shouldn't he? Public opinion saw no cruelty, but merely righteousness in such a proceeding, and they were both accordingly burned alive in March 1612.

It was one of the clerkly James's customs to issue proclamations. Among the first of these was a warning issued against the encroachments of the Jesuits, advising them of a date by which they must have decamped from his kingdom and country. Another very forcibly recommended unanimity of religion—that is to say, complete uniformity of ceremony. A bold priest, Burgess by name, preached a sermon in the King's presence, soon after this, on the insignificance of ceremonies. They resembled, he said, the glass of the Roman Senator, which was not worth a man's life or subsistence. Augustus, having been invited to a feast by this Senator, was greeted on his arrival by terrible cries. A slave, who had broken some costly glass, was about to be thrown into the fishpond. The Emperor bade them defer the punishment until he had inquired of his host whether he had glass worth a man's life. Upon the Senator answering that he possessed glass worth a province, Augustus asked to see it, and smashing it into fragments, remarked, " Better that it should all perish than that one man should die." " I leave the application to your Majesty."

The proclamations continued undiminished, however, and it became a favourite amusement of James to issue edicts forbidding lawful trades. This was the cause of much discontent, and appeal was made to the Lord Chief Justice. In 1610 two questions were laid before Coke : whether the King could prohibit the erection of new houses in London by proclamation (a naïve notification had been issued with a view to preventing the "overdevelopment" of the capital), or forbid the manufacture of starch (in allusion to a manifesto limiting the uses of wheat to purposes of food). The answer was returned that the King had neither power to create offences by proclamation, nor make trades, which did not legally subject themselves to judicial control, liable to punishment by the Star Chamber. After this ensued a temporary respite from edicts levying fines or threatening imprisonment.

The dissensions between King and People became so violent that they soon led to a complete rupture between James and the House of Commons, which would not submit to his high-handed levying and collecting of taxes in order to squander the money on his own pleasures and caprices. James, who required £500,000 to pay his debts, was made to endure a speech in Parliament concerning the prodigality of himself and favourites. An insulting rumour added that it had been said in the House that the King must pack all the Scots in his household back to the country whence they came. James, losing all patience, prorogued Parliament, and finally dissolved it in February 1611.

This was the beginning of a conflict between the Crown and the People which lasted throughout James's lifetime, causing the Great Revolution under his son, and being only finally extinguished seventy-eight years afterwards by the offer from both Houses of the Crown to William of Orange.

It was to no purpose that the King's revenues were increased year by year, by illegal taxation too: nothing sufficed. In February 1611 he divided £34,000 among six favourites, five of whom were Scotch. In the March of the same year he made Carr Viscount Rochester and a peer of England. For the first time in English history a Scot took his seat in the House of Lords, and a Scot, moreover, who had done his best to inflame the King against the Commons.

To relieve its pecuniary distress the Court hit upon the expedient of selling baronetcies. Every knight or squire possessed of money or estates to the value of a hundred a year could become a baronet, provided he were willing to disburse £1080 (a sum sufficient to support thirty infantry-men in Ireland for three years) in three yearly payments to the State coffers. This contrivance brought no very great relief, however. Either the extravagance was too reckless, or the seekers after titles were not sufficiently numerous.

Things had gone so far in 1614, that, in spite of the hitherto unheard-of sale of Crown property, James was at his wits' end for want of money. He owed £680,000, not to mention a yearly deficit of £200,000. The garrisons in Holland were on the point of mutinying for their pay, and the fleet was in much the same condition. Fortresses were falling into ruins for want of repair, and English Ambassadors abroad were fruitlessly writing home for money. It was once more decided to summon Parliament. In spite of the most shameless packing, however, the Commons came in with a strong Opposition; and they had much to complain of. The King, among other things, had given Lord Harrington the exclusive right of coining copper money, in return for his having lent him £300,000 at his daughter's wedding. He had also granted a monopoly of the manufacture of glass, and had given the sole right of trade with France to a single company.

The Upper House declined to meet the Lower on a common ground of procedure, and when Bishop Neile, one of the greatest sycophants the royal influence possessed in the Lords, permitted himself some offensive strictures on the Commons, such a storm broke loose among the latter that one member (an aristocrat), abused the courtiers as "spaniels" towards the King and "wolves" towards the people, and another went so far as to warn the Scotch favourites that the Sicilian Vespers might find a parallel in England.

James, who, in a lengthy peroration, had attempted to influence the Commons in his favour, saw that he had nothing to hope from them and dissolved Parliament in the following year.

In order to free him from debt, and to contrive, if possible, some means of supplying the sums swallowed up by the Government and Court, a scheme was devised of inducing private citizens to send money to the King, apparently of their own free will. The bishops inaugurated it by offering James their Church plate and other valuables. This example was followed by all who hoped or expected favours from the court; and a great number of people sent money to the Treasury at Whitehall. Thus the idea obtained that James should issue a summons for all England to follow this example. It seemed, at first, as if this self-taxation would bring in a good round sum. The King asked the city for a loan of £100,000, and it replied (very differently to the response it had made to Elizabeth) that they would rather give £10,000 than lend £100,000. In the course of little over a month £34,000 came in, but with that the stream ceased. Government wrote fruitlessly to all the counties and their officials, &c., to renew the summons. The sheriffs unanimously replied that if the King were to summon Parliament he would experience no difficulty in getting money. During two whole months only £500 came in. Fresh appeals were made and renewed pressure attempted without obtaining the desired results.

The luckless Raleigh, who had heard of these things in his prison, but was without adequate information from the outside world, wrote a pamphlet on the prerogatives of Parliament, full of good advice to the King, whom he assumed to be personally guiltless of the abuses his ministers practised in his name. He naïvely looked for his freedom in return for the tract, which naturally was suppressed.

The notorious Peckham case was another cause of popular ill-humour. In the course of this trial, a man who had been greatly exasperated by clerical and official demeanour, and had expressed himself indiscreetly thereon, was subjected to repeated torture on the pretext of a sermon which had never been preached or printed, but which an examination of his house had brought to light. Bacon degraded himself by urging on the executioners at the rack—a form of torture which had been abolished in common law, but was still considered legitimately applicable in political cases.

That James was personally cruel is shown, amongst other things, by his frequent pardons on the scaffold. He kept such men as Cobham, Grey, and Markham waiting two hours with the axe hanging over their heads, undergoing all the tortures of death, before they were informed that their execution had been deferred. The times, however, were as cruel as he. Through all the published letters of that period runs incessant mention of hanging, racking, breaking on the wheel, half hanging, and executions, without the least emotion being expressed. Any death gave invariable rise to suspicions of poison. Even when the King lost his eldest son, it was stubbornly believed that he had rid himself of him from jealousy of his popularity. As every death was attributed to foul play, so every disease or sickness was assigned to witchcraft. Sorcerers and witches were condemned and despised, but believed in, nevertheless, even by such men as Philip Sidney's friend, Fulk Greville, Lord Brook and Chancellor of the Exchequer under James. He obviously fully credits the witchcraft of which he speaks so disdainfully in his work, " Five Years of King James's Government."

IV

THE CUSTOMS OF THE COURT

THE tone of the Court was vicious throughout. Relations between the sexes were much looser than would have been expected under a king who, in general, troubled himself little about women. We find a description in Sir Dudley Carleton's letters of a bridal adventure, which ended in the King going in night-gear to awaken the bride next morning and remaining with her some time, "in or upon the bed, chuse which you will believe." James spoke of the Queen in public notices as "Our dearest bedfellow." In the half-imbecile, half-obscene correspondence between James and Carr's successor, Buckingham, the latter signs himself, "Your dog," while James addresses him as "Dog Steenie." The King even calls the solemn Cecil, "little beagle;" and the Queen, writing to Buckingham to beg him intercede with the King for Raleigh's life, addresses him as "my kind dog."

With personal dignity, all decency also was set aside. Even the elder Disraeli, James's principal admirer and apologist, acknowledges that the morals of the Court were appalling, and that these courtiers, who passed their days in absolute idleness and preposterous luxury, were stained by infamous vices. He quotes Drayton's lines from the "Mooncalf," descriptive of a lady and gentleman of this circle—

"He's too much woman, and she's too much man."

Neither does he deny the contemporary Arthur Wilson's account of many young girls of good family, who, reduced to poverty by their parents' luxurious lives, looked upon their beauty as so much capital. They came up to London in order to put themselves up for sale, obtained large pensions for life, and ultimately married prominent and wealthy men. They were considered sensible, well-bred women, and were even looked upon as *esprits forts*. The conversation of the men was so profligate, that the following sentiment, less decently expressed, must have been frequently heard: "I would rather that one should believe I possessed a lady's favours, though I did not, than really possess them when none knew thereof."

Gondomar, the Spanish envoy, played an important part at the Court of King James. Don Diego Sarmiento de Acuña, Count of Gondomar, was one of the first diplomatists of Spain. He must have lacked the intuitions of a statesman, in so far as he flattered himself that England could be brought back to Roman Catholicism, but he was a past-master in the art of managing men.   He knew how to awe by rare firmness of decision and how to win by exemplary suppleness ; he knew when to speak and when to be silent ; and, finally, he understood how to further his master's aims by the most intelligent means.   He had as free access to James as any English courtier, having acquired it by lively sallies and by talking bad Latin, in order to give the King an opportunity of correcting him.

Ladies of rank crowded on to their balconies to attract this man's attention as he rode or drove to his house ; and it appears, says Disraeli, that any one of them would have sold her favours for a good round sum.   Noticeable among these ladies of title, says Wilson, were many who owned some pre-tensions to wit, or had charming daughters or pretty nieces, whose presence attracted many men to their houses.   The follow-ing anecdote made considerable noise at the time, and has been variously repeated.   In Drury Lane, Gondomar, one day, passed the house of a charming widow, a certain Lady Jacob.   He saluted her, and was amazed to find that in return to his greeting she merely moved her mouth, which she opened, indeed, to a very great extent.   He was profoundly astonished by this lack of courtesy, but reflected that she had probably been overtaken by a fit of the gapes.   The same thing occurring, however, on the following day, he sent one of his retinue to inform her that English ladies were usually more gracious than to return his greeting in such an outrageous manner.   She replied, that being aware that he had acquired several good graces for a handsome sum, she had wished to prove to him that she also had a mouth which could be stopped in the same fashion.   Whereupon he took the hint, and immediately despatched her a present.

In all this, however, the women merely followed the example of the men.   The English Ambassador at Madrid had long been aware of, and profited by, the possibility of buying the secrets of the Spanish Government at comparatively reasonable prices.   In May 1613, however, he discovered that Spain, in the same manner, annually paid large sums to a whole series of eminent persons in England.   He saw, to his disgust, the name of the English Admiral, Sir William Monson, among the pensioners of Spain, and learned, to his consternation, that the late Chancellor of the Exchequer, Lord Salisbury, had been in her pay up to the moment of his death.   In the following December he obtained a complete list of men enjoying Spanish pay, and was thunder-struck on reading the names of men whose integrity he had never doubted, and who were filling the highest offices of state.   Not daring to trust the secret to paper, correspondence by no means being considered inviolable in those days, he applied for per-mission to bring the disgraceful information to James in person.

V

ARABELLA STUART AND WILLIAM SEYMOUR

AN event occurring in the royal family (concerning which Gardiner observes that, in our day, such a thing would rouse the wrath of the British people from one end of the kingdom to the other) serves to illustrate both the heartlessness of the King and the lawless condition of the people.

Arabella Stuart, who was King James's cousin, had possessed her own appanage from the time of Queen Elizabeth. She had her apartments in the Palace, and associated with the Queen's ladies. Her letters show a refined and lovable woman's soul, absolutely untroubled by any political ambition. She says in a letter to her uncle Shrewsbury that she wishes to refute the apparent impossibility of a young woman's being able to preserve her purity and innocence among the follies with which a court surrounds her. She is alluding, amongst other things, to one of the eternal masquerades through which the Queen and her ladies racketed, attired, upon this occasion, "as sea nymphs or nereids, to the great delight of all beholders" (Arthur Wilson's "History of Great Britain," 1633). She kept apart as much as possible from this whirl of gaiety, and the various foreign potentates who applied for her hand were all dismissed. She would not, she said, wed a man whom she did not know. Nevertheless it was rumoured that she intended to marry some foreign prince who would enforce her rights to the English throne. James sent her to the Tower at Christmas 1609 on account of this report, and summoned the Council. The misunderstanding was cleared up, and she was hastily set at liberty, James expressly assuring her that he would have no objection to her marrying a subject.

A few weeks after she learned to know and love the man to whom she devoted herself with a passion and fidelity which recalls that of Imogen for Posthumus in Shakespeare's *Cymbeline*. This was young William Seymour, a son of Lord Beauchamp, one of the first noblemen in England. He was received in her apartments, and obtained her promise in February, the King's assurance to Arabella giving them every security for the future. Nevertheless, the young Princess's choice could not have fallen more unfortunately. Lord Beauchamp was the son of the Earl of Hertford and Catherine Grey, the inheritress of the Suffolk rights to the throne. The Earl's eldest son was still alive, and William Seymour had no claim to the crown at the moment; but the fact that his brother might die childless made him an always possible pretender. The Suffolk claims had been recognised by Act of Parliament, and the Parliament which had acknowledged James was powerless to change the succession. In the face of this notorious fact, James ignored the consideration that neither Seymour and Arabella, nor any one else, wanted to deprive him of the throne in favour of the young pair. Both were summoned before the Council and examined.

Seymour was made to renounce all thought of marriage with Arabella, and the young couple did not see each other for three months. In May 1610, however, they were secretly married.

When the news reached James's ears in July, he was furious. Arabella was detained in custody at Lambeth, and Seymour was sent to the Tower.

Arabella strove in vain to touch the King's heart. Great sympathy was felt in London, however, for the young couple, and secret meetings were permitted them by their gaolers. When the correspondence between them was discovered, Arabella was commanded to travel to Durham and put herself under the care of its Bishop. On her refusal to quit her apartments, she was carried away by force. Falling ill on the journey, she was given permission to pause by the way, and, attiring herself like one of Shakespeare's heroines, she seized the opportunity to escape. She drew on a pair of French trousers over her skirt, put on a man's coat and high boots, wore a manly wig with long curls over her hair, set a low-flapped black hat upon her head, threw a short cloak around her, and fastened a small sword at her side. Thus disguised, she fled by horse to Blackwall, where a French ship awaited her and Lord Seymour, the latter having arranged his escape for the same time. An accident prevented their meeting, and Arabella's friends, growing impatient, insisted, in spite of her protests, on setting out at once. When Seymour arrived next day, he learned to his disappointment, that the ship had set sail. He succeeded, however, in getting put over to Ostend. Meanwhile, Arabella, a few miles from Calais, induced the captain to lay-to for an hour or so to give Seymour an opportunity of overtaking them. They were here surprised by an English cruiser, which had been sent from Dover to capture the fugitives, and Arabella was brought back to the Tower. When she implored pardon, James brutally replied that she had eaten forbidden fruit, and must pay the price of her disobedience. Despair deprived her of her reason, and she died miserably, after five years of imprisonment. Not until after her death was her husband permitted to return to England.

VI

ROCHESTER AND LADY ESSEX

IT was Rochester who was the real ruler of England all this time. He was the acknowledged favourite; to him every suitor applied and from him came every reward. He was made head of the Privy Council after the death of Lord Dunbar, and was nominated Lord High Treasurer of Scotland, a title which gave him great prestige in his native country. He was also made Baron Brandspech, and, in accordance with the general expectation, Viscount Rochester and Knight of the Garter. The only decided opposition he had to encounter was that of young Prince Henry, the nation's darling, who could not endure his arrogant way, and was, moreover, his rival in fair ladies' favours. After the death of the Prince, Rochester was more powerful than ever. As principal Secretary, Carr managed all the King's correspondence, and on more than one occasion he answered letters without consulting either King or Council. The King, if he was aware of this, had reached such a pitch of infatuation that he submitted to everything. Carr was given a new title in 1613 and the Viscount Rochester was made Earl of Somerset. In 1614 the King made him Lord Chamberlain "because he loved him better than all men living." In the interim he had been appointed Keeper of the Seals and Warden of the Cinque Ports.

It was from such a height as this that he fell, and the circumstances of his overthrow form perhaps the most interesting events, from a psychological point of view, of James' reign. They made a great impression on contemporary minds, and occupy a large space in the letters of the period—letters in which Shakespeare's name is never mentioned and of whose very existence their historico-polemical writers do not seem to have been aware.

It was one of James's ambitions on his coming to England to put an end to the feuds and dissensions which were rife among the great families. To this end he arranged a match between Essex's son, and a daughter of the house which had ruined his father and driven him to death. In January 1608, accordingly, the fourteen-year-old Earl was married to the Lady Frances Howard, just thirteen years of age, and he thus became allied with the powerful houses of Howard and Cecil. Mr. Pory wrote to Sir Robert Cotton on the occasion of the marriage, "The bride-

groom carried himself as gravely and as gracefully as if he were
of his father's age."

The Church in those times sanctioned these marriages between
children, but every sense of fitness demanded that they should be
immediately parted. Young Essex was sent on foreign travel,
and did not return to claim his bride until he was eighteen. He
was a solidly built youth, possessed of a heavy and imperturbably
calm disposition. Frances, on the other hand, was obstinately
and stormily passionate in both her likes and dislikes. She had
been brought up by a coarse and covetous mother, and early corrupted by contact with the vices of the Court. She took a deep
dislike to her youthful bridegroom from the first and refused to live
with him. Her relations, however, compelled her to accompany
him to his estate, Chartley.

She had previously attracted the attention of both Prince Henry
and the favourite Rochester. Expecting more from Rochester,
as a contemporary document explains, than from the unprofitable
attentions of the Prince, she chose the former, a fact which can
hardly have failed to augment the ill-will already existing between
the King's son and the King's friend. From the moment of her
choice all the passionate intensity of her nature was concentrated
upon avoiding any intercourse with her husband and in assuring
Rochester that his jealousy on that score was groundless.

She chose for her confidante a certain Mrs. Turner, a doctor's
widow, who, after leading a dissipated life, was settling down to a
reputation for witchcraft. Lady Essex begged some potion of her
which should chill the Earl's ardour, and this not working to her
satisfaction, she wrote the following letter to her priestess, which
was later produced at the trial and made public by Fulk Greville :—

" Sweet Turner, as thou hast been hitherto, so art thou all my
hopes of good in this world. My Lord is lusty as ever he was,
and hath complained to my brother Howard, that hee hath not
layne with mee, nor used mee as his wife. This makes me mad,
since of all men I loath him, because he is the only obstacle and
hindrance, that I shall never enjoy him whom I love."

Upon the Earl's complaining a second time, the two applied
to a Dr. Forman, quack and reputed sorcerer, for some means of
causing an aversion (frigidity *quoad hanc*) in the Earl. The
mountebank obligingly performed all manner of hocus-pocus with
wax dolls, &c., and these in their turn failing, Lady Essex wrote
to him :—

" Sweet Father, although I have found you ready at all times
to further mee, yet must I still crave your helpe; wherefore I
beseech you to remember that you keepe the doores close, and
that you still retaine the Lord with mee and his affection towards
mee. I have no cause but to be confident in you, though the
world be against mee; yet heaven failes mee not; many are the
troubles I sustaine, the doggednesse of my Lord, the crossenesse

of my enemies, and the subversion of my fortunes, unlesse you by your wisdome doe deliver mee out of the midst of this wildernesse, which I entreat for God's sake. From Chartley.—Your affectionate loving daughter,   FRANCES ESSEX."

In the beginning of the year 1613, a woman named Mary Woods accused Lady Essex of attempting to bribe her to poison the Earl. The accusation came to nothing, however, and the Countess soon afterwards tried a new tack. It was now three years since her husband's return from abroad, and if she could succeed in convincing the Court that the marriage had never been consummated there was some chance of its being declared void. Having won her father and her utterly unscrupulous uncle, the powerful Lord Northampton, to her side, she induced the latter, who played Pandarus to this Cressida, to represent the situation to the King. James, loving Rochester as much as ever, and taking a pleasure in completing the happiness of those he loved, lent a willing ear. Northampton and Suffolk both took the matter up warmly, clearly seeing how advantageous an alliance with Carr, whom they had hitherto regarded as an enemy, would be to their plans. A meeting between the relatives of both parties was arranged. It consisted of the Earls of Northampton and Suffolk on Lady Essex's side, and the Earl of Southampton and Lord Knollys on her husband's. Essex, while resolved not to make any declaration which might prove an obstacle to his marrying again, fully conceded that he was not qualified to be this particular lady's husband. A commission of clergy and lawyers was therefore appointed to inquire into the matter.

A committee was nominated of six midwives and ten Godfearing matrons of rank, who had all borne children, to ascertain if Lady Essex was, as she asserted, a virgin. The lady's modesty insisted upon being closely veiled during the examination, which naturally gave rise to a rumour that another woman had been substituted.

The examination, which terminated in favour of the plaintiff, convinced none but those who had undertaken it, and was the occasion of much coarse-grained jesting.

With considerable impudence, Lady Essex maintained that her husband had been deprived of his manhood by witchcraft; but she was careful not to mention either Dr. Forman or herself as the instigators of this sorcery. Several members of the commission were prepared beforehand to declare the marriage void, it having been made worth their while to fall in with the wishes of the King and his favourite. Archbishop Abbot, however, an independent spirit, insisted from the first that it was utterly improbable that witchcraft could produce the assigned result, and urged that in accommodating the Countess they were establishing a precedent of which any childless wife could take advantage. The votes being equal, Abbot petitioned the King to allow his withdrawal. James, however, appointed two new members, both bishops, instead, and thus made the votes 7 to 5 in favour of "nullity." Abbot, as the result of his protest, became for a while the most popular man in England. Bishop Neile, who had always been despised, sank still lower in the public esteem, and Bishop Bilson of Winchester, of whom better things had been expected, was overwhelmed with ridicule. His son, whom the King knighted in order to reward his father, was acclaimed by general consent, Sir Nullity Bilson.

Throughout his whole career, and in his late relations with Lady Essex, Rochester had been guided by an intimate and capable adviser, Sir Thomas Overbury. He had assisted Rochester in the composition of his love-letters to the Countess, and he knew a great deal too much about the secret meetings, which he had himself arranged, between the lovers at Paternoster Row, Hammersmith, &c. When he learned that Rochester intended to supplement the connection by marriage, he strove by every means in his power to prevent it. He had been accustomed to dictate to his master in everything, but Rochester had now grown restive, and was resolved, by fair means or foul, on freeing himself from this control. To this end the King was given to understand that it was a common jest that Rochester managed the King, but Overbury ruled Rochester. In order to get rid of him in an honourable manner, he was appointed to some official post abroad. Overbury, however, whose ambition bound him to England, detected that this was but a mild form of banishment, and strove to excuse himself, finally declining outright. This was considered a breach of a subject's duty by James, and, upon the advice of the favourite, Overbury was sent to the Tower. Rochester now began to play a double game, and while assuring the prisoner that he was doing his utmost to obtain his release, he was, in reality, concentrating all his influence upon keeping him where he was. It was necessary to befool Overbury into thinking he had reason to be grateful to him, in case the prisoner should one day be released, and should wish to reveal all that Rochester was most anxious to keep concealed.

It was commanded from the first that Overbury should have no contact whatever with the outside world, an order which speaks for itself. When, however, the Lieutenant of the Tower, Sir William Wood, interpreted these directions so literally that he refused Rochester's own messengers access, it became necessary to replace him by the more amenable Sir Gervase Helwys.

Lady Essex, who was not the woman for half measures, preferred to make certain of Overbury once for all, and was determined that he should never leave the Tower alive. For this purpose she again applied to Mrs. Turner, who was well supplied with means serviceable to the occasion. The first thing necessary was to assure themselves of the man to whose immediate care the prisoner was intrusted. Lady Essex applied to Sir Thomas Monson, Master of the Tower Armoury, and through his influence Helwys was induced to dismiss Overbury's attendant and supply his place with Richard Weston, a former servant of Anne Turner.

This man was instructed by Mrs. Turner to meet Lady Essex at Whitehall, and to receive from her a little phial whose contents were to be mixed with the prisoner's food. Meeting Helwys on his way to Overbury's cell, and supposing him to be initiated into the secret, Weston consulted him as to the best way of administering the poison. Helwys, horror-stricken, prevailed upon him to throw away the contents of the phial. He was in too much awe of the Howard family to venture an accusation, and Weston at his instigation told Lady Essex that the poison had been duly administered, and that the prisoner's health was failing in consequence. Overbury was, in truth, suffering greatly from the frustration of his hopes of release, and he naïvely requested Rochester to send him an emetic in order that the King, hearing of his sickness, might be moved to compassion. It is not known what kind of medicament Rochester sent, nor whether he was aware of Lady Essex's attempt, but he seems to have played his own hand on this occasion.

On finding that Overbury, in spite of his steadily failing health, still continued to live, Lady Frances renewed her activity. Rochester was sending sweetmeats, jellies, and wines to the prisoner, and Lady Essex mixed poison with all these condiments, quite unconscious of the fact that Helwys, now upon the alert, took care that none of them should reach the prisoner. Losing all patience, she looked round for some more certain means than this poison, which worked with such astonishing and irritating deliberation. Learning that the apothecary Franklin was attending Overbury, she bribed his boy to give the sick man a poisoned injection. This was done, and the prisoner died in the Tower on the following day. Northampton immediately spread about a report that Sir Thomas Overbury had by no means led such a secluded life in the Tower as was generally supposed, but had by his dissolute life there contracted a disease of which he died. The rumour was generally believed, but that some suspicions were entertained can be seen in the letters of the times. John Chamberlain, writing to Sir Dudley Carleton on the 14th October 1613, speaks of Overbury's death as being caused by this disease, " or something worse."

Thus the last obstacle was cleared from the path which led this brilliant pair to the altar. Lady Frances was happy, and much farther removed from any feeling of remorse than Lady Macbeth. The King was full of affection for her, and, in order that she might not be wanting her title of Countess, Rochester was made Earl of Somerset. The wedding was celebrated with inordinate pomp on

the 26th December 1613. The bride had the assurance to appear
with maidenly hair unbound upon her shoulders. John Chamberlain, writing to Mrs. Alice Carleton, December 30th, says, "She
was married in her hair, and led to the chapel by her bridemen,
a Duke of Saxony that is here, and the Earl of Northampton, her
great-uncle." The wedding was celebrated in the Chapel Royal,
in the same place and by the same bishop who had solemnised
the previous marriage. King, Queen, and Archbishop were all
present, not to mention those of the nobility who wished to
stand well with the King and his favourite, and rich gifts were
brought by all. Gondomar, wishing to show himself attentive to
so highly favoured a pair, sent them some magnificent jewels.
The City of London, the Merchant Adventurers, the East India
Company, and the Customs sent each their present of precious
metals of great value. Gold, silver, and jewels were showered upon
them throughout the first half of January 1614. Bacon, though
personally no admirer of Somerset, naturally did not hold back.
It is very significantly remarked in a letter from John Chamberlain to Sir Dudley Carleton, December 23, 1613, " Sir Francis
Bacon prepares a masque to honour the marriage, which will
stand him in about £2000, and though he have been offered some
help by the House, and especially by Mr. Solicitor, Sir Henry
Yelverton, who would have sent him £500, yet he would not
accept it, but offers them the whole charge with the honour." A
few years later it is Bacon who conducts the poisoning case
against Rochester.

The day following the wedding the King sent a message to
the Lord Mayor, inviting him to arrange a fête for Lord and Lady
Somerset. The City vainly endeavoured to excuse itself on the
ground of insufficient space, but the King himself suggested a
remedy, and it was arranged that the guests should go in procession from Westminster to the City, the gentlemen on horseback and the ladies in carriages. The bride was pleased to
consider her carriage suitable to the occasion, but not being satisfied with her horses, she sent to borrow Lord Winwood's. He,
replying that it did not beseem so great a lady to borrow, gallantly
begged her acceptance of the horses as a gift.

Macaulay has likened this Court to that of Nero, and Swinburne has added that these celebrations recall the bridals of
Sporus and Locusta. Chapman had already inscribed to
Rochester two of the dedicatory sonnets which accompanied
the last books of his translation of the Iliad, and filled them with
absurdly exaggerated praise of the Viscount's "heroic virtues."
He now wrote his "Andromeda Liberata" in glorification of the
nuptials, and on his being attacked on that score, he retorted
with his exceedingly naïve "Defence of Perseus and Andromeda."

Life with Lady Frances could have no beneficial effect upon
Somerset's character. Nothing was magnificent enough for him,

2 I

and he was constantly importing new fashions in order to please his master and his wife. That ingenuously moralising historian, Arthur Wilson, complains bitterly of his appearance, his curled and perfumed locks, smooth shaven face and bare neck, and the golden embroideries lavished upon his attire. His only occupation was to solicit estates and money of the King. The subjects supplied him handsomely, for every petitioner paid tribute to Somerset. How much he received in this manner is uncertain, but he spent not less than £90,000 a year. It may be said to his credit, that he never, as did the later favourites, sought to tamper with the law, and he now and then displayed some generosity, but it was the exactions of his Howard connections which ruined him. The Council's most honourable members, amongst whom was Shakespeare's patron, Pembroke, saw with indignation that he predisposed the King in favour of their rivals.

His successor appeared in 1614. George Villiers, a young, handsome man of lively disposition, was promoted step by step, yet not too hastily, for fear of wounding Somerset's feelings. His presence at Court, however, was exceedingly disagreeable to the latter, who treated his rival with cold insolence, and seized every opportunity of humbling him. Somerset's passionate temper and arrogant disposition soon betrayed him into treating the King with similar superciliousness. He was rebuked by James, and a temporary reconciliation was effected; but how far Carr was from the enjoyment of a clear conscience is shown by his soliciting a general pardon, such as Wolsey had received from Henry VIII., from the King at this time, which was to include every possible offence, not forgetting murder. This, he pointed out to James, was in case his enemies should attempt to destroy him by false accusations after the King's death. James was willing, but Lord Ellesmere refused to apply the great seal to the document in question. The King's wrath was great but unavailing. Ellesmere fell upon his knees, but refused to affix the seal.

Soon after this Somerset experienced the need of this comprehensive absolution which he had failed to secure. The apothecary's boy, who had administered the injection to Overbury, fell dangerously ill at Flushing, and, wishing to ease his burdened soul, confessed the murder to Lord Winwood. Helwys was examined, Weston was examined, and Lord and Lady Somerset were soon implicated in the case. As soon as Somerset heard that he was accused, he quitted the King, with whom he was staying at Royston, and started for London in order to clear himself. The King, by this time, was profoundly weary of his old favourite, and entirely taken up by his new. To give some idea of James's dissimulation, we will quote Sir Anthony Weldon's account, as an eye-witness, of the parting between the King and Somerset. "The Earle when he kissed his hand, the King hung about his neck, slabbering his cheeks, saying, 'For God's sake, when shall I see thee again ?   On my soul, I shall neither eat nor sleep until you come again.'   The Earle told him, on Monday (this being on the Friday).   'For God's sake, let me,' said the King.   'Shall I, shall I;' then lolled about his neck.   'Then, for God's sake, give thy lady this kiss for me.'   In the same manner at the stayres' head, at the middle of the stayres, and at the stayres' foot.   The Earl was not in his coach when the King used these very words, 'I shall never see his face more.'"

Short work was made of the subordinate culprits.   Mrs. Turner, Weston, Helwys, and the apothecary Franklin, were all declared guilty and hanged.   The Countess bore testimony to her husband's innocence, and he went to the Tower with the collar of the Garter and the George about his neck.   He threatened that if he were brought to trial he would betray secrets which contained an accusation against the King—contemporary letters show that this was understood to mean that he would confess to having poisoned Prince Henry at the King's instigation; but he abandoned this accusation later, and conducted his defence with dignity, denying all complicity in the murder.   The Countess was less self-possessed.   The judgment hall was filled with spectators, and the Earl of Essex amongst them was seated exactly opposite her.   As the accusation was read, she trembled and turned pale, and when Weston's name was reached, she covered her face with her fan.   When, according to custom, she was asked if she acknowledged herself guilty, she could but answer, Yes.   She was condemned to death, and to the question whether she had anything further to add, replied that she would say nothing to palliate her guilt, but prayed the King's mercy.   Somerset was also unanimously declared guilty.

The King pardoned them both.   He could hardly send to the scaffold the man who had so long been his most intimate friend, neither could he well despatch thither the daughter of his Chancellor of the Exchequer.   But although Somerset steadily maintained his innocence, both he and his wife were sent to the Tower.

In the letters written at the time of the trial, as much mention is made of Sir George Villiers as of Somerset.   The new favourite has been ill for some time, "not without suspicion of smallpox, which if it had fallen out *actum erat de amicitia*.   But it proves otherwise, and we say there is much casting about how to make him a great man, and that he shall now be made of the Garter," &c.

He was soon made Cupbearer, Chamberlain, Master of the Horse, Marquis of Buckingham, and Keeper of the Great Seal, and he retained his pernicious influence well into the reign of Charles the First.   It is highly characteristic of James that he was now as anxious to procure Villiers Raleigh's old estate, Sherborne, from the imprisoned Somerset as he had been to wrest it from the imprisoned Raleigh for Somerset.   He must have regarded it as a lawful "morrowing gift," so inextricably had it become associated with a rising favourite in his mind. Somerset was given to understand that he would obtain a free pardon, together with the restitution of the rest of his properties, if he would secure the now all-powerful Villiers' protection by relinquishing Sherborne in his favour. On his obstinately refusing, he and Lady Somerset were left to languish for six long years in the Tower.[1]

[1] Arthur Wilson: "The History of Great Britain, being the Life and Reign of James the First," 1653. Sir A. Weldon: "A Cat may look upon a King," London, 1652. The author of "Memoirs of Sophia Dorothea": "The Court and Times of James the First, illustrated by Authentic Letters," 2 vols., London, 1848. Fulk Greville: "The Five Years of King James." "Secret History of the Court of James the First," edited by Sir Walter Scott, 2 vols., Edinburgh, 1811. "An Inquiry into the Literary and Political Character of James the First," by the author of "Curiosities of Literature," London, 1816. Samuel R. Gardiner: "History of England from the Accession of James I. to the Outbreak of the Civil War," vol. ii., London, 1883. Edmond Gosse: "Raleigh," London, 1886. "The Court and Character of King James, Written and taken by Sir A. W(eldon), being an Eye and Ear Witness," London, 1650. Aulicus Coquinariæ: "A Vindication in Answer to a Pamphlet entitled 'The Court and Character of King James,'" London, 1650.

VII

CONTEMPT OF WOMEN—TROILUS AND CRESSIDA

In order to give a complete picture, it was necessary to trace events down to the years in which external happenings ceased to work upon Shakespeare's mind. He died in the same year that the Lady Arabella perished in the Tower, and when the scandal of the Somerset trial was beginning to fade from the public mind. It is obviously impossible to point to any one cause which could have made an especially deep impression on his inner life. All we can say with certainty is, that the general atmosphere of the times, of the corrupt condition of morals here described, could hardly fail to leave some mark on a disposition which, just at this time, was susceptible and irritable to the highest degree. If, as we maintain, there now ensued a period during which his melancholy was prone to dwell upon the darkest side of life ; if he shows, in these years, a sickly tendency to imbibe poison from everything ; and if all his observation and experience seem to result in a contempt of mankind, so did the general condition of society afford ample nourishment for the mood of scorn for human nature.

In the merely external, Shakespeare's life cannot at this time have undergone any great catastrophe. He was now (1607) forty-three years of age. As soon as the play was over, between five and six of an afternoon, he stepped into one of the Thames boats and was set across the river to his house, where his books and work awaited him. He studied much, making himself familiar with the works of his cotemporaries, plunging anew into Plutarch, reading Chaucer and Gower, and pondering over More's *Utopia.* He worked as hard as ever. Neither the rehearsal in the morning nor the play at mid-day had power to weary him. He read through old dramatic manuscripts to see if new treatment could revive them into use, and returned to long-laid-by manuscripts of his own to work upon them afresh.

He attended to business at the same time, received the rents of his houses at Stratford, collected his tithes from the same place, and watched the lawsuits in which the purchase of these tithes had involved him. He had obtained the object of his existence, so far as the possession of property was concerned ; but never had he been so downcast and dispirited, never had he felt so keenly the emptiness of life.

So long as Shakespeare was young, the general condition of society and the ways and worth of men had troubled him less. Then, except for the feeling of belonging to a despised caste and the increasing spread of Puritanism, he was at peace with his surroundings. Now he saw more sharply the true outlines of his times and his world, and perceived more clearly that eternal infirmity of human nature, which at all times only waits for a propitious climate in order to develop itself.

The last work which had lain ready on his table was *Antony and Cleopatra.* He had there, for the second time, given his impression of the subversion of a world.

There was a pendant to this war of the East (which was in reality waged for Cleopatra's sake), a war fought by all the countries of the Mediterranean for the possession of a loose woman; the most famous of all wars, the old Trojan war, set going by a " cuckold and carried on for a whore," so it will shortly be described by a scandalous buffoon, whom Shakespeare uses, so to speak, in his own name. Here was stuff for a tragi-comedy of right bitter sort.

From childhood he, and every one else, had been filled with the fame and glory of this war. All its heroes were models of bravery, magnanimity, wisdom, friendship, and fidelity, as if such things existed! For the first time in his life he feels a desire to mock—to shout "Bah!" straight out of his heart—to turn the wrong side out, the true side.

Menelaus and Helen—what a ridiculous couple! The wretched head of horned cattle moves heaven and earth, causes thousands of men to be slain, and all that he may have his damaged beauty back again.[1] Menelaus stood too low for his satire, however. Shakespeare himself had never felt thus. Neither was it in his humour to portray a woman who, like Helen, had openly left one man for another, a husband for a lover—there was none of woman's special duplicity in that. The transfer from one to another, which alone was of interest to him, in her case was already past and gone. Helen's destiny is settled before the drama begins. There is no play, no inner variety in her character, no dramatic situation between her in Troy and Menelaus without.

But in the old legends of Troy which sagas and folk-tales had handed down to him, he found, in miniature, the plot whereon the whole war turned. Cressida, a rejuvenated Helen; Troilus, the simpleton who loved her, and whom she betrayed; and round about them grouped all those archetypes of subtlety, wisdom, and strength—that venerable old twaddler Nestor, and that sly fox

---

[1] Heine, some hundreds of years later, expresses the same feeling in his
" O König Wiswamatra,
O welch ein Ochs bist du,
Dass du so viel kämpfest und brüssest
Und Alles für eine Kuh !"

Ulysses, &c. Here was something which urged him on to representation. Here was a plot which chimed in with his mood.

Shakespeare had no interest in delineating that *bellâtre*, Prince Paris; he had felt him as little as he had Menelaus. But he had many a time felt as Troilus did—the honest soul, the honourable fool, who was simple enough to believe in a woman's constancy. And he knew well, too well, that Lady Cressida, with the alluring ways, the nimble wit, the warm blood, speaking lawful passion with (to not too true an ear) the lawful modesty of speech. She would rather be desired than confer, would rather be loved than love, says "yes" with a "no" yet upon her lips, and flames up at the least suspicion of her truth. Not that she is false. Oh, no! why false? We believe in her as her lover believes in her, and as she believes in herself—until she leaves him for the Greek camp. Then she has scarcely turned her back upon him than she loses her heart to the first she meets, and her constancy fails at the first proof to which it is put.

All his life through these two forms had preoccupied his imagination. In *Lucretia*, he coupled Troilus with Hector among Trojan heroes. In the fourth act of the *Merchant of Venice*, he made Lorenzo say:

> "In such a night
> Troilus, methinks, mounted the Trojan walls,
> And sighed his soul towards the Grecian tents
> Where Cressid lay."

In *Henry V.*, Pistol included Doll Tearsheet among "Cressid's kind," making Doll doubly ridiculous by classing her with the Trojan maid of far-famed charm. In *Much Ado About Nothing*, (Act v.), Benedict called Troilus "the first employer of Pandars." In *As You Like It* (Act iv.), Rosalind jested about him, and yet yielded him a certain recognition. Protesting that no man ever yet died for love, she said, "Troilus had his brains dashed out with a Grecian club, yet did what he could to die before, *and he is one of the patterns of love.*" In *Twelfth Night* and in *All's Well that Ends Well*, the Fool and Lafeu both jested about Pandarus and his ill-famed zeal in bringing Troilus and Cressida together.

Slowly, like the Hamlet tradition, this subject had been growing ripe in Shakespeare's mind. It had hitherto lived in his imagination in much the same form in which it had been handled by his compatriots. By Chaucer, first and foremost, who in his *Troilus and Cressida* (about 1360) had translated, elaborated, and enlarged Boccaccio's beautiful poem, *Filostrato*. But neither Chaucer nor any other Englishman who had translated or reproduced the subject (such as Lydgate, 1460, who restored Guido delle Columne's *Historia Trojana*, or Caxton, who in 1471 published a translation of Raoul le Fevre's *Recueil des Histoires de Troyes*) had found in it any material for satire. Especially had none of its earlier elaborators found any fault with the character of Cressida. Not the poets once. Chaucer founded his heroine in all essentials upon Boccaccio's. He, who was the first to gather the material into a poetic whole, had no intention of presenting his heroine in an unfavourable light. He wished to give expression, as he openly declares, to his own devotion to his lady-love in his description of Troilus's passion for Cressida. The old Trouvère, Benoit de St. Maure, and his *Histoire de la Guerre de Troie* (about 1160), was undoubtedly his model. It is from him he received the impression that Griseida (into whom he transforms Benoit's Briseida) gradually falls a victim to the seductions of Diomedes, in whose company she leaves Troy, and little by little grows untrue to Troilus. He adds a stanza to this effect, on the inconstancy of women.[1] It was not to be expected that Boccaccio should kneel before women with the platonic love and devout worship of Dante and Petrarch. Beatrice is a mystical, Laura an earthly ideal. Griseida is a young lady from the Court of Naples, such as it was then. A young, lovable, and frail woman of flesh and blood. But only frail, never base, and very far from being a coquette. Boccaccio never forgets that he has dedicated the poem to his love and that she also left the place where they had dwelt together, for one where he durst not follow her. He says clearly that in the portrayal of Griseida's charms he has drawn a picture of his love, but he refrains with consummate tact from driving the comparison further.

Chaucer, as little as Boccaccio, found anything in the relations of the lovers to satirise. He intends, to the best of his abilities, to prove their love as innocent and lawful as possible. He paints it with a naïve and enraptured simplicity, which proves how far he is from mockery.[2] He does not even rave over Cressida's faithlessness to Troilus; she is excused, she trembles and hesitates before she falls. Inconstancy is forced upon her by the overwhelming might of hard circumstance.

There is nothing in these two poets that can compare with the passionate heat and hatred, the boundless bitterness with which Shakespeare delineates and pursues his Cressida. His mood is the more remarkable that he in no wise paints her as unlovable

---

[1] "Giovine donna è mobile, e vogliosa
E negli amanti molti, e sua bellezza
Estima più che allo specchio, e pomposa
Ha vanagloria di sua giovinezza ;
La qual quanto piacevole e vezzosa
E più, cotanto più seco l'apprezza
Virtù non sente, nè conoscimento,
Volubil sempre come foglia al vento."

[2] " Her armes smale, her streghte bak and softe,
Her sides long, fleshly, smothe, and white,
He gan to stroke ; and good thrift bad ful oft.
Her snowish throte, her brestes round and lite :
Thus in this hevene he gan him to delite,
And then withal a thousand times her kiste
That what to dou for joie unnethe he wiste."

or corrupt; she is merely a shallow, frivolous, sensual, pleasure-loving coquette.

She does little, on the whole, to call for such severity of judgment. She is a mere child and beginner in comparison with Cleopatra, for instance, who, for all that, is not so unmercifully condemned. But Shakespeare has aggravated and pointed every circumstance until Cressida becomes odious, and rouses only aversion. The change from love to treachery, from Troilus to Diomedes, is in no earlier poet effected with such rapidity. Whenever Shakespeare expresses by the mouth of one or another of his characters the estimate in which he intends his audience to hold her, one is astounded by the bitterness of the hatred he discloses. It is especially noticeable in the scene (Act iv.) in which Cressida comes to the Greek camp and is greeted by the kings with a kiss.

At this point Cressida has as yet offended in nothing. She has, out of pure, vehement love for him, passed such a night with Troilus as Juliet did with Romeo, persuaded to it by Pandarus, as Juliet was by her nurse. Now she accepts and returns the kiss wherewith the Greek chieftains bid her welcome. We may re-mark, in parenthesis, that at that time there was no impropriety in such a greeting. In William Brenchley Rye's " England as seen by Foreigners in the Days of Elizabeth and James the First," are found, under the heading " England and Englishmen," the following notes by Samuel Riechel, a merchant from Ulm :—
" Item, when a foreigner or an inhabitant goes to a citizen's house on business, or is invited as a guest, and having entered therein, he is received by the master of the house, the lady, or the daughter, and by them welcomed ; he has even the right to take them by the arm and kiss them, which is the custom of the country; and if any one does not do so, it is regarded and imputed as ignorance and ill-breeding on his part."

For all that, Ulysses, who sees through her at the first glance, breaks out on occasion of this kiss which Cressida returns :

> " Fie, fie upon her,
> There's language in her eye, her cheek, her lips,
> Nay, her foot speaks, her wanton spirit looks out
> At every joint and motive of her body.
> Oh, these encounterers, so glib of tongue,
> That give occasion welcome ere it comes,
> And wide unclasp the tables of their thoughts
> To every ticklish reader ! Set them down
> For sluttish spoils of opportunity,
> And daughters of the game."

So Shakespeare causes his heroine to be described, and doubt-less it is his own last word about her. Immediately before her he had portrayed Cleopatra. When we remember the position occupied in his drama by the Egyptian queen, whom he, for all

that, has stamped as the most dangerous of all dangerous co-
quettes, we can only marvel at the distance his spiritual nature
has traversed since then.

There was in Shakespeare's disposition, as we have already
remarked, a deep and extraordinary tendency to submissive admiration and worship. Many of his flowing lyrics spring from
this source. Recall his humility of attitude before the objects of
this admiration, before Henry V., for example, and his adoration for the friend in the Sonnets. We still find this need of
giving lyrical and ecstatic expression to his hero-worship in
Antony and Cleopatra. He by no means undertakes a defence
of the desolating temptress, but with what glamour he surrounds
her ! What eulogies he lavishes upon her ! She stands in an
aureole of the adulation of all the other characters in the drama.
At the time Shakespeare wrote this great tragedy, he had still
so much of romantic enthusiasm remaining to him that he found
it natural to let her live and die gloriously. Let be that she was
a sorceress, still she fascinates.

What a change ! Shakespeare, who had hitherto worshipped
women, has become a misogamist. This mood, forgotten since
his early youth, rises up again in hundredfold strength, and his
very soul overflows in scorn for the sex.

What is the cause ? Has anything befallen him—anything
new ? Upon what and whom does he think ? Does he speak
out of new and recent experience, or is it the old sorrow from the
time of the Sonnets, of which he made use in the construction
of Cleopatra's character, and is this the same grief which has
taken new shape in his mind and is turning sour ? is it this
which has grown increasingly bitter until it corrodes ?

There are two types of artist soul. There is the one which
needs many varying experiences and constantly changing models,
and which instantly gives a poetic form to every fresh incident.
There is the other which requires amazingly few outside elements
to fertilise it, and for which a single life circumstance, inscribed
with sufficient force, can furnish a whole wealth of ever-changing
thought and modes of expression. Sören Kierkegaard among
writers, and Max Klinger among painters, are both great examples
of the latter type.

To which did Shakespeare belong ? His many-sidedness and
fertility is incontrovertible, and every particular points to the use
of a multiplicity of models. But for all that, his groups of feminine
characters can frequently be traced back to an original type, and
therefore, most likely, to a single model. When one momentous
incident of a poet's life is known, we are very apt to relate to it
everything in his works which could possibly have any connection
with it. In this manner the French literary and critical world
most obstinately found traces of Alfred de Musset's life with
George Sand in every expression of melancholy or complaint of
desolation in his poems. In his biography of his brother, how-

ever, Paul de Musset has revealed the fact that the "December Night," which seems so obvious a supplement to the "May Night" that turns upon George Sand, was really written in quite another spirit, to a totally different woman. Also, the character delineated in the "Letter to Lamartine," which was generally believed to be that of the famous poetess, had in reality nothing whatever to do with her.

It is quite possible, therefore, that this last woman's character, instead of being only a variant of the Cleopatra type, was a product of a new, fiery, and scorching impression of feminine inconstancy and worthlessness. We are too entirely ignorant of the circumstances of the poet's life to venture any decided opinion, all we can say is, that incidents and novel experiences are not absolutely necessary as an explanation. There is a remote possibility that the first sketch of the play was already written in 1603, in which case it would be more than likely that the dark lady was once more his prototype. On the other hand, it may be, as already suggested, that in a productive soul one circumstance will take the place of many, and an experience which at first seemed wholly tragic may, in the rapid inner development of genius, come to wholly change its character. He has suffered under it; it has sucked his heart's blood and left him a beaten man on his path through life. He has sought to embody it in serious and worthy forms, until suddenly it stands before him as a burlesque. His misery no longer seems a cruel destiny, but a well-merited punishment for immoderate stupidity, and this bitter mood has sought relief in such scornful laughter as that whose discord strikes so harshly in *Troilus and Cressida.*

We can imagine that Shakespeare began by worshipping his lady-love, complaining of her coldness and hardness, celebrating her fingers in song, cursing her faithlessness, and feeling himself driven nearly wild with grief at the false position in which she had placed him; this is the standpoint of the Sonnets. In the course of years the fever had stormed itself out, but the memory of the enchantment was still visibly fresh, and his mind pictured the loved one as a marvellous phenomenon, half queen, half gipsy, alluring and repellant, true and false, strong and weak, a siren and a mystery; this is the standpoint of *Antony and Cleopatra.* Then, possibly, when life had sobered him down, when he had cooled, as we all do cool in the hardening ice of experience, he suddenly and sharply realised the insanity of an exotic enthusiasm for so worthless an object. He looks upon this condition, which invariably begins with self-deception and must of necessity end in disillusionment, as a disgraceful and tremendous absurdity; and his wrath over wasted feelings and wasted time and suffering, over the degradation and humiliation of its self-deception, and ultimately the treason itself, seeks final and supreme relief in the outburst, "What a farce!" which is in itself the germ of *Troilus and Cressida.*

VIII

TROILUS AND CRESSIDA—THE HISTORICAL MATERIAL.

IN the twenty-fourth book of the Iliad Homer makes his solitary mention of Troilus as a son whom Priam had lost before the opening of the poem. The old King says:

> "O me, accursed man,
> All my good sons are gone, my light the shades Cimmerian
> Have swallowed from me. I have lost Mestor, surnamed the Fair,
> Troilus, that ready knight at arms, that made his field repair
> Ever so prompt and joyfully."

This is all the great old world poet says of the king's son, whose fame in the Middle Ages outshone Hector's own. This brief mention of an early death stirred the imagination and set fancy at work. The cyclic poets expanded the hint and developed Troilus into a handsome youth who fell by Achilles' lance. It had become the custom under Imperial Rome to derive the empire from the Trojans, and the theory gave birth to many fabrications, professing to emanate from eye-witnesses of the war.

Yet it was not before the time of Constantine the Great, that a description was given which quite displaced Homer during the Middle Ages. This was Dictys Cretensis' book, *De Bello Trojano*, translated from the original Greek into Latin. The translator, a certain Quintus Septimius, informs us that Dictys was a brother in arms of Idomeneus, and at his prince's suggestion wrote this book in Phœnician characters, and afterwards caused it to be buried with him. An earthquake in the time of Nero brought it to light. The translator is evidently simple enough to believe in the truth of this account. A more daring forgery was issued about 635, after the fall of the Western Empire of Rome. The author is supposed to be a certain Dares Phrygius, who was one of Hector's counsellors, and who wrote the Iliad before Homer. The title of this book also is *De Bello Trojano*, and it professes to have been translated into Latin by Cornelius Nepos, who is said to have found the manuscript at Athens, "where, in his day, Homer was considered half mad" because he had depicted gods and men as carrying on a war with one another. Troilus is the most prominent hero of the book, which is a wretched compilation of far-fetched reminiscences.

Dares, however, became the fountain-head for all mediæval storytellers, first and foremost among them being Benoit de St. Maure, troubadour to Henry II. of England. Of his poem, containing 30,000 verses, only fragments have ever been printed. As a genuine Trouvère of the early half of the twelfth century, he has adorned his ancient material with sumptuous descriptions of towns, palaces, and accoutrements. He enters, so far as he is able, into the spiritual life of his hero, and supplies him with what, according to the notions of his times, he could not possibly lack—a love motive. He represents Briseis, Achilles' vaunted love, as the daughter of Kalchas, whom, following the example of Dares, he makes a Trojan. Briseida, who is beloved by Troilus, returns to Troy after her father goes over to the Greeks. When Kalchas wishes to regain his daughter, she is exchanged, as in Shakespeare's drama, for the prisoner Antenor. Diomedes is sent by the Greeks to escort her, and Briseida falls a victim to his seductive arts. Many of the incidents in Shakespeare's play are to be found in Benoit—that Diomedes is experienced in women, for example; that Briseis gives him a favour wherewith to adorn his lance; that he dismounts Troilus and sends his horse to his lady-love, and that Troilus inveighs against her broken faith, &c.

Now it can be traced how, in the further development of the theme, one writer after another adds some feature which Shakespeare in his turn still further elaborates. Guido de Colonna (or delle Columne), a judge at Messina in 1287, retranslates Benoit de St. Maure into barbarous Latin, making no acknowledgment of his source, and transforming Achilles into a raw, bloodthirsty barbarian.

Boccaccio, who prefers significant names, and the title of whose poem, *Filostrato*, signifies "one struck to earth by love," changes Briseida into Cryseida (thus in old editions), in order that her name may mean "the golden," and he it is who adds Pandarus, the "all-giver," who aids Troilus in his love affairs. He is Cryseida's kinsman and is evidently sympathetic all through.[1]

It is Chaucer who first submits the character of Pandarus to an important change, and makes it the transition point of the Pandarus we find in Shakespeare. In his poem Troilus's young friend has become the elderly kinsman of Creseyde, and he brings the young pair together, mostly out of looseness. It is he who persuades the young maiden and leads her astray by means of lying impostures. It was not Chaucer's intention, as it was Shakespeare's, to make

---

[1] Troilus says to him :

> "Non m'hai piccola cosa tu donata
> Ne me a piccola cosa donato hai
> La vita mia ti fia sempre obligata
> In l'hai da morte in via suscitata."

the old fellow odious. His *rôle* is not carried out with the cynical and repulsive lowness of Shakespeare's character. Chaucer endeavours to ward off any painful impression by making the shameless old rascal the wit of his poem. He did not achieve his object; his readers saw only the procurer in Pandarus, whose name became thenceforward a by-word in the English language, and it was as such that Shakespeare drew the character in downright, unmistakable disgust.[1]

We have yet other sources, Latin, French, and English, for the details of the drama. From Ovid's *Metamorphoses*, for example (which Shakespeare must have known from childhood), he took the idea of making Ajax almost an idiot in his conceited stupidity. It is in the third book of the *Metamorphoses* that Ulysses, fighting with Ajax for Achilles' weapon, overwhelms his opponent with biting sarcasms.[2] Shakespeare found the name of Thersites in the same book, with a word concerning his *rôle* as lampooner of princes.

We may doubt whether Shakespeare knew Lydgate's *Book of Troy*. Most of his details with regard to the siege are taken from an old writing translated from the French and published by Wynkyn de Worde in 1503. Here, for example, is the parade of heroes, the talk of King Neoptolemus being no son of Achilles, and the corrupted names of the six gates of Troy—Dardane, Timbria, Helias, Chetas, Troyen, and Antenorides. Here also he would find the name of Hector's horse, Galathea, the archer who calls upon the Greeks, the bastard Margarelon, Cassandra's warning to Hector, the glove Cressida gives away, and Troilus's idea that a man is not called upon to be merciful in war, but should take a victory as he may.[3]

We cannot tell if Shakespeare was further indebted to some old dramatic writings, whereof only the names have survived to us. In 1515, a "Komedy" called the *Story of Troylus and Pandor* was played before Henry VIII. On New Year's Day, 1572, a play about Ajax and Ulisses was performed at Windsor Castle, and another in 1584 concerning Agamemnon and Ulisses.[4] In Henslowe's Daybook for April and May 1599

---

[1] *Jahrbuch der Deutschen Shakespearegesellschaft*, iii. 252, and vi. 169. Francesco de Sanctis: *Historia della letterature italiana*, i. 308.

[2] " Huic modo ne prosit, quod, uti est, hebes esse, videtur.
　　Artis opus tantæ rudis et sine pectore miles
　　Indueret?
　　Ajacis stolidi Danais Sollertia prosit
　　Tu vires sine mente geris, mihi cura futuri
　　Tu pugnare potes, pugnandi tempora mecum
　　Eligit Atrides. In tantum corpore prodes."
　　　　　　　　　　　　　　　Met. xiii. 135, 290, 327, 360.

[3] Halliwell-Phillips: *Memoranda on Troilus and Cressida*. 1880. (Only twenty copies.)

[4] "Ajax and Ulisses shoven on New Yeares day at nighte by the children of Wynsor.—The history of Agamemnon and Ulisses presented and enacted before her Majestie by the Earle of Oxenford his boyes on St. Johns daie at night at Grenewiche, 1584."

we see that the poets Dekker and Henry Chettle (Dickers and
Harey Cheattel, in his amusing orthography) wrote a piece, at his
invitation, for the Lord Admiral's troupe, *Troeyles and creasse-
day*. In May he lends them a sum of money on it, changing its
title to *A tragedy about Agamemnon*. It is finally entered at
the Stationers' Hall in February 1603 as a piece entitled *Troilus
and Cresseda*, "as it was played by the Lord Chamberlain's men "[1]
(Shakespeare's company). The fact that in Shakespeare's drama,
as we have it, rhyme is introduced in various parts of the dialogue,
and several other details of versification, seems to point to the
possibility that the so-called piece was in reality Shakespeare's
first sketch of the play. It is one of Fleay's tediously worked out
theories that the drama was produced in three different parts,
with an interval of from twelve to thirteen years between each.
He is quite regardless of the fact that the parts are absolutely
inseparable, and is evidently entirely innocent of the manner of
growth of poems. He also totally ignores such important evidence as that of the preface to the oldest edition, 1609, which
positively asserts that the piece has never hitherto been played.
It is, of course, possible that this edition, like most of its kind,
was unauthorised, but even then the writer of the preface would
scarcely lie about a fact which could be so easily verified, and
which, moreover, he was not in the least interested in falsifying.

---

[1] " Entred for his (Master Robertes') copie in full court holden this day to print
when he hath gotten sufficient aucthority for yt the Booke of Troilus and Cresseda, as
it is acted by my Lord Chamberlen's men."

IX

SHAKESPEARE AND CHAPMAN—SHAKESPEARE
AND HOMER

WE have now apparently exhausted the literary sources of this mysterious and so little understood work. But we have not, for all that, solved the fundamental question which has occupied so many brains and pens. Was it Shakespeare's intention to ridicule Homer? Did he know Homer?

To a Dane, *Troilus and Cressida* recalls the mockery Holberg's *Ulysses von Ithacia* makes of the Homeric material, just as the *Ulysses* reminds us of Shakespeare's play. *Troilus and Cressida* seems to have represented to the English poet much what Holberg's play did to him, a satire, namely, on the absurdities the Gothic and Anglo-Saxon understanding (*i.e.* narrow-mindedness) found in Homer. It is sufficiently remarkable that Shakespeare should have written a travesty which could, in spite of many reservations, be classed with *Ulysses von Ithacia*. As far as Holberg is concerned, the explanation is simple enough. His is the taste of the enlightened age, and the ancient civilisation's noble naïveté viewed in the light of dry rationalism, filled him with amazement and laughter. But what has Shakespeare to do with rationalism? His was the very time of the renaissance of that old world civilisation, the moment of its resurrection. How came he to scorn it?

The general working of the public mind towards the ancient Greeks had prompted Elizabeth to write a commentary on Plato and to translate the Dialogues of Socrates; but Shakespeare's knowledge of Greek was defective, and thus it was that he, as playwright, represented the popular trend, in contradistinction to the numerous other poets, who, like Ben Jonson, prided themselves on their erudition.

Moreover, like the Romans, and subsequently the Italians and French, the Englishmen of his day believed themselves to be descended from those ancient Trojans, whom Virgil, as true Roman, had glorified at the expense of the Greeks. The England of Shakespeare's time took a pride in her Trojan forefathers, and we find evidence in other of his works that he, as English patriot, sided with the Trojans in the old battles of Ilion, and was, consequently, prejudiced against the Greek heroes. In my opinion, however, all this has little to do with the point at issue. We have already found it probable that Chapman was the poet whose intimacy with Pembroke roused Shakespeare's jealousy, making him feel slighted and neglected, and causing him so much melancholy suffering. I am not ignorant of the arguments which have been brought forward in support of the theory that the rival poet was not Chapman but Daniel, nor of what Miss Charlotte Stopes and G. A. Leigh have to say on the subject of Minto and Tyler.[1] I do not, however, consider that they have been able to refute the strong evidence in favour of its being no other than Chapman who was the poet of Shakespeare's Sonnets 78–86.

In the year 1598 Chapman had just published the first seven books of his *Iliad*, namely, the first, second, seventh, eighth, ninth, tenth, and eleventh of Homer. The remaining books, followed by a complete *Odyssey*, were not published until 1611, two years after the first appearance of *Troilus and Cressida*. To render the comparatively unknown Homer into good English verse was an achievement worthy of the acknowledgments Chapman received. His translation is to this day, in spite of its faults, the best that England possesses. Keats himself has written a sonnet in praise of it.

How great a reputation Chapman enjoyed as a dramatist may be seen in the dedication of John Webster's tragedy *The White Divel* (1612), at the close of which he says: "Detraction is the sworn friend to ignorance. For mine owne part, I have ever truly cherisht my good opinion of other men's worthy labours, especially of that full and haightened stile of Maister Chapman. The labour'd and understanding workes of Maister Johnson: The no less worthy composures of the both worthy and excellent Maister Beamont and Maister Fletcher: and lastly (without wrong last to be named), the right happy and copious industry of Mr. Shakespeare, Mr. Decker and Mr. Heywood." As will have been noticed, Chapman's name heads the list, while Shakespeare's comes at the bottom in conjunction with such insignificant men as Decker and Heywood!

Nevertheless (or possibly on that account) there is little doubt that Shakespeare found Chapman personally antipathetic. His style was unequalled for arrogance and pedantry; he was insufferably vain of his learning, and not a whit less conceited of the divine inspiration he, as poet, must necessarily possess. Even the most ardent of his modern admirers admits that his own poems are both grotesque and wearisome, and Shakespeare must certainly have suffered under the miserable conclusion Chapman added to Marlowe's beautiful *Hero and Leander*, a poem that Shakespeare himself so greatly admired. Take only the

[1] *Jahrbuch der Deutschen Shakespearegesellschaft*, xxv. p. 196 ; *Westminster Review*, Feb. 1897.

fragment of introductory prose which prefaces his translation of
Homer, and try to wade through it. Short as it is, it is impossible. Read but the confused garrulity and impossible imagery
of the dedication in 1598, and could a more shocking collection
of mediæval philology be found outside the two pages he writes
about Homer?

Swinburne, who loves him, says of his style: " Demosthenes,
according to report, taught himself to speak with pebbles in his
mouth; but it is presumable that he also learnt to dispense with
their aid before he stood up against Æschines or Hyperides on
any great occasion of public oratory. Our philosophic poet, on
the other hand, before addressing such audience as he may find,
is careful always to fill his mouth till the jaws are stretched well-
nigh to bursting with the largest, roughest, and most angular of
polygonal flintstones that can be hewn or dug out of the mine of
language; and as fast as one voluminous sentence or unwieldy
paragraph has emptied his mouth of the first batch of barbarisms,
he is no less careful to refill it before proceeding to a fresh de-
livery." [1] The comparison is strikingly exact.

It is this incomprehensible style which made Chapman's
readers so few in number, and caused his frequent complaints of
being slighted and neglected. As Swinburne jestingly says of him:

> " We understand a fury in his words,
> But not his words."

Even in his fine translation of Homer, he is unable to forego his
tendency to obscurity, and constrained and inflated expression.
It is universally admitted that even a translation must take some
colouring from its translator, and no man in England was less
Hellenic than Chapman. Swinburne has rightly observed that
his temperament was more Icelandic than Greek, that he handled
the sacred vessels of Greek art with the substantial grasp of the
barbarian, and when he would reproduce Homer he gave rather
the stride of a giant than the step of a god.

In all probability it was the grief Shakespeare felt at seeing
Chapman selected by Pembroke, added to the ill-humour caused
by the elder poet's arrogance and clumsy pedantry, which goaded
him into wanton opposition to the inevitable enthusiasm for the
Homeric world and its heroes.

And so he gave his bitter mood full play.

He touches upon the *Iliad's* most beautiful and most powerful
elements, Achilles' wrath, the friendship between Achilles and
Patroclus, the question of Helen being delivered to the Greeks,
the attempt to goad Achilles into renewing the conflict, Hector
and Andromache's farewell, and Hector's death, but only to profane and ridicule all.

It was a curious coincidence that Shakespeare should lay

[1] A. C. Swinburne : *Essay on Chapman.*

hands on this material just at the most despondent period of his life; for nowhere could we well receive a deeper impression of modern crudeness and decadence, and never could we meet with a fuller expression of German-Gothic innate barbarism in relation to Hellenism than when we see this great poet of the Northern Renaissance make free with the poetry of the old world.

Let us recall, for instance, the friendship, the brotherhood, existing between Achilles and Patroclus as it is drawn by Homer, and then see what an abomination Shakespeare, under the influence of his own times, makes of it.[1] He causes Thersites to spit upon the connection, and by not allowing any one to protest, so full of loathing for humanity has he become, leaves us to suppose his version to be correct.

How refined and Greek is Homer's treatment of Helen's position. There is no hint there of the modern ridicule of Menelaus; he is equally worthy, equally "beloved by the gods," and still the same mighty hero, if his wife has been abducted. Nor is there any scorn for Helen, only worship for her marvellous beauty, which even the old men upon the walls turn their heads to watch, only compassion for her fate and sympathy with her sufferings. And now, here, this eternal mockery of Menelaus as a deserted husband, these endless good and bad jests on his lot, this barbaric laughter over Helen as unchaste!

Thersites is made the mouthpiece of most of it. Shakespeare found his name in Ovid, and a description of his person in Homer, in one of the books first translated by Chapman :—

> "——All sate, and audience gave,
> Thersites only would speak all. A most disordered store
> Of words he foolishly poured out, of which his mind held more
> Than it could manage; anything with which he could procure
> Laughter, he never could contain. He should have yet been sure
> To touch no kings; t' oppose their states becomes not jesters' parts,
> But he the filthiest fellow was of all that had deserts
> In Troy's brave siege. He was squint-eyed, and lame of either foot;
> So crook-backed that he had no breast; sharp-headed where did shoot
> (Here and there spersed) thin mossy hair. He most of all envied
> Ulysses and Æacides, whom yet his spleen would chide."

---

[1] "*Patroclus.* No more words, Thersites; peace!

"*Thersites.* I will hold my peace when Achilles' brach bids me, shall I?" (Act ii. sc. 1.)

"*Thersites.* Prithee, be silent, boy; I profit not by thy talk: thou art thought to be Achilles' male varlet.

"*Patroclus.* Male varlet, you rogue! What's that?

"*Thersites.* Why, his masculine whore. Now the rotten diseases of the South, the guts-griping, ruptures, catarrhs, loads o' gravel i' the back, lethargies, cold palsies, raw eyes, dirt rotten livers, wheezing lungs, bladders full of impostume, sciaticas, lime-kilns i' the palm, incurable bone-ache, and the rivalled fee-simple of the tetter, take and take again all such preposterous discoveries." (Act v. sc. 2.)

The argument which has been brought forward to prove that Shakespeare could not have known this description creating the character of Thersites is worthless. It has been considered impossible that he, who knew so well how to turn all material to account, should not have profited, in that case, by the famous scene where Odysseus beats Thersites. As a matter of fact, Shakespeare did so, and with much humour, only it is Ajax who is the chastiser, while Thersites exclaims (Act ii. sc. 3): "He beats me, and I rail at him. O worthy satisfaction! would it were otherwise; that I could beat him, while he railed at me."

Clearly enough, the character of the witty, malicious lampooner made an impression upon Shakespeare, and he, probably following the example of earlier plays, transformed him into a clown, and made him act as chorus accompanying the action of the play. Such, obviously, was the Fool in *Lear;* but how different is the melancholy, emotional satire to which King Lear's faithful companion in distress gives vent from the flaying, scorching scorn, the stream of fierce invective wherewith Thersites overwhelms every one and everything.

One cannot but see that these lampoons of Menelaus and Helen represent Shakespeare's own feeling, partly because Thersites is undoubtedly used as a kind of Satyr-chorus, and partly because the dispassionate and unprejudiced characters of the drama express themselves in harmony with him.

Notice, for instance, this reply of Thersites (Act ii. sc. 3):

"After this, the vengeance upon the whole camp! or, rather, the bone-ache! for that, methinks, is the curse upon those that war for a placket. . . . ."
"Here is such patchery, such juggling, and such knavery! all the argument is a cuckold and a whore; a good quarrel to draw emulous factions and bleed to death upon. Now the dry serpigo on the subject and war and lechery confound all!"

Or read this description of Menelaus (Act v. sc. 1):

"And the goodly transformation of Jupiter there, his brother the bull, the primitive statue and oblique memorial of cuckolds; a thrifty shoeing-horn in a chain, hanging at his brother's leg—to what form but that he is, should wit larded with malice, and malice forced with wit, turn him to? To an ass, were nothing; he is both ass and ox; to an ox, were nothing; he is both ox and ass. To be a dog, a mule, a cat, a fitchew, a toad, a lizard, an owl, a puttock, or a herring without a roe, I would not care; but to be Menelaus! I would conspire against destiny. Ask me not what I would be if I were not Thersites; for I care not to be the louse of a lazar, so I were not Menelaus."

One can by no means accept this as merely the outburst of a brawling slave's hatred of his superiors, for the entirely unpre-

judiced Diomedes expresses himself in the same spirit to Paris
(Act iv. sc. 1):

> "*Paris.* And tell me, noble Diomede, faith, tell me true,
> Even in the soul of sound good fellowship,
> Who, in your thoughts, merits fair Helen best,
> Myself or Menelaus.
> *Diomedes.* Both alike :
> He merits well to have her that doth seek her,
> Not making any scruple of her soilure,
> With such a hell of pain and world of charge ;
> And you as well to keep her, that defend her,
> Not palating her dishonour,
> With such a costly load of wealth and friends :
> He, like a puling cuckold, would drink up
> The lees and dregs of a flat tamed piece ;
> You, like a lecher, out of whorish loins
> Are pleased to breed out your inheritors :
> Both merits poised, each weighs nor less nor more ;
> But he as he, the heavier for a whore.
> *Paris.* You are too bitter to your countrywoman.
> *Diomedes.* She's bitter to her country : hear me, Paris :
> For every false drop in her bawdy veins
> A Grecian's life hath sunk ; for every scruple
> Of her contaminated carrion weight
> A Trojan hath been slain : since she could speak
> She hath not given so many good words breath
> As for her Greeks and Trojans have suffered death."

In the *Iliad* these forms represent the outcome of the imagination of the noblest people of the Mediterranean shores, unaffected
by religious terrors and alcohol ; they are bright, glad, reverential
fantasies, born in a warm sun under a deep blue sky. From
Shakespeare they step forth travestied by the gloom and bitterness of a great poet of a Northern race, of a stock civilised by
Christianity, not by culture ; a stock which, despite all the efforts
of the Renaissance to give new birth to heathendom, has become,
once for all, disciplined and habituated to look upon the senses
as tempters which lead down into the mire ; to which the pleasurable is the forbidden and sexual attraction a disgrace.

How significant it is that Shakespeare only sees Greek love
as scourged by the lash of venereal diseases. Throughout the
entire play a pestilential breath of innuendo is blown with outbursts of cursing, all centering on a contagion which first showed
itself some thousand years after the Homeric times. As Homeric
friendships are bestialised, so is Greek love profaned to suit
modern circumstances. To Thersites, the Greek princes are,
every one of them, scandalous rakes. "Here's Agamemnon, an
honest fellow enough, and one that loves quails, but he has not as
much brain as earwax" (Act v. sc. 1). "That same Diomed's a

false-hearted rogue, a most unjust knave. . . . They say he keeps a Trojan drab and uses the traitor Calchas' tent.—Nothing but lechery; all incontinent varlets" (Act v. sc. 1). Achilles, that "idol of idiot worshippers," that "full dish of fool," has Queen Hecuba's daughter as a concubine, and has treacherously promised her to leave his fellow-countrymen in the lurch. "Patroclus will give me anything for the intelligence of this whore: the parrot will not do more for an almond than he for a commodious drab. Lechery, lechery still, nothing else holds fashion." Of Menelaus and Paris, "cuckold and cuckold-maker," enough has already been said. Helen has been sternly condemned, and of Cressida with her two adorers, Troilus and Diomedes, "How the devil luxury, with his fat rump and potato-fingers, tickles these two together! Fry lechery, fry" (Act v. sc. 2).

It is clear that the Christian conception of faithlessness in love has displaced the old Hellenic innocence and naïveté. How fervent is Achilles' love for Briseis in Homer; how honest, warm, and indignant he is when he asks Agamemnon's messengers if among the children of men only the Atrides love their wives, and he himself answers that every man who is brave and of good understanding loves and shelters his wife, as he of his inmost heart loved and would shelter Briseis, prisoner of war though she was. None the less does Homer tell us how immediately after Achilles has ended his speech and dismissed his guests, he stretches himself upon his couch, "in the inner room of his tent, richly wrought, and that fair lady by his side that he from Lesbos brought, bright Diomeda." It never occurs to the Greek poet that this implies any faithlessness to the absent Briseis, but Shakespeare's standard is thoroughly and mediævally rigorous.

On two points the comparison between Homer and Shakespeare is inevitable. The first is the farewell between Hector and Andromache. There is nothing finer in Greek poetry (which is to say, any poetry) than this tragic idyl, so profoundly human and movingly beautiful as it is. The pure womanliness which out of deep grief and pain utters a complaint without weakness, and expresses without sentimentality a boundless love poured out upon this one object: "Thy life makes still my father be, my mother, brother, and besides thou art my husband too. Most loved, most worthy."

In contrast to this womanliness stands the man's strength, untouched by harshness, stirred by the deepest tenderness, but fixed in immovable determination. The picture of the child, too, frightened by the nodding plumes upon his father's helm, until Hector sets the casque upon the ground and kisses the tears from the eyes of his boy. The scene takes place in the sixth book of the *Iliad*, and could not have been known to Shakespeare, inasmuch as it was as yet untranslated by Chapman. See what he sets in its place:

"*Andromache.* Unarm, unarm, and do not fight to-day.
Hector. You train me to offend you : get you in :
By all the everlasting gods I'll go !
Andromache. My dreams will, sure, prove ominous to the day.
Hector. No more, I say."

This is the harshness of a mediæval duke; the golden dust is brushed from the wings of the Greek Psyche. If Harald Hardrada, as chieftain of the Varangians, ever gave a thought to the spirit of Greek art, as he passed with his troops through the streets of Constantinople, he must have looked upon it thus, despising the ancient Hellenes because he found the modern cowardly and effeminate.

Shakespeare had no particular place and no particular people in his mind when he wrote this play ; he simply robbed the finest scenes of their beauty, because his mind, at that time, had elected to dwell upon the lowest and basest side of human nature.

The second point is the mission to Achilles, told in the ninth book of the *Iliad.* It was translated and published by Chapman in 1598, and must certainly have been known to Shakespeare.[1] This book is one of the few finished works of art which have been produced upon this earth. The Greek Epos itself contains nothing more consummate than its delineation of character, the contrast between the arrogant and the intellectual, the polished and the humorous, the interplay of personality from the highest pathos to the reiterated twaddle of the old man. Achilles' wrath, Nestor's experience, Odysseus' subtle tact, Phœnix's good-natured rambling, the wounded pride of the Hellenic emissaries, are all gathered together in the endeavour to induce Achilles to quit his tent.

Contrast this with the burlesque attempt to provoke that cowardly snob and raw dunce of an Achilles out of his exclusiveness, by passing him by without returning his greeting or seeming conscious of his existence ; this same Achilles, who falls upon Hector with his myrmidons and scoundrelly murders him, just as the hero, wearied by battle, has taken off his helmet and laid aside his sword. It reads like the invention of a mediæval barbarian. But Shakespeare is neither mediæval nor a barbarian. No, he has written it down out of a bitterness so deep that he has felt hero-worship, like love, to be an illusion of the senses. As the phantasy of first love is absurd, and Troilus's loyalty towards its object ridiculous, so is the honour of our forefathers and of war in general a delusion. Shakespeare now suspects the most assured reputations ; he believes that if Achilles really lived at all, he was most probably a stupid and vainglorious boaster,

---

[1] The expression "by Jove multi potent," Act iv., sc. 5, is taken from Chapman. This is the only time it is used by Shakespeare.

just as Helen must have been a hussy by no means worthy of the turmoil which was made about her.

As he distorted Achilles into an absurdity, so he wrenched all other personalities into caricatures. Gervinus has justly remarked that Shakespeare here acts very much as his Patroclus does when he mimics Agamemnon's loftiness and Nestor's weakness, for Achilles' delectation (Act i. sc. 3). We feel in the delineation of Nestor that Anglo-Saxon master-hand which seizes upon the unsightly details which the Greek ignores:

> " He coughs and spits,
> And with a palsy fumbling on his gorget,
> Shakes in and out the rivet."

And we recognise in the allusion to the mimicry of Agamemnon that cheap estimate of an actor's profession, which, with a contempt for the whole guild of poets, is discernible throughout Shakespeare's works, in spite of his efforts to raise both callings in the eyes of the public.[1]

Nestor is overwhelmed with ridicule, and is made to declare, at the close of the first act, that he will hide his silver beard in a golden beaver, and will maintain in duel with Hector that his own long-dead wife was as great a beauty and as chaste a wife as Hector's—grandmother.

Ulysses, who is intended to represent the wise man of the play, is as trivial of mind as the rest. There was a certain amount of grandeur in the way Iago handled Othello, Rodrigo, and Cassio, as though they were mere puppets in his hands; but there is none in the sport Ulysses makes of those swaggering numskulls, Achilles and Ajax. The bitterness which breathes out of all that Shakespeare writes at this period has found gratification in making Ulysses not one whit more sublime than the fools with whom he plays.

Amongst German critics, Gervinus has characterised *Troilus and Cressida* as a good-naturedly humorous play. No description could be more unlikely. Seldom has a poet been less good-natured than Shakespeare here. No less impossible is the theory (also nourished in Gervinus' imagination) that the poet of the English Renaissance was offended by the loose ethics of Homeric

---

[1] " And, like a strutting player, whose conceit
Lies in his hamstring, and doth think it rich
To hear the wooden dialogue and sound
'Twixt his stretched footing and the scaffoldage,
Such to be pitied and o'er-wrested seeming
He acts thy greatness in."

And the passage previously quoted from *Macbeth* :

" Life's but . . . . . a poor player,
That struts and frets his hour upon the stage,
And then is heard no more."

Also the 110th Sonnet.

poetry. Shakespeare most certainly was never so moral as this moralising German critic (and what German critic is not moralising) would have him to be. It is not a sense of the ethics of Homer, but a feeling for his poetry that is lacking. In Shakespeare's time men took too much pleasure in classical culture to appreciate the antique naïveté. It was not until the beginning of the nineteenth century, when popular poetry once more began to be universally honoured, that Homer displaced Virgil in the popular estimation. Even Goethe preferred Virgil to Homer. Gervinus is equally wide of the mark when, in his anxiety to prove *Troilus and Cressida* a purely literary satire, he hazards the assertion that Shakespeare never intended here to "hold up a mirror to his times;"[1] for it is precisely his own times, and no other, that were in his mind when he wrote this play.

[1] " Sein gutmüthiges humoristisches Spiel."—" So kann allerdings aus der ganzen Darstellung die naheliegende Wahrzeit gezogen werden : dass die erhabenste Dichtung ohne streng sittlichen Grundlagen nicht das sei, wozu sie befähigt und berufen ist."—" Gewiss würde er dies Stück nicht unter die rechnen wollen, die der Zeit einen Spiegel vorhalten."—Gervinus · *Shakespeare*, iv. 22, 31, 32.

X

SCORN OF WOMAN'S GUILE AND PUBLIC STUPIDITY

TROILUS AND CRESSIDA first appeared in 1609 in two editions, one of which is introduced by a remarkable and diverting preface, entitled "A never writer to an ever reader, News." It says:—

"Eternall reader, you have heere a new play, never stal'd with the stage, never clapper-clawd with the palmes of the Vulgar, and yet passing full of the palme comicall; for it is a birth of your brain, that never undertooke anything comicall, vainely: And were but the vaine names of commedies changde for the titles of Commodities, or of Playes for Pleas; you should see all those grand censors, that now stile them such vanities, flocke to them for the maine grace of their gravities: especially this author's Commedies, that are so framed to the life, that they serve for the most common Commentaries, of all the actions of our lives, shewing such a dexteritie, and power of witte, that the most displeased with playes are pleased with his comedies. And all such dull and heavy-witted worldlings, as were never capable of the witte of a commedie, coming by report of them to his representations, have found that witte there, that they never found in themselves, and have parted better witted than they came: feeling an edge of witte set upon them, more than ever they dreamed they had brain to grind it on. So much and such sauvred salt of witte is in his Commedies, that they seem (for their height of pleasure) to be borne in that sea that brought forth Venus. Amongst all there is none more witty than this. And had I time I would comment upon it, though I know it needs it not (for so much as will make you think your testerne well bestowed), but for so much worth, as ever poore I know to be stuft in it. It deserves such a labour, as well as the best Commedy in Terence or Plautus. And believe this, that when he is gone, and his Commedies out of sale, you will scramble for them and set up a new English inquisition. Take this for a warning, and at the perrill of your pleasures losse, and judgements, refuse not nor like this the less for not being sullied with the smoaky breath of the multitude; but thanke fortune for the scape it hath made amongst you. Since by the grand possessors wills I believe you should have prayed for them rather than been prayed. And so I leave all such to be prayed for (for the state of their witte's health) that will not praise it. VALE."

How remarkable a comprehension of Shakespeare's work this old-time preface shows, how clear-sighted an enthusiasm, and how just a perception of his position in the future.

The play was again published in 1623 in folio, and under conditions which betray the publisher's perplexity as to its classification. It is altogether missing from the list of contents, in which the plays are arranged under three headings, comedies, histories, and tragedies. It is thrust, unpaged, into the middle of the book, between the histories and the tragedies, between *Henry VIII.* and *Coriolanus*, probably because the editor mistakenly deemed it to contain more of history and of tragedy than of comedy. Of all Shakespeare's works, it is *Troilus and Cressida* which most nearly approaches the *Don Quixote* of Cervantes.

It is a proof of the stultifying effect of the too close attention of philological critics to metrical peculiarities (peculiarities which a poet can always accommodate as he thinks proper) upon the finer psychological sense, that either the whole or a greater part of *Troilus and Cressida* has been taken for the work of Shakespeare's youth, and has been attributed to the *Romeo and Juliet* period. This view has been taken by L. Moland and C. d'Hericault in their *Nouvelles Françaises du 14ᵐᵉ Siècle*, and not a few undiscerning biographers of Shakespeare.

The contrast between the two plays is remarkable and instructive. *Romeo and Juliet* is a genuine work of youth, a product of truth and faith. *Troilus and Cressida* is the outcome of the disillusionment, suspicion, and bitterness of ripe manhood. The critics have been deceived by the apparently astonishing youthfulness of parts of *Troilus and Cressida*, some upon the ground of its occasional euphuisms and bombast (evidently satirical), others by the enthusiasm of youth and absorption in love which some of Troilus's replies express; for instance:

> "I tell thee I am mad
> In Cressid's love: thou answer'st 'She is fair,'
> Pour'st in the open ulcer of my heart
> Her eyes, her hair, her cheek, her gait, her voice," &c.

In his most ardent raptures there sounds a note of ridicule.[1] All this is a complete inversion of *Romeo and Juliet*. His youthful tragedy portrayed a woman so staunchly true in love that she is driven thereby to a bitter death. *Troilus and Cressida* deals with a woman whose constancy fails at the first proof. There is no abyss between the soul and the senses in *Romeo and Juliet;* the two melt into one in fullest harmony. But it is the lower side of love's ideal nature which is parodied in *Troilus*

---

[1] Troilus's euphuisms:—
> "I was about to tell thee: when my heart
> As wedgèd with a sigh, would rive in twain,
> Lest Hector or my father should perceive me,
> I have, as when the sun doth light a storm,
> Buried this sigh in wrinkle of a smile" (Act i. sc. 1).
> "——O gentle Pandarus,
> From Cupid's shoulder pluck his painted wings,
> And fly with me to Cressid" (Act iii. sc. 2).

and Cressida, and causes it to resemble the flippant accompaniment to the serenade in Mozart's *Don Juan,* which caricatures the sentimentality of the text.

It is true that there is a chivalrous fine feeling and sensual tenderness in Troilus's love, which seems to foreshadow, as it were, that which some centuries later found such full expression in Keats. But the melancholy of Shakespeare's matured perception sets its iron tooth in everything at this period of his life, and he looks upon absorption in love as senseless and laughable. He shows us how blindly Troilus runs into the snare, giddy with happiness and uplifted to the heavens, and how the next moment he awakes from his intoxication, betrayed; but he shows it without sympathy, coldly. Therefore, the play never once arouses any true emotion, since Troilus himself never really interests. The piece blazes out, but imparts no warmth. Shakespeare wrote it thus, and therefore, while *Troilus and Cressida* will find many readers who will admire it, few will love it.

Shakespeare deliberately made Cressida sensually attractive, but spiritually repulsive and unclean. She has desire for Troilus, but no love. She is among those who are born experienced; she knows how to inflame, win, and keep men enchained, but the honourable love of a man is useless to her. At the same time she is one of those who easily find their master. Any man who is not imposed upon by her airs, who sees through her mock-prudish rebuffs, subdues her without difficulty. All her sagacity amounted to, after all, was that Troilus would continue ardent so long as she said "No;" that men, in short, value the unattainable and what is won with difficulty,—the wisdom of any commonplace coquette. Never has Shakespeare represented coquetry as so void of charming qualities.

Cressida is never modest even when she is most prudish; she understands a jest, even bold and libertine ones, and she will bandy them with enjoyment. With all her kittenish charm she is uninteresting, and, in spite of her hot blood, she betrays the coldest selfishness. She is neither ridiculous nor unlovely, but as little is she beautiful; in no other of Shakespeare's characters is the sensual attraction exercised by a woman so completely shorn of its poetry.

Her uncle Pandarus is as experienced as she is in the art of exciting by alternately thrusting forward and holding back. He has been named a demoralised Polonius, and the epithet is good. He is an old voluptuary, who finds his amusement in playing the spy and go-between, now that more active pleasures are denied to him. The cynical enjoyment with which Shakespeare (in spite of his contempt for him) has drawn him is very characteristic of this period of his life. Pandarus is clever enough, and often witty, but there is no enjoyment of his wit; he is as comical, base, and shameless as Falstaff himself, but he never calls forth the abstract sympathy we feel for the latter. Nothing makes amends for his vileness, nor for that of Thersites, nor for that of any other character in the whole play. Here, as in other plays, *Timon of Athens* in particular, is shown that deep-seated Anglo-Saxon vein which, according to the popular estimate, Shakespeare entirely lacked,— that vein in which flows the life-blood of Swift's, Hogarth's, and even some of Byron's principal works, and it shows how, after all, there was some sympathy between the Merrie England of those days and the later Land of Spleen.

We have noticed the harsh strength of Ulysses' judgment of Cressida, and in the decisive scene, in which Troilus is the unseen witness of Cressida's perfidy, are written words so weighty and so full of emotion that we feel Shakespeare's very soul speaks in them.

Diomedes begs Cressida for the scarf which Troilus has given her.

> " *Diomedes.* I had your heart before, this follows it.
> *Troilus (aside).* I did swear patience.
> *Cressida.* You shall not have it, Diomed, faith you shall not :
> I'll give you something else.
> *Diomedes.* I will have this : whose was it ?
> *Cressida.* It is no matter.
> *Diomedes.* Come, tell me whose it was ?
> *Cressida. 'Twas one that loved me better than you will,*
> *But, now you have it, take it.*"

And the bit of feminine psychology which Shakespeare has given in Cressida's farewell to Diomedes :

> " Good-night : I prithee, come.
> Troilus, farewell ! one eye yet looks on thee,
> *But with my heart the other eye doth see.*
> Ah, poor our sex ! This fault in us I find,
> The error of our eye directs our mind."

And the terrible words Shakespeare puts into Troilus's mouth when he tries so desperately to shake off the impression, and deny the possibility of what he has seen :

> " *Ulysses.* Why stay we, then ?
> *Troilus.* To make a recordation to my soul
> Of every syllable that here was spoken.
> But if I tell how these two did co-act,
> Shall I not lie in publishing this truth ?
> Sith yet there is a credence in my heart,
> An esperance so obstinately strong,
> That doth invert the attest of eyes and ears,
> As if those organs had deceptious functions
> Created only to calum iate.
> Was Cressid here ?

> *Ulysses.* I cannot conjure, Trojan.
> *Troilus.* She was not, sure.
> *Ulysses.* Most sure she was.
> *Troilus.* Why, my negation hath no taste of madness.
> *Ulysses.* Nor mine, my lord. Cressid was here but now
> *Troilus.* Let it not be believed for womanhood !
> *Think, we had mothers* : do not give advantage
> To stubborn critics, apt, without a theme,
> For depravation, to square this general sex
> By Cressid's rule ; rather think this not Cressid.
> *Ulysses.* What hath she done, prince, that can soil our
>   mothers ?
> *Troilus.* Nothing at all, unless that that were she."

Not only Troilus, but the whole play has here become permeated by Ulysses' conception of Cressida, and in this despairing
outburst, "Think, we had mothers," is the pith of the piece
uttered forth with terrible clearness.

Yet Troilus and Cressida by no means represent the whole of
the play. In order to counterbalance the slightness of the action,
the bombastic speech, the railing abuse, and the heavy bitter
Juvenal-like satire of his drama, Shakespeare has interpolated
some serious and thoughtful utterances in which some of the
fruits of his abundant experience are expressed in weighty and
concise form.

Achilles, and more especially Ulysses, give vent to profound
political and psychological reflections, entirely regardless of the
fact that the one is a thoughtless blockhead, and the other is a
crafty and unsympathetic nature, the mere negative pole of
Troilus, cold as he is warm, cunning as he is naïve. These
remarkable and thoughtful utterances, not in the least in harmony
with their characters, stand in direct contradiction to the whole
play and its farcical treatment, but they are none the less notable
for that. This singular inconsistency is one of the many in which
this incongruous play is so rich, and it is these very contradictions
which make it attractive, insomuch as they reveal the conflicting
moods from which it sprang. They arrest the attention like the
irregular features of a face whose expression varies between irony,
satire, melancholy, and profundity.

Ulysses, who is represented as the sole statesman among the
Greeks, degrades himself by low flattery of the idiotic Ajax,
servilely referring to him as "this thrice worthy and right valiant
lord," who should not soil the victory he has won by going as
messenger to Achilles' tent, and he persuades the princes to pass
Achilles by without greeting him. On this occasion Achilles,
who is otherwise but a braggart, dolt, coward, and scoundrel,
surprises us by a succession of outbursts, in each of which he
gives voice to as deep and bitter knowledge of human nature as
does Timon of Athens himself.

> " What, am I poor of late?
> 'Tis certain greatness once fall'n out with Fortune
> Must fall out with men too : what the declined is
> He shall as soon read in the eyes of others,
> As feel in his own fall.
>
> .   .   .   .
>
> And not a man, for being simply man,
> Hath any honour, but honour for those honours
> That are without him, as place, riches, favour,
> Prizes of accident as oft as merit :
> Which when they fall, as being slippery standers,
> The love that leaned on them is slippery too,
> Do one pluck down another, and together
> Die in the fall."

Ulysses now enters upon a thoughtful conversation with Achilles, calling his attention to the fact that no man, however highly advanced he may be, has any real knowledge of his worth until he has received the judgment of others and observed their attitude towards him.   Achilles answers him a happy and per-intent analogy on principles of pure philosophical reasonings, and Ulysses continues :

> " That no man is the lord of anything
> Till he communicate his parts to others ;
> Nor doth he of himself know them for aught
> Till he behold them formed in the applause
> Where they're extended : who like an arch reverberates
> The voice again, or, like a gate of steel
> Fronting the sun, receives and renders back
> His figure and his heart."

Achilles interrupts a long discourse, ending with a thrust at Ajax, with the question " What, are my deeds forgot ? " and the remarkable answer he receives reveals, to an observant reader, one of the sources of the bitterness and pessimism of the play.   It can scarcely be doubted that Shakespeare at this time felt himself ousted from the popular favour by younger and less worthy men : we know that immediately after his death he was eclipsed by Fletcher.   He is absorbed by a feeling of the ingratitude of man and the injustice of what is called the way of the world.   We found the first traces of this feeling in the words of Bertram's dead father, quoted by the King in *All's Well that Ends Well*, and here it breaks out in full force in a reply whose very weak pretext is that of showing Achilles how ill advised he is to rest upon his laurels :

> " Time hath, my lord, a wallet on his back,
> Wherein he puts alms for oblivion,
> A great-sized monster of ingratitudes :
> Those scraps are good deeds past, which are devoured

As fast as they are made, forgot as soon
As done : perseverance dear, my lord,
Keeps honour bright : to have done is to hang
Quite out of fashion, like a rusty mail.
In monumental mockery.   Take the instant way ;
For honour travels in a strait so narrow,
Where but one goes abreast : keep then the path ;
For emulation hath a thousand sons
That one by one pursue : if you give way,
Or hedge aside from the direct forthright,
Like to an entered tide, they all rush by
And leave you hindmost ;
Or like a gallant horse fall'n in first rank,
Lie there for pavement to the abject rear,
O'errun and trampled on : then what they do in present,
Though less than yours in past, must o'ertop yours ;
For time is like a fashionable host,
That slightly shakes his parting guest by the hand,
And with his arms outstretched, as he would fly,
Grasps in the comer ; welcome ever smiles,
And farewell goes out sighing.   Oh, let not virtue seek
Remuneration for the thing it was ;
For beauty, wit,
High birth, vigour of bone, desert in service,
Love, friendship, charity are subjects all
To envious and calumniating time.
One touch of nature makes the whole world kin,
That all with one consent praise new-born gauds,
Though they are made and moulded of things past ;
And give to dust that is a little gilt
More land than gilt o'erdusted."

How plainly is one of the sources betrayed here of the black waters of bitterness which bubble up in *Troilus and Cressida*, a bitterness which spares neither man nor woman, war nor love, hero nor lover, and which springs in part from woman's guile, in part from the undoubted stupidity of the English public.   In the latter part of the conversation between Ulysses and Achilles the former has some renowned words on the direction of the state—its ideal government, that is to say.   The incongruity between the circumstance of utterance and the utterance itself is nowhere more striking in this play than here.   Ulysses tells Achilles that they all know why he refuses to take part in the battle ; every one is well aware that he is in love with Priam's daughter ; and when Achilles exclaims in amazement at finding the secrets of his private life disclosed, Ulysses, with a solemnity inconsistent with the triviality of the subject and the grim ways of espionage, gives the almost mystical and too profound answer :

> " Is that a wonder?
> The providence that's in a watchful state

Knows almost every grain of Pluto's gold,
Finds bottom in the uncomprehensive deeps,
Keeps place with thought, and almost, like the gods,
Does thoughts unveil in their dumb cradles.
There is a mystery—with whom relation
Durst never meddle—in the soul of state;
Which hath an operation more divine
Than breath or pen can give expression to."

He then turns abruptly to the subject of Achilles's amours with Polyxena being common talk, and seeks to provoke the lover into joining the combat by telling him that it has become a common jest that Achilles has conquered Hector's sister, but that Ajax has subdued Hector himself, and then ends his speech with the following obscure allusion to the relation between Achilles and Ajax:—

" Farewell, my lord. I as your lover speak:
The fool slides o'er the ice that you should break." [1]

In spite of the strange inconsistency of all these political allusions, they are of the greatest interest to us, inasmuch as they so clearly indicate Shakespeare's next great work, the Roman tragedy of *Coriolanus* (1608).

Ulysses makes steady protest against the vulgar error that it is the gross work, and not the guiding spirit, which is decisive in war and politics. He complains of the abuse Achilles and Thersites heap upon the leaders of the campaign (Act i. sc. 3):

" They tax our policy and call it cowardice,
Count wisdom as no member of the war,
Forestall prescience, and esteem no act
But that of hand: the still and mental parts
That do contrive how many hands shall strike
When fitness calls them on, and know by measure
Of their observant toil the enemies' weight—
Why, this hath not a finger's dignity," &c.

It is, of course, Thersites who has taken the lead; the light wit and deep humour of the earlier clowns is displaced in him by the frantic outbursts of a contemptible scamp. Throughout, Thersites

[1] F. Halliwell-Phillips has published, concerning these last two lines, a miniature book, *The Fool and the Ice*, London, 1883. He explains that a whole little history lies behind this curious simile. When Lord Chandos's Company played at Evesham, near Stratford (before 1600), a country fool there, Jack Miller by name, became so infatuated with their clown that he wanted to run away with them, and had, consequently, to be locked up. He saw from the window, however, that the company was preparing to depart, and springing out, sped, in spite of the danger, over forty yards of ice so thin that it would not bear a piece of brick which was laid upon it. (First told in a little book by the player Robert Arnim, afterwards one of Shakespeare's colleagues. It was published in 1603 under the title " Foole upon Foole, or Sixe Sortes of Sottes, by Colonnico del Mondo Snuffe," clown at the Globe Theatre.)

is intended as a caricature of the envious and worthless (if sharp-sighted) plebeian, of whose wit Shakespeare has need for the complete scourging of an arrogant and corrupt aristocracy, but whose politics are the subject of his utter disgust and scorn. As the haughty intelligence of Ulysses seems to foreshadow Prospero, but without his bright supernatural clearness, so does Thersites seem to be a preliminary sketch for Caliban, barring his heavy, earthy, grotesque clumsiness. The character more immediately allied to that of Thersites, however, is not Caliban, but that grim cynic Apemantus in *Timon of Athens.*

Still more significant than the previously quoted lines is the speech in which Ulysses (Act i. sc. 3) develops a political view which was obviously Shakespeare's own, and which is soon to be proclaimed in *Coriolanus.* Its point of view proceeds from the conviction, expressed in our day by Nietzsche, that the distance between man and man must on no account be bridged over, and is introduced by a half-astronomical, half-astrological explanation of the Ptolemaic system :

> " The heavens themselves, the planets, and this centre
> Observe degree, priority, and place,
> Insisture, course, proportion, season, form,
> Office and custom, in all line of order ;
> And therefore is the glorious planet Sol
> In noble eminence enthroned and sphered
> Amidst the others ; whose med'cinable eye
> Corrects the ill aspects of planets evil,
> And posts, like the commandment of a king,
> Sans check to good and bad : but when the planets
> In evil mixture to disorder wander,
> What plagues and what portents ! what mutiny !
> What raging of the sea ! frights, changes, horrors,
> Divert and crack, rend and deracinate
> The unity and married calm of states
> Quite from their fixture "

The remainder of the passage has become a fixed ingredient of English Shakespearian anthologies, and carries us on directly in to *Coriolanus :*

> " Oh, when degree is shaked,
> Which is the ladder to all high designs,
> Then enterprise is sick. . . .
> Take but degree away, untune that string,
> And hark, what discord follows ! each thing meets
> In mere oppugnancy : the bounded waters
> Should lift their bosoms higher than the shores,
> And make a sop of all this solid globe :
> Strength should be lord of imbecility,
> And the rude son should strike the father dead.
> Force should be right ; or rather right and wrong,

Between whose endless jar justice resides,
Should lose their names, and so should justice too.

.   .   .   .

This chaos, when degree is suffocate,
Follows the choking.
And this neglection of degree it is
That by a pace goes backward, with a purpose
It hath to climb. The general's disdained
By him one step below, he by the next,
That next by him beneath. . . .
. . . It grows to an envious fever
Of pale and bloodless emulation."

Shakespeare has so often emphasised the superiority of real merit to outside show, that he needs no vindication from a charge of worship of mere rank and station. What he here expresses is merely that inherently aristocratic point of view which we recognised in his early works, and which has intensified with increasing years. It was from the first founded upon a conviction that only among an hereditary aristocracy, under a well-established monarchy, was any patronage of his art and profession possible, and the opinion, steadily nourished by the enmity of the middle classes, will soon be expressed with extraordinary vehemence in *Coriolanus.*

Troilus and Cressida, then, which seems at first sight to be a romantic play founded on an old world subject, is in reality, despite its embellishments, a satire on the ancient material, and a parody of romanticism itself. It cannot therefore be classed with the attempts made by other great poets to resuscitate the old Greek personalities. Racine's *Iphigenia in Aulis* and Goethe's *Iphigenia in Tauris,* were written in serious earnestness, although neither of them approximated closely to the old world of tradition. Racine's Greeks are courtly Frenchmen from the salons, and Goethe's are German princes and princesses, of humane and classic culture, who attitudinise like the figures in a painting by Raphael Mengs. It may be said that Shakespeare's Hector, who quotes Aristotle, and his Lord Achilles, with his spurs and long sword, are as much noblemen of the Renaissance as Racine's Seigneur Achilles is a courtier in periwig and red-heeled shoes. But Racine meant no satire, while Shakespeare most deliberately caricatured. All turns to discord under his touch ; love is betrayed, heroes are murdered, constancy ridiculed, levity and coarseness triumph, and no gleam of better things shines out at the end. The play closes with an indecent jest of the loathsome Pandar's.

XI

DEATH OF SHAKESPEARE'S MOTHER—CORIOLANUS —HATRED OF THE MASSES

SHAKESPEARE'S mother was buried on the 9th of September 1608. He had travelled about the country of late, playing with his company, from the middle of May until far into the autumn, during which period court and aristocracy were absent from the capital. It is not certain whether he had returned to London at this time or not, but he hastened to Stratford on hearing of his mother's death, and must have stayed some time on his property, "New Place," after attending her funeral; for we find him still at Stratford on the 16th of October. On that day he stands godfather to the son of a friend of his youth, Henry Walker, an alderman of the borough, who is mentioned in Shakespeare's will.

The death of a mother is always a mournfully irreparable loss, often the saddest a man can sustain. We can realise how deeply it would go to Shakespeare's heart when we remember the capacity for profound and passionate feeling with which nature had blessed and cursed him. We know little of his mother; but judging from that affinity which generally exists between famous sons and their mothers, we may suppose that she was no ordinary woman. Mary Arden, who belonged to an old and honourable family, which traced its descent (perhaps justly) back to the days of Edward the Confessor, represented the haughty patrician element of the Shakespeare family. Her ancestors had borne their coat of arms for centuries, and the son would be proud of his mother for this among other reasons, just as the mother would be proud of her son.

In the midst of the prevailing gloom and bitterness of his spirit, this fresh blow fell upon him, and, out of his weariness of life as his surroundings and experiences showed it to him, recalled this one mainstay to him—his mother. He remembered all she had been to him for forty-four years, and the thoughts of the man and the dreams of the poet were thus led to dwell upon the significance in a man's life of this unique form, comparable to no other—his mother.

Thus it was that, although his genius must follow the path it had entered upon and pursue it to the end, we find, in the midst of all that was low and base in his next work, this one sublime mother-form, the proudest and most highly-wrought that he has drawn, Volumnia.

The *Tragedy of Coriolanus* was first published in 1623, in folio edition, but 1608 is the generally accepted date of its production, partly because a speech in Ben Jonson's *The Silent Woman* (1609) seems to indicate a reminiscence of *Coriolanus*, and partly because many different critics concur in the opinion that its style and versification point to that year.

How came this work to emerge from the depths of all the discontent, despondency, hatred of life, and contempt for humanity which went at this time to make up Shakespeare's soul? He was angry and soured, and the sources of his embittered feelings are embodied in his plays, seeking outlet, now under one, now under another form. In *Troilus and Cressida* it was the relation of the sexes; here it is social conditions and politics.

His point of view is as personal as it well could be. Shakespeare's aversion to the mob was based upon his contempt for their discrimination, but it had its deepest roots in the purely physical repugnance of his artist nerves to their plebeian atmosphere. It was obvious in *Troilus and Cressida* that the irritation with public stupidity was at its height. He now, for the third time, finds in his Plutarch a subject which not only responds to the mood of the moment, but also gives him an opportunity for portraying a notable mother; and he is irresistibly drawn to give his material dramatic style.

It is the old traditional story of Coriolanus, great man and great general, who, in the remote days of Roman antiquity, became involved in such hopeless conflict with the populace of his native city, and was so roughly dealt with by them in return, that he was driven, in his bitterness, to reckless deeds.

Plutarch, however, was by no means prejudiced against the people, and the subject had to be entirely re-fashioned by Shakespeare before it would harmonise with his mood. The historian may be guilty of serious contradictions in matters of detail, but he endeavours, to the best of his ability, to enter into the circumstances of times which were of hoary antiquity, even to him. The main drift of his narrative is to the effect that Coriolanus had already attained to great authority and influence in the city, when the Senate, which represented the wealth of the community, came into collision with the masses. The people were overridden by usurers, the law was terribly severe upon debtors, and the poor were subjected to incessant distraint; their few possessions were sold, and men who had fought bravely for their country and were covered with honourable scars were frequently imprisoned. In the recent war with the Sabines the patricians had been forced to promise the people better treatment in the future, but the moment the war was over they broke their word, and distraint and imprisonment went on as before. After this the plebeians refused to come forward at the conscription, and the patricians, in spite of the opposition of Coriolanus, were compelled to yield.

Shakespeare was evidently incapable of forming any idea of the free citizenship of olden days, still less of that period of ferment during which the Roman people united to form a vigorous political party, a civic and military power combined, which proved the nucleus round which the great Roman Empire eventually shaped itself — a power of which J. L. Heiberg's words on thought might have been predicted: " It will conquer the world, nothing less."

Much the same thing was occurring in Shakespeare's own time, and, under his very eyes, as it were, the English people were initiating their struggle for self-government. But they who constituted the Opposition were antagonistic to him and his art, and he looked without sympathy upon their conflict. Thus it was that those proud and self-reliant plebeians, who exiled themselves to Mons Sacer sooner than submit to the yoke of the patricians, represented no more to him than did that London mob which was daily before his eyes. To him the Tribunes of the People were but political agitators of the lowest type, mere personifications of the envy of the masses, and representatives of their stupidity and their brute force of numbers. Ignoring every incident which shed a favourable light upon the plebeians, he seized upon every instance of popular folly which could be found in Plutarch's account of a later revolt, in order to incorporate it in his scornful delineation. Again and again he insists, by means of his hero's passionate invective, on the cowardice of the people, and that in the face of Plutarch's explicit testimony to their bravery. His detestation of the mass thrived upon this reiterated accentuation of the wretched pusillanimity of the plebeians, which went hand-in-hand with a rebellious hatred for their benefactors.

Was it Shakespeare's intention to allude to the strained relations existing between James and his Parliament? Does Coriolanus represent an aristocratically-minded poet's side-glance at the political situation in England? I fancy it does. Heaven knows there was little resemblance between the amazingly craven and vacillating James and the haughty, resolute hero of Roman tradition, who fought a whole garrison single-handed. Nor was it personal resemblance which suggested the comparison, but a general conception of the situation as between a beneficent power on the one hand and the people on the other. He regarded the latter wholly as mob, and looked upon their struggle for freedom as mutiny, pure and simple.

It is hard to have to say it, but the more one studies Shakespeare with reference to contemporary history, the more is one struck by the evident necessity he felt, in spite of the undoubted disgust with which King and Court inspired him, for seeking the support of the kingly power against his adversaries. Many are the unmistakable, though discreet and delicate, compliments he addresses to the monarch.

It was even before his accession that we detected, in *Hamlet*, the first glance in the direction of James. The accentuation of Hamlet's relations with the players is not without its acknowledgments and appeal to the Scottish monarch. In *Measure for Measure* the stress laid upon the Duke's doubly careful watch over all that transpires in Vienna during the apparent neglect of his absence was undoubtedly intended to excuse James's somewhat cowardly desertion of London, immediately after his coronation, for the whole time the plague raged there. We find this feeling again in *Coriolanus*, and again in *The Tempest*, which was written for the wedding festivities of the Princess Elizabeth and the Elector Palatine, and which contains, under cover of the sagacious Prospero, many subtle and dainty, but utterly undeserved, compliments to the wise and learned King James. There is a striking analogy between the relations of Molière to Louis XIV. and those of Shakespeare to his king. Both great men had the religious prejudices of the people against them; both, as poets of the royal theatre, had to make some show of subservience, but Molière could feel a more sincere admiration for his Louis than could Shakespeare for his James.

In an otherwise masterly review of *The Tempest* in the *Universal Review* for 1889, Richard Garnett has called *Coriolanus* a reflection of a Conservative's view of James's struggle with the Parliament. This is an exaggeration, which leads him to raise the question as to whether the play owed its origin to the first conflict with the House, or the second in 1614. He pronounces for the latter, and thus arrives at an opinion, held by himself alone, that *Coriolanus* was Shakespeare's last work.

The argument on which he bases this view proves, on closer inspection, to be entirely worthless. Some lines in the fifth Act (sc. 5) run as follows:

"Think with thyself
How much more unfortunate than all living women
Are we come thither."

In the older editions of North's translations of Plutarch (1595 and 1603) it stands thus: "How much more *unfortunately* than all the women living," the form *unfortunate* of the tragedy not appearing until the edition of 1612. This circumstance was detected by Halliwell-Phillips, and led him and Garnett to the conclusion that Shakespeare used the edition of 1612, and cannot therefore have written his drama before that year. When we consider how very slight the deviation is, and how it was practically necessitated by the metre, we see what a poor criterion it is of the date of production. Moreover, precisely the opposite conclusion might be drawn from a comparison of North's translation with other details of the play. In the fourth Act (sc. 5) we find, for example:

> "——For if
> I had feared death, of all men i' the world
> I would have 'voided thee; but *in mere spite*
> To be quit of those my banishers
> Stand I before thee here."

In the 1579 and 1595 editions of North it stands thus: "For if I had feared death, I would not have come thither to have put myself in hazard, but prickt forward *with spite*."

In all later editions the italicised words are omitted, "with desire to be revenged" being substituted in their stead. According to this method, a very much earlier date might be assumed for *Coriolanus*, but both arguments are equally worthless.

We have, therefore, no occasion to abandon 1608 on that ground, and we have certainly no need to do so for the sake of a fanciful approximation of the position of Coriolanus to that of James at the dissolution of Parliament in 1614.

Thus much, at any rate, can be declared with absolute certainty, that the anti-democratic spirit and passion of the play sprang from no momentary political situation, but from Shakespeare's heart of hearts. We have watched its growth with the passing of years. A detestation of the mob, a positive hatred of the mass as mass, can be traced in the faltering efforts of his early youth. We may see its workings in what is undoubtedly Shakespeare's own description of Jack Cade's rebellion in the *Second Part of Henry VI.*, and we divine it again in the conspicuous absence of all allusion to Magna Charta displayed in *King John.*

We have already stated that Shakespeare's aristocratic contempt for the mob had its root in a purely physical aversion for the atmosphere of the "people." We need but to glance through his works to find the proof of it. In the *Second Part of Henry VI.* (Act iv. sc. 7) Dick entreats Cade "that the laws of England may come out of his mouth;" whereupon Smith remarks aside: "It will be stinking law; for his breath stinks with eating toasted cheese." And again in Casca's description of Cæsar's demeanour when he refuses the crown at the Lupercalian festival: "He put it the third time by, and still he refused it; the rabblement hooted and clapped their chapped hands, and threw up their sweaty nightcaps, and *uttered such a deal of stinking breath* because Cæsar refused the crown, that it had almost choked Cæsar; for he swooned and fell down at it: and for mine own part, I durst not laugh for fear of opening my lips and receiving the bad air" (*Julius Cæsar*, Act i. sc. 2).

Also the words in which Cleopatra (in the last scene of the play) expresses her horror of being taken in Octavius Cæsar's triumph to Rome:

> " Now, Iras, what thinkest thou?
> Thou, an Egyptian puppet, shalt be shown
> In Rome as well as I : mechanic slaves,
> With greasy aprons, rules, and hammers, shall
> Uplift us to the view ; *in their thick breaths,*
> *Rank of gross diet, shall we be enclosed*
> *And forced to drink their vapour.*"

All Shakespeare's principal characters display this shrinking from the mob, although motives of interest may induce them to keep it concealed. When Richard II., having banished Boling-broke, describes the latter's farewell to the people, he says (*Richard II.*, Act i. sc. 4):

> " Ourself and Bushy, Bagot here and Green,
> Observed his courtship to the common people ;
> How did he seem to dive into their hearts
> With humble and familiar courtesy,
> Wooing poor craftsmen with the craft of smiles
> And patient underbearing of his fortune,
> As 'twere to banish their effects with him.
> Off goes his bonnet to an oyster-wench,
> A brace of draymen bid God-speed him well,
> And had the tribute of his supple knee,
> With ' Thanks, my countrymen, my loving friends.' "

The number of these passages proves that it was, in plain words, their evil smell which repelled Shakespeare. He was the true artist in this respect too, and more sensitive to noxious fumes than any woman. At the present period of his life this particular distaste has grown to a violent aversion. The good qualities and virtues of the people do not exist for him; he believes their sufferings to be either imaginary or induced by their own faults. Their struggles are ridiculous to him, and their rights a fiction; their true characteristics are accessibility to flattery and ingratitude towards their benefactors; and their only real passion is an innate, deep, and concentrated hatred of their superiors; but all these qualities are merged in this chief crime: they *stink*.

> " *Cor.* For the mutable *rank-scented* many, let them
> Regard me as I do not flatter, and
> Therein behold themselves " (Act iii. sc. 1).
>   " *Brutus.* I heard him swear,
> Were he to stand for consul, never would he
> Appear i' the market-place, nor on him put
> The napless vesture of humility ;
> Nor, showing as the manner is, his wounds
> To the people, beg their *stinking breaths* " (Act ii. sc. 1).

When Coriolanus is banished by the people, he turns upon them with the outburst :

> " You common cry of curs ! *whose breath I hate*
> As reek o' the rotten fens, whose loves I prize
> As the dead carcases of unburied men
> That do corrupt my air " (Act iii. sc. 3).

When old Menenius, Coriolanus's enthusiastic admirer, hears that the banished man has gone over to the Volscians, he says to the People's Tribunes :

> " You have made good work,
> You and your apron-men : you that stood so much
> Upon the voice of occupation and
> The breath of *garlic-eaters !* " (Act iv. sc. 6).

And a little farther on :

> " Here come the clusters.
> And is Aufidius with him ?   You are they
> That made the air unwholesome when you cast
> Your *stinking* greasy caps up, hooting at
> Coriolanus' exile."

If we seek to know how Shakespeare came by this non-political but purely sensuous contempt for the people, we must search for the reason among the experiences of his own daily life.   Where but in the course of his connection with the theatre would he come into contact with those whom he looked upon as human vermin ?   He suffered under the perpetual obligation of writing, staging, and acting his dramas with a view to pleasing the Great Public.   His finest and best had always most difficulty in making its way, and hence the bitter words in *Hamlet* about the " excellent play" which " was never acted, or, if it was, not above once ; for the play, I remember, pleased not the *million*."

Into this epithet, "the million," Shakespeare has condensed his contempt for the masses as art critics.   Even the poets, and they are many, who have been honest and ardent political democrats, have seldom extended their belief in the majority to a faith in its capacity for appraising their art.   The most liberal-minded of them all well know that the opinion of a connoisseur is worth more than the judgment of a hundred thousand ignoramuses.   With Shakespeare, however, his artist's scorn for the capacity of the many did not confine itself to the sphere of Art, but included the world beyond.   As, year after year, his glance fell from the stage upon the flat caps covering the unkempt hair of the crowding heads down there in the open yard which constituted the pit, his sentiments grew increasingly contemptuous towards " the groundlings."   These unwashed citizens, " the understanding gentlemen of the ground," as Ben Jonson nicknamed them, were attired in unlovely black smocks and goatskin jerkins, which had none too pleasant an odour. They were called "nutcrackers" from their habit of everlastingly cracking nuts and throwing the shells upon the stage. Tossing about apple-peel, corks, sausage ends, and small pebbles was another of their amusements. Tobacco, ale, and apple vendors forced their way among them, and even before the curtain was lifted a reek of tobacco-smoke and beer rose from the crowd impatiently waiting for the prima donna to be shaved. The fashionable folk of the stage and boxes, whom they hated, and with whom they were ever seeking occasion to brawl, called them *stinkards*. Abuse was flung backwards and forwards between them, and the pit threw apples and dirt, and even went so far as to spit on to the stage. In the *Gull's Hornebooke* (1609) Dekker says: "The stage, like time, will bring you to most perfect light and lay you open: neither are you to be hunted from thence, though the *scarecrows* in the *yard* hoot at you, hiss at you, spit on you." As late as 1614 the prologue to an old comedy, *The Hog has lost his Pearl*, says:

> "We may be pelted off for what we know,
>   With apples, eggs, or stones, from *those below*."

Who knows if Shakespeare was better satisfied with the less rowdy portion of his audience? Art was not the sole attraction of the theatre. We read in an old book on English plays:—— "In the play-houses at London it is the fashion of youthes to go first into the *yarde* and carry their eye through every gallery; then, like unto ravens, when they spy the carrion, thither they fly and press as near to the fairest as they can."[1] These fine gentlemen, who sat or reclined at full length on the stage, were probably as much occupied with their ladies as the less well-to-do theatre-goers. We know that they occasionally watched the play as Hamlet did, with their heads in their mistresses' laps, for the position is described in Fletcher's *Queen of Corinth* (Act i. sc. 2):

> "For the fair courtier, the woman's man,
>   That tells my lady stories, dissolves riddles,
>   Ushers her to her coach, *lies at her feet*
>   *At solemn masques, applauding what she laughs at*."

Dekker (*Gull's Hornebooke*) informs us that keen card-playing went on amongst some of the spectators, while others read, drank, or smoked tobacco. Christopher Marlowe has an epigram on this last practice, and Ben Jonson complains in his *Bartholomew Fair* of "those who accommodate gentlemen with tobacco at our theatres." He gives an elaborate description in his play,

---

[1] *Plays confuted in Five several Actions*, by Stephen Gosson, 1580.

The Case is Altered, of the manner in which capricious lordlings conducted themselves at the performance of a new piece :—

"And they have such a habit of dislike in all things, that they will approve nothing, be it never so conceited or elaborate ; but sit dispersed, making faces and spitting, wagging their upright ears, and cry, filthy, filthy ; simply uttering their own condition, and using their wryed countenances instead of a vice, to turn the good aspects of all that shall sit near them, from what they behold" (Act ii. sc. 6).

The fact that women's parts were invariably played by young men may have contributed to the general rowdyism of the play-going public, although, on the other hand, it must have been conducive to greater morality on the part of those directly connected with the theatre.   It was surely a real amelioration of Shakespeare's fate that the difficulties with which he had to struggle were not increased by that enthralling and ravishing evil which bears the name of actress.[1]

The notion of feminine characters being taken by a woman was so foreign to England that the individual who ascertained the use of forks in Italy, discovered the existence of actresses at the same time and in the same place.   Coryate writes from Venice in July 1608 :—"Here I observed certaine things that I never saw before ; for I saw women act, a thing I never saw before, though I have heard that it hath been sometimes used in London ; and they performed it with as good a grace, action, gestures, and whatsoever convenient for a player, as I ever saw any masculine actor."   It was not until forty-four years after Shakespeare's death that a woman stepped on to the English stage.   We know precisely when and in what play she appeared.   On the 8th of December 1660 the part of Desdemona was taken by an Englishwoman.   The prologue read upon this occasion is still in existence.[2]

A theatrical audience of those days was, to Shakespeare's eyes at any rate, an uncultivated horde, and it was this crowd

---

[1] It is therefore a droll error into which the otherwise admirable writer, Professor Fr. Paulson, falls in his essay, *Hamlet die Tragedie des Pessimismus* (*Deutsche Rundschau*, vol. lix. p. 243), when he remarks as a proof of the sensuality of Hamlet's nature : "Man erinnere sich nur seiner Intimität mit den Schauspielern ; als sie ankommen, fällt sein Blick sogleich auf die Füsse der *Schauspielerin.*"

[2] "A Prologue to introduce the first woman that came to act on this stage, in the tragedy called *The Moor of Venice :*"—

> " I come unknown to any of the rest
> To tell you news ; I saw the lady drest.
> The woman plays to day ; mistake me not,
> No man in gown or page in petticoat :
> A woman to my knowledge, yet I can't
> If I should die, make affidavit on't. . . .
> 'Tis possible a virtuous woman may
> Abhor all sorts of looseness and yet play,
> Play on the stage when all eyes are upon her.
> Shall we count that a crime. France counts an honour ?"

which represented to him "the people." He may have looked upon them in his youth with a certain amount of goodwill and forbearance, but they had become entirely odious to him now. It was undoubtedly the constant spectacle of the "*understanders*," and the atmosphere of their exhalations, which caused his scorn to flame so fiercely over democratic movements and their leaders, and all that ingratitude and lack of perception which, to him, represented "the people."

With his necessarily slight historical knowledge and insight, Shakespeare would look upon the old days of both Rome and England in precisely the same light in which he saw his own times. His first Roman drama testifies to his innately anti-democratic tendencies. He seized with avidity upon every instance in Plutarch of the stupidity and brutality of the masses. Recall, for example, the scene in which the mob murders Cinna, the poet, for no better reason than its fury against Cinna, the conspirator (*Julius Cæsar*, Act iii. sc. 3):

" *Third Citizen.* Your name, sir, truly.
" *Cinna.* Truly my name is Cinna.
" *First Citizen.* Tear him to pieces ; he's a conspirator.
" *Cinna.* I am Cinna the poet. I am Cinna the poet.
" *Fourth Citizen.* Tear him for his bad verses. Tear him for his bad verses.
" *Cinna.* I am not Cinna the conspirator.
" *Fourth Citizen.* It is no matter, his name's Cinna ; pluck but his name out of his heart, and turn him going.
" *Third Citizen.* Tear him, tear him ! "

All four citizens are alike in their bloodthirsty fury. Shakespeare displays the same aristocratic contempt for the fickle crowd, whose opinion wavers with every speaker ; witness its complete change of front immediately after Antony's oration. It was this feeling, possibly, which was at the bottom of his want of success in dealing with Cæsar. He probably found Cæsar antipathetic, not on the ground of his subversion of a republican form of government, but as leader of the Roman democracy. Shakespeare sympathised with the conspiracy of the nobles against him because all popular rule—even that which was guided by genius—was repugnant to him, inasmuch as it was power exercised, directly or indirectly, by an ignorant herd.

This point of view meets us again and again in *Coriolanus ;* and whereas, in his earlier plays, it was only occasionally and, as it were, accidentally expressed, it has now grown and strengthened into deliberate utterance.

I am aware that, generally speaking, neither English nor German critics will agree with me in this. Englishmen, to whom Shakespeare is not only their national poet, but the voice of wisdom itself, will, as a rule, see nothing in his poetry but a love of all that is simple, just, and true. They consider that due attention, on the whole, has been paid to the rights of the people in this play; that it contains the essence, as it were, of all that can be urged in favour of either democracy or aristocracy, and that Shakespeare himself was impartial. His hero is by no means, they say, represented in a favourable light; he is ruined by his pride, which, degenerating into unbearable arrogance, causes him to commit the crime of turning his arms against his country, and brings him to a miserable end. His relations with his mother represent the sole instance in which the inhuman, anti-social intractability of Coriolanus' character relaxes and softens; otherwise he is hard and unlovable throughout. The Roman people, on the other hand, are represented as good and amiable in the main; they are certainly somewhat inconstant, but Coriolanus is no less fickle than they, and certainly less excusable. That plebeian greed of plunder which so exasperated Marcius at Corioli is common to the private soldier of all times. No, they say, Shakespeare was totally unprejudiced, or, if he had a prefer-ence, it was for old Menenius, the free-spoken, patriotic soul who always turns a cheerfully humorous side to the people, even when he sees their faults most plainly.

I am simply repeating here a view of the matter actually expressed by eminent English and American critics—a view which, presumably therefore, represents that of the English-speaking public in general.[1]

In Germany also—more particularly at the time when Shake-speare's dramas were interpreted by liberal professors, who in-voluntarily brought them into harmony with their own ideas and those of the period—many attempts were made to prove that Shakespeare was absolutely impartial in political matters. Some even sought to make him a Liberal after the fashion of those who, early in this century, went by that name in Central Europe.

We have no interest, however, in re-fashioning Shakespeare. It is enough for us if our perception is fine and keen enough to recognise him in his works, and we must actually put on blinders not to see on which side Shakespeare's sympathies lie here. He is only too much of one mind with the senators who say that "poor suitors have strong breaths," and Coriolanus, who is never refuted or contradicted, says no more than what the poet in his own person would endorse.

In the first scene of the play, immediately following Menenius' well-known parable of the belly and the other members of the body, Marcius appears and fiercely advocates the view Menenius has humorously expressed:

---

[1] See *Shakespeare's Tragedy of Coriolanus*, by the Rev. Henry N. Hudson, Professor of Shakespeare at Boston University. Boston, 1881.

" He that will give good words to thee will flatter
Beneath abhorring.   What would you have, you curs,
That like not peace nor war ?   He that trusts to you,
Where he should find you lions, finds you hares ;
Where foxes, geese ; you are no surer, no,
Than is the coal of fire upon the ice,
Or hailstone in the sun.   Your virtue is
To make him worthy whose offence subdues him,
And curse that justice did it.   Who deserves greatness,
Deserves your hate ; and your affections are
A sick man's appetite, who desires most that
Which would increase his coil . . .
. . . Hang ye !   Trust ye !
With every minute you do change a mind ;
And call him noble that was now your hate,
Him vile that was your garland."

The facts of the play bear out every statement here made by
Coriolanus, including the one that the plebeians are only brave
with their tongues, and run as soon as it comes to blows.   They
turn tail on the first encounter with the Volscians.

" *Marcius.*   All the contagion of the south light on you,
You shames of Rome !   You herd of—Boils and plagues
Plaster you o'er ! that you may be abhorred
Farther than seen, and one infest another
Against the wind a mile !   You souls of geese,
That bear the shapes of men, how have you run
From slaves that apes would beat !   Pluto and hell !
All hurt behind ; backs red and faces pale
With flight and agu'd fear ! " (Act i. sc. 4).

By dint of threatening to draw his sword upon the runaways,
he succeeds in driving them back to the attack, compels the
enemy to retreat, and forces himself single-handed, like a demigod or very god of war, through the gates of the town, which
close upon him before his comrades can follow.   When he comes
forth again, bleeding, and the town is taken, his wrath thunders
afresh on finding that the only idea of the soldiery is to secure
as much booty as possible :

" See here these movers, that do prize their hours
At a crack'd drachm !   Cushions, leaden spoons,
Irons of a doit, doublets that hangmen would
Bury with those that wore them, these base slaves,
Ere yet the fight be done, pack up :—Down with them ! "

As far as Coriolanus is concerned the popular party is simply
the body of those who " cannot rule nor ever will be ruled " (Act
iii. sc. 1).   The majority of nobles are too weak to venture to
oppose the people's tribunes as they should, but Coriolanus,
perceiving the danger of allowing these men to gain influence in

the government of the city, courageously, if imprudently, braves
their hatred in order to thwart and repress them (Act iii. sc. 1).

> "*First Senator.* No more words, we beseech you
>   *Coriolanus.* How! no more?
> As for my country I have shed my blood,
> Not fearing outward force, so shall my lungs
> Coin words till their decay, against those measels,
> Which we disdain should tetter us, yet sought
> The very way to catch them."

He further asserts that the people had not deserved the
recent distribution of corn, for they had attempted to evade the
summons to arms, and during the war they chiefly displayed
their courage in mutinying. They had brought groundless
accusations against the senate, and it was contemptible to allow
them, out of fear of their numbers, any share in the government.
His last words upon the subject are:

> ". . . This double worship,
> Where one part does disdain with cause, the other
> Insult without all reason; where gentry, title, wisdom,
> Cannot conclude but by the yea and no
> Of general ignorance,—it must omit
> Real necessities, and give way the while
> To unstable slightness: purpose so barr'd it follows,
> Nothing is done to purpose. . . . "

So, in *Troilus and Cressida*, would Ulysses, who represents
all that is truly wise in statesmanship, have spoken. There is no
humane consideration for the oppressed condition of the poor, no
just recognition of the right of those who bear the burden to
have a voice in its distribution. That Shakespeare held the same
political views as Coriolanus is amply shown by the fact that
the most dissimilar characters approve of them in every particular, excepting only the violent and defiant manner in which
they are expressed. Menenius' description of the tribunes of the
people is not a whit less scathing than that of Marcius.

"Our very priests must become mockers, if they shall encounter
such ridiculous subjects as you are. When you speak best unto
the purpose, it is not worth the wagging of your beards; and
your beards deserve not so honourable a grave as to stuff a
butcher's cushion, or to be entombed in an ass's pack-saddle.
Yet you must be saying, Marcius is proud, who, in a cheap estimation, is worth all your predecessors since Deucalion" (Act ii.
sc. 1).

When Coriolanus's freedom of speech has procured his banishment, Menenius exclaims in admiration (Act iii. sc. 1):

> " *His nature is too noble for this world:*
> He would not flatter Neptune for his trident,
> Or Jove for 's power to thunder. His heart's his mouth."

Thus he is exiled for his virtues, not for his failings, and at heart they all agree with Menenius. When Coriolanus has gone over to the enemy, and their one anxiety is to appease his wrath, Cominius expresses the same view of the culpability of people and tribunes towards him (Act iv. sc. 4) :

> " Who shall ask it ?
> The tribunes cannot do 't for shame ; the people
> Deserve such pity of him as the wolf
> Does of the shepherd."

Even the voice of one of the two serving-men of the Capitol exalts Coriolanus and justifies his scorn for the love or hatred of the people, the ignorant, bewildered masses—

" . . . So that, if they love, they know not why, they hate upon no better a ground : therefore for Coriolanus neither to care whether they love or hate him manifests the true knowledge he has of their dispositions ; and out of his noble carelessness lets them plainly see 't " (Act ii. sc. 2).

This is almost too well expressed for a servant ; we perceive that the poet has taken no particular pains to disguise his own voice. The same man tells how well Coriolanus has deserved of his country ; he did not rise, as some do, by standing hat in hand and bowing himself into favour with the people :

" . . . But he hath so planted his honours in their eyes and his actions in their hearts, that for their tongues to be silent and not confess so much were a kind of ungrateful injury ; to report otherwise were a malice, that giving itself to lie, would pluck reproof and rebuke from every ear that heard it."

This uncultured mind bears the same testimony as that of the most refined and intelligent patricians to the greatness of the hero. It is not difficult, I think, to follow the mental processes from which this work evolved. When Shakespeare came to reflect on what had constituted his chief gladness here on earth and made his melancholy life endurable to him, he found that his one lasting, if not too freely flowing, source of pleasure had been the friendship and appreciation of one or two noble and nobly-minded gentlemen.

For the people he felt nothing but scorn, and he was now, more than ever, incapable of seeing them as an aggregation of separate individualities, they were merged in the brutality which distinguished them in the mass. Humanity in general was to him not millions of individuals, but a few great entities amidst millions of non-entities. He saw more and more clearly that the existence of these few illustrious men was all that made life worth living, and the belief gave impetus to that hero-worship which had been characteristic of his early youth. Formerly, however, this wor-

ship had lacked its present polemical quality. The fact that
Coriolanus was a great warrior made no particular impression on
Shakespeare at this period; it was quite incidental, and he included it simply because he must. It was not the soldier that he
wished to glorify but the demigod. His present impression of
the circumstances and conditions of life is this: there must of
necessity be formed around the solitary great ones of this earth a
conspiracy of envy and hatred raised by the small and mean. As
Coriolanus says, "Who deserves greatness, deserves your hate."

Owing to this turn of thought, Shakespeare found fewer
heroes to worship; but his worship became the more intense,
and appears in this play in greater force than ever before. The
patricians, who have a proper understanding of his merit, regard
Coriolanus with a species of lover-like enthusiasm, a sort of
adoration. When Marcius's mother tells Menenius that she has
had a letter from her son, and adds, "And I think there's one at
home for you," Menenius cries:

"I will make my very house reel to-night: a letter for me!
"*Virgilia.* Yes, certain, there's a letter for you; I saw't.
"*Menenius.* A letter for me! It gives me an estate of seven years'
health; in which time I will make a lip at the physician: the most
sovereign prescription in Galen is but empiricutic, and, to this preserva-
tive, of no better report than a horse-drench" (Act ii. sc. 1).

So speaks his friend; we will now listen to his bitterest enemy,
Aufidius, the man whom he has defeated and humiliated in battle
after battle, who hates him, and vows that neither temple nor prayer
of priest, nor any of those things which usually restrain a man's
wrath, shall prevail to soften him. He has sworn that wherever
he may find his enemy, be it even on his own hearth, he will
wash his hands in his heart's blood. But when Marcius forsakes
Rome, and repairing to the Volscians, actually seeks Aufidius in
his own home, upon his own hearth, we hear only the admiration
and genuine enthusiasm which the sound of his voice and the
mere majesty of his presence calls forth in the adversary who
would gladly hate him, and still more gladly despise him if he
could.

> "O Marcius, Marcius!
> Each word thou hast spoke hath weeded from my heart
> A root of ancient envy. If Jupiter
> Should from yond cloud speak divine things,
> And say ''Tis true,' I'd not believe them more
> Than thee, all noble Marcius. Let me twine
> Mine arms about that body, where against
> My grained ash an hundred times hath broke,
> And scarred the moon with splinters: here I clip
> The anvil of my sword, and do contest
> As hotly and as nobly with thy love,
> As ever in ambitious strength I did

Contend against thy valour. Know thou first,
I loved the maid I married; never man
Sighed truer breath; but that I see thee here,
Thou noble thing! more dances my rapt heart
Than when I first my wedded mistress saw
Bestride my threshold " (Act iv. sc. 5).

We have, then, in this play an almost wildly enthusiastic hero-worship upon a background of equally unqualified contempt for the populace. It is something different, however, from the humble devotion of his younger days to alien greatness (as in *Henry V.*), and is founded rather on an overpowering and defiant consciousness of his own worth and superiority.

The reader must recall the fact that his contemporaries looked upon Shakespeare not so much as a poet who earned his living as an actor, but as an actor who occasionally wrote plays. We must also remember that the profession of an actor was but lightly esteemed in those days, and the work of a dramatist was considered as a kind of inferior poetry, which scarcely ranked as literature. Probably most of Shakespeare's intimates considered his small narrative poems—his *Venus and Adonis*, his *Lucretia*, &c.—his real claim to notoriety, and they would regret that for the sake of money he had joined the ranks of the thousand and one dramatic writers. We are told in the dedication of *Histrio Mastix* (1634), that the playwrights of the day took no trouble with what they wrote, but covetously pillaged from old and new sources, "chronicles, legends, and romances."

Shakespeare did not even publish his own plays, but submitted to their appropriation by grasping booksellers, who published them with such a mutilation of the text, that it must have been a perfect terror to him to look at them. This mishandling of his plays would be so obnoxious to him, that it was not likely he would care to possess any copies. He was in much the same position in this respect as the modern author, who, unprotected by any law of international copyright, sees his works mangled and mutilated in foreign languages.

He would doubtless enjoy a certain amount of popularity, but he remained to the last an actor among actors (not even then in the first rank with Burbage) and a poet among poets. Never once did it occur to any of his contemporaries that he stood alone, and that all the others taken together were as nothing in comparison with him.

He lived and died one of the many.

That his spirit rose in silent but passionate rebellion against this judgment is obvious. Were there moments in which he clearly felt and keenly recognised his greatness? It must have been so, and these moments had grown more frequent of late. Were there also times when he said to himself, "Five hundred, a thousand years hence, my name will still be known to mankind and my plays read"?　We cannot say; it hardly seems probable, or he would surely have contended for the right to publish his own works.　We cannot doubt that he believed himself worthy at this time of such lasting fame, but he had, as we can well understand, no faith at all that future generations would see more clearly, judge more truly, and appraise more justly than his contemporaries.　He had no idea of historical evolution, his belief was rather that the culture of his native country was rapidly declining.　He had watched the growth of narrow-minded prejudice, had seen the triumphant progress of that pious stupidity which condemned his art as a wile of the devil; and his detestation of the mass of men, past, present, and to come, made him equally indifferent to their praise or blame. Therefore it pleased him to express this indifference through the medium of Coriolanus, the man who turns his back upon the senate when it eulogises him, and of whom Plutarch tells us that the one thing for which he valued his fame was the pleasure it gave his mother.　Yet Shakespeare makes him say (Act i. sc. 9):

> " My mother,
> Who has a charter to extol her blood,
> When she does praise me grieves me."

Shakespeare has now broken with the judgments of mankind. He dwells on the cold heights above the snow-line, beyond human praise or blame, beyond the joys of fame and the perils of celebrity, breathing that keen atmosphere of indifference in which the soul hovers, upheld by scorn.

Some few on this earth are men, the rest are *spawn*, as Menenius calls them; and so Shakespeare sympathises with Coriolanus and honours him, endowing him with Cordelia's hatred of unworthy flattery, even placing her very words in his mouth (Act ii. sc. 2):

> " But your people
> I love them as they weigh."

Therefore it is he equips his hero with the same stern devotion to truth with which, later in the century, Molière endows his Alceste, but, instead of in the semi-farcical, it is in the wholly heroic manner (Act iii. sc. 3):

> " Let them pronounce the steep Tarpeian death,
> Vagabond exile, flaying, pent to linger
> But with a grain a day.　I would not buy
> Their mercy at the price of one fair word."

We see Shakespeare's whole soul with Coriolanus when he cannot bring himself to ask the Consulate of the people in requital of his services.　Let them freely give him his reward, but that he should have to ask for it—torture!

When his friends insist upon his conforming to custom and appearing in person as applicant, Shakespeare, who has hitherto followed Plutarch step by step, here diverges, in order to represent this step as being excessively disagreeable to Marcius. According to the Greek historian, Coriolanus at once proceeds with a splendid retinue to the Forum, and there displays the wounds he has received in the recent wars; but Shakespeare's hero cannot bring himself to boast of his exploits to the people, nor to appeal to their admiration and compassion by making an exhibition of his wounds:

> " I cannot
> Put on the gown, stand naked, and entreat them,
> For my wounds' sake, to give their suffrage : please you
> That I may pass this doing " (Act ii. sc. 2).

He finally yields, but has hardly set foot in the Forum before he begins to curse at the position in which he has placed himself:

> "What must I say?
> 'I pray, sir'—Plague upon't! I cannot bring
> My tongue to such a pace :—'Look, sir, my wounds!
> I got them in my country's service when
> Some certain of your brethren roared and ran
> From the noise of our own drums '" (Act ii. sc. 3).

He makes an effort to control himself, and, turning brusquely to the nearest bystanders, he addresses them with ill-concealed irony. On being asked what has induced him to stand for the Consulate, he hastily and rashly replies:

> " Mine own desert.
> " *Second Citizen.* Your own desert!
> " *Coriolanus.* Ay, but not mine own desire.
> " *Third Citizen.* How not your own desire?
> "*Coriolanus.* No, sir, 'twas never my desire to trouble the poor with begging."

Having secured a few votes in this remarkably tactless manner, he exclaims:

> " Most sweet voices!
> Better to die, better to starve,
> Than crave the hire which first we do deserve."

When the intrigues of the tribunes succeed in inducing the people to revoke his election, he so far forgets himself in his fury at the insult that they are enabled to pronounce sentence of banishment against him. He then bursts into an outbreak of taunts and threats: "You common cry of curs! I banish *you!*" —which recalls how some thousand years later another chosen of the people and subsequent object of democratic jealousy, Gambetta, thundered at the noisy assembly at Belleville: "Cowardly brood! I will follow you up into your very dens."

The nature of the material and the whole conception of the play required that the pride of Coriolanus should occasionally be expressed with repellant arrogance. But we feel, through all the intentional artistic exaggeration of the hero's self-esteem, how there arose in Shakespeare's own soul, from the depth of his stormy contempt for humanity, a pride immeasurably pure and steadfast.

XII

CORIOLANUS AS A DRAMA

THE tragedy of *Coriolanus* is constructed strictly according to rule; the plot is simple and powerful, and is developed, with steadily increasing interest, to a logical climax. With the exception of *Othello*, Shakespeare has never treated his material in a more simply intelligible fashion. It is the tragedy of an inviolably truthful personality in a world of small-minded folk; the tragedy of the punishment a reckless egoism incurs when it is betrayed into setting its own pride above duty to state and fatherland.

Shakespeare's aristocratic sympathies did not blind him to Coriolanus' unjustifiable crime and its inevitable consequences. Infuriated by his banishment, the great soldier goes over to the enemies of Rome and leads the Volscian army against his native city, plundering and terrifying as he goes. He spurns the humble entreaties of his friends, and only yields to the women of the city when, led by his mother and his wife, they come to implore mercy and peace.

Coriolanus' fierce outburst when the name of traitor is flung at him proves that Shakespeare did not look upon treason as a pardonable crime:

> " The fires of the lowest hell fold in your people !
> Call me their traitor !—Thou injurious tribune !
> Within thine eyes sat twenty thousand deaths,
> In thy hands clutched as many millions, in
> Thy lying tongue both numbers, I would say
> ' Thou liest,' unto thee, with a voice as free
> As I do pray the gods " (Act iii. sc. 3).

Immediately after this his outraged pride leads him to commit the very crime he has so wrathfully disclaimed. No consideration for his country or fellow-citizens can restrain him. The forces which arrest his vengeance are the mother he has worshipped all his life and the wife he tenderly loves. He knows that it is himself he is offering up when he sacrifices his rancour on the altar of his family. The Volscians will never forgive him for delivering up their triumph to Rome after he had practically delivered up Rome to them. And so he perishes, finally overtaken by Aufidius' long-accumulated jealousy acting through the disappointed rage of the Volscians. In Plutarch Shakespeare found his plot and the chief characters of his play ready to hand. He added the individuality of the tribunes and of Menenius (with the exception of the parable of the belly). Virgilia, who is little more than a name in the original, Shakespeare has transformed by one of his own wonderful touches into a woman whose chief charm lies in the quiet gentleness of her nature. " My gracious silence, hail!" thus Marcius greets her (Act ii. sc. 1), and she is exhaustively defined in the exclamation. Her principal utterances, as well as Volumnia's most important speeches, are mere versifications of Plutarch's prose, and this is why these women have so much genuinely Roman blood in their veins. Volumnia is the true Roman matron of the days of the Republic. Shakespeare has wrought her character with special care, and her rich and powerful personality is not without its darker side. Her kinship with her son is perceptible in all her ways and words. She is more prone, as a woman, to employ, or at least approve of, dissimulation, but her nature is not a whit less defiantly haughty. Her first thought may be jesuitical; her second is always violent:

> " *Vol.* Oh, sir, sir, sir,
> I would have had you put your power well on,
> Before you had worn it out.
> *Cor.*   Let go.
> *Vol.* You might have been enough the man you are, ·
> With striving less to be so: lesser had been
> The thwartings of your dispositions, *if*
> *You had not showed them how ye were disposed*
> *Ere they lacked power to cross you.*
> *Cor.*   Let them hang.
> *Vol. Ay, and burn too* " (Act iii. sc. 2).

When matters come to a climax, she shows no more discretion in her treatment of the tribunes than did her son, but displays precisely the same power of vituperation. On reading her speeches we realise the satisfaction and relief it was to Shakespeare to vent himself in furious invectives through the medium of his dramatic creations :

> " *Vol.* . . . Hadst thou foxship
> To banish him that struck more blows for Rome
> Than thou hast spoken words ?
> *Sic.*   O blessèd heavens !
> *Vol.* More noble blows, than ever thou wise words ;
> And for Rome's good. I'll tell thee what ; yet go :
> Nay, but thou shalt stay too : I would my son
> Were in Arabia, and thy tribe before him,
> His good sword in his hand " (Act iv. sc. 2).

A comparison between Volumnia's final appeal to her son in the last act and the speech as it is given in Plutarch is of the greatest interest. Shakespeare has followed his author step by step, but has enriched him by the addition of the most artlessly human touches :

> " There's no man in the world
> More bound to's mother ; yet here he lets me prate
> Like one i' the stocks. Thou hast never in thy life
> Showed thy dear mother any courtesy ;
> When she, (poor hen !) fond of no second brood,
> Has clucked thee to the wars and safely home,
> Loaden with honour " (Act v. sc. 3).

How the stern, soldierly bearing of the woman is softened by these touches with which Shakespeare has embellished her portrait !

The diction both here and throughout the play is that of Shakespeare's most matured period ; but never before had he used bolder similes, shown more independence in his method of expression, nor condensed so much thought and feeling into so few lines. We have already drawn attention to the masterly handling of his material—a handling, however, which by no means precludes the intrusion of several extravagances, some heroic, some simply childish.

The hero's bodily strength and courage, for example, are strained to the mythical. He forces his way single-handed into a hostile town, holds his own there against a whole army, and finally makes good his retreat, wounded but not subdued. Even Bible tradition, in which divine aid comes to the rescue, cannot furnish forth such deeds. Neither Samson's escape from Gaza (Judges xvi.) nor David's from Keilah (1 Sam. xxiii.) can compare with this amazing exploit.

Equally unlikely is the foolishly defiant and arrogant attitude assumed by the senate, and more especially by Coriolanus, towards the plebeian party. Upon what do the nobles rely to support them in such an attitude ? They have already been compelled to yield the political power of tribuneship, and it never even occurred to them to defy the sentence of banishment pronounced by these same tribunes. How comes it then that they seize every opportunity to taunt and scorn ? How is it that these patricians, who have spoken so many brave words, make so poor a show of resistance when the Volscians are at their gates ? They are so steeped in party spirit that their first thought, when defeat comes upon them, is to rejoice in the confusion and discomfiture the plebeians have brought upon themselves, and finally, abandoning all self-respect, they crawl to the feet of their exasperated conqueror.

The confusion of Shakespeare's authority in this part of the story would account for much.[1] According to Plutarch, Coriolanus, in the course of his victorious march from one Latin town to another, plunders the plebeians, but spares the patricians. A sudden change of public opinion occurs in Rome during his siege of Lavinium, and the popular party desires to recall Coriolanus, but the senate refuses—why, we are not told. The enemy is close upon them before a parley is agreed upon. Coriolanus offers easy terms, the admission of the Volscians to the Latin Federation being the chief stipulation. Despite the general feeling of discouragement in Rome, the senate answers haughtily that Romans will never yield to fear, and the Volscians must first lay down their arms if they desire to obtain a " favour." Directly after this defiance they make the most abject submission, and send their women as suppliants to the hostile camp.

While Shakespeare's Coriolanus has none of this consideration for his former friends, his patricians are as cowardly and incapable as the historian's. Cominius, Titus Lartius, and the others, who are originally represented as valiant men, make a very poor show at the end. Several, in short, of Plutarch's abundant contradictions have found their way into Shakespeare's play; they mark the beginning of a certain inconsequence which henceforward betrays itself in his work. From this point onwards his plays are no longer as highly finished as formerly.

I am not alluding here to the inconsistencies of his hero, for they only serve to give life and truth to his character, and the poet either represented them unconsciously, or was too ingenuous to avoid them ; witness the reflection made by Coriolanus at the very moment of his rebellious disinclination to ask the suffrages of the people :

> " Custom calls me to't ;
> What custom wills, in all things should we do't,
> The dust on antique time would lie unswept,
> And mountainous error be too highly heapt
> For truth to o'er-peer " (Act ii. sc. 3).

Coriolanus is utterly unconscious that this speech of his strikes at the very root of that ultra-conservatism which he affects. The very thing he has refused to understand is, that if we invariably followed custom, the follies of the past would never be swept away, nor the rocks which hinder our progress burst asunder. To Coriolanus, what is customary is right, and he never realises the fact that his disdain for the tribunes and people has led him into a politically untenable position. We are by no means sure that Shakespeare's perceptions in this case were any keener than his hero's ; but, consciously or unconsciously, it is this very inconsistency in Coriolanus' character which makes it so vividly lifelike.

[1] The matter is interestingly discussed in Kreyssig's instructive and sympathetic work : *Vorlesungen über Shakespeare,* 1859, vol. ii. p. 110.

Troilus and Cressida overflowed with contempt for the feminine sex as such, for love as a comical or pitiable sensuality, for mock heroics and sham military glory. *Coriolanus* is brimful of scorn for the masses; for the stupidity, fickleness, and cowardice of the ignorant, slavish souls, and for the baseness of their leaders.

But the passionate disdain possessing Shakespeare's soul is destined to a stronger and wilder outburst in the work he next takes in hand. The outbreak in *Timon* is against no one sex, no one caste, no one nation or fraction of humanity; it is the result of an overwhelming contempt, which excepts nothing and no one, but embraces the whole human race.

XIII

TIMON OF ATHENS—HATRED OF MANKIND

TIMON OF ATHENS has come down to us in a pitiable condition. The text is in a terrible state, and there are, not only between one scene and another, but between one page and another, such radical differences in the style and general spirit of the play as to preclude the possibility of its having been the work of one man. The threads of the story are often entirely disconnected, and circumstances occur (or are referred to) for which we were in no way prepared. The best part of the versification is distinctly Shakespearian, and contains all that wealth of thought which was characteristic of this period of his life; but the other parts are careless, discordant, and desperately monotonous. The prose dialogue especially jars, thrust as it is, with its long-winded straining after effect, into scenes which are otherwise compact and vigorous.

All Shakespeare students of the present day concur in the opinion that *Timon of Athens*, like *Pericles*, is but a great fragment from the master-hand.

The *Lyfe of Timon of Athens* was printed for the first time in the old folio edition of 1623. Careful examination shows us that the first pages of the play of *Timon* (which is inserted between *Romeo and Juliet* and *Julius Cæsar*) are numbered 80, 81, 82, 81, instead of 78, 79, 80, 81, and end at page 98. The names of the actors, for which in no other case is more than the necessary space allowed, here occupy the whole of page 99, and page 100 is left blank. *Julius Cæsar* begins upon the next page, which is numbered 109. Fleay noticed that *Troilus and Cressida*, which, as we remarked, is unnumbered, would exactly fill the pages 78 to 108. By some error, which furnishes us with another hint, the second and third pages of this play are numbered 79 and 80. Obviously it was the publisher's original intention to include *Troilus and Cressida* among the tragedies. On its being subsequently observed that there was nothing really tragic about the play, they cast about, since *Julius Cæsar* was already printed, for another tragedy which would as nearly as possible fill the vacant space.

Shakespeare found the material for *Timon of Athens* in the course of his reading for *Antony and Cleopatra*. There is, in

Plutarch's "Life of Antony," a brief sketch of Timon and his mis-anthropy, his relations with Alcibiades and the Cynic Apemantus, the anecdote of the fig-tree, and the two epitaphs. The subject evidently attracted Shakespeare by its harmony with his own distraught and excited frame of mind at the time. He was soon absorbed in it, and in some form or another he made acquaintance with Lucian's hitherto untranslated dialogue *Timon*, which contained many incidents giving fulness to the story, and from which he appropriated the discovery of the treasure, the consequent return of the parasitic friends, and Timon's scornful treatment of them.

Shakespeare probably found these details in some old play on the same subject. Dyce published, in 1842, an old drama on Timon which had been found in manuscript, and was judged by Steevens to date from 1600, or thereabouts. It seems to have been written for some academic circle, and in it we find the faithful steward and the farewell banquet with which the third act closes. In the older drama, instead of warm water, Timon throws stones, painted to resemble artichokes, at his guests. Some trace of these stones may be found in these lines in Shakespeare's play:

> " *Second Lord.* Lord Timon's mad.
> *Third Lord.* I feel't upon my bones.
> *Fourth Lord.* One day he gives us diamonds, next day stones."

In the old play, when Timon finds the gold, and his faithless mistress and friends flock around him once more, he repulses them, crying:

> " Why vexe yee me, yee Furies? I protest,
> and all the Gods to witnesse invocate,
> I doe abhorre the titles of a friende,
> of father, or companion. I curse
> the aire yee breathe, I lothe to breathe that air."

He naïvely intimates a change of mind in the epilogue:

> " I now am left alone: this rascall route
> hath left my side. What's this? I feele through out
> a sodeine change: my fury doth abate,
> my hearte grows milde and lays aside its hate;"

and concludes with a still more ingenuous appeal for applause:

> " Let loving hands, loude sounding in the ayre,
> cause Timon to the citty to repaire."

We have no proof that Shakespeare was acquainted with this particular work. He probably used some other contemporary play, belonging to the theatre, which had proved a failure in its original form, and which both his company and his own inclinations urged him to thoroughly recast. It was not so entirely rewritten, however, that we can look upon the play as actually the work of Shakespeare—there are too many traces of another and a feebler hand; but the vital, lyrical, powerful pathos is his, and his alone.

There are two theories on this subject. Fleay, in his well-known and thorough investigation of the matter, endeavours to prove that the original scheme was Shakespeare's, but that some inferior hand amplified it for acting purposes. Fleay selected all the indubitably Shakespearian portions, and had them printed as a separate play, contending that it not only included all that was of any value (which will scarcely be disputed), but that, on the score of intelligibility, none of the rejected speeches were needed.[1] Swinburne, who scarcely ever agrees with Fleay, also shares the belief that Shakespeare· used no ready-made groundwork for his play. His first opinion was that *Timon of Athens* was interrupted by Shakespeare's premature death, but later he inclined to the theory that, after working upon it for some time, the poet laid it aside as being little suited to dramatic treatment. Swinburne does not undervalue the work done by Shakespeare on that account, but remarks, on the contrary, that, had Juvenal been gifted with the inspiration of Æschylus, he might have written just such another tragedy as the fourth act of the drama.[2]

The theory that Shakespeare made use of a finished play which he only partially rewrote, leaving the rest in its clumsy imperfection, was originally propounded by the English critics Sympson and Knight. It was first attacked and afterwards eagerly supported by Delius, who gives the reasons for his change of opinion at great length.[3] H. A. Evans, the commentator of the Irving edition, also shares this latter view. There is no dispute between the two parties concerning the portions written by Shakespeare; the contention is simply this: Did Shakespeare remodel another man's play, or did another man complete his?

As Fleay's attempt to construct a connected and intelligible play from the Shakespearian fragments failed, because a great part of the weak and spurious matter is absolutely necessary to the coherence of the whole, it certainly seems more reasonable to accept Shakespeare as the reviser. Some of the English critics incline to the opinion that the inferior scenes were the work of the contemporary poets George Wilkins and John Day.

After a lapse of nearly 300 years it is impossible to give any decided opinion on the matter, more especially for a critic whose mother tongue is not English. In these days of occultism and

---

[1] *New Shakespeare Society's Transactions*, 1874, pp. 130–194.
[2] Swinburne: *A Study of Shakespeare*, pp. 212–215.
[3] *Jarbuch der deutschen Shakespearegesellschaʼt*, iii. pp. 334–361.

spiritualism the simplest way out of the difficulty would be for some of those favoured individuals, who hold communion with the other world by means of small tables and pencils, to induce Shakespeare himself to settle the matter once for all. Meanwhile we must be content with probabilities. To those who only know the work through translations, or to those who, like Gervinus and Kreyssig, the German critics, have not devoted sufficient attention to the language, the necessity of assuming a second writer may not be so obvious. It is not impossible, of course, that the feeble, prosy, and longwinded parts were written by Shakespeare, roughly sketched in such a fit of despondency and utter indifference to detail that he could not force himself to revise, re-write, and condense; but the possibility is an exceedingly remote one. We know how finely Shakespeare generally constructed his plays, even in the first rough draft.

The drama, as it stands, presents the picture of a thoughtlessly and extravagantly open-handed nature, whose one unfailing pleasure is to give. King Lear only gave away his possessions once, and then in his old age and to his daughters; but Timon daily bestows money and jewels upon all and sundry. At the opening of the play he is, without appearing to be personally luxurious, living in the midst of all the voluptuousness with which a Mæcenas, in the gayest of all the world's gay capitals, could surround himself. Artists and merchants flock round the generous patron who pays them more than they ask. A chorus of sycophants sing his praises day and night. It is but natural that, under those circumstances, a carelessly good-natured temperament should look upon society as a circle for the exchange of friendly services, which it is equally honourable to render or receive.

He pays no heed to the faithful steward who warns him that this life cannot last. He no more disturbs himself about the melting of his money from his coffers than if he were living in a communistic society with the general wealth at his disposal.

At last the tide of fortune turns. His coffers are empty; the steward is no longer able to find him money to fling away, and Timon must go a borrowing in his turn. Almost before the report of his ruin has had time to spread, bills come pouring in, and his impatient creditors, yesterday his comrades, send messengers for their money. All his requests for a loan are refused by his former friends—one on the ground of his own poverty, while another professes to be offended because he was not applied to in the first instance, and a third will not even lend a portion of the large sums Timon has but lately lavished upon him.

Timon has hitherto been one of fortune's favourites, but now the true nature of the world is suddenly revealed to him, as it was to Hamlet and King Lear. Like theirs, but far more harshly and bitterly, his former confiding simplicity is replaced by frantic pessimism. Wishing to show his false friends all the contempt he feels for them, Timon invites them to a final banquet, and they, supposing that he has recovered his wealth, attend with excuses on their lips for their recent behaviour. The table is sumptuously spread, but the covered dishes contain only warm water, which Timon disdainfully flings in the faces of his guests.

He cuts himself adrift from all intercourse with mankind, and retreats to the woods to lead the solitary life of a Stoic. The half-jesting retirement of Jaques in *As You Like It*, and his dismissal of all who trouble his solitude, are here carried out in grim earnest.

It is not for long that he remains poor, for he has hardly begun to dig for the roots on which he lives than he finds treasure buried in the earth. Unlike Lucian's misanthrope, who rejoices in the possession of gold as a means of securing a life free from care, Shakespeare's Timon sickens at the sight of his wealth. Neither does he care for the honourable amends made by his countrymen. We learn it so late in the day that we can scarcely believe that Timon was formerly a skilful general, who had done good service to his country. This feature is taken from Lucian, and the character of the luxurious Mæcenas would have gained in interest and nobility if this trait had been impressed upon us earlier in the play. The senate, meanwhile, being threatened with war, offers Timon the sole command. He proudly rejects the overtures made by these misers and usurers in purple, and even remains unsoftened by the faithful devotion of his steward. He anathematises every one and all things, and returns to his cave to die by his own hand.

The non-Shakespearian elements of the play do not prevent his genius and master-hand from pervading the whole, and it is easy to see how this work grew out of the one immediately preceding it, to trace the connecting links between the two plays.

When Coriolanus is exasperated by the ingratitude of the plebeians, he joins the enemies of his country and people, and becomes the assailant of his native city. When Timon falls a victim to the thanklessness of those he has loaded with benefits, his hatred embraces the whole human race. The contrast is very suggestive. The despair of Coriolanus is of an active kind, driving him to deeds and placing him at the head of an army. Timon's is of the passive sort: he merely curses and shuns mankind. It is not until the discovery of the treasure determines him to use his wealth in spreading corruption and misery that his hatred takes a semi-practical form. This contrast was not an element of the drama until Shakespeare made it so.

The whole conduct of his Alcibiades forms a complete parallel to that of Coriolanus, and here again the connection between the two plays is obvious. Shakespeare found a brief account of the mutual relations of Timon and Alcibiades in North's translation of Plutarch's "Life of Antony," together with a description of Timon's good-will towards the general on account of the calamities that he foresaw he would bring upon the Athenians. The name of Alcibiades would not recall to Shakespeare, as it does to us, the most glorious period of Greek culture, and such names as Pericles, Aristophanes, and Plato—he generally gives Latin names to his Greeks, such as Lucius, Flavius, Servilius, &c.; nor did it represent to him the unrivalled subtlety, charm, instability, and reckless extravagance of the man. He would read Plutarch's comparison of Alcibiades and Coriolanus, in which the Greek and Roman generals are considered homogeneous, and for Shakespeare Alcibiades was merely the soldier and commander; on that account he let him occupy much the same relation to Timon that Fortinbras did to Hamlet.

Where Timon merely hates, Alcibiades seizes his weapons; and when Timon curses indiscriminately, Alcibiades punishes severely but deliberately. He does not tear down the city walls and put every tenth citizen to the sword, as he is invited to do; he only seeks vengeance on his personal enemies and those whom he considers guilty. But Timon, like Hamlet, generalises his bitter experiences, and loathes everything that bears the form or name of man. When Athens sends to entreat him to take the command and save the city from the violence of Alcibiades, he is harder and colder, and a hundred times more bitterly relentless, than Coriolanus, who, after all, could bow to entreaty, or than Alcibiades, who is satisfied with a strictly limited vengeance. Timon's loathing of life and hatred of humanity is consistent throughout.

Like *Coriolanus*, this play was undoubtedly written in a frame of mind which prompted Shakespeare less to abandon himself to the waves of imagination than to dwell upon the worthlessness of mankind, and the scornful branding of the contemptible. There is even less inventiveness here than in *Coriolanus:* the plot is not only simple, it is scanty—more appropriate to a parable or didactic poem than a drama. Most of the characters are merely abstractly representative of their class or profession, *e.g.* the Poet, the Painter, the servants, the false friends, the flatterers, the creditors and mistresses. They are simply employed to give prominence to the principal figure, or rather, to a great lyrical outburst of bitterness, scorn, and execration.

In the poet's description of his work in the first scene of the play, Shakespeare has indicated his point of view with unusual precision:

> " I have, in this rough work, shaped out a man
> Whom this beneath world doth embrace and hug
> With amplest entertainment. . . .
> . . . His large fortune,
> Upon his good and gracious nature hanging,

Subdues and properties to his love and tendance
All sorts of hearts."

He unfolds an allegory in which Fortune is represented as enthroned upon a high and pleasant hill, from whose base all kinds of people are struggling upwards to better their condition:

" Amongst them all
Whose eyes are on this sovereign lady fixed,
One do I personate of lord Timon's fame,
Whom Fortune with her ivory hand wafts to her;
Whose present grace to present slaves and servants
Translates his rivals."

The Painter justly observes that the allegory of the hill and the enthroned Fortune could be equally well expressed in a picture as a poem, but the Poet continues:

" When Fortune, in her shift and change of mood,
Spurns down her late beloved, all his dependants,
Which laboured after him to the mountain's top,
Even on their knees and hands, let him slip down,
Not one accompanying his declining foot."

Shakespeare has defined his purpose here as clearly as did Daudet, some hundreds of years later, in the first chapter of his *Sappho*, in which the whole course of the story is symbolised in the ever-increasing difficulty with which the hero mounts the stairs, carrying the heroine to the highest story of the house in which he lives. The bitterness of Shakespeare's mood is shown in the distinct indication that the Poet and the Painter, rogues and toadies as they are, stand in the first ranks of their professions, and cannot, therefore, claim the excuse of poverty. It is significant of the dramatist's low opinion of his fellow-craftsmen —not one of them is mentioned in his will—that he should make his Poet most eloquent in condemnation of his own peculiar faults. Hence Timon's ejaculation in the last act:

" Must thou needs stand for a villain in thine own work
Wilt thou whip thine own faults in other men ? "

In *Timon*, as in *Coriolanus*, Shakespeare put his own thoughts and feelings into the mouths of the various characters of the play. Falseness and ingratitude are the subjects of the most frequent allusion. They were uppermost in the poet's mind at the time, and the changes are rung upon these vices by the Epicurean and the Cynic, by servants and strangers, before and after the climax. Even the fickle Poet serves, as we have seen, as spokesman for the all-prevailing idea; and the Painter, who is every whit as worthless, says with droll irony (Act v. sc. 1):

" Promising is the very air o' the time : it opens the eyes of expectation : performance is ever the duller for his act; and, but in the
plainer and simpler kind of people, the deed of saying is quite out of
use. To promise is most courtly and fashionable : performance is a
kind of will or testament, which argues a great sickness in his judgment that makes it."

If there was one thing Shakespeare loathed above another, it
was the lifeless ceremony which disguises hollowness and fraud.
Early in the play (Act i. sc. 2) Timon says to his guests :

> " Nay, my lords,
> Ceremony was but devised at first
> To set a gloss on faint deeds, hollow welcomes,
> Recanting goodness, sorry ere 'tis shown ;
> But where there is true friendship, there needs none."

Although Apemantus is the converse of Timon at every point—
coarse where he is refined, mean where he is generous, and base
where he is noble—yet in his first monologue the Cynic also
strikes the keynote of the piece (Act i. sc. 2) :

> " We make ourselves fools, to disport ourselves ;
> And spend our flatteries, to drink those men
> Upon whose age we void it up again,
> With poisonous spite and envy.
> Who lives, that's not depravèd or depraves ?
> Who dies, that bears not one spurn to their graves
> Of their friend's gift ? "

The first stranger says in a speech, whose monotony betrays
the fact that it was not entirely Shakespeare's although he has
retouched it in several places (notably the italicised lines) :

> " Who can call him
> His friend that dips in the same dish ? for, in
> My knowing, Timon hath been this lord's father,
> And kept his credit with his purse ;
> Supported his estate ; nay, Timon's money
> Has paid his men their wages : *he ne'er drinks,*
> *But Timon's silver treads upon his lip ;*
> And yet, (oh, see the monstrousness of man
> When he looks out in an ungrateful shape !)
> He does deny him in respect of his,
> What charitable men afford to beggars " (Act iii. sc. 2).

Finally, like the serving-man in the Capitol, who expresses
his approval of Coriolanus' self-conceit, Timon's servant, when
his application for a loan is refused, says :

" The devil knew not what he did when he made man politic; he
crossed himself by 't : and I cannot think but, in the end, the villainies

of men will set him clear. How fairly this lord strives to appear foul! takes virtuous copies to be wicked; *like those that, under hot, ardent zeal, would set whole realms on fire.*"

This direct, unmistakable attack upon Puritanism has a remarkable effect coming from the lips of a Grecian servant, and we may gather from it some idea of the general aim of all these outbursts against hypocrisy.

We must now, with a view to defining the non-Shakespearian elements of the play, devote some attention to its dual authorship. In the first act it is particularly the prose dialogues between Apemantus and others which seem unworthy of Shakespeare. The repartee is laconic but laboured—not always witty, though invariably bitter and disdainful. The style somewhat resembles that of the colloquies between Diogenes and Alexander in Lyly's *Alexander and Campaspe*. The first of Apemantus' conversations might have been written by Shakespeare—it seems to have some sort of continuity with the utterances of Thersites in *Troilus and Cressida*—but the second has every appearance of being either an interpolation by a strange hand, or a scene which Shakespeare had forgotten to score out. Flavius's monologue (Act i. sc. 2) never came from Shakespeare's pen in this form. Its marked contrast to the rest shows that it might be the outcome of notes taken by some blundering shorthand writer among the audience.

The long conversation, in the second act, between Apemantus, the Fool, Caphis, and various servants, was, in all probability, written by an alien hand. It contains nothing but idle chatter devised to amuse the gallery, and it introduces characters who seem about to take some standing in the play, but who vanish immediately, leaving no trace. A Page comes with messages and letters from the mistress of a brothel, to which the Fool appears to belong, but we are told nothing of the contents of these letters, whose addresses the bearer is unable to read.

In the third act there is much that is feeble and irrelevant, together with an aimless unrest which incessantly pervades the stage. It is not until the banqueting scene towards the end of the act that Shakespeare makes his presence felt in the storm which bursts from Timon's lips. The powerful fourth act displays Shakespeare at his best and strongest; there is very little here which could be attributed to alien sources. I cannot understand the decision with which English critics (including a poet like Tennyson) have condemned as spurious Flavius's monologue at the close of the second scene. Its drift is that of the speech in the following scene, in which he expresses the whole spirit of the play in one line: "What viler things upon the earth than friends!" Although there is evidently some confusion in the third scene (for example, the intimation of the Poet's and Painter's appearance long before they really arrive), I cannot agree with Fleay that Shakespeare had no share in the passage contained between the lines, "Where liest o' nights, Timon?" and "Thou art the cap of all the fools alive."

One speech in particular betrays the master-hand. It is that in which Timon expresses the wish that Apemantus's desire to become a beast among beasts may be fulfilled:

" If thou wert the lion, the fox would beguile thee: if thou wert the lamb, the fox would eat thee: if thou wert the fox, the lion would suspect thee when, peradventure, thou wert accused by the ass: if thou wert the ass, thy dulness would torment thee: and still thou livedst but as a breakfast to the wolf: if thou wert the wolf, thy greediness would afflict thee, and oft thou shouldst hazard thy life for thy dinner."

There is as much knowledge of life here as in a concentrated essence of all Lafontaine's fables.

The last scenes of the fifth act were evidently never revised by Shakespeare. It is a comical incongruity that makes the soldier who, we are expressly told, is unable to read, capable of distinguishing Timon's tomb, and even of having the forethought to take a wax impression of the words. There is also an amalgamation of the two contradictory inscriptions, of which the first tells us that the dead man wishes to remain nameless and unknown, while the last two lines begin with the declaration, "Here lie I, Timon." Notwithstanding the shocking condition of the text, the repeatedly occurring confusion of the action, and the evident marks of an alien hand, Shakespeare's leading idea and dominant purpose is never for a moment obscured. Much in *Timon* reminds us of *King Lear*, the injudiciously distributed benefits and the ingratitude of their recipients are the same, but in the former the bitterness and virulence are tenfold greater, and the genius incontestably less. Lear is supported in his misfortunes by the brave and manly Kent, the faithful Fool, that truest of all true hearts, Cordelia, her husband, the valiant King of France. There is but one who remains faithful to Timon, a servant, which in those days meant a slave, whose self-sacrificing devotion forces his master, sorely against his will, to except one man from his universal vituperation. In his own class he does not meet with a single honestly devoted heart, either man's or woman's; he has no daughter, as Lear; no mother, as Coriolanus; no friend, not one.

How far more fortunate was Antony! It is a corrupt world in the process of dissolution that we find in *Antony and Cleopatra*. Most of it is rotten or false, but the passion binding the two principal characters together by its magic is entirely genuine. Perdican's profound speech in De Musset's " *On ne badine pas avec l'amour* " applies both to them and the whole play: " Tous les hommes sont menteurs, inconstants, faux, bavards, hypocrites,

orgueilleux; toutes les femmes sont artificieuses, perfides, vani-
teuses; le monde n'est qu'un égout sans fond; mais il y au monde
une chose sainte et sublime, c'est l'union de deux de ces êtres
imparfaits." This simple fact, that Antony and Cleopatra love
one another, ennobles and purifies them both, and consoles us,
the spectators, for the disaster their passion brings upon them.
Timon has no mistress, no relation with the other sex, only contempt for it.

There is a significant revelation of the crudity and stupidity
with which, even before the end of the seventeenth century,
Shakespeare's admirers made free with him, in an adaptation
which Shadwell published in 1678 under the title "The History
of Timon the Man Hater into a Play." In this Timon is represented as deserting his mistress Evandra, by whom he is
passionately loved to the last. This introduction of a sympathetic woman's character naturally secured the play a success
which was never attained by Shakespeare's hero, a solitary
misanthrope alone with his bitterness. Shakespeare has intentionally veiled the defects of nature and judgment which deprive
Timon to some extent of our sympathy, both in his prosperity
and his misfortunes. He had never in his bright days attached
himself so warmly to any heart that he felt it beat in unison with
his own. Had he ever been powerfully drawn to a single friend,
he would not have squandered his possessions so lightly on all
the world. Because he only loved mankind in the mass, he now
hates them in the mass. He never, now as then, shows any
powers of discrimination.

Shakespeare merely used him as a well-known example of the
punishment simple-minded trustfulness brings upon itself; his
indiscretion is the outcome of native nobility, and his wrath is
perfectly justifiable. We feel that Timon possesses the poet's
sympathy and compassion, even when his abhorrence of humanity
passes the bounds of hatred, and becomes a passion for its
annihilation. Timon turns hermit in order to escape from the
sight of human beings, and this misanthropy is no mere mask
worn to conceal his despair at the loss of this world's goods,
since it stands the test of the finding of the treasure. He no
longer looks upon wealth as the means of procuring pleasure, but
only as an instrument of vengeance. It is for that, and that alone,
that he rejoices when the "yellow glittering, precious gold" falls
into his hands:

> "Why, this
> Will lug your priests and servants from your sides,
> . . . Make the hoar leprosy adored, place thieves
> And give them title, knee, and approbation
> With senators on the bench; this is it
> That makes the wappened widow wed again;
> She whom the spital-house and ulcerous sores

Would cast the gorge at, this embalms and spices
To the April day again" (Act iv. sc. 3).

When Alcibiades, who was formerly on friendly terms with
him and has retained some kindly feeling towards him, disturbs
his solitude by a visit, Timon receives him with the exclamation:

> "The canker gnaw thy heart
> For showing me again the eyes of man!
> *Alcibiades.* What is thy name? Is man so hateful to thee
> That art thyself a man?
> *Timon.* I am Misanthropos, and hate mankind.
> For thy part, I do wish thou wert a dog
> That I might love thee something" (Act iv. sc. 3).

So might old Schopenhauer, with his loathing for men and
his love for dogs, have expressed himself. Timon explains this
hatred as the result of a dispassionate insight into the worthlessness of human nature:

> "For every guise of fortune
> Is smoothed by that below: the learned pate
> Ducks to the golden fool: all is oblique;
> There's nothing level in our cursèd natures
> But direct villany."

When Alcibiades, who appears in company with two hetæræ,
addresses Timon in friendly fashion, the latter turns to abuse one
of the women, declaring that she carries more destruction with
her than the soldier does in his sword. She retorts, and he rails
at her in the fashion of *Troilus and Cressida*. In his eyes the
wanton woman is merely the disseminator of disease, and he
expresses the hope that she may bring many a young man to
sickness and misery. Alcibiades offers to serve him:

> "Noble Timon,
> What friendship may I do thee?
> *Timon.* None, but to maintain my opinion.
> *Alcibiades.* What is it, Timon?
> *Timon.* Promise me friendship, but perform none."

When Alcibiades informs him that he is leading his army
against Athens, Timon prays that the gods will give him the
victory, in order that he may exterminate the people root and
branch, and himself afterwards. He gives him gold for his war,
and conjures him to rage like a pestilence:

> "Let not thy sword skip one:
> Pity not honoured age for his white beard;
> He is an usurer: strike me the counterfeit matron,
> It is her habit only that is honest,
> Herself's a bawd: let not the virgin's cheek

Make soft thy trenchant sword; for those milk paps
That through the window bars bore at men's eyes
Are not within the leaf of pity writ,
But set them down horrible traitors: spare not the babe,
Whose dimpled smile from fools exhaust their mercy;
Think it a bastard, whom the oracle
Hath doubtfully pronounced thy throat shall cut,
And mince it sans remorse: swear against objects;
Put armour on thine ears and on thine eyes;
Whose proofs, nor yells of mothers, maids, nor babes,
Nor sight of priests in holy vestments bleeding,
Shall pierce a jot.   There's gold to pay thy soldiers:
Make large confusion: and, thy fury spent,
Confounded be thyself" (Act iv. sc. 3).

The women, seeing his wealth, immediately beg him for gold, and he answers, "Hold up, you sluts, your aprons mountant." They are not to swear, for their oaths are worthless, but they are to go on deceiving, and being "whores still," they are to seduce him to attempts to convert them, and to deck their own thin hair with the hair of corpses, that of hanged women preferably; they are to paint and rouge until they themselves lie dead: "Paint till a horse may mire upon your face."

They shout to him for more gold; they will "do anything for gold."   Timon answers them in words which Shakespeare, for all the pathos of his youth, has never surpassed, words whose frenzied scathing has never been equalled:

" Consumptions sow
In hollow bones of men: strike their sharp shins,
And mar men's spurring; crack the lawyer's voice,
That he may never more false title plead,
Nor sound his quillets shrilly: hoar the flamen,
That scolds against the quality of flesh,
And not believes himself: down with the nose,
Down with it flat: take the bridge quite away
Of him that, his particular to foresee,
Smells from the general weal: make curled-pate ruffians bald,
And let the unscarred ruffians of the war
Derive some pain from you: plague all;
That your activity may defeat and quell
The source of all erection.   There's more gold:
Do you damn others, and let this damn you,
And ditches grave you all.
Phrynia and Timandra. More counsel with more gold, bounteous Timon."

The passion in this is overpowering.   One need only compare it with Lucian to realise the fire that Shakespeare has put into the old Greek, whose reflections are only savage in substance, being absolutely tame in expression—"The name of misanthrope shall sound sweetest in my ears, and my characteristics shall be peevishness, harshness, rudeness, hostility towards men," &c. Compare this scene with the latter part of Plutarch's *Alcibiades*, to which we know Shakespeare had referred, and see what the poet's acrimony has made of Timandra, the faithful mistress who follows Alcibiades to Phrygia. They are together when his murderess sets fire to the house, and it is Timandra who enshrouds his body in the most costly material she possesses, and gives him as splendid a funeral as her isolated position can secure.

Apemantus follows close upon Alcibiades, and after he is driven away, two bandits appear, attracted by the report of the treasure. Timon welcomes them, crying, " Rascal thieves, here's gold." He adds good advice to the money. They are to drink wine until it drives them mad, so they may, perchance, escape hanging; they are to put no trust in physicians, whose antidotes are poisons; when they can, they are to kill as well as steal. Theft is universal, the law itself being only made to conceal robbery:

> " Rob one another. There's more gold. Cut throats.
> All that you meet are thieves: to Athens go ;
> Break open shops ; *nothing can you steal*
> *But thieves do lose it."*

The worthy Proudhon himself has not set forth more plainly his axiom, " Property is theft."

When the Senate appeals to Timon for his assistance as general and statesman, he first professes sympathy, then cries:

> " If Alcibiades kill my countrymen,
> Let Alcibiades know this of Timon,
> That Timon cares not."

He may sack Athens, pull old men by the beard, and give the sacred virgins over to the mercies of the soldiery. Timon cares as little as the soldier's knife recks of the throats it cuts. The most worthless blade in Alcibiades' camp is more valued by him than any life in Athens. All feeling for country, home, even for the helpless, has utterly perished.

Shakespeare borrows a final touch from Plutarch, which, in his hand, becomes a masterpiece of bloodthirsty irony. He declares he does not, as they suppose, rejoice in the general desolation ; his countrymen shall once more enjoy his hospitality. A fig-tree grows by his cave, which it is his intention to cut down ; but before it is felled, any friend of his, high or low, who wishes to escape the horrors of a siege, is welcome to come and hang himself. He next announces that his grave is prepared, and they that seek him may come thither and find an oracle in his tombstone, then :

> " Lips, let sour words go by and language end :
> What is amiss, plague and infection mend !
> Graves only be man's works and death their gain !
> Sun, hide thy beams ! Timon hath done his reign."

These are his last words.　May pestilence rage amongst men ! May it infect and destroy so long as there is a man left to dig a grave !　May the world be annihilated as Timon is about to annihilate himself.　The light of the sun will presently be extinguished for him ; let it be extinguished for all !

This is not Othello's sorrow over the power of evil to wreck the happiness of noble hearts, nor King Lear's wail over the ever-threatening possibilities and the heaped-up miseries of life : it is an angry bitterness, caused by ingratitude, which has grown so great that it darkens the sky of life and causes the thunder to roll with such threatening peals as we have never heard even in Shakespeare.　All that he has lived through in these last years, and all that he has suffered from the baseness of other men, is concentrated in this colossal figure of the desperate man-hater, whose wild rhetoric is like a dark essence of blood and gall drawn off to relieve suffering.

XIV

CONVALESCENCE—TRANSFORMATION—
THE NEW TYPE

THE last, wildest words of this bitter outbreak had been spoken. The dark cloud had burst and the skies were slowly clearing.

It seems as though the blackest of his griefs had been lightened in the utterance, and now that the steady *crescendo* had burst into its most furious *forte*, he breathed more freely again. He had said his say; Timon had called for the extinction of humanity by plague, sexual disease, slaughter, and suicide. The powers of cursing could go no farther.

Shakespeare has shouted himself hoarse and his fury is spent. The fever is over and convalescence has set in. The darkened sun shines out once more, and the gloomy sky shines blue again.

How and why! Who shall say?

In all the obscurity of Shakespeare's life-history, nowhere do we feel our ignorance of his personal experiences more acutely than here. Some have sought an explanation in the resignation which comes with advancing years, and of which we certainly catch glimpses in his latest works. But Shakespeare neither was, nor felt himself, old at forty-five; and the word resignation is meaningless in connection with this marvellous softening of his long exasperated mood. It is more than a mere reconciliation; it is a revival of that free and lambent imagination which has lain so long in what seemed to be its death-swoon. There is no play of fancy in resignation.

Once more he finds life worth living, the earth beautiful, enchantingly, fantastically attractive, and those who dwell upon it worthy of his love.

In the purely external circumstances no change has occurred. The political outlook in England is the same, and it is not likely that he would be greatly stirred by events such as the assassination of Henry IV. of France in 1610 and the consequent expulsion of the Jesuits from Great Britain. Details—like the decree forbidding English Catholics (Recusants) from coming within ten miles of the Court, and James's removal of his mother's bones and their pompous re-interment in Westminster Abbey—could have little effect upon Shakespeare.

What has personally befallen him that has had such power to

re-attune his spirit and lead it back from discord to the old melody and harmony? Surely we are now brought face to face with one of the decisive crises of his life.

Let us anticipate the works yet to be written—*Pericles, Cymbeline, Winter's Tale,* and *The Tempest.*

In this last splendid period of his life's glowing September, his dramatic activity, bearing about it the clear transparent atmosphere of early autumn, is more richly varied now than it has ever been.

What figures occupy the most prominent place in the poet's sumptuous harvest-home but the young, womanly forms of Marina, Imogen, Perdita, and Miranda. These girlish and forsaken creatures are lost and found again, suffer grievous wrongs, and are in no case cherished as they deserve; but their charm, purity, and nobility of nature triumph over everything.

They must have had their prototypes or type.

A new world has opened out to Shakespeare, but it would be profitless to spend much time on more or less probable conjectures concerning how and by whom it was revealed. We will, therefore, only lightly touch upon the possibility that Shakespeare, after and during the violent crisis of his loathing for humanity, was gradually reconciled to life by some young and womanly nobility of soul, and by all the poetry which surrounds it and follows in its train.

All these youthful women are akin, and are sharply separated from the heroines of his former plays. They are half-real, half-imaginary. The charm of youth and fantastic romance shines round them like a halo; the foulness of life has no power to defile them. They are self-reliant without being endowed with the buoyant spirit of his earlier adventurous maidens, and they are gentle without being overshadowed by the pathetic mournfulness of his sacrificial victims. Not one comes to a tragic end, and not one ever utters a jest, but all are holy in the poet's eyes.

The situations of Marina and Perdita are very similar; both are castaways, apparently fatherless and motherless, left solitary amidst dangerous or pitiable circumstances. Imogen is suspected and her life threatened, like Marina's, and although she is suspected and sentenced to death by her nearest and dearest, her strength never falters, and even her love for her unworthy husband is unimpaired.

Miranda is deprived of her rank and condemned to the solitude of a desert island, but is sheltered even there by a father's watchful care. There is indeed a half-fatherly tenderness in the delineation of Miranda, and the conception of the native charm of a young girl as a wonderful mystery of nature. Neither Molière's Agnes nor Shakespeare's Miranda have ever looked upon the face of a young man before they meet the one they love, but Agnes possesses only the artificially-preserved ignorance and innocence which disappear like dew before the sun of love. To Shakespeare, Miranda appears like a being from another world, an ideal of pure spiritual womanhood and maidenly passion, before which he almost kneels in worship.

Let us glance back at Shakespeare's gallery of women. There are the viragoes of his youth, bloodthirsty women like Tamora, guilty and powerful ones like Margaret of Anjou, and later, Lady Macbeth, Goneril, and Regan; there are feeble women like Anne in Richard III., and shrews like Katharine and Adriana, in whom we seem to detect a reminiscence of the wife at Stratford.

Then we have the passionately loving, like Julia in *Two Gentlemen of Verona*, Venus, Titania, Helena in *All's Well that Ends Well*, and, above all, Juliet. There are the charmingly witty and often frolicsome young girls, like Rosaline in *Love's Labour's Lost*, Portia in the *Merchant of Venice*, Beatrice, Viola, and Rosalind.

Then the simply-minded, deeply-feeling, silent natures, with an element of tragedy about them, pre-ordained to destruction— Ophelia, Desdemona, Cordelia. After these come the merely sensual types of his bitter mood—Cleopatra and Cressida.

And now, lastly, the young girl, drawn with the ripened man's rapture over her youth, and a certain passion of admiration.[1] She had been lost to him, as Marina to her father Pericles, and Perdita to her father Leontes. He feels for her the same fatherly tenderness which his last incarnation, the magician Prospero, feels for his daughter Miranda.

He had taken a greater burden of life upon himself in the past than he well could bear, and he now lays its heaviest portion aside. No more tragedies! No more historical dramas! No more of the horrors of realism! In their stead a fantastic reflection of life, with all the changes and chances of fairy-tale and legend! A framework of fanciful poetry woven around the charming seriousness of the youthful woman and the serious charm of the young girl.

It works like a vision from another world, an enchantment set in surroundings as dream-like as itself. A ship in the open sea off Mitylene; a strange, delightful, ocean-encircled Bohemia; a lonely, magically-protected island; a Britain, where kings of the Roman period and Italians of the sixteenth century meet young princes who dwell in woodland caves and have never seen the face of woman.

---

[1] In Mrs. Jameson's charming old book, *Shakespeare's Female Characters*, she has grouped his women in an arbitrary manner. Disregarding all chronological sequence, she divides twenty-three characters into four groups:—1. Characters of Intellect. 2. Characters of Passion and Imagination. 3. Characters of the Affections. 4. Historical characters. Heine characterises forty-five feminine figures in his *Shakespeare's Mädchen und Frauen*, but the last twenty-one are only distinguished by a few quotations, and he makes no attempt at any deeper interpretation, historical or psychological.

Thus he gradually returns to those brighter moods of his youth from which the fairy dances of the *Midsummer Night's Dream* had evolved, or that unknown Forest of Arden in which cypresses grew and lions prowled, and happy youth and mirthful maidenhood carelessly roamed. Only the spirit of frolic has departed, while free play is given to a fancy unhampered by the laws of reality, and much earnest discernment lies behind the untrammelled sport of imagination. He waves the magician's wand and reality vanishes, now, as formerly. But the light heart has grown sorrowful, and its mirth is no more than a faint smile. He offers the daydreams of a lonely spirit now, rich but evanescent visions, occupying in all a period of from four to five years.

Then Prospero buries his magic wand a fathom deep in the earth for ever.

XV

PERICLES—COLLABORATION WITH WILKINS AND ROWLEY—SHAKESPEARE AND CORNEILLE

SEVENFOLD darkness surrounds Shakespeare's productions in that transition period during which morbid distrust was giving way to the brighter view of life we find in his later plays. We possess a brief series of plays: *Timon of Athens* and *Pericles*, which are plainly only partially his work, and *Henry VIII.* and *The Two Noble Kinsmen*, of which we may confidently assert that Shakespeare had nothing to do with them beyond the insertion of single important speeches and the addition of a few valuable touches.

He had not adapted other men's work since his novitiate, neither had he blended his own intellectual produce with alien and inferior efforts. What is the reason of such an association suddenly and repeatedly occurring now? I will state my view of the matter without any circumlocution or criticism of the opinion of others. We noticed in *Coriolanus* that Shakespeare's changed attitude towards humanity had also affected his attitude towards his art. A certain carelessness of execution had made itself felt. His steadily increasing despair of finding any virtue or worth in the world, and the ever-growing resentment against the coarseness and thanklessness of men, were accompanied by his corresponding indifference and negligence as a dramatist.

We have followed Shakespeare through his early struggles and youthful happiness to the great and serious epoch of his life, and through the anything but brief period of gloom to its crisis in the wild outburst of *Timon of Athens;* after which we recognised the first symptoms of convalescence. A perspective of not too profoundly serious nor realistic dramas has opened out before us, whose freely playing fantasy proves that Shakespeare is once more reconciled to life.

It stands to reason that this reconciliation was not effected by any sudden change, and Shakespeare would not immediately return to the old striving after perfection in his profession—did not do so, in fact, until that very last work in which he laid aside his art for ever. We saw that he had strained too much at life, and he now realises that he has done the same with art. Either he no longer taxes his strength to the uttermost when he writes, or he has lost that power for which no task was too heavy, no horror too terrible to depict. From this moment we feel a foreboding that this mighty genius will lay down his pen some years before his life is to end, and we realise that his mind is being gradually withdrawn from the theatre. He has already ceased to act; soon he will have ceased to write for the stage. He longs for rest, for solitude, away from the town, far into the country, away from his life's battlefield to the quietude of his birthplace, there to pass his remaining years and die.

He may have reasoned thus: For whom should he write? Where were they for whom he had written the plays of his youth? They were dead or far away; he had lost sight of them and they of him—how long does any warm sympathy with a productive intellect usually last? With his ever-increasing indifference to fame, he shrank more and more from the exertion entailed by laborious planning and careful execution, and as little did he care whether the work he did was known by his or another man's name. In his utter contempt for what the crowd did or did not believe about him, he allowed piratical booksellers to publish one worthless play after another with his immortal name upon the title-page—*Sir John Oldcastle* in 1600, *The London Prodigal* in 1605, *A Yorkshire Tragedy* in 1608, *Lord Cromwell* in 1613—and he either obscured or permitted others to obscure his work by associating it with the feeble or affected productions of younger and inferior men. We saw in *Timon*, as we shall presently see in *Pericles* and other plays, how the lines drawn by his master-hand have been blurred by others, traced by clumsy and unsteady fingers. It is not always easy to distinguish whether it was Shakespeare who began the play and wearied of his work half-way through, as Michael Angelo so frequently did, carelessly looking on at its completion by another hand, or whether he had the attempts of others lying before him and hid his own poetical strength and greatness in these fungus growths of childish versification and unhealthy prose, leaving it to chance whether the future generations, to whom he never gave much thought, would be able to distinguish his part in them. It may be that he treated his work for the theatre much as a modern author does when he makes over his ideas to a collaborator, or writes anonymously in a newspaper or periodical. He believes that among his friends are three or four who will recognise his style, and if they do not (as frequently happens) it is no great matter.

On the title-page of the first quarto edition of *Pericles*, in 1609, are these words: "The late, and much admired play called Pericles, Prince of Tyre. . . . By William Shakespeare." "The late" —the play cannot have been acted before 1608, for there is no contemporary mention of it before that date, whereas from

1609 onwards it is frequently noticed. "The much admired play"—everything witnesses to the truth of these words.[1]

Many contemporary references testify to the favour the play enjoyed. In an anonymous poem, *Pimlyco, or Runne Redcap* (1609), Pericles is mentioned as the new play which gentle and simple crowd to see:

> " Amazde I stood, to see a Crowd
> Of civill Throats stretched out so lowd
> (As at a New Play). All the Roomes
> Did swarm with Gentiles mix'd with Groomes,
> So that I truly thought all These
> Came to see *Shore* or *Pericles*."

The previously mentioned prologue (p. 539) to Robert Tailor's *The Hog has Lost his Pearl* (1614) cannot wish the play anything better than that it may succeed as well as *Pericles*:

> " And if it prove so happy as to please,
> Weele say 'tis fortunate like *Pericles*."

In 1629, Ben Jonson, exasperated by the utter failure of his play *The New Inn*, affords evidence, in the ode addressed to himself which accompanies the drama, of the persistent popularity of *Pericles*:

> " No doubt some mouldy tale
> Like Pericles, and stale
> As the shrieves crusts and nasty as his fish—
> Scraps out of every dish
> Thrown forth and raked into the common tub,
> May keep up the Play-club."

In Sheppard's poem, *The Times displayed in Six Sestyads*. Shakespeare is said to equal Sophocles and surpass Aristophanes, and all for *Pericles'* sake:

> " With Sophocles we may
> Compare great Shakespeare: Aristophanes
> Never like him his Fancy could display,
> Witness the *Prince of Tyre, his Pericles*."

This play was not included in the First Folio edition, probably because the editors could not come to an agreement with the original publisher; for these pirates were protected by law as soon as the book was entered at Stationers' Hall. During Shakespeare's lifetime and after his death it was one of the most popular of English dramas.

[1] The complete title runs thus :—"The late, and much admired Play, called Pericles, Prince of Tyre, with the true Relation of the whole History, adventures, and fortunes of the said Prince: As also, The no lesse strange and worthy accidents, in the Birth and Life of his Daughter MARIANA. As it hath been diuers and sundry times acted by his Maiesties Seruants, at the Globe on the Bancside. By William Shakespeare. Imprinted at London for Henry Gosson, and are to be sold at the Signe of the Sunne in Paternoster Row. 1609."

Pericles was formerly considered one of Shakespeare's earliest works, an opinion held strangely enough by Karl Elze in our own day. But all English critics now believe, what Hallam was the first to discover, that the language of such parts of it as were written by Shakespeare belongs in style to his latest period, and it is unanimously declared to have been written somewhere about the year 1608, after *Antony and Cleopatra* and before *Cymbeline* and *The Tempest*. (See, for example, P. Z. Round's introduction to the Irving edition, or Furnival's *Triar Table of the order of Shakespeare's Plays*, reprinted in Dowden and elsewhere.) My own opinion of course is, that *Pericles* follows naturally upon *Coriolanus* and *Timon of Athens*, and forms an appropriate overture to the succeeding fantastically idyllic plays. The reader will have noticed that, unlike Dowden and Furnivall, I have not been able to assign so early a date for the whole series of pessimistic dramas as 1608 would imply.[1] I assume that certain portions of *Pericles* were forming in Shakespeare's mind even in the midst of the venom to which he was giving vent for the last time in *Timon of Athens*. In such periods of violent upheaval there may be an undercurrent to the surface-current in the mind of a poet as well as in another man's, and it is this undercurrent which will presently gain strength and become the prevalent mood.

The intelligent reader will have realised that all this dating of Shakespeare's pessimistic works can only be approximate. I am inclined to advance them a year, because I fancy I can trace a connection between *Coriolanus* and Shakespeare's own thoughts of his mother, who died in 1608. But a son does not only think of his mother at the moment she is taken from him, and the fear of losing her in the illness which probably preceded her death may have recalled his mother's image to Shakespeare's mind with special force long before he actually lost her. Here, is in all cases where it is not expressly mentioned, the reader is requested to see an underlying Perhaps or Possibly, and to add one where he feels the need of it. Only the main lines of the sequence are at all certain. Where external criterions are missing, the internal alone cannot determine the question of a year or a month. As far as *Pericles* is concerned, we do possess some guide, for it is most unlikely that Shakespeare's share in the play would be added after it was performed in 1608, especially in the face of the assurance on the title-page.

The work as it has come down to us is not in reality a drama at all, but an incompletely dramatised epic poem. We are taken back to the childhood of dramatic art. The prologue to each act

---

[1] The Triar Table determines their order thus :—

Troilus and Cressida	.	.	.	.	.	1606–7
Antony and Cleopatra	.	.	.	.	.	1606–7
Coriolanus	.	.	.	.	.	1607–8
Timon of Athens	,	.	.	.	.	1607–8

and the various explanatory passages interpolated throughout the play are supposed to be spoken by the old English poet John Gower, who had treated the subject in narrative verse about the year 1390. He introduces the play to the audience and explains it, as it were, with his pointer. Anything that cannot well be acted he narrates, or has represented in dumb-show. He speaks in the old octosyllabic rhymed iambics, which, as a rule, however, do not rhyme:

> " To sing a song that old was *sung*
> From ashes ancient Gower has *come*,
> Assuming man's *infirmities*,
> To glad your ears and please your *eyes.*"

And in the last lines of the prologue to the fourth act:

> " Dionyza doth *appear*,
> With Leonine a *murderer.*"

He jestingly alludes to the fact that the play includes nearly the whole of Pericles' life, from youth to old age. Marina is born at the beginning of the third act, and is about to be married at the close of the fifth. Nothing could well be farther from that unity of time and place which was attempted in France at a later period. The first act is laid at Antioch, Tyre, and Tarsus; the second in Pentapolis, on the sea-shore, in a corridor of Simonides' palace, and lastly in a hall of state. The third act opens on board ship and continues in the house of Cerimon at Ephesus. The fourth act begins with an open place near the sea-shore and ends in a brothel at Mitylene; the fifth, on Pericles' ship off Mitylene, ending in the Temple of Diana at Ephesus. There is as little unity of action as of time and place about the play; its disconnected details are merely held together by the individuality of the principal characters, and there is neither rhyme nor reason in its various incidents; pure chance seems to rule all. The reader will seek in vain for any intention—I do not mean moral, but any fundamental idea in the play. Gower certainly institutes a con trast between an immoral princess at the beginning of the play and a virtuous one at the close, but this moral contrast has no connection with the intermediate acts.

Pericles was an old and very popular subject. Its earliest form was probably that of a Greek romance of the fifth century, of which a Latin translation is still extant. It was translated into various languages during the Middle Ages, and one version has found its way into the *Gesta Romanorum*. In the twelfth century it was incorporated by Godfrey of Viterbo in his great *Chronicle*. John Gower, who adapts it in the eighth book of his *Confessio Amantis*, gives Godfrey as his authority. The Latin tale was translated into English by Lawrence Twine in 1576, under the title of *The Patterne of Paynfull Aduentures*, a second edition of which was published in 1607. In all but the English adaptations the hero's name is given as Apollonius of Tyre. There can be no doubt that Shakespeare's play was based upon the 1607 edition, and this in itself is sufficient to refute the antiquated notion that his part in it belonged to his youthful period. It was on the substance of this play, and doubtless also upon Shakespeare's share in it, that George Wilkins founded the romance he published in 1608 under the title of *The Painfull Adventures of Pericles Prince of Tyre, Being the true history of the Play of Pericles as it was lately presented by the worthy and ancient John Gower.* The fact that Wilkins, in the dedication of his book, which is a mere abstract of Twine and the play, calls it "a poor infant of my braine," and the still more remarkable similarity of the style and metrical structure of the first act of *Pericles* with Wilkins' own play, *The Miseries of enforced Marriage*, would seem to point to him as the author of the extraneous portions of *Pericles.* In both dramas a quantity of disconnected material has been brought together in a long-drawn-out play, destitute of dramatic situations or interest, and in both we find the same jarring and awkward inversions of words. The incidents of the *Enforced Marriage* recall some of the non-Shakespearian elements of *Timon;* here, also, we are shown a spendthrift, evidently in possession of the sympathies of his author, by whom he is considered a victim. The mingling of prose, blank verse, and clumsily-introduced couplets with the same rhymes constantly recurring, reminds us of those acts and scenes in which Shakespeare had no part. Fleay observes that 195 rhymed lines occur in the two first acts of *Pericles*, and only fourteen in the last three, so marked is the contrast of style between the two parts, and he notices that this frequency of rhyme corresponds closely to the method of George Wilkins' own work. Both he and Boyle agree with Delius, who was the first to express the opinion, that Wilkins is the author of the first two acts. By dint of comparisons of style, Fleay came to the conclusion that Gower's two speeches in five-footed iambics, before and after Scenes 5 and 6 (which differ so markedly in form and language from his other monologues), were written by William Rowley, who had been associated in the previous year with Wilkins and Day in the production of a wretched melodrama, *The Travels of Three English Brothers.* His attempt, however, to ascribe to Rowley the two prose scenes which take place in the brothel is made more on moral than æsthetic grounds, and can have very little weight. My own opinion is that they were entirely written by Shakespeare. They are plainly presupposed in certain passages which are unmistakably Shakespearian ; they accord with that general view of life from which he is but now beginning to escape, and they markedly recall the corresponding scenes in *Measure for Measure.*

It is impossible to ascertain the precise circumstances under which the play was produced. Some critics have maintained that it originally began with what is now the third act, and that Shakespeare, having lain it aside, gave Wilkins and Rowley permission to complete it for the stage. But in reality the two men wrote the play in collaboration and disposed of it to Shakespeare's company, which in turn submitted it to the poet, who worked upon such parts as appealed to his imagination. As the play now belonged to the theatre, and Wilkins was not at liberty to publish it, he forestalled the booksellers by bringing it out as a story, taking all the credit of invention and execution upon himself.

Never was a drama contrived out of more unlikely material. The name of the knightly Prince of Tyre is changed, probably because it did not suit the metre, from Apollonius to Pericles, which was corrupted from the Pyrocles of Sidney's *Arcadia*. He comes to Antioch to risk his life on the solution of a riddle. According to his success or failure he is to be rewarded by the Princess's hand or death. The riddle betrays to him the abominable fact that the Princess is living in incest with her own father. He withdraws from the contest, and flies from the country to escape the wrath of the wicked prince, who is even more certain to slay him for success than for failure. He returns to Tyre, but feeling insecure even there, he falls into a state of melancholy, and quits his kingdom to escape the pursuit of Antiochus.

Arriving at Tarsus at a time when its inhabitants are suffering from famine, he succours them with corn from his ships. Soon afterwards he is wrecked off Pentapolis and cast ashore. His armour is dragged out of the sea in fishermen's nets, and Pericles takes part in a knightly tournament. The king's daughter, Thaisa, falls in love with him at first sight, as did Nausicaa with Odysseus. She ignores all the young knights around her for the sake of this noble stranger, who has suffered shipwreck and so many other misfortunes. She will marry him or none; he shines in comparison with the others as a precious stone beside glass. Pericles weds Thaisa, and bears her away with him on his ship. They are overtaken by a storm, during which Thaisa dies in giving birth to a daughter. The superstition of the sailors requires that her corpse shall be immediately thrown into the sea. The coffin drifts ashore at Ephesus, where Thaisa reawakes to life unharmed. The newborn child is left by Pericles to be nursed at Tarsus. As Marina grows up, her foster-mother determines to kill her because she outshines her daughter. Pirates land and prevent the murder; carrying off Marina, they sell her to the mistress of a brothel in Mitylene. She preserves her purity amidst these horrible surroundings, and, finding a protector, gains her release. She is taken on board Pericles' ship that she may charm away his melancholy. A recognition ensues, and, in obedience to a sign from Diana, they sail to Ephesus; the husband is reunited to his wife and the newly-found daughter to her mother.

This is the dramatically impossible canvas which Shakespeare undertook to retouch and finish. That he should have made the first sketch of the play, as Fleay so warmly maintains, seems very improbable upon a careful study of the plot. To write such a beginning to an already finished end would have been an almost impossible task for Wilkins and his collaborator, involving a terribly active vigilance; for the setting of the Shakespearian scenes, Gower's prologues, interludes, and epilogues, &c., is a frame of their own making. Everything favours the theory that it was Shakespeare who undertook to shape a half- or wholly-finished piece of patchwork.

He hardly touched the first two acts, but they contain some traces of his pen—the delicacy with which the incest of the Princess is treated, for example, and Thaisa's timid, almost mute, though suddenly-aroused love for him who at first glance seems to her the chief of men. The scene between the three fishermen, with which the second act opens, owns some turns which speak of Shakespeare, especially where a fisherman says that the avaricious rich are the whales "o' the land, who never leave gaping till they've swallowed the whole parish, church, steeple, bells, and all," and another replies, "But, master, if I had been the sexton, I would have been that day in the belfry."

" *Second Fisherman.* Why, man?

" *Third Fisherman.* Because he should have swallowed me too: and when I had been in his belly, I would have kept such a jangling of the bells, that he should never have left till he cast bells, steeple, church, and parish up again."

It is not impossible, however, that these gleams of Shakespearian wit are mere imitations of his manner. But, on the other hand, the obvious mimicry of the *Midsummer Night's Dream* in Gower's prologue to the third act is commonplace and clumsy enough:

> " Now sleep yslaked hath the rout;
> No din but snores the house about.
>
> .   .   .   .   .
>
> The cat, with eyne of burning coal,
> Now couches fore the mouse's hole;
> And crickets sing at the oven's mouth,
> E'er the blither for their drouth."

Compare this with Puck's:

> " Now the wasted brands do glow,
> Whilst the screech-owl, screeching loud," &c.

An awkwardly introduced pantomime interrupts the prologue, which is tediously renewed; then suddenly, like a voice from another world, a rich, full tone breaks in upon the feeble drivel, and we hear Shakespeare's own voice in unmistakable and royal power:

> " Thou God of this great vast, rebuke these surges,
> Which wash both heaven and hell; and thou, that hast
> Upon the winds command, bind them in brass,
> Having called them from the deep! Oh, still
> Thy deafening, dreadful thunders; gently quench
> Thy nimble, sulphurous flashes!—Oh, how, Lychorida,
> How does my queen?—Thou stormest venomously:
> Wilt thou spit all thyself? The seaman's whistle
> Is as a whisper in the ears of death,
> Unheard." . . .

The nurse brings the tiny new-born babe, saying:

> " Here is a thing too young for such a place,
> Who, if it had conceit, would die, as I
> Am like to do: take in your arms this piece
> Of your dead queen.
> > *Pericles.*   How, how Lychorida!
> > *Lychorida.* Patience, good sir; do not assist the storm
> Here's all that is left living of your queen,
> A little daughter: for the sake of it,
> Be manly and take comfort."

The sailors enter, and, after a brief, masterly conversation, full of the raging storm and the struggle to save the ship, they superstitiously demand that the queen, who has but this instant drawn her last breath, should be thrown overboard. The king is compelled to yield, and turning a last look upon her, says:

> " A terrible childbed hast thou had, my dear;
> No light, no fire: the unfriendly elements
> Forgot thee utterly; nor have I time
> To give thee hallowed to thy grave, but straight
> Must cast thee, scarcely coffined, in the ooze;
> Where, for a monument upon thy bones,
> And e'er-remaining lamps, the belching whale
> And humming water must o'erwhelm thy corse,
> Lying with simple shells."

He gives orders to change the course of the ship and make for Tarsus, because " the babe cannot hold out to Tyrus." There is so mighty a breath of storm and raging seas, such rolling of thunder and flashing of lightning in these scenes, that nothing in English poetry, not excepting Shakespeare's *Tempest* itself, nor Byron's and Shelley's descriptions of Nature, can surpass it.

The storm blows and howls, hisses and screams, till the sound of the boatswain's whistle is lost in the raging of the elements. These scenes are famous and beloved among that seafaring folk for whom they were written, and who know the subject-matter so well.

The effect is tremendously heightened by the struggles of human passion amidst the fury of the elements. The tender and strong grief expressed in Pericles' subdued lament for Thaisa is not drowned by the storm; it sounds a clear, spiritual note of contrast with the raging of the sea. And how touching is Pericles' greeting to his new-born child:

> " Now, mild may be thy life !
> For a more blustrous birth had never babe :
> Quiet and gentle thy conditions, for
> Thou art the rudeliest welcomed to this world
> That ever was prince's child.   Happy what follows !
> Thou hast as chiding a nativity
> As fire, air, water, earth, and heaven can make,
> To herald thee from the womb." . . .

Although Wilkins' tale follows the course of the play very faithfully, there are but two points in which the resemblance between them extends to a similarity of wording. The first of these occurs in the second act, which was Wilkins' own work, and the second here. In his tale Wilkins says:

" Poor inch of nature !   Thou art as rudely welcome to the world as ever princess' babe was, and hast as chiding a nativity as fire, air, earth, and water can afford thee."

Even more striking than the identity of words is the exclamation " Poor inch of nature ! " It is so entirely Shakespearian that we are tempted to believe it must have been accidentally omitted in the manuscripts from which the first edition was printed.

It is not until the birth of Marina in the third act that Shakespeare really takes the play in hand. Why ? Because it is only now that it begins to have any interest for him. It is the development of this character, this tender image of youthful charm and noble purity, which attracts him to the task.

How Shakespearian is the scene in which Marina is found strewing flowers on the grave of her dead nurse just before Dionyza sends her away to be murdered; it foreshadows two scenes in plays which are shortly to follow—the two brothers laying flowers on the supposed corpse of Fidelio in *Cymbeline*, and Perdita, disguised as a shepherdess, distributing all kinds of blossoms to the two strangers and her guests in *The Winter's Tale*.

Marina says (Act iv. sc. 1):

> " No, I will rob Tellus of her weed
> To strew thy green with flowers : the yellows, blues,
> The purple violets, and marigolds,
> Shall as a carpet hang upon thy grave
> While summer-days do last.—Ay me ! poor maid,
> Born in a tempest, when my mother died,
> This world to me is like a lasting storm,
> Whirring me from my friends."

The words are simple, and not especially remarkable in themselves, but they are of the greatest importance as symptoms. They are the first mild tones escaping from an instrument which has long yielded only harsh and jarring sounds. There is nothing like them in the dramas of Shakespeare's despairing mood.

When, weary and sad, he consented to re-write parts of this *Pericles*, it was that he might embody the feeling by which he is now possessed. Pericles is a romantic Ulysses, a far-travelled, sorely tried, much-enduring man, who has, little by little, lost all that was dear to him. When first we meet him, he is threatened with death because he has correctly solved a horrible riddle of life. How symbolic this ! and he is thus made cautious and introspective, restless and depressed. There is a touch of melancholy about him from the first, accompanied by an indifference to danger ; later, when his distrust of men has been aroused, this characteristic despondency becomes intensified, and gives an appearance of depth of thought and feeling. His sensitive nature, brave enough in the midst of storm and shipwreck, sinks deeper and deeper into a depression which becomes almost melancholia. Feeling solitary and forsaken, he allows no one to approach him, pays no heed when he is spoken to, but sits, silent and stern, brooding over his griefs (Act iv. sc. 1). Then Marina comes into his life. When she is first brought on board, she tries to attract his attention by her sweet, modest play and song; then she speaks to him, but is rebuffed, even angrily repulsed, until the gentle narrative of the circumstances of her birth and the misfortunes which have pursued her arrests the king's attention. The restoration of his daughter produces a sudden change from anguished melancholy to subdued happiness.

So, as a poet, had Shakespeare of late withdrawn from the world, and in just such a manner he looked upon men and their sympathy until the appearance of Marina and her sisters in his poetry.

It is probable that Shakespeare wrote the part of Pericles for Burbage, but there is much of himself in it. The two men had more in common than one would be apt to suppose from the only too well-known story of their rivalry on a certain intimate occasion. It is just such trivial anecdotes as this that make their way and are remembered.

Shakespeare has spiritualised Pericles; Marina, in his hands, is a glorified being, who is scarcely grown up before her charm and rare qualities rouse envy and hatred. We first see her strewing flowers on a grave, and immediately after this we listen to her attempt to disarm the man who has undertaken to murder her. She proves herself as innocent as the Queen Dagmar of the ancient ballad. She "never spake bad word nor did ill turn to any living creature." She never killed a mouse or hurt a fly; once she trod upon a worm against her will and wept for it. No human creature could be cast in gentler mould, and truth and nobility unite with this mildness to shed, as it were, a halo round her.

When, after rebuffing and rejecting her, Pericles has gradually softened towards Marina, he asks her where she was born and who provided the rich raiment she is wearing. She replies that if she were to tell the story of her life none would believe her, and she prefers to remain silent. Pericles urges her:

> "Prithee, speak:
> Falseness cannot come from thee; for thou look'st
> Modest as Justice, and thou seem'st a palace
> For the crowned Truth to dwell in; I will believe thee.
>
> .   .   .   .
>
> Tell thy story;
> If thine considered prove the thousandth part
> Of my endurance, thou art a man, and I
> Have suffered like a girl: yet thou dost look
> Like Patience gazing on kings' graves, and smiling
> Extremity out of act."

All this rich imagery brings Marina before us with the nobility of character which is so fitly expressed in her outward seeming. It is Pericles himself who feels like a buried prince, and it is he who has need of her patient sympathy, that the violence of his grief may be softened by her smile. It is all very dramatically effective. The old Greek tragedies frequently relied on these scenes of recovery and recognition, and they never failed to produce their effect. The dialogue here is softly subdued, it is no painting in strong burning colours that we are shown, but a delicately blended pastel. In order to gain an insight into Shakespeare's humour at the time *As You Like It* and *Twelfth Night* were written, the reader was asked to think of a day on which he felt especially well and strong and sensible that all his bodily organs were in a healthy condition,—one of those days in which there is a festive feeling in the sunshine, a gentle caress in the air.

To enter into his mood in a similar manner now you would

need to recall some day of convalescence, when health is just returning after a long and severe illness. You are still so weak that you shrink from any exertion, and, though no longer ill, you are as yet far from being well; your walk is unsteady, and the grasp of your hand is weak. But the senses are keener than usual, and in little much is seen; one gleam of sunshine in the room has more power to cheer and enliven than a whole landscape bathed in sunshine at another time. The twitter of a bird in the garden, just a few chirps, has more meaning than a whole chorus of nightingales by moonlight at other moments. A single pink in a glass gives as much pleasure as a whole conservatory of exotic plants. You are grateful for a trifle, touched by friendliness, and easily moved to admiration. He who has but just returned to life has an appreciative spirit.

As Shakespeare, with the greater susceptibility of genius, was more keenly alive to the joyousness of youth, so more intensely than others he felt the quiet, half-sad pleasures of convalescence.

' Wishing to accentuate the sublime innocence of Marina's nature, he submits it to the grimmest test, and gives it the blackest foil one could well imagine. The gently nurtured girl is sold by pirates to a brothel, and the delineation of the inmates of the house, and Marina's bearing towards them and their customers, occupies the greater part of the fourth act.

As we have already said, we can see no reason why Fleay should reject these scenes as non-Shakespearian. When this critic (whose reputation has suffered by his arbitrariness and inconsistency) does not venture to ascribe them to Wilkins, and yet will not admit them to be Shakespeare's, he is in reality pandering to the narrow-mindedness of the clergyman, who insists that any art which is to be recognised shall only be allowed to overstep the bounds of propriety in a humorously jocose manner. These scenes, so bluntly true to nature in the vile picture they set before us, are limned in just that Caravaggio colouring which distinguished Shakespeare's work during the period which is now about to close. Marina's utterances, the best he has put into her mouth, are animated by a sublimity which recalls Jesus' answers to his persecutors. Finally, the whole *personnel* is exactly that of *Measure for Measure*, whose genuineness no one has ever disputed. There is also an occasional resemblance of situation. Isabella, in her robes of spotless purity, offers precisely the same contrast to the world of pimps and panders who riot through the play that Marina does here to the woman of the brothel and her servants.

After all that he had suffered, it was hardly possible Shakespeare would relapse into the romantic, mediæval worship of woman as woman. But his natural rectitude of spirit soon led him to make exceptions from the general condemnation which he was inclined for a time to pass upon the sex; and now that his soul's health was returning to him, he felt drawn, after having

dwelt solely upon women of the merely sensual type, to place a
halo round the head of the young girl, and so he brings her
with unspotted innocence out of the most terrible situations.

When she sees that she is locked into the house, she says:

> " Alack that Leonine was so slack, so slow !
> He should have struck, not spoke ; or that these pirates,
> Not enough barbarous, had but o'erboard thrown me
> For to seek my mother !
> *Bawd.* Why lament you, pretty one ?
> *Marina.* That I am pretty.
> *Bawd.* Come, the gods have done their part in you.
> *Marina.* I accuse them not.
> *Bawd.* You are 'light into my hands, where you are like to
> live.
> *Marina.* The more my fault
> To 'scape his hands where I was like to die.
> . . . Are you a woman ?
> *Bawd.* What would you have me be, an I be not a woman ?   •
> *Marina.* An honest woman, or not a woman."

The governor Lysimachus seeks the house, and is left alone
with Marina.   He begins :

> " Now, pretty one, how long have you been at this trade ?
> *Marina.* What trade, sir ?
> *Lysimachus.* Why, I cannot name't but I shall offend.
> *Marina.* I cannot be offended with my trade.   Please you to
> name it.
> *Lysimachus.* How long have you been of this profession ?
> *Marina.* E'er since I can remember.
> *Lysimachus.* Did you go to't so young?   Were you a gamester at
> five or at seven ?
> *Marina.* Earlier too, sir, if now I be one.
> *Lysimachus.* Why, the house you dwell in proclaims you to be a
> creature of sale.
> *Marina.* Do you know this house to be a place of such resort, and
> will come into't?   I hear say you are of honourable parts, and are the
> governor of this place.
> *Lysimachus.* Why, hath your principal made known unto you who
> I am ?
> *Marina.* Who is my principal ?
> *Lysimachus.* Why, your herb-woman ; she that sets seeds and roots
> of shame and iniquity.   Oh, you have heard something of my power,
> and so stand aloof for more serious wooing. . . . Come, bring me to
> some private place : come, come.
> *Marina.* If you were born to honour, show it now ;
> If put upon you, make the judgment good
> That thought you worthy of it."

Lysimachus is arrested by her words and his purpose changed.
He gives her gold, bids her persevere in the ways of purity, and

prays the gods will strengthen her. She succeeds in obtaining her freedom and in supporting herself by her talents. The lasting impression she had made on the governor in her degradation is proved by his sending for her to charm King Pericles' melancholy, and later he aspires to her hand.

The scenes quoted do not give an intellectual equivalent for all that has been dared in order to produce them, but they bear witness to the desire Shakespeare felt of painting youthful womanly purity shining whitely in a very snake-pit of vice, and the spirit in which it is accomplished is that of both Shakespeare and the Renaissance.

At a somewhat earlier period such a subject would have assumed, in England, the form of a *Morality*, an allegorical religious play, in which the steadfastness of the virtuous woman would have triumphed over *Vice*. At a somewhat later period, in France, it would have been a Christian drama, in which heathen wickedness and incredulity were put to confusion by the youthful believer. Shakespeare carries it back to the days of Diana; his virtue and vice are alike heathen, owning no connection with church or creed.

Thirty-seven years later, during the minority of Louis XIV., Pierre Corneille made use of a very similar subject in his but little-known tragedy, *Théodore, Vierge et Martyre*. The scene is laid in the same place in which *Pericles* begins, in Antioch during the reign of Diocletian.

Marcella, the wicked wife of the governor of the province, determines that her daughter Flavia shall marry the object of her passion, Placidus. He, however, has no thought but for the Princess Theodora, a descendant of the old Syrian kings. Theodora is a Christian, and these are the times of Christian persecution. In order to revenge herself upon the young girl and estrange Placidus from her, Marcella causes her to be confined in just such another house as that into which Marina was sold.

The dramatic interest would naturally lie in the development of Theodora's feelings when she finds herself abandoned to her fate. But the chaste young girl will not, and cannot, express in words the horror she must feel; and in any case the laws of propriety would not allow her to do so on the French stage. Corneille avoided the difficulty by exchanging action for narrative. Various false or incomplete accounts of what has taken place keep the audience in anxious expectation.

Placidus is told that Theodora's sentence has been commuted to one of simple banishment. He breathes again. Then he hears that Theodora has actually been taken to the house; that Didymus, her Christian admirer, bribed the soldiers to allow him to enter first, and that shortly afterwards he returned, covering his face with his cloak as though ashamed.

He is furious. The third announcement informs him that it was Theodora who came out disguised in Didymus's clothes. Placidus' rage now gives way to agonising jealousy. He believes that Theodora has yielded willingly to Didymus, and he suffers tortures. Finally we learn the truth. Didymus himself tells how he rescued Theodora unharmed; he is a Christian, and expects to die. "Live thou without jealousy," he says to Placidus; "I can endure the death penalty." "Alas!" answers Placidus, "how can I be other than jealous, knowing that this glorious creature owes more than life to thee. Thou hast given thy life to save her honour; how can I but envy thy happiness!" Both Theodora and Didymus are martyred, and the pagan lover, who did nothing to help his love, is left alone with his shame.

The sole contrast intended here is between the noble qualities developed by the Christian faith and that baseness which was considered inseparable from heathendom.

Two things arrest our attention in this comparison: firstly, the superiority of the English drama, which openly represents all things on the stage, even such subjects as are only passingly alluded to by society; and, secondly, the marked difference in the spirit of that Old England of the Renaissance from the all-pervading Christianism of the early classic period in "most Christian" France.

The calm dignity of Marina's innocence has none of that taint of the confessional which was plainly obnoxious to Shakespeare, and which neither the mediæval plays before him, nor Corneille and Calderon after, could escape. Corneille's Theodora is a saint by profession and a martyr from choice. She gives herself up to her enemies at the end of the play, because she has been assured by supernatural revelation that she will not again be imprisoned in the house from which she has just escaped. Shakespeare's Marina, the tenderly and carefully outlined sketch of the type which is presently to wholly possess his imagination, is purely human in her innate nobility of nature.

It is deeply interesting to trace in this sombre yet fantastically romantic play of *Pericles* the germs of all his succeeding works.

Marina and her mother, long lost and late recovered by a sorrowing king, are the preliminary studies for Perdita and Hermione in *A Winter's Tale*. Perdita, as her name tells us, is lost and is living, ignorant of her parentage, in a strange country. Marina's flower-strewing suggests Perdita's distribution of blossoms, accompanied by words which reveal a profound understanding of flower-nature, and Hermione is recovered by Leontes as is Thaisa by Pericles.

The wicked stepmother in *Cymbeline* corresponds to the wicked foster-mother in *Pericles*. She hates Imogen as Dionyza hates Marina. Pisanio is supposed to have murdered her as Leonine is believed to have slain Marina, and Cymbeline recovers both sons and daughter as Pericles his wife and child.

The tendency to substitute some easy process of explanation, such as melodramatic music or supernatural revelation, in the place of severe dramatic technique, which appears at this time, betrays a certain weariness of the demands of the art. Diana appears to the slumbering Pericles as Jupiter does to Posthumus in *Cymbeline*.

But it is for *The Tempest* that *Pericles* more especially prepares us. The attitude of the melancholy prince towards his daughter seems to foreshadow that of the noble Prospero towards his child Miranda. Prospero is also living in exile from his home. But it is Cerimon who approaches more nearly in character to Prospero. Note his great speech:

> "I held it ever,
> Virtue and cunning were endowments greater
> Than nobleness and riches: careless heirs
> May the two latter darken and expend;
> But immortality attends the former,
> Making a man a god. 'Tis known I ever
> Have studied physic, through which secret art,
> By turning o'er authorities, I have,
> Together with my practice, made familiar
> To me and to my aid the blest infusions
> That dwell in vegetives, in metals, stones;
> And I can speak of the disturbances
> That Nature works, and of her cures; which doth give me
> A more content in course of true delight
> Than to be thirsty after tottering honour
> Or tie my treasure up in silken bags,
> To please the fool and death" (Act iii. sc. 2).

The position in which Thaisa and Pericles stand in the second act towards the angry father, who has in reality no serious objection to their union, closely resembles that of Ferdinand and Miranda before the feigned wrath of Prospero. Most notable of all is the preliminary sketch we find in *Pericles* of the tempest which ushers in the play of that name. Over and above the resemblance between the storm scenes, we have Marina's description of the hurricane during which she was born (*Pericles*, Act iv. sc. 1), and Ariel's description of the shipwreck (*Tempest*, Act i. sc. 2).

Many other slight touches prove a relationship between the two plays. In *The Tempest* (Act ii. sc. 1), as in *Pericles* (Act v. sc. 1), we have soothing slumbrous music and mention of harpies (*Tempest*, Act iii. sc. 3, and *Pericles*, Act iv. sc. 3). The words "virgin knot," so charmingly used by Marina:

> "If fires be hot, knives sharp, or waters deep,
> Untied I still my virgin knot will keep" (Act iv. sc. 2),

are also employed by Prospero in reference to Miranda in *The Tempest* (Act iv. sc. 1); and it will be observed that these are the only two instances in which they occur in Shakespeare.

Thus the germs of all his latest works lie in this unjustly neglected and despised play, which has suffered under a double disadvantage: it is not entirely Shakespeare's work, and in such portions of it as are his own there exist, in the dark shadow cast by her hideous surroundings about Marina, traces of that gloomy mood from which he was but just emerging. But for all that, whether we look upon it as a contribution to Shakespeare's biography or as a poem, this beautiful and remarkable fragment, *Pericles*, is a work of the greatest interest.[1]

---

[1] Delius: *Ueber Shakespeare's Pericles, Prince of Tyre. Jahrbuch der deutschen Shakespeare-Gesellschaft*, iii. 175-205; F. G. Fleay: *On the Play of Pericles. The New Shakspere Society's Transactions*, 1874, 195-254; Swinburne: *A Study of Shakespeare*, p. 206; Gervinus: *Shakespeare*, vol. i. 187, and Elze: *Shakespeare*, p. 409, still believe *Pericles* to be a work of Shakespeare's youth.

XVI

FRANCIS BEAUMONT AND JOHN FLETCHER

IT was a comparatively easy task to distinguish Shakespeare's part in *Timon of Athens* and *Pericles*, for it consisted of all that was important in either play. The identity of the men who collaborated with him seems to have been decided by pure chance, and is of little interest to us now-a-days. It is a different matter, however, in the case of two other dramas of this period which have been associated with Shakespeare's name—*The Two Noble Kinsmen* and *Henry VIII.*—for his part in them is unimportant, in one almost imperceptible, in fact. Their real author was a young man just coming into notice, who afterwards became one of the most famous dramatists of the day, and can hardly have been indifferent to Shakespeare. The question, therefore, of their mutual relations and the origin of their collaboration is one of the greatest interest.

A drama entitled *Philaster* had been played at the Globe Theatre in 1608 with extraordinary success. It was the joint work of two young men, Francis Beaumont, aged 22, and John Fletcher, aged 28. The play made their reputation, and they found themselves famous from the moment of its representation. A would-be amusing, but in reality rather dull play of Fletcher's, *The Woman-Hater*, had been put on the stage in 1606-7. It contained some good comic parts, but nothing that gave promise of the poet's later works.

After this triumph with *Philaster*, the two friends produced in 1610 or 1611 their masterpiece, *The Maid's Tragedy*, and their scarcely less admired *A King and no King*. This joint activity continued until the death of Beaumont in 1615. During the remaining ten years of his life Fletcher wrote alone, with the single exception of a play produced in collaboration with Rowley, and attained to a fame which probably eclipsed Shakespeare's in these last years of his life, as it certainly did immediately after his death. Dryden remarks, in his well-known *Essay of Dramatic Poetry* (1668), "Their plays are now the most pleasant and frequent entertainments of the stage, two of them being acted through the year for one of Shakespeare's or Jonson's." This statement seems somewhat exaggerated if we compare it with the entries in Pepys' Diary; still, we know that Shakespeare's fame was completely

2 P

eclipsed towards the end of the century by that of Ben Jonson. Samuel Butler not only prefers the latter, but speaks as though his superiority was universally admitted.[1]

The two new poets were neither learned proletaires, like Peele, Greene, and Marlowe, nor of the middle classes, like Shakespeare and Ben Jonson, but were both of good family. Fletcher's father was a high-placed ecclesiastic, much experienced in the courts of Elizabeth and James, and Beaumont was the son of a Justice of Common Pleas, and related to families of some standing. One great source of their popularity lay in the fact that they were thus enabled to reproduce to perfection the manners of the fine gentleman, his general dissipation, and his quick repartee.

Francis Beaumont was born somewhere about the year 1586, at Grace Dieu in Leicestershire. His family numbered among those of the legal aristocracy, and many of its members were noted for poetical propensities and abilities; there were no fewer than three poets by name of Beaumont living at the time of Francis' death. The future dramatist was entered at ten years of age as a gentleman-commoner at Broadgate Hall, Oxford. He early left the university for London, where he was made a member of the Inner Temple. His legal studies appear to have sat lightly upon him, and he seems to have devoted himself principally to the composition of those plays and masques which were so frequently performed by the various legal colleges of those days. In 1613 he wrote the masque which was performed by the legal institutions of the Inner Temple and Gray's Inn in honour of the Princess Elizabeth's marriage with the Elector-Palatine.

It seems to have been a mutual enthusiasm for Jonson's *Volpone* (1605) which brought Beaumont and Fletcher together, and united them in a brotherly friendship and fellowship in work of which history affords few parallels. Aubrey, to whom we are indebted for a number of anecdotes about Shakespeare, gives the following vivid picture of their life: "They lived together on the Bankside, not far from the playhouse; both batchelors lay together, had one wench in the house between them, which they did so admire; the same cloathes and cloake, etc., between them."

The two friends soon set to work, and appear to have planned out the dramas together, each finally working out the scenes most suited to his talents. An anecdote related by Winstanley seems to indicate such a method. One day while they were thus apportioning their parts in a tavern they frequented, a man standing at the door overheard the exclamation, "I will undertake to kill the king;" suspecting some treasonable conspiracy, he gave information, with the result that both poets were arrested. In support of the veracity of this anecdote, George Darley observes that a similar incident occurs in Fletcher's *Woman-Hater* (Act v. sc. 2). Great bitterness is certainly expressed in this play on the

[1] See Richard Garnett : *The Age of Dryden*, p. 249.

subject of informers ; witness the very unflattering sketch of their ways and manners in the third scene of the second act.

In whatsoever fashion *The Two Noble Kinsmen* may have originally been written, the joint-authors must have finally revised it in company and obliterated to the best of their ability the distinguishing marks of their very different styles. Otherwise it would not offer, now that we are in possession of works executed by each separately, the present difficulty of apportioning to each the honour due to him.

There was no lack of difference, especially of a metrical nature, about their styles. As far as we can judge, Beaumont's was the gift for tragedy ; he had less wit and less skill than Fletcher, but he was more genuinely inspired, richer in feeling, and more daring in invention than his brother poet. His noble head is encircled by a halo of sadness, for, like Marlowe and Shelley, two of England's greatest poets, he died before he had completed his thirtieth year.

Beaumont was a devoted admirer of Ben Jonson, and a constant frequenter of that "Mermaid Tavern" whose literary and social gatherings have been celebrated in his poetical epistle to the object of his admiration. His passionate regard for the author of *Volpone* is shown in a poem addressed to him upon the subject, in which he exalts Jonson's art and the charm of his comedy above all that any other poet (thereby including Shakespeare) had ever produced for the English stage. Jonson replies with his ode "To Mr. Francis Beaumont," in which he reciprocates the admiring attention by a declaration of the warmest affection, and expresses himself "not worth the least indulgent thought thy pen drops forth," assuring his friend that he envies him his greater talent. According to Dryden, Jonson submitted everything he wrote to Beaumont's criticism as long as the young man was alive, and even gave him his manuscripts to correct.

While Beaumont's name is thus associated with Jonson, Fletcher's forms a constellation in conjunction with that of Shakespeare.

John Fletcher was born in December 1579, at Rye in Sussex, and was therefore fifteen years younger than the great poet with whom he is said to have collaborated more than once. His father, the Dean of Peterborough, was successively promoted through the bishoprics of Bristol and Worcester to that of London. He was a handsome, eloquent man, with a luxurious temperament, inclined to display and pleasure of all kinds. Every inch a courtier, all his thoughts were concentrated upon gaining, retaining, or recovering the royal favour.

One episode of his life of an impressively dramatic and historic interest, calculated to make the strongest impression on the imagination of an embryo tragic poet, must have been often related by him to his young son. Dr. Richard Fletcher was the divine appointed by Government to attend on Mary Stuart at the time of her execution, and was therefore both spectator and participator in the closing scene of the Scottish Cleopatra's life.·

When he approached the Queen in the great hall hung with black, and invited her, as he was in duty bound to do, to unite with him in prayer, she turned her back upon him.

"Madam," he began with a low obeisance, "the Queen's most excellent majesty. Madam, the Queen's most excellent majesty." Thrice he commenced his sentence, wanting words to pursue it. When he repeated the words a fourth time she cut him short.

"Mr. Dean," she said, "I am a Catholic, and must die a Catholic. It is useless to attempt to move me, and your prayers will avail me little."

"Change your opinion, madam," he cried, his tongue being loosed at last. "Repent of your sins, settle your faith in Christ, by Him to be saved."

"Trouble not yourself further, Mr. Dean," she answered. "I am settled in my own faith, for which I mean to shed my blood."

"I am sorry, madam," said Shrewsbury, "to see you so addicted to Popery!"[1]

Slowly and carefully her ladies removed her veil so as not to disturb the arrangement of her hair. They took off her long black robe, and she stood then in a skirt of scarlet velvet; they removed the black bodice, and revealed one of scarlet silk. Sobbing, they drew on her scarlet sleeves and placed scarlet slippers upon her feet. It was like a transformation scene in a theatre when the proud woman stood suddenly dressed in scarlet in the black funeral hall. When her women wept and wailed she said to them, "*Ne criez pas vous, j'ai promis pour vous. Adieu, au revoir*, and praying in a loud voice, *In te Domine confido*, she laid her head upon the block. It was impossible that Richard Fletcher should ever forget the inflexible resolution and indomitable courage displayed by the great actress, nor was he likely to forget the terrible mingling of horror with pure burlesque in the final scene. In his agitation, the executioner missed his aim, and a weak blow fell upon the handkerchief with which the Queen's eyes were bound, inflicting a slight wound upon her cheek. The second blow left the severed head hanging by a piece of skin, which the executioner cut as he drew back the axe. Then Dr. Fletcher witnessed a second transformation, as marvellous as any ever produced by a magician's wand: the great mass of thick false hair fell from the head. The Queen who had knelt before the block possessed all the ripened charm and dignified beauty of maturity; the head held up by the executioner to the gaze of the little company was that of a grey,

---

[1] Froude: *History of England*, vol. xii. p. 254.

wrinkled, old woman.[1] Could anything in the world have given young Fletcher a keener insight into the horrors of tragic catastrophe, the solemnity of death, and the blending of the terrible with the utterly grotesque which life's most supreme moments occasionally produce? It must have acted like a call and incitement to the creation of tragic and burlesque theatrical effect.

John Fletcher was educated at Cambridge, and probably came to London shortly before Beaumont, to try his fortune as a dramatic writer. His first success was with *Philaster, or Love lies Bleeding*, in 1608. Shakespeare must have witnessed its triumphant performance with strangely mingled feelings, for it could but strike him as being in many ways an echo of his own work. In so far as he is wrongfully deprived of his throne, Prince Philaster occupies much the same position as Hamlet, and several of his speeches to the king are markedly in the style of the Danish Prince of Shakespeare's play. Thus, in the opening scene of the first act:

> "*King.* Sure he's possess'd.
> *Philaster.* Yes, with my father's spirit: It's true, O king
> A dangerous spirit. Now he tells me, king,
> I was a king's heir, bids me be a king;
> And whispers to me, these are all my subjects.
> 'Tis strange he will not let me sleep, but dives
> Into my fancy, and there gives me shapes that kneel
> And do me service, cry me 'King.'
> But I'll oppose him, he's a factious spirit,
> And will undo me. Noble sir, your hand,
> I am your servant.
> *King.* Away, I do not like this," &c.

The king, however, has nothing to fear from Philaster, for the prince loves and is beloved by the monarch's daughter, Arethusa, whom her father intends to wed to that arrogant braggart, Prince Pharamond of Spain. Philaster, all unknown to himself, is beloved by Euphrasia, the daughter of the courtier Cleon. Disguised as a page she enters the prince's service under the name of Bellario, and displays a devotion which no trial can shake, not even that of carrying love-letters between Philaster and Arethusa, nor of being transferred to the service of the latter that she may be at hand in case of need. Euphrasia's situation and feelings resemble those of Viola in *Twelfth Night*, but the comedy of Shakespeare's play here becomes serious and romantic tragedy. *Philaster* must have reminded Shakespeare yet more forcibly of another of his plays, and one to which the second half of the title, *i.e.*, *Love lies Bleeding*, would have been applicable, for in the course of the piece Philaster and Arethusa are brought into a situation which is a counterpart of that of Othello and Desdemona.

---

[1] J. St. Loe Strachey: *Beaumont and Fletcher*, vol. i. p. **xv.**

It happens in the following manner. The princess treats Pharamond with as much coldness as she dares, allowing her betrothed none of the privileges which he may claim after marriage. Pharamond, who naïvely confides to the audience that his temperament will not stand such treatment, is sympathised with by an exceedingly accommodating court lady. Her name is Megra; she is one of those wanton fair ones whom Fletcher excelled in portraying, and is closely akin to the Chloe of his charming play *The Faithful Shepherd*. The time and place of this assignation being betrayed, the king, enraged at the insult offered to his daughter, breaks in upon them and overwhelms Megra with cruel and coarse abuse. She, on her part, threatens that if her name is publicly disgraced, she will reveal all she knows of a much too tender friendship between the princess and a handsome page lately taken into her service.

The king, finding that Bellario is actually attendant upon Arethusa, believes the slander and insists upon his instant dismissal. The courtiers, who, in common with the people, love Philaster and look to him to dethrone the king and rule in his stead, have watched this obstacle of his passion for the princess with no great favour. They hasten to report the rumour to him. Dion, Euphrasia-Bellario's own father, mendaciously asserts that he has surprised the lovers together. No use is made of this incident, nor of any of the opportunities offered by Euphrasia's disguise, which remains a secret even from the audience until the last scene of the play. Philaster in a jealous frenzy draws his sword upon Bellario and drives him away. The page instinctively guesses that Philaster is caught in the meshes of some intrigue, but does not divine its nature. Her parting words might have been addressed by Desdemona to Othello :

> "But through these tears,
> Shed at my hopeless parting, I can see
> A world of treason practised upon you,
> And her, and me."

Just as Desdemona, suspecting nothing, warmly pleads Cassio's cause with Othello, so Arethusa laments to Philaster that she has been forced to dismiss his cherished messenger of love :

> " O cruel!
> Are you hard-hearted too? Who shall now tell you
> How much I loved you? Who shall swear it to you,
> And weep the tears I send? Who shall now bring you
> Letters, rings, bracelets? lose his health in service?
> Wake tedious nights in stories of your praise?" (Act iii. sc. 2).

Philaster suffers the same agonies as the Moor of Venice, but being of a naturally gentle disposition, he only answers her in terms hardly to be surpassed for mournful and pathetic beauty. Later, coming upon the princess and her page, who have met by chance in a wood, he is so carried away by jealousy that he draws his sword first upon Arethusa and then upon Bellario. The page takes the blow without a murmur, and goes willingly to prison in place of Philaster for the attempt upon the princess's life. The devotion of Desdemona is thus reproduced in both these maidens, and finds in both a striking expression. All comes right eventually. A revolution places Philaster upon the throne, the women who love him recover from their wounds, and the discovery of Bellario's sex puts an end to all scandal. Philaster marries his beloved, and she, even more magnanimous than the queen in De Musset's *Carmosine*, closes the play with an invitation to Bellario-Euphrasia to share their life:

> " Come, live with me ;
> Live free as I do. She that loves my lord,
> Cursed be the wife that hates her."

In spite of its many echoes from his own plays, Shakespeare cannot have failed to appreciate the talent displayed in this drama. The gentleness and charm of the women in the works of both young poets must have appealed to him, offering as they did so marked a contrast to those of Chapman and Marlowe, neither of whom had any appreciation of womanliness or power to depict it. The best of Chapman's tragedies can have contained little that would attract Shakespeare. *The Conspiracy and Tragedy of Charles Duke of Byron, Marshall of France*, was rather a ten-act epic than a drama. His comedies, too, even *Eastward Hoe*, with its wonderful picture of the London of the day to which Ben Jonson and Marston contributed their share, must have repelled him by a realism which he always avoided in his own work. Beaumont and Fletcher laid their scenes in Sicily or rather in some imaginary country, whose abstract poetry, more in accordance with the Romance nation's manner of representing men and their passions, cannot have been unsympathetic to Shakespeare, especially at this period of his life.

A King and no King, the play which in all probability immediately succeeded *Philaster*, contains the same merits and defects as the latter, and here also Shakespeare might find reminiscences of his own work. When the king's mother kneels before her son, and is raised by him (Act iii. sc. 1), we are reminded of Volumnia kneeling to Coriolanus, and we feel that the same scene was in the mind of the two young poets. The comic character of the play is one Bessus, a soldier by profession, and an arrant coward in spite of his captaincy. He is a braggart, liar, and, if occasion offers, a pander, being equally diverting in all these capacities. Considerable humour is displayed in the elaboration of his character, but the mighty figure of Falstaff is plainly discernible in the background. The authors even go to the length of appropriating some distinctly Falstaffian expressions. A fencing-master says of Bessus (Act iv. sc. 3) :

"It showed discretion, the better part of valour." [1]

In *Philaster* we were shown a strong passion consumed by groundless jealousy. In *A King and no King* we have a still stronger passion, that of the young Arbaces for Princess Panthea, leading to confusion and disaster. Throughout the whole play Arbaces never doubts for a moment that they are brother and sister. The secret of his birth is not discovered until the last scene, just as Bellario's sex is not made known until the end of *Philaster*. Spaconia discovers that King Tigranes, who is as her very life to her, is in love with Panthea ; whereupon she assumes much the same position towards him that Euphrasia did towards her love. But there is profounder study of character in the new play. Arbaces, a mixture of vanity and boastfulness with really excellent qualities, makes an extremely complex personality, though not an unnatural or unsympathetic one, and we are given a study of complicated passion in no way inferior to that in Racine's *Phèdre*, the instinct of love violently and irresistibly aroused, but constantly met by the fear and horror of incest. The subject is treated with great pathos and power of language. [2]

---

[1] It is Falstaff who says in the *First Part of Henry IV.* (Act v. sc. 4), "The better part of valour is discretion." This parallel has been overlooked both in Ingleby's *Shakespeare's Century of Praise* and in Furnivall's *Fresh Allusions to Shakespeare.*

[2]   "Know I have lost
The only difference betwixt man and beast,
My reason.

                    PANTHEA.

Heaven forbid !

                    ARBACES.

Nay, it is gone,
And I am left as far without a bound
As the wide ocean that obeys the winds ;
Each sudden passion throws me where it lists,
And overwhelms all that oppose my will.
I have beheld thee with a lustful eye ;
My heart is set on wickedness, to act
Such sins with thee as I have been afraid
To think of. . . . .
I have lived
To conquer men, and now am overthrown
Only by words, brother and sister. Where
Have those words dwelling ? I will find 'em out
And utterly destroy 'em ; but they are
Not to be grasped. . . . .
Accursed man !
Thou bought'st thy reason at too dear a rate ;

In 1609–10 Fletcher reached the zenith of his fame as sole author and as collaborator with Beaumont. That sweet and fresh pastoral play *The Faithful Shepherdess*, Fletcher's unassisted work, must have been written before the spring of 1610, for Sir William Skipworth, to whom, amongst others, it is dedicated, died in the May of that year. The theme was peculiarly suited to the fresh and delicate grace of Fletcher's lyrical gift, and here again Shakespeare may have perceived a distinct imitation of his *Midsummer Night's Dream*. Here also the lovers are metamorphosed, and Perigot embraces Amaryllis in the form of Amoret, believing her to be his love; he also wounds Amoret as Philaster wounds Arethusa. A still earlier version of the play may be found in Spenser's *Shepherd's Calendar*. Darley has observed that Fletcher imitated several lines from the same source, and among them, oddly enough, some which had been appropriated by Spenser from Chaucer, whose verses greatly surpass either of the later poets in charm. In *The Faithful Shepherdess*, for example, we have (v. 5):

> " Sort all your shepherds from the lazy clowns
> That feed their heifers in the budded brooms."

In Spenser's *Shepherd's Calendar* it stands:

> " So loytering live you, little herd grooms,
> Keeping your beasts in the budded brooms."

But in Chaucer's *House of Fame* we find the following verse (iii. 133):

> " And many a floite and litlyng home
> And pipis made of grenè corne
> As have these litel herdè-groomes
> That kepen bestis in the bromes."

Fletcher's principal source, however, was, as the title tells us, Guarini's *Pastor Fido*.

The Faithful Shepherdess is a charming idyl, too airy and delicate to have an immediate success with his own generation, but it may be read with pleasure to this day, and has secured lasting fame to its author. Ben Jonson's later but also admirable pastoral play, *The Sad Shepherd*, is the English poem of that period which most resembles it.

Immediately after the production of this little tragi-comedy Fletcher offered to the Globe Theatre the most remarkable work

> For thou hast all thy actions bounded in
> With curious rules, where every beast is free ;
> What is there that acknowledges a kindred
> But wretched man ?   Who ever saw the bull
> Fearfully leave the heifer that he liked
> Because they had one dam ?"

which had resulted from the combined labours of himself and Francis Beaumont—*The Maid's Tragedy.*

The first act opens with the preparations for a wedding festivity. The king has commanded the worthy and distinguished Lord Amintor to break off his engagement to the gentle and devoted Aspasia and to marry Evadne, the beautiful sister of his dearest friend and comrade, the great general Melantius. Amintor, to whom the king's command is sacred, and who is, moreover, strongly attracted by Evadne, breaks with Aspasia, dear as she is to him. We witness Aspasia's deep grief, the outburst of rage on the part of her father (the cowardly Calianax), and the performance of the masque on the eve of the wedding, in which some of the poets' sweetest lyrics are to be found.

The second act represents the wedding-night. The disrobing of the bride by her friends, and all the fun and banter attendant on the occasion, form the introduction. Then follows, between bridegroom and bride, the first great scene of the play, as boldly dramatic as any written by Shakespeare before or Webster after this date. Amintor approaches Evadne with tender words, she gently repulses him. He strives to disarm what he supposes to be her bashfulness, but she tells him calmly and coldly that she will never be his. Still he does not understand, and now urges her with impatient desire. Then she rises, like a serpent about to sting, and coldly hisses that she is, and will continue to be, the king's mistress, that the marriage has merely been arranged by him as a screen for his relations with her. The fury and thirst for revenge which seizes Amintor when he realises this outrage gives way to a desperate comprehension that it is the king who has dishonoured him; to a subject the person of the king is inviolable.

The third act opens with an audacious visit from the king on the following morning. With cool patronage he asks Amintor if the night has given him satisfaction. Amintor replies composedly, and answers the king's more particular inquiries quite in the style of the happy husband. It is now the king's turn to be disconcerted. He sends for Evadne and violently accuses her of treachery, against which she, of course, passionately protests. The king, beside himself with rage, sends for Amintor; he is furiously attacked by Evadne for his falsehoods, and the king brutally explains the situation and the part the husband is expected to play. This double scene is written in a masterly fashion, with a strong sense of dramatic effect, but the rest of the act is worthless, being chiefly composed of dialogues between Amintor and Melantius, who learns the truth about his sister from his friend. The two are perpetually drawing upon each other and sheathing their swords again; firstly, because Melantius will not believe in his sister's shame; secondly, because Amintor will not allow Melantius to seek any revenge which will reveal his dishonour.

It all reads like a weak imitation of the Spanish dramatists before Calderon.

The fourth act presents another series of effective scenes. The brother accuses the sister of her infamy, and when she coldly denies everything he threatens her with his sword, until she vows that she will take bloody vengeance on the cruel and vicious king who has brought about her degradation. Then the suddenly converted Evadne falls upon her knees and implores her husband's forgiveness, which he, seeing how bitterly she repents the life she has been living, accords. This is followed by a particularly well-imagined scene, in which the ridiculous old Calianax, who hates Melantius, denounces him to the king for his attempt to persuade him, Calianax, to give up the city he held for the monarch. In spite of its truth, Melantius listens to the accusation quite imperturbably, and succeeds in giving it the appearance of being merely the ramblings of an old dotard.

In the fifth act is a skilfully prepared Judith scene—the second great scene of the play. Evadne goes to the king's chamber, passing through the anteroom, which resounds with the profligate jests of the courtiers. The authors linger with a certain voluptuous cruelty over the scene between the king, who does not awake from his sleep until his hands have been tied to the bed, and the woman who has been his mistress, and who now tortures him with scathing words before she murders him. The remaining scenes are marred by their excessive sensationalism. Aspasia, disguised as her brother, seeks Amintor, from whom she can no longer be separated. He receives her with warm cordiality, but she taunts, strikes, and even kicks him, wishing to attain, if possible, the happiness of dying by his hand. He finally loses patience and draws his sword upon her, seeing too late that it is his beloved whom he has slain. Evadne now appears, red-handed and glowing with love, but Amintor repulses her with horror, she is stained with that greatest of all crimes, regicide. She kills herself in despair, and Amintor also dies by his own hand.

Aspasia is the perpetually slighted young woman who appears always resigned and gentle, in all Beaumont and Fletcher's plays. The old coward Calianax is another of their standing characters. The brotherhood between Melantius and Amintor possesses, in spite of its occasional artificiality, some interest for us, as does the corresponding friendship in the *Two Noble Kinsmen*, from the fact that the mutual relations between the authors evidently served as the prototype in both cases. Evadne's character, if not completely intelligible, is entirely *hors ligne*, and most admirably suited to dramatic treatment. The play indeed is a model of everything which dramatic and theatrical treatment requires, and was well calculated to impress an audience for whom Shakespeare's art was too refined.

We cannot, therefore, be surprised that the friend and fellow-craftsman of the two poets, who was the first to publish a collected edition of their works after their death, should write the following words without fear of contradiction : "But to mention them is to throw a cloud upon all former names and benight posterity; this book being, without flattery, the greatest monument of the scene that time and humanity have produced, and must live, not only the crown and sole reputation of our own, but the stain of all other nations and languages" (Shirley's address to the reader).

XVII

SHAKESPEARE AND FLETCHER—THE TWO NOBLE KINSMEN AND HENRY VIII.

IN the year 1684 a drama was published for the first time under the following title:

" *The Two Noble Kinsmen ;* presented at the Blackfriars, by the King's Maiesties Servants, with great applause.   Written by the memorable Worthies of their time $\left\{ \begin{array}{l} \text{Mr. } \textit{John Fletcher} \text{ and} \\ \text{Mr. } \textit{William Shakespeare} \end{array} \right\}$ Gent: Printed at *London* by *Tho. Cotes* for *John Waterson,* and are to be sold at the signe of the *Crown* in Paul's Churchyard."

This play was not included in the First Folio edition of Beaumont and Fletcher (1647), but it appeared in the second (1679). Even supposing the editors of the First Folio edition of Shakespeare's works to have entertained no doubt of his share in it, it would probably remain in Fletcher's possession until his death in 1625, and would therefore be inaccessible to them.

The play is of no particular value; it is far inferior to Fletcher's best work, and not to be compared with any of Shakespeare's completed dramas.   Nevertheless, many eminent critics of this century have found distinct traces in this play of the styles of both greater and lesser poet.

Like that of *Troilus and Cressida,* the theme found its way from the pages of an old-world poet, Statius' *Thebaide* in this case, into those of Boccaccio, and through him it came to Chaucer. Under the form given it by the latter it proved the foundation of several dramas of the reigns of Elizabeth and James.[1] Most of the essential details of *The Two Noble Kinsmen* may be found in Boccaccio's *La Teseide.*

It is a tale of two devoted friends, both suddenly seized by a romantic passion for a woman whom they have watched walking in a garden from the window of the tower in which they are held prisoners of war.   Their friendship is shattered, each claiming the exclusive right to the affections of this lady, who is the Duke's sister Emilia.   One of the friends is set at liberty upon

---

[1] A careful study of the plot may be found in Theodor Bierfreund's book : *Palamon og Arcite,* 1891.

the express condition of his quitting the country for ever. His irresistible longing for the fair one, however, draws him back to live disguised in her neighbourhood. The second friend escapes from prison, and meeting the first, engages him in a duel, which is interrupted by Duke Theseus. They explain their position to him, and their passion for his sister. The Duke arranges a formal tournament between the suitors; Emilia's hand is to reward the victor, and the vanquished is to suffer death. The conqueror, however, is fatally injured by a fall from his horse, and it is the defeated man who marries the princess.

There can be no reasonable question of the traces of Fletcher's hand in this play, for in it we find not only his easily recognised metrical style, but many features peculiar to his poorer work—the lax composition which permits of two plots running side by side with no connection between them, a tendency to merely theatrical effect and entirely motiveless action, contrived to surprise the audience at the cost of psychology, and finally his conception of virtue and vice in the relations between man and woman. To Fletcher, chastity meant entire abstinence, and side by side with this "chastity" he places, and delineates with relish, an immodest and purely sensual passion. Thus Emilia talks of her "chastity," and the jailer's daughter alludes to her passion for Palamon in terms which are repulsively shameless. When Shakespeare's women love, they are neither chaste in this fashion nor passionate in this fashion. They are sympathetically and reverentially drawn as loving only one man and loving him faithfully, whereas the affections of Fletcher's heroines veer round as suddenly as we saw Evadne's veer in *The Maid's Tragedy*. Therefore it is possible for him to portray such women as Emilia, who during the tournament loves first one and then the other of her suitors as his chances of victory are in the ascendant. That it contains many reminiscences of Shakespeare is no argument against Fletcher's responsibility for the greater part of the play, but quite the contrary; we have already seen how many of these traces are to be found even among his best works. In the *Two Noble Kinsmen* we find echoes from *The Midsummer Night's Dream*, from *Julius Cæsar* (the quarrel between Brutus and Cassio), and, above all, a tasteless and offensive imitation of Ophelia's madness, when the jailer's daughter goes crazy for fear while seeking Palamon in the wood at night, and in her raving and singing later in the play. Shakespeare never repeated without excelling, and certainly never parodied himself in this fashion.[1]

Shakespeare evidently had no part in the planning of the play. There is no originality in it, and if we do obtain a glimpse of some sort of life's philosophy, it is certainly not his.

---

[1] A similar opinion is skilfully maintained by Bierfreund, but I cannot agree with his main contention that Shakespeare had no part in this play whatever.

Swinburne's surmise that the play was sketched by Shakespeare and completed by Fletcher, can therefore hardly be correct. Among other arguments, we may mention that the part in which, according to Swinburne's own opinion, Shakespeare's hand is most traceable, is the conclusion, which is hardly likely to have been written first.

Can any part of the play be ascribed to Shakespeare ?   Gardiner and Delius believe not, and the Danish critics a few years ago shared the same scarcely justifiable opinion.   Bierfreund is uninfluenced by the fact that many of the most eminent English critics hold a contrary view, but such a circumstance should impose the very closest study of the play on the part of foreign critics.   In my case this has led me to the conclusion that although the drama was planned and the greater part executed by Fletcher, he had Shakespeare's assistance in finishing the work.   We can hardly imagine that Shakespeare vouchsafed his help from any motive but that of interest in, and a friendly feeling for, the younger poet, who had submitted his work to him and appealed for his assistance.

It would but weary the reader to go through the work from beginning to end to show how the seal of Shakespeare's style is stamped upon it.   The traces of his pen are most frequent in the opening act ; the appeal of the first queen to Theseus ("We are three queens," &c.), in the introductory scene, for example.   These lines possess all the rhythm peculiar to the productions of the last years of the poet's life ; and how boldly figurative and genuinely Shakespearian in expression is the same queen's fanciful expression :

> " Dowagers, take hands ;
> Let us be widows to our woes ; delay
> Commends us to a famishing hope."

Theseus' last speech in this act (the summing up of the situation and circumstances) reminds us of Hamlet's monologue, " The whips and scorns of life, the oppressors' wrongs," &c., and Ulysses' beauty, wit, high birth," &c.

> "Since I have known frights, fury, friends' behests,
> Love's provocations, zeal, a mistress' task,
> Desire of liberty, a fever, madness." . . .

Mere imitations must not be confounded with Shakespeare's own style, however.   The passage in which Emilia speaks of the ardent and tender friendship that united her to her dead friend Flavina, which in England has been mistakenly admired as Shakespeare's work, is in reality a poor copy of the passage in the *Midsummer Night's Dream* (Act iii. sc. 2) where Helena describes the love between herself and Hermia.   The unhealthy affection here set forth bears Fletcher's stamp upon it, and is made particularly unpleasant by the use Emilia makes of the word "innocent."

We are again sensible of Shakespeare's touch in the monologue spoken by the jailer's daughter, which constitutes the second scene of the third act. Note the picturesque expression, "In me has grief slain fear," and many others. From the moment she goes out of her mind down to the last word she utters, Shakespeare has neither part nor lot in those speeches whose uncouth imitation of his style must have been singularly offensive to him.

The greater part of the first scene of the fifth act is undoubtedly Shakespeare's. Theseus' first speech is superb, and Arcite's address to the knights and invocation of Mars is delightful. The lines at the close of the play have also a Shakespearian ring about them, especially the words so much admired by Swinburne:

> "That nought could buy
> Dear love but loss of dear love."

But there is no deeper, no intellectual interest for us in all this. Shakespeare had nothing to do with the psychology, or rather want of it, in this play.[1]

Had he any greater share in *Henry VIII.?* The play was first published in the Folio edition of 1623, where it closes the series of Historical Plays. The first four acts are founded on Holinshed's Chronicle, and the last upon Fox's *Acts and Monuments of the Church*, commonly known as the *Book of Martyrs*. The authors were also directly or indirectly indebted to a book which at that date only existed in manuscript, George Cavendish's *Relics of Cardinal Wolsey*, which had been largely drawn upon by Holinshed and Hall. The earliest reference to a play of Henry VIII. may be found in the Stationers' Hall Registry for the 12th of February 1604–5, where the "Enterlude for K. Henry VIII." is entered; but this refers to Rowley's worthless and fanatically Protestant play "*When you see mee you know mee.*" The next mention of such a drama occurs in the well-known oft-quoted letters concerning the burning of the Globe Theatre on the 29th of June 1613. In an epistle from Thomas Larkin to Sir Thomas Pickering, dated "This last of June 1613," we read: "No longer since than yesterday, while Burbege's company were acting at the Globe the play of Henry VIII., and there shooting off certain chambers in way of triumph, the fire catched and there burnt so furiously, as it consumed the whole house, all in less than two hours, the people having enough to do to save themselves." Also Sir Henry Wotton in a letter to his nephews, dated the 6th of July 1613, writes: "Now let matters of state sleep, I will entertain you

---

[1] Compare Hickson, Fleay, and Furnivall upon the subject of *The Two Noble Kinsmen. New Shakspere Society's Transactions*, 1874. R. Boyle maintains that he can trace Massinger's hand in the play.

at the present with what happened at the Bankside. The king's
players had a new play, called All is True, representing some principal pieces of the reign of Henry VIII., which was set forth with
many extraordinary circumstances of pomp and majesty, even to the
matting of the stage; the knights of the Order, with their Georges
and Garter, the guards with their embroidered coats and the like;
sufficient, in Truth, within a while to make greatness very familiar
if not ridiculous. Now King Henry making a masque at the Cardinal Wolsey's House, and certain canons being shot off at his
entrance, some of the paper, or other stuff wherewith one of them
was stopped, did light on the thatch, where being thought at first
but an idle smoak, and their eyes more attentive to the show, it
kindled inwardly and ran round like a train, consuming within
less than an hour the whole House to the very grounds."

The emphatic and thrice repeated assertion of the prologue
that all that is about to be represented is *the truth*, taken in conjunction with other details, proves that the play described is our
Henry VIII., and at that date, therefore, a new work.

Although never very highly esteemed, it was not until somewhere about the year 1850 that it was ever doubted that *Henry
VIII.* was entirely written by Shakespeare. It would now be
impossible to find any one holding such an opinion; some of the
most competent critics, indeed, maintain that Shakespeare had
nothing whatever to do with it.[1]

That keen observer, Emerson, alluding to *Henry VIII.* in
his book *Representative Men* draws attention to the two entirely
different rhythms of its verse—one that is Shakespearian, and
another much inferior. Almost simultaneously, Spedding published an article in the *Gentleman's Magazine* for August 1856
(afterwards reprinted under the title "Who Wrote Shakespeare's
Henry VIII?"), in which he points out these differing rhythms,
affirming one of them to be Fletcher's. Furnivall and Fleay declared themselves of the same opinion in 1874. To understand this
criticism, the reader must bear in mind the following simple evolution of English five-footed iambics. The language does not possess
what Scandinavians call feminine rhymes, alternating and contrasting with the masculine. The first attempt to break the monotony
of the blank verse simply consisted in the addition of an extra
syllable to the original ten—*double ending*. The proportion
of these lengthened lines in Shakespeare's *Henry V.* is 18 in

---

[1] In his prefatory treatise to the *Leopold Shakspere* (136 quarto pages),
F. J. Furnivall has dealt with this play as being in part Shakespeare's. Now he is
of a different opinion, and in a copy of the book presented by him to me, he has
written on the margin against *Henry VIII.* "Not Shakspere's." Arthur Symons,
who edits and prefaces the play in the Irving edition, told me that he now inclines,
on account of its metrical structure, to the belief that Shakespeare had no share in it.
P. A. Daniels, the erudite editor of so many Shakespearian quartos, said that he had
arrived at no decision respecting its authorship, and characteristically added that the
identity was a matter of indifference to him so long as the play was good. This is
not the psychological standpoint.

100. Ben Jonson long adhered to the old regular construction, but finally yielded to the newer fashion. Fletcher constantly used the eleven-syllabled lines, employing them indeed so regularly and consciously that he is betrayed into a certain monotonous mannerism. Instance the following from *The Wild Goose Chase*:

> " I would I were a woman, sir, to fit you,
> As there be such, no doubt, may engine you too,
> May with a countermine blow up your valour.
> But in good faith, sir, we are both too honest ;
> And the plague is, we cannot be persuaded ;
> For look you, if we thought it were a glory
> To be the last of all your lovely ladies." . . .

This will also show that Fletcher did not, as a rule, allow the idea to overlap from one line to the next.

In Shakespeare's later works the proportion of eleven-syllabled lines is 33 in 100; in Massinger it is 40, and in Fletcher 50 to 80, or even more. Again, Shakespeare made use, with ever-increasing frequency, of *enjambement* or "run on" lines. This style is particularly noticeable in the passionate dramas of his bitter period, and the growing habit of employing them led to the more and more frequent appearance of lines ending with an adverb, article, or preposition (light and weaking endings). There may be a hundred such in his later plays ; there are, for instance, 130 in *Cymbeline*. This feature became an extravagance with his successors. Massinger, whose dramas are considerably shorter than Shakespeare's, has from 150 to 170 of these weak endings in each play.

In comparison with Shakespeare's work there is an effeminate ring about Fletcher's verse, and his was the Corinthian, if Shakespeare's was the Ionic style. Separate and unalloyed, it would be impossible to mistake them, but it is a very different matter when they are blended together in one and the same work as in *Henry VIII*. And here again the problem offered by the *Two Noble Kinsmen* presents itself. Did Shakespeare leave the play unfinished, and was it completed by Fletcher after his death ? or did he help Fletcher by writing or re-writing certain scenes of his play ? The first supposition is an utter impossibility, as far as I am concerned. The planning of the drama was not Shakespeare's ; never in his life did anything so shapeless come from his pen. Is any part of the play due to him ? In spite of the verdicts of Furnivall and Symons, I think so. In the first place, we are not justified in ignoring the testimony borne by Heminge and Condell in the First Folio edition. We have always hitherto taken for granted that they were better qualified to judge of the authenticity of a play than we of the present day ; not one of the plays accepted by them has since been rejected by posterity, and we need a very good reason for making an exception of *Henry VIII.* The sole pretext we can offer is the weakness of the whole play, including those portions of which we are in doubt. But this weakness cannot in any way be considered as decisive. Here, working with another man, Shakespeare did not put forth his full strength, exercise all his powers, nor give free play to his imagination. Of this, *Henry VIII.* is not the only example. Moreover, there are strong points of resemblance between those parts of the play which the majority of English critics ascribe to him and works of the same period which were unmistakably his and his alone.

So far back as 1765, Samuel Johnson, who never doubted that the whole play was due to Shakespeare, remarked that the poet's genius seemed to rise and set with Queen Katharine, and that any one might have invented and written the rest. In 1850 James Spedding, moved thereto by some suggestive criticism by Tennyson, came to the conclusion already mentioned, that only certain parts were written by Shakespeare, and that the remainder was due to Fletcher. This opinion was confirmed by Samuel Hickson, who remarked that he had arrived at the same decision three or four years previously, and even with the same results as far as the separate scenes were concerned. This theory was, after a careful examination of the metrical structure, still further corroborated by Fleay.

That the general scheme of the drama was not due to Shakespeare is self-evident. Spedding observed how utterly ineffective the play is as a whole, how the interest collapses instead of increasing, and how the sympathy aroused in the audience is in steady opposition to the actual development of events. The centre of interest in the first act is undeniably Queen Katharine, and, although the deference due to so recent a king as Elizabeth's father forbade too plain speaking, the audience is clearly given to understand that the monarch's passion for Anne Boleyn was really at the bottom of his conscientious scruples concerning the wedlock in which he had lived for twenty years. Notwithstanding this, the spectators are expected to feel joy and satisfaction when Anne is solemnly crowned queen, and actual triumph when she gives birth to a daughter. In the last act we have the impeachment of Archbishop Cranmer, his acquittal by the king, and his appointment to the godfathership of Elizabeth, all of which has no connection whatever with the real action of the play. Wolsey, one of the two chief characters, the evil principle in opposition to the good Queen Katharine, disappears before her, not even surviving the close of the third act. The whole play, in fact, resolves itself into a succession of spectacular effects, processions, songs, dances, and music. We are shown a great assembly of the State Council in connection with Buckingham's trial; a great festival in Wolsey's palace, with masquerade and dance; the great trial scene, with England's queen at the bar; a great coronation scene, with canopy, crown jewels, and flourish of trumpets; the dying Katharine's vision of dancing angels, with golden vizards and palm branches in their hands; and lastly, the great christening scene in the palace, with another procession of canopy, trumpets, and heralds.

An invisible writing inscribes on every page the words *Written to order.* In all probability it was a hurriedly written piece, hastily put together for performance at the court gaieties in honour of the Princess Elizabeth's marriage. It was for those festivities that Beaumont's little play, *The Masque of the Inner Temple and Gray's Inn,* and Shakespeare's own masterpiece, *The Tempest,* were written. Shakespeare's part in *Henry VIII.* is limited to Act i. sc. 1 and 2, Act ii. sc. 3 and sc. 4, Act iii. sc. 2 as far as Wolsey's first monologue, "What should this mean," and Act v. sc. 1 and 4.

This play cannot be classed with Shakespeare's other historical dramas, for, as we have already observed, its events were of too recent occurrence to allow of a strictly veracious treatment. How was it possible to tell the truth about Henry VIII., that coarse and cruel Bluebeard, with his six wives? Did he not inaugurate the Reformation, and was he not the father of Queen Elizabeth? As little could the material interests which furthered the Reformation be represented on the stage, or the various religious and political aspects of the Reformation itself. Fettered and bound as he was by a hundred different considerations, Shakespeare acquitted himself of his difficult task with tact and skill. When Henry, immediately after his encounter with the beauteous court lady, began, after all those years, to feel scruples on the score of his marriage with his brother's wife, Shakespeare, without making him a hypocrite, allows us to perceive how the new passion acted as a spur to his conscience. The character of Wolsey is founded upon the Chronicle, and the clever parvenu's bold, unscrupulous, yet withal self-controlled nature, is indicated by a few light touches. Fletcher has spoiled the character by the introduction of the badly-written monologues uttered by Wolsey after his fall. We recognise the voice of the clergyman's son in their feeble, pastoral strain. The picture of Anne Boleyn, delicately outlined by Shakespeare, was also put out of drawing later in the play by Fletcher. All the light of the piece, however, is concentrated around the figure of the repudiated Catholic queen, Katharine of Arragon, for in her (as he found her character in the Chronicle) Shakespeare recognised a variant of his present all-absorbing type—the noble and neglected woman. She closely resembles the misjudged Queen Hermione, so unjustly separated from her husband and thrown into prison in the *Winter's Tale.* As in *Cymbeline* Imogen still loves Posthumus although he has cast her off, so Katharine continues to love the man who has wronged her.

Shakespeare has hardly put a word into the mouth of the Queen which may not be found in the Chronicle, but he has created a character of mingled charm and distinction, a union of Castilian pride with extreme simplicity, of inflexible resolution with gentlest resignation, and of a quick temper with a sincere piety, through which the temper sometimes shows. He has drawn with a caressing touch the figure of a queen neither beautiful nor brilliant, but true—true to the core, proud of her birth and queenly rank, but softer than wax in the hands of her royal lord, whom she loves after twenty-four years of married life as dearly as on her wedding-day. Her letters show how devoted and lovable she was, and in them she addresses Henry as "Your Grace, my husband, my Henry," and signs herself "Your humble wife and true servant." In those scenes in which it has fallen to Fletcher's lot to represent the Queen, he has adhered faithfully to Shakespeare's conception of her, which was virtually that of the Chronicle. Even in the hour of her death, Katharine does not forget to rebuke and punish the messenger who has failed in due respect by omitting to kneel; but she forgives her enemy the Cardinal and sends the King this last greeting:

> "Remember me
> In all humility unto his highness :
> Say his long trouble now is passing
> Out of the world : tell him in death I bless'd him,
> For so I will.—Mine eyes grow dim."

Her stately dignity resembles that of Hermione, but she differs from the latter in her pride of race and piety. Hermione is neither pious nor proud; neither was Shakespeare. We find a little proof of his detestation of sectarianism even in the pompous play of *Henry VIII.* In the third scene of the fifth act the porter exclaims of the inquisitive multitude crowding to watch the christening procession:

"There are the youths that thunder at the playhouse and fight for bitten apples ; that no audience but the Tribulation of Tower Hill or the limbs of Limehouse, their dear brothers, are able to endure."

Limehouse was an artisan house in London; there also the foreigners settled, and it resounded with the strife of religious sects. It is amusing to note how Shakespeare contrived to have a fling at his detested *groundlings* and his Puritan enemies at one and the same time.

As we all know, the drama closes with Cranmer's lengthy and flattering prediction of the greatness of Elizabeth and James, which is marred by the monotony of Fletcher's worst mannerisms. Shakespeare clearly had no share in this tirade, which makes all the more strange the part it has played in the discussions which have been carried on with so little psychology relative to Shakespeare's religious and denominational standpoint. How many times has the prophecy that under Elizabeth "God shall be truly known" been quoted in support of the great poet's firmly Protestant convictions? Yet the line was evidently never written by him, and not a single turn of thought in the whole of this lengthy speech owns any suggestion of his pathos and style. It is only here and there in the play that we obtain a glimpse of Shakespeare, and then he is fettered and hampered by collaboration with another man and by an uncongenial task, to which only a great exertion of his genius could here and there impart any dramatic interest.

XVIII

CYMBELINE—THE THEME—THE POINT OF DEPARTURE—
THE MORAL — THE IDYLL — IMOGEN — SHAKESPEARE
AND GOETHE—SHAKESPEARE AND CALDERON

IN *Cymbeline* Shakespeare is once more sole master of his
material, and he works it up into such a many-coloured web as no
loom but his can produce. Here, too, we find a certain offhand
carelessness of technique. The exposition is perfunctory; the
preliminaries of the action are conveyed to us in a scene of pure
narrative. The comic passages are, as a rule, weak, the mirth-
moving device being for one of the other characters to ridicule or
parody in asides the utterances of the coarse and vain Prince
Cloten. In the middle of the play (iii. 3), a poorly-written monologue gives us a sort of supplementary exposition, necessary to
the understanding of the plot. Finally, the dramatic knot is loosed
by means of a *deus ex machinâ*, Jupiter, "upon his eagle back'd,"
appearing to the sleeping Posthumus, and leaving with him an
oracular "label," in which, as though to bear witness to the poet's
"small Latin," the deity childishly derives *mulier* from *mollis aer*,
or "tender air." But, in spite of all this, Shakespeare is here
once more at the height of his poetic greatness; the convalescent
has recovered all his strength. He has thrown his whole soul
into the creation of his heroine, and has so enchased this Imogen,
this pearl among women, that all her excellences show to the best
advantage, and the setting is not unworthy of the jewel.

As in Cleopatra and Cressida we had woman determined solely
by her sex, so in Imogen we have an embodiment of the highest
possible characteristics of womanhood—untainted health of soul,
unshaken fortitude, constancy that withstands all trials, inexhaustible forbearance, unclouded intelligence, love that never
wavers, and unquenchable radiance of spirit. She, like Marina,
is cast into the snake-pit of the world. She is slandered, and not,
like Desdemona, at second or third hand, but by the very man
who boasts of her favours and supports his boast with seemingly
incontrovertible proofs. Like Cordelia, she is misjudged; but
whereas Cordelia is merely driven from her father's presence
along with the man of her choice, Imogen is doomed to death
by her cruelly-deceived husband, whom alone she adores; and

through it all she preserves her love for him unweakened and unchanged.

Strange—very strange! In Imogen we find the fullest, deepest love that Shakespeare has ever placed in a woman's breast, and that although *Cymbeline* follows close upon plays which were filled to the brim with contempt for womankind. He believed, then, in such love, so impassioned, so immovable, so humble—believed in it now? He had, then, observed or encountered such a love—encountered it at this point of his life?

Even a poet has scant enough opportunities of observing love. Love is a rare thing, much rarer than the world pretends, and when it exists, it is apt to be sparing of words. Did he simply fall back on his own experiences, his own inward sensations, his knowledge of his own heart, and, transposing his feelings from the major to the minor key, place them on a woman's lips? Or did he love at this moment, and was he himself thus beloved at the end of the fifth decade of his life? The probability is, doubtless, that he wrote from some quite fresh experience, though it does not follow that the experience was actually his own. It is not often that women love men of his mental habit and stature with such intensity of passion. The rule will always be that a Molière shall find himself cast aside for some Comte de Guiche, a Shakespeare for some Earl of Pembroke. Thus we cannot with any certainty conclude that he himself was the object of the passion which had revived his faith in a woman's power of complete and unconditional absorption in love for one man, and for him alone. In the first place, had the experience been his own, he would scarcely have left London so soon. Yet the probability is that he must just about this time have gained some clear and personal insight into an ideal love. In the public sphere, too, it is not unlikely that Arabella Stuart's undaunted passion for Lord William Seymour, so cruelly punished by King James, may have afforded the model for Imogen's devotion to Leonatus Posthumus in defiance of the will of King Cymbeline.

Cymbeline was first printed in the Folio of 1623. The earliest mention of it occurs in the *Booke of Plaies and Notes thereof* kept by the above-mentioned astrologer and magician, Dr. Simon Forman. He was present, he says, at a performance of *A Winter's Tale* on May 15, 1611, and at the same time he sketches the plot of *Cymbeline*, but unfortunately does not give the date of the performance. In all probability it was quite recent; the play was no doubt written in the course of 1610, while the fate of Arabella Stuart was still fresh in the poet's mind. Forman died in September 1611.

In depth and variety of colouring, in richness of matter, profundity of thought, and heedlessness of conventional canons, *Cymbeline* has few rivals among Shakespeare's plays. Fascinating as it is, however, this tragi-comedy has never been very popular on the stage. The great public, indeed, has neither studied nor understood it.

In none of his works has Shakespeare played greater havoc with chronology. He jumbles up the ages with superb indifference. The period purports to be that of Augustus, yet we are introduced to English, French, and Italian cavaliers, and hear them talk of pistol-shooting and playing bowls and cards. The list of characters ends thus—"Lords, ladies, Roman senators, tribunes, apparitions, a soothsayer, a Dutch gentleman, a Spanish gentleman, musicians, officers, captains, soldiers, messengers, and other attendants." Was there ever such a farrago?

What did Shakespeare mean by this play? is the question that now confronts us. My readers are aware that I never, in the first instance, try to answer this question directly. The fundamental point is, What impelled him to write? how did he arrive at the theme? When that is answered, the rest follows almost as a matter of course.

Where, then, is the starting-point of this seeming tangle? We find it on resolving the material of the play into its component parts.

There are three easily distinguishable elements in the action.

In his great storehouse of English history, Holinshed, Shakespeare found some account of a King Kymbeline or Cimbeline, who is said to have been educated at Rome, and there knighted by the Emperor Augustus, under whom he served in several campaigns. He is stated to have stood so high in the Emperor's favour that "he was at liberty to pay his tribute or not" as he chose. He reigned thirty-five years, was buried in London, and left two sons, Guiderius and Arviragus. The name Imogen occurs in Holinshed's story of Brutus and Locrine. In the tragedy of *Locrine*, dating from 1595, Imogen is mentioned as the wife of Brutus.

Although Cymbeline, says Holinshed, is declared by most authorities to have lived at unbroken peace with Rome, yet some Roman writers affirm that the Britons having refused to pay tribute when Augustus came to the throne, that Emperor, in the tenth year after the death of Julius Cæsar, "made prouision to passe with an armie ouer into Britaine." He is said, however, to have altered his mind; so that the Roman descent upon Britain under Caius Lucius is an invention of the poet's.

In Boccaccio's *Decameron*, again (Book II. Novel 9), Shakespeare found the story of the faithful Ginevra, of which this is the substance :—At a tavern in Paris, a company of Italian merchants, after supper one evening, fall to discussing their wives. Three of them have but a poor opinion of their ladies' virtue, but one, Bernabo Lomellini of Genoa, maintains that his wife would resist any possible temptation, however long he had been absent from her. A certain Ambrogiuolo lays a heavy wager with him on the point, and betakes himself to Genoa, but finds Bernabo's confidence fully justified. He hits upon the scheme of concealing himself in a chest which is conveyed into the lady's bedroom. In the middle of the night he raises the lid. "He crept quietly forth, and stood in the room, where a candle was burning. By its light, he carefully examined the furnishing of the apartment, the pictures, and other objects of note, and fixed them in his memory. Then he approached the bed, and when he saw that both she and a little child who lay beside her were sleeping soundly, he uncovered her and beheld that her beauty in nowise consisted in her attire. But he could not discover any mark whereby to convince her husband, save one which she had under the left breast; it was a birth-mark around which there grew certain yellow hairs." Then he takes from one of her chests a purse and a night-gown, together with certain rings and belts, and conceals them in his own hiding-place. He hastens back to Paris, summons the merchants together, and boasts of having won the wager. The description of the room makes little impression on Bernabo, who remarks that all this he may have learnt by bribing a chambermaid; but when the birth-mark is described, he feels as though a dagger had been plunged into his heart. He despatches a servant with a letter to his wife, requesting her to meet him at a country-house some twenty miles from Genoa, and at the same time orders the servant to murder her on the way. The lady receives the letter with great joy, and next morning takes horse to ride with the servant to the country-house. Loathing his task, the man consents to spare her, gives her a suit of male attire, and suffers her to escape, bringing his master false tidings of her death, and producing her clothes in witness of it. Ginevra, dressed as a man, enters the service of a Spanish nobleman, and accompanies him to Alexandria, whither he goes to convey to the Sultan a present of certain rare falcons. The Sultan notices the pretty youth in his train, and makes him (or rather her) his favourite. In the market-place of Acre she chances upon a booth in the Venetian bazaar where Ambrogiuolo has displayed for sale, among other wares, the purse and belt he stole from her. On her inquiring where he got them, he replies that they were given him by his mistress, the Lady Ginevra. She persuades him to come to Alexandria, manages to bring her husband thither also, and makes them both appear before the Sultan. The truth is brought to light and the liar shamed; but he does not escape so easily as Iachimo in the play. He who had falsely boasted of a lady's favour, and thereby brought her to ruin, is, with true mediæval consistency, allotted the punishment he deserves: "Wherefore the Sultan commanded that Ambrogiuolo should be led forth to a high place in the city, and should there be bound to a stake in the full glare of the sunshine, and smeared all over with honey, and should not be set free till his body fell to pieces by its own decay. So that he was not alone stung to death in unspeakable torments by flies, wasps, and hornets, which greatly abound in that country, but also devoured to the last particle of his flesh. His white bones, held together by the sinews alone, stood there unremoved for a long time, a terror and a warning to all."

These two tales—of the wars between Rome and heathen Britain, and of the slander, peril, and rescue of Ginevra—were in themselves totally unconnected. Shakespeare welded them by making Ginevra, whom he calls Imogen, a daughter of King Cymbeline by his first marriage, and therefore next in succession to the crown of Britain.

There remains a third element in the play—the story of Belarius, his banishment, his flight with the king's sons, his solitary life in the forest with the two youths, the coming of Imogen, and so forth. All this is the fruit of Shakespeare's free invention, slightly stimulated, perhaps, by a story in the *Decameron* (Book II. Novel 8). It is in this invented portion, studied in its relation of complement and contrast to the rest, that we shall find an un-mistakable index to the moods, sentiments, and ideas under the influence of which he chose this subject and shaped it to his ends.

I conceive the situation in this wise : the mood he has been living through, the mood which has left its freshest impress on his mind, is one in which life in human society seems unendurable, and especially life in a large town and at a court. Never before had he felt so keenly and indignantly what a court really is. Stupidity, coarseness, weakness, and falsehood flourish in courts, and carry all before them. Cymbeline is stupid and weak, Cloten is stupid and coarse, the queen is false.

Here the best men are banished, like Belarius and Posthumus; here the best woman is foully wronged, like Imogen. Here the high-born murderess sits in the seat of the mighty—the queen herself deals in poisons, and demands deadly " compounds " of her physicians. Corruption reaches its height at courts ; but in great towns as a whole, wherever multitudes of men are gathered together, it is impossible even for the best to keep himself above reproach. The weapons used against him—lies, slanders, and perfidy—force him to employ whatever means he can in self-defence. Let us then turn our backs on the town, and seek an idyllic existence in the country, in the lonely woodland places.

This note recurs persistently in all the works of Shakespeare's latest period. Timon longed to escape from Athens and make the solitudes echo with his invectives. Here Belarius and the king's two sons live secluded in a romantic wilderness ; and we shall presently find Florizel and Perdita surrounded by the autumnal beauty of a rustic festival, and Prospero dwelling with Miranda on a lovely uninhabited island.

When Shakespeare, in early years, had conjured up visions of a fantastic life in sylvan solitudes, it was simply because it amused him to place his Rosalinds and Celias in surroundings worthy of their exquisiteness, ideal Ardennes, or perhaps we should say ideal Forests of Arden like that in which, as a boy, he had learnt to read the secrets of Nature. In these regions, exempt from the cares of the working-day world, young men and maidens passed their days together in happy idleness, pensive or blithesome, laughing or loving. The forest was simply a republic created by Nature herself for a witty and amorous *élite* of the most brilliant cavaliers and ladies he had known, or rather had bodied forth in his own image that he might live in the company of his peers. The air resounded with songs and sighs and kisses, with word-plays and laughter. It was a dreamland, a paradise of dainty lovers.

How differently does he now conceive of the solitude of the country! It has become to him the one thing in life, the refuge, the sanctuary. It means for him an atmosphere of purity, the home of spiritual health, the stronghold of innocence, the one safe retreat for whoso would flee from the pestilence of falsehood and perfidy that rages in courts and cities.

There no one can escape it. But now, we must observe, Shakespeare no longer regards this contagion of untruth and unfaith with the eyes of a Timon. He now looks down from higher and clearer altitudes.

It is true that no one can keep his life wholly free from false-hood, deceit, and violence towards others. But neither falsehood nor deceit, nor even violence is always and inevitably a crime; it is often a necessity, a legitimate weapon, a right. At bottom, Shakespeare had always held that there were no such things as unconditional duties and absolute prohibitions. He had never, for example, questioned Hamlet's right to kill the king, scarcely even his right to run his sword through Polonius. Nevertheless he had hitherto been unable to conquer a feeling of indignation and disgust when he saw around him nothing but breaches of the simplest moral laws. Now, on the other hand, the dim divina-tions of his earlier years crystallised in his mind into a coherent body of thought to this effect: no commandment is unconditional; it is not in the observance or non-observance of an external fiat that the merit of an action, to say nothing of a character, consists; everything depends upon the volitional substance into which the individual, as a responsible agent, transmutes the formal impera-tive at the moment of decision.

In other words, Shakespeare now sees clearly that the ethics of intention are the only true, the only possible ethics.

Imogen says (iv. 2):

> "If I do lie, and do
> No harm by it, though the gods hear, I hope
> They'll pardon it."

Pisanio says in his soliloquy (iii. 5):

> " Thou bidd'st me to my loss : for, true to thee,
> Were to prove false, which I will never be
> To him that is most true."

And he hits the nail on the head when he characterises him-self in these words (iv. 3):

> " Wherein I am false, I am honest; not true, to be true."

That is to say, he lies and deceives because he cannot help it; but his character is none the worse, nay, all the better on that account.   He disobeys his master, and thereby merits his gratitude; he hoodwinks Cloten, and therein he does well.

In the same way, all the nobler characters fly in the face of accepted moral laws.   Imogen disobeys her father and braves his wrath, and even his curse, because she will not renounce the husband of her choice.   So, too, she afterwards deceives the young men in the forest by appearing in male attire and under an assumed name—untruthfully, and yet with a higher truth, calling herself Fidele, the faithful one.   So, too, the upright Belarius robs the king of both his sons, but thereby saves them for him and for the country; and during their whole boy-hood he puts them off, for their own good, with false accounts of things.   So, too, the honest physician deceives the queen, whose wickedness he has divined, by giving her an opiate in place of a poison, and thereby baffling her attempt at murder. So, too, Guiderius acts rightly in taking the law into his own hands, and answering Cloten's insults by killing him at sight and cutting off his head.   He thus, without knowing it, prevents the brutish idiot's intended violence to Imogen.

Thus all the good characters commit acts of deception, violence, and falsehood, or even live their whole life under false colours, without in the least derogating from their moral worth. They touch evil without defilement, even if they suffer and now and then feel themselves insecure in their strained relations to truth and right.

Beyond all doubt, it must have been actual and intimate experience that first darkened Shakespeare's view of life, and then opened his eyes again to its brighter aspects.   But it is the idea which he here indirectly expresses that seems to have played the essential and decisive part in uplifting his spirit above the mood of mere hatred and contempt for humanity : the realisa-tion that the quality of a given act depends rather on the agent than on the act itself.   Although it be true, for example, that falsehood and deceit encounter us on every hand, it does not necessarily follow that human nature is utterly corrupt.   Neither deceit nor any other course of action in conflict with moral law is absolutely and unconditionally wrong. The majority, indeed, of those who speak falsely and act unlawfully are an ignoble crew; but even the best, the noblest, may systematically transgress the moral law and be good and noble still. This is the meaning of moral self-government; the only true morality consists in following out our own ends, by our own means, and on our own responsibility. The only real and binding laws are those which we lay down for ourselves, and it is the breach of these laws alone that degrades us.

Seen from this point of view, the world puts on a less gloomy aspect. The poet is no longer impelled by a spiritual necessity to bring down his curtain to the notes of the trump of doom, to make all voyages end in shipwreck, all dramas issue in annihilation, or even to leaven the tragedy of life with consistent scorn and execration for humanity at large.

In his present frame of mind there is a touch of weary tolerance. He no longer cares to dwell upon the harsh realities of life; he seeks distraction in dreaming. And he dreams of retribution, of the suppression of the utterly vile (the queen dies, Cloten is killed), of letting mercy season justice in the treatment of certain human beasts of prey (Iachimo), and of preserving a little circle, a chosen few, whom neither the errors into which passion has led them, nor the acts of deceit and violence they have committed in self-defence, render unworthy of our sympathies. Life on earth is still worth living so long as there are women like Imogen and men like her brothers. She, indeed, is an ideal, and they creatures of romance; but their existence is a condition-precedent of poetry.

It is to this fertilising mist of feeling, this productive trend of thought, that the play owes its origin.

Shakespeare has so far taken heart again that he can give us something more and something better than poetical fragments or plays which, like his recent ones, produce a powerful but harsh effect. He will once more unroll a large, various, and many-coloured panorama.

The action of *Cymbeline*, like that of *Lear*, is only nominally located in pre-Christian England. There is not the slightest attempt at representation of the period, and the barbarism depicted is mediæval rather than antique. For the rest, the starting-point of *Cymbeline* vaguely resembles that of *Lear*. Cymbeline is causelessly estranged from Imogen, as Lear is from Cordelia; there is something in Cymbeline's weakness and folly that recalls the unreason of Lear. But in the older play everything is tragically designed and in the great manner, whereas here the whole action is devised with a happy end in view.

The consort of this pitiful king is a crafty and ambitious

woman, who, by alternately flattering and defying him, has got him entirely under her thumb. She says herself (i. 2):—

> " I never do him wrong
> But he does buy my injuries to be friends,
> Pays dear for my offences."

In other words, she knows that she can always find her profit in a scene of reconciliation. Her object is to make Imogen the wife of Cloten, her son by a former marriage, and thus to secure for him the succession to the throne. This scheme of hers is the original source of all the misfortunes which overwhelm the heroine. For Imogen loves Posthumus, in spite of his poverty a paragon among men, and cannot be induced to renounce the husband she has chosen. Therefore the play opens with the banishment of Posthumus.

The characters and incidents of Shakespeare's own invention give perspective to the play, the underplot forming a parallel to the main action, as the story of Gloucester and his cruel son forms a parallel to that of Lear and his heartless daughters. Belarius, a soldier and statesman, has twenty years ago fallen into unmerited disgrace with Cymbeline, who, listening to the voice of calumny, has outlawed him with the same unreasoning passion with which he now sends Posthumus into exile. In revenge for this wrong, Belarius has carried off Cymbeline's two sons, who have ever since lived with him in a lonely place among the mountains, believing him to be their father. To them comes Imogen in her hour of need, disguised as a boy, and is received with the utmost warmth and tenderness by the brothers, who do not know her, and whom she does not know. One of them, Guiderius, kills Cloten, who insulted and challenged him. Both the young men take up arms to meet the Roman invaders, and, together with Belarius and Posthumus, they save their father's kingdom.

Gervinus has acutely and justly remarked that the fundamental contrast expressed in their story, as in Cymbeline's political situation, in Imogen's relation to Posthumus and Pisanio's relation to them both, is precisely the dual contrast expressed in the English words *true* and *false*—*true* meaning at once "veracious" and "faithful" (ideas which, in the play, shade off into each other), while *false*, in like manner, means both "mendacious" and "faithless."

Life at court is beset with treacherous quicksands. The king is stupid, passionate, perpetually misguided; the queen is a wily murderess; and between them stands her son, Cloten, one of Shakespeare's most original figures, a true creation of genius, without a rival in all the poet's long gallery of fools and dullards. His stupid inefficiency and undisguised malignity have nothing in common with his mother's hypocritical and supple craft; he takes after her in worthlessness alone.

For the sake of an inartistic stage effect, Shakespeare has endowed him with a bodily frame indistinguishable from that of the handsome Posthumus, leaving it to his head alone to express the world-wide difference between them. But how admirably has the poet characterised the dolt and boor by making him shoot forth his words with an explosive stammer! With profound humour and delicate observation, he has endowed him with the loftiest notions of his own dignity, and given him no shadow of doubt as to his rights. There are no bounds to his vanity, his coarseness, his bestiality. If words could do it, not a word of his but would wound others to the quick. And not only his words, but his intents are of the most malignant; he would outrage Imogen at Milford Haven and "spurn her home" to her father. His stupidity, fortunately, renders him less dangerous, and with delicate art Shakespeare has managed to make him from first to last produce a comic effect, thereby softening the painful impression of the portraiture. We take pleasure in him as in Caliban, whom he foreshadows, and who had the same designs upon Miranda as he upon Imogen. We might even describe Caliban as Cloten developed into a type, a symbol.

It is such personages as these that compose the world which Belarius depicts to Guiderius and Arviragus (iii. 3), when the two youths repine against the inactivity of their lonely forest life, and yearn to plunge into the social turmoil and "drink delight of battle with their peers:"

> " How you speak !
> Did you but know the city's usuries,
> And felt them knowingly: the art o' the court,
> As hard to leave as keep; whose top to climb
> Is certain falling, or so slippery, that
> The fear's as bad as falling: the toil o' the war,
> A pain that only seems to seek out danger
> I' the name of fame and honour; which dies i' the search,
> And hath as oft a slanderous epitaph
> As record of fair act; nay, many times
> Doth ill deserve by doing well; what's worse,
> Must court'sy at the censure.—O boys! this story
> The world may read in me."

Amid these surroundings two personages have grown up whom Shakespeare would have us regard as beings of a loftier order.

He has taken all possible pains, from the very first scene of the play, to inspire the spectator with the highest conception of Posthumus. One nobleman speaks of him to another in terms such as, in bygone days, the poet had applied to Henry Percy:

> " He liv'd in court
> (Which rare it is to do) most prais'd, most lov'd;
> A sample to the youngest, to the more mature

> A glass that feated them; and to the graver
> A child that guided dotards."

A little farther on, Iachimo says of him to Imogen (i. 6):

> " He sits 'mongst men like a descended god;
> He hath a kind of honour sets him off
> More than a mortal seeming;"

and finally, at the close of the play (v. 5), " He was the best of all, amongst the rar'st of good ones "—an appreciation which it is a pity Iachimo did not arrive at a little sooner, as it might have prevented him from committing his villainies. Shakespeare throws into relief the dignity and repose of Posthumus, and his self-possession when the king denounces and banishes him. We see that he obeys because he regards it as unavoidable, though he has set at naught the king's will in relation to Imogen. In the compulsory haste of his leave-taking, he shows himself penetrated with a sense of his inferiority to her, and appeals to us by the way in which he tempers the loftiness of his bearing towards the outer world with a graceful humility towards his wife. It is rather surprising that he never for a moment seems to think of carrying Imogen with him into exile. This passivity is probably explained by her reluctance to take any step not absolutely forced upon her, that should render more difficult an eventual reconciliation. He will wait for better times, and long and hope for them.

As he is on the point of departure, Cloten forces himself upon him, insults and challenges him. He remains unruffled, ignores the challenge, contemptuously turns his back upon the oaf, and calmly leaves him to entertain the courtiers with boasts of his own valour and the cowardice of Posthumus, well knowing that no one will believe him.

The character, then, is well sketched out. But his mediæval fable compelled Shakespeare to introduce traits which, in the light of our humaner age, seem inconsistent and inadmissible. No man with any decency of feeling would in our days make such a wager as his; no man would give a stranger, and one, moreover, who is to all appearance a vain and quite unscrupulous woman-hunter, the warmest and most insistent letter of recommendation to his wife; and still less would any one give the same man an unwritten license to employ every means in his power to shake her virtue, simply in order to enjoy his discomfiture when all his arts shall have failed. And even if we could forgive or excuse such conduct in Posthumus, we cannot possibly extend our tolerance to his easy credulity when Iachimo boasts of his conquest, his insane fury against Imogen, and the base falsehood of the letter he sends her in order to facilitate Pisanio's murderous task. Even in the worst of cases we do not admit a man's right to have a woman assassinated because she has forgotten her love for him. They

2 R

thought otherwise in the days of the Renaissance; they did not look so closely into the plots of the old *novelle*, and were content, in the domain of romance, with traditional views of right and duty.

Nevertheless, Shakespeare has done what he could to mitigate the painful impression produced by Posthumus's conduct. Long before he knows that Iachimo has deceived him, he repents of his cruel deed, bitterly deplores that Pisanio has (as he thinks) obeyed him, and speaks in the warmest terms of Imogen's worth. He says, for instance (v. 4):

> "For Imogen's dear life take mine; and though
> 'Tis not so dear, yet 'tis a life."

He imposes upon himself the sternest penance. He comes to England with the Roman army, and then, nameless and disguised as a peasant, fights against the invaders. Together with Belarius and the king's sons, he is instrumental in staying the flight of the Britons, freeing Cymbeline, who has already been taken prisoner, winning the battle, and saving the kingdom. This done, he once more assumes his Roman garb, and seeks death at the hands of his countrymen, whose saviour he has been. He is taken prisoner and brought before the king, when all is cleared up.

From the moment he sets foot on English ground, there is in his course of action a more high-pitched and overstrained idealism than we are apt to find in Shakespeare's heroes—a craving for self-imposed expiation. Still the character fails to strike us as the perfect whole the poet would fain make of it. Posthumus impresses us, not as a favourite of the gods, but as a man whose penitence is as unbridled and excessive as his blind passion.

Far other is the case of Imogen. In her perfection is indeed attained. She is the noblest and most adorable womanly figure Shakespeare has ever drawn, and at the same time the most various. He has drawn spiritual women before her—Desdemona, Cordelia—but the secret of their being could be expressed in two words. He has also drawn brilliant women—Beatrice, Rosalind —whereas Imogen is not brilliant at all. Nevertheless she is designed and depicted as incomparable among her sex—" she is alone the Arabian bird." We see her in the most various situations, and she is equal to them all. We see her exposed to trial after trial, each harder than the last, and she emerges from them all, not only scatheless, but with her rare and enchanting qualities thrown into ever stronger relief.

At the very outset she gives proof of perfect self-command in her relation to her weak and passionate father, her false and venomous stepmother. The treasure of tenderness that fills her soul betrays itself in her parting from Posthumus, in her passionate regret that she could not give him one kiss more, and in the fervour with which she reproaches Pisanio for having left the shore before his master's ship had quite sunk below the horizon. During his absence her thoughts are unceasingly fixed on him. She repels with firmness the advances of her clownish wooer, Cloten. Brought face to face with Iachimo, she first receives him graciously, then sees through him at once when he begins to speak ill of Posthumus, and finally treats him with princely dignity when he has excused his offensive speeches as nothing but an ill-timed jest.

Next comes the bedroom scene, in which she falls asleep, and Iachimo, as she slumbers, paints for us her exquisite purity. Then we have her disdainful dismissal of Cloten; her reception of the letter from Posthumus; her calm confronting (as it seems) of certain death; her exquisite communion with her brothers; her death-like sleep and horrorstruck awakening beside the body which she takes to be her husband's; her denunciations of Pisanio as the supposed murderer; and, finally, the moment of reunion— all scenes which are pearls of Shakespeare's art, the rarest jewels in his diadem, never outshone in the poetry of any nation.

He depicts her as born for happiness, but early inured to suffering, and therefore calm and collected. When Posthumus is banished, she acquiesces in the separation; she will live in the memory of her love. Every one commiserates her; herself, she scarcely complains. She wishes no evil to her enemies; at the end, when the detestable queen is dead, she laments her father's bereavement, little dreaming that nothing but the death of the murderess could have saved her father's life.

Only one relation in life can stir her to passionate utterance— her relation to Posthumus. When she takes leave of him she says (i. 2):

> "You must be gone;
> And I shall here abide the hourly shot
> Of angry eyes; not comforted to live,
> But that there is this jewel in the world,
> That I may see again."

And to his farewell she replies:

> "Nay, stay a little.
> Were you but riding forth to air yourself,
> Such parting were too petty."

When he is gone she cries:

> "There cannot be a pinch in death
> More sharp than this is."

Her father's upbraidings leave her cold:

> "I am senseless of your wrath; a touch more rare
> Subdues all pangs, all fears."

To his continued reproaches she only replies with a rapturous eulogy of Posthumus:

> "He is
> A man worth any woman; overbuys me
> Almost the sum he pays."

And her passion deepens after her husband's departure. She envies the handkerchief he has kissed; she laments that she could not watch his receding ship; she would have "broke her eye-strings" to see the last of it. He has been torn away from her while she had yet "most pretty things to say;" how she would think of him and beg him to think of her at three fixed hours of every day; and she would have made him swear not to forget her for any "she of Italy." He was gone before she could give him the parting kiss which she had set " betwixt two charming words."

She is devoid of ambition. She would willingly exchange her royal station for idyllic happiness in a country retreat such as that for which Shakespeare is now longing. When Posthumus has left her she exclaims (i. 2):

> "Would I were
> A neatherd's daughter, and my Leonatus
> Our neighbour shepherd's son!"

In other words, she sighs for the lot in life which we shall find in *The Winter's Tale* apportioned to Prince Florizel and Princess Perdita. In the same spirit she reflects before the coming of Iachimo (i. 7):

> " Blessed be those,
> How mean soe'er, that have their honest wills,
> Which seasons comfort."

And then when Iachimo ("little Iago") slanders Posthumus to her, as he will presently slander her to Posthumus, how different is her conduct from her husband's! She has turned pale at his entrance, at Pisanio's mere announcement of a nobleman from Rome with letters from her lord. To Iachimo's first whispers of Posthumus's infidelity, she merely answers:

> "My lord, I fear,
> Has forgot Britain."

But when Iachimo proceeds to draw a gloating picture of her husband's debaucheries, and offers himself as an instrument for her revenge upon the faithless one, she replies with the exclamation:

> "What, ho, Pisanio!"

She summons her servant; she has seen all she wants of this Italian.

Even when she says nothing she fills the scene, as when,

having gone to rest, she lies in bed reading, dismisses her attendant, closes the book and falls asleep. How wonderfully has Shakespeare brought home to us the atmosphere of purity in this sleeping-chamber by means of the passionate words he places in the mouth of Iachimo (ii. 2):

> "Cytherea,
> How bravely thou becom'st thy bed! fresh lily,
> And whiter than the sheets! That I might touch!
> But kiss; one kiss!—Rubies unparagon'd,
> How dearly they do't!—'Tis her breathing that
> Perfumes the chamber thus."

The influence of this scene — interpreting as it does the overpowering impression that emanates even from the material surroundings of exquisite womanhood, the almost magical glamour of purity and loveliness combined — may in all probability be traced in the rapture expressed by Goethe's Faust when he and Mephistopheles enter Gretchen's chamber. Iachimo is here the love-sick Faust and the malign Mephistopheles in one. Remember Faust's outburst:

> "Willkommen, süsser Dämmerschein,
> Der Du dies Heiligthum durchwebst
> Ergreif mein Herz, du süsse Liebespein,
> Die Du vom Thau der Hoffnung schmachtend lebst!
> Wie athmet hier Gefühl der Stille."

Despite the difference between the two situations, there can be no doubt that the one has influenced the other.[1]

As though in ecstasy over this incomparable creation, Shakespeare once more bursts forth into song. Once and again he pays her lyric homage; here in Cloten's morning song, "Hark, hark, the lark at heaven's gate sings," and afterwards in the dirge her brother's chant over what they believe to be her dead body.

Shakespeare makes her lose her self-control for the first time when Cloten ventures to speak disparagingly of her husband, calling him a "base wretch," a beggar "foster'd with cold dishes, with scraps o' the court," "a hilding for a livery," and so on.

---

[1] Scarcely any poet has been more followed in modern times than Shakespeare. We have already drawn attention to the by no means accidental resemblances in Voltaire, Goethe, and Schiller, and we have further instances. Schiller's *Die Jungfrau von Orleans* is markedly indebted to the first part of *Henry VI*. The scene between the maid and the Duke of Burgundy (ii. 10) is fashioned after the corresponding scene in Shakespeare (iii. 3), and that between the maid and her father in Schiller (iv. 11) answers to Shakespeare's (v. 4). The apothecary in Oehlenschläger's *Aladdin* is borrowed from the apothecary in *Romeo and Juliet*. In Björnstjerne's Björnson's *Maria Stuart* (ii. 2) Ruthven rises from a sick bed to totter into the conspirators with Knox, and take the more eager share in the plot to murder Rizzio, as the sick Ligarius makes his way to Brutus (*Julius Cæsar*, ii. 1) to join the conspiracy to murder Cæsar.

Then she bursts forth into words of more than masculine violence, and almost as opprobrious as Cloten's own (ii. 3):

> " Profane fellow !
> Wert thou the son of Jupiter, and no more
> But what thou art besides, thou wert too base
> To be his groom : thou wert dignified enough,
> Even to the point of envy, if 't were made
> Comparative for your virtues, to be styl'd
> The under-hangman of his kingdom, and hated
> For being preferr'd so well."

It is in the same flush of anger that she speaks the words which first sting Cloten to comic fury, and then inspire him with his hideous design. Leonatus' meanest garment, she says, is " dearer in her respect " than Cloten's whole person—an expression which rankles in the mind of the noxious dullard, until at last it drives him out of his senses.

New charm and new nobility breathe around her in the scene in which she receives the letter from her husband, designed to lure her to her death. First all her enthusiasm, and then all her passion, blaze forth and burn with the clearest flame. Hear this (iii. 2):

> " *Pisanio.* Madam, here is a letter from my lord.
> *Imogen.* Who? thy lord? that is my lord : Leonatus.
> O learn'd indeed were that astronomer
> That knew the stars as I his characters ;
> He'd lay the future open.—You good gods,
> Let what is here contain'd relish of love,
> Of my lord's health, of his content,—yet not,
> That we two are asunder,—let that grieve him :
> Some griefs are medicinable ; that is one of them,
> For it doth physic love :—of his content,
> All but in that !—Good wax, thy leave.—Bless'd be
> You bees, that make these locks of counsel ! "

She reads that her lord appoints a meeting-place at Milford Haven, little dreaming that she is summoned there only to be murdered :

> " O for a horse with wings !—Hear'st thou, Pisanio ?
> He is at Milford Haven : read, and tell me
> How far 'tis thither. If one of mean affairs
> May plod it in a week, why may not I
> Glide thither in a day ?—Then, true Pisanio,
> (Who long'st, like me, to see thy lord ; who long'st,—
> O let me 'bate !—but not like me ;—yet long'st,—
> But in a fainter kind :—O not like me,
> For mine's beyond beyond) say, and speak thick,
> (Love's counsellor should fill the bores of hearing,
> To the smothering of the sense), how far it is
> To this same blessed Milford : and, by the way,

Tell me how Wales was made so happy as
To inherit such a haven : but, first of all,
How we may steal from hence ; and, for the gap
That we shall make in time, from our hencegoing
And our return, to excuse : but first, how get hence :
Why should excuse be born or e'er begot ?
We'll talk of that hereafter. . . . Prithee, speak,
How many score of miles may we well ride
'Twixt hour and hour ?
 Pis. One score, 'twixt sun and sun,
Madam's, enough for you : [*Aside*] and too much too.
 Imo. Why, one that rode to 's execution, man,
Could never go so slow ; I have heard of riding wagers,
Where horses have been nimbler than the sands
That run i' the clock's behalf. But this is foolery :
Go bid my woman feign a sickness."

These outbursts are beyond all praise; but quite on a level
with them stands her answer when Pisanio shows her Posthumus's letter to him, denouncing her with the foulest epithets, and
the whole extent of her misfortune becomes clear to her. It is
then she utters the words (iii. 4) which Sören Kierkegaard admired so deeply :

" False to his bed ! what is it to be false ?
To lie in watch there and to think on him ?
To weep 'twixt clock and clock ? if sleep charge nature
To break it with a fearful dream of him
And cry myself awake ? that's false to's bed, is it ? "

It is very characteristic that she never for a moment believes
that Posthumus can really think it possible she should have given
herself to another. She seeks another explanation for his inexplicable conduct :

" Some jay of Italy,
Whose mother was her painting, hath betray'd him."

This is scant comfort to her, however, and she implores
Pisanio, who would spare her, to strike, for life has now lost all
value for her. As she is baring her breast to the blow, she speaks
these admirable words :

" Come, here's my heart :
Something's afore 't :—soft, soft ! we'll no defence ;
Obedient as the scabbard.—What is here ?
The scriptures of the loyal Leonatus,
All turn'd to heresy ? Away, away,
Corrupters of my faith ! you shall no more
Be stomachers to my heart."

With the same intentness, or rather with the same tenderness,
has Shakespeare, all through the play, imbued himself with her
spirit, never losing touch of her for a moment, but lovingly filling

in trait upon trait, until at last he represents her, half in jest, as the sun of the play. The king says in the concluding scene:

> "See,
> Posthumus anchors upon Imogen;
> And she, like harmless lightning, throws her eye
> On him, her brothers, me, her master, hitting
> Each object with a joy: the counterchange
> Is severally in all."

Early in the play Imogen expressed the wish that she were a neatherd's daughter, and Leonatus a shepherd's son. Later, when, clad in manly attire, she chances upon the lonely forest cave in which her brothers dwell, she feels completely at ease in their neighbourhood, and in the primitive life for which she has always longed—as Shakespeare longs for it now. The brothers are happy with her, and she with them. She says (Act iii. sc. 6).

> "Pardon me, gods!
> I'd change my sex to be companions with them,
> Since Leonatus's false."

And later (Act iv. sc. 2):

> "These are kind creatures. Gods! what lies I have heard!
> Our courtiers say all's savage but at court."

Belarius exclaims in the same spirit (Act iii. sc. 3):

> "Oh, this life
> Is nobler than attending for a check,
> Richer than doing nothing for a bauble,
> Prouder than rustling in unpaid for silk."

The princes, in whom the royal soldierly blood asserts itself in a thirst for adventure, reply in a contrary strain:

> "*Guiderius.*   Haply this life is best
> If quiet life be best; sweeter to you
> That have a sharper known; well corresponding
> With your stiff age; but unto us it is
> A call of ignorance, travelling a-bed;
> A prison for a debtor, that not dares
> To stride a limit."

And his brother adds:

> "What should we speak of
> When we are as old as you? When we shall hear
> The rain and wind beat dark December.
> . . . . We have seen nothing;
> We are beastly."

Shakespeare has diffused a marvellous poetry throughout this forest idyl; a matchless freshness and primitive charm pervade the whole. In this period of detestation for the abortions of culture, the poet has beguiled himself by picturing a life far from all civilisation, an innately noble youth in a natural state, and he depicts two young men who have seen nothing of life and never looked upon the face of woman; whose days have been passed in the pursuit of game, and who, like the Homeric warriors, prepared and cooked with their own hands the spoil procured by their bows and arrows. But their race shines through, and they prove of better stock than we should have looked for in the sons of the contemptible Cymbeline. Their instincts all tend towards the noble and princely ideal.

In the Spanish drama, which twenty-five years later received such an impetus under Calderon, it became a leading motive to portray young men and women brought up in solitude without having seen a single being of the other sex, and without knowledge of their rank and parentage. Thus in Calderon's *Life is a Dream* (*La vida es sueño*) of 1635, we are shown a king's son leading a solitary life in utter ignorance of his royal descent. He is seized by a passionate love on his first meeting with mankind, and is crudely violent in the face of any opposition, but, like the princes in *Cymbeline*, the seeds of majesty are lying dormant and the princely instincts spring readily into life. In the play *En esta vida todo as verdad y todo es mentira* of 1647, a faithful servant carries off the emperor's son from the pursuit of a tyrant, and seeks refuge in a mountain cave of Sicily. He also takes charge of a base-born son of the tyrant, and the two lads are brought up together. They see no one but their foster-father, are clad in the skins of animals and live upon game and fruit. When the tyrant appears to claim his child and slay the emperor's son, none can tell him which is which, and neither threats nor entreaties can prevail upon the servant to yield the secret. Here, as in *Life is a Dream*, the first glimpse of a woman rouses instant love in both young men. In *A Daughter of the Air* (*La hija del ayre*) of 1664, Semiramis is brought up by an old priest, as Miranda is by Prospero in *The Tempest*. Like all these beings reared in solitude remote from the turmoil of life, Semiramis nourishes an impatient longing to be out in the world. In the two plays of 1672, *Eco y Narciso* and *El monstruo de los jardines*, Calderon employs a variation of the same idea. Narcissus in the one and Achilles in the other are brought up in solitude in order that we may see all the emotions aroused, especially those of love and jealousy, in a being so primitive that it cannot even name its own sensations.

In this episode, and throughout this last period of his poetry, Shakespeare entered a realm which the imagination of the Latin races immediately seized upon and made their own. But in all their dramatic poetry of this nature they never surpassed that of the English poet.

He refrained entirely from the erotic in this idyl, and instead of the demands of a lover's passion, he portrayed unconscious brotherly love offered to a sister disguised as a boy. Imogen and the two strong-natured, high-minded youths dwell charmingly together, but their companionship is destroyed in the bud when Imogen, after having drunk the narcotic supplied by the physician to the queen instead of poison, lies as one dead. A gently touching element is introduced into this moving play when the two brothers bear her forth and sing over her bier. We witness a burial without rites or ceremonies, requiems or church formalities, an attempt being made to fill their place with spon-taneous natural symbols. A similar attempt was made by Goethe in the double chorus sung over Mignon's body in *Wilhelm Meister* (Book VIII. chap. viii.). Imogen's head is laid towards the east, and the brothers sing over her the beautiful duet which their father had taught them at the burial of their mother. Its rhythm contains the germ of all that later became Shelley's poetry.

The first verse runs :

> " Fear no more the heat of sun,
> Nor the furious winter's rages ;
> Thou thy worldly task hast done,
> Home art gone and ta'en thy wages :
> Golden lads and girls all must
> As chimney-sweeper, come to dust." [1]

The concluding verses, in which the voices are heard first in solo and then in duets, form a wonderful harmony of metric and poetic art.

This idyl, in which he found and expressed his reawakened love for the heart of Nature, has been worked out by Shakespeare with especial tenderness. He by no means intended to represent a flight from scorn of mankind as a thing desirable in itself, but merely to depict solitude as a refuge for the weary, and existence in the country as a happiness for those who have done with life.

As a drama, *Cymbeline* contains more of the nature of intrigue than any earlier play. There is no little skill displayed in the way Pisanio misleads Cloten by showing him Posthumus's letter, and where Imogen takes the headless Cloten, attired in Posthumus's clothes, for her murdered husband. The mythological dream vision seems to have been interpolated for use at court festivities. The explanatory tablet left by Jupiter, and the king's joyful out-burst in the last scene, " Am I a mother to the birth of three ? " prove that even at his fullest and ripest Shakespeare was never securely possessed of an unfailing good taste, but such trifling errors of judgment are more than counterbalanced by the over-flowing richness of the fairylike poetry of this drama.

---

[1] It is somewhat remarkable that Guiderius and Arviragus should know anything about chimney-sweepers.

XIX

WE are now about to see Shakespeare enthralled and reinspired
by the glamour of fairy tale and romance.

The *Winter's Tale* was first printed in the Folio of 1623, but,
as we have already mentioned, an entry in Dr. Simon Forman's
diary informs us that he saw it played at the Globe Theatre on
the 15th of May 1611. A notice in the official diary of Sir Henry
Herbert, Master of the Revels, goes to prove that at that date the
play was quite new. "For the king's players. An olde playe
called Winter's Tale, formerly allowed of by Sir George Bucke,
and likewyse by mee on Mr. Hemmings his word that nothing
profane was added or reformed, though the allowed book was
missinge; and therefore I returned itt without fee this 19th of
August 1623." The Sir George Bucke mentioned here did not
receive his official appointment as censor until August 1610.
Therefore it was probably one of the first performances of the
Winter's Tale at which Forman was present in the spring
of 1611.

We have already drawn attention to Ben Jonson's little fling
at the play in the introduction to his *Bartholomew's Fair* in 1614.

The play was founded on a romance of Robert Greene's,
published in 1588 under the title of "Pandosto, the Triumph
of Time," and was re-named half-a-century later "The Historie
of Dorastus and Fawnia." So popular was it, that it was printed
again and again. We know of at least seventeen editions, and in
all likelihood there were more.

Shakespeare had adapted Lodge's *Rosalynde* in his earlier
pastoral play, *As You Like It*, very soon after its publication
in 1590. It is significant that this other tale, with its peculiar
blending of the pathetic and idyllic, should only now, though it
must have long been familiar to him, strike him as suitable for
dramatic treatment. Karl Elze's theory that Shakespeare had
adapted the story in some earlier work, which Greene had in
his mind when he wrote his famous and violent accusation of
plagiarism, cannot be considered as more than a random con-

jecture. Greene's attack was sufficiently accounted for by that remodelling and adaptation of older works which was practised by the young poet from the very first, and it clearly aimed at *Henry VI.*

Shakespeare, who could not, of course, use Greene's title, called his play *A Winter's Tale;* a title which would convey an impression, at that time, of a serious and touching or exciting story, and he plainly strove for a dream-like and fantastic effect in his work. Mamillius says, when he begins his little story (Act ii. sc. 1), "A sad tale's best for winter," and in three different places the romantic impossibility of the plot is impressed upon the audience. In the description of the discovery of Perdita we are warned that "this news, which is called true, is so like an old tale, that the verity of it is in strong suspicion" (Act v. sc. 2).

The geographical extravagances are those of the romance; it was Greene who surrounded Bohemia with the sea and transferred the Oracle of Delphi to the Island of Delphos. But Shakespeare contributed the anachronisms; it was he who made the oracle exist contemporaneously with Russia as an empire, who made Hermione a daughter of a Russian Emperor and caused her statue to be executed by Giulio Romano. The religion of the play is decidedly vague, the very characters themselves seem to forget at times what they are, one moment figuring as Christians, and the next worshipping Jupiter and Proserpina. In the same play in which a pilgrimage is made to Delphi to obtain an oracle, a shepherd lad says there is "but one puritan amongst them, and he sings songs to hornpipes" (Act iv. sc. 2). All this is unintentional, no doubt, but it greatly adds to the general fairy tale effect.

We do not know why Shakespeare transposed the localities. In Greene's book the tragedy of the play occurs in Bohemia, and the idyllic part in Sicily; in the drama the situations are reversed. It might be that Bohemia seemed to him a more suitable country for the exposure of an infant than the better known and more thickly populated island of the Mediterranean.

All the main features of the play are drawn from Greene, first and foremost the king's unreasonable jealousy because his wife, at his own urgent request, invites Polixenes to prolong his stay and speaks to him in friendly fashion. Among the grounds of jealousy enumerated by Greene was the naïve and dramatically unsuitable one that Bellaria, in her desire to please and obey her husband by showing every attention to his guest, frequently entered his bed-chamber to ascertain if anything was needed there.[1] Greene's queen really dies when she is cast off by the king in his jealous madness, but this tragic episode, which

---

[1] *The Historie of Dorastus and Fawnia.* Shakespeare's Library. T. P. Collins. Vol. i. p. 7.

would have deprived him of his reconciliation scene, was not adopted by Shakespeare. He did, however, include and amplify the death of Mamillius, their little son, who pines away from sorrow for the king's harsh treatment of his mother. Mamillius is one of the gems of the play; a finer sketch of a gifted, large-hearted child could not be. We can but feel that Shakespeare, in drawing this picture of the young boy and his early death, must once again have had his own little son in his mind, and that it was of him he was thinking when he makes Polixenes say of his young prince (Act i. sc. 2):

> " If at home, sir,
> He's all my exercise, my mirth, my matter;
> Now my sworn friend, and then mine enemy;
> My parasite, my soldier, statesman, all:
> He makes a July's day short as December;
> And with his varying childness, cures in me
> Thoughts that would thick my blood."
> *Leontes.* So stands this squire
> Offic'd with me."

The father's tone towards little Mamillius is at first a jesting one.

> " Mamillius, art thou my boy?"
> *Mamillius.* Ay, my good lord.
> *Leontes.* Why, that's my bawcock. What, hast smutch'd thy nose?
> They say it is a copy out of mine."

Later, when jealousy grows upon him, he cries:

> " Come, sir page,
> Look on me with your welkin eye: sweet villain!
> Most dear'st! my collop!—Can thy dam?—may'st be?"

The children of the French poets of the middle and end of that century were never childlike. They would have made a little prince destined to a sad and early death talk solemnly and maturely, like little Joas in Racine's *Athelie;* but Shakespeare had no hesitation in letting his princeling talk like a real child. He says to the lady-in-waiting who offers to play with him:

> " No, I'll none of you.
> 1*st Lady.* Why, my sweet lord?
> *Mamillius.* You'll kiss me hard, and speak to me as if
> I were a baby still."

He announces that he likes another lady better because her eyebrows are black and fine; and he knows that eyebrows are most becoming when they are shaped like a half-moon, and look as though drawn with a pen.

" *2nd Lady.* Who taught you this?
    Mamillius. I learn'd it out of women's faces. Pray, now
What colour are your eyebrows?
    1st Lady. Blue, my lord.
    Mam. Nay, that's a mock; I have seen a lady's nose
That has been blue, but not her eyebrows."

The tale he is about to tell is cut short by the entrance of the
furious king.

During the trial scene, which forms a parallel to that in *Henry
VIII.*, tidings are brought of the prince's death (Act iii. sc. 1):

" ——whose honourable thoughts
(Thoughts too high for one so tender) cleft the heart
That could conceive a gross and foolish fire
Blemished his gracious dam."

In Greene's tale the death of the child causes that of his mother,
but in the play, where it follows immediately upon the king's
defiant rejection of the oracle, it effects a sudden revulsion of
feeling in him as a punishment direct from Heaven. Shakespeare
allowed Hermione to be merely reported dead because his mood at
this time required that the play should end happily. That Mami-
lius seems to pass entirely out of every one's memory is only
another proof of a fact we have already touched upon, namely,
Shakespeare's negligent style of work in these last years of his
working life. The poet, however, is careful to keep Hermione
well in mind; she is brought before us in the vision Antigonus
sees shortly before his death, and she is preserved during sixteen
years of solitude that she may be restored to us at the last. It is,
indeed, chiefly by her personality that the two markedly distinct
parts of this wasp-waisted play are held together.

Although, as in Pericles, there is more of an epic than a dramatic character about the work, it possesses a certain unity of tone
and feeling. As a painting may contain two comparatively unconnected groups which are yet united by a general harmony of
line and colouring, so, in this apparently disconnected plot, there
is an all-pervading poetic harmony which we may call the tone or
spirit of the play. Shakespeare was careful from the first that
its melancholy should not grow to such an incurable gloom as to
prevent our enjoyment of the charming scenes between Florizel and
Perdita at the sheep-shearing festival, or the thievish tricks of the
rascal Autolycus. The poet sought to make each chord of feeling
struck during the play melt away in the gentle strain of reconciliation at the close. If Hermione had returned to the king at once,
which would have been the most natural course of events, the play
would have ended with the third act. She therefore disappears,
finally returning to life and the embrace of the weeping Leontes
in the semblance of a statue.

Looked upon from a purely abstract point of view, as though it were a musical composition, the play might be considered in the light of a soul's history. Beginning with powerful emotions, suspense and dread; with terrible mistakes entailing deserved and undeserved suffering, it leads to a despair which in turn gradually yields to forgetfulness and levity ; but not lastingly. Once alone with its helpless grief and hopeless repentance, the heart still finds in its innermost sanctuary the memory which, death-doomed and petrified, has yet been faithfully guarded and cherished unscathed until, ransomed by tears, it consents to live once more. The play has its meaning and moral just as a symphony may have, neither more nor less. It would be absurd to seek for a psychological reason for Hermione's prolonged concealment. She reappears at the end because her presence is required, as the final chord is needed in music or the completing arabesque in a drawing.

Among Shakespeare's additions in the first part of the play we find the characters of the noble and resolute Paulina and her weakly good-natured husband. Paulina, who has been overlooked by both Mrs. Jameson and Heine in their descriptions of Shakespeare's feminine characters, is one of the most admirable and original figures he has put upon the stage. She has more courage than ten men, and possesses that natural eloquence and power of pathos which determined honesty and sound common sense can bestow upon a woman. She would go through fire and water for the queen whom she loves and trusts. She is untouched by sentimentality; there is as little of the erotic as there is of repugnance in her attitude towards her husband. Her treatment of the king's jealous frenzy reminds us of Emilia in *Othello*, but the resemblance ends there. In Paulina there is a vein of that rare metal which we only find in excellent women of this not essentially feminine type. We meet it again in the nineteenth century in the character of Christiana Oehlenschläger as we see it in Hauch's beautiful commemorative poem.

The rustic fête in the second part of the play, with the conversations between Florizel and Perdita, is entirely Shakespeare's work; above all is the diverting figure of Autolycus his own peculiar property.

In Greene's tale the king falls violently in love with his daughter when she is restored to him a grown woman, and he kills himself in despair when she is wedded to her lover. Shakespeare rejected this stupid and ugly feature ; his ending is all pure harmony.

Here, as in *Cymbeline*, we see the poet compelled by the nature of his theme to dwell upon the disastrous effects of jealousy. This is the third time he treats of such suspicions driving to madness. Othello was the first great example, then Posthumus, and now Leontes.

The case of Leontes is so far unique that no one has suggested causes of jealousy, nor slandered Hermione to him. His own coarse and foolish imaginings alone are to blame. This variation of the vice was evidently intended to darken the background against which womanly high-mindedness and blamelessness were to shine forth.

Mrs. Jameson has charmingly said that Hermione combines such rare virtues as "dignity without pride, love without passion, and tenderness without weakness." As queen, wife, and mother, there is a majestic lovableness about her, a grand and gracious simplicity, a natural self-control, the proverb, "Still waters run deep," being eminently applicable to her. Her gentle dignity contrasts well with Paulina's enthusiastic intrepidity, and her noble reticence with Paulina's free outspokenness. Her attitude and language during the trial scene are superb, far outshining Queen Katherine's on a similar occasion. Her nature, the ideal Englishwoman's nature, all meekness and submissiveness, rises in dignified protest. She is brief in her self-defence; life has no value for her since she has lost her husband's love, since her little son has been removed from her as though she were plague-stricken, and her new-born daughter "from her breast, the innocent milk in its most innocent mouth, haled out to murder." Her only desire is to vindicate her honour, yet the first words of this cruelly accused and shamefully treated woman are full of pity for the remorse which Leontes will some day suffer. Her language is that of innocent fortitude. When about to be taken to prison she says:

> "There's some ill planet reigns :
> I must be patient till the heavens look
> With an aspect more favourable.   Good my lords,
> I am not prone to weeping, as our sex
> Commonly are ; the want of which vain dew
> Perchance shall dry your pities : but I have
> That honourable grief lodged here which burns
> Worse than tears drown."

She bids her women not weep until she has deserved imprisonment; then indeed their tears will have cause to flow.

In the second half of the *Winter's Tale* we are surrounded by a fresh and charming country, and shown a picture of rustic happiness and well-being. No one was less influenced by the sentimental vagaries of the fantastic pastorals of the day than Shakespeare. He had drawn in Corin and Phebe, in *As You Like It*, an extremely natural, and therefore not particularly poetical, shepherd and shepherdess; and the herdsmen in the *Winter's Tale* are no beautiful languishing souls. They do not write sonnets and madrigals, but drink ale and eat pies and dance. The hostess serves her guests with a face that is "o' fire with labour and the thing she took to quench it." The clowns' heads are full of the prices of wool; they have no thought for roses and nightingales, and their simplicity is rather comical than touching. They are more than overmatched by the light-fingered Autolycus, who educates them by means of ballads, and eases them of their purses at the same time. He is a Jack-of-all-trades, has travelled the country with a monkey, been a process-server, bailiff, and servant to Prince Florizel; he has gone about with a puppet-show playing the Prodigal Son; finally, he marries a tinker's wife and settles down as a confirmed rogue. He is the clown of the piece—roguish, genial, witty, and always master of the situation. In spite of the fact that Shakespeare seized every opportunity to flout the lower classes, that he always gave a satirical and repellent picture of them as a mass, yet their natural wit, good sense, and kind-heartedness are always portrayed in his clowns with a sympathetic touch. Before his time, the buffoon was never an inherent part of the play; he came on and danced his jig without any connection with the plot, and was, in fact, merely intended to amuse the uneducated portion of the audience and make them laugh. Shakespeare was the first to incorporate him into the plot, and to endow him, not merely with the jester's wit, but with the higher faculties and feelings of the Fool in *Lear*, or the gay humour of the vagabond pedlar, Autolycus.

The clown in the *Winter's Tale* is the drollest and sharpest of knaves, and is employed to unravel the knot in the story. He it is who transports the old shepherd and his son from Bohemia to the court of King Leontes in Sicily.

The ludicrous features of rustic society, however, are quite overpowered by the kind-heartedness which stamps every word coming from the lips of these worthy country folk, and prepares us for the appearance of Perdita in their midst.

She has been adopted out of compassion, and, with her gold, proves a source of prosperity to her adoptive parents. Thus she grows up without feeling the pressure of poverty or servitude. She wins the prince's heart by the beauty of her youth, and when we first see her she is attired in all her splendour as queen of a rural festival. Modest and charming as she is, she shows the courage of a true princess in face of the difficulties and hardships she must encounter for the sake of her love.

She is one of Shakespeare's cherished children, and he has endowed her with his favourite trait—a distaste for anything artificial or unnatural. Not even to improve the flowers in her garden will she employ the art of special means of cultivation. She will not have the rich blooms of " carnations and streaked gillyflowers " there; they do not thrive and she will not plant them. When Polixenes asks why she disdains them, she replies (Act iv. sc. 3):

> " For I have heard it said
> There is an art which in their piedness shares
> With great creating nature."

To which Polixenes makes the profound response :

> "Say there be ;
> Yet nature is made better by no mean,
> But nature makes that mean : so over that art
> Which you say adds to nature is an art
> That nature makes.   You see, sweet maid, we marry
> A gentler scion to the wildest stock,
> And make conceive a bark of baser kind
> By bud of nobler race ; this is an art
> Which does mend nature,—change it rather ; but
> The art itself is nature."

These are the most profound and subtle words that could well be spoken on the subject of the relations between nature and culture ; the clearest repudiation of that gospel of naturalism against which the figure of Caliban and the ridicule cast upon Gonzalo's Utopia in *The Tempest* are protests.   Perdita herself is one of those chosen flowers which are the product of that true culture which preserves and ennobles nature.

They are also words of genuine wisdom on the relative positions of nature and art.   Shakespeare's art was that of nature itself, and in this short speech we possess his æsthetic confession of faith.

His ideal was a poetry which strayed neither in matter nor manner from what Hamlet calls "the modesty of nature."   Although he did not wholly succeed in escaping its infection, Shakespeare invariably pursued the artificial taste of the times with gibes.   From the days when he made merry at the expense of Euphuisms in *Love's Labour's Lost* and Falstaff, until now, when he puts such affectedly poetical language in the mouths of his courtiers in the *Winter's Tale*, he has always ridiculed it vigorously.

In the first scene of the play Camillo says in praise of Mamillius :

> "They that went on crutches before he was born desire still their life to see him a man.

Whereupon Archidamus sarcastically inquires :

> " Would they else be content to die ? "

and Camillo is forced to laughingly confess :

> " Yes, if there were no other excuse why they should desire to live."

Still more absurd is the style in which the Third Gentleman describes, in the last scene of the play, the meeting between the king and his long-lost daughter and the aspect of the spectators. He says of Paulina :

"She had one eye declined for the loss of her husband, another elevated that the oracle was fulfilled.[1]

This comical diction reaches a climax in the following expressions:

"One of the prettiest touches of all, and that *which angled for mine eyes, caught water though not the fish*, was when at the relation of the queen's death, with the manner how she came to't, bravely confessed and lamented by the king, how attentiveness wounded his daughter; till, from one sign of dolour to another, she did, with an ' Alas,' I would fain say, *bleed tears*, for I am sure my heart wept blood.   Who was most marble there changed colour; some swooned, all sorrowed: if all the world could have seen 't *the woe had been universal.*"

That Shakespeare's æsthetic sense did not sanction such expressions as these of the Third Gentleman scarcely needs stating. Perdita's language is that of nature itself.   So great is her dislike of artificiality, that she will not even plant gardener's flowers in her garden, saying:

> "No more than were I painted I would wish
> This youth should say 'twere well, and only therefore
> Desire to breed by me."

Nowhere is Shakespeare's knowledge of nature more charmingly displayed than in her speeches.   It is not only the poetic expression that is so wonderful in Perdita's distribution of flowers; it is the intimacy shown with their habits.   She says (Act iv. sc. 3):

> "Hot lavender, mints, savory, marjoram;
> The marigold, that goes to bed wi' the sun
> And with him rises weeping."

How well she knows that in England the daffodils bloom as early as February and March, while the swallow does not come till April:

> "—— O Proserpina,
> For the flowers now that, frighted, thou lett'st fall
> From Dis's waggon ! daffodils,
> That come before the swallow dares, and take
> The winds of March with beauty; violets dim,
> But sweeter than the lids of Juno's eyes
> Or Cytherea's breath; pale primroses,
> That die unmarried, ere they can behold
> Bright Phœbus in his strength—a malady
> Most incident to maids; bold oxlips and

---

[1] Julius Lange positively asserts that these expressions are not to be taken as an intentional jest on the part of Shakespeare, but are to be regarded as part of his style ("said in sober earnest," to quote his own words), and he makes them the pretext of an attack upon the "then, as now, idolised Shakespeare—in whose works, after all, we find more high-sounding and highly-coloured words than any meaning or real understanding of life." (Tilskueren, 1895, p. 699.)

> The crown imperial ; lilies of all kinds,
> The flower-de-luce being one ! Oh, these I lack
> To make you garlands of, and my sweet friend,
> To strew him o'er and o'er !
>   *Florizel.* What, like a corse ?
>   *Perdita.* No, like a bank for love to lie and play on :
> Not like a corse ; or if, not to be buried,
> But quick and in mine arms." . . .

Florizel's answer describes her with a lover's eloquence :

> " What you do
> Still betters what is done.   When you speak, sweet,
> I'd have you do it ever : when you sing,
> I'd have you buy and sell so, so give alms,
> Pray so, and, for the ordering your affairs,
> To sing them too." . . .

Her charm is equalled by her pride and resolution.   When the king threatens to have her " beauty scratched with briars " if she dares retain her hold upon his son, although she believes all is lost, she says :

> " I was not much afraid ; for once or twice
> I was about to speak and tell him plainly,
> The self-same sun that shines upon his court
> Hides not his visage from our cottage, but
> Looks on alike." . . .

The delineation of the love between Florizel and Perdita is marked by certain features not to be found in Shakespeare's youthful works, but which reappear with Ferdinand and Miranda in *The Tempest*.   There is a certain remoteness from the world about it, a tenderness for those who are still yearning and hoping for happiness and a renunciation of any expectation as far as himself is concerned.   He stands outside and beyond it all now.   In the old days the poet stood on a level, as it were, with the love he was portraying ; now he looks upon it from above with a fatherly eye.

As in *Cymbeline*, the court is here placed in contrast with idyllic life, and shown as the abode of cruelty, stupidity, and vice. Even the better of the two kings, Polixenes, is rough and harsh, and Leontes, whom we are not to look upon as criminal, but only as misled by his miserable suspicions, offers a true picture of the princely attitude and princely behaviour of the time of the Renaissance, during the sixteenth century in Italy and about a century later in England.   It was with good reason that Belarius said in *Cymbeline* (Act iii. sc. 3) :

> " And we will fear no poison, which attends
> In place of greater state."

We see that the thoughts of the king immediately turn to poison when he believes that his wife has deceived him, and we also see that the courtier in whom he confides has all the means ready to hand (Act i. sc. 2):

> "And thou . . .
> . . . might'st bespice a cup,
> To give mine enemy a lasting wink;
> Which draught to me were cordial.
>   *Camillo.*   Sir, my lord,
> I could do this, and that with no rash potion,
> But with a lingering dram that should not work
> Maliciously like poison."

When, to escape committing this crime, Camillo takes flight with Polixenes, and the king has to be content with wreaking his vengeance on the hapless Hermione and her infant, he returns again and again to the thought of having them burned:

> "Say that she were gone,
> Given to the fire, a moiety of my rest
> Might come to me again."

Then the command with regard to the child:

> "Hence with it, and, together with the dam,
> Commit them to the fire!" (Act ii. sc. 3).

Paulina shall share their fate for daring to oppose him:

> "I'll ha' thee burnt!"

When she is gone, he repeats his order for the burning of the infant·

> "Take it hence
> And see it instantly consumed with fire. . . .
> . . . If thou refuse,
> And wilt encounter with my wrath, say so;
> The bastard brains with these my proper hands
> Shall I dash out.   Go, take it to the fire!"

We can see that Shakespeare had no intention of allowing the drama to become mawkish by giving too free scope to the humours of a pastoral play.

The resemblance between the sufferings of the infant Perdita, put ashore on the coast of Bohemia during a tempest, and those of the infant Marina, born during a storm at sea, is accentuated by lines which markedly recall a well-known passage in *Pericles.* In the *Winter's Tale* we have (Act iii. sc. 3):

> "Thou'rt like to have
> A lullaby too rough: I never saw
> The heavens so dim by day.   A savage clamour!" [1]

---

[1] In *Pericles:*
> "For thou'rt the rudliest welcome to this world
> That e'er was prince's child."

The impression designedly produced upon the audience, that all this is not serious earnest, enables Shakespeare to approach more nearly to tragic dissonance than would otherwise be permissible in a work of this kind. The atmosphere of fairy tale, so skilfully breathed here and there throughout the play, carries with it a certain playfulness of expression which gives a touch of raillery to incidents which would otherwise be horrible. Playfulness it is, and we once more obtain a glimpse of this quality which has so long deserted Shakespeare. It would be difficult to find a more roguish bit of drollery than the old shepherd's monologue on finding the child (Act iii. sc. 3):

"A pretty one; a very pretty one: sure, some 'scape: though I am not bookish, yet I can read waiting-gentlewoman in the 'scape. This has been some stair-work, some trunk-work, some behind-door-work: they were warmer that got this than the poor thing is here."

The same tone is preserved in the young shepherd's account of how he saw Antigonus torn to pieces by a bear. Impossible to feel horror-stricken or solemn over this:

"And then for the land-service, to see how the bear tore out his shoulder-bone; how he cried to me for help, and said his name was Antigonus, a nobleman. But to make an end of the ship, to see how the sea flap-dragoned it; but first how the poor souls roared, and the sea mocked them; and how the poor gentleman roared, and the bear mocked him, both roaring louder than sea or weather."

It does not seem very likely that the unfortunate man's chief anxiety while the bear was tearing him to pieces would be to inform the shepherd of his name and rank. He forgot to add his age, although, through a slip on Shakespeare's part, the old shepherd knows without being told that Antigonus was aged.

Shakespeare did not concentrate his whole strength on this play either. He took no great pains to reduce his scattered materials to order, and, as if in defiance of those classically cultivated people who demanded unity of time and place, he allowed sixteen years to elapse between two acts, leaving us on the voyage between Sicily and Bohemia, between reality and wonderland. In other words, he has freely improvised on his instrument upon a given poetic theme; he has painted purely decoratively, content with a general harmony of colour and unity of tone, without giving much thought to any ultimate meaning.

XX

THE TEMPEST—WRITTEN FOR THE PRINCESS
ELIZABETH'S WEDDING

IT is a different matter with that rich, fantastic wonder-poem, *The Tempest*, on which Shakespeare concentrated for the last time all the powers of his mind. Everything here is ordered and concise, and so inspired with thought that we seem to be standing face to face with the poet's idea. In spite of all its boldness of imagination, the dramatic order and condensation are such that the whole complies with the severest rules of Aristotle, the action of the entire play occupying in reality only three hours.

Owing to a notice by the Master of the Revels concerning a performance of the play at Whitehall in 1611, the date 1610–11 was long accepted as the year of its production. This memorandum is, however, a forgery, and the sole bit of reliable information we possess of *The Tempest*, before its appearance in the Folio edition of 1613, is a notice in Vertue's Manuscripts of a performance at court in February 1613, as one of the festivities celebrating the Princess Elizabeth's wedding. We can prove that this was its first performance and that it was written expressly for the occasion.

The Princess Elizabeth had been educated at Combe Abbey, far from the impure atmosphere of the court, under the care of Lord and Lady Harrington, an honourable and right-minded couple. When returned to her parents at the age of fifteen, she was distinguished by a charm and dignity beyond her years, and soon became the special favourite of her brother Henry, then seventeen years of age. Claimants for her hand were not long in appearing. The Prince of Piedmont was among the first, but the Pope would not consent to a marriage between a Catholic potentate and a Protestant princess. The next wooer was no less a person than Gustavus Adolphus, and his suit was rejected because James refused to bestow his daughter upon the enemy of his friend and brother-in-law, Christian IV. of Denmark. As early as December 1611 negotiations were entered upon on behalf of Prince Frederick V., who had just succeeded his father as Elector of the Palatinate. There was much to be said in favour of an alliance with a son of the man who had stood at the head of the Protestant League in Germany, and in May 1612 a preliminary contract of betrothal was signed. In the August of the same year an ambassador from the young Elector came to England. Meanwhile the first suitor, strongly supported by the Queen's Catholic sympathies, had reappeared. The King of Spain had also made some overtures, but they had fallen through on account of their implying the conversion of the Princess to the Catholic faith. It was the Elector Frederick, therefore, who was finally victorious in the contest, and matters were soon so far settled that he could set out on his journey to England. He was very popular there by reason of his Protestantism, and he arrived at Gravesend amid general rejoicing. He sailed up to Whitehall on the 22nd of October, and was enthusiastically greeted by the crowd. King James received him warmly, and presented him with a ring worth eighteen hundred pounds. He was ardently supported by the young Prince of Wales, who announced his intention of following his sister on her wedding-tour to Germany, where it was his secret purpose to look for a bride for himself, regardless of political intrigue.

The Elector Palatine was a remarkably handsome and pre-possessing young man. Born on the 16th of August 1596, he was at this time just sixteen years of age, and nothing in his conduct suggested the unmanly and contemptible character he displayed eight years later, when he, as King of Bohemia, lost the battle of Prague through a drunken revel. The contemporary English accounts of him abound with his praise. He made an excellent impression everywhere, and we read of his dignified and princely behaviour in a letter from John Chamberlain to Sir Dudley Carleton, dated 22nd October 1612: "He hath a train of very sober and well-fashioned gentlemen, his whole number is not above 170, servants and all, being limited by the King not to exceed." The condition of the exchequer would not permit of any unnecessary extravagance, and in less than a month after the wedding the whole retinue appointed to attend on the Prince during his stay in England was dismissed—a slight which the young Princess took very much to heart.

The much beloved Prince Henry was far from well at the time of his future brother-in-law's arrival in London. He had injured himself by violent bodily exercise during the unusually hot summer, and had ruined his digestion by eating great quantities of fruit. We now know that the illness by which he was attacked was typhus fever, and it appears that not many days after he was convalescent he incurred a severe relapse by playing tennis in the cold open air with no more clothing on the upper part of his body than a shirt.

High-minded, enlightened, and honourable as he was, Prince Henry was the idol and hope of the English nation. Queen Anne had taken the Prince, while he was yet a boy, to visit Raleigh at the Tower, soon after the illustrious prisoner had been forced to abandon those hopes of the Admiralship of the Danish fleet which he had based on the visit of Christian the Fourth to England. Prince Henry had been intimate with Raleigh since 1610, and is reported to have said, " No man but my father would have kept such a bird in a cage ! " He had, with great difficulty, obtained from the King a promise that Raleigh should be released at Christmas 1612—a promise which was never kept.

On the morning of the 6th of November the Prince's condition was declared hopeless. The Queen sent to the Tower for a bottle of Raleigh's famous cordial, which she believed to have once saved her own life, and in which Raleigh himself placed the greatest faith. He despatched it with a message that it would save the Prince's life, unless he were dying of poison. It only availed to ease his death struggles, however, and, barely nineteen years of age, he died before the day was out.

Never before in the history of England had such hopes been fixed and such affection lavished on an heir-apparent, and we can realise how great would be the grief of the entire nation for his loss. According to the manner of the times, it was generally supposed that he had been poisoned. John Chamberlain, writing to Sir Dudley Carleton, says that grave doubts were entertained, but adds that no traces of poison were found when the body was opened on the second day. The editor of these letters, however (author of the *Memoirs of Sophia Dorothea*), remarks : " There is nothing conclusive in this ; for, in the first place, there were poisons which left no trace of their presence ; and, in the next, if the effects of poisoning had been visible, the physicians would have been afraid to say so. More than one writer has ventured to assert that the atrocious crime was perpetrated with the connivance of the king, whose notorious jealousy of the popular young prince at this period, and foolish fondness for his brother Charles, induced a wretch well known to have been guilty of similar practices—the King's favourite, Viscount Rochester—to cause the prince to be secretly put out of the way." It was hoped by all who objected to the marriage of the Princess to the German Elector that Prince Henry's death would stand in the way of the wedding, for it could hardly be celebrated at a time of such deep mourning. The Elector, however, had come over to England on purpose to be married, and it was not possible to delay the ceremony long. The final marriage contract was signed by the King on the 17th of November, and the formal betrothal took place on the 27th of the same month. The wedding was postponed, but only until February. Sir Thomas Lake writes on the 6th of January that mourning is given up, and the wedding festivities are arranged.

The bride of seventeen was solemnly united to the bridegroom of sixteen to the general gratification of the court, on the 14th of

February, in the presence of many spectators. On the 18th of the same month John Chamberlain writes to Mrs. Carleton: "The bridegroom and bride were both in a suit of cloth of silver, richly embroidered with silver, her train carried up by thirteen young ladies, or lord's daughters at least, besides five or six more that could not come near it. These were all in the same livery with the bride, though not so rich. The bride was married in her hair, that hung down long, with an exceeding rich coronet on her head, which the King valued at a million of crowns."

The bridegroom, with the King and Prince Charles, took part in a tournament of the wedding, and earned great applause in the evening by a display of his splendid horsemanship (*Court and Times of James the First*). In Wilson's *Contemporary History* (p. 64) we read of the bride: "Her vestments were white, the emblem of Innocency, her hair dishevel'd, hanging down her back at length, an ornament of Virginity; a crown of pure gold upon her head, the cognizance of Majesty, being all beset with precious gems, shining liking a constellation, her train supported by twelve young ladies in white garments, so adorned with jewels that her passage looked like a milky way."

Among the various plays chosen for performance at court during these wedding festivities was *The Tempest*, and we shall see that it was written expressly for the occasion.

It is hardly necessary to confute Hunter's theory, argued at great length, that the play dates from 1596. One fact alone will sufficiently prove its absurdity, namely, that use is made in the play of a passage from Florio's translation of Montaigne, which was not published until 1603. Nor is there any foundation for Karl Elze's opinion (also lengthily set forth) that *The Tempest* was written by 1604. The metre shows that it belongs to Shakespeare's latest period. It has a proportion of 33 in the 100 of eleven-syllabled lines, whereas *Antony and Cleopatra*, written long after 1604, has but 25, and *As You Like It*, of the year 1600, only 12 in the 100.

We have another fragment of internal evidence against the play having been written before 1610. In May 1609 Sir George Somer's fleet was scattered by a storm in mid-ocean while on its way to Virginia. The admiral's ship, driven out of its course, was blown by the gale unto the Bermudas. After all hope had been abandoned, the vessel was saved by being stranded between two rocks in just such a bay as that to which Ariel guides the king's ship in *The Tempest*. A little book was written on the subject of this shipwreck, and the adventures connected with it, by Sylvester Jourdan, and was published in 1610 under the title, "Discovery of the Bermudas, otherwise called, The Isle of Devils." The storm and the peril of the admiral's ship are described; the vessel had sprung a leak, and the sailors were falling asleep at the pumps out of sheer exhaustion when she grounded. They found the island (hitherto regarded as enchanted) uninhabited, the air mild, and the soil remarkably fertile.

Shakespeare borrowed several details from this book, the name of Bermoothes, mentioned by Ariel in the first act, for instance; and his only reason for not following the narrative in detail was his desire to lay the scene in an island of the Mediterranean.

The play, then, was written for the royal wedding in 1613. This date was first surmised by Tieck, and later declared probable by Johan Meissner, being finally confirmed by Richard Garnett in the *Universal Review* of 1889. The latter maintains and proves that *The Tempest* was written for a private audience on the occasion of a wedding; that the nature of the audience and the identity of the wedding are determined by unmistakable references to the personality of the bridegroom, to the early death of Prince Henry, and to the qualities which King James prided himself on possessing, and for which he loved to be praised. Over and above all this, there is internal evidence for the year 1613, and none for any other date.

The play is much shorter than the generality of Shakespeare's dramas, there being only 2000 lines in *The Tempest* against the average 3000. It was not permitted to take up too much of the King's time nor of that of his guests; moreover, the play had to be written and learned and put on the stage all within the course of, at most, a few months. Thus there was every inducement to make it short.

Not being written for performance in an ordinary theatre, it was desirable to have as few changes of scene as possible, and in this respect *The Tempest* is unique among Shakespeare's plays. After the opening scene on the deck of the ship, no change of scenery whatever is necessary, although the action transpires on different parts of the island. The occasion of the play made it equally desirable to avoid change of costume, and of this there is actually none, except where Prospero attires himself in ducal robes at the close of the play, and even this he effects on the stage with the assistance of Ariel. We have already referred to the compression of the play, which, instead of extending, as is usual with Shakespeare, over a long period, or even (as in *Pericles* and *The Winter's Tale*) over a whole lifetime, merely occupies three hours, not much longer than was required for the performance of the play.

In spite of its brevity, two masques, of the kind generally represented before royalty on such occasions, are introduced into the play. The pantomime and ballet, with its transformations, are much more elaborate than would have been necessary if the scene was only there for its own sake. "Enter several strange Shapes, bringing in a banquet; they dance about it with gentle actions of salutation; and inviting the king, &c., to eat, they depart. Thunder and lightning. Enter Ariel, like a harpy; claps his wings upon the table, and with a quaint device the banquet vanishes." King James had, as we know, a fancy for all manner of stage machinery, and Inigo Jones contrived quantities of it for use at court festivities.

Still more suggestive is the great wedding masque, which, with its mythological figures, Juno, Ceres, and Iris, occupies nearly the whole of the fourth act. If it were not that *The Tempest* was written for a bridal performance, this masque would be condemned, so extraneous is it to the plot, as a later interpolation, and as such, indeed, it was considered by Karl Elze. Without it, however, the fourth act dwindles to nothing, and the ballet is obviously required to give it its proper length. Moreover, masque and play are inseparably connected by the famous lines, "and like the baseless fabric of this vision," &c. It has been attributed, without sufficient reason, to Beaumont; but even supposing him to have composed it, it must have been planned by the author of the play and written to his order, and it affords unmistakable proof that *The Tempest* was composed as an occasional play for the diversion of princes and courtiers. The audience must have been in possession of circumstances justifying the introduction of the masque, and those circumstances could not be anything but a wedding. We may now assert with absolute certainty that *The Tempest* was performed on the occasion of the Princess Elizabeth's wedding. They would not revive an old play, originally written for the stage, for such a purpose, still less would they use one which had been composed for a previous wedding. Shakespeare would never allow anything unsuitable to be performed; moreover, at no former marriage would such a play have been appropriate. The fact that it was one of the king's musicians who composed the music for Ariel's songs, " Full fathom five " in the first act, and "Where the bee sucks" in the last, renders it still more probable that this of the court was its first performance. Everything indicates a royal wedding.

We find many flattering allusions in this play to King James, who could not possibly be neglected on such an occasion as that of his daughter's bridal. When Prospero, explaining his position to his daughter (Act i. sc. 2), tells how he was foremost among all the dukes for dignity and knowledge of the liberal arts, his special study, and how, absorbed in secret studies, he grew a stranger to his state, his speech conveys that interpretation of James's position and character which he himself favoured, and implies, at the same time, that the possession of these qualities was the cause of his unpopularity. Possibly there was a touch of well-concealed irony in all this. Garnett, indeed, finds an intentional dramatic satire in the crustiness and self-sufficiency of the character, proving that even the development of the highest human qualities is attended by drawbacks. But this is carrying the parallel between the characteristics of Prospero and James too far. Garnett can truly say, however, that just such a prince as Prospero, wise, humane, peace-loving, pursuing distant aims which none but he could realise or fathom; independent of counsellors and more than a match for his enemies in sagacity, holding himself in reserve until the decisive moment and then taking effective action, a devoted student of every lawful science but a sworn foe to the black art, did James imagine himself to be, and as such did he love to be represented.

We have seen with what mingled feelings the King and court would prepare for the Princess's wedding. The grief for Prince Henry's death was still so fresh that all rejoicing must be overshadowed by it. A noisy joyous play would have been out of place, while, upon the other hand, it would not do to destroy all festive feeling by directly recalling the loss the royal family and the nation had so lately sustained. Shakespeare performed this difficult task with admirable tact and good feeling. He alluded to the death of the Prince, but in such a manner that grief was lost in joy. Until the last act of the play the youthful Prince Ferdinand is believed by his father and the courtiers to be dead, and frequent expression is given to their sorrow over their supposed loss. The Prince is not the son of Prospero, but of Alonso, and the sonless Duke finds a son in Ferdinand, as James found one in the Elector Palatine.

The fact that these guarded allusions to Prince Henry's death are found throughout the play prove that it must have been written after the 6th of November, and, since it was evidently performed before the wedding, which was celebrated on the 14th of February, we may see how little time was needed by Shakespeare in which to produce a work actually brimming over with genius, and how far he was from being enfeebled or exhausted when, in this play, he bade farewell for ever to his art and his position in London.

The entire drama is permeated by the atmosphere of that age of discovery and struggling colonists. It has been admirably shown by Watkins Lloyd that all the topics and problems it deals with correspond to the colonisation of Virginia—the marvels brought to light by the discovery of new countries and new races; by the wonderful falsehoods, and still more wonderful truths, of travellers concerning natural phenomena and the superstitions arising from them. Sea perils and shipwreck, the power that lies in such calamities to provoke remorse for crimes committed; the quarrels and mutinies of colonists, the struggles of their leaders to preserve their authority; theories on the civilisation and government of new countries, the reappearance of old world vices on a new soil, the contrast between the reasoning powers of man and those of the savage; and lastly, all the demands made upon the activity, promptitude, and energy of the conquerors.

The date of the first Virginian settlement was May 1607, and it then consisted of 107 colonists. The Virginia Company was not founded until 1609 and very little was known about it before 1610. Not before 1612 could they write home, " Our colony is now seven hundred strong." These circumstances all seem to point to 1612–13 as the period during which *The Tempest* was produced.

XXI

SOURCES OF THE TEMPEST

WE possess no knowledge of any one particular source from which *The Tempest* might have been drawn, but it seems probable that Shakespeare constructed his drama upon some already existing foundation. A childishly old-fashioned play by Jacob Ayrer, *Comedia von der schönen Sidea*, seems to have been founded upon a variant of the story used by Shakespeare.[1] Ayrer died in 1605, and his work, therefore, cannot have owed anything to that of the great dramatist. The similarity between the two plays is confined to the relations between Prospero and Alonso, and Ferdinand and Miranda. In the German play we have a banished sovereign, his daughter, and a captive prince, who is compelled to atone for his audacity in making love to the daughter by carrying and cutting firewood. He promises his beloved she shall be queen, and attempting to draw his sword upon his father-in-law, is rendered powerless by magic. There is no real resemblance between the dramas. It is, of course, possible that Dowland, or some other English actor, might have introduced the *Sidea* from Germany, but Shakespeare did not know German, and in any case the play was too poor a one to interest him. Moreover, since we know that Ayrer did occasionally copy English works, we may safely conclude that both dramatists were indebted to some earlier English source. There is nothing specially original about the above incidents. In Greene's *Friar Bacon*, four men make fruitless efforts to draw swords held in their scabbards by magic, and *The Tempest* would naturally possess traits in common with other plays representing sorcery upon the stage. In Marlowe's drama, *Dr. Faustus*, for instance, the hero punishes his would-be murderers by making them wallow in filth (*Faustus*, Act iv. sc. 2), just as Prospero drives Caliban, Trinculo, and Stephano into the marsh and leaves them there up to their chins in mire (*Tempest*, Act iv.).

It is a most arbitrary and unreasonable supposition of Meissner's that Shakespeare borrowed his wedding masque from the one performed at Prince Henry's christening, in which also Juno, Ceres, and Iris appear. Shakespeare was never

---

[1] Jacob Ayrer : *Opera Theatricum.* Nurnburg, 1618. L. Tieck : *Deutsches Theater*, i. p. 323. Albert Cohn : *Shakespeare in Germany*, ii. pp. 1–75.

so lacking in inventive power that he needed to unearth a description of an old play which had been acted before King James at Stirling Castle some nineteen years previously. We know that the masque itself was not yet in print.

It was an early and correct observation that various minor details of *The Tempest* were taken from different books of travel. Shakespeare found the name of Setebos, and, possibly, the first idea of Caliban himself, in an account of Magellan's voyage to the south pole in Eden's *Historye of Travaile in East and West Indies* (1577). From Raleigh's *Discovery of the large, rich, and bewtiful Empire of Guiana* (1596) he took the fable of the men whose heads stood upon their breasts. Raleigh writes that, though this may be an invention, he is inclined to believe it true, because every child in the provinces of Arromai and Canuri maintains that their mouths were in the middle of their breasts.[1] (See Gonzalo's speech in *The Tempest*, Act iii. sc. 2.)

It was Hunter who first suggested that Shakespeare might have taken some hints from Ariosto. It is possible that he had in mind some stanzas from the 43rd canto of *Orlando Furioso*. The 15th and 14th contain a faint foreshadowing, as it were, of Prospero and Miranda, and the 187th stanza alludes to the power of witchcraft to raise storms and calm seas again. The *Orlando* had been translated into English by Harrington, but, as we have already observed, Shakespeare was fully qualified to read it in the original. Too much, however, has already been made of these trivial, nay, utterly insignificant coincidences.[2]

It is far more remarkable that the famous and beautiful passage (Act iv.) proclaiming the transitoriness of all earthly things—a passage which seems to be a mournful epitome of the philosophy of Shakespeare's last years of productiveness—may be an easy adaptation of an inferior and quite unknown poet

---

[1] " Or that there were such men
Whose heads stood in their breasts? which now we find,
Each putter-out of five for one will bring us
Good warrant of."

[2] We read of the old man :

" Nella nostra cittade era un uom saggio
Di tutte l' arti oltre ogni creder dotto."

Of his arrangements for his daughter, due to the bad character of his wife, we are told :

" Fuor del commercio popolo la invola,
Ed ove piu solingo il luogo vede,
Questo amplo e bel palagio e ricco tanto
Fece fare a demonj per incanto."

Of the storm, which, by the way, is not raised by the said old man, but by a hermit, we are merely told :

" E facea alcuno effetto soprumano

.   .   .   .   .

Fermare il vento ad un segno di croce
E far tranquillo il mar quando è più atroce."

of his day.   When the spirit play conjured up by Prospero has
vanished he says:

> "These our actors,
> As I foretold you, were all spirits, and
> Are melted into air, into thin air,
> And, like the baseless fabric of this vision,
> The cloud-capp'd towers, the gorgeous palaces,
> The solemn temples, the great globe itself,
> Yea, all which it inherit, shall dissolve,
> And, like this insubstantial pageant faded,
> Leave not a rack behind.   We are such stuff
> As dreams are made on, and our little life
> Is rounded with a sleep."

In Count Stirling's tragedy of *Darius*, published in London,
1604, the following verses occur:

> " Let Greatness of her glassy scepters vaunt,
> Not scepters, no, but reeds, soon bruis'd, soon broken;
> And let this worldly pomp our wits enchant,
> All fades, and scarcely leaves behind a token.
> Those golden palaces, those gorgeous halls,
> With furniture superfluously fair,
> Those stately courts, those sky-encount'ring walls,
> Evanish all like vapours in the air."

History could scarcely afford a more striking proof that in
art the style is all, subject and meaning being of comparatively
small importance.   Stirling's verses are by no means bad, nor
even poor, and their decidedly pleasing rhymes express, in very
similar words, exactly the same idea we find in Shakespeare's
lines, and were, moreover, their precursors.   Nevertheless, both
they and the name of their author would be utterly forgotten long
since if Shakespeare had not, by a marvellous touch or two,
transformed them into a few lines of blank verse which will hold
their own in the memory of man as long as the English language
lasts.

As Meissner[1] pointed out, Shakespeare was indebted to
Frampton's translation of Marco Polo (1579) for one or two
suggestive hints.   For example, we read in Frampton of the
desert of Lob in Asia: " You shall heare in the ayre, the
sound of *Tabers and other instruments*, to putte the travellers in
feare, and to make them lose their way, and to depart their company and loose themselves: and by that meanes many doe die,
being deceived so, by evill spirits, that make these soundes, and
also doe call diverse of the travellers *by their names*."   Compare
this with Caliban's words in *The Tempest* (Act iii. sc. 2):

---

[1] Johan Meissner: *Untersuchungen über Shakespeare's Sturm.*

"The isle is full of noises,
Sounds, and sweet airs, that give delight and hurt not.
Sometimes a *thousand twangling instruments*
Will hum about mine ears, and sometimes voices."

And Trinculo's subsequent jesting remark, which evidently refers
to the accompaniment of a clown's morris dance: "I would I
could see this *tabourer;* he lays it on." Compare also Alonso's
lament (Act iii. sc. 3):

"Oh, it is monstrous, monstrous!
Methought the billows spoke and told me of it;
The winds did sing it to me, and the thunder,
That deep and dreadful organ-pipe, pronounced
The name of Prospero: it did bass my trespass."

Shakespeare may have found the first suggestions of Caliban
and Ariel in Greene's *Friar Bacon*. In the ninth scene of this
play, two necromancers, Bungay and Vandermast, dispute as to
which possess the greater power, the pyromantic (fire) spirits or
the geomantic (earth) spirits. The fire spirits, says Bungay, are
mere transparent shadows that float past us like heralds, while
the spirits of earth are strong enough to burst rocks asunder.
Vandermast maintains that earth spirits are dull, as befits their
place of abode. They are coarse and earthly, less intelligent
than other spirits, and thus it is they are at the service of
jugglers, witches, and common sorcerers. But the fine spirits
are mighty and swift, their power is far-reaching.

A more direct suggestion of Ariel's charming ways was
probably found by Shakespeare at the close of the already
mentioned *Faithful Shepherdess*, written by his young friend
Fletcher. In it the satyr offers his services to the beautiful
Corin in terms which recall Ariel's speech to Prospero (Act i.
sc. 2):

"All hail, great master! grave sir, hail! I come
To answer thy best pleasure; be't to fly,
To swim, to dive into the fire, to ride
On the curled clouds, to thy strong bidding task
Ariel and all his quality."

Fletcher's satyr makes the same offer:

"Tell me, sweetest,
What new service now is meetest
For a satyr? Shall I stray
In the middle air, and stay
The sailing rack, or nimbly take
Hold by the moon, and gently make
Suit to the pale queen of night
For a beam to give thee light?

2 T

Shall I dive into the sea,
And bring thee coral, making way
Through the rising waves that fall
In snowy fleeces?" &c.

But a much more striking example of Shakespeare's taste and talent for adaptation is presented by Prospero's farewell speech to the elves (Act v. sc. 1), "Ye elves of hills, brooks," &c. Warburton was the first to draw attention to the fact that this speech, in which Shakespeare bids farewell to his art, and tells, through the medium of Prospero's marvellous eloquence, of all that he has accomplished, was founded upon the great incantation in Ovid's *Metamorphoses* (vii. 197–219), where, after the conquest of the golden fleece, Medea, at Jason's request, invokes the spirits of night to obtain the prolongation of his old father's life. A comparison of the text plainly proves Shakespeare's indebtedness to Golding's translation of the Latin work:

"Ye Ayres and Windes: *ye Elues of Hilles, of Brooks, of Woods alone,*
Of standing Lakes, and of the Night approche ye everyone
Through helpe of whom (the crooked bankes much wondring at the thing)
I haue compelled streames to run cleane backward to their spring.
By charmes I make the calme seas rough, and make the rough seas playne,
And cover all the Skie with clouds and chase them thence againe.
By charmes I raise and lay the windes and burst the Viper's iaw,
And from the bowels of the earth both stones and trees do draw.
Whole woods and Forrests I remoouve: I make the Mountains shake,
And euen the earth it selfe to grone and fearefully to quake.
I call up dead men from their graues, and thee, O lightsome Moone,
I darken oft, though beaten brass abate thy perill soone.
Our Sorcerie dimmes the Morning faire, and darkes the Sun at Noone.

. . . .

Among the earth-bred brothers you a mortall warre did set
And brought asleepe the Dragon fell whose eyes were neuer shet."

The corresponding lines in *The Tempest* run:

" *Ye elves of hills, brooks, standing lakes, and groves ;*
And ye that on the sands with printless foot
Do chase the ebbing Neptune, and do fly him
When he comes back; you . . . . .
. . . . *by whose aid—*
Weak masters though ye be—*I have bedimm'd*
The noontide sun, call'd forth the mutinous winds,
And twixt the green sea and the azur'd vault
Set roaring war : to the dread-rattling thunder
Have I given fire, and rifted Jove's stout oak

With his own bolt: *the strong-bas'd promontory*
Have I made shake ; and by the spurs *pluck'd up*
The pine and cedar : graves at my command
Have wak'd their sleepers, op'd and let 'em forth
By my so potent art."

The words employed in addressing the elves are actually the same. Medea's power to raise and calm the waves becomes the elfin chase of and flight from the advancing and retreating billows. Both Medea and Prospero proclaim their power to overcloud the sky and darken the sun, to raise winds and shatter trees, tearing them up by the roots. They can make the very mountains tremble, and can compel the grave to give up its dead.

The names Prospero and Stephano may be found in Ben Jonson's *Every Man in his Humour* (1595). Prospero was also the name of a riding-master well known in the London of Shakepeare's day.

Malone has suggested that the name " Caliban " was derived from " cannibal." Although the creature displays no tendency towards cannibalism, it is possible that Shakespeare had this term for a man-eater in his mind when he invented the name; it is even probable, seeing that the passage in Montaigne from which he drew Gonzalo's Utopia is contained in a chapter headed " Les Cannibales." Furness, who has inaugurated such an admirable edition of Shakespeare, considers this surmise an improbable one. He and Th. Elze incline to the belief that the name was derived from Calibia, a town in the neighbourhood of Tunis, but the connection is scarcely more obvious. Shakespeare found the name Ariel in Isaiah xxix. 1, the name of a city in which David dwelt, and he doubtless appropriated it on account of its similarity in sound to both English and Latin words for air.

We now seem to have exhausted all the available literary sources of *The Tempest*, and we need only add that Dryden and Davenant, in their abominable adaptation of the play (published in London 1670), made free use of Calderon's already mentioned " En esta vida todo es vertad y todo es mentira," and thus provided the Miranda, who has never seen a young man, with a counterpart in Hippolyto, who has never seen the face of woman.

XXII

THE TEMPEST AS A PLAY—SHAKESPEARE AND PROSPERO—FAREWELL TO ART

ALTHOUGH, taken from the point of view of a play, *The Tempest* is lacking in dramatic interest, the entire work is so marvellously rich in poetry and so inspired by imagination, that it forms a whole little world in itself, and holds the reader captive by that power which sheer perfection possesses to enthrall.

If the ordinary being desires to obtain a salutary impression of his own insignificance and an ennobling one of the sublimity of true genius, he need only study this last of Shakespeare's masterpieces. In the majority of cases the result will be prostrate admiration.

Shakespeare gave freer rein to his imagination in this play than he had allowed himself since the days of the *Midsummer Night's Dream* and the *First Part of Henry IV*. He felt able, indeed compelled to do this; and, in spite of the restraint imposed upon him by the occasion for which it was written, he devoted his whole individuality to the task with greater force than he had done for years. The play contains far more of the nature of a confession than was usual at this period. Never, with the exception of *Hamlet* and *Timon*, had Shakespeare been so personal.

It may be said that, in a manner, *The Tempest* was a continuation of his gloomy period; once again he treated of black ingratitude and cunning and violence practised upon a good man.

Prospero, Duke of Milan, absorbed in scientific study, and finding his real dukedom in his library, imprudently intrusted the direction of his little state to his brother Antonio. The latter, betraying his trust, won over to his side all the officers of state appointed by Prospero, entered into an alliance with the Duke's enemy, Alonso, King of Naples, and reduced the hitherto free state of Milan to a condition of vassalage. Then, with the assistance of Alonso and his brother Sebastian, Antonio attacked and dethroned Prospero. The Duke, with his little three-year-old daughter, was carried out some leagues to sea, placed in a rotten old hull, and abandoned. A Neapolitan noble, Gonzalo, compassionately supplied them with provisions, clothes, and, above all, the precious books upon which Prospero's supernatural powers depended. The boat was driven ashore upon an island whose one inhabitant, the aboriginal Caliban, was reduced to subjection by means of the control exercised over the spirit world by the banished man. Here, then, Prospero dwelt in peace and solitude, devoting himself to the culture of his mind, the enjoyment of nature, and the careful education of his daughter Miranda, who received such a training as seldom falls to the lot of a princess.

Twelve years have passed, and Miranda is just fifteen when the play begins. Prospero is aware that his star has reached its zenith and that his old enemies are in his power. The King of Naples has married his daughter, Claribel, to the King of Tunis, and the wedding has been celebrated, oddly enough, at the home of the bridegroom; but then it was probably the first time in history that a Christian King of Naples had bestowed his daughter upon a Mohammedan. Alonso, with all his train, including his brother and the usurper of Milan, is on his homeward voyage when Prospero raises the storm which drives them on his island. After being sufficiently bewildered and humiliated, they are finally forgiven, and the King's son, purified by the trials through which he has passed, is, as Prospero has all along intended that he should be, united to Miranda.

It was evidently Shakespeare's intention in *The Tempest* to give a picture of mankind as he now saw it, and we are shown something quite new in him, a typical representation of the different phases of humanity.

In Caliban we have the primitive man, the aboriginal, the animal which has just evolved into the first rough stages of the human being. In Prospero we are given the highest development of Nature, the man of the future, the superhuman man of spirit.

We have seen that Shakespeare roughly planned such a character some years back, in the faintly outlined sketch of Cerimon in *Pericles* (*ante*, p. 591). Prospero is the fulfilment of the promise contained in Cerimon's principal speech, a man, namely, who can compel to his uses all the beneficent powers dwelling in metals, stones, and plants. He is a creature of princely mould, who has subdued outward Nature, has brought his own turbulent inner self under perfect control, and has overpowered the bitterness caused by the wrongs he has suffered in the harmony emanating from his own richly spiritual life.

Prospero, like all Shakespeare's heroes and heroines of this last decade—Pericles, Imogen, and Hermione no less than Lear and Timon—suffers grievous wrong. He is even more sinned against than Timon, has suffered more and lost more through ingratitude. He has not squandered his substance like the misanthrope, but, absorbed in occupations of a higher nature, he has neglected his worldly interests and fallen a victim to his own careless trustfulness

The injustice offered to Imogen and Hermione was not so detestable in its origin as that suffered by Prospero; the wrong done them sprang from misguided love, and was therefore easier to condone. The crime against the Duke was actuated by such low motives as envy and covetousness.

Tried by suffering, Prospero proves its strengthening qualities. Far from succumbing to the blow, it is not until it has fallen that he displays his true, far-reaching, and terrible power, and becomes the great irresistible magician which Shakespeare himself had so long been. His power is not understood by his daughter, who is but a child, but it is felt by his enemies. He plays with them as he pleases, compels them to repent their past treatment of him, and then pardons them with a calmness of superiority to which Timon could never have attained, but which is far from being that all-obliterating tenderness with which Imogen and Hermione forgive remorseful sinners.

There is less of charity towards the offenders in Prospero's absolution than that element of contempt which has so long and so exclusively filled Shakespeare's soul. His forgiveness, the oblivion of a scornful indifference, is not so much that of the strong man who knows his power to crush if need be, as that of the wisdom which is no longer affected by outward circumstance.

Richard Garnett aptly observes, in his critical introduction to the play in the "Irving Edition," that Prospero finds it easy to forgive because, in his secret soul, he sets very little value on the dukedom he has lost, and is, therefore, roused to very little indignation by the treachery which deprived him of it. His daughter's happiness is the sole thing which greatly interests him now, and he carries his indifference to worldly matters so far that, without any outward compulsion, he breaks his magic wand and casts his books into the sea. Resuming his place among the ranks of ordinary men, he retains nothing but his inalienable treasure of experience and reflection. I quote the following passage from Garnett on account of its remarkable correspondence with the general conception of Shakespeare's development set forth in this book.

"That this Quixotic height of magnanimity should not surprise, that it should seem quite in keeping with the character, proves how deeply this character has been drawn from Shakespeare's own nature. Prospero is not Shakespeare, but the play is in a certain measure autobiographical. . . . It shows us more than anything else what the discipline of life had made of Shakespeare at fifty—a fruit too fully matured to be suffered to hang much longer on the tree. Conscious superiority untinged by arrogance, genial scorn for the mean and base, mercifulness into which contempt entered very largely, serenity excluding passionate affection while admitting tenderness, intellect overtopping morality but in no way blighting or perverting it—such are the mental features of him in whose development the man of the world kept pace with the poet, and who now shone as the consummate perfection of both."

In other words, it is Shakespeare's own nature which overflows into Prospero, and thus the magician represents not merely the noble-minded great man, but the genius, imaginatively delineated, not, as in *Hamlet*, psychologically analysed. Audibly and visibly does Prospero's genius manifest itself, visible and audible also the inward and outward opposition he combats.

The two figures in which this spiritual power and this resistance are embodied are the most admirable productions of an artist's powers in this or any other age. Ariel is a supernatural, Caliban a bestially natural being, and both have been endowed with a human soul. They were not seen, but created.

Prospero is the master-mind, the man of the future, as shown by his control over the forces of Nature. He passes as a magician, and Shakespeare found his prototype, as far as external accessories were concerned, in a scholar of mark and man of high principles, Dr. Dee, who died in 1607. This Dr. Dee believed himself possessed of powers to conjure up spirits, good and bad, and on this account enjoyed a great reputation in his day. A man owning but a small share of the scientific knowledge of our times would inevitably have been regarded as a powerful magician at that date. In the creation of Prospero, therefore, Shakespeare unconsciously anticipated the results of time. He not merely gave him a magic wand, but created a poetical embodiment of the forces of Nature as his attendant spirit. In accordance with the method described in the *Midsummer Night's Dream* he gave life to Ariel:

> "The poet's eye, in fine frenzy rolling,
> Doth glance from heaven to earth, from earth to heaven :
> And as imagination bodies forth
> The forms of things unknown, the poet's pen
> Turns them to shapes and gives to airy nothings
> A local habitation and a name.
> Such tricks hath strong imagination,
> That if it would but apprehend some joy,
> It comprehends the bringer of that joy."

Ariel is just such a harbinger of joy ; from the moment he appears we are content and assured of pleasurable impressions. In the whole record of poetry he is the one good spirit who arrests and affects us as a living being. He is a non-christian angel, a sprite, an elf, the messenger of Prospero's thought, the fulfiller of his will through the elementary spirits subject to the great magician's power. He is the emblem of Shakespeare's own genius, that "affable, familiar ghost" (as Shakespeare expresses it in his 86th sonnet) which Chapman boasted of possessing. His longing for freedom after prolonged servitude has a peculiar and touching significance as a symbol of the yearning of the poet's own genius for rest.

Ariel possesses that power of omnipresence and all those constantly varying forms which are the special gift of imagination. He skims along the foam, flies on the keen north wind, and burrows in the frozen earth. Now he is a fire spirit spreading terror as he flashes in cloven flame, encircling the mast and playing about the rigging of the vessel, or as one great bolt hurls himself to strike with all the power and speed of lightning. Now again, he is a mermaid, seen in fitful glimpses, and chanting alluring songs. He sounds the magic music of the air, he mimics the monotonous splashing of the waves, or barks like a dog and crows like a cock. In every essence of his nature as well as name he is a spirit of the air, a mirage, a hallucination of light and sound. He is a bird, a harpy, and finds his way through the darkness of night to fetch dew from the enchanted Bermudas. Faithful and zealous servant of the good, he terrifies, bewilders, and befools the wicked. He is compounded of charm and delicacy, and is as swift and bright as lightning.

He was formerly in the service of the witch Sycorax, but, incurring her displeasure, was imprisoned by her in the rift of a cloven pine. There he was held in suffering many years, until delivered at last by Prospero's supernatural powers. He serves the magician in return for his release, but never ceases to long for his promised freedom. Although a creature of the air, he is capable of compassion, and can understand a sentiment of devotion which he does not actually feel. His subject condition is painful to him, and he looks forward with joy to the hour of liberty. Spirit of fire and air as he is, his essence exhales itself in music and mischievous pranks.

Caliban, on the other hand, is of the earth earthy, a kind of land-fish, a being formed of heavy and gross materials, who was raised by Prospero from the condition of an animal to that of a human being, without, however, being really civilised. Prospero made much of the creature at first, caressed him and gave him to drink of water mixed with the juice of berries; taught him the art of speech and how to name the greater and the lesser light, and lodged him in his cell. But from the moment Caliban's savage instinct prompted him to attempt the violation of Miranda, Prospero treated him as a slave and made him serve as such. Strangely enough, however, Shakespeare has made him no prosaically raw being, untouched by the poetry of the enchanted island. The vulgar new-comers, Trinculo and Stephano, speak in prose, but Caliban's utterances are always rhythmic; indeed, many of the most exquisitely melodious lines in the play fall from the lips of this poor animal. They sound like an echo from the time he lived within the magic circle and was the constant companion of Prospero and Miranda.

But since, from being their fellow, he has been degraded to their slave, all gratitude for former benefits has disappeared from his mind ; and he now employs the language they have taught him in cursing the master who has robbed him, the original inhabitant, of his birthright. His is the hatred of the savage for his civilised conquerors.

We have seen that the abhorrence Shakespeare felt for the vices of the court and fashionable life inclined him during these later years to dream of some natural life far from all civilisation (*Cymbeline*). But his instinct was too sure and his judgment too sound to allow of his ever believing, with the Utopists of his day, that the natural primitive state of man was one of innocence and nobility of soul in the golden age of prehistoric times. Caliban is a protest against this very theory, and Shakespeare distinctly ridicules all such fanaticism in the lines copied from Montaigne, and placed in Gonzalo's mouth, concerning the organisation of an ideal commonwealth ; without commerce, law, or letters, without riches or poverty, without corn, oil, or wine, and without work of any kind, but a happy idleness for all.

Caliban represents the primitive, the prehistoric man ; yet, such as he is, a poetically inclined philosopher of our day has discovered in him the features of the eternal plebeian. It is instructive to witness with how few reservations Renan was enabled to modernise the type, and shown how, tidied up and washed and interpreted as the dull fickle democracy, Caliban was as capable as the old aristocratic-religious despotism of sounding a conservative note, of protecting the arts and graciously patronising the sciences, &c.

Shakespeare's Caliban was the offspring of Sycorax and begotten by the Devil himself. With such a pedigree he could hardly be expected to rise to any height of angelic goodness and purity. He is, in reality, more of an elemental power than a human being; and therefore rouses neither indignation nor contempt in the mind of the audience, but genuine amusement. Invented, and drawn with masterly humour, he represents the savage natives found by the English in America, upon whom they bestowed the blessings of civilisation in the form of strong drink. There is not only wit but profound significance in the scene (Act ii. sc. 2) in which Caliban, who at first takes Trinculo and Stephano for two spirits sent by Prospero to torment him, allows himself to be persuaded that Trinculo is the Man in the Moon, shown to him by Miranda on beautiful moonlight nights, and forthwith worships him as his god, because he alone possesses the bottle with the heavenly liquor which has been put to the creature's lips, and given him his first taste of the wonderful intoxication produced by fire-water.

Midway between these symbols of the highest culture and of Nature in its crudest form Shakespeare has placed a young girl, as noble in body and soul as her father, and yet so purely and simply a child of Nature that she unhesitatingly follows her instincts, including that of love. She is the counterpart of the masculine ideal in Prospero, being all that is admirable in woman ; hence her name, Miranda. To preserve her absolutely unspotted and fresh, Shakespeare has made her almost as young as his Juliet; and to still further accentuate the impression of maidenly immaculateness, she has grown up without seeing a single youth of the other sex, a trait which was used and abused by the Spaniards later in the same century. Hence the wondering admiration of the first meeting between Ferdinand and Miranda :

> "What ! is't a spirit ?
> Lord, how it looks about ! Believe me, sir,
> It carries a brave form. But 'tis a spirit."

When her father denies this she says :

> " I might call him
> A thing divine, for nothing natural
> I ever saw so noble."

And Ferdinand :

> " My prime request,
> Which I do last pronounce, is, O you wonder !
> If you be maid or no ? "

It is Prospero, whose greatness shows no less in his power over human beings than over the forces of Nature, who has brought these two together, and who, although assuming displeasure at their mutual attraction, causes all which concerns them to follow the exact course his will has marked out.

He sees into the soul of mankind with as sure an eye as Shakespeare himself, and plays the part of Providence to his surroundings as incontestably as did the poet to the beings of his own creation.

When Prospero shows the young people to his guests, they are playing chess, and there would seem to be a touch of symbol in the fact that they are playing, not only because they wish to do so, but because they must. There is, moreover, something almost personal in the way Prospero trains and admonishes the loving couple. Garnett is inclined to infer from the repeated exhortations to Ferdinand to restrain the impulse of his blood until the wedding-hour has struck, that the play was acted some days before the royal wedding ceremony. But if these warnings were intended for the Elector in his capacity of bridegroom, they were a piece of tasteless impertinence. No, it is far more likely that, as before suggested, they contain a melancholy confession, a purely personal reminiscence. Shakespeare cannot be accused of any excessive severity in such questions of morals. We saw in *Measure for Measure* that he considered the connection between the two lovers, for which they are to be so severely punished, was to the full as good as marriage, although entered upon without ceremonies. It was no mere formalism which spoke here, but bitter experience. Now that he was already, in thought, on his way back to Stratford, and was living in anticipation of what awaited him there, Shakespeare was reminded of how he and Anne Hathaway forestalled their ceremonial union, and he spoke of the punishment following on such actions as a curse, which he knew:

> " Barren hate,
> Sour-eyed disdain and discord shall bestrew
> The union of your bed with weeds so loathly
> That you shall hate it both " (Act iv. sc. 1).

As already observed, Shakespeare appropriated from some source or another the incident of the youthful suitor being obliged to submit to the trial of carrying and piling wood. It almost seems that his motive in including such an incident was to show that it is man's great and noble privilege to serve out of love. To Caliban all service is slavery; throughout the whole play he roars for freedom, and never so loudly as when he is drunk. For Ariel, too, all bondage, even that of a higher being, is mere torment. Man alone finds pleasure in the servitude of love. Thus Ferdinand bears uncomplainingly, and even gladly, for Miranda's sake, the burden laid upon him (Act iii. sc. 1):

> " I am in my condition
> A prince, Miranda, I do think, a king.
>
> . . . . . .
>
> The very instant that I saw you, did
> My heart fly to your service ; there resides
> To make me slave to it."

She shares this feeling :

> " I am your wife if you will marry me !
> If not, I'll die your maid ; to be your fellow
> You may deny me ; but I'll be your servant
> Whether you will or no."

It is a feeling of the same nature which impels Prospero to return to Milan to fulfil his duty towards the state whose government he has so long neglected.

There are certain analogies between *The Tempest* and the *Midsummer Night's Dream*. In both we are shown a fantastic world in which heavenly powers make sport of earthly fools. Caliban discovering a god in the drunken Trinculo reminds us of Titania's amorous worship of Bottom. Both are wedding-plays, and yet what a difference ! The *Midsummer Night's Dream* was one of Shakespeare's earliest independent poetical works, written at the age of twenty-six, and his first great success. *The Tempest* was written as a farewell to art and the artist's life, just before the completion of his forty-ninth year, and everything in the play bespeaks the touch of autumn.

The scenery is autumnal throughout, and the time is that of the autumn equinox with its storms and shipwrecks. With noticeable care all the plants named, even those occurring merely in similes, are such flowers and fruit, &c., as appear in the fall of the year in a northern landscape. The climate is harsh and northerly in spite of the southern situation of the island and the southern names. Even the utterances of the goddesses, the blessing of Ceres, for example, show that the season is late September—thus answering to Shakespeare's time of life and frame of mind.

No means of intensifying this impression are neglected. The utter sadness of Prospero's famous words describing the trackless disappearance of all earthly things harmonises with the time of year and with his underlying thought—"We are such stuff as dreams are made on:" a deep sleep, from which we awaken to life, and again, deep sleep hereafter. What a personal note it is in the last scene of the play where Prospero says :

> " And thence retire me to my Milan, where
> Every third thought shall be my grave."

How we feel that Stratford was the poet's Milan, just as Ariel's longing for freedom was the yearning of the poet's genius for rest. He has had enough of the burden of work, enough of the toilsome necromancy of imagination, enough of art, enough of the life of the town. A deep sense of the vanity of all things has laid its hold upon him, he believes in no future and expects no results from the work of a lifetime.

> " Our revels now are ended. These our actors
> . . . . . . were all spirits and
> are melted into air, into thin air."

Like Prospero, he had sacrificed his position to his art, and, like him, he had dwelt upon an enchanted island in the ocean of life. He had been its lord and master, with dominion over spirits, with the spirit of the air as his servant, and the spirit of the earth as his slave. At his will graves had opened, and by his magic art the heroes of the past had lived again. The words with which Prospero opens the fifth act come, despite all gloomy thoughts of death and wearied hopes of rest, straight from Shakespeare's own lips :

> " Now does my project gather to a head ;
> My charms crack not ; my spirits obey ; and time
> Goes upright with his carriage."

All will soon be accomplished and Ariel's hour of deliverance is nigh. The parting of the master from his genius is not without a touch of melancholy:

> " My dainty Ariel ! *I shall miss thee,*
> But yet thou shalt have freedom."

Prospero has determined in his heart to renounce all his magical powers :

> " To the elements
> Be free, and fare thee well ! "

He has taken leave of all his elves by name, and now utters words whose personal application has never been approached by any character hitherto set upon the stage by Shakespeare :

> " But this rough service
> I here abjure, and, when I have required
> Some heavenly music, which even now I do,
> . . . . . . I'll break my staff,
> Bury it certain fathoms in the earth,
> And deeper than did ever plummet sound
> I'll drown my book."

Solemn music is heard, and Shakespeare has bidden farewell to his art.

Collaboration in *Henry VIII.* and the production and staging of *The Tempest* were the last manifestations of his dramatic activity. In all probability he only waited for the close of the court festivities before carrying out his plan of leaving London and returning to Stratford ; and Ben Jonson's foolish thrust at *those who beget tales, tempests, and such like drolleries*, would not find him in town. When we drew attention to his efforts to increase his capital, and his purchase of houses and land at Stratford, we showed that, even at that early period, he hoped eventually to quit the metropolis, to give up the theatre and literature and to spend the last years of his life in the country. Even supposing him to have delayed his departure until after the performance of *The Tempest*, an event which happened only four months later would have supplied the final inducement to leave. In the month of June 1613 a fire broke out, as we know, at the Globe Theatre during a performance of *Henry VIII.*, and the whole building was burned to the ground. Thus the scene of his activity for so many long years disappeared, as it were, in smoke, leaving no trace behind. He was probably part owner of the stage properties and costumes, which were all consumed. In any case, the flames devoured all the manuscripts of his plays then in the possession of the theatre, a priceless treasure—for him surely a painful, and for us an irreparable, loss.

XXIII

THE RIDE TO STRATFORD

THAT must have been a momentous day in Shakespeare's life on which, after giving up his house in London, he mounted his horse and rode back to Stratford-on-Avon to take up his abode there for good.

He would recall that day in 1585 when, twenty-eight years younger, with his life lying before him veiled in the mists of expectation and uncertainty, he set out from Stratford to London to try his fortunes in the great city. Then his heart beat high, and he must have felt towards his horse much as the Dauphin did in *Henry V.* (Act iii. sc. 7) when he said, "When I bestride him I soar, I am a hawk: he trots the air; the earth sings when he touches it, the basest horn of his hoof is more musical than the pipe of Hermes."

Life lay behind him now. His hopes had been fulfilled in many ways; he was famous, he had raised himself a degree in the social scale, above all he was rich, but for all that he was not happy.

The great town, in which he had spent the better part of a lifetime, had not so succeeded in attaching him to it that he would feel any pain in leaving it. There was neither man nor woman there so dear to him as to make society preferable to solitude, and the crowded life of London to the seclusion of the country and an existence passed in the midst of family and Nature.

He had toiled enough, his working days were over, and now, at last, the cloud should be lifted from his name which had so long been cast upon it by his profession. It was nine years since he had actually appeared upon the stage, since he had made over his parts to others, and now he had ceased to take any pleasure in his pen. None of those were left for whom he had cared to write plays and put them upon the stage; the new generation and present frequenters of the theatre were strangers to him. There was no one in London who would heed his leaving it, no friends to induce him to stay, no farewell banquet to be given in his honour.

He would remember his first arrival in London, and how, according to the custom of all poor travellers, he sold his horse at Smithfield. He could, if he wished, keep many horses now, but no power could renew the joyous mood of twenty-one. Then the wind had played with the long curls hanging below his hat, now he was elderly and bald.

The journey from London to Stratford took three days. He would put up at the inns at which he was accustomed to stay on his yearly journey to and fro, and where he was always greeted as a welcome guest, and given a bed with snow-white sheets, for which travellers on foot were charged an extra penny, but which he, as rider, enjoyed gratis. The hostess at Oxford, pretty Mistress Davenant, would give him a specially cordial greeting. The two were old and good friends. Little William, born in 1606, and now seven years old, possessed a certain, perhaps accidental, resemblance of feature to the guest.

As Shakespeare rode on, Stratford, so well known and yet, as settled home, so new, would (as Hamlet says) rise "before his mind's eye." A life of daily companionship with his wife was to begin afresh after a break of twenty-eight years. She was now fifty-seven, and consequently much older, in proportion, than her husband of forty-nine than when they were lovers and newly married, the one under and the other somewhat over twenty. There could be no intellectual bond between them after so long a separation, and their married life was but an empty form.

Of their two daughters, Susanna, the elder, was now thirty, and had been married for six years to Dr. John Hall, a respected physician at Stratford. Judith, the younger daughter, was twenty-eight and unmarried.

The Halls, with their little five-year-old daughter, lived in a picturesque house in Old Stratford, at that time surrounded by woods. Mrs. Shakespeare and Judith lived at New Place, and the spirit prevailing in both establishments was not the spirit of Shakespeare.

Not only the town of Stratford, but his own home and family were desperately pious and puritanical. That power which had been most inimical to him in London, which had dishonoured his profession, and with which he had been at war during all the years of his dramatic activity; that very power against which he had striven, sometimes by open attack, more often by cautious insinuation, had triumphed in his native town behind his back and taken complete possession of his only home.

The closing of the theatre, which did not occur in London until the Puritans had completely gained the upper hand many years later, had already been anticipated in Stratford. The performance of those plays at which Shakespeare in his youth had made acquaintance with the men, his future brother professionals, with whom he sought refuge in London, was strictly forbidden. So long ago as 1602 the town council had carried a resolution that no performance of play or interlude should be permitted in the Guildhall, that long, low building with its eight small-paned windows. It was the only place in Stratford suitable for such a purpose, and was connected with many of Shakespeare's memories. Directly above the long narrow hall, on the first floor, was the school which he had attended daily as a child. Into the hall itself he had awesomely penetrated the day the glories of a theatre were first displayed before his childish eyes. And now eleven years had passed since that wise Council had decreed that any alderman or citizen giving his consent to the representation of plays in this building should be fined ten shillings for every infringement of the prohibition. This not proving a sufficient deterrent, the fine was raised in 1612 from ten shillings to the extravagant sum of £10, equivalent to about £50 in our day. Fifty pounds for allowing a play to be performed in the only hall in the town suitable for the purpose! This was rank fanaticism!

Moreover, it was a fanaticism which had found its way into his own home. That strong tendency to Puritanism which was so marked among his descendants until the race died out, had already developed in his family. His wife was extremely religious, as is often the case with women whose youthful conduct has not been too circumspect. When she captured her boy husband of eighteen, her blood was as warm as his, but now she was vastly his superior in matters of religion. Neither could he look for any real intellectual companionship from his daughters. Susanna was pious, her husband still more so. Judith was as ignorant as a child. Thus he must pay the penalty of his long absence from home and his utter neglect of the education of his girls.

It was to no happy harmony of thought and feeling, therefore, that the poet could look forward as he rode away from his dramatic fairyland to the simplicities of domestic life. The only attractions existing for him there were his position as a gentleman, the satisfaction of no longer being obliged to act and write for money, and the pleasure of living on and roaming about his own property. The very fact that he did go back to Stratford with the little there was to attract him there proves how slight a hold London had taken upon him, and with what a feeling of loneliness, and (now that the bitterness was past) with what indifference, he bade farewell to the metropolis, its inhabitants and its pleasures.

It was the quietude of Stratford which attracted him, its leisure, the emptiness of its dirty streets, its remoteness from the busy world. What he really longed for was Nature, the Nature with which he had lived in such intimate companionship in his early youth, which he had missed so terribly while writing *As You Like It* and its fellow-plays, and from which he had so long been separated.

Far more than human beings was it the gardens which he had bought and planted there which drew him back to his native town—the gardens and trees on which he looked from his windows at New Place.

XXIV

STRATFORD-UPON-AVON

HE was home again. Home once more, where he knew every
road and path, every house and field, every tree and bush. The
silence of the empty streets struck him afresh as his footsteps
echoed down them, and the river Avon shone bright and still
between the willows bending down to the water's edge. He had
shot many a deer in the neighbourhood of that stream, and it
was by its banks that Jaques, in *As You Like It*, had sat as
he watched the wounded stag that sighed as though its leathern
coat would burst, while the big round tears coursed down its
innocent nose. The fine arched bridge was erected in the time
of Henry VIII. by the same Sir Hugh Clopton who had built
New Place, the house which Shakespeare had bought, and been
obliged to restore before his family could live in it.

Close by the river stood the avenue leading to the beautiful
Gothic church of the Holy Trinity, with its slender spire and
handsome windows. Within were the graves and monuments
of the neighbouring gentry, and there, so much sooner than he
could possibly have dreamed, was Shakespeare himself to lie.

Passing through Church Street, he would come upon the
Guild Chapel, a fine square building, from whose tower rang
the weekly bells calling to Sunday-morning service. He remembered those bells from of old, and now they would be constantly sounding in his ears, for New Place lay just across
the road. Soon they would be tolling his own funeral knell.
Directly adjoining the chapel stood the timbered building which
represented both Guildhall and school. Once it had seemed
large and spacious ; how small and mean it looked now ! It
was more satisfactory to glance on to the corner where his
large garden and green lawns stood, and his eye would rest
affectionately upon the mulberry-tree his own hands had planted.
Ten steps from his door lay the tavern, quaint and low, and how
familiar ! Not the first time would it be that he had sat at that
table, the largest, it was said, that had ever been cut in England
from a single piece of wood. He would at least find something
to drink there, and a game of draughts or dice. With a sigh he
realised that this tavern was likely to prove his chief refuge from
his loneliness.

2 U

Every spot was rich in memories. Five minutes' walk would bring him to Henley Street, where he had played as a child, and where stood the old house in which he was born. He would enter; there was the kitchen, which had been the living room as well in his parents' time; near the entry was the woman's store-room, and above, the sleeping-room in which he was born. How little he dreamed that this spot was to become a place of pil-grimage for the whole Anglo-Saxon race—nay, for the whole civilised world.

He would take the road to Shottery, along which he had walked times out of number in his youth—for had not he and Anne Hathaway kept their trysts there? Right and left rose the high hedges separating the fields. Trees, standing singly or in groups, were scattered about the country, and the road, lined with elms, beeches, and willows, wound its way through the undulating country lying between Stratford and Shottery. Half-an-hour's walk would bring him to Anne Hathaway's cottage, with the moss-grown roof. He would enter, and look once more upon the wooden bench in the chimney-corner on which he and she had sat in their ardent youth. How long ago it all seemed! There was the old fifteenth-century bed in which Anne's parents had slept, with her, as a child, at their feet. The mattress was nothing but a straw palliasse, but the bedstead was beautifully carved with figures in the old style. When, a year or two later, he bequeathed to his wife "the second best bed," did he remem-ber that this bed was already hers, I wonder?

Another day he would make his way as far as Warwick and its castle. The town was not unlike that of Stratford; it had the same timbered houses, but here the two great towers of the castle rose and predominated over the beautiful scenery. How vividly the past would rise up before him as he stood on the bridge and gazed up at the castle. He would remember his own youthful dreams concerning it, and the forms he had conjured up from their graves to people it afresh. There was the Earl of Warwick, who enumerated all the proofs of Gloucester's violent death in *Henry VI.*, and that other Earl in the *Second Part of Henry IV.* (Act iii. sc. 1) into whose mouth he had put words whose truth he was now proving:

> "There is a history in all men's lives
> Figuring the nature of the times deceased."

Charlcote House he would see too. He had stood as a culprit before its master once, and had suffered the bitterest humiliation of his life, one so deep that it had driven him away from home, and had thus been the means of leading him to success and prosperity in London.

How strange it was to be here again where every one knew and greeted him. In London he had been swallowed up in the crowd. How familiar, too, the homely provincial version of his name, with the abbreviated first syllable. In town that first syllable was always long, a pronunciation which left no doubt as to the etymology of the name.[1] It was on account of these differing pronunciations that he had, while in London, changed the spelling of his name. He had always written it *Shakspere*, but in town it had from the first (the dedication of *Venus and Adonis* and *The Rape of Lucrece*) been printed *Shakespeare:* a spelling always followed by the various publishers of the quarto editions of his dramas, only one adopting the orthography *Shakspeare*.[2]

Every one knew him, and he must exchange a word with all—with the ploughman in the field, the farmer's wife in her poultry-yard, the mason on the scaffolding, the fish-dealer at his stall, the cobbler in his workshop, and the butcher in the slaughter-house. How well he could talk to each, for no human occupation, however humble, was unfamiliar to him. He had a thorough acquaintance from of old with the butcher's trade. It had formed a part of his father's business, and his early tragedies contain many a proof of his familiarity with it. The Second and Third Parts of *Henry VI.* are full of similes drawn from it.[3]

There was hardly any trade, calling, or position in life which he did not understand as if he had been born to it. Doubtless the

---

[1] In 1875 Charles Mackay made an attempt, in the *Athenæum*, to prove a Celtic origin for the name, deriving it from *seac* = dry, and *speir* = shanks, thus dry or long shanks. If we take into consideration the numerous other names and nicknames of the day which began with Shake—Shake-buckler, Shake-launce, Shake-shaft, &c., this explanation does not seem very probable. Another argument in favour of its Anglo-Saxon origin and simple meaning, *Spearshaker*, is the contemporaneous existence of the Italian surname Crollalanza.

[2] It may be mentioned that there were no less than fifty-five different ways of writing the name at that time. It is well known that such spellings were quite arbitrary. In Shakespeare's wedding contract, for example, we have the version *Shagspere*.

[3] " And as the butcher takes away the calf,
And binds the wretch and beats it when it strays,
Bearing it to the bloody slaughter-house " (II. iii. 1).

" Who finds the heifer dead and bleeding fresh,
And sees fast by a butcher with an axe,
But will suspect 'twas he that made the slaughter " (II. iii. 2).

" *Holland.* And Dick the butcher.
" *Bevis.* Then is sin struck down like an ox and iniquity's throat cut like a calf " (II. iv. 2).

" *Cade.* They fell before thee like sheep and oxen, and thou behavedst thyself as if thou hadst been in thine own slaughter-house " (II. iv. 3).

" So first the harmless sheep doth yield his fleece,
And next his throat unto the butcher's knife " (III. v. 6).

In *As You Like It* (ii. 2) Rosalind says, using a simile drawn from the same trade: " This way will I take upon me to wash your liver clean as a sound sheep's heart, that there shall be not one spot of love in it."

See Alfred C. Calmon, who in *Fact and Fiction about Shakespeare* has been very successful in pointing out the numerous reminiscences of Stratford to be found in Shakespeare's plays.

simple folk of his native town respected him as much for his sound judgment and universal knowledge as for his wealth and property. It would be too much to expect that they should recognise anything more and greater in him.

Many years ago, at the outset of his career as a dramatist, he had made a defeated king praise a country life for its simplicity and freedom from care (*Third Part of Henry VI.*, ii. 5):

> "O God! methinks it were a happy life
> To be no better than a homely swain;
> To sit upon a hill, as I do now,
> To carve out dials quaintly, point by point,
> Thereby to see the minutes how they run,
> How many make the hour full complete;
> How many hours bring about the day;
> How many days will finish up the year;
> How many years a mortal man may live.
> When this is known, then to divide the times:
> So many hours must I tend my flock;
> So many hours must I take my rest;
> So many hours must I contemplate;
> So many hours must I sport myself;
> So many days my ewes have been with young;
> So many weeks ere the poor fools will yean;
> So many years ere I shall shear the fleece:
> So minutes, hours, days, months and years,
> Passed over to the end they were created,
> Would bring white hairs and a quiet grave.'

In just such a regular monotony were Shakespeare's own days now to pass.

XXV

THE LAST YEARS OF SHAKESPEARE'S LIFE

DID Shakespeare find that peace and contentment at Stratford which he sought? From one thing and another we are almost forced to conclude he did not. His own family seem to have looked upon him in the light of a returned artist-bohemian, of a man whose past career and present religious principles were anything but a credit to them. Elze and others believe, indeed, that, like Byron's descendants at a later date, Shakespeare's family considered him a stain upon their reputation. This surmise may be correct, but there is no very great foundation for it.

It has long been inferred, from the fact that he made her his heiress, that Susanna was Shakespeare's favourite daughter. She was probably the individual to whom he felt most drawn in Stratford; but we must not conclude too much from a testamentary disposition. It was plainly the poet's intention to entail his property, and his original desire was that his little son Hamnet, as bearer and continuer of the name, should succeed to everything. Upon the death of the son, the elder daughter would naturally take his place.

It is not conceivable that Susanna could have any real understanding of, or sympathy with, her father. Her very epitaph places her in direct contrast with him in matters of religion, distinctly maintaining that though she was gifted above her sex, which she owed partly to her father, she was also wise with regard to her soul's salvation, and that was entirely due to Him whose happiness she was now sharing. Shakespeare had none of the credit for that.[1] Her natural inclination to bigoted piety was confirmed and augmented by the influence of her husband, whose sectarian zeal and narrow-minded hatred of Catholicism are plainly shown in such of his journals and books as have been preserved. We can fancy how Shakespeare's depth and delicacy of feeling must have suffered under all this. It is even possible that Susanna and her husband may have burned, on the score of what they considered his irreligious principles, any

[1] "Witty above her sexe, but that's not all,
Wise to salvation was good Mistress Hall,
Something of Shakespeare was in that, but this
Wholly of him with whom she's now in blisse."

677

papers that Shakespeare left behind, as Byron's family destroyed his memoirs. This would explain their total disappearance, which, after all, is no more strange than the utter absence of any manuscripts belonging to Beaumont or Fletcher, or any other dramatic writer of the period.

The younger daughter, Judith, could not even write her own name, and signed her mark with a quaint little flourish when she was married. It is clearly impossible, therefore, that she could have taken any interest in her father's manuscripts. In the seventeenth century it was no very liberal education that a poet's daughter received; even Milton's eldest daughter, at a much later period, was unable to write. Susanna could just inscribe her own name, but that seems to have been the limit of her literary accomplishments. Her utter indifference to all such matters would sufficiently account for the destruction of her father's papers, and this surmise is confirmed by a remarkable statement made in his preface by Dr. John Cooke, the editor of her husband's papers. Whilst serving as army surgeon during the Civil War, he was stationed at Stratford to defend the bridge over the Avon. One of his men, lately an assistant of Dr. Hall's, told him that the books and manuscripts left by the doctor were still in existence, and offered to accompany him to the widow's house in search of them. Cooke examined the books, and Mrs. Hall informed him that she had others which had belonged to her husband's partner, and had cost a considerable sum. He replied that if the books pleased him he would be willing to pay the original price. She then produced them, and they proved to be the very book from which we are quoting, and some others' all ready for printing. Cooke, who knew Dr. Hall's handwriting, told her that at least one of these books was her husband's, and showed her the writing. She denied it, and finding that his persistence was giving offence, he paid the sum she named and carried off the books.

This extract proves that Susanna neither knew her husband's handwriting nor recognised his own books. So entirely lacking was she in any interest in intellectual matters, that she, a rich woman, set no greater value on her husband's works than to sell them for a trifle on the first opportunity that offered.

We can draw a tolerably reliable inference from this anecdote of the interest she was likely to take in any written or printed papers left by her father. In all probability she did not even take the trouble to burn them, but either threw them away or sold them as waste paper.

If we reflect that Susanna, born in better circumstances and better educated than her mother, must have been decidedly her superior, we can see how little Shakespeare's wife, now well stricken in years, could have understood or appreciated her husband. She undoubtedly preferred sermons to plays, and both her heart and house were always open to itinerant Puritan preachers.   Of this we possess reliable information.

Shakespeare returned to London during the winter of 1614. Letters have been preserved from his cousin Thomas Greene, the town-clerk, proving that he was in the capital on the 16th of November and the 23rd of December.   This visit of his is interesting in two ways, for we know that Shakespeare, capable man of business as he was, was defending the rights of his fellow-citizens against the country gentry; and we also know the use his family made of his absence.

The town records of Stratford show that Shakespeare's family was entertaining a travelling Puritan preacher just at this time, for, according to custom, the town presented this man with a quart of sack and a quart of claret, and we read in the municipal accounts: "*Item, for one quart of sack and one quart of clarett wine geven to a preacher at the New Place, xxd.*"

It is a significant fact that his family should be entertaining a member of the sect Shakespeare held to be peculiarly inimical to himself whilst he, the master of the house, was absent on business.

Probably his family never saw one of his plays performed, nor even read such of them as were printed in the pirated editions.

Anne Hathaway's cottage, which stands unchanged, though the roof is gradually falling in, was visited by the present writer in 1895.   An old woman lived in it, the last of the Hathaways.   She was sitting on a chair opposite the *courtship bench*, on which, according to tradition, the lovers used to sit.   In the family Bible, lying open before her, she pointed with pride to a long list of names inscribed by the Hathaways during hundreds of years, and forming a kind of genealogical tree.   The room was filled with all manner of pictures of William Shakespeare and Anne Hathaway, with relics of the poet, and of famous actors and critics of his plays.   The old woman, who lived among and by these comparatively valueless treasures, explained the meaning and story of each thing, but to the cautiously ventured inquiry whether she had ever read anything by this same Shakespeare who surrounded her on every side, and on whose memory she was actually living, she returned the somewhat astonished reply, " Read anything of him !   No, I read my Bible."   If this female Hathaway has never read anything of Shakespeare, was Anne, who must have been far behind this last scion of her race in general and certainly Shakespearian culture, likely ever to have done so ?

Seeing that his own family had no great opinion of him, we can hardly be surprised that, in spite of his wealth and his oft-mentioned kindliness of disposition, he was hardly appreciated by the upper ten of Stratford's 1500 citizens.   Although he was one of its richest inhabitants, he was never appointed to one of the public offices of the town during the years of his residence there.

There were few with whom he could associate in the little town. The most frequently alluded to of his Stratford acquaintances was a certain John Combe (steward of Ambrose, Earl of Warwick), a man of low repute as tax-collector and worse as money-lender and usurer. That he figured as a philanthropist in his will does not prove very much, but he must have been better than his reputation, or he would surely never have been one of Shakespeare's companions. Tradition tells that the poet and Combe not only spent much time together in their own houses, but were also in the habit of passing their evenings in the tavern (now called the Falcon) which lay just across the road. Here, then, the mighty genius, stranded in a little country town, sat at the same great table which stands there to-day, tossing dice and emptying his glass in company with a country bumpkin of doubtful reputation.

Tradition further adds that it was one of Shakespeare's few amusements to compose ironical epitaphs for his acquaintances, and he is said to have written an exceedingly contemptuous one upon John Combe in his character of usurer and extortioner. This epitaph, however, which has survived to us in various forms, is proved to have been printed, with its many variations, as early as 1608. It was probably only assigned to Shakespeare in the same manner that all the Danish witticisms of the following century were attributed to Wessel. John Combe died in 1614, leaving Shakespeare a legacy of five pounds. If he was the best of Shakespeare's Stratford associates, we can figure to ourselves the rest.

His chief companionship must have been that of Nature.

Wiser and more profound than any other in Voltaire's *Candide* is its closing utterance, "*Il faut cultiver notre jardin.*" Candide and his friends, at the end of the story, come across a Turk who, absolutely indifferent to all that is occurring in Constantinople, is entirely absorbed in the cultivation of his garden. The only communication he holds with the capital is to send thither for sale the fruit that he grows. This Turk's philosophy of life makes a great impression upon Voltaire's hero, who has known and experienced the dangers and difficulties of nearly every human lot, and his constant refrain throughout the last pages of the book is, "*Je sais qu'il faut cultiver notre jardin.*" "You are right," answers another character; "let us work and give up brooding; only work makes life bearable." When Pangloss undertakes, for the last time, to prove how wonderfully everything is linked together in this best of all possible worlds, Candide adds the final apostrophe, "Well said! but we must cultivate our gardens."

This was the thought which was now singing its meagre, sad little melody in Shakespeare's soul.

His two gardens stretched from New Place down to the Avon; the larger had one fault—it only communicated by a narrow lane with the bit of ground that lay directly round the house, two small properties on the Chapel Lane side intervening between house and garden. The smaller garden was probably given up to flowers, the larger to the cultivation of fruit. Warwickshire is especially noted for its apples.

Thus Shakespeare could now improve the quality of his own fruit by that process of grafting which Polixenes had so lately taught Perdita in the *Winter's Tale*. He could now, as did the gardener long ago in *Richard II.*, bid his assistants bind up the dangling apricots and prop the bending branches.

He had planted the famous mulberry-tree with his own hand, and it stood until the Rev. Francis Gastrell, who owned New Place in 1756, cut it down in a fit of exasperation with the crowds who requested admission to see it. Any one who has visited Stratford knows of the endless pieces of furniture and little boxes which were made from its wood. Garrick, who revived Shakespeare upon the stage, sat under it in 1744; and when, in 1769, he was presented with the freedom of the city, the casket in which the charter was enclosed was made from a portion of the tree. In the same year, when, on the occasion of Shakespeare's Jubilee, he sang his song, *Shakespeare's Mulberry-Tree*, he held in his hand a goblet made from its wood.

A serious attempt was made in Shakespeare's time to introduce the breeding of silkworms at Stratford, and the planting of the mulberry-tree may have had some connection with this experiment.

Not even the ruins of New Place are in existence to-day, but only the site where the house once stood, and the old well in the yard, which is so overgrown with ivy that the windlass looks like a handle of greenery. The foundation-stones of the boundary wall are covered with earth and grass, and form a sort of embankment towards the road. The gardens, however, are much as they were in Shakespeare's day; the larger is spacious and beautiful. Wandering there of an autumn afternoon, when the leaves are beginning to turn faintly golden, a strange feeling comes over one —a feeling belonging to the place, from which it is very difficult to tear oneself away.

One seems to see him walking with grave stateliness there, clad in scarlet, with the broad white collar falling over the sleeveless black tunic. We see the hand which has written so many ill-understood and insufficiently appreciated masterpieces binding up branches or lopping off stray tendrils, while the sunlight sparkles on the plain gold signet ring with its initials, W.S., which is still in our possession.

The numerous portraits and the famous death-masque discovered in Germany are all forgeries. The only genuine likenesses are the bad engraving by Droeshout prefixed to the first Folio and the poorly executed coloured bust by the Dutchman Gerhard Johnson on the monument in the Church of the Holy Trinity, which was probably done from a death-masque. It may be added that a painting was discovered at Stratford eight years ago, which purports to be the original of Droeshout's engraving, and the genuineness of which is still a matter of dispute.[1]

It holds us captive, this head with the healthy, full, red lips, the slight brownish moustache, the fine, high, poet's brow, with the reddish hair growing naturally and becomingly at the sides. The expression is speaking; Shakespeare must surely have looked like this. Even if the painting should prove a forgery, an imitation of Droeshout's work instead of its original, it will still retain an artistic and psychological value possessed by none of the other portraits. As he looks out at us from the canvas, we seem to see him as he was in those last years at Stratford, chatting with the townsfolk and "cultivating his garden."[2]

[1] In the Halliwell-Phillips collection of Shakespearian rarities, stored at the Safe Deposit, Chancery Lane, there was a copy of the print which, according to the catalogue of the collection, is in its original proof condition, before it was altered by "an inferior hand." As traces of what is called the "inferior hand" are to be found in the painting, it would seem that the latter was copied from the print. (See John Corbin: *Two Undescribed Portraits of Shakespeare. Harper's New Monthly Magazine.*)

[2] R. E. Hunter: *Shakespeare and Stratford.* 1864. Halliwell-Phillips: *Brief Guide to the Gardens.* 1863. G. L. Lee: *Shakespeare's Home and Rural Life.* 1874. W. H. H.: *Stratford-upon-Avon. Historic Stratford.* 1893. *The Home and Haunts of Shakespeare,* with an Introduction by H. H. Furness. 1892. Karl Elze: *Shakespeare,* chap. viii.

XXVI

SHAKESPEARE'S DEATH

ON the 9th of July 1614 a terrible calamity fell upon the little
town in which Shakespeare dwelt, and a great fire destroyed no
less than fifty-four houses, besides various barns and stables. In
spite of a prohibitive law, the houses of most of the poorer citizens
were thatched with straw, which proved, of course, highly inflammable. Doubtless Shakespeare, whose house was spared,
contributed generously towards the alleviation of the general
distress.

In March 1612, Shakespeare, jointly with Will Johnson, a wine
merchant, John Jackson, and his friend and editor John Heminge,
bought a house at Blackfriars in London. The deed of purchase
which is still in existence in the British Museum, bears Shakespeare's authentic signature written above the first of the appended
seals. His name above and in the body of the document has a
different spelling. This property must have necessitated a certain
amount of attention, and probably occasioned more than one
journey up to town. The already mentioned sojourn there at the
close of the year 1614 was not one of these, however. Shakespeare's object then was the fulfilment of a commission intrusted
to him by his fellow-townsfolk.

For more than a century past, the great families had been
enclosing all the land they could seize, and their parks and preserves began to usurp the old common lands and hunting-grounds,
their object being to crush the mediæval custom of the whole community's joint interest in agriculture and cattle-rearing. A steady
withdrawal of land from agricultural purposes went on, and the
peasant classes were growing gradually poorer as the large landowners arbitrarily raised the prices of meat and wool. Under
these circumstances the country people naturally did their best to
prevent the enclosure of land.

In 1614 Shakespeare's native 'town was agitated by a proposal
to enclose and parcel out the common land of Old Stratford and
Welcombe. That Shakespeare was averse to this plan and determined to oppose it we learn from an utterance of his preserved in
the memoranda of his cousin, Thomas Greene, which have been
published by Halliwell-Phillips. According to these, Shakespeare
said to his cousin that *he was not able to bear the enclosing of*

Welcombe. We also learn that he concluded an agreement on the 28th of October, on behalf of his cousin and himself, with a certain William Replingham of Great Harborough, an ardent supporter of the enclosure project. Replingham thereby pledged himself to indemnify the persons concerned for any loss or injury entailed upon them by the enclosure. Shakespeare was also induced to plead the cause of his fellow-townsmen in London, the Stratford town council sending Thomas Greene thither to beg him to use all his influence for the benefit of the town, which had already suffered grievous loss through the fire. That Greene fulfilled his commission is proved by his letter to the council of the 17th of November 1614, in which he says he received reassuring intelligence from Shakespeare, and that both the poet and his son-in-law, Dr. Hall, believe that the dreaded plan will never be carried into execution.[1]

They were right. In 1618, in answer to a petition from the corporation, Government decreed that no enclosure was to be made, and gave orders that any fences already erected for that purpose were to be pulled down.

The year 1615 seems to have passed quietly enough in that country solitude and peace which Shakespeare had so long desired.

He must have been taken seriously ill in January 1616, for above the actual date of his will, *March 25th*, stands that of *January*, as though he had begun to draw it up, and then, feeling better, had postponed his intention of making a will.

The last event of any importance in Shakespeare's life took place on the 10th of February 1616; on that day his daughter Judith was married. She was no longer quite young, being thirty-one, and it was no very brilliant match she made. The bridegroom, Thomas Quiney, was a tavern-keeper and vintner in Stratford, and a son of the Richard Quiney who applied eighteen years before to his "loving countryman," William Shakespeare, for a loan of £30. Thomas Quiney was four years younger than his bride, therefore the maxim of *Twelfth Night*, "Let still the woman take an elder than herself," was as little heeded in his daughter's case as it had been in Shakespeare's own. A vintner in a town the size of Stratford is not likely to have been either a very wealthy man or one of such education that Shakespeare would take any pleasure in his society.

The last wedding festivity in which Shakespeare had taken part was the ideally royal marriage of Ferdinand and Miranda.

---

[1] The passage runs: "My cosen Shakespeare comyng yesterday to town, I went to see him, how he did. He told me that they assured him they ment to inclose no further than to Gospell Bush, and so upp straight (leavyng out part of the dyngles to the ffield) to the gate in Clopton hedg, and take in Salisburyes peece; and that they mean in Aprill to survey the land, and then to give satisfaccion, and not before; and he and Mr. Hall say they think ther will be nothyng done at all."

Also C. M. Ingleby: *Shakespeare and the Welcombe Enclosures*, 1883.

What a contrast was this of Judith and her vintner! It was prose after poetry.

Ben Jonson and Michael Drayton are supposed to have come down for the wedding, but of this we have no certain information. The supposition rests entirely on the following brief statement, written at least fifty years afterwards by the rector of Stratford, John Ward. "Shakespeare, Drayton, and Ben Jhonson had a merry meeting, and, it seems, drank too hard, for Shakespeare died of a feavour there contracted." He does not say that this merry meeting was held at the time of the wedding, but the probabilities are that it was. Drayton was a Warwickshire man, and possessed intimate friends in the neighbourhood of Stratford. Ben Jonson may have been invited in return for his having asked Shakespeare to stand as godfather to one of his children. There are good grounds for the surmise that in any case the wine was supplied by the son-in-law, and that the silver-gilt bowl bequeathed to Judith was used upon this occasion.

It was childish of the cleric to connect this little drinking party with Shakespeare's illness. The tradition of Shakespeare's liking for a good glass was rife in Stratford as late as the eighteenth century. Numerous pictures of the crab-apple tree preserve the legend that Shakespeare started off for Bidford one youthful day for the sake of the lively topers he had heard dwelt there, and the tale runs that he drank so hard he had to lie down under the *crab-tree* on his way home, and sleep for several hours. The story repeated by Ward probably originated in these reports. All we know for certain is that some days after the wedding Shakespeare was taken ill.

Several circumstances tend to prove that the poet was attacked by typhus fever. Stratford, with its low, damp situation and its filthy roads, was a regular typhus trap in those days. Halliwell-Phillips has published a list of enactments and penalties promulgated by the magistrates with a view to the clearing of the streets. They extend into the latter half of the eighteenth century, and that there are none for the years in question is accounted for by the fact that the documents for 1605–1646 are missing. Even so late as the Shakespeare Jubilee in 1769, Garrick, who was fêted by the town on this occasion, described it as "the most dirty, unseemly, ill-pav'd, wretched-looking town in all Britain." Chapel Lane, towards which Shakespeare's house fronted, was one of the unhealthiest streets in the town. It hardly possessed a house, being but a medley of sheds and stables with an open drain running down the middle of the street. It was small wonder that the place was constantly visited by pestilential epidemics, and little was known in those days of any laws of hygiene, and as little of any treatment for typhus. Shakespeare's son-in-law, who was probably his doctor, knew of no remedy for it, as his journals prove.

Shakespeare drew up his will on the 25th of March.   As we have already said, it is still in existence, and is reproduced in facsimile in the twenty-fourth volume of the German Shakespeare Year-book.

The fact that it was dictated, and the extreme shakiness of the signature at the foot of the three lengthily detailed folio pages, prove that Shakespeare was very ill when his will was made.

His daughter Susanna is the principal heiress.   Judith receives £150 ready money and £150 more after the lapse of three years, under certain conditions.   These are the principal bequests. Joan Hart, his sister, is remembered in various ways.   She is to receive five pounds in ready money and all his clothes.   Her three sons are separately mentioned, although Shakespeare cannot remember the baptismal name of the second, and are to have five pounds each.   To his granddaughter, Elizabeth Hall, he leaves his silver plate.   Ten pounds is to go to the poor of Stratford, and his sword to Thomas Combe.   Various good burghers of the town, including Hamlet Sadler, after whom Shakespeare's son was named, are left twenty-six shillings and eightpence each, wherewith to buy a ring in memory of the deceased.   A line inserted later bequeaths a similar sum for a similar purpose to the three actors with whom Shakespeare was most intimately associated in his late company, and whom he calls "my comrades"—John Heminge, Richard Burbage, and Henry Condell. As is well known, it is to the first and last of these three that we owe the first Folio edition, containing nineteen of Shakespeare's plays which would otherwise have been lost to us.

A peculiar psychological interest attaches to the following features of the will.

In the first place, the much discussed and remarkable fact that in making his last will Shakespeare apparently entirely forgot his wife.   Not until it was completed and read aloud to him did he remember that she, who would receive, of course, the legal widow's share, should at least be named; and then, between the last lines, he has inserted: "*Item, I gyve unto my wief my second best bed with the furniture.*"   The poverty of the gift is the more obvious when we recall how Shakespeare's father-in-law remembered his wife in his will.

It is also significant, more especially as it was contrary to the custom of the times, that not a single member of Mrs. Shakespeare's family was mentioned in the will.   The name Hathaway does not occur, although it is frequently mentioned in the wills of Shakespeare's descendants; in that of Thomas Nash, for instance, and of Susanna's daughter Elizabeth, who became Lady Barnard by her second marriage.   The inference is plain, that Shakespeare was on very unfriendly terms with his wife's family.

The next peculiarity is that Shakespeare never refers to his position as a dramatic writer, nor makes any allusion to books, manuscripts, or papers of any kind, as forming part of his property. This absence of all concern for his poetical reputation is in complete accord with the sovereign contempt for posthumous fame which we have already observed in him.

Finally, it is not without significance that there was neither poet nor author mentioned among those to whom Shakespeare left money for the purchase of that ordinary token of friendship, a ring to be worn as a memento. It would seem as though he felt himself under no obligation to any of his fellow-authors, and had nothing to thank them for. This neglect is quite in harmony with the contempt he always displayed for his brother craftsmen when he had occasion to represent them upon the stage. He may have been willing enough to drink in company with Ben Jonson, the honest and envious friend of so many years' standing, but he had no more depth of affection for him than for any other of the dramatists and lyric poets among whom his lot had been cast. As Byron says of Childe Harold—he was one among them, not of them.

He lingered on for four weeks, and then he died.

He had probably completed his fifty-second year the day before, thus dying at the same age as Molière and Napoleon. He had lived long enough to finish his work, and the mighty turbulent river of his life came to an end among the sands, in the daily drop, drop, drop.[1]

A monument was erected by his family in Stratford church before the year 1623. Below the bust is an inscription, probably of Dr. Hall's composition. The first two lines liken him, in badly constructed Latin, to a Nestor for judgment, a Socrates for genius, and a Virgil for art.[2]

We could imagine a more appropriate epitaph.

---

[1] It is not altogether correct to say that Shakespeare died on the same day as Cervantes. True, they both died on the 23rd of April 1616, but the Gregorian calendar was then in use in Spain, while England was still reckoning by the Julian ; there is an actual difference of ten days therefore

[2] " Judicio Pylium, genio Socratem arte Maronem,
Terra tegit, populus moeret, Olympus habet."

XXVII

CONCLUSION

EVEN a long human life is so brief and fugitive that it seems little short of a miracle that it can leave traces behind which endure through centuries. The millions die and sink into oblivion and their deeds die with them. A few thousands so far conquer death as to leave their names to be a burden to the memories of school-children, but convey little else to posterity. But some few master-minds remain, and among them Shakespeare ranks with Leonardo and Michael Angelo. He was hardly laid in his grave than he rose from it again. Of all the great names of this earth, none is more certain of immortality than that of Shakespeare.

An English poet of this century has written:

> " Revolving years have flitted on,
>   Corroding Time has done its worst,
> Pilgrim and worshipper have gone
>   From Avon's shrine to shrines of dust ;
> But Shakespeare lives unrivall'd still
>   And unapproached by mortal mind,
> The giant of Parnassus' hill,
>   The pride, the monarch of mankind."

The monarch of mankind! they are proud words those, but they do not altogether over-estimate the truth. He is by no means the only king in the intellectual world, but his power is unlimited by time or space. From the moment his life's history ceases his far greater history begins. We find its first records in Great Britain, and consequently in North America; then it spread among the German-speaking peoples and the whole Teutonic race, on through the Scandinavian countries to the Finns and the Sclavonic races. We find his influence in France, Spain, and Italy; and now, in the nineteenth century, it may be traced over the whole civilised world.

His writings are translated into every tongue and all the languages of the earth do him honour.

Not only have his works influenced the minds of readers in every country, but they have moulded the spiritual lives of thinkers, writers and poets; no mortal man, from the time of the Renaissance to our own day, has caused such upheavals and revivals in the literatures of different nations. Intellectual revolutions have emanated from his outspoken boldness and his eternal youth, and have been quelled again by his sanity, his moderation, and his eternal wisdom.

It would be far easier to enumerate the great men who have known him and owed him nothing than to reckon up the names of those who are far more indebted to him than they can say. All the real intellectual life of England since his day has been stamped by his genius, all her creative spirits have imbibed their life's nourishment from his works. Modern German intellectual life is based, through Lessing, upon him. Goethe and Schiller are unimaginable without him. His influence is felt in France through Voltaire, Victor Hugo, and Alfred de Vigny. Ludovic Vitet and Alfred de Musset were from the very first inspired by him. Not only the drama in Russia and Poland felt his influence, but the inmost spiritual life of the Sclavonic story-tellers and brooders is fashioned after the pattern of his imperishable creations. From the moment of the regeneration of poetry in the North he was reverenced by Ewald, Oehlenschläger, Bredahl, and Hauch, and he is not without his influence upon Björnson and Ibsen.

This book was not written with the intention of describing Shakespeare's triumphant progress through the world, nor of telling the tale of his world-wide dominion. Its purpose was to declare and prove that Shakespeare is not thirty-six plays and a few poems jumbled together and read pêle-mêle, but a man who felt and thought, rejoiced and suffered, brooded, dreamed, and created.

Far too long has it been the custom to say, "We know nothing about Shakespeare;" or, "An octavo page would contain all our knowledge of him." Even Swinburne has written of the intangibility of his personality in his works. Such assertions have been carried so far that a wretched group of dilettanti has been bold enough, in Europe and America, to deny William Shakespeare the right to his own life-work, to give to another the honour due to his genius, and to bespatter him and his invulnerable name with an insane abuse which has re-echoed through every land.

It is to refute this idea of Shakespeare's impersonality, and to indignantly repel an ignorant and arrogant attack upon one of the greatest benefactors of the human race, that the present attempt has been made.

It is the author's opinion that, given the possession of forty-five important works by any man, it is entirely our own fault if we know nothing whatever about him. The poet has incorporated his whole individuality in these writings, and there, if we can read aright, we shall find him.

2 X

The William Shakespeare who was born at Stratford-on-Avon in the reign of Queen Elizabeth, who lived and wrote in London in her reign and that of James, who ascended into heaven in his comedies and descended into hell in his tragedies, and died at the age of fifty-two in his native town, rises a wonderful personality in grand and distinct outlines, with all the vivid colouring of life from the pages of his books, before the eyes of all who read them with an open, receptive mind, with sanity of judgment and simple susceptibility to the power of genius.

INDEX

2 Y

THE END

Printed by BALLANTYNE, HANSON & Co.
Edinburgh & London

www.ingramcontent.com/pod-product-compliance
Lightning Source LLC
Chambersburg PA
CBHW030918020726
47498CB00001B/19